THE BARON'S CLOAK

THE BARON'S CLOAK

A History of the Russian Empire
in War and Revolution

WILLARD SUNDERLAND

CORNELL UNIVERSITY PRESS
ITHACA AND LONDON

First published 2014 by Cornell University Press

Printed in the United States of America

Library of Congress Cataloging-in-Publication Data

Sunderland, Willard, 1965– author.
    The baron's cloak : a history of the Russian Empire in war and revolution /
Willard Sunderland.
        pages cm
    Includes bibliographical references and index.
    ISBN 978-0-8014-5270-3 (cloth : alk. paper)
  1. Ungern-Sternberg, Roman, 1885–1921. 2. Generals—Russia—
Biography. 3. Generals—Soviet Union—Biography. 4. Soviet Union—
History—Revolution, 1917–1921. 5. Siberia (Russia)—History—
Revolution, 1917–1921. 6. Mongolia—History, Military—20th century.
7. Russia—Description and travel. 8. Soviet Union—Description and
travel. I. Title.
    DK254.U5S86   2014
    947.08'3092—dc23
    [B]   2013045239

Cornell University Press strives to use environmentally responsible suppliers
and materials to the fullest extent possible in the publishing of its books.
Such materials include vegetable-based, low-VOC inks and acid-free papers
that are recycled, totally chlorine-free, or partly composed of nonwood fibers.
For further information, visit our website at www.cornellpress.cornell.edu.

Cloth printing   10 9 8 7 6 5 4 3 2 1

For HM

In the beginning, all the arrangements for building
the Tower of Babel were in fairly good order.
—FRANZ KAFKA, "THE CITY COAT OF ARMS"

CONTENTS

MAPS

PREFACE

When I was a boy I would play at collecting countries in my family's atlas with the span of my hands, marveling at their curious shapes as I tallied up and compared their respective sizes. Like all school kids, I knew, of course, that the USSR was the biggest of them all, but the fact seemed all the more remarkable somehow because I could never get my fingers across it. No matter where I started, Leningrad or Kamchatka, the lumpy oblong of the country stretched farther still. There was always more to go.

It was about halfway through my work on this book when I realized that it, too, is an attempt to come to terms with the vastness of Russia. When I began my research, my plan was to write about Baron von Ungern-Sternberg much as others had, telling his evocative story for its own sake. But as I read more deeply, I began to see how widely he had lived and traveled, and the sources I was finding seemed to reveal at least as much about the Russian Empire as they did about him, if not more, while the fate of the country was certainly no less gripping or meaningful. Why then not enlist him as a guide, using his life to open up the empire's sprawling patchwork of regions and peoples, and especially the connections between them in a momentous time? And so, this is the turn that led me here, to this book rather than to another.

Of course, an approach like this seems all but fated to fall short. How couldn't it? The scales are too incongruous; a single life on the one hand, a vast empire on the other. Yet at the same time, one of the great pleasures of being a historian is to take up precisely this kind of problem. It's the chance to tinker with perspectives, to seek the particular in the general and vice versa, and to adjust and readjust the fittings between them in the search for meaning. In truth, working on a small scale is no less daunting than working on a larger one—both demand a reckoning with incompleteness. The tiny details of an hour can be as fraught to re-create as a year, the fullness of a garden plot as unsurveyable as a continent. Considered in this light, perhaps using a life to take the measure of an empire is not such a faulty notion, or at least no more faulty than any other method one might pursue. One still ends up taking in a great span, even if, inevitably, something remains out of reach.

UNGERN'S LIFE: A TIMELINE

1886	Born in Graz, Austria, then part of the Habsburg Empire.
1888–1890	Family moves to Tiflis (now Tbilisi), then the capital of the Russian imperial region of the Caucasus (Kavkaz), where Ungern's father has a position in the regional administration.
1890–1902	Spends his boyhood years in Estland, now Estonia, then a province of the Russian Empire. Ungern's parents divorce. His mother soon remarries and Ungern moves to his stepfather's estate at Jerwakant in the countryside near the port of Reval (now Tallinn), the capital of the province. In 1900, he leaves the estate for boarding school in Reval.
1903–1905	Military school in St. Petersburg. Withdraws from school because of poor performance.
1905–1906	Volunteers for service as a private in the Russo-Japanese War. Spends several months in Manchuria in northern China, though by the time he arrives the fighting is effectively over.
1906–1908	Returns to military school in St. Petersburg. Graduates in 1908.
1908–1910	Assumes his first army post as a lieutenant in the Trans-Baikal Cossack Host, serving on the Sino-Russian border.
1910–1913	Transfers to new post with the Amur Cossacks located some 500 miles east on the Amur River. Stories tell that he had to leave his original post because of a duel.

1913	Resigns from the army and travels to the region of Kobdo in far western Mongolia hoping to serve as a volunteer among the Mongol forces that are fighting the Chinese after the Mongol declaration of independence. The local Russian authorities in Kobdo reject the plan.
1914–1917	Re-enlists with army shortly after the Great War begins. Fights in East Prussia, Poland, the Carpathians, and northern Persia. Earns numerous commendations for bravery. Also court-martialed for "conduct unbecoming an officer" and sentenced to three months in the stockade. Appears to be serving in northern Persia at the time of the February Revolution.
1917–1920	Commits to fighting the Bolsheviks after their takeover in October 1917. Serves in the Trans-Baikal and along the Chinese Eastern Railway (CER) in northern Manchuria as a commander in the forces of his friend and fellow Trans-Baikal Cossack, the warlord Ataman Grigorii Semenov.
Sept./Oct. 1920	The Mongolian campaign begins. Ungern moves the Asiatic Division into Mongolia after the Red Army advances on the Trans-Baikal.
Feb. 1921	His force takes the Mongolian capital of Urga.
May 1921	Launches attack on the Reds in Siberia near the border town of Kiakhta.
Aug. 1921	Captured by Reds in north-central Mongolia.
Sept. 1921	Tried and executed in Novonikolaevsk, now Novosibirsk.

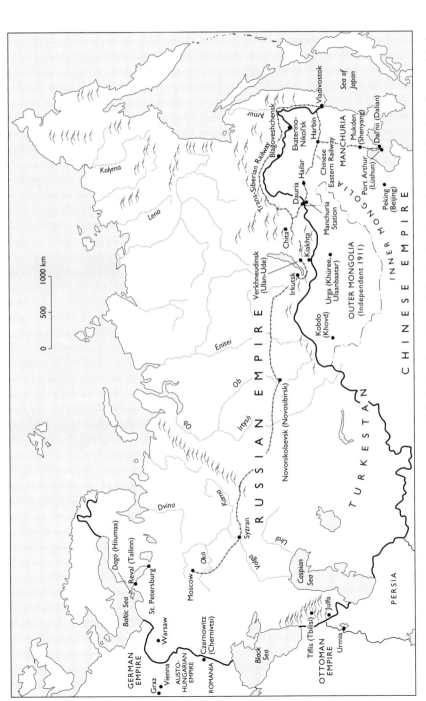

Map 1. The Russian Empire, ca. 1914. The points on this map mark the key locations of Ungern's Eurasian life. Born in Austria and shot thirty-five years later in central Siberia, most of his life in between was spent on Russia's far-flung eastern and western frontiers.

THE BARON'S CLOAK

INTRODUCTION

No ideas but in things!
—WILLIAM CARLOS WILLIAMS. "A Sort of a Song"

On either September 15 or 16, 1921, Ungern took off his cloak. Or perhaps someone took it from him. Shortly after that he was shot.

The cloak, technically speaking, is a *deel,* the traditional dress of Mongolian nomads. With a wide base and narrow collar, it runs about four feet from top to bottom, with two broad sleeves almost as long as the garment itself hanging from the sides. We can tell that this particular deel belonged to someone important because of the color, a rich shade of orangey-gold usually reserved for nobles, and the fact that it is made of silk rather than more ordinary wool or cotton. The embroidered roundels running across the front and back also suggest a certain refinement. Yet for all this, only one thing about the cloak is truly unusual. Sewn to the shoulders are two faded gray-green European-style army epaulettes. They seem out of place, as if stitched on after the fact. Each bears the mark of two small stars and the initials "A. S." in Cyrillic lettering.[1]

To see the deel today we have to go to the Central Museum of the Armed Forces in Moscow. Over the years it has hung in the museum's public galleries, though on the day I visited, I found it in the office of Tat'iana Sergeevna Leonova, the friendly director of the material objects collections, who was keeping it in her closet while the exhibit halls were being renovated. Tat'iana Sergeevna also showed me a yellowed inventory card from 1939 when the museum first acquired the deel as a "trophy of the Red Army from the period of the civil war." According to the card, the garment was in poor condition, and spreading it out on a small table, the signs of wear and repair became obvious. "They say he wore it all the time in Mongolia, you know," Tat'iana Sergeevna said to me as we leaned in a little to take a closer look.

* * *

We have only a handful of photographs of Ungern wearing his deel, though two in particular offer a good place to begin his story. In the first, he appears seated, deel-clad, in a wallpapered room. From the documents, we know that his full name is Baron Roman Feodorovich von Ungern-Sternberg and that he is a tsarist military officer and member of the Baltic German aristocracy, one of the favored elites of the old Russian Empire. We know, too, that he is thirty-five years old and a war hero, a fact advertised by the medal on his chest, the St. George's Cross, the imperial army's highest medal for valor. Finally, his moustache also tells us something: bushy and caterpillar-thick, it's the kind favored by the men of the Cossack regiments, the special frontier forces he has served with for years on the eastern borders of the empire. Posing here, he seems healthy and relaxed, despite the circumstances. The date of the photo is September 1 or 2, 1921, the location, Irkutsk, a city near Lake Baikal in Eastern Siberia. He had been captured a little over a week earlier in northern Mongolia by a unit of Red Army partisans. Though he was interrogated right away, he has been brought to Irkutsk now for further questioning.

At the time of his capture, Ungern was one of the last White commanders still fighting the Bolsheviks, also known as the communists or the Reds, in the brutal civil war that began raging in Russia shortly after the Bolsheviks seized power in October 1917. For most of the war his base was the Trans-Baikal region, some 500 miles to the east of Irkutsk, but when the Red Army began closing in on the area in the fall of 1920, he moved south into neighboring Mongolia, where he flushed out the Chinese republicans who were occupying the country at the time and quickly established himself as a kind of imported warlord, his power resting on his so-called Asiatic Division—a multinational cavalry force made up of Russians, Buryats, Ukrainians, Tatars, Bashkirs, Mongols, Chinese, and Japanese, among others. It was around this time that he began wearing his brightly colored deel. The idea, he says, was to make himself more visible to his troops in the field.

The interrogators already know this and much of the rest of what Ungern is telling them, in part because they have been following events in Mongolia closely over the preceding months but also because Red Army troops have captured copies of letters and other papers from his time in power in Urga (now Ulaanbaatar), the Mongolian capital, including his so-called Order No. 15, a curious document amounting to a cross between a combat order and a spiritual-political manifesto that he distributed to his troops a little earlier that spring.

I.1. Ungern in captivity in Irkutsk, September 1 or 2, 1921. Courtesy
State Central Museum of Contemporary History, Moscow.

During the interrogations, Ungern admits that he had had ambitious plans
in Mongolia. In taking over the country, his hope had been to launch a sweeping series of restorations, beginning with the restoration of the Mongolian ruler,
the Bogda, who had just recently been deposed by the republican Chinese.
(Ungern, in fact, formally reinstalled him shortly after taking Urga.) With this
accomplished, he then imagined resurrecting the fallen dynasty of the Qing
in China and the Romanovs in Russia, while also creating a vast new domain
at the center of the continent—what he described as a "central Mongolian
empire" (*sredinnoe mongol'skoe tsarstvo*)—that would unite the Mongols and

other nomads of the steppe under the Bogda, who would then dutifully pledge his own allegiance to the great "Manchu khan" in Beijing. The empires of old had come apart, but he, Ungern, would cobble them back together again.

He relates all of this matter-of-factly, but it's clear there is something mystical about him, as if he senses a deeper spiritual purpose at work in the events of the time. Indeed, as he sees it, the world is in the grips of a great existential crisis, a final reckoning being battled out between the white and yellow races on the one hand, and revolution and tradition on the other. For the moment, the revolutionaries have the upper hand. The twin "infections" of godlessness and socialism, both relayed from Europe, have destroyed Russia and are corrupting Asia as well—the best proof of it being the Chinese republicans who toppled the Qing in 1911 and, in his view, are no better than the Bolsheviks. Yet he is convinced that a turning point is just ahead. Soon the madness will ebb and the peoples of Asia, having returned to their senses, will rise up to destroy the revolution. Thus rather than any sort of "peril," the "yellows" represent the salvation everyone is waiting for, mankind's last hope for deliverance.

Of course, despite these portentous visions for humanity at large, things for Ungern himself have not worked out so well, and as the interrogators quiz him about the unraveling of his campaign, he is as candid about this as he is about everything else. He explains that, though he managed to take Urga, his position in the town was always vulnerable and, as a result, he could do little more than initiate his plans. He was also restless, impatient to get back to fighting the Reds. So, in late May, with most of his great restorationist project in Mongolia and China still hanging in the air, he decided to leave Urga and plunge into a new attack against Siberia, leading his division up to the border at Kiakhta under a brilliant yellow banner emblazoned with the monogram of Michael II, the brother of the former tsar Nicholas II, whom Ungern saw as the country's rightful ruler.

Almost immediately, however, the new campaign turned into a fateful mistake. The assault at Kiakhta was thrown back by the Red Army, forcing Ungern to continue his fight in the steppes and hills of the border zone without a strong base behind him. Then two months later came a final turn for the worse as a group of his officers mutinied and tried to kill him. He survived the coup but was caught by a Red patrol shortly thereafter.

In fact, it's because of this betrayal, he says, that he is willing to talk so openly. His own men having turned against him, there seems little point in hiding anything. Thus when the interrogators confront him with the multiple executions and other abuses carried out by the division as well as his own standing orders "to eliminate Jews and communists together with their families," he readily acknowledges the charges. As he sees it, the Jews caused the revolution, so they deserve whatever they get, and it's clear to him that Reds and Jews are essentially interchangeable, two sides of the same dirty coin. The interrogators also press him about the harsh punishments he meted out to his own men during the campaign, officers included. He admits to this as well.

The second photo continues the story. It is now some two weeks later, September 15, and we have moved a thousand miles west to the hardscrabble railway town of Novonikolaevsk (today, Novosibirsk), where Ungern has been brought for his trial, a show trial to be exact, since the event has been planned as an act of political theater and the outcome is not in doubt. In fact, Novonikolaevsk, far removed from where he fought in the war, has been selected for the occasion because it is the newly proclaimed "capital of Red Siberia" and the Communist government knows that a trial here will draw more attention. This photo shows him standing upright, flanked by two Red Army guards, a commissar behind him. We see now that he has the typical build of a cavalry officer: tall and lanky. Though he still wears his St. George's Cross, the thick cloth belt that would have run around his waist has been removed as a precaution against a suicide attempt. Without it, the garment seems to pour down from him like an ill-fitting drape.

The first photograph is our earliest physical proof of Ungern wearing his improvised uniform; the second, the last. Not long after the latter photo was taken, the court in Novonikolaevsk delivered its verdict, and either later that day or the next he was shot.

Everyday objects have a way of speaking to us, of revealing their owners in ways we—and they—might not expect. This is the case here as well. Though fitted with his epaulettes and cut to his height and frame, Ungern's deel was more than his alone—it also belonged to the multicultural world of the Russian Empire, and if he came to wear it, it is because he, too, was shaped by the myriad cross-cultural combinations and contradictions of his diverse imperial home. In fact, once we go looking for the empire in Ungern's story, we find it everywhere, at every stage and locale. Even the people who took the cloak from him that day in Novonikolaevsk were working within its shadow in their own complicated way.

* * *

This book is a study of the Russian Empire told through Ungern's life. One might choose other lives to do this, but Ungern's is more useful than most because he leads us into places and questions we rarely consider together.

Most studies of the empire focus on a region or a problem, or some combination of the two. The advantage of this approach is that it helps expose the many complexities of imperial life that tend to fall away when we make broad generalizations, while at the same time underscoring a basic truth: the empire was always defined by difference. No two imperial regions were the same, nor were they treated the same way. Even policies intended to have a more universal

I.2. At the trial in Novonikolaevsk, now Novosibirsk. Courtesy State Archive of Novosibirsk Oblast.

application rarely played out that way in practice. The traditional imperial order was a puzzle of accommodations made between the tsars and the different peoples of the realm, reflecting the alternating stages of the empire's history and its varied physical and cultural environments. The norm in this sense was no norm. Every part of the empire was an empire of its own.

Yet for all the importance of this basic observation, whenever we emphasize too much the singularity of the empire's individual pieces, we lose sight of the fact that the various parts did, in fact, fit together. Though stunningly diverse, the far-flung worlds of the empire were never truly separate. Instead ideas, goods, and people moved between them, tying them together into an incongruous whole. Many imperial subjects spent their lives in just one part of the state, enmeshed in the bonds of their local worlds. But numerous others knew the country on much broader terms, and the number of these people only increased as time went on.

Ungern was one of those people, and using his life to study the empire is, in effect, a way to capture this reality: to take in a picture of the country as a great sprawling piece, its disparate classes, peoples, and regions stitched together unevenly, even awkwardly, but nonetheless together. At the same time, his life coincided with the unraveling of the empire, and his experience opens up this reality for us as well. His moment of power in Mongolia was a direct consequence of imperial collapse, and his life before then unfolded in the midst of the many contradictions and fissures that made up the empire's awkward togetherness. He thus offers us a way to consider two of the most fundamental questions one could ask of any of the world's "vanished kingdoms," tsarist Russia included: what special bonds allowed these states to hold together, and why and how, at certain critical moments, did these bonds weaken and fall apart?[2]

The answers to these questions in Russia's case are more complicated than any single life could explain. But the basic premise of this book is that the personal experience of empire nonetheless has much to tell us about the bigger picture. Surveying empires from the great vantage of policies, structures, or ideologies, as historians usually do, we perceive one set of truths, but stepping into the shoes of imperial people, we see another.[3]

* * *

Ungern was an imperial person in the most basic of respects. Born in the sleepy provincial town of Graz in the Habsburg Empire and shot thirty-five years later in Western Siberia, his life in between was one of repeated movement across imperial spaces: first to the Caucasus and Estland (now Estonia), where he grew up; then St. Petersburg, where he completed officer training school; Manchuria, where he served as a private-volunteer in the Russo-Japanese War; and after his graduation, various points in the Trans-Baikal, the Amur, and the newly independent, formerly Chinese-ruled region of Outer Mongolia, where he served as an officer in the army's Cossack regiments. As World War I began, he returned to the European side of the country and fought on all the Russian fronts of the war, from East Prussia to northern Persia. Then during the revolutionary year of 1917, he moved back again to the Trans-Baikal, where became a commander under the warlord Ataman Semenov (the "A. S." of his epaulettes).

As Ungern moved within the circuits that bound up Russia's Eurasian world, he took on the habits of his various environments. He knew at least five languages: German, French, and Russian perfectly, as well as some Mongolian and Chinese. He was raised as a Lutheran but gravitated over time to a mix of mystical Christianity and Buddhism, while at the same time consulting with soothsayers and, as best we can tell, feeling comfortable enough with Russian

Orthodoxy to be married (to a Chinese Christian convert) in a Russian church in Harbin. Born into the ruling class as a Baltic baron, he spent most of his adult years among the Trans-Baikal Cossacks, who represented another sort of imperial order, much more plebeian than the barons but just as multicultural in their way. He absorbed imperial ideologies, including anti-Semitism and a fascination for Asia. Last but not least, he was very much a denizen of borders, living around the edges of the country and moving into neighboring empires easily and frequently. In that sense, he was not merely an imperial person but a transimperial one as well.

Yet what makes Ungern useful as a guide to the empire is not his highly imperial personal profile alone, but also his timing. His life coincided with the most decisive era of the empire's modern history. Born in the mid-1880s, he grew up in the midst of what turned out to be the tsars' last great push to modernize and tighten up their country. His was the age of Russification and the Trans-Siberian, of imperialist excitement then disappointment in East Asia, and also of nationalism and recurring questions about how and whether the different peoples of the empire should live together. The Revolution of 1905, which he experienced as a young cadet in St. Petersburg, was the first clear indication of how explosive these questions could become, and how hard they would be to resolve. Then came the terrific violence and dislocation of the Great War and the February Revolution, which overwhelmed the monarchy and opened the door to the unraveling of the empire, and finally the October Revolution and the civil war that confirmed the empire's end.

Thus within the span of his lifetime, just thirty-some years, the tsarist world passed from possibility to extinction. Ungern himself seems to have been unmoored by this great transformation, to the point, apparently, of wanting to turn back the clock entirely. Ironically, however, despite his intense devotion to the empire, what he represented most by the time of the Mongolian campaign was not the resurrection of the old imperial order but rather the chaotic rise of the nonstate frontier that filled the vacuum left by the empire's collapse, and if he failed in his ambitious plans, it was at least in part because he was unable to convert the frontier's volatile form of power into something more permanent. Instead, again ironically, it was his enemies, the Bolsheviks, who ultimately managed to do this. Though they despised the empire in every way and were committed to destroying it, they nonetheless did the most to bring it back by erecting their new imperial order—the USSR—on the smoking remains of the old.

· · ·

Though my book traces the path of Ungern's life, it is meant as a microhistory rather than a biography. In a biography, the objective is to tell a life story, and, because of this, even when biographers take a broad approach to their subjects, as the good ones usually do, they nonetheless make the life the priority. In the end, it's the unique qualities and special value or significance of the individual person that they are seeking to explain. In a microhistory, by contrast, the method often involves the telling of a life, but the life itself is mostly a tool. The goal is to use it to explain something else, something larger.[4]

Though an obscure figure in the grand sweep of the Russian Revolution, Ungern has received a fair amount of attention from historians and other writers because of the extremism and exoticism of the Mongolian campaign: the killings, the mysticism, the imperial dreams, the deel. Even before his death he had begun to be described as the "mad baron of Mongolia" and by other variants on the madness theme, and this way of seeing him has persisted over the years, creating a small international library of mostly sensational Ungerniana.[5] Despite these various studies, we still know little about him if only because there is, in fact, very little to know. With the exception of the letters and orders of the Mongolian period, he left virtually nothing in his own hand, making it almost impossible "to climb into his head" in search of the interior world biographers usually hope to find.[6] His talkative interrogation transcripts are an exception. Indeed, for most of his life he barely appears in the sources at all, just the faintest traces in now long-forgotten schoolbooks and military files.

As I reconstruct his life in the chapters that follow, I try to bring the limited sources we have about him into the story so that you, the reader, can judge how I have reached my conclusions. I explore the anecdotes that are often repeated about him, trying to see how well they match up with the firmer things we know. My research took me to many of the sites of his life, so I bring my sense of these places into the text as well, using my impressions of what they look like today to help imagine how they might have been in his time. Finally, because it is so hard to resist, on those occasions when the sources run out and all one can do is to guess at what Ungern might have been thinking, I, too, take the plunge and make a few speculations of my own (judiciously, of course).

At the same time, my focus is less on Ungern than on the empire around him, and approached this way, the fact that we rarely get a good look at him is not necessarily a problem. We might wish that he would tell us more about what he was thinking or doing at different moments, yet we don't really need him to. We just need him to lead us into his surroundings, and we can make him do this relatively easily. With a simple turn of our camera, we can transform him from a poor biographical subject into a revealing microhistorical one.[7]

This is what I have tried to do here, to reposition the way we look at Ungern so that he can help us make sense of the complicated experience of the empire in a remarkable time. His usefulness for this approach is tied in part to the fact that he lived in so many places. To capture this breadth of experience, each of the chapters of the book is centered on a key site or region of his life, starting with Graz and ending with Novonikolaevsk, allowing us to transit between them as he did, in succession, one after the other.

By providing this geographical frame, I hope to impart a sense of the great horizontal connectedness of the empire, revealing both the varying ties that bound it to its neighbors, such as the empires of Europe and China, as well as its internal linkages. Indeed, a key argument of the book is that these knots of connection, both internal and external, help to explain how the empire "worked" as well as how it fell apart, and what then allowed the Bolsheviks to reassemble it, albeit partially and under different terms, after the revolution.

Ungern's greatest value for a microhistory of the empire, however, is that he takes us into the complicated questions of his time. In each of the locations of his life we see a snapshot of the imperial machinery: the government's policies, the dynamics of local society, the intertwining of cultures, all of which gives us a feel for the empire's paradoxical combination of strength and weakness. Russia's rulers in the late imperial era were conservative modernizers whose basic goal was to strengthen the state by making it more coherent and, where necessary, more national—that is, more Russian—seeking, in effect, to finally create the single imperial space that had never truly existed before. This difficult undertaking, however, only added contradictions and tensions to a society that was already brimming with them. As a member of the nobility and the officer corps, two of the most important pillars of the old regime, Ungern lived at the heart of this complexity. That he was a Russianized Baltic German whose life unfolded largely on the edges of the empire rather than at the center only reinforced this, for it was precisely in the borderlands and in their complicated pathways of cross-cultural contact that the country's challenges as a multinational home were posed most sharply.

In fact, the recurring features of Ungern's life turn out to have been the great questions of the last stage of the empire's history: the problem of borders, how they should be drawn, and who should live within them. Ungern moved easily within and between empires. In that sense, he reminds us of the striking liquidity of his age of transcontinental railroads, mass migrations, and global capital flows. At the same time, everywhere he moved he encountered the uncertainties produced by mobility, questions about who belonged and who didn't within a given community, as well as the changing relationships between centers and peripheries, nations and empires, "East" and "West." In fact, over the course of his life the borders he lived around so repeatedly were themselves in movement, waxing and waning in importance, disappearing and then reappearing in new places. These borders became sites of enormous bloodshed as well as great creativity, places for killing and for imagining. Getting down to the personal level we see how these paradoxical mixtures came about and their equally paradoxical consequences.

Ungern's passage through the complexities of his time is ultimately a disturbing story. It is hard to know exactly when his inclination toward violence and extremism began, though the Great War must have played a formative part. Certainly by the end of his life these habits had become second nature, as he ordered executions easily and was confident in his hatreds. The only excuse we can make for him is that this was also true of many others around him, including the Bolsheviks, who were just as dedicated in their extremism as he was, only in a different key. He doesn't stand for the old empire any more than they do or than any single person could, but all the actors of the revolution were shaped by the same imperial milieu and, in particular, by the way it came apart, so in that sense if we study the questions and relationships of the empire we are sure to see something of how this came to be.

*   *   *

Here again the deel serves as a kind of touchstone. As we move with Ungern from one place to the next, his experiences adding up around us, we come to understand why his cross-cultural uniform might have spoken to him. Even before he knew anything about Mongolia, he was already familiar with the complicated politics of transiting between cultures and frontiers. The cloak also reflected the stark choices one had to make during the revolution. In 1917, embittered soldiers furiously tore the epaulettes from their officers' shoulders, seeing them as hated symbols of the old order. Horrified by the unraveling of the army symbolized by this kind of fury, White officers like Ungern made a point of putting their epaulettes back on. The Red Army, by contrast, did not.

In fact, it must have been at least in part to highlight this difference, and even to mock him for it, that the authorities in Novonikolaevsk kept him in his deel for the trial. There he was, on stage for the whole world to see, pathetic shoulder boards and all: the wretched, eccentric representative of an outmoded world, about to get the revolutionary comeuppance he so richly deserved.

Once the verdict came in, did his executioners think much about the cloak as they took it from him? Did he?

CHAPTER 1

GRAZ

Yes! I know from where I have sprung!
—Friedrich Nietzsche. *The Gay Science*

The Mansion District

Leechgasse begins just beyond the limits of the Inner Town (*Innere Stadt*), the early core of Graz once bounded by the city wall. From there, the street runs east, away from the old town, cutting a swath for about a mile through the comfortable residential area of Geidorf. Baron Nikolai Roman Max von Ungern-Sternberg was born on this street, in house Number 5, on January 10, 1886.[1]

The details of the day are unknown, but we know at least that he entered the world among his own kind. Of the twenty-six houses that stood on the street that year, nine were owned by nobles of one rank or another—barons, counts, hereditary knights (*Rittern*), or simply "vons." Josephine von Degrazia lived at Number 24, Count Bardeau lived at Number 1, *Ritter* Wilhelm von Artens and his wife Elise von Edle resided at Number 7.[2] Other well-born folk clustered along nearby streets, including elegant Elisabethstrasse, a newly laid out boulevard of stately apartment houses and walled gardens.[3]

Graz began in the late medieval period as the outpost of colonists who drifted down to the Southern Alps from what is today southern Germany. The region then, like all of Austria, was a marchland (*Mark*), an uncertain frontier where the new German arrivals mixed with Slavs and Magyars. (Slovenia today is just a short train ride away.) The region around Graz, Styria (*Steiermark* in German), still reflects the history of the frontier in its name, as does the town: "Graz" comes from an old Slavonic word for small castle or fortification (*gradets*).

Today most of the Slavic influences are gone, but there is still a castle. It looms over the city on the top of a 1,200-foot hill, the Schlossberg (literally: the Castle Mount).[4] Looking down from the high ramparts, you see the Mur River running slightly to the west. Ungern's old neighborhood extends to the east. And just below, pinched between the Mur and the foot of the hill, lies the old town, a dense warren of red-roofed storybook-style stone houses and churches, punctuated in places by the small openings of market squares. From high up, the old heart of the city is a picturesque jumble. The lines of Geidorf, by comparison, are more even. In Ungern's time, the contrast would have been all the more striking. At once superbly modern and comfortably conservative, it was the suburb of the upper class, a quiet mansion district (*Villenviertel*) where people of means could seek their refuge from both the old and the new.

In Graz, as in much of Europe in the nineteenth century, the new began with the railroad, which arrived in 1844. Right behind the train came other heralds of modern times: a police force, a trolley system (first horse-drawn, then electric), inspectors, tax collectors, clerks, and growing numbers of students, decked out in their frock coats and short caps, who crowded into the town's new commercial and technical schools as well as the old sixteenth-century university. Factories and workers appeared, along with the so-called *Grossbürgertum*—wealthy merchants, lawyers, doctors, entrepreneurs—who installed themselves as city fathers and busily remade Graz into their vision of a modern city.

New districts spread out across the Mur. The old city walls were cleared. The population climbed. By 1883, the town had become the fourth largest city in Austria, home to close to a hundred thousand people, more than twice the number that had lived there just forty years earlier.[5] The only thing that did not change much was the town's ethnic and religious profile. Much as it had been since the time of the Counter-Reformation, Graz remained overwhelmingly German and Catholic. Jews and Protestants were small minorities. Slovenes, the largest non-German group in the city, made up less than 10 percent of the population.[6]

What would the noble types of Leechgasse have thought of the changing city around them? We can guess that they would have been impressed but also perhaps a little wary. Like their peers elsewhere in the Habsburg Empire and across the continent, the bluebloods of Graz were specialists of stability rather than transformation. For centuries, they had admired the view from the peak of Europe's pyramid, enjoying the gifts of a social system that codified what seemed to be a God-given link between birth on the one hand and authority and wealth on the other. According to this system, nobles were nobles because

Graz.

Graz: Hauptplatz mit Blick auf den Schloßberg.

1.1. Graz's main square in the 1880s. The Schlossberg and its distinctive clock tower (the *Uhrturm*)
loom in the background. Reproduced from P. K. Rosseger et al., *Wanderungen durch
Steiermark und Kärnten* (Stuttgard, n.d.), 93.

their fathers and forefathers had been nobles before them, and because they
were nobles, they owned land and dictated terms to every one else. They controlled the very top of the pyramid, which meant that they dominated the base
as well. Practically speaking, not even kings or queens stood above the nobles
since monarchs, too, depended on the highest nobles for their power.[7] The presumption of noble control was remarkably enduring, standing largely unchal-
lenged for centuries. Whenever Europeans lower in the pyramid grew tired of
bearing the weight of the people above them, rebellions flared. But the upheav-
als almost never challenged the nobles' right to rule. Instead, the rebels made
a point of brutally killing the nobles they detested for ruling badly. The rebels
were then themselves invariably brutally crushed, or they agreed to concede,
and the system reverted to form. It wasn't until the 1700s when the philosophes
and revolutionaries of the Enlightenment began to denounce what they called
the conjoined evils of "slavery, feudalism, and heredity" that the structure of
noble privilege showed the first signs of cracking.[8]

Yet once the cracks appeared, the structure weakened quickly. A number of nobles lost their heads (literally) in the French Revolution. Many more survived but saw their political and economic influence diminished by the great changes that swept through the continent in the 1800s. Industrialization created new wealth outside the noble class. Slow but noticeable democratization—the opening of parliaments, the expansion of suffrage—diluted the nobles' political clout. The pyramid that the wellborn of Europe had dominated for so long suddenly seemed to be flattening out. "Aristocracies," wrote the British critic Matthew Arnold in 1869, "are for epochs of concentration." "In epochs of expansion, such as our own . . . [they] appear bewildered and helpless."[9] By the end of the century, with the growth of working-class and middle-class politics, the nobility's most ardent critics were confident that their bell had begun to toll. The lords and ladies, it seemed, were finished.

Reports of the death of the nobility, however, turned out to be premature. For even as the world changes, much stays the same, and so it was with the nobles. The old social pyramid of Europe had indeed begun to flatten out, but the traditional hierarchy did not collapse in one go, and many nobles used their privilege to adjust to the developments around them. As a result, even at the end of the nineteenth century, all across Europe titled men from the oldest families continued to rule governments and armies. They remained the largest landowners. The most adaptive and enterprising nobles became successful industrialists and bankers. Others made careers in the new business of (limited) electoral politics. Most important, the nobility as a group held onto a powerful sense of corporate identity.[10] Though divided by wealth and rank and increasingly influenced by the new industrial bourgeoisie gaining power around them, most nobles thought of themselves as members of a separate society—the denizens of a special universe with its own expectations, habits, and moral sensibilities.

This was especially true of the aristocracy, the richest and oldest of the noble families. The highest born of Europe married each other, attended each other's clubs, balls, and funerals, looked after their friends and relatives in business and government, and shared a common attachment to the manor (or castle) lifestyle.[11] They patrolled their lineages by keeping their own scrupulously maintained genealogies and tracked each other's comings and goings in the society pages. This rarified aristocratic world lasted largely intact up to the Great War and even beyond.[12]

In the Habsburg Empire in the 1880s, the unrivaled focus of noble life was Vienna. All the highest families had residences there, most of them nestled in the old center of the city, close to the emperor's palace, the baroque-styled Hofburg, encircled by winding cobblestone streets and the gently greening bronzes of glorious monarchs. In the elegant mansions and boardrooms of the great city, the *Hoffähig* (literally: "those presentable at court") made the quiet

arrangements that had worked for centuries to keep them in charge, while turning the city at the same time into their playground—a "never-ending vortex" of
"festivities, balls and concerts, riding exhibitions and parades, gala theatrical
performances, and garden parties," as one nostalgic princess remembered.[13]

Compared with Vienna, the noble globe of Graz turned far more slowly.
Most of the town's titled families were locals with estates in the nearby countryside. Others were tourists from around Europe who moved to the town for
the summer or winter seasons, where they rented apartments or took suites
at the Erzherzog Johann on the Hauptplatz, Graz's most genteel hotel. Still others were retirees—privileged pensioners from the Habsburg civil service and
officer corps who came to the banks of the Mur "to seek the gentle comfort
of their repose." Travel writers and guide books of the late nineteenth century proudly described the town as "Pensionopolis" and remarked on the high
density of retired generals.[14]

By the 1880s, the nobles' influence over politics in Graz had been largely
replaced by the new power of the *Grossbürgertum*. But the counts, barons,
and vons still lent a certain tone. They patronized theaters and horse races,
attended lectures at the university and local scholarly societies, endowed the
town's churches and charities. On spring afternoons, noble families enjoyed
coffee and ice cream at the Café Wirth in the city park near the base of the
Schlossberg. During the New Year's holidays and the carnival season that followed (*Fasching*), they danced and drank at hotel ballrooms or one another's
mansions.[15] Around the time of Ungern's birth, during the snowy days of early
January 1886, local papers reported a rash of traffic accidents as horse-drawn
sleighs and cabs ferried the town's finer residents from one New Year's event
to the next.[16]

The Transnationals

Though we move through numerous worlds in life, we begin with one. The
noble world of Graz was Ungern's first society. His family left the city when he
was just three years old, well before Graz could have had a meaningful impact.
Yet even in these earliest years, it mattered where he lived. Ungern seems to
have maintained a connection to Austria over the rest of his life. He returned to
visit Graz as a boy. His maternal grandmother lived there permanently in her
last decades (she died in 1925). His younger brother Constantin made his life
in Shanghai after the Russian Revolution but returned to Austria in the 1930s,
dying in Vienna at the end of World War II. And as the anti-Bolshevik front in
Eastern Siberia eroded around him in 1920, Ungern himself appears to have
considered returning to his "homeland," but the Austrians refused him a visa.[17]

Leechgasse 5 no longer exists. The house, renumbered later as 21, was torn
down in the 1960s to make way for a squat beige office building. In photographs

taken just before the demolition, we see a weathered but imposing two-story stone home with wrought-iron balconies and the traces of elegant carvings along the windows and soffits. The other late Habsburg-era homes that still stand on the street have a similar look—handsome two- and three-story urban mansions with high portals and terraces, some of them still presiding over leafy lots that once contained landscaped paths, small fountains, and gazebos.[18] These were comfortable residences for large families and squads of "staff." The Ungern-Sternbergs' villa would have been home to at least eleven people: five servants (possibly more)—a cook, maid, caretaker, nanny, and coachman—and six lords and ladies: baby Ungern, his older sister Constance (aged two), his parents, his maternal grandmother Amélie, and his mother's younger brother, also his godfather, Baron Max von Wimpffen.

Through his parents, Ungern was tied to the Germanic nobilities of Europe. Ungern's mother, Sophie Charlotte von Wimpffen (1861–1907), came from an old noble family with roots in Wimpffen am Neckar, a small medieval-era spa town in the wine country of Baden-Württemberg in southern Germany.[19] Beginning in the late eighteenth century, members of the Wimpffen clan acquired lands in the Habsburg Empire, and Sophie Charlotte's branch of the family appears to have had relatives in Austria by the mid-1800s. In a registry of Styrian landowners from 1873, her father and a maternal uncle are listed as the owners of a small estate of mostly "mountain pasture" (*Alpen*) not far from Graz.[20]

It's not clear if Ungern's mother grew up on the Austrian estate, but her ties to Styria must explain why the family was living in Graz at the time of Ungern's birth. At least three Wimpffen lines were established in Austria then. The most prominent were counts (*Grafen*), members of the empire's high nobility (*Hochadel*) and part of so-called court society, the highest tier of some four hundred noble families with access to the imperial court in Vienna.[21] These Wimpffens were true magnates, with large estates in Styria as well as other regions of Austria and the empire. Ungern's mother's family were barons (*Freiherrn*), one rank below the counts. They owned far less land and, in keeping with the snobby bias of court society, had noticeably lower status.[22] Ungern's grandmother was a widow by the time of his birth. The family appears to have been renting the house on Leechgasse. They then moved and rented another house just one street over when Ungern's younger brother was born two years later.

Ungern's father was from a more prominent family. Theodor IV Leonhard Rudolf von Ungern-Sternberg (1857–1918/23) was a descendant of one of the most recognized aristocratic clans of the Russian Baltic whose ancestry stretched to the thirteenth century, when the first Sternberg came to medieval Livonia as a knight in the service of the northern crusades.[23] Over time, the family expanded, both in number and in wealth, and by the mid-1800s seven branches of Ungern-Sternbergs stretched out across the eastern Baltic region from Kurland in the south, north around the Gulf of Riga, to the provinces

Map 2. Central Europe, late nineteenth century. Though Ungern's mother came from southern Germany and his father from the Russian imperial province of Estland, the family was living in Austria-Hungary when he was born. How they met is unclear, but their transimperial life was not unusual for aristocrats of the time.

of Livland and Estland. Theodor's family came from the northern tip of this band of aristocratic settlement, with roots on the small island of Dagö (now Hiiumaa) in Estland province.

The Ungern-Sternbergs of Estland were members of the so-called original nobility (*Uradel*) made up of the seventy-five oldest families in the province.

Their name was listed on the First Register (*Matrikel*) of the provincial nobility along with other storied families: the Rosens, Stackelbergs, Meyendorffs, Pahlens, Taubes, Wrangels, Uexkulls;[24] and their crest hung in the nave of the main Protestant cathedral in Reval (now Tallinn), the head city of the province. Ungern's father's family was neither the wealthiest of the Estland nobles nor even the wealthiest of the Ungern-Sternbergs, but they certainly benefited from the general halo of their name. The clan's ancestors had worked in Russian service since the tsars annexed the Baltic lands in the early 1700s. (An Ungern-Sternberg had handed over the keys of Reval to Peter the Great.) Even within the much larger Russian nobility, the Ungern-Sternbergs were known as one of the most esteemed houses of the state.

We do not know how or where Ungern's parents met, though their Baltic German/Austrian German union was not unusual. The most important concerns of the marriage market of the Germanic aristocracy in the late nineteenth century were rank and wealth. Religion mattered, but one could always convert or make other accommodations, as many spouses did. In the case of Ungern's parents, both families were Protestant. They were also old (in the sense of having long genealogies), landed, and baronial—"nobility of birth" (*Geburtsadel*) rather than "nobility of money" (*Geldadel*).

The only thing less than completely ordinary about the union between Theodor and Sophie was that elite Baltic German nobles rarely married outside their own narrow range of Baltic German families, a practice that allowed them to concentrate their wealth and political patronage all the more tightly within a small and powerful circle.[25] (This also led to accusations of excessive inbreeding.) But Theodor was the fourth son in his family, so his parents would probably have been less concerned about this issue in his case. As for Sophie Charlotte's parents, given their family's relatively lesser standing within the Austrian nobility, a groom from the venerable Ungern-Sternbergs would likely have seemed a promising match. In any case, for both families the fact that their children had found partners from another empire would have seemed entirely unremarkable.

This was because by the late nineteenth century the aristocratic world of Europe was fundamentally multinational—an "antipasto" of peoples jumbled together.[26] Leafing through the bulging volumes of the *Almanach de Gotha*, the preeminent registry of the old aristocracy, one finds page after page of international partnerships—marriages between families from Austria and Italy, Italy and France, Britain and Germany, Germany and Sweden. Even the large majority of aristocratic families that married within their own national set were devoted cosmopolitans whose lifestyles tended to combine "the French language, the English hunt, and the Prussian monocle."[27]

Cultural borrowing of this sort was in fact so much a norm that it also became a value. The primary allegiance of the well-bred male aristocrat was to the family name and honor. The second was to the monarch, who, as Aristocrat

Number One, was regarded as the essential guardian of the class. Beyond that, however, the most meaningful loyalty was to a general sense of nobleness, a noble way of life that was based on knowing foreign languages (English and French, first and foremost), traveling to the cultured spots of the continent, and sharing the habits and tastes of transnational society. The class ideal thus favored a kind of rooted (rather than rootless) cosmopolitanism. The model aristocrat was supposed to be from the manor but of the world.[28]

Among these worldly aristocrats, the Germans were arguably the most transnational of all. That is, more than many of their continental peers, their lives tended to "transcend [the borders] of any one nation-state, empire, or politically defined territory."[29] In the late nineteenth century, German speakers were divided between four countries—Germany, Switzerland, the Habsburg Empire, and Russia—but ties between the Germanic nobilities of these states were close and often personal. Ungern grew up within the folds of these connections.

His father and all his paternal uncles attended German universities before returning home to pursue business or service paths in the Russian Empire. His mother's relatives had branches in both Germany and Austria. And his maternal grandmother was of Swiss-Italian origin, though she was born in Munich. All of them crossed borders easily and frequently. If the various members of the two sides of Ungern's family had ever gathered for a Sunday picnic, their accents would have stood out, but they would have understood each other's High German (*Hochdeutsch*) perfectly—or they might have switched to French. (Ungern later claimed in Mongolia that French was his best language.) And as they prattled away over the clinking of the china that their servants pulled from the picnic baskets, they would have shared a common digest of European news, high culture, and aristocratic gossip.

Coming up with a precise term to describe how aristocrats like the Ungern-Sternbergs and Wimpffens saw themselves is difficult. They were obviously Europeans in the sense of belonging to "the vicinage of Europe"—a continental neighborhood that by their time had long possessed a clear cultural identity.[30] They were subjects of the Habsburg and Russian empires, with state passports in their travel bags. And they were also people with deep attachments to their respective "subnational places"—Styria and Estland.[31] In the heavy, leather-bound book that records Ungern's baptism in the Protestant Church of the Savior in Graz in April 1886, his mother and father are defined by their titles, religion, and the specific location of their birth rather than by categories of nationality.[32] And yet, along with these identities, both Sophie and Theodor would certainly have seen themselves as Germans—not in the sense of being nationals of a German state but rather as members of a broader German world (*Deutschtum*), defined by German "speech culture" (*Sprachkultur*) and *Kultur* more generally. Baron Otto von Taube, born just a few years before Ungern and a neighbor of the family's in Estland, described his fellow Baltic aristocrats as people "rooted in their local place (*Heimat*)—in the estate, in the soil . . . and in a German essence or spirit (*Geist*)...which is the product of the German language."[33]

Even in the late nineteenth century, this transnational lifestyle still seemed natural enough. One might live outside of "Germany proper" (variously defined) yet still define oneself as German. One could float within a fluid universe of cosmopolitan aristocrats and still have one's feet firmly planted in the ancestral manor. Yet at the same time, things were changing. National ideas were starting to pressure aristocrats to make hard choices. Europe in the 1880s was a continent of "nationalizing states." Some of these states were new creations—Italy, Germany, Bulgaria, for example. Others like Great Britain, France, Spain, and the Habsburg and Romanov empires were much older. But all of them were affected by the "rapidly rising prestige...of the national idea." And so too were communities within these countries—the Poles and the Irish, for example—who aspired to create (or re-create) states of their own.[34] In 1774, Johann Gottfried Herder, an early prophet of the cultural nation, had declared that "every nation contains its center of happiness within itself."[35] A century later this sort of thinking had become old hat. Almost every one assumed that being happy did indeed mean being national (and vice versa), and earnest work was well underway to make the nation as happy as possible.

As it turned out, however, the road to national contentment was far from easy. Across Europe, various nations claimed the same territory; others had no territory at all; almost every national group, according to at least one of its neighbors, appeared to have its history wrong; and no single nation or state was as homogenous or cohesive as its leaders wanted it to be. Because of their diffusion across the broad center of the continent, German speakers found themselves caught in all of these complications—from all sides. As a result, wherever they lived, they quickly became the focus of "German questions."

In the new Prussian-centered German Empire (*Kaiserreich*) created in 1871, the "German question" seemed simple enough. The national territory had been cobbled together out of a patchwork of duchies and principalities. Now the territory's population had to be forged into a single "German people" (*Deutsches Volk*). Part of this work would require getting the "new" Germans to think about themselves differently. They would need updated versions of history, new monuments, new institutions to strengthen their bonds. But part of the work would also mean assimilating (or expelling) inhabitants who were not German enough, in particular, the country's various minorities of Alsatians, Danes, and Poles. Some influential nationalists went further still: They dreamed of building a "Greater Germany" with borders that would encompass not only the Germans of the *Reich* but also all the German speakers of the continent, from the southern Alps to the eastern Baltic. This vision was inherently dangerous since it essentially meant going to war to claim Germans who were currently the subjects of other empires, but to these patriots at least, even war was a small price to pay for national fulfillment.[36]

In the land of Ungern's birth, however, the "German question" looked quite different. Like the Prussians, the Austrian rulers of the Habsburg Empire were Germans in a cultural sense, but they were very much runners up in the German world. The Habsburgs had lost a costly war with the Prussians in 1866, and though they had managed to keep their state from being cobbled into the new German Reich they had obvious reasons for not being ardent supporters of a broader German cause on the international stage.

On the domestic front, they were just as hesitant. Unlike the new Germany, the Habsburg Empire was not even remotely a German-dominated state. Germans made up the largest share of the civil service and officer corps, and German was the language of high culture and administration. But the state's formal title after 1867 was the Dual Monarchy of Austria-Hungary, reflecting the country's division into two parts, with two separate parliaments and administrations linked by a limited common government and a monarch who was at once emperor of Austria and king of Hungary (among other titles). Within the "motley mixture of peoples" that made up the two sides of the empire, Germans amounted to less than a quarter of the population. Even in the "Austrian" part of the state (Cisleithania), which included regions such as Bohemia, Slovenia, Galicia, and the Tyrol, German speakers did not exceed 40 percent.[37]

Given the diversity of the realm, promoting German nationalism—or any nationalism—was risky business. But more to the point, the Habsburgs were not inclined to promote nationalism because they were not nationalists. Emperor Franz Joseph (r. 1848–1916) saw himself as the "father" of all eleven of the officially recognized national groups in his state and, like a good, old-fashioned dynast, he was quite happy to have his subjects sing the state anthem in all eleven languages.[38] "The emperor's dream," as the historian Timothy Snyder has put it, "was of an empire of peoples devoted to their ruler, *despite* nationalism. Nationalism was inevitable, national unification was inevitable, but it need not weaken the Habsburgs."[39]

In fact, the Habsburg order in the 1880s was itself so nonnationalist (even unnationalist) in its orientation that it showed little interest in the practice (much beloved by nation-states) of telling people what nation they belong to. A Supreme Court decision from 1881 made a point of stressing that the central government should not be permitted to decide matters of "national status": "To the single person, adherence to a . . . national group is essentially a matter of feeling," the court concluded. "Therefore [an individual] shall be considered a member of that national group to which he says he belongs according to his own declaration."[40] In other words, as far as the highest Habsburg court was concerned, nationality was personal rather than political. One was German (or Hungarian or Serbian) only if one wanted to be.

Not surprisingly, this sort of national agnosticism did not sit well with Austrian German nationalists. As they saw it, the Germans were the ruling people

of the Habsburg state—the *Herrenvolk*—and their culture needed to be promoted, especially in places like Bohemia where Germans were "drowning in a
Slavic sea."[41] The government also had to do more to check the Magyarization
being pursued by the Hungarians in their half of the country. Indeed, there was
a gathering sense not only among self-appointed "guardians of the nation" but
also among educated Austrians and Europeans more generally that the country's "German element" was losing ground. In 1880, a census of language use
in the empire revealed that far fewer people spoke German than most German
speakers had assumed, and the upsetting findings of the census coincided with
the election of a "pro-Slavic" parliament.[42]

Austrian Germans in the 1880s were anxious, and national slights—or at
least perceived national slights—were common. One British writer tells the
story of a Count von Falkenstein from the mixed German-Italian region of Tyrol who tried to buy a train ticket from Roveredo to Botzen. The count asked
for his fare at the station in German as he had always done, only to find himself
rebuffed by the stiff wind of national prickliness. "'Botzen?,' the Italian clerk
responded. 'Don't know the place.... I presume you mean 'Bolzano.'"[43]

Austria's earliest German national program was drafted by a small circle
of intellectuals in Linz in 1882. But by the 1890s, Graz had overtaken Linz
as the country's "semi-official [headquarters] for the exponents of German-
ism."[44] Nationalist writers found it easy to publish in the city, using the platform offered by sympathetic local newspapers. Student groups and charities
began adding the adjectives "German" (*deutsch*) or "national" (*völkisch*) to
their names. Ethnographers fanned out from the university to document the
"warm-hearted (*gemütlich*) German inhabitants of Styria." And local authorities projected an image of Graz as an appealingly national antidote to overly
multinational Vienna—a modern Austrian German city with its own *Ring-
straße,* opera house, and grand city hall but without the capital's (in their view)
off-putting "goulash" of Jews, Slavs, and foreigners.[45] "We hope," wrote Graz's
main *völkisch* daily in 1884, "that our city shall never cease to call itself—and
will forever remain—purely German."[46]

Sleepy, provincial Graz can thus be seen as one of the unlikely pressure
points of European modernity. By the late 1880s the town stood like a series of
open questions posed to the future: Was it right for states to be multinational in
an age of nationalism? What was the proper relationship between unity and diversity? What kind of unity should one strive for? Should one even strive for it at
all? Aristocratic families like the Ungern-Sternbergs and the Wimpffens found
themselves in the middle of these conundrums. For centuries their variety of
highborn cosmopolitanism had been so natural as to be uncontroversial. But
even as Ungern burbled in his baby clothes, the landscape was changing. What
seemed natural now—increasingly—was to be national, and anything else was
potentially suspect. To the nationalists, German or otherwise, the countless

counts, earls, and barons of Europe who remained supra- or multinational in their habits were not just laughable anachronisms—they were "amphibians," untrustworthy types who were neither one thing nor the other.[47] "Cosmopolitanism is a crime," intoned the Russian nationalist Vasilii Rozanov, speaking for xenophobes across the continent. "It's a mutt that will eat anything" (*nichem ne brezguet*).[48]

The transnational, cosmopolitan Ungern-Sternbergs left Graz for Russia sometime in early 1889. Grandmother Amélie went with them, as did the new family member, Constantin, who was born in Graz in October 1888.[49] In departing Austria for Russia, the family stepped out of one thicket of imperial dilemmas and into another.

CHAPTER 2

ESTLAND

"All this detail—these memories of our country world of childhood ... of wood and meadow, pond and hill."
—THOMAS MANN, *Dr. Faustus*

The Subcontractors

Hiiumaa Island lies twelve miles off the western coast of Estonia in the Baltic Sea. In the late nineteenth century, this small outcrop of windswept rock was one of the westernmost fringes of the Russian Empire, closer to Stockholm and Gotland than St. Petersburg. Today the ferry crossing from the Estonian mainland takes just an hour and a half, but the island still feels like an isolated place.

Thick birch and pine forests cover much of the land. One sees few cars or people. Here and there the pointy steeples of Lutheran churches poke up amid the treetops. The Ungern-Sternberg clan used to own properties throughout Hiiumaa, including a sizeable two-story house in the small port of Kärdla, the largest town on the island. The plain white house (current address: Number 8, Factory Square [Vabrikuväljak]) is long and broad, topped with a high red-tiled roof. Behind the rear veranda runs a wide area of trees and lawn known as Parunipark—the Baron's Park. Today the building is home to the Hiiumaa history museum.[1]

Ungern's father grew up in the house at Kärdla, though he and his family would have known it by the German name of Kertel. The Germans also called the island Dagö rather than Hiiumaa. The double names reflect the fact that the island then was divided between two disproportionate communities.

A small number of German nobles owned most of the land, while Estonian commoners made up most of the inhabitants. In practice, this meant that the Estonians worked for the Germans. Ungern's grandfather, Robert Eginhard von Ungern-Sternberg, rented out farmland to Estonian peasants. Estonian servants tended his house and grounds, and several hundred more "peasant proletarians" worked in the textile factory that he owned near Kertel harbor. By the time of his death in 1898, the factory was a prosperous complex that included a Lutheran chapel, a clinic, a volunteer fire department, a post and telegraph office, a credit union, a choral society, neatly laid out worker houses, "one school for [the children of] the German factory managers, [and] two schools for the Estonian population."[2]

The division on the island reflected the norm on the mainland. The Russian Baltic consisted of three provinces—Estland, Livland, and Curland—whose collective borders roughly coincide with the modern states of Estonia and Latvia. Estland, the smallest and most northerly of the group, like the others (and like faraway Styria), was a frontier of German conquest and settlement in the late Middle Ages. German bishops and knights came to wage holy war against the "heathen" Estonians, receiving land and indulgences from the Church in return. German merchants followed, making their profits on trade with the crusader castle towns whose rounded turrets and pitched roofs still dot the coasts and inland waterways.[3]

As centuries passed, the region changed hands repeatedly. Denmark ruled part of the area for a period, then the Livonian Order, Poland, Sweden, and finally the Russian Empire, which annexed all of Estland and the eastern Baltic from the Swedes in the early eighteenth century. In every case, however, regardless of which higher power claimed the area, deals were struck, and it was the German speakers—German merchants in the towns and German knights overall—who remained in charge. They were the rulers. The Estonians, by contrast, were the exploited. Categorized by the German lords and burghers as socially inferior "non-Germans" (*Undeutsche*), they were barred from the guilds and noble associations and turned into a rural underclass. Until 1816–1819, they were enserfed.[4]

Such was the curious world of the Russian Empire in the middle decades of the nineteenth century. Estland at the time had been a part of the empire for approximately one hundred and fifty years, but little about it was "Russian" in a meaningful sense. Germans made up the ruling class, the population was overwhelmingly Estonian, and with the exception of a few Russian officials and military men in the provincial capital of Reval (Estonian: Tallinn; Russian: Revel'), signs of Russian power were few and far between. Yet what seems odd to us now—a Russian imperial province ruled by Germans—was a commonplace then. The Russians, like many empire-builders before them, took advantage of the services of local elites to reinforce their power as they expanded their state into non-Russian areas. At the heart of the relationship was

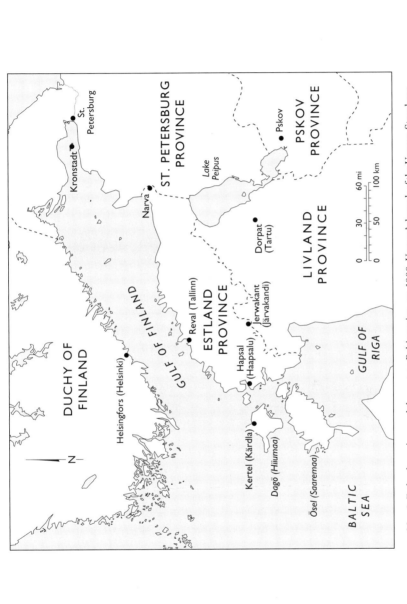

Map 3. Estland province and the eastern Baltic region, ca. 1900. Ungern's branch of the Ungern-Sternberg clan had historic ties to Hiiumaa Island (known to the Germans as Dagö) located just off the Estonian coast. Though Ungern surely spent time on the island as a boy, his home during his childhood years was his stepfather's estate at Jerwakant just south of Reval (now Tallinn).

a simple quid pro quo. The native nobles were allowed to keep their lands and privileges. They were incorporated on an equal footing within the ranks of the Russian nobility. They were, in effect, bought off. And in return, they pledged their loyalty to the tsar.

In the process, the non-Russian nobles became de facto subcontractors for the empire. They continued to run their affairs under Russian power much as they had done before—only now their domains belonged to the empire and they ran them in the name of the tsar. In Estland and the other provinces of the Russian Baltic, the subcontractors who did the bidding of the Russian emperor were the German barons, the descendents of the knights.

For centuries, the cultural foreignness of these particular subcontractors hadn't been much of a problem. The barons had been largely left to their own devices in looking after the Baltic, and the Russian imperial establishment had been largely happy with their services. The abiding rule of imperial life was economic and cultural autonomy offered in return for political obedience. But in the 1880s, for a variety of reasons, the terms of the contract began to change. The barons found themselves faced with new expectations, and the consequences for Ungern's life—and for the history of the empire—would be enormous.

"May the Stones Speak to You"

Ungern would spend most of his childhood in Estland, but as the family left Graz, they moved first to the Caucasus.

Baltic noblemen in the nineteenth century were expected to have an "occupation" (*Besitz*), a career that kept them busy and productive and did honor to the family name. For most barons, this meant devoting themselves to running their estates or serving in their local government and estate associations. A notable minority entered Russian state service or the military, where they often rose to the highest ranks. By the end of the nineteenth century, law, medicine, even business had become acceptable pursuits. Ungern's grandfather, the successful entrepreneur, had an "occupation" and would have expected the same of his four male children. His oldest son entered the Russian Foreign Ministry. The second became a naval officer. The third followed the patriarch and took over the family factory and estates. And Ungern's father, Theodor, became a scholar, which by his time had also become a respectable vocation.[5]

Theodor's specialty was geology—rocks and soils. After earning his doctorate at the University of Leipzig in 1881, he spent the next years on expeditions and intermittent government assignments. In the spring of 1887, leaving the family behind in Graz, he traveled to the Crimea to survey wine production for the Russian Ministry of State Domains.[6] Two years later a post opened in the Russian Caucasus and the family moved with him, making their home in Tiflis (Tbilisi), now the capital of Georgia but then the headquarters of what the Russians call the Trans-Caucasus (*Zakavkaz'e*), including most of modern-day Georgia, Armenia, and Azerbaijan. Theodor worked in the administration of the Russian viceroy and had the formal title of special assignments official (*chinovnik osobykh poruchenii*), though it's not clear what he did in his post. All we find in the genealogy books are the barest outlines of his life in the region. We know that he "scaled Mount Elbrus twice" and "went on numerous scientific travels to Transcaucasia, Persia, and Asiatic Turkey."[7] The private world of the family, however, is all but locked away.

Reading between the lines, though, it's easy enough to imagine the young Ungern-Sternbergs as typical aristocratic colonials—the naturalist of means and his family, enjoying the exotic Orient while serving the empire. Theodor knew Russian. Sophie Charlotte did not, though she would have found plenty of Russians in her set to speak with in French. There were also other Baltic Germans serving with Theodor in the Russian administration, either as civilian officials or in the military. They would have mixed together in a small colonial community. There is a photograph of Ungern from those years. In it we see a boy with long bangs, about age four, dressed in the cloak of a local Cossack (*cherkeska*), a common tourist get-up of the period.

The family spent two years in Tiflis. During that time, Ungern's older sister Constance died. She was not quite six years old.[8] We know nothing about how she died, or how her death affected Ungern's parents. They had lost another daughter, Florence, their first child, at the age of two even before Ungern was born, and the death of young children was a fact of life then, even in the wealthiest families. But we can imagine that the sadness of her death might have made other troubles worse.

The Ungern-Sternbergs were not a happy couple. They carried the high debt that was a common strain for late nineteenth-century Baltic nobles.[9] Ungern's father was also frequently absent. Baron Otto von Taube, who lived near the family in Estland in the 1880s and 1890s, recalls in his memoirs that Sophie Charlotte was "lively" and "utterly gracious," "with the most beautiful brown eyes in the world." Theodor, by contrast, was "short . . . ugly, and mean-spirited." (Taube admits that Ungern's mother was his first boyhood crush, which may explain why he didn't much care for her husband.) In Taube's opinion, Theodor's extended travels damaged the relationship.[10] Another friend recalled that Sophie Charlotte "suffered greatly" in her marriage.[11] All we know for certain is that young Constance died in October 1889, and the couple divorced almost exactly two years later.

The file on the divorce is located in the Estonian Historical Archives in Tartu. It's a slim folder of brown and yellowed pages, many of them covered over with official stamps and the almost indecipherable scrawls of lawyers and

2.1. Ungern as a boy in a cherkeska, early 1890s. Reproduced from Witold
St. Michałowski, *Testament Barona* (Warsaw, 1972), opposite p. 32.

clerks running like plumes along the margins. In keeping with the traditional
subcontracting norms of the empire, divorces were handled by the immediate religious authority in question—in this case, the Estland Consistory of the
Evangelical Lutheran Church—which then made its decision and passed its
ruling up the imperial line of command to the Ministry of the Interior in
St. Petersburg. Most of the documents are in German: neatly penned letters
between the spouses and their counselors, or petitions submitted in the name
of the tsar, the standard protocol of the time.[12]

In the late nineteenth century, the grounds allowed for separation by the Lutheran Church were extensive, ranging from insanity to incompatibility. As a result, divorce among Baltic Germans, in particular Baltic German nobles, was unusual but not unheard of.[13] In the case of the Ungern-Sternbergs, the only hint at a cause for the dissolution is a cryptic reference Theodor makes to the couple's enduring unhappiness: "wounds that cannot heal."[14] Sophie Charlotte for her part explained to the consistory that she tried to visit Theodor but that "he refused to receive [her]," implying that it was the husband who took the initiative to end the marriage, though this may have been simply a legal pretext for initiating the divorce proceedings.[15] Nothing in the file indicates any rancor or contentiousness.

The authorities awarded custody of the children to Sophie Charlotte, which was unusual for the time, though this decision, too, is not explained in the documents.[16] In fact, perhaps the only thing clear about the divorce is that it set Ungern's parents onto opposite paths. At first, Theodor returned to the Caucasus and continued his scientific travels, but within a few years he fell into legal and financial trouble in Europe and by 1899 was diagnosed as "mentally unsound" (*umalishennyi*) and confined to a sanatorium on the Estland coast. This could have been a case of what we would describe today as depression, or it could have been something even more serious. The paperwork on Theodor's confinement does not describe his symptoms in any detail. Ever the transnational, before falling ill he married an Englishwoman in London and together they had a daughter in Montreux. It is not clear how much contact he had with his sons in their boyhood. His ultimate end is also a mystery. The genealogies offer no information on where or how he died or even a clear date for his death, just a span of years: 1918/1923.[17]

Sophie Charlotte, by contrast, stayed in place. After the divorce, she rented a manor in central Estland with her mother and the two boys. During this time, she was courted by a neighbor, a widower, Baron Oskar von Hoyningen-Huene. In 1894 they married, and the family moved to Hoyningen-Huene's estate at Jerwakant (Estonian: Järvakandi) in the woodsy countryside about forty miles south of Reval. Sophie Charlotte had three children with her new husband, and appears to have become a traditional Estland baroness. She died in Reval in 1907 at the age of forty-six.[18]

Ungern grew up at Jerwakant, and we can assume that it was the place that most influenced him as a boy. During his childhood, the Baltic barons were a social class suspended between two ages. Many of them had one foot in the modernity of the late nineteenth century, the world of industrial technology, capitalist business, nationalist politics, and increasingly "democratic" social relations. The Russian Empire, like the other states of Europe, was changing rapidly at the time, and the barons, for better and for worse, signed on for this transformation.

Yet they were also as a whole profoundly conservative—traditionalists in the literal sense of the world. So they kept their other foot in their ancestral estates—the *Rittergut* or more simply the *Gut*—where the order of things was much more predictable. Here they lived in great manor houses and cultivated what one contemporary called their "sense [of themselves] as masters" (*Herrenbewuβtsein*).[19] Life on the *Gut* was not immune from the world outside. German nobles in the Baltic like nobles elsewhere had to contend with the economic change that was reaching the countryside—rising costs of labor and land, rising indebtedness, market pressures on their crops and manufactures, state regulations. But the rural estate was nonetheless a kind of refuge—the nobleman's idyll, a seat in the world but also above it.

Serfdom was abolished in Estonian areas during the 1820s, but the Estonian serfs were freed without land, which kept them closely tied to their former owners. Even in the time of Ungern's boyhood, almost 70 percent of land in the province still remained in the hands of a tiny number of German lords, and social distinctions remained stark.[20] There was a quasi-feudal feel to the world of the countryside, accentuated by the divide of ethnicity. The peasants, all Estonian, worked in the fields. The landlords, all German, supervised and collected rents. The barons saw themselves quite literally as knights, rewarded by God (and the tsar) with power over the peasants by virtue of their bloodline. The peasants spoke Estonian. The lords spoke German. The peasants paid rent to their ex-masters sometimes with cash but often in kind, echoing the old ways of the feudal economy. As late as the turn of the 1900s, the barons continued to enjoy feudal-era privileges—the exclusive right to make and sell liquor, for example.[21] By Ungern's time, almost everyone in both communities was Lutheran, but even their common faith was marked by a social divide. In the Ungern-Sternbergs' church at Pühalepa on Hiiumaa Island, for example, the German barons sat up front in special pews, while the Estonian peasants prayed behind them.

This was the slowly modernizing yet still deeply traditional world of Jerwakant in Ungern's youth. Today the old manor house is a ruin—a shell of crumbling walls with trees growing up where the floors would have been. Like many Estland manors, the building was burned to the ground during the Revolution of 1905 and never rebuilt. But photographs prior to the destruction show a grand neoclassical stone palace looming at the end of a long lane bordered by trees and gardens. Beyond the manor house were acres of woods, fields, and pastureland, dotted here and there with outbuildings, including high stone windmills, one of which still towers today over the nearby road to Tallinn. Baron Hoyningen-Huene, Ungern's stepfather, operated a dairy, distillery, and glass works on the estate.[22] By the early 1910s, over two hundred people lived on the manor lands, most of them Estonian peasant workers and servants along with a few German overseers.[23]

Ungern left no recollections of his boyhood at Jerwakant, but we can glimpse something of the life of the home through the memoirs of Baron Otto von Taube, whose family sold the estate to Hoyningen-Huene. (This is the same Taube who had a crush on Ungern's mother.) Taube describes a broad ceremonial stairway soaring up from the grand entrance of the home; a great hall (known simply as *der Saal*) for dances and banquets; suites of family rooms covered, according to the fashion of the late nineteenth century, with oriental carpets; display cases full of old weapons and family artifacts; walls adorned with ancestral portraits and family crests.[24]

In the Taube's home as well as those of most baronial families, the mother was the much-beloved "soul of the house," doting on her children. She ran the business of the household, overseeing a platoon of servants. Fathers were more distant, both physically and emotionally. Often busy on or away from the estate, children saw them less, and they tended to be treated with respect, even awe, rather than love. Lutheran values of order, discipline, and duty were the norm.[25]

Households are not straightforward ideological statements. It is a mistake to assume that certain kinds of families inevitably produce a certain type of identity or set of convictions. Yet in every household we find an ideology of sorts, some reflection of an idealized world of social relations, some sense of right and wrong, a way of marking and reinforcing the differences between "us" and "them," whoever the "them" might be. To appreciate the world of Ungern's boyhood we have to imagine the ideology of his home as he would have known it—not as a formal set of rules but as a tone, a guiding sense. The home of a baronial family in his time, to one degree or another, was a special preserve. The barons saw themselves as a people apart. They were above the Estonians, yet separate from the Russians. And their homes were the capsules that contained the rare substance of this specialness, their supposedly unique devotion to tradition, culture, honor, taste, and history.

At Jerwakant, this sense of exclusivity was stamped on the building itself. The founder of the estate in the early nineteenth century had had his workmen etch a quotation from the *Aeneid* in Latin in giant letters across the manor's façade—*Saxa te loquuntur,* "May the Stones Speak to You"—that still appeared on the house in Ungern's time.[26] We have no idea what he thought of this lofty exhortation, or if he thought about it at all. It may have simply blended in, as unremarkable as anything else about the manor in his boyish eyes. But even in this ordinariness we can feel something of the barons' view of the world, and some of this must have stuck with him. He would have known from this early point in his life that his people were the ones who lived in homes inscribed like monuments, that they were the special kind who honored tradition and gave commands.

2.2. Jerwakant manor house, ca. 1900. Ungern spent much of his boyhood in this grand home in the
Estland countryside not far from Reval. Barely visible here, the lofty inscription from Virgil
runs across the main portal. Reproduced from *Eesti mõisad: 250 fotot aastaist 1860–1939*
(Ants Hein, comp.) (Tallinn, 2004), 176.

Growing up in what the Germans called the *Landsche*—the countryside—
there was never any confusion about where one fit. One paid calls on other
Germans, either on nearby estates or in town, the closest being the provincial
capital of Reval, only a short ride away by rail. (Every noble family of any station kept a city house in addition to their country manor.) Education in the
home was likewise thoroughly German, with an emphasis on the rigorous exposure to *Kultur*—the high realm of "intellectual, artistic, and religious facts."[27]

The Estonians, though close, were always separate. Baron Taube recalled
having an Estonian nanny and learning Estonian fairy tales from his German
mother. He played with Estonian village boys as a child but grew distant from
them as he entered adolescence. There was certainly no hint of equality with
the Estonians as seen from the barons' side. As for Russians, there weren't
many in the vicinity, yet Taube studied Russian with a tutor at home because,
as subjects of the Russian Empire, his father insisted that his children learn the
state language. Plus, Taube's extended family included Russian relatives and
connections.[28]

In fact, many Baltic nobles had ties to Russia, Estland nobles especially.
Though the typical Estland baron and baroness spent much of their lives in the
virtually Russianless world of the Baltic countryside, a large share had Russian relations or spouses and regularly sojourned in Russia proper. A small
but consistent minority of barons attended elite schools in St. Petersburg (as
Ungern would) and went on to careers that took them across the empire before
they returned to the manor to retire. By 1914, 74 of Estland's 104 noble families
were Russified to the point of having identifiable Russian branches.[29]

Even families that rarely intermarried with Russian clans still pointed them-selves toward Russia in small but meaningful ways, such as by taking Russian names. The Ungern-Sternbergs tended to marry other Baltic German nobles—Rennenkampfs, Hoyningen-Huenes, Stackelbergs, Rosens, Manteuffels. Most of their children became Roberts, Rolfs, Julies, and Maries. But some Russian names appear in the lists—Ol'ga, Tat'iana, Mikhail. Ungern's paternal grand-mother was Natalia von Rennenkampf. The mixed Russo-German style of Un-gern's birth name—Nikolai Roman Max—was also not uncommon.

For the Estland barons, the connection to Russia was central to their ethos as subcontractors. The degree of actual attachment varied, however. Some lords developed intimate ties to Russia and identified with it completely. Many others saw it as a backward and alien country that should consider itself lucky to have the more cultured Germans as its subjects.[30] But closeness in the sense of cultural belonging or even sympathy was not required from the barons in any case. For the better part of two hundred years, the overriding concern be-tween the Russians and the barons was devotion to the tsar, and the fundamen-tal presumption of the contract on both sides was that the nationality of the devotee was secondary to the devotion itself. This began to change in the last decades of the nineteenth century in part because nationality changed but even more because notions of devotion did as well.

Russification

Like most boys of his class, Ungern received his early schooling at home. Then in the spring of 1900 at the age of fourteen he was sent off the estate and into the world to attend Russian-language high school in Reval.

Had he been born even ten years earlier, he would almost surely have fol-lowed a different path. His schooling on the estate would have lasted until about age twelve, and after that he would likely have spent his entire middle and high-school career not in Russian schools but in German ones, either in Reval, Riga, or other Baltic towns. This was the route taken by Ungern's father, uncles, grandfather, and stepfather, as well as most Estland noble boys up to the 1880s.[31] But Ungern came of age in a different era. By his teenage years, German-language middle and high schools in the Baltic had been closed, and the choice facing baronial parents was clear. They could keep tutoring their children on the estate, send them to school in Germany, enroll them (at high cost) in one of the few German-language schools that remained open in St. Petersburg, or send them into the Russian system.

The closing of German schools was only one of the imperial initiatives that changed life for the Baltic barons beginning in the 1880s. Over the course of the decade, Russian became the language of business in all draft offices in the region, most courts, and most municipal offices. In 1889, the old German-run judicial system in the region was overhauled to conform to Russian standards, and in 1892 the Baltic provinces ceased to be considered "specially governed" regions and were placed instead under the "general laws of the empire." Russian police and newly appointed Estonian officials entered the countryside, replacing the local power of the German lords and pastors. Increased funding went to support Orthodox congregations and schools, and Orthodox proselytizers fanned out to claim wavering Lutherans. In the early 1890s, Dorpat University, the only non-Russian university in the empire and the unrivaled "higher school of life" for the baronial class, received a Russian name and curriculum, and German fraternity brothers were instructed to wear Russian student uniforms. Of the key public institutions of Baltic noble life, only the nobles' corporate assemblies—the *Ritterschaften*—remained relatively unchanged.[32]

The new approach to the Baltic Germans, and to Baltic nobles in particular, was part of the Russian Empire's response to its own version of the "German question." In addition to the Baltic Germans, other Germans lived in the Volga region and southern Russia as well as in the capitals of St. Petersburg and Moscow. Historically all of these communities, though distinct from one another, had been equally favored by the Russian system. But by the 1870s, wary of the "Germanizing tendencies" of the new Germany and inspired by their own rising nationalism, influential Russians began to rethink their position. Russian publicists questioned why Germans seemed to be better off than ordinary Russian folk—was it due to German exploitation? Russian clerics fumed about what they saw as the undeserved privileges of German churches in an Orthodox empire. And Russian officials wondered how much the hearts of Russia's Germans were stirred by connections to their German brothers across the border, reflecting the government's growing concern with imperial communities (Poles, Jews, Muslim Tatars) that might be drawn to "alternative centers of attraction" in foreign states.[33] By the 1880s, the tsar on the throne was a Germanophobe (Alexander III, r. 1881–1894), and the course toward Russification was set.

But Russification in the Baltic, as in other parts of the empire, was in fact a number of Russifications at once. On the one hand, it was an openly punitive policy motivated by Russian national resentment. As one Russian official huffed in 1898, German nobles in Livland "looked down on Russians" and dismissed the country as "a land of barbarians."[34] Russification was thus a tool of vindication—a means of showing the barons who was truly boss. Yet it was also a tool for supporting (within limits) the Estonians and Latvians and for standardizing administration and procedure to make the state work more effectively (from the center's point of view).[35]

Russian policies were thus ideological as well as practical, and, while they were discriminatory, they were not *only* discriminatory. The watchword of the day was state unity. As one Russian official intoned in 1891,

The Baltic provinces today are living through a remarkable moment. Though incorporated as a part of [Russia] since 1710, never once in all this time has the region truly belonged. Now at last, these lands are joining the fold of our common fatherland, and a new era is dawning. From this time forward, the history of the Baltic shall be bound to the common history of the entire expansive Russian state![36]

In pursuing state unity, the tsarist government never realistically intended to turn the many diverse peoples of the empire into Russians in a cultural sense, though some Russian nationalists certainly dreamed of this in the long term. Instead, the objective was to make diversity more workable. Russification in this sense was the late imperial state's awkward, overbearing solution to the dilemma of being multinational in a national age. Though seen by almost all of its detractors and some of its promoters as a nationalist policy, Russification was in fact an imperial one. Its ultimate purpose was to repair and improve the country as an empire rather than reengineer it into a Russian nation-state.

Not surprisingly, however, these subtleties did not matter much to the Baltic barons. As they saw it, they were the victims of "an unadulterated policy of assimilation," and they complained bitterly about what they took as an assault on "our independent authority, our historical distinctiveness (*Eigenart*), [and] our German essence."[37] There were passionate cries of "better dead than Slav!," as well as heated accusations that "the Slavic-Asiatic racial instinct" had diminished the citadels of *Kultur* and that "the Great Russian idea" was being imposed through an unhealthy combination of "Orthodoxy, nihilism, red tape, paper rubles, liquor, and dynamite."[38] "It is tragic," wrote Count Alexander von Keyserling, a neighbor of the Hoyningen-Huenes, in 1890, capturing the mood of the times, "but all that remains is exodus or death."[39]

In fact, some Baltic barons did emigrate—mostly to Germany. A few resisted by organizing underground German-language schools, or by refusing to submit official paperwork in Russian. Others retreated into the private and still intensely German worlds of home and family.[40] But most nobles, like most burghers, adjusted to the changes. The German lords, unlike Polish nobles in the western provinces, for example, where Russification laws were far stricter, were allowed to retain their land, and, precisely because they remained noble landowners, they continued to be seen—and to see themselves—as the useful partners of a conservative government. Indeed, in keeping with the imperial logic of Russification, it was still acceptable for the barons to be German—they just had to be more Russian about doing so.

The adaptive nobles sent their children to Russian schools. Ungern's road to Russia began at the Nicholas the First Gymnasium, which was located in Reval's Lower Town (*Unterstadt*), not far from the port and right up against the base of the steep hill that contains the Upper Town (*Oberstadt*), the medieval core of the city. In Ungern's time (much as today), the Upper Town was known as the Cathedral Mount (*Domberg* or simply the *Dom;* Estonian: *Toompea;* Russian: *Vyshgorod*) after the original German church built on the hill in the crusader era. This was traditionally the noble district, and until the 1880s it was an exclusive German power zone. Many blueblood families had residences on the hill, including a number of Ungern-Sternbergs and Hoyningen-Huenes, and the hilltop was also home to the assembly hall of the Estland *Ritterschaft,* the provincial governor's palace, and the great protestant cathedral church (*Domkirche*), the unrivaled headquarters of Estland Lutheranism, with its towering baroque steeple.[41]

In the 1880s Russian officials started moving into addresses on the Dom, and in 1894 a massive, onion-domed neo-Muscovite Orthodox cathedral began going up not far from the *Domkirche.* To make their point all the clearer, the Russians named their new church in honor of Prince Aleksandr Nevsky, "heroic defender of the frontier" whose victories over the "the godless Germans" in the thirteenth century made him the ultimate Russification saint.[42] Today the heights of Tallinn's old town remain dominated by this German-Russian contest of onion domes and spires.

The Lower Town was more diverse. Reval grew quickly in the late nineteenth century as factories and port traffic expanded, turning the city into a vibrant economic center and "a pearl in the crown of our expansive fatherland."[43] The population (roughly sixty thousand in 1897), historically dominated by German burghers, became a more complicated mix of German, Russian, and Estonian merchants, professionals, craftsmen, soldiers, officials, servants, and factory workers, most of whom lived either in the neighborhoods clustered below the Dom or farther out in newer industrial suburbs.[44]

The Nicholas Gymnasium was the oldest existing high school in Reval at the time. Traditionally it had groomed the sons of the city's German middle classes, but in the era of Russification the school's population changed.[45] Ungern attended the gymnasium from 1900 to 1902, and of the fifty or so boys in his class, 54 percent were Germans, 24 percent were Estonian, 12 percent were Russian, and 4 percent were of "Jewish nationality," while 38 percent were nobles, 48 percent came from "the urban estates," 6 percent were from clerical families, and about 5 percent were peasants. Almost 80 percent of his classmates were Lutheran.[46] The teachers included Germans and a few Estonians, but most, in complete contrast with the students, were Russians, including the principal, Grigorii Ianchevetskii, a noted conservative pedagogue and enthusiastic champion of the local "Russian cause" (*russkoe delo*)[47]

Ianchevetskii ran his domain according to the strict norms of the times. Detailed regulations laid out when pupils could go to bed, when they had to rise, when and with whom they could go to the theater, and the length of their haircuts. (Some students lived directly under the principal's supervision in the school's small boardinghouse, though most lived with parents or relatives or, like Ungern, rented private rooms.)

The curriculum was classical—Ungern attended Latin class five out of six days a week—with a heavy emphasis on the humanities and "the interior development of personality" that the "humanistic ideal" implied. In fact, much as the Prussian prototype on which the Russian version was based, the curriculum at schools like the Nicholas Gymnasium was supposed to be "as non-utilitarian as possible" because the goal was to produce elite "men of strong character" rather than (as critics saw it) "real people" with practical skills. Exams were frequent. Punishments were swift and public.[48]

Of all the work done at the school, however, the most important arguably was the cultivation of patriotism. Like Jean-Jacques Rousseau a century earlier, Russia's educational leaders in the fin de siècle were convinced that one of the essential tasks of education was to turn children into patriots "by inclination, by passion, [and] by necessity."[49] Consequently, schools like the Nicholas Gymnasium became laboratories for designing the Russia-centered patriotic community envisioned by the Russification regime. Students of "different nationalities" took their classes together in Russian. They sang "God Save the Tsar" in Russian at morning assembly. Yet at the same time, in accordance with imperial practicality (if not toleration), all the boys during Ungern's years at the school also studied German as a standard element in the curriculum, and Estonian boys were permitted two special classes of Estonian per week (for an extra fee). Each of the three Christian communities at the school—Orthodox, Protestant, and Catholic—received religious instruction (*zakon bozhii*) in their own faith. (No such course was offered to Jews, however.)[50]

The spirit of the school was intensely Russian, but one wonders how much of the spirit Ungern and his classmates actually understood. "Most pupils not only do not think in Russian," lamented the principal in his annual report for 1902, "but, regrettably, they also do not even speak [the language]. And this is despite [our] best efforts . . . to ensure that students speak nothing but Russian at school and as much as possible outside of it as well."[51]

The administration's frustration with this situation reflects the fact that Russification, like many Russian bureaucratic initiatives of the tsarist era (and later), was shaped by a worldview of paper-based social engineering that took the plan rather than reality as the starting point. As Prince Sergei Shakhovskoi, the Russifying governor of Estland, noted in 1885, "When it comes to the Germans, I believe it's best to act with great, stunning blows and not get lost in the details," such as the detail, for example, that almost no one in Estland— Germans or Estonians—knew Russian when the Russian schooling laws went into effect.[52]

Свидѣтельство.

Симъ свидѣтельствую ученику 4-го класса Ревельской Гимназіи Императора Николая I Роману Унгернъ-Штернбергъ по его личной просьбѣ, что онъ вслѣдствіе ненормально протекшаго воспаленія легкихъ на правой сторонѣ и правой грудной плевы, которымъ онъ заболѣлъ въ Ноябрѣ мѣсяцѣ 1900-го года, въ Январѣ с.г. для леченія былъ посланъ на югъ, гдѣ остался до конца Мая м. с.г.

Докторъ медицины Эд. фонъ Самсонъ.

Ревель, 16-го Августа 1901 г.

2.3. Doctor's note, Reval, 1901. This note from the files of the Nicholas the First Gymnasium indicates that Ungern missed five months of school in 1901 due to complications from a bout with pneumonia. He apparently spent the time in "the south" (most likely the Black Sea coast) where he was sent for the milder climate.
Courtesy Estonian Historical Archives, Tartu.

Ungern was undoubtedly in this group. His grade sheets show that he received failing marks in Russian language (ones and twos on a five-point scale)
and was a poor student overall: During the 1901–1902 academic year, his av-
erages placed him in the bottom 5 percent of the fifty boys in his section, and
in the third quarter of the year he earned the dubious distinction of being the
absolute worst student in his group.

Besides the poor grades, the school records from Reval reveal the first
glimpse we have of Ungern's personality. As a fifteen-year-old boy, he was constantly getting in trouble. His grade sheets are full of entries for "reprimands"
(*vzyskaniia*) for "laziness and lack of application" as well as "prankstering"
inside and outside of class.[53] Was Ungern acting up because he couldn't understand much of what was going on? Was he bored? We know that the mix of
his personality contained streaks of impetuousness and willful disobedience.
He could be dismissively presumptuous as well as moody and withdrawn. We
see these qualities more clearly close to the end of his life. To say that we find
the first signs of them in his grade book from Reval is tempting, though it is
only a guess.

Yet for all of his misbehavior and wretched grades, Ungern was clearly a
bright boy. According to the recollections of relatives, though "the terror of his
teachers," he was also curious. At some point in his teenage years, he became
"passionately interested in philosophy," to the point of ripping out the chapters
of philosophy books so that he could carry them in his pockets "for easier reading."[54] One family friend remembered that he admired Dostoevsky. "Tolstoy,"
by contrast, "seemed far too tame."[55]

Regardless of his reading habits, by the time he reached adolescence
Ungern was very much a product of competing influences and diverse combinations of his transnational imperial world. He was the son of Baltic German/
Austrian German parents but was given a Russo-German name. He grew up
on a German manor in a Russian-ruled state but lived surrounded by Estonians. He spoke German as his native language but Russian (as best he could)
in public. He was Lutheran yet attended school with Catholics, Orthodox, and
Jews. In addition, he was a European cosmopolitan—or at least he was profoundly shaped by European culture, both through the influence of his parents
and maternal grandmother and through his travels to visit relatives in Europe
and his classical European education.

If Ungern identified with Russia at this point in his life, it was probably
only superficially. His school was Russian, and his teachers did their best to
impart Russian state patriotism to their mostly non-Russian pupils. The tsar
he was taught to revere was Russian, as were the new monolingual street signs
that began going up in Reval when he was there. (The earlier signs had been in
German *and* Russian; now they were in Russian alone.) Baltic German teen-
agers in his time also enjoyed the chic of sprinkling their *baltisch* speech with

Russian words.[56] But for all this, it is hard to see how Russia could have shaped him much by his teenage years.

Ungern was a Russian subject, but the terms of his connection to the empire were still those of a Baltic German subcontractor. Russification was supposed to create another order of belonging. As the Russian minister of justice declared to a multinational audience of dignitaries in Reval in 1895, "The Russian cause ... requires people who are more than Russian in name only, or merely because they are [Russian] subjects. It requires people who are Russian in their actions and convictions."[57] Put another way, what the empire now sought from its non-Russian subcontractors was the special devotion of state love, which was at once something more and something different from the dutiful service and polite allegiance most of them had previously provided.

As a member of the first generation of Russification, Ungern would indeed become one of those non-Russians who developed a closer attachment to Russia, though it is too simple to conclude that he did so by government design. We are shaped into who we become by the mysterious interplay between what is possible and what we hope for. In Ungern's case, it is impossible to know what he wished for at the age of fifteen, though his dismal grades and dedication to misbehavior had the inevitable effect of making some outcomes more likely than others.

More specifically, it made it highly *unlikely* that he could stay in school. And so it came to pass that in April 1902, at the start of Easter recess, before he had the chance to finish the year at the bottom of the class (or to be expelled), and probably with the hope of straightening out his behavior, Ungern's mother withdrew him from the Nicholas Gymnasium and sent him to military school in St. Petersburg.[58]

CHAPTER 3

ST. PETERSBURG, MANCHURIA, ST. PETERSBURG

"The errors of young men are the ruin of business"
—FRANCIS BACON. "Of Youth and Beauty"

Into the Cosmopolis

During the age of Peter the Great, the Russians began to call their country an empire (*imperiia*). The new name was part of a great change. Inspired by the mercantile powers of England, Holland, and Sweden, the tsar and his lieutenants forced the Muscovite boyars to turn toward northern Europe, and a series of adjustments quickly followed. Pantaloons replaced kaftans. Beards were shaved. Wives and daughters were instructed to enter "society." Weapons, taxes, maps, and government offices were transformed or copied to match the European style. And all of this lodged itself in the new state name. *Imperiia* was a Latinate borrowing—a touchstone to the glory, breadth, and martial achievement of ancient Rome, the Rome of the original Caesars. Prior to the eighteenth century, the Rome that had most weighed on the mind of the Russians was the "second Rome" of Constantinople. To plot his path toward Europe, Peter inverted the Roman precedence. The West began to take over the East.

St. Petersburg, the new capital that Peter ordered into being on the Baltic Sea, was the epitome of the new Western-leaning *imperiia*. It was a Russian city built in the European style yet, like every great imperial center, ancient Rome most of all, it was also a purposefully diverse place—a cosmopolis defined by the mixings of multiple cultures.[1] By 1903, the year of Ungern's arrival, roughly one-fifth of the city's 1.4 million residents were non-Russians, some of them new migrants, others with deep roots going back to the time of the city's founding.[2] Foreign shop signs dotted the façades of Nevskii Prospekt, the city's greatest avenue. Houses of imperial finance loomed over the Fontanka. The city was home to Polish charities, French bookstores, German, Estonian, and Finnish language schools, Jewish workers' clubs, Georgian cafés, a Turkish bath, and a range of Christian churches. A Moorish-style synagogue opened in the early 1890s. By the 1910s, the city added a mosque and a Buddhist temple.[3]

The cosmopolitan landscape meant that Ungern was not out of place. Germans—from the Baltic and elsewhere—were the largest non-Russian community in the city, and the road he took to the capital had been traveled by many Estland boys before him. But the sight of the city must have been remarkable all the same—the great palaces lining the Neva and the canals, the forest of smokestacks towering over the workers' suburbs, the electric trams—introduced in 1907—clanging their way past the crowds on Nevskii.

St. Petersburg was ten times the size of Reval, at once more Russian, more diverse, and more vibrant. It was the essential gear of the imperial clockwork and ground zero for the country's lurching transformation into a modern society. Perhaps it is not surprising then that it was here that Ungern began the conversion that would turn him into a more culturally Russianized and devoted sort of imperial subject—the kind of subject who lived for the empire rather than simply lived within it. At the same time, even in the great imperial melting pot, this new orientation was not a foregone conclusion. The move toward Russianness, like any process of cultural change, might occur in degrees or not at all, and it was invariably ambiguous, a question of mixing and nesting identities rather than mechanically throwing out an old worldview and replacing it with a new one.

The dynamics producing this sort of change were also complicated. Heavy-handed Russification was only one way to turn non-Russians into Russians, and it was rarely effective—not only because coercion often produced alienation and resistance but also because the imposition itself was never absolute. The late tsarist government aimed to Russify, but the way it went about it was clumsy and uneven. Policies directed toward Poles and Finns, for example, were different from those targeting Volga Tatars or native peoples in Siberia. Even in a single Russified setting, such as Ungern's school in Reval, no single rule applied to all. And as a state program, Russification was a boom lowered on groups. By contrast, the act of becoming Russian—Russianization—was unavoidably personal.

Ungern never recorded what happened in his case, but it's easy to imagine that his pro-Russian turn was as much voluntary as required. On the one hand, it made sense for him to begin to identify more strongly with Russia in St. Petersburg, and he undoubtedly experienced the adjustment as a natural process.

On the other, by going to military school, he found himself in precisely the kind of institution that never doubted for a moment that he *would identify* with Russia. All the boys did. No other option was allowed.

"I Don't Have to Stand in One Place"

Ungern's introduction to the military began at the College of Naval Cadets (*Morskoi Kadetskii Korpus*). His parents probably chose to send him there because of family ties. One of his uncles on his father's side was a naval officer, and at least eleven Ungern-Sternbergs had attended the school over its long history, including an ensign stationed at the nearby naval base of Kronstadt.[4] (Some Hoyningen-Huenes were also alumni.) But even without the family connections, the school was the right place to go. Only "hereditary nobles" and/ or "sons of officers of the fleet" could attend, making it a good address for a baron. It was also well-known as a no-nonsense establishment, which surely made it appealing to the weary parents of an unruly schoolboy.[5] Between the summer of 1902 and the following spring, Ungern took special courses at a private tutoring school in Reval. He then passed his entrance exams and enrolled in the Naval College on May 5, 1903.[6] He was seventeen years old.

Ungern's fellow cadets were seven hundred boys aged thirteen through nineteen, all of whom lived and studied, along with the staff, in the college's hulking neoclassical complex on Vasil'evskii Island in the heart of St. Petersburg, a short distance across the Neva from the Winter Palace.[7] The building still stands today—long, austere, imposing, the look one expects of a military school.[8] The mission of the college was to produce the cream of the imperial navy, so the curriculum was both technical and social. Cadets studied French, Russian history, religion, trigonometry, astronomy, naval architecture, and theoretical mechanics. When they weren't in class, they drilled, fenced, and practiced calisthenics. In the summer, they trained on cruises in the Baltic. As winter approached, they prepared for the annual college ball by taking required dancing lessons.[9]

The school had close connections to the court. Senior cadets (*michmany*), like their peers at the city's other military schools, performed guard duty at the Winter Palace, and Tsar Nicholas and members of the royal family routinely visited the college and its training ships as they cruised the Baltic. Everywhere you turned, the college clicked with devotion to "Tsar, Faith, and Fatherland." As one of Ungern's classmates recalled, "If the sovereign had commanded us to hurl ourselves out the window, we surely would have done so."[10]

The cultivation of this sort of devotion was a fundamental goal of the tsarist military establishment. The Russian high command, following the German lead, had recognized the need to train a new sort of officer—"the new

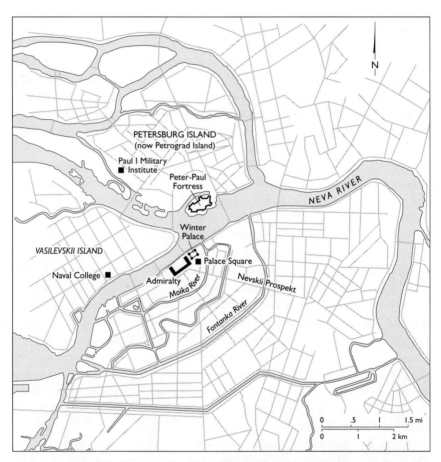

Map 4. St. Petersburg (center) ca. 1900. Ungern received his officer training at two of the Russian empire's most prestigious military institutions. Both are still military schools today.

man, the military technician"—since at least 1870, but preparation of this sort in the Russian military was uneven at best, and in the cadet schools—as opposed to the higher institutes and academies—it was virtually nonexistent.[11] Instead, even in Ungern's time, the focus of cadet education was on discipline and rote learning. Officers were not taught to think as much as to answer correctly and obey. As the superintendent Vice-Admiral Grigorii Chukhnin reminded his pupils (including Ungern) at an assembly in May 1904, "Remember dear cadets…without laws or rules, there can be no society and no protections for the individual.…Therefore, make this a truth to live by: learn to obey [your superiors] and to master yourself."[12] Chukhnin had a reputation as a martinet—his nickname in the fleet was "Little Greg the Enforcer" (*Grishka-katorzhnyi*).[13] By all accounts, during his tenure at the school he enforced all he could.

In matters of nationality, however, no real enforcement was required. Most of the cadets were Russian. The curriculum was taught in Russian, just as it was at all the empire's officers' schools, and Orthodox ritual and rhetoric were pervasive features of everyday life. The Russian world of the school was fully in keeping with the government's view that the Russians as the "predominant people of the empire" should naturally predominate in running and shaping the military.[14]

Beginning in 1888, quotas were introduced to restrict the overall share of non-Russians in the officer corps. Yet at the same time, they were never excluded. At any one time up to 20 percent of officers tended to be of non-Russian origin, with Poles and Germans—especially Baltic German noblemen—

3.1. Naval cadets during a riding lesson in St. Petersburg, early 1900s. Reproduced from *Voennaia stolitsa rossiiskoi imperii: v fotografiiakh kontsa xix—nachala xx vekov* (St. Petersburg, 2004), 110–11, pl. 117.

making up the largest share of non-Russians at most ranks.[15] This meant that military educators like Chukhnin found themselves charged with a potentially contradictory mission. They ran what were essentially Russian schools, but their students included a good number of non-Russians—even non-Orthodox non-Russians—and the pedagogical goal was *not* to create Russian nationalists but rather patriots of the tsar. Even in an age of seemingly overbearing Russification, the ideal cadet was Russian in form, tsarist in content.

Of the 148 boys in Ungern's college regiment (*rota*) in 1903, about 80 percent had Russian surnames, with some Ukrainians and Belorussians among them. (Both these groups were considered "Russian" by the government.) The rest were German (including two other barons and two untitled "vons") and were likely Baltic German Protestants.[16] Only two nationalities were effectively barred from the school: Polish Catholics and Jews. Anti-Polish restrictions went into effect after the Polish Revolt of 1863, and though Poles were never formally excluded from cadet schools, they faced barriers that made their admission virtually impossible.[17] Jews, by contrast, were simply banned outright. Jewish conscripts and volunteers served in the ranks—in fact, they were required by law to submit to the draft. But in keeping with the anti-Semitic prejudices of the high command, the only way a Jew could enter officer school was by converting to Orthodoxy.[18]

For all of these reasons, the Russification regime of the Naval College—and the capital military establishment in general—differed sharply from what Ungern had known in Reval. The college's overwhelmingly Russian environment made it only natural to expect that non-Russian cadets would quickly acquire a Russian cultural orientation. Admiral Chukhnin noted the challenge of teaching boys "of diverse views and backgrounds who come [to the school] from the far-flung corners of our expansive fatherland." And at least one incident occurred during Ungern's time at the school in which a German student was punished for making "a highly blasphemous statement, injurious to Russian Orthodox sentiment" during religion class—presumably Lutheran religion class since this would have been offered (in Russian) to Lutheran cadets.[19] But otherwise, no expressions of concern about language, religion, or national politics appear in the school records from the years of Ungern's attendance. The issue was apparently moot.

Becoming more Russian must have been an issue for Ungern personally since it involved so much schoolwork in the Russian language. But it is hard to imagine that he would have seen any point in resisting the process. Becoming more Russian did not require becoming less German. There were other Germans around him at the school, and the school's main concern was not rooting out German culture as much as instilling imperial devotion.

Rather than any questions about nationality, by far the greater challenge for Ungern—and for most of his peers—must have been simply adapting to the rigorous routine of the college itself. Students ate together at regular hours from the same revolving menu. Their dorms were Spartan. They drilled incessantly. Their teachers were dull, the courses duller. Any cadet who veered even slightly from the rule faced "confinement" (*arest*) of one duration and severity or another. The superintendent concluded that most of the boys "absolutely loathed" the college leadership. The staff's opinion of their students seems to have been equally dim.[20]

At first, Ungern did well enough in his classes, but by his third semester he had grown either bored or angry (or both) and, in a repeat of the situation in Reval, his grades began to slump. By the fall of 1904, he had sunk close to the bottom of the 168 students in his class.[21] His marks in "conduct" were especially terrible. In just a year and a half, he managed to be cited for forty-two violations, including oversleeping, missing class, fighting, smoking, returning late from leave, failing to keep his hair at "regulation length," and losing his documents.[22] (This is not the whole list.) He was also flip to his superiors. Once while on watch during a training cruise, he wandered away from his post. When the duty officer caught him and demanded an explanation, he apparently replied: "I'm not some sort of manservant. I don't have to stand in one place."[23]

By early 1905, the college had clearly had enough. The family was cabled to withdraw their miserable teenager immediately or face the certainty of expulsion. The withdrawal request arrived from Jerwakant a few days later, and on February 18, 1905, Ungern left the school.[24]

The Railroad and the War

As Ungern slid toward his second consecutive academic disaster, great events were unfolding just outside the window. Five weeks before he left the school, troops fired into a crowd of workers that had gathered in the large square in front of the Winter Palace. The workers carried icons and portraits of the tsar as well as a petition begging Nicholas to review their grievances: "We, the workers of St. Petersburg, our wives, our children, and our aged, helpless parents, come to Thee, O Sire, to seek justice and protection." The massacre—Bloody Sunday—shocked the country and turned into the first eruption of what became the 1905 Revolution.[25]

The revolution was the furious expression of all the uneven consequences of the empire's modernization over the preceding decades. All the resentments of Russian society exploded—of poor against rich, soldiers against officers, national groups against one another, liberals against conservatives, radicals against every one, and almost every one against the government. The tsarist regime managed to survive, but not before promising a parliament (the national Duma) and other concessions and enduring nearly two years of more or less continuous upheaval. During the chaotic days of mid-January, Ungern was surrounded by the first clashes of this great conflagration. He must have seen the soldiers and workers milling in the streets near the college. The school itself went into lockdown. Senior students collected rifles from the armory and took up posts on the rooftops.[26]

The fierce anger of the revolution was also fueled by the government's failures in an unpopular war with Japan that had begun a year earlier when the Japanese made a surprise attack on a Russian fleet resting in the Manchurian naval base of Port Arthur. The war's cause was imperialism. Japan was a new imperial power, Russia a much older one. But both were intent on expanding their influence in East Asia. The great prize was China—or rather parts of the Chinese periphery, its ports and northern borderlands—that the weak Qing Dynasty in Beijing (Peking) no longer seemed able to control.

Japan defeated the Qing in the Sino-Japanese War of 1894–1895 and became the dominant power in Korea. Russia established its influence in the northern Chinese region of Manchuria. But both countries envied each other's claims, which made conflict of some kind all but inevitable. When the war began in early 1904, the presumption on the part of the tsarist court and most every one else was that Russia—the power with the larger army, the larger navy, the *European* power—would win handily. Instead, the conflict dragged on for almost two years and Russia lost every major engagement and ultimately the war itself.

Two months after leaving the Naval College, against the backdrop of the revolution and the war, Ungern made a fateful decision: he volunteered for the army. While his exact motivations are unclear, with a war on, he must have signed up in the hopes of seeing action. The "great contest" with Japan was a fixture of daily life at the college during his last year—the tsar visited the school shortly after the declaration of war in order to commission the graduating class and prayers for victory were read at morning assembly. In the early going when enthusiasm ran high, Ungern, like all the cadets, would have seen columns of volunteers filing through the city streets on their way to the troop trains.[27] At the same time, it is also likely that he signed up at least in part for personal reasons: he may have been bored. According to a laconic entry in his college conduct book, relations with his stepfather were "difficult."[28] One assumes his latest scholastic debacle only made things worse.

Indeed, perhaps the young Ungern was looking for a measure of redemption. Perhaps going away to war was a chance for him to prove himself in a way that he hadn't been able to in school. (He also had a role model to follow since his father had done much the same thing in 1877 when he interrupted his studies to sign up to fight the Turks.) What seems likely in any case is that he was motivated both by duty and patriotism and by a drive for adventure and war—an urge to be in the action. These two vines of his character would grow together, curlicue-like, for the rest of his life, pulling him into the tsarist system and ultimately, by 1921, into imperial plans of his own.

Two weeks after his enlistment, Ungern found himself on his way to Manchuria, traveling in a troop train pounding along the Trans-Siberian. Though the full length of the great 5,000-mile railway would not be completed until 1916, the Trans-Siberian was still the most obvious material cause of the war. Even before construction began, the Japanese recognized the threat it posed to their interests. As Chancellor Yamagata Aritomo put it in 1888, "The day that a Trans-Siberian railway is completed will be the day crisis comes to Korea, and when crisis comes to Korea, the entire Orient will face upheaval."[29]

Japanese concerns grew when the Russians obtained permission from the Chinese to build a spur that would split off from the main Trans-Siberian and run on a giant 1,000-mile slant through Manchuria. By cutting across Chinese territory, the Chinese Eastern Railway (CER; Chinese: *Zhong Dong Tie Lu*), as this line came to be called, shortened Russia's road to the Pacific by close to 350 miles, allowing trains to reach the sea far faster (and more cheaply) than if they stayed solely on Russian territory.[30] (The Russians would eventually complete the longer track on their side of the border—the so-called Amur Railway. They simply saw the advantage of the shortcut through Manchuria and thus completed the CER first.) Naturally, the Japanese also saw the clear advantage that the CER gave to the Russians, and not long after it became operational, they attacked.

The Trans-Siberian, including the CER, ultimately fell far short of being the magical "road to power" that its enthusiastic supporters had hoped it would be.[31] The line had just one track, which limited the traffic it could carry, and speeds had to be kept low for long distances (often no more than 10 to 15 miles per hour) because of shoddy construction or difficult terrain, or both. Until late 1904, trains had to be unloaded and ferried across Lake Baikal by steamer (or on rails laid over the ice) before starting again on the other side. The railway was also hugely expensive and once the war began became even less efficient. As the Russian commander General Aleksei Kuropatkin reported to the tsar in the fall of 1904, "Our reinforcements arrive in driblets. Supplies dispatched in the spring are still on the line."[32] The train's influence on the battle fronts was profound—without it, the Russians could not even have fielded a credible army in the Far East. But its contribution to the outcome of the conflict, for obvious reasons, was much less glorious than expected.

The impact on the empire more generally, however, was unmistakable. As construction unfolded over the mid-1890s and early 1900s, millions of peasant settlers squeezed onto the railway to relocate to Siberia, or what was often simply called "Russia beyond the Urals" (*Rossiia za Uralom*) or "Asian Russia" (*Aziatskaia Rossiia*). Telegraph lines running along the track flashed news from one end of the country to the other. And the train bred a sense of optimism about the country—a rush of technological enthusiasm that echoed the heady mood that had buoyed the Americans and Canadians as they built their transcontinental lines a generation earlier.[33] The Trans-Siberian, it seemed, was

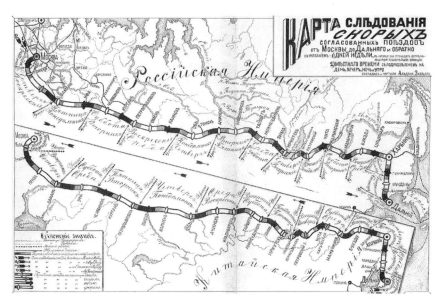

3.2. Map of the far-eastern express trains, 1903. Maps like this helped to elide the enormous distance between Moscow and China, bringing the Far East ever closer in the Russian imagination. Courtesy www.transsib.ru.

Russia's trampoline, bouncing it into the forefront of the world. The line was pulling Siberia into the "general cultural and economic orbit of the empire,"[34] Russifying the "alien East" by carting in wagonloads of Russian settlers, and creating a true "all-Russian economy" by transforming the Far East into a "vast new market for Russian industry."[35] To metric enthusiasts, the great vector even promised to deliver the country from its archaic habit of measuring everything according to its own scale of poods, versts, fathoms, and buckets. It was only a matter of time before the train delivered "the Kilogram...to the Pacific Ocean."[36]

Much of this excitement was overheated. The practical unifying effects of the Trans-Siberian were still years away. But the mental shift it produced began to shape people right away. Before the railway, travel between the western and eastern poles of the empire took weeks or months, either by horse and barge across the continent or by oceangoing steamship from the Black Sea through Suez and around India and China. Yet with the train, the fastest trip—the Moscow-Dal'nii express—took just nine days.

Maps of the railway from the early 1900s made the immense distance between Moscow and Manchuria look like it barely mattered at all.[37] The train's impact in this sense was Einsteinian: it redrew the accepted parameters of reality and produced a true "transformation of the dimensions of life and thought."[38] The faraway drew closer. The exotic came more into view. Steamy

geopolitical dreams—and fears—filled the air as Russians pondered the implications of being much closer to East Asia than they had ever seemed before.

Ungern's generation, the first generation of Russification, was also the first
to live within this new East Asian orientation, which in turn was reinforcing the
overall interconnectedness of the empire. For men and women of his time, the
fate of Far Eastern cities like Harbin and Vladivostok seemed palpably linked
to the futures of old western capitals like Helsingfors (Helsinki) and Warsaw, if
only because one could now move between them relatively easily. Stories about
them lay side-by-side in every newspaper. Though the Russo-Japanese War
ended up being a disaster for the Russians, ironically it only confirmed and
reinforced this new reality. Thanks to the Trans-Siberian, the empire began a
rapid Asian turn that made the East more relevant to the West, and vice versa.

"The Manchurian Side"

Ungern enlisted as a "private-volunteer" with the 91st Dvinsk Infantry Regiment in Reval on May 10, 1905. The 91st did not deploy to the front but instead
put new conscripts and reservists through crash-course training before ship-
ping them out east to join other regiments. In Ungern's case, this meant leaving
for Manchuria on May 21—just eleven days after his enlistment.[39] His group
of about sixty men traveled east by train, most likely first to St. Petersburg,
then Moscow, then to the Volga crossing at Syzran' and onward on the Trans-
Siberian across the Urals into Western Siberia. From there, they proceeded
over the Yenisei River into Eastern Siberia, then around Lake Baikal on the
newly completed Circum-Baikal Line, before finally turning south after Chita
onto the Trans-Baikal Line that cut down through the Trans-Baikal Region
(*Zabaikal'skaia oblast'*) toward the CER. After passing into Chinese territory
at Manchuria Station (Russian: *Man'chzhuria*; Chinese: *Manzhouli*), they then
crossed the final 600 miles to Harbin, the capital of Russian Manchuria. The
trip, given the traffic clogging the line, took about three weeks. By war's end,
over a million soldiers moved to the front along this route.[40] According to his
personnel file, sometime after reaching Irkutsk on the western side of Lake
Baikal, Ungern was formally handed off to his new regiment: the 12th Velikie
Luki.

By early June when Ungern reached the regiment's positions in the low hills
of central Manchuria just north of Mukden (today: Shenyang), the war was
effectively over.[41] The Japanese had destroyed the Russian fleet in mid-May
and, with both sides worn down, peace talks had begun. The ceasefire meant
that the soldiers on both sides had little more to do than hold their ground.
Ungern earned a medal for his service in the campaign. Many writers later
assumed that this meant he saw combat. In fact, there was no fighting by the

3.3. Russian troops leaving Reval for the Russo-Japanese War in 1904. Ungern volunteered for military service in Reval a year or so after this photo and may well have marched in a formation like this on his way to the troop train. The Domberg appears in the background. Reproduced from *Vana Tallinn: Ehitised Ja Inimesed* (Toomas Karjahärm, comp.) (Tallinn, 2007), 124.

time he arrived. Instead the men spent their time repairing fortifications and bridges, posting guard, and drilling. Or they simply waited. During the summer monsoons, the cascading rains turned everything into mud and made it hard to do much of anything.

According to the official history of the Velikie Luki, the soldiers were disappointed. They "longed" for the war to continue so that they could "pay the enemy back for Mukden and Tsushima."[42] One often reads this kind of thing in official histories of lost wars—the men wanted to keep fighting, the politicians forced them to stop. Perhaps this was the case in this instance, but if it was, it was surely only partially so. Yet in Ungern's case, he undoubtedly *did* want the war to go on. We can imagine his frustration—he had crossed the country to join the "great contest," but the contest, cruelly for him, had stopped just before he arrived. He then had to endure being stuck in Manchuria for half a year *after* the signing of the peace. Because of delays in withdrawing the army and revolutionary "disturbances" on the railway, the regiment didn't get back to European Russia until February 1906.[43]

The eight months that Ungern spent on "the Manchurian side" (M*an'chzhurshchina*), as the soldiers called it, introduced him to a new world. Based on the terms of their agreement with the Chinese, the Russians (in their view) had "absolute and exclusive rights of administration" over a narrow strip of territory surrounding the CER—the so-called alienated corridor (*po-losa otchuzhdeniia*).[44] Beyond the strip were the vast spaces of Manchuria, mostly barren steppes in the north and more thickly settled farmlands in the south.[45] Inside it, by contrast, was a de facto Russian colony, a "state within a state...with its own territory, authorities, and head of government"—that is, the director of the CER.[46]

Most Russian settlements within the corridor were small railway towns like Manchuria Station with perhaps a few thousand people, often next to or surrounded by Chinese villages. But in the middle was the colonial boomtown of Harbin, a bustling commercial and administrative center that straddled the intersection of the main CER and a trunk line that ran south to the Liaodong Peninsula and the strategic ports of Dal'nii (literally: Faraway; Chinese: Dalian) and Port Arthur (now: Lüshun). The Sungari River (Chinese: Songhua) also connected the city to the Amur lands in the north. Like Shanghai and other foreign "treaty ports," Harbin was a "dual city," at once Russian and Chinese, with a European-style Russian quarter of broad avenues and squares laid out next to a densely packed Chinese district, each with its separate jurisdictions.[47]

Ungern may never have gotten a good look at a Japanese soldier. His regiment faced the enemy lines, but the more ordinary interactions by the time he arrived would have been with Chinese peasants whose settlements surrounded the Russian positions. Ungern would have marched through local villages, with their pent-roofed, dun-colored houses, temples, and ancestor shrines. By the summer, he would have seen mule-drawn Manchurian "great carts" (Chinese: *da che*) hauling the soybean crop, and shallow-draft junks poling their way along the muddy Liao and Sungari rivers. The roads at the time would also have been clogged with refugees taking advantage of the ceasefire to return to their homes.

A tiny minority of the rural folk around where he was stationed in central Manchuria were Sinicized native peoples such as Manchus and Daurs, but the overwhelming majority were ethnic Chinese (Han). At the time of the Russo-Japanese War, Manchuria, which the Qing referred to as the Three Northeastern Provinces or simply, the Northeast (*Dongbei san sheng, Dongbei*), was in the midst of a long (and ambiguous) historical transformation from a Manchu borderland to a Chinese region,[48] and just two years after the war ended, the administration of the entire area was reorganized and ceased to be treated as a borderland at all.[49]

It is impossible to know what Ungern thought of the new peoples and cultures he was seeing. He was nineteen when he arrived in Manchuria. This was his first exposure to Asia, his first encounter with his country's far-reaching claims and influences over the lands of the Far East. Russian views of the peoples of East Asia were diverse, as were the East Asians themselves. But if there was a single overriding view it was that "Orientals" were inferior. Though the

3.4. Russian soldiers passing through Mukden (now Shenyang) in central Manchuria. Ungern was deployed not far from this city and would surely have seen scenes like this during his time in the war. Reproduced from the Library of Congress, LC-USZ62-103623.

Russians' identification with Europe *in* Europe was complicated, when it came to Asia, they tended to view themselves in European terms. They were the moderns, the bearers of civilization, representatives of the world of industry, enterprise, science, Christianity, law. Asian peoples, by contrast, were at best backward and oppressed, at worst cunning, dirty, and godless. Even comparatively positive stereotypes of "Asiatics" as spiritual or wise rested on the assumption that these traits, while admirable, mattered less than others in the modern world.[50]

Much of the Russian understanding of East Asia at the time was molded by race. The tsarist colony in Manchuria never became an "overtly racial regime" on the order of the Cape Colony or the Jim Crow South, for example.[51] But like their European and American counterparts, educated Russians saw the world through a lens of race that presumed white superiority. To numerous writers, the Chinese were a massive "yellow torrent" waiting to crash over Siberia, while Tsar Nicholas described the Japanese as "monkeys" and "yellow-faced dwarves," and almost everyone acknowledged a supposedly obvious "yellow peril" (*zheltaia opasnost'*), all close enough to the way that Westerners talked about these things for Russian and Western views to appear largely interchangeable.[52] These attitudes were obvious in the lead-up to the Russo-Japanese War, though they persisted afterward as well since, if anything, the Japanese victory only increased the level of anxiety. Anti-"yellow" prejudice would surround Ungern again when he served in the Amur region in the 1910s.

Not all Russians saw "the East" so dimly, however. In fact, some took the polar opposite view, including a small but highly placed group of intellectuals and enthusiasts known as the Asianists (*Vostochniki*), who interpreted their country's long-running relationship with Asia as unique and inspiring. As they saw it, Russia was itself an Asian country with roots going back to "ancient Scythia," and the Russian people were, if not Asians themselves, then at least far closer to them than other Europeans because of their long history of racial intermixing. The country thus needed to celebrate its common bonds with the "yellows" rather than rejecting their cultures as supposedly inferior.[53]

Of course, even this more "positive" view was still condescending. Indeed, the Asianists were just as imperialist as the broader culture around them, only in a slightly different vein. As they saw it, the Russians' longstanding bond with Asia meant that they were also the bearers of a special colonizing mission. Unlike Westerners who disdained and exploited Asian peoples, the Russians were benevolent elder brothers who intuitively understood and respected their values (such as monarchism and traditionalism). They knew the Asians better, and, as a result, they would help them better. As the mystical, Buddhist-loving Prince Esper Ukhtomskii put it in 1900, "There is nothing easier for Russians than getting along with Asiatics."[54]

By the time of the Mongolian campaign in 1920–1921, Ungern may well have borrowed something from this line of thinking. His Bolshevik interrogators describe him as being drawn to "Eastern culture" in every way, "including the food," and his writings from the time reflect the curious mixture of paternalism and cross-cultural redemption that we find in Ukhtomskii and other Asianists.[55] In a sense, he even outdid the Asianists in Orientophilia. While clearly fascinated with the East, they nonetheless identified with Russia and what they saw as its special Asian destiny, whereas Ungern ultimately came to reject Russia as completely degraded by the revolutionary corruptions of the West.

In this respect, he had more in common by the end of his life with post–World War I figures like the writer-philosopher Oswald Spengler, whose famous *Decline of the West* described Europe at the time as nothing more than "an empty sound," or the American émigré Ezra Pound, who dismissed it as "an old bitch gone in the teeth," "a botched civilization."[56] For Ungern, then, it wasn't just that he felt drawn to Asia; he was also completely repelled by

Europe, and by revolutionary Russia as a part of it. The "white race," in his view, was finished. It wasn't going to do anything for the "yellows." Instead it was the "yellows" who would save the whites.

But how much of this could have been in his thoughts in Manchuria in 1905? Some inkling of it perhaps, but with no record of his thoughts at the time, all we can say with relative certainty is that the Asia that surrounded him at that moment would surely have seemed at least as mundane and ordinary as it did evocative and inspiring. We know for one that the policies of the Russian army in Manchuria were much more practical than sentimental. The troops had orders to treat the Chinese fairly, which only made sense given how much the army depended on them for food, shelter, and labor. At the same time, however, it's clear that the high command never stopped seeing them as potentially suspect. The country folk might look like simple farmers, but couldn't they also be spies or bandits? Though the Qing remained formally neutral during the war, tsarist commanders simply assumed that, as "Asiatics," they naturally favored the Japanese. When Chinese villagers fled or were forced to evacuate, Russian troops often looted their homes, "looking for food, clothing, and women."[57]

For the rank-and-file soldiers marching around Ungern, the "yellows" they met in Manchuria must have appeared starkly different from themselves. Peasant settlers and Cossacks routinely looked down on the Chinese as "idol worshippers" (*idolopoklonniki*) and "unchristians" (*nekhristy*).[58] Similar prejudices flourished elsewhere, including Harbin, where a local expression seemed to say it all: "100 rubles is not money, 50 miles is no distance, and a Chinaman is not a person."[59]

"The Highest Tier according to Conduct"

What did Ungern make of all this? All that we can be sure of is that something happened in the Far East that changed his life. We know this because of what he did when the war ended. Though he returned to St. Petersburg to continue training to be an officer, in every other particular he broke with the past. He switched from the navy to the army. His grades and conduct improved. Most important, he figured out a way to stay in school and graduate in the normal two-year term. On June 15, 1908, with the tsar presiding over the ceremony, Ungern was handed his epaulettes as an officer in the Russian imperial army.[60] For his first post, he then proceeded to choose a Cossack regiment on the Chinese border.

When Ungern resumed his studies in St. Petersburg in the spring of 1906, the country was still rumbling with the effects of the revolution. The empire's first parliament—the Duma—was convening in keeping with the promise made by the tsar a few months earlier in October after the country had been brought to a virtual standstill by a great statewide strike. Newspapers roiled with political discussion. Workers still protested periodically. Peasants from the Ukraine to the Volga had begun a turn toward open rebellion, torching the houses of landlords, seizing noble land. The violence of the revolution in the countryside would continue in fits and starts for another year.

Just two months before Ungern's return from Manchuria, the violence had also reached his family. In December 1905 Jerwakant was looted and burned, sacked by a crowd of peasants along with workers from Reval, one of close to two hundred manors destroyed in the Baltic during what the barons called "the Time of the Fires." (The Hoyningen-Huenes were able to flee the house shortly before the mob arrived, but they had to leave everything behind, including Sophie Charlotte's "beautiful silver.") The army together with German "self-defense" units followed up by organizing sweeps known as "punitive expeditions" to round up "criminal elements"—in fact any persons who seemed like they might have had a hand in the mayhem or were unlucky enough to be in the wrong place at the wrong time. Field courts delivered swift sentences. Roughly nine hundred people were executed in the Baltic before the unrest was put down, with many more exiled to Siberia.[61]

The uncertainty of the times also affected the military. The shock of Russia's defeat in the war with Japan and the rash of mutinies that swept through the army during the conflict produced a bitter critique of military leadership, both within educated society and the military itself. Officers in particular wrote openly about their poor training and the need to improve military education. The cadet schools were derided for being either too harsh or too soft on their "white-gloved" charges, and the military institutes (*voennye uchilishcha*)—the more advanced officer training schools that represented the next rung up in the system—seemed just as deficient, offering an education that seemed at once superficial and out-of-date, narrowly technical and overly frivolous. (The 1905 Revolution marked a low point of enthusiasm for mandatory dancing lessons.)[62]

Worst of all, the institutes were accused of doing their students, known as "yunkers" (*iunkera*), a disservice by instilling them with an overweening sense of entitlement and reinforcing the idea that they were somehow separate from the rest of society. As one officer wrote,

> Everywhere else in the world, people see an army officer as a professional, as some one whose training gives him the skills necessary for his particular line of work. They expect him to know how to do his job, much as they would any engineer, doctor, lawyer, or professor. It's only in our country that people seem to think their military men need to be a separate breed of people (*osobaia poroda liudei*) with their own unique cultivation and their own ethics and sense of duty.[63]

To reform-minded officers and even some conservatives, what postrevolutionary Russia needed instead was a professional, fit, sensible "modern officer" more in step with the country's changing society.[64]

As far as the high command was concerned, the officer of the future also needed to be more reliably Russian. The Revolution of 1905 ended up raging as much in the borderlands of the empire as in the center. The burning of Jerwakant, in this sense, was symbolic of a range of ethnic tensions, all of which convinced a number of generals that the army needed to consider making a great transition. Rather than continuing to be a multiethnic imperial force, it needed to transform itself into something closer to a national army, a true "nation at arms" to be led by Russian officers who knew "how to fight for all that is Russian" (*za vse russkoe*).[65]

In keeping with this idea, the high command established a commission that looked into the question and proposed expanding the range of restrictions affecting non-Russian officers, including, for the first time, introducing limits on the number of Lutherans in the corps, which de facto meant introducing limits on the number of Russian Germans. According to the proposed plan, all the national groups in the empire would be ranked according to their perceived degree of loyalty to the government. Non-Russian officers would be banned from serving in their home regions in order to guard against the possibility of their joining up with their fellow nationals against the Russians. Even Russian officers with spouses from suspect groups—Armenians, Poles, and Jews, in particular—would face restrictions.[66]

In the end, however, despite such proposals, the officer corps did not change much. The share of non-Russians remained largely the same through to the end of the old regime. Indeed, many of the high commission's suggestions were purposefully shelved, in part because the General Staff realized they would be too messy to introduce, but also because they concluded that non-Russian nationality was, in fact, not really a problem. Scores of colonels and generals might have German or Georgian surnames, but this was just the surface. They were otherwise completely Russified—or at least this is how it seemed to the high command.

Indeed, one of the abiding articles of faith of the tsarist military elite in its last decade was the sense that merely serving in the army was enough to produce Russification, and it was this perception, paradoxically, that helped keep the institution diverse. The specifics of nationality, according to authorities like General Anton Denikin, "had no effect on the friendly course of regimental life." Army life made "ethnic differences" irrelevant—they simply "faded away."[67] There was thus no need to legislate against diversity because diversity—at least in a meaningful sense—was going to disappear in any case.

All this is to say that there is no indication in the files that Ungern had any trouble returning to officer school as a Baltic German Lutheran. Thanks to his voluntary enlistment during the war, his prior academic record was overlooked, and in October 1906 he was admitted to the Paul the First Military Institute (*Pavlovskoe voennoe uchilishche*) located on Great Savior Street (*Bol'shaia Spasskaia ul.*) on the Petersburg Side in central St. Petersburg, not far from the Peter and Paul Fortress and less than a mile from the Naval College.[68]

Like the Naval College, Ungern's new school was an elite establishment whose students were overwhelmingly either hereditary nobles or the sons of officers (or both);[69] and the surroundings were the same: the same grand neo-classical complex, the same long hallways with squeaky parquet floors and walls larded with the portraits of tsars and generals, the same vast courtyard where the yunkers marched and drilled incessantly.[70] Like the college, the mood of the school was also austere. A cadet just a few years senior to Ungern recalled that there was "no such thing as fun at the institute."[71] With the exception of leave, the only break from the numbing routine of class and drill was summer training at the nearby suburban military camp of Krasnoe Selo (Beautiful Village), where at least the young men were allowed to scream and charge.[72]

Ungern earned the equivalent of a "C" average in his classes, which for him was a breakthrough.[73] He also completely reformed his behavior. While a number of his classmates were cited for failing to properly salute their superiors or returning from leave "in a drunken state with an unbuttoned overcoat," Ungern managed to maintain a spotless record and ultimately graduated in the "highest tier according to conduct."[74]

We can also assume that he continued his Russian turn. According to school records, 90 percent of his fellow yunkers were Russian Orthodox, as were all of the officer-instructors.[75] In that sense, Ungern would have stood out as a German island in a Russian sea. But by the same token, one wonders how German he would have seemed by at this time in any case. Though he had a double-barreled German surname and took Lutheran rather than Orthodox religion class, he would have appeared Russian enough in most other ways. After four years of military school and almost a year in army service, his spoken Russian must have been completely fluent.

Indeed, to the high command a non-Russian cadet like Ungern would probably have seemed a fine example of the army's supposedly special Russianizing power. At the same time, it is unlikely that his Germanness would have been wiped away during his time at the institute. Instead, it's more probable that rather than losing or rejecting his former identity, he simply continued adopting another, becoming, in effect, a cross-cultural hybrid with attachments to both cultures.

This sort of cultural in-betweenness was a common condition of imperial life, though the particulars necessarily varied enormously from person to person. In part, this was due to the enormous diversity of the empire. Every social environment within the country allowed for potentially different combinations of language, faith, and social practices. But it also reflects the fact that the late tsarist state never proposed a single way for its subjects to be multicultural—or even unicultural, for that matter. Unlike the Bolsheviks, who invented the ideal of a new Soviet man, the old regime—precisely because it was an old regime—never developed an equivalent tsarist imperial man as an ideal type. Imperial subjecthood remained relatively flexible during the Duma years that followed 1905, even with all the official prejudice of the Russification laws and the clamor against "borderland types" (*okraintsy*) on the part of Russian nationalists.[76] The formula for imperial belonging would tighten with the coming of the Great War, but that was still in the future.

Yunkers chose their postgraduation postings based on class rank. Students at the top of the class were allowed to pick first and usually opted to continue their education at one of the elite military academies or to join a prestigious guards' regiment. (The valedictorian of Ungern's class, for example, chose a post with the Finnish Life Guards.)[77] Given that Ungern found himself over a hundred spots farther down the list, however, his options were less lofty. The average students around him tended to choose infantry regiments in European Russia, where most of the army was stationed, with posts near big cities like Warsaw, Odessa, Riga, and Moscow going first. A smaller share selected destinations in the Caucasus, Central Asia, and Siberia. According to family lore, Ungern loved to ride and wanted to serve in the cavalry—his superiors would later describe him as a talented horseman—so he chose a posting with a Cossack Host: the Trans-Baikal Cossacks, whose regiments faced the border with the Qing Empire in the regions of Outer Mongolia and northeastern Manchuria.[78]

Things might have been different. His initial preference seems to have been for a posting with the Siberian Cossack Host near the town of Chimkent, in what is today southeastern Kazakhstan. Just a few days later, however, this assignment was changed. Scrolling down the typed list of yunkers' postings, we see the original entry crossed out and the new one scratched in by hand above it.[79]

It's unclear why Ungern made the switch, or even whether it was his own decision.[80] Was the opening in Central Asia withdrawn? Did he reconsider and opt for something closer to Manchuria because of his service there during the war? All we know for sure is that with the stroke of a pen, his life shifted onto a different path. By moving from Turkestan to Eastern Siberia, the army's newest officer was heading farther east, like the empire itself.

Like his fellow classmates assigned to the Asian half of the empire, Ungern received an extra month's leave following graduation. After that, he had fifteen days to report to his post.[81]

CHAPTER 4

BEYOND THE BAIKAL

"Why is your Siberia so cold?"
"Such is God's will!" answers the coachman.
—ANTON CHEKHOV. *From Siberia*

Toward Asia

Russians in Ungern's time were used to thinking of their country as divided into two uneven parts: European Russia (*Evropeiskaia Rossiia*) on the western side of the Ural Mountains, home to the historical core of the state and its great cities, and Asian Russia (*Aziatskaia Rossiia*) stretching out to the east, more than twice as vast as the western side but far less developed.

The famous chemist Dmitri Mendeleev explained the contrast between the two halves as a tale of two centers: the center of the empire's population, which he situated in a corner of Tambov province not far from Moscow, and the center of the country's "inhabitable area"—that is, the center of all the territory outside of the far north of the state—which he pinpointed some 1,300 miles to the east near the town of Omsk in Western Siberia.[1] Connecting the two points, as he saw it, was a simple reality. The Russians lived overwhelmingly in the western end of their homeland, but the territory *available* to them lay overwhelmingly in the east, which meant, necessarily, that over time they would be drawn to the east as well. In fact, Mendeleev argued that this eastward shift was a "law" of history that had already been unfolding incrementally for centuries. Tambov was thus destined to meet up with Omsk. If anything, the rendezvous would simply come all the faster now that the country had finally begun to race ahead at the speed of the locomotive and the steamboat.

It's easier to see what Mendeleev had in mind when we imagine the kind of map he might have used for his projections.[2] On the western side, we find the well-blackened circles of St. Petersburg and Moscow and the myriad points of lesser cities, towns, and villages—a world of dots of all sizes. Turning east, however, the dots mostly disappear. A few black circles nestle in the oasis heartland of Central Asia. Vladivostok stands guard in the Far East. Besides this, though, what stands out most is a thin strip of points running unevenly across the far southern portion of the region. This is the human shadow of the Trans-Siberian, the narrow trace, in effect, of the momentous colonizing movement Mendeleev was talking about. As he and other supporters of the railway had predicted, the great line was indeed pulling Tambov to Omsk, but it was doing so by the slenderest of threads. The Siberia that most Russians knew, if they knew it at all, was the train. Beyond it lay a sprawling, largely vacant wilderness.

Ungern was twenty-two years old when he set out for the far side of the Urals. In a photo taken shortly before his deployment, he appears tall and lanky, fair-haired, with a young man's wispy moustache. Staring confidently into the camera and dressed smartly in his new Trans-Baikaler uniform, he has the look of youthful possibility and composed military manliness that one finds in countless officer graduation portraits of the time.[3] Having crossed the country a few years earlier to join the Russo-Japanese War, he would have known that he was about to leave the well-dotted side of the map for the almost un-dotted one. All of Siberia was sparsely populated then, but the more rugged and distant part of the region between the Yenisei River and the Amur—what the Russians refer to as Eastern Siberia—had fewer people than the western half, and Ungern's destination within Eastern Siberia—the region east of Lake Baikal—had fewer still.

The Russian conquest of Siberia began in the 1580s under Ivan the Terrible. The Cossack Ermak Timofeevich, leading an army of mercenaries in the pay of a mining magnate, toppled the Khan of Kuchum and claimed (at least temporarily) his khanate for the tsar. But this was only the western part of Western Siberia. It took the Muscovites another generation to cross the vast and difficult distances to Lake Baikal, subjugating new peoples as they went. When they reached the Baikal in the early seventeenth century, they found one of Earth's natural wonders, the world's deepest lake, teeming, as the explorers put it, with "fish of all sorts and beasts of the sea."[4] Nearby the newcomers also found local peoples—semi-nomadic Buryats and Tungus (Evenks). Over the following hundred years, they alternatively parlayed and bludgeoned these groups into submission, gradually bringing the entire region "under the tsar's high hand."[5]

As the Russians built up their presence on the Baikal, they settled most thickly on the western side. Irkutsk, the largest city in Eastern Siberia by Ungern's time, was founded just west of the lake, having begun as a Muscovite

4.1. Ungern, around the time of his graduation from the Paul the First Military School.
This photo shows the young graduate in his new Trans-Baikal Host uniform.
Having just received his officer's epaulettes, he is about to head east.
Reproduced from Nikolai von Essen (comp.), *Nachrichten über
das Geschlecht Ungern-Sternberg*, Vol.4, *Urkunden–
Stammtafeln–Ahnentafeln–Porträts*
(Tartu, 1939), pl. 14.

fort on the Angara River in the midst of the wooded-steppes of the Western
Buryats. By comparison, the region across the lake to the southeast, what the
Russians called at first *Dauria* ("the land of the Daurs") and later *Zabaikal'e*
(literally: "the land beyond the Baikal") was always less inhabited.[6] Buryats
and Tungus lived here as well, though because of the broader prairie land in
this part of the Baikal zone, they were more thoroughly nomadic than their
cousins in the west. (The early Russian documents refer to them as "horse
people.") The Russians in the region were also far fewer—for centuries little
more than a dusting of peasants, townsmen, Cossacks, and convicts. Around
the time of Ungern's arrival, even with a rising tide of settlers carried in by
the railroad, the entire Trans-Baikal region (*Zabaikal'skaia oblast'*), a territory
bigger than Germany and just a little smaller than the Hapsburg Empire, had a
population less than half the size of St. Petersburg.[7]

What would have drawn Ungern to this distant frontier? Most of his contemporaries never visited the Trans-Baikal. Even today the region seems remote to people from the European side of the country. Yet Ungern's coming of age coincided with rising interest in Siberia and the empire's far eastern peripheries. The war with Japan was a part of this eastern turn—even a product of it in a very basic sense—but the turn involved more than geopolitics alone. Poets and artists like the Orientophiles (*Vostokofily*) took up Asian themes. Spiritualists evoked the "mysteries" of Asian religion. Scholars of different sorts fanned out toward the Pacific with their instruments and notebooks. And the public followed the progress of eastern colonization in the newspapers.[8] For centuries, Siberia had seemed little more than a distant icebox. Now, thanks in part to the magic filament of the railway, it was becoming a source of fascination and anticipation, the empire's "house of riches," its latest "land of the future."[9]

Ungern must have been affected by this broad Asian turn, though the decision to start his career in the Trans-Baikal was probably influenced at least as much by his service in Manchuria during the war and by the role models right around him, including numerous Baltic Germans who viewed the country's eastern frontier as a "spacious field" for proving themselves and "acquiring position and character."[10] Though "going east" never became the near obligatory rite for them that the "grand continental tour" had been for English lords in the eighteenth century, it was common enough. The empire was home to multiple societies in miniature moving in predictable cycles: long-distance merchants and brokers, Orthodox and Muslim pilgrims, radicals sent in and out of exile, civilian officials, military men. A subset of Baltic Germans, most of them from the army or civil service, made up another of these mobile imperial communities. They grew up and received their educations in the western half of the country and then went east before (usually) coming back again.

We find this pattern in the Ungern-Sternberg clan, where a number of Ungern's close and distant relations traveled in or wrote about "the East." (Some relations on his mother's side, the Wimpffens, did as well, including his uncle and godfather, Max, who published a study of Buddhism.) Neighbors like the von Keyserlings, who lived just down the road from Jerwakant, in particular, the venerable naturalist Count Alexander von Keyserling and his grandson, Hermann, a boyhood friend of Ungern's who later became a philosopher-mystic in Germany, took long Asian travels. Ungern even had a direct tie to Asian service in the person of his great uncle, General Paul von Rennenkampf, a hero of the war with Japan who began his career with the Trans-Baikal Host and would later command the first army corps Ungern served in during World War I.[11]

Given these circumstances, perhaps it's not surprising that a young baron would have sought to start his career on a remote frontier like the Trans-Baikal. It was the sort of usefully faraway place where one could gain experience and stand out. People back home would talk about you. And who better to serve with at the edge of the empire than the Cossacks, the empire's ultimate frontiersmen?

"The Most Special Sort of Russians"

The origins of the Cossacks go back to the fourteenth century when bands of roamers and runaways began establishing isolated enclaves in different parts of the great unclaimed grasslands south of Muscovy. (The term "Cossack" derives from a Turkic word for "freebooter" or "outlaw.") For centuries, these slowly forming communities lived by their own codes and developed a fiercely independent culture, sometimes allying themselves with Moscow and the other powerful states around them, sometimes flaunting their disobedience.

By Ungern's time, however, the so-called age of Cossack freedom (*volia*) had long since passed. The Russian empire defeated its rivals for the steppe by the end of the eighteenth century and over the years that followed it gradually but relentlessly transformed the Cossack world, eliminating the groups it didn't like (such as the Zaporozhians of central Ukraine, for example) and re-organizing the rest as frontier cavalry forces known as Hosts (*voisko;* plural: *voiska*). In the process, Cossack men became a species of farmer-soldier, their lives divided between working their homesteads and patrolling the frontier, while Cossacks overall became a social estate (*soslovie*) alongside others within the Russian system.[12]

In 1908, the year that Ungern entered the Cossack domain, eleven Hosts with a combined population of some eight million people stood guard along stretches of the empire's roughly 4,500-mile border between the Black Sea and the Pacific.[13] Some of the Hosts—like those centered around the Don and Terek rivers in southern Russia—were heirs to the old independent Cossacks of Muscovite times. But most, including the five centered in the Asian half of the country, were more recent creations. As the empire pushed into Siberia and beyond, the tsars enlisted Cossacks to defend the country's expanding frontiers, and when no Cossacks were on hand in the vicinity, they simply created new ones by decree.

To start a new Host, families from existing ones usually found themselves forcibly relocated to the new frontier, with local peasant colonists and, depending on the region, native peoples drummed in on site to join them. The new Host would then be granted land by the state, while individual Cossacks grabbed whatever additional land they could for themselves by "right of occupation" (*po zakhvatu*). The approach worked well enough, and Cossacks seemed useful enough, that the process was repeated several times over.

The history of the Trans-Baikal Host followed this general pattern.[14] The first Cossacks came to the region from other parts of Siberia in the mid-1600s at the head of expeditions dispatched by the court to explore the territory and claim whatever local peoples they found as new subjects. Typically this involved the Cossacks offering the Siberian natives what they described as "presents" (metal cups and knives, glass beads, cloth) so that the locals would in turn give them furs, which the Cossacks then conveniently interpreted as "tribute" (*yasak*).[15] Not surprisingly, to the natives, this looked more like trade than political subjugation, which led to a certain amount of confusion.

Raids and killings flashed between the various sides when the trade-like tribute broke down. There were also confrontations with the Qing in nearby Mongolia and Manchuria, who resented the Russian encroachments. In the process, Cossack blockhouses were besieged and torched, and early Russian claims to the region of the Amur River, whose headwaters began just to the east, were rebuffed. But the Muscovite grip on the Trans-Baikal nonetheless tightened over time, and the number of Cossacks in the region slowly grew as new "service people" signed on along with willing (or forcibly recruited) Buryats and Tungus.

The various Russian and native Cossack groups created through this incremental process of incorporation established themselves in a winding string of small fortified outposts (*ostrogi*) on the "Dauria side" south and east of the Baikal, between the Selenga and Argun rivers, facing the agreed-upon border with the Qing Empire.[16] Then, in 1851, after not doing much at all with these communities for the better part of two hundred years, the government dramatically increased their numbers by forcing local peasants to enroll and placed all of them—the old and the more recent—under the authority of a new, overarching Trans-Baikal Host.

The creation of the new Host was motivated by the purest sort of geo-politics. Just a decade after it was founded, using well-timed saber rattling, the tsarist government pressured the Qing into giving up the northern banks of the Amur and Ussuri rivers, bringing what is now the entire Russian Far East into Russian hands and making good on the expansion that they had failed to achieve two centuries earlier. The grand designer of this revanchism was Lieutenant General Nikolai Murav'ev, governor-general of Eastern Siberia at the time and an outspoken proponent of Russia's "Pacific destiny." Not uncoincidentally, Murav'ev was also the driving force behind the creation of the Host, and the close relationship between Russian imperialism and the Host that began in his time continued until the end of the empire. In 1900, Trans-Baikal regiments moved into Manchuria to help put down the Boxer Rebellion, staying on afterward to guard the Chinese Eastern Railway. (Ungern's great uncle Paul von Rennenkampf was there at the time as well.) In the war with Japan, the Trans-Baikalers fought in Manchuria and Korea, and after the peace, they figured prominently in the General Staff's various scenarios for what might come next.[17]

The campaigns took a heavy toll on the Host's economy. Every Cossack deployed faraway meant one less worker on the farm, and given that Cossack families were expected to provide horses and supplies for their fighting men, the material costs of service quickly added up. As one Cossack lament from 1907 put it, "Oh, how bitter our sadness/ No more tears have we to shed/ This treacherous twentieth century/ Such misery it has bred."[18] Trans-Baikal commanders also worried about the cost of a more general sort of decline. Drink and permissiveness had set in in the settlements. Schools were failing. "Our young children can't recite even the most basic prayers or the titles of the tsar or the name of their settlement commander (*stanichnyi ataman*), while the older ones seem to know nothing of the land of their birth (*rodina*) or of our Cossack history."[19]

In addition to these woes, there were doubts about the Cossacks' worthiness as a fighting force. By the early twentieth century, it was clear to the War Ministry that Hosts everywhere were in trouble. Though designed as would-be "self-financing institutions," they seemed to have little hope of making the revenue needed to outfit their men for war in an industrial age, and so a slow if inconsistent move began to try to solve the problem by folding the Hosts more completely into the regular structures of the army.[20]

Yet the Cossacks continued to have admirers, not least because of the place they'd come to occupy in the Russian historical imagination. By Ungern's time, the unruly Cossacks of yesteryear had been cleaned up and repackaged as romantic heroes thanks to the writings of Pushkin, Gogol', and Tolstoy, all of whom had become required reading in every high school curriculum. Their manly panache leapt off of the canvases of artists like Ilya Repin and Vasilii Surikov. Cossack daring even starred in the first successful Russian film, *Stenka Razin,* which (in eight dramatic minutes) told the doomed love story of a seventeenth-century Cossack rebel.[21] Ungern must have been exposed to this Cossack lore and, like many adventurous young men of his time, could well have dreamed of joining imaginary horsemen on their fierce rides through the frontier.

The army, meanwhile, had its own Cossack myth. Though the high command was well aware of the financial and logistical problems facing the Hosts, they had little interest in getting rid of them (this would happen later with great brutality under the Bolsheviks). Instead, they wanted to reform them to make them more effective. In fact, to the Hosts' most committed supporters, the Cossacks did not need much reform at all, only a redoubling of their traditional "warrior spirit" and dedication to the crown. Nicholas II, for one, idolized his Cossack regiments, trusting them as his most loyal soldiers, the unbending wall that had protected the monarchy from the tide of revolution that almost destroyed it in 1905. (In fact, this argument became perhaps the most important one for maintaining the Cossacks as a special force.) Cossacks themselves took pride in what they called the "Cossack way"—a euphemism for everything that seemed to make them "the most special sort of Russians, sharply different from the rest of the empire's estates."[22]

And indeed, much about the Cossacks was different, down to the small details. Cossack ranks and designations were tinged with the exotic patina of the past—*ataman* for Cossack leader, *khorunzhi* for junior lieutenant, *stanitsa* for Cossack settlement. Even the term "Host" was archaic and peculiar, used only in regard to Cossack forces rather than other divisions of the military. Cossacks were allowed to grow their hair longer than their counterparts in the regular army. They had their own headgear—the *papakha,* a tall cylindrical hat made of black-dyed sheep's wool—as well as a special sword, the razor-sharp, slightly curved Cossack saber (*shashka*), which they carried, when riding, slung across their backs on a hanger.[23] They had their own courts and customs, their own credo of service.

By the time Ungern joined them, regardless of their problems, it's fair to say that the Trans-Baikal Cossacks were just as impressed with their distinctiveness—and jealous of their prerogatives—as any of the other Hosts of the empire. As the authors of a cheap pocketbook of Host tales and songs reminded their readers: "Be proud, *Zabaikal'tsy,* for, thanks to the tsar's boundless grace, you belong to the great Cossack family."[24]

With the Aliens on a Sea of Grass

Ungern stepped off the Trans-Siberian to report for duty at Host headquarters in Chita, the largest city in the Trans-Baikal, on July 27, 1908.[25] From there he proceeded to his post with the 2nd Company of the 1st Argun Regiment in Military Sector 2, with quarters in the small outpost of Ust'-Narynsk. The Host then was divided into four sectors, each responsible for a parcel of the Chinese border. Sector 2 faced the border on the Argun River, and Ust'-Narynsk was located on the river itself, not far from the modern town of Zabaikal'sk, roughly 300 miles southeast of Chita.

The outpost was formally administered by the larger settlement of Tsagan-Oluevskaya (today: Tsagan-Oluy), the site of the closest regiment office and located farther in behind the border. (Tsagan-Oluevskaya was also quite close to Dauria, were Ungern would later serve during the civil war.) In 1908, this larger settlement had a population of just over forty-five hundred people, including five hundred active-duty Cossacks. Ust'-Narynsk would have been much smaller—perhaps just a hundred residents, probably less.[26] This tiny place, not even a dot on the map of the empire, would be Ungern's home for the next year and a half.[27]

The land all around was steppe—rolling grassy prairie. Ungern would have first seen the area in high summer, dried brown by the sun. The contrast with the northern part of the Trans-Baikal would have been striking. Chita, then as now the major transit hub of the region, lies in the midst of high hills covered in evergreens and deciduous larch and birch, a continuation of the hilly, forested landscape that makes up most of Eastern Siberia. Even in summer, with all the dirt and dust of a rumbling industrial center, there is a greenness to the city. But leaving Chita by train toward the Chinese border, you watch the heights of the hills gradually diminish, as if a great hand were slowly pressing down the elevations. By the time you arrive in the zone of the old Cossack settlements, the hills have become low-rolling grassy knobs, and the woods have disappeared. The steppe is at its gentlest in the spring when the swelling rises become covered in a lush carpet of tufted grasses and blossoming forbs and wild flowers—"a sea of green without end."[28] Winters and summers, by contrast, are harsh, either impossibly cold or achingly hot.

In 1908 the Trans-Baikal Cossacks had a population of just under 240,000 people, about one-third of the population of the Trans-Baikal *oblast'* as a whole. Roughly a tenth of the Host was made up of males of service age (from nineteen to thirty-seven years old) who rotated through phases of duty along and behind the border.[29] The steppes were too dry for much farming, so the base of the economy was in livestock: sheep, cattle, goats, horses. Each Cossack was expected to provide his own fully outfitted mount, which meant that the horses were especially prized, both on the Cossack homesteads and in the

4.2. Chinese Junction (Kitaiskii raz"ezd; now: Tarskaia), about seventy miles east of Chita. The Trans-Baikal spur splits off here from the main Trans-Siberian line to make its way down to the Chinese border and the CER. Ungern would have passed through this junction countless times. Courtesy www.ruscarts.ru.

Host's large reserve herds.[30] Most of the animals were of the short, hardy Mongolian type, though the breed was known by the Cossacks as their own "Trans-Baikal horse." The markings and names of the animals are scrupulously noted in the Host's papers: "Mamai," "Mars," "Athos," "Friend," "Turtunai," "Kermek," "Janissary," "Jaguar," "Spider," "Serb."[31] If the family stories are true and Ungern had indeed wanted to ride, he had come to the right place. He had arrived in the land of the horse.

He had also joined a very different sort of imperial environment. The Trans-Baikalers were engineered by the state to serve the cause of Russian imperialism, but they were just as much the products of a less directed sort of imperial history. Cossacks lived among Buryats and Tungus, whose cultures had adapted to the grasslands as nomadic pastoralists. The Buryats are a Mongol people. The Tungus, in linguistic terms, are most closely related to Manchus. When the Russians first reached the Trans-Baikal, both groups were shamanists, but beginning in the late 1600s the Buryats, following the Mongols, converted to Lamaist Buddhism, and most of the Tungus of the steppe converted thereafter to either Orthodoxy or Buddhism, though shamanist beliefs never entirely disappeared. Of the two communities, the Buryats were by far the more numerous. By Ungern's time, they outnumbered the so-called "Horse Tungus" by a little more than three to one and over the centuries had strongly "Buryatized" their culture.[32]

The Trans-Baikalers were deeply influenced by both groups. Roughly 12 percent of the Cossacks were Tungus and Buryats, making the Host a fundamentally multiethnic and multiconfessional society.[33] Thirty-three Lamaist temples (Buriat: *datsan*) operated on Host lands together with ninety churches. Relatively few non-Russian Cossacks lived in Ungern's sector, but Buryat *ulus* (nomadic encampments) dotted the Aga steppe that rolled just behind the sector settlements, and Tungus occupied two areas to the north and east.

Russian and native worlds were thickly interwoven. Russian was the official language of the Host, but the Cossacks' everyday speech was laced with words drawn from Tungus and Buryat, and it was common for native Russian speakers to know the other languages. Buddhists and Orthodox revered the same local shrines and saints (St. Nicholas to Lamaist Buryats was *Khutuktu Mikola*—Nicholas the Reincarnated Lama), and paid their priests the same way—with money, sheep, furs, bread. Everyone (Russians included) turned to shamans whenever it seemed useful, such as when plagues struck their flocks. In Cossack towns like Aksha, Buryats and Russians went together to the local music hall.[34]

Intermarriages were common—of Buryats and Tungus with one another, and of Russians with both groups—which then had the natural effect of producing mixed-race children. According to one observer, there were three dominant "types" in the Trans-Baikal: Slavs, Buryats, and "mestizos" (*metisy*).[35] Not

4.3. Trans-Baikal Cossack, probably a Buryat or Tungus, late 1890s. Note the curved saber and the tall cylindrical hat known as a papakha. Reproduced from *Chasovye otechestva: iz istorii rossiiskogo kazachestva; katalog vystavki* (St. Petersburg, 2006), 90, no. 100.

surprisingly, the long history of getting along in this particular way affected physical appearances. As a government report put it in 1899, "The Russians [here] possess unique physical characteristics that [make them] quite different from the Russian national type that predominates in European Russia." In fact, in the authors' view, there was a distinct "Trans-Baikal type" created from the "well-established fusion" of Russian and native "elements."[36] Ordinary Russians in the region referred to the process more directly as "going Buryat" (*bratskovat'*—from the old Russian term for Buryats—*bratskie*, or *bratskie liudi*) and called Russian-native mixed-race people *karymy*, from the Buryat/Mongol word *kharym*, meaning "foreign" or "of another birth."[37]

The same sort of mixing took place between the Cossacks and the Mongols and Chinese across the Qing border—or more precisely, across *one* of the borders. For there were, in fact, two borders where Ungern was serving, one relatively new and the harbinger of things to come, the other much older and seemingly destined to fade out. The most obvious signs of the modern border were in Manchuria Station, the nearby railway town located just inside Qing territory and the first station on the CER that one reached from the Russian side. (Ungern had passed through here earlier on his way to and from the Russo-Japanese War, and the town would loom large in his life in the civil war to come.) Russian guards and customs inspectors worked here as well as veterinary officials and doctors who checked Russia-bound travelers and livestock for plague and other diseases.[38] Qing officials also had their offices in the town. Manchuria Station was home, in effect, to much of the bureaucratic machinery of an international border that we now see as ordinary and familiar.

In the early twentieth century, however, this sort of border was still relatively new, a product of the intertwined and growing dynamics of nationalism and state power. As European societies became more integrated over the course of the 1800s, they defined themselves all the more against foreign societies, and their governments stepped all the deeper into the role of gatekeepers. Borders—and the laws and procedures reinforcing them—became the real and metaphorical ramparts of the country. They had to be well-guarded, the nation behind them well-protected. In keeping with this logic, states increasingly monopolized the powers of admission and exclusion. Understandings of citizenship and subjecthood grew more tightly defined. Passports and other identity documents proliferated. Migration quotas, sanitary inspections, and customs declarations followed. By the end of the century, this new complex of institutions and practices, having begun in Europe, multiplied into an international norm. "Watchtowers, passport stamps, and serious men" began lining up along borders wherever governments were able.[39]

But the arrival of this new sort of border did not erase what had been there before, at least not in the Trans-Baikal. On the platform at Manchuria Station, watching first the Russian officials then the Chinese make their checks (or vice versa), one could feel the separation—or at least the intention of separation—that modern border crossings are supposed to convey. But just a few miles away, at Ungern's outpost on the river, the separation was much harder to see. There, in keeping with longstanding traditions, Cossacks and other locals would travel regularly back and forth across the Argun. The headmen of settlements like Ust'-Narynsk brokered agreements with Mongols and their Manchu commanders to cut hay, chop wood, and graze their flocks on the Qing side. They crossed over to fish for sturgeon and carp from the Chinese bank. They traded knives, salt, livestock. And they visited the camps of their Mongolian counterparts on special feast days, which is when the economic arrangements were typically struck. ("Renting abroad" tended to be cheaper than renting on the Russian side, which helps to explain the popularity of the practice.) Chinese military agricultural settlements (*jun tun*) were also appearing in the Argun area at the time, bringing in Han soldier-farmers. The Cossacks would have had contacts with them as well.[40]

In addition to these ordinary cross-border ties, Trans-Baikal Cossacks provided escorts for the mails to and from Chinese territory, and guarded Russian government offices in Manchuria Station as well as the state's consulates in Outer Mongolia and the country's principal diplomatic mission in Beijing (Peking). Visitors to the Trans-Baikal around the turn of the century found it strange that so many Russian Cossacks could speak perfect Buryat and Mongolian without knowing how to either read or write in their own language, though given the Cossacks' intense connections with the Mongolian world, it would have been even more surprising if things had been the other way around.

Of course, what surprised Russian observers most was not that cross-cultural mixing would occur. The surprise had to do with the *outcome* of the mixing. As people of a supposedly higher culture, it was simply assumed that the Russians would be the ones doing the influencing. The reverse sort of cultural flow, however, was more problematic. Cossacks were Russians—indeed, they were supposed to be quite special Russians, bearers of the national spirit. Buryats and Tungus, meanwhile, were seen as "aliens" (*inorodtsy;* literally: "people of a different birth")—members of a huge and ill-defined category of non-Russians that educated society considered fundamentally different from their own nationality.

By Ungern's time, the term *inorodtsy* was increasingly used as a catchall to describe all of the empire's national minorities. To certain Russian nationalists, Ungern himself would have been considered an alien. But the original and still more common usage applied more narrowly to the empire's diverse array of "eastern peoples" whose overriding common trait was their supposed backwardness in comparison with the Russians.[41] The aliens, in effect, were the equivalent of the "colonials" of Europe's overseas empires—groups that appeared to fall short by praying to the wrong god, living in tents rather than houses, having "primitive" habits, or, increasingly, simply having the wrong skin color.

Ordinary Russians, including Cossacks, were lauded by Russian patriots for their "remarkable knack in getting along" with these backward peoples—Russian settlers, the Russians liked to remind themselves, were not arrogant racists like British colonists, for example. But then again, most educated Russians were clearly dismayed when they saw good Russian folk fall too much under the sway of what they considered to be "lesser tribes." Russians who "went native" raised doubts about the integrity and strength of Russian national identity and led to questions about who was really in charge.[42]

This ambivalence about the virtues of diversity was also deeply imprinted in official policy. The late tsarist state was an imperial order torn in two directions. On the one hand, the government embraced and even celebrated the diversity of the empire. The greatest proof was the imperial showcase of St. Petersburg with its mosque, synagogue, Buddhist temple, and diverse array of Christian churches. Yet on the other hand, as a regime intent on charting an imperial course through a national age, it had obvious reasons for viewing certain types of diversity as a problem. The fundamental tension of this situation created the complicated logic of Russification, which was the state's attempt to build a more obviously Russian-oriented—and therefore, by extension—more manageable sort of imperial diversity.

The place of the eastern aliens in the new empire of Russification depended on who one was talking about (some groups appeared more problematic than others—Muslims, for example). In the Trans-Baikal during Ungern's service, the local "alien question" was not as fraught as elsewhere in Asian Russia and certainly much less than in the western part of the country. Buryats and Tungus were not seen as threats like the Poles, most of whom seemed congenitally disloyal, or the Baltic Germans, whose loyalty was at least potentially suspect. Nor were they feared like Chinese migrants in the Russian Far East, who were taken as the cusp of a great "yellow wave" about to crash down on the empire. And they were certainly not regarded as cunning and dangerous like the Jews, who, even in an empire "where every one except the tsar . . . belonged to a group that was, one way or another, discriminated against," were arguably the most discriminated of all.[43] Instead, the "aliens" of the Baikal region seemed docile "children of nature"—the kind of backward, largely harmless primitives who deserved Russification as a gift rather than a punishment.

In his new home on the Argun, Ungern thus found himself in a different environment of Russification than those that he had known in Estland or St. Petersburg, reflecting the fact that every region of the empire—even every local or institutional setting—was defined by its own mix of ethnicity, history, and geography, which in turn affected the way in which Russian authorities interpreted their interest. The state's policies were not necessarily any gentler in the Trans-Baikal than elsewhere. And by and large they conformed to the same general objective—that is, the goal was "the systematic unification in material, spiritual, and intellectual terms...of the aliens with the Russian element."[44] But the empire's officials pursued their work among the Buryats and Tungus with a presumption of benevolence. The prevailing view, in effect, was that the government was doing these backward peoples a favor. The national resentment and anxiety that helped to drive anti-German measures in the Baltic, for example, was virtually absent in the Trans-Baikal. Here the mood was less one of angst than of dutiful imperialist paternalism.

In 1904, in keeping with this ethos, the government replaced the Eastern Buryats' autonomous steppe councils (*stepnye dumy*) with a Russian-style county administration headed by a special "alien agent" (*inorodcheskii upravnik*). Officials began surveying and reapportioning Buryat pastures, turning over whatever "excess" land they found to incoming Russian settlers. (Nomads in the Trans-Baikal, much as elsewhere, were invariably seen to have more land than they needed.) Russian-language schools multiplied. Orthodox missionary work expanded.[45]

Not surprisingly, these initiatives were not well received by the native peoples they were supposed to improve. According to the Buryat scholar Tsyben Zhamtsarano, who traveled throughout the Baikal region in the early years of the century, ordinary Buryats were convinced that their "Russian masters" were bent on milking them "like dairy cows." Buryat students resented the Russification measures and organized reading circles and protests in 1905, rallying behind slogans like "Everyone for our people! Everyone for the Buryats!" (In keeping with the complexity of the situation, however, the students expressed their grievances in Russian rather than their own language.)[46]

There were also critiques of the government for not doing enough. Self-appointed Russian advocates for the aliens, agreeing that modernization overall was a good thing, complained that native peoples were given too few doctors and schools. Russian priests pointed out that the Orthodox mission in the Trans-Baikal was starved for funds, whereas "the lamas" somehow managed to come up with enough money to build "stunning temples." And Cossacks from Ungern's sector grumbled that Buryat nomads got away with grazing their flocks on Host land because, unlike the Russians "who have family names,...many aliens still use only given names," and, as a result, were almost impossible to track down.[47] The effects of Russification on the ground, in other words, were inconsistent, even haphazard. Some aspects of life changed. Much else stayed the same.

By far the greatest long-term change in the Trans-Baikal was the rise in Russian colonization. In the thirty years before 1917, the age of the so-called Great Siberian Migration, some five million peasants resettled to the region from the European side of the country, with roughly half the total arriving between just 1907 and 1914.[48] During this period, Siberia became the fastest-growing region in the country, at once a bustling and chaotic frontier of new settlement as well as the government's premier proving ground for the new empire it imagined for itself.[49] State investments in Asian colonization, feeble at first, rose steadily after the turn of the century and especially after 1907 when Petr Stolypin, an ardent champion of colonization—in particular, colonization by ethnic Russians—became prime minister.

By the time Ungern arrived on the Argun, the Resettlement Administration, the state's newly established colonization agency, oversaw a vast colonization enterprise throughout Asian Russia. Administration officials surveyed lands and doled out village plots, issued cheap guidebooks for peasant land scouts, and operated "settler relay camps." Stolypin toured the colonization kingdom himself in the late summer and fall of 1910, writing back to the tsar with ecstatic impressions: "Your Majesty... Siberia is developing marvelously (*rastet skazochno*).... And the settlers overall are a wonderful, strong colonizing element... very inclined to the monarchy, with a true, deeply Russian outlook."[50]

The greatest share of the new settlement was taking place in Western Siberia and what is now northern Kazakhstan, in a band running roughly 50 miles to either side of the Trans-Siberian. (These were mostly the areas Stolypin visited.) By comparison, the new dots appearing on the map "beyond the Baikal" were far fewer, but the effects were clear nonetheless. Chita became a boomtown. Prices shot up. The official gazette of the region carried announcements of newly opened settlement plots and posted the visiting hours of local resettlement offices. On maps of the border zone, new markings appeared—the color-coded squares and rectangles of so-called resettlement sections (*pereselencheskie uchastki*) measured in the thousands of acres, carved out of what had once been Cossack and native lands.[51]

Beyond the expectation that settlement would be good for overall development and push nomads like the Eastern Buryats toward sedentarization, hopes also ran high that a new tide of Russians would reduce "the undesirable consequences, from the state's point of view, of Russian mixing with the alien element."[52] Even at the very dawn of the Great Siberian Migration, well before it swelled into the huge tide it would become, one of Siberia's most prolific publicists looked forward to the coming of new settlers, hailing them as culture bearers who would "reinforce the Russian element," building up its "steadfastness and endurance." "Where aliens have predominated, Russians have grown weak and begun to disappear." The injection of new "Russian life" would turn this around.[53] Colonization in the Trans-Baikal would thus Russify the natives, while Russifying the Russians as well.

"The Most Disastrous Sort of Historical Error"

Such was the empire that surrounded Ungern in the Trans-Baikal—old yet new, traditional yet changing. Almost nothing about the social world he found on the Argun would have been familiar to him. There were no Germans to speak of, no Lutherans, no aristocrats, none of the pomp and circumstance he had regularly seen in the capital, not even much of a money economy. Very few of his fellow officers were noble graduates of elite military institutes. Instead, most were themselves Cossacks who had attended more modest training schools (*iunkerskie uchilishcha*) in provincial cities like Irkutsk or Orenburg and then returned to the Host for their service.[54] In fact, Cossack-born officers tended to criticize "non-native" ones (*neprirodnye*) like Ungern for showing up without knowing the Cossacks "any better than they know the Red Indians of Mayne Reid or [James Fennimore] Cooper."[55] Officers from elite schools, for their part, tended to look down on their provincial counterparts.[56] One wonders how well Ungern was accepted by his peers, at least initially. He was a true outsider.

Yet he must have wanted to fit in. Something must have fired his imagination in the Trans-Baikal since the region went on to play such an oversized role in his life. He would return here during the civil war, and it's hard not to believe that it was now, during the period of his first encounter, that he began the move toward Mongolia that would culminate in the Mongolian campaign. Living in his outpost on the Argun as a young officer, like every one else, he would have gone back and forth across the river. He would have spun his first Buddhist prayer wheel and seen his first shaman's lodge, small shacks draped with the skins of fox and bear. He would have learned the art of sitting in Buryat or Mongolian tents for hours sipping tea steeped with salt, fried butter, and sheep's fat.[57] He must have learned some Mongolian or Buryat and perhaps some Chinese (Mandarin) and Manchu, enough at least to do his work on the border.

Ungern may have reflected on the curiousness of the situation he found himself in—a Baltic German transnational cosmopolitan aristocrat serving in the Russian army with a corps of semi-Russian, semi-Buryatized cavalrymen on a section of the Chinese border that was, in fact, only a border for certain people and not really much of one for others. Though, then again, if he never reflected on such things, this, too, would not have been surprising. The curious pathways of the Russian Empire seem odd to us now because we are so far removed from them. But Ungern lived in a time when the unusual was normal.

We have almost no information on his duties during his time on the Argun. Based on Host files, we know that his company had clashes with khunkhuzy (from the Chinese *hong huzi*, meaning "red beards"), gangs of outlaws working in the Argun region who sometimes carried off stock or horses from the Cossack settlements. (Similar outlaw groups worked the Amur as well.) His record also indicates that his detachment "provided assistance to local civilian authorities" on at least one occasion, though the incident in question is unclear.[58] Our only official view of him in this period of his life is as a name on lists—rosters of the men who made up his company and of the officers who borrowed money against the Host's "capital reserves," their debts neatly recorded down to the fraction of a kopeck. (By the end of his service on the Argun, Ungern appears to have owed 85 rubles.)[59] His interior world—the world of his thoughts—is completely invisible.

Given his philosophical bent and interest in Dostoyevsky, did he while away any hours on the Argun reading *The Brothers Karamazov* or *Crime and Punishment?* Did he take along any Nietzsche? Dostoyevsky served as a gateway to Nietzsche for numerous readers of Ungern's generation, and Nietzsche's influence was arguably at its peak at the very time that Ungern was moving to the Trans-Baikal. Though we have no record of his ever reading the "philosopher with a hammer," it is easy to imagine him being drawn to Nietzsche's view of the world, especially his rejection of conventional authority and rationalism and his admiration for "powerful souls."[60] In a survey of cadet reading habits from Ungern's time in school, a few students identified Nietzsche as their favorite writer.[61]

The idea that Ungern might have read Dostoyevsky or Nietzsche on the Argun is pure guesswork, of course, but there is at least circumstantial evidence to suggest he read another book while he was there. In the spring of 1908, a few months before his arrival, the military district HQ in Irkutsk instructed the Trans-Baikal ataman to help his officers obtain a book called *The Psychology of Socialism* by the French scholar Gustave Le Bon.[62] A sharp critique of socialism that had just appeared in Russian translation, the work offered what the high command described as the "correct perspective" on the socialist movement, and the goal of assigning it, naturally, was to reinforce this perspective among the officers and, with their help, to then drum it into the men.[63]

The order about the book makes no mention of 1905, but the high command must have had the revolution on their mind when they assigned it. The upheaval in the Trans-Baikal had been as violent and divisive as anywhere in the empire. Even before the Host's forces had completed their withdrawal from the war theater in Manchuria, a number of regiments were rushed home to put down "disturbances" along the Trans-Siberian, including an armed uprising in Chita that led (briefly) to revolutionaries taking over the town center and proclaiming the creation of a "Chita Republic." (In one of the curious twists of Ungern's story, his great-uncle Paul von Rennenkampf was the officer assigned to suppress the uprising.) Hundreds of deaths, deportations, and executions ensued. While Cossacks helped stamp out the revolt, many of them sympathized with the other side, and in 1907 the Host elected a pro-socialist as their deputy to the Third Duma.[64]

It must have seemed, then, like an opportune time to assign a book like *The Psychology of Socialism.* By the time it appeared, Le Bon was already well-known for his trenchant criticisms of the dark sides of modernity, which, as he saw it, were too often drowned out in the noisy enthusiasm for progress and civilization that also defined the times. In his first best-seller, *The Crowd,* he had argued, in fact, that the changes of modern life were dragging the world toward degeneration rather than progress, Exhibit A being the rise of "the crowd"—that is, of mass politics and all the irrationality and hysteria that seemed to accompany it. "Merely by joining an organized crowd," he wrote at the time, "a man slips several rungs down the ladder of civilization. As an individual, he might be quite cultivated; in a crowd . . . he becomes a barbarian."[65]

The new book essentially reprised this argument by making the case against socialism as the worst of the mass movements of the age, a "false religion" peddled by cynical "high priests"—that is, the socialist intellectuals—who harped on about equality but whose true goal was to gin up the crowd to gain support and take power. Indeed, given the irrational tenor of the times, he fully expected them to succeed in taking over somewhere. The only hope for avoiding this, in fact, was to lock them up right away, while at the same time borrowing from their approach. The socialists might be disgusting opportunists, but they were at least savvy: they knew that politics in the modern age had become an art of mass manipulation. What was the point any more of appealing to reason? All the crowd really wanted was magic and spectacle. Levelheaded people had to come to their senses and realize this as well.[66]

Reading Le Bon's book today, over a hundred years later, parts of it seem remarkably prescient—the manipulation of mass sentiment through propaganda indeed became one of the disturbing hallmarks of twentieth-century politics. Yet the army's decision to assign the book in Ungern's time is still curious if only because it offers almost no way out of the problem. As Le Bon sees it, the fight is already all but over. Drunk on the absurd mythologies of the socialists, "the masses" are more than ready to follow them over the cliff into "the most disastrous sort of . . . historical error," the naive assumption that history and tradition are so meaningless that one can simply do away with them whenever one pleases.[67] The seed of socialism's victory thus starts in human weakness. Man will be duped because, in fact, he *wants* to be duped. His irrationalism will be his destruction.

Did Ungern read Le Bon's book? This is one of those difficult moments that come up when writing a history. It is tempting to believe that he did. The message meshes so perfectly with what we see of his thinking by the time of the Mongolian campaign that it would be cruelly ironic if he had not. Knowing that his superiors wanted him to read the book makes the idea all the more tantalizing. Yet we have no proof, so the most we can do is imagine.

One thing seems likely, however: if Ungern did read it, it almost certainly would have spoken to him. After all, he, too, had felt the mayhem of revolution—the chaos of Bloody Sunday in St. Petersburg, his family's stories of the burning of Jerwakant, perhaps even his great-uncle's tales of putting down the revolt in Chita. Turning Le Bon's pages—*if* he turned them—Ungern might

have experienced that sense of recognition that sometimes comes over us when
we read a book, the feeling that what the author is saying must be true because it
matches our own experience, it's our life, it's what we already know.

> The fate of the first people to witness the triumph of socialism can be summed
> up in a few lines. Everything will begin, of course, with the pillaging and then
> shooting of thousands of employers, businessmen, and capitalists—in short,
> anyone considered an exploiter. Intelligence and ability will be replaced by the
> rule of mediocrity. Equality of servitude will be established everywhere. The
> dream of socialism thus achieved, heaven will descend and eternal bliss shall
> reign on earth.
>   Oh but no!...It will be a hell. A terrible hell shall be our fate.[68]

CHAPTER 5

THE BLACK DRAGON RIVER

Our hair is without fragrance. We wear a sword on our hips:
Sound the sword on the shield!

—RICHARD SCHAUKAL. *Das Buch der Tage und Träume*

The Officer's Way

Ungern left the Trans-Baikal Cossacks in early 1910. The exact circumstances are unclear, but the explanation we usually hear is that he was forced out because of a duel. According to one writer, it was a drunken sword fight rather than a formal standoff, and at least one author places the event a few years later in the Amur region rather than in the Trans-Baikal. The single most important point that seems to carry over from one version to the next is that Ungern was wounded in the head during the contest and that the injury went on to give him migraines for the rest of his life. His interrogators in 1921 described him as having a scar on his forehead, adding in their notes that it came from "a duel in the East," presumably because Ungern told them so.[1]

His new post was with the next Host over—the Amur Cossacks whose headquarters were located in the town of Blagoveshchensk on the Amur River some 400 miles east of his home on the Argun. According to another story from the period, Ungern apparently dared his regiment mates that he would make the journey to Blagoveshchensk by horse, crossing into Chinese territory and then cutting through the mountains of the Greater Khingan range that separates Mongolia from northwestern Manchuria. The ride would be a test of man against nature—all Ungern would take with him was a hunting dog and a rifle.

(In some versions of the story, he also brings a falcon.)[2] The more common way to reach Blagoveshchensk—more comfortable but far less direct—was to stay on the Russian side, traveling first by train north to the main Trans-Siberian line then across to Sretensk on the Shilka River and then farther east from there by steamboat, following the Shilka as it flows down to the Amur. (The Amur Railway, the easternmost section of the Trans-Siberian, was still under construction at the time, so taking the train the whole way was not yet possible.)

What are we to make of these stories? We first hear them in the memoirs of men who met or served with Ungern at the earliest a few years later. One assumes they heard them from him firsthand, but we can't be sure, and none of them knew him in 1910.[3] Meanwhile, all the army records show us are two dates: his withdrawal from the Trans-Baikal Host in February 1910 and his enlistment on the Amur some two months later.[4] With nothing to confirm what he was doing in between, all we can say for certain about the duel and the trek is that they *might* have happened. At the same time, the stories seem to ring true, both because they fit with what we know so far of his temperament, which has been proof enough for most writers, but also because they seem in sync with the culture that surrounded him, the values and presumptions of the tsarist officer corps, which was now his element and would remain his spiritual home for the rest of his life.

At the time Ungern left the Trans-Baikal, the Russian army was the largest military force in the world, with an active duty roster of close to 1.2 million men. Of this total, about forty-five thousand—just under 4 percent—were officers. Traditionally the corps had been a preserve of the noble class, but in Ungern's time, a slow yet profound change was underway. Princes, counts, and barons continued to dominate the highest ranks, but more and more junior officers and "noncoms" (*unter-ofitsery*) were of nonnoble origin, reflecting two developments—one, the army was allowing more commoners to get officer's training because it needed more officers than the nobility could provide, and two, more nobles were choosing careers other than the army. In the two years between 1911 and 1912, the proportion of officers "of noble birth" slipped by 3 percent. By 1912, they accounted for less than half the corps.[5]

In social terms, young officers like Ungern operated within a paradoxical world. On the one hand, there was the mundane reality of their posts. Most found themselves assigned to humdrum garrison towns where they lived and ate together in common officer quarters. (Officers were banned from marrying before the age of twenty-eight, so the only ones with families around were usually considerably older.) Pay was low, the work often tedious—a succession of drills and recordkeeping. With little to do, "entertainment" tended to come down to a few familiar pastimes: syphoning off money from the regiment, gambling, visiting prostitutes, and, last but not least, drinking, usually heavily, in keeping with what one officer described as "our Slavic expansiveness."[6]

5.1. *Officer Life*, 1908. Military journals like this could be found in regimental libraries around the empire. The cover here shows a Cossack bivouac in Manchuria during the war with Japan. Courtesy Russian National Library, St. Petersburg.

Yet on the other hand, the ideal that young officers were taught to venerate was lofty in the extreme. The man of the corps was supposed to be a paragon of virtue, a modern knight in khaki—gracious to women, smart in appearance, crisply dutiful, and guided by an unfailing sense of honor, all traits associated with older self-conceptions of the European gentleman. In keeping with this inspiring image, Russian officers were told (and told themselves), even as they were downing vodka and playing cards, that they represented the empire's finest breed, a cut above not only the soldiers beneath them but also broader civilian society. (As we saw earlier, Russian military reformers hotly criticized this sort of thinking in the era after the war with Japan, but the prejudices nonetheless persisted in the corps through to the fall the old regime and the civil war as well.)

Duels were a part of the officer's ambivalent circumstances. In Ungern's time, they were a legal occurrence, sanctioned by a change in the military code from the early 1890s. Prior to that, they had been banned for decades, but the practice had remained common enough that the high command decided to legalize it in order to bring it into the open and regulate it. The symbolism was also important. Dueling was an aristocratic ritual associated with the ethos of the honorable nobleman-warrior. By reviving the practice in the 1890s, the army was, in effect, taking a small step to try to hold on to the past, retrofitting a noble tradition to an officer corps that was no longer as noble as before.[7]

The Military Dueling Code (*duel'nyi kodeks*) classified insults according to a scale ranging from upsetting but harmless expressions of "impoliteness" to full-fledged "acts of aggression." When an officer felt he had been offended seriously enough to warrant a duel, he was required to take his request to his commanding officer who would then refer it to a special Court of Honor (*sud chesti*) made up of fellow officers in the regiment whose role was to interpret the case in light of the code and determine whether a duel could indeed proceed. In theory, the courts had the power to rule against a duel, and this did indeed occur, but more often than not they approved the requests they received because duels were seen as a positive reflection on the level of honor in the regiment.[8]

In fact, the pressure to encourage dueling tended to be so great that when the courts showed any sort of leniency, it was taken as an embarrassment. In the Amur Military District in 1914, for example, a Court of Honor initially approved a duel but later allowed the officer who had committed the insult to leave the regiment before the duel took place, which then led to a howl of complaint from the district's commander: "Upon review of this matter, I have come to the upsetting conclusion that the court has failed to uphold the necessary high principles. Decency and morality appear to be declining among our officers. More and more we see philistine, petty bourgeois attitudes creeping into the corps."[9]

Officers in Cossack regiments differed in certain ways from the general officer population. By Ungern's time, for one, many officers in the Hosts were themselves Cossacks, like the men they commanded, so the social divide between officers and soldiers was somewhat less pronounced in Cossack regiments than in the broader army. Cossack officers also tended to spend their careers in their home Hosts in contrast to regular infantry or cavalry officers who might shuffle for years between posts in different regiments, sometimes from one end of the country to the other. The relative stability of Cossack service had the effect of reinforcing the view among Cossack officers that their first allegiance was to their ancestral Hosts and their fellow Cossacks rather than to the army as a whole.

Yet otherwise, Cossack officers were wholly in step with the ethos of social distinction and manly honor that suffused the broader corps, the only difference being the tendency to embroider these general values with their own Cossack touch. As they saw it, the Cossacks were the only true "warrior estate," the only group in the empire raised from boyhood to serve in arms. Unlike ordinary army regiments that might be stationed deep inside the country, Cossacks were always on the frontier, just across from "their future opponents," a mere gunshot away from battle.[10] And rather than fancy cavalry guards, as one Cossack writer put it, they were hardy horsemen, "men of simple habits, with little need for comfort, less fussy, physically tougher and more resilient...than regular officers."[11]

In other words, if Ungern did indeed fight a duel, even an "unofficial" one, and then leave the regiment by setting out alone through the wilderness, we can see, to a degree, how this could have made sense according to the values of his world. Both the duel and the trek were outlandish in one regard, yet conformist in another, because each of them reflected norms of masculine behavior upheld within the officer class. We can even see Ungern's actions—if indeed they occurred—as the distillation of a romanticized Cossack ideal. Ungern was the man of honor standing up for his integrity, the resilient frontiersman surviving by his wits in the wilderness, the knight-errant seeking feats to prove his character. Each of these registers of manly conduct was a curious throwback to earlier times, the echo of old ideals. They were strangely out of step with a modernizing empire of technocrats, transcontinental railways, and colonization plans, yet at the same time they suited the nostalgia of the aristocratic and military elite. They also evoked some of the conservative bravado of the tsarist system itself.

By the time Ungern took up his new post, it seems fair to assume that he had melded with the norms of the officer's society that surrounded him. We hear something of this in the performance review he received from his company commander in 1912, his second full year after arriving on the Amur:

Rank, First Name, Surname:...Junior Lieutenant (*khorunzhii*) Baron Roman Ungern-Sternberg....Extensive experience in the ranks. Rides well and with flair (*likho*), inclined toward cavalry work. Enjoys service in the field. Strong intellect. Reads not only military but also general literature, in which he is well served by his knowledge of several languages. Morally beyond reproach. Well-loved by his comrades. Possesses a gentle character and a kind heart.[12]

"Third Company Is Coming Along Nicely"

The Amur River, the ninth longest in the world, is the creation of two major tributaries—the Argun and the Shilka. The rivers meet near the village of Pokrovka at the eastern edge of the Trans-Baikal, and the Amur flows from there some 1,700 miles to the Pacific, eventually spilling into the ocean across from the great island of Sakhalin. Over its long and bending course, the river runs unevenly, widening, then narrowing, then widening again, and passing through a collage of landscapes—forest, steppe, marshland, mountains. Much of the Amur, which the Chinese call the Black Dragon River (*Heilongjiang*), ices over in the winter months, the thaw coming in some places as late as early May.[13]

In Ungern's time, when the river was open, steam-powered paddleboats, barges, timber rafts, and square-rigged Chinese junks would have plied between the banks.[14] The traffic was thickest near the towns, though settlements overall were rare, especially on the Russian side. In 1910 Blagoveshchensk, the capital of the Amur region (*Amurskaia oblast'*), which was located on the so-called Middle Amur, the central section of the river, had a population of about 70,000 people, whereas the population of the region numbered just 140,000, giving the territory as a whole a density of well under one person per square mile.[15] Beyond a narrow strip close to the river, much of the territory of the region was, in effect, a wilderness—desolate in winter, teeming with midges and mosquitoes in the summer. As late as the 1890s, Siberian tigers still prowled on the outskirts of towns. "What a country for sportsmen!" was the famous explorer Fridtjof Nansen's first impression when he visited the upper reaches of the river in the fall of 1913.[16]

Yet the wilderness was changing. In the early twentieth century, the Amur region was a colonization zone, an old frontier in the process of becoming new again. Much like the Trans-Baikal, the first Russians to reach the Amur were Cossack explorers who arrived in the region in the mid-seventeenth century with instructions from the tsar to locate precious minerals, furs, and tribute-paying peoples along the valley of a great river that they still knew only as the Shilka (or Shikar/Shilkara). (Early reports painted the whole area of the Amur as an El Dorado of sturgeon and grain—a region "beautiful and abundant.")[17] But these first Russian pioneers found themselves forced out within just a few decades by the nomadic Manchus (Jurchens), who at the very time the Muscovites were arriving on the Amur were themselves invading and taking over northern and central China on their way to establishing a new imperial order—the Qing dynasty (*Da Qing:* literally, the dynasty of the great clearness)—that would rule the Chinese Empire for the next 250 years.[18]

At the heart of the contest between the Muscovites and the Qing were the scattered Tungusic and Mongol peoples of the broader Amur region—Barga Mongols, Daurs, Oroqen (Orochon), and Solon in the Upper and Middle Amur; Hehe/Nanai (Golds) and Gilyak (Nivkh) near the lower courses of the river and along the Ussuri, the greatest of the rivers that flow into the Amur as it bends toward the Pacific.[19] The Russians aimed to make these varied tribal groups into Russian subjects, but the Qing already claimed them as their own and consequently dismissed the newly arrived "hairy barbarians" as little more than poachers. As Emperor Kangxi informed his emissaries as they left for talks with the Muscovites in 1688,

> The Lo-ch'a [general term for "demons" or foreigners] have invaded our frontier territory....They have occupied...the lands of our subjects....[Of these] the territory of the Black Dragon River is the most important, [for by descending] the Black Dragon River...to its mouth, the Lo-ch'a can reach the sea....Therefore...it is our opinion that [neither the Black Dragon River nor any of its tributaries] can be abandoned to the Lo-ch'a....If the Lo-ch'a agree to all our demands, we shall return their fugitives as well as the prisoners captured by our grand army....We shall join with [the Lo-ch'a] to draw the limits of the boundaries, and we shall grant them trade. But if they do not agree, we shall not talk peace with them.[20]

The new Manchu rulers of China were far more powerful on the Amur than the Muscovites, so the Lo-ch'a did indeed submit. In 1689, they agreed to abandon their claims to the northern (left) bank of the Amur, destroyed their forts, and retreated to the Trans-Baikal.[21]

By the mid-1800s, however, the situation had changed completely. The Qing were now the weaker party. In 1842, they were defeated in the First Opium War and found themselves forced to accept the humiliating Treaty of Nanking (Nanjing), conceding trading terms, reparations, and territory (Hong Kong Island) to the British. Then on the heels of this embarrassment came the eruption of a massive peasant uprising—the Taiping Rebellion—that consumed the center and south of the country and threatened to topple the dynasty. Knowing the Qing were vulnerable and distracted, the Russians took advantage to reassert their claims. Ships dispatched by the tsar sailed up the Amur from the Pacific. Poets and capitalists sang of a future "Siberian Mississippi." Cossacks were mustered. Flags were planted.[22]

Faced with few good options, the Qing gave in to Russian demands to redraw the border, and the result, codified in a series of treaties, was the largest territorial concession of the Qing period. Between 1858 and 1860, the Chinese signed away all the lands north of the Amur and east of the Ussuri to the tsarist state—an immense area of some 360,000 square miles, a vastness that made Hong Kong look like "a pinprick."[23] The lands in question were home to a thin dusting of indigenous peoples and only barely known in the capital. The Qing therefore reasonably concluded that they could surrender the territory temporarily "to pacify the bestial heart of the barbarians" and then reacquire it later, but this was not to be. The dynasty was overthrown in the 1911 Revolution, and the Amur and Ussuri regions ended up passing to Russia for good.[24]

The leader of the charge to acquire what would become known as the Russian Far East was Governor-General of Eastern Siberia Nikolai Murav'ev. This was the same Murav'ev who had created the Trans-Baikal Host just a few years earlier and who would soon become better known as *Count* Murav'ev-*Amurskii*, and immortalized as the "conqueror of the Amur" in monuments up and down the Russian side of the river.[25] Given the remoteness of the Amur region and what seemed to be the obvious lesson of the Chinese experience, Murav'ev was convinced that the first thing the Russians had to do with their new territory was to "occupy it as quickly as possible."[26] To do this, the easiest course was to simply repeat what had worked so well before. He thus urged the tsar to create a new Cossack force to settle the area. The tsar agreed, and the result was the founding of the Amur Cossack Host.[27]

For the bodies to staff his new creation, Murav'ev turned to the Trans-Baikal. This made sense—the *Zabaikal'tsy*, already under his command, were the closest Cossacks on hand. To make the relocation seem attractive, the government promised inducements, but the families that moved to the Amur in the late 1850s (roughly fourteen thousand individuals in all) still had to be chosen by lot and, when this failed, by force. They then received minimal supplies (plus tax exemptions) and found themselves dropped off in small parties on the desolate riverbank, evenly spaced out at intervals of roughly 20 miles along the huge watery course of the new border.

Murav'ev was bullish, though cautious, about the undertaking. "Do what you can to make the whole Amur ours," he reportedly told a party of Cossack settlers on the upper reaches of the river in 1858. "Just don't do anything on the right bank for now. In time, we'll take that side of the river as well, but for now settle on the left."[28] Something of the hopefulness and Christian enthusiasm of the moment was captured in the name of what would become the capital of the region: Blagoveshchensk in Russian means "good news."[29]

Not surprisingly, despite the official optimism, many of the early pioneers died, unable to survive the harsh winters or provide for themselves until the annual visit of the supply barge in the spring. Others "went wild" or "degenerated...overcome by the implacable enemy of nature," according to one description from the time.[30] During the next fifty years, the state bolstered

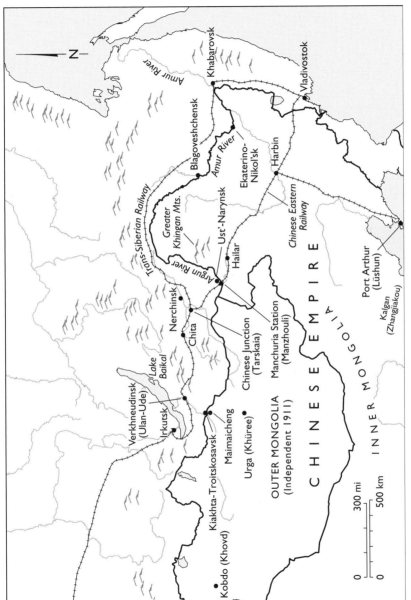

Map 5. The Trans-Baikal region and the Russian Far East, early 1900s

these meager beginnings with additional resettlements, though the Cossack presence in the region always remained much fainter than in the Trans-Baikal and infinitesimal compared with the more populous Hosts of European Russia. In 1889, the Cossacks on the Ussuri were hived off to form a Host of their own, and at the time of Ungern's service, the Amur and the Ussuri Hosts were by far the two smallest in the empire—just thirty-four thousand and twenty-five thousand people, respectively.[31] The lands set aside for these Hosts hugged the rivers for huge stretches, but their populations were tiny.

One of these small settlements was Ungern's new home—Ekaterino-Nikol'sk, located directly on the Amur in the middle course of the river, about 330 miles south of Blagoveshchensk. The *stanitsa* was established in 1858 by Cossacks dropped off the river barge in the initial wave of Cossack colonization. (The settlement was named in honor of Murav'ev's wife, the Countess Ekaterina Nikolaevna Murav'eva.) By the time Ungern arrived, Ekaterino-Nikol'sk, known as the "Fair Lady of the Amur" (*Krasavitsa Amura*) for its picturesque location on a bluff overlooking the river, had grown into a district center—the largest settlement in its immediate vicinity, with a population of about fourteen hundred people.[32]

Thanks to a detailed survey from 1912, we know that the residents of Ekaterino-Nikol'sk were all Orthodox. Roughly 50 percent of the men and 14 percent of the women were literate. A third of the houses had iron roofs, the rest were thatch. The settlement had a church and a two-year primary school. Most families planted between 13 and 25 acres of grain, devoting the rest of their lands to pasture and hayfields. They kept cows, pigs, and close to one thousand horses. For cash, most supplemented their farming by selling firewood, which they cut in the thickly forested hills of the Bureya range that loomed nearby and then sold to the hungry steamboats that worked the river.[33]

On a Russian map of the area from the same period, we see Ekaterino-Nikol'sk sitting in the midst of a small cluster of Cossack settlements and farms (*khutora*). Immediately to the east lies the "old settler" village of Blagoslovennoe (Blessed). ("Old settler" was a term Russians used to describe peasant colonists who were already established on the land for several generations.) Slightly farther east down the river, we see the villages of more recent peasant migrants, known as "new settlers" (*novosely*). Behind Ekaterino-Nikol'sk, in the hills that roll away from the river, appear the mining camps of the Amur Mining District and dirt roads leading up toward the Amur Railway, about 60 miles away, running roughly parallel to the water.[34]

The active-duty Cossacks stationed at Ekaterino-Nikol'sk belonged to the Third Company of the First Count Murav'ev-Amurskii Regiment. Quartered in barracks near the settlement, the men of Third Company spent most of their days on patrol, checking papers and searching boats on the river. Through the year, they also participated in exercises and training camps where they drilled and conducted war games.[35] During the roughly two and a half years that Ungern served on the river, he was assigned to provide defense training for settler parties and took part in at least four "punitive expeditions," which may refer to suppressing miners' strikes in the area or organizing searches for runaway convicts. (One "expedition" was to nearby Yakutsk oblast', also a region with numerous mines and convict stations.) In 1912, he was promoted to the rank of senior lieutenant (*sotnik*).[36] In December of that same year, the regiment commander inspected Ekaterino-Nikol'sk and later wrote to thank Ungern and the other officers for their efforts. "The work of Third Company is coming along nicely.…The Cossacks appear healthy and fit. The horses are nicely fattened for the winter."[37]

Right across the Amur from Ekaterino-Nikol'sk was the Qing Empire, or more specifically the Chinese province of Heilongjiang in northern Manchuria. In practical terms, the dynamic of the border here was similar to what Ungern had known on the Argun. Cossack posts stood on one bank, Qing military and customs posts faced them from the other. The same ordinary traffic of people and goods shuttled across the water (or the ice). Chinese migrant workers heading for mines on the Russian side got their passes stamped at the crossing at Ekaterino-Nikol'sk. Chinese smugglers brought over cheap Chinese vodka, which obliging Cossacks then surreptitiously delivered to purchasers on the Russian bank. (In some cases, Cossacks served as armed escorts for the smugglers.)[38]

Because of the lack of roads, the principal line of communication was the river, which meant that settlements on either side of the Amur tended to be more connected to each other than they were to the villages of their own countrymen located away from the water. Chinese and Russians hopped rides on the same boats. Chinese villagers fled to the Russian bank when local *hong huzi* raided their homes because it was easier to cross the river than to make it to safety anywhere else on the Qing side.[39] When the *hong huzi* attacked the Russian bank, as they sometimes did, Cossacks had standing permission to cross over and give pursuit on Qing territory. According to a report by the Amur Region Border Commissar in 1913, *stanitsa* commanders generally enjoyed "good neighborly relations" with their Chinese counterparts, whom they saw frequently. Everyone knew the local Russo-Chinese pidgin. Much as on the Argun, Russians living on the Amur brokered arrangements to cut hay and timber across the water on the Qing side.[40]

Yet the Amur border, like every border area, was also shaped by its own dynamic, reflecting the specific history and geography of the region, and in this sense, the world that surrounded Ekaterino-Nikol'sk was indeed different from the one Ungern had known in the Trans-Baikal. The Qing territories that fronted the Argun—the Hulunbuir area of Heilongjiang province, also known as Barga—were very sparsely populated. With the exception of CER station towns like Manchuria Station and Hailar, which had Chinese residents, the Chinese colonization overall was light and the few inhabitants beyond the towns were nomads—Barga (Bargut) Mongols, in particular. (The region today forms part of China's Inner Mongolian Autonomous Region.)[41]

On the Amur, by contrast, the concentration of population was much thicker, and the residents were overwhelmingly ethnic Chinese (Han)—for the most part, Chinese peasants actively courted to settle the open spaces of Manchuria by the Qing government. For centuries, the Qing had forbidden Chinese agricultural settlement in what they called the Northeast (*Dongbei*), but by the latter part of the nineteenth century, they reversed course and opened colonization offices in order "to move people to strengthen the border." Between 1820 and 1910, settlement in Heilongjiang skyrocketed by over 1,100 percent. By 1912, the year that the Qing dynasty finally collapsed, the population of Manchuria as a whole, which included Heilongjiang and two other provinces, had climbed to eighteen million people.[42]

Though the relative growth was much smaller, the Russian side of the river, of course, was changing too. Blagoveshchensk's population more than doubled in the first decade of the twentieth century. Every spring tens of thousands of workers poured into the region from Siberia and European Russia to labor in the gold mines and on the Amur Railway. (These seasonal visitors became some of the Chinese bootleggers' most dedicated customers.) "New settler" villages multiplied rapidly. And the local civil service also grew as "scores of specialists" under contract with the government's newly established Amur Expedition—a kind of regional development taskforce—arrived on the river to measure "colonizing capacity" and fit out the "economic corridor" of the railroad.[43] Things were good enough that local peasants started wearing felt hats "like town folk" and bought up newfangled American farm machines.[44] "All along the Amur, and in Blagoveshchensk in particular, business is hopping," wrote one local correspondent in 1910.[45]

Yet for all the dynamism, it was hard by this time to find unabashed optimists about Russia's overall position in the Far East. The same writer who applauded the roaring tempo of change on the river lamented that the country's efforts at development seemed constantly undercut by "our usual lack of organization" (*bezsistemnost'*).[46] Indeed, for most Russians, the disaster of the Russo-Japanese War still fresh in their minds, the view from the Amur appeared at best ambiguous. On the one hand, much as before, few of them doubted that their country *deserved* to rule over Asia. Educated Russians, by and large, were easily as presumptuous as any of the imperialists of the age, including the Americans, who, though relative newcomers, were actively expanding their influence in China and had taken over the Philippines after the Spanish-American War.[47] Yet on the other hand, the Russians felt vulnerable in a way that Westerners did not because their country's geography placed them directly in the region. They were there, exposed to all the dangers and uncertainties—the possibility of a new contest with Japan, or the fear of what might come from the "huge ocean wave of colonization" they saw unfolding just across from them on the opposite bank of the river.[48]

"Life grows here not by the day but by the hour," the military governor of the Amur wrote to St. Petersburg in early 1912. "And yet every year fifteen times more colonists settle in Heilongjiang than in our Amur region." "The Chinaman has awakened," the governor added, clearly implying that this was not a good thing for Russian interests.[49] Even before the Revolution of 1911 that would sweep away the Qing, Russian observers described an air of "nervousness, uncertainty, and indeterminacy" hanging over the region. "Surrounded on all sides by hostile forces, one wonders whether we might indeed be nothing more than temporary guests on this frontier...."[50]

The Thin Russian Line

The fear of losing the Far East was one of the great anxieties preoccupying Russia's leaders in the last decade of tsarist rule. The fear never completely paralyzed life in the region, and different Russians responded to it differently. Perhaps even calling it a fear is not quite right; it was more an apprehensiveness, a nagging sense of being outnumbered and surrounded, or, for ordinary workers and small-scale merchants, of feeling economically trapped. Yet regardless of what we might call it, the feeling was pervasive, and it deeply shaped the Russian imperial community that Ungern joined on the river.

By the 1910s, disease, emigration, and acculturation had reduced the native Tungusic and Mongol reindeer herders and hunter-fishermen of the Amur to just a few thousand individuals. The military governor even went so far as to declare in 1914 that "practically speaking, we no longer have indigenous peoples left in [our] territory."[51] Indeed, one of the most striking things about the Amur in Ungern's time is that almost everyone who lived there (like Ungern) had recently come from somewhere else. Even more than most parts of Asian Russia, the Amur resembled a mini-America, a place almost exclusively made up of immigrants or their close descendents.

The majority of these transplants were Slavs (Russians and "Little Russians"), but a large minority, at least 10 to12 percent of the population, was made up of people the Russians described as "yellows" (*zheltye*): Koreans and especially the much more numerous Chinese. With the exception of some well-established Chinese merchants, almost all of these Asian residents were seasonal traders and laborers (Chinese: *huagong;* Russian: *otkhodniki*) who crossed over for periods to work on the Russian side. Most were men, and virtually none were Russian subjects.[52] In practice, the term "yellows" applied

5.2. The wharf at Reinovo on the northern section of the Amur River. Reproduced from *Amurskaia zheleznaia doroga: Postroika zapadnoi chasti
amurskoi zheleznoi dorogi, 1908–1913* (Moscow, 1913), 280.

to foreigners. "Yellows" who became subjects of the empire were considered
"aliens" like the other non-Russian eastern peoples of the region.

Thus by the 1910s, state policymakers on the Amur, unlike their counterparts in many other borderlands of the empire, did not worry much about the
problem of Russifying native "aliens." As they saw it, the local "alien question"
had become largely irrelevant. Instead, Russification on the Amur was primar-
ily a matter of migration and, in particular, of using migration to generate development and create a more manageably "Russian" imperial region.

From the time of the territory's incorporation into the empire, the tsarist
government had taken a generally accommodating approach to Chinese
migration. Russian settlement was sparse, and Chinese workers and traders
provided a cheap and readily available source of goods and labor. (Not uncoincidentally, the Qing adopted a pro-emigration stance around the same time
because they began to see a plus for themselves in having large numbers of
their subjects living outside the state.)[53] But all of this was precarious. Russians tended to resent their dependence on "yellow labor" (*zheltyi trud*), and
as the age of Russification wore on, tsarist planners dreamed of taking "decisive
measures" "to defend the region against the…onslaught of the yellow race."[54]
As Nikolai L'iudvigovich Gondatti, the future head of the Amur Expedition
and governor-general, succinctly put it in 1908: "The Far East must be Russian and for Russians only" (*russkii i tol'ko dlia russkikh*)[55] The man Gondatti
replaced, Governor-General Pavel Fridrikhovich Unterberger, agreed, though
he expressed it slightly differently: "I'd rather see our lands go empty than have
them occupied by the yellow element."[56]

Ungern arrived on the river just as "the struggle against the Yellow Peril was
heating up" (*v pol'nom razgare*).[57] Between 1907 and 1913, in keeping with a
broad international reaction against Chinese immigration, the empire's laws
changed toward restricting Chinese migrants. Fees, fines, and deportations
increased. Most important, "foreign subjects," which effectively meant the

Chinese, were banned from working on "state projects" like the Amur Railway, whose construction was formally approved by the Third Duma in 1908.[58] (Up to this point, Chinese laborers had made up the bulk of the workers on the Trans-Siberian and in state-owned mines in the Far East.) At the same time, in the summer of 1909, Premier Stolypin created a special cabinet-level committee to supervise Far Eastern colonization.[59] The Amur Expedition, staffed with teams of colonization experts, was formed a few months later. In that same year and into 1910, peasant resettlements (mostly from Ukrainian areas) rose dramatically.[60] Meanwhile, the number of Chinese migrants—at least those entering the region legally with state-issued passes—noticeably slumped.[61]

This drive to "build Russia on the Amur," as it was often called, not surprisingly proved to be full of contradictions and curious consequences. On the one hand, state policy and the public's generally anxious mood reflected and encouraged anti-Asian racism. East Asians were considered dirty and untrustworthy, their food foul. Zoning laws increasingly moved them into special "China" and "Korea towns" in Russian Far Eastern cities. (Blagoveshchensk, for example, acquired an official "Chinese quarter" in 1910.)[62] In that same year, plague broke out in Manchuria and tsarist authorities immediately identified all Chinese subjects as potential carriers, leading to a raft of anti-Chinese measures in the name of public health.[63] There was also a good deal of everyday anti-Chinese violence and discrimination.[64] By far the worst violence had occurred some ten years before Ungern's arrival, during the tense days of the Boxer Rebellion, when local Russians and Cossack troops drove the Chinese out of Blagoveshchensk and across the river to the Qing side. In the general panic, some five thousand Chinese were drowned, shot, or hacked to death with axes before they even reached the water.[65]

The general anti-Asian phobia affected not only Asians, however. Alongside efforts to reduce Chinese migration and expand Russian settlement, the government also imposed limits on Jews in the Far East. Jews were arguably the most discriminated minority in the empire. In European Russia, with the exception of visible communities in St. Petersburg and Moscow, they were largely confined to a so-called Pale of Settlement (*cherta osedlosti*) stretching from the Baltic to the Black Sea. Beginning in the 1860s, however, they were permitted (with certain restrictions) to live in Siberia and the Far East. By Ungern's time, synagogues had appeared in all the larger Far Eastern towns (including Blagoveshchensk), and Harbin, the nearby "capital of the CER" in northern Manchuria, was known for its sizeable Jewish minority.[66]

But by 1909, even this relative openness was curtailed. New Jewish settlement in Far Eastern regions was banned and orders went out to deport any illegal arrivals "as promptly as possible."[67] In the Far East, Judeophobia and anti-"yellow" prejudice ran together in officials like Governor-General Gondatti, who saw both groups as equally pernicious threats to "Russian labor." (In the case of the Jews, this required some remarkable paranoia, given the fact that their presence in the Far East never amounted to more than even 0.6 percent of the region's population.)[68]

Fear thus ran through much of imperial policy on the Amur, which then helps to explain why prejudices as seemingly different as anti-"yellow" racism and anti-Semitism could work together. Both the virtually invisible Jews and the more obvious "yellows," in particular the Chinese, provoked anxiety and seemed to reinforce the impression of a region under threat. The far eastern and far western edges of the empire were curiously similar in this respect. Russification in the west was also shaped by fear. In the Baltic, the threat began with the Germans. In Poland and the western provinces, it was the Poles and the Jews. Much like the Amur, Russia's international borders in the west had become "sites of zero-sum population politics" where imperial authorities on all sides worried constantly about the coming and going of "unreliable" groups.[69] In Russian Poland, there was "de-Polonizing energy." On the Amur, the turn was toward de-Sinicization.[70]

These parallels of imperial policy from west to east make sense, for the two ends of the state were sustained by living connections. Life on one border influenced approaches to the other. Anti-Jewish directives raced from west to east by telegraph. Anti-Semitic officials traveled back and forth by train, taking the experiences and prejudices of one frontier with them as they were reassigned to another. One of the great ironies of the late imperial period is that the new connectivity of the empire that was doing so much to integrate and standardize the country was at the same time spreading and reproducing habits of discrimination and anxiety that would ultimately help to pull it apart. Another irony is that so many of the men leading the charge for discriminatory Russification were themselves not entirely Russian to begin with—governors Gondatti and Unterberger are a case in point.

But it would be going too far to imagine the Amur region in the early 1910s as a place where Russians or anyone else spent much time pondering the empire's unsustainable tensions. During Ungern's service on the river, he must have witnessed the casual anti-Chinese prejudice that we know was a part of everyday life. As a Cossack officer, he may have participated in searches for "illegal" Jews in Blagoveshchensk and other Far Eastern towns. Yet like everyone else on the Amur, he also lived within webs of much more benign cross-cultural contacts.

In addition to dealing with Chinese during his patrols along the river, we know from the Host records that a Chinese laundry washed the Cossacks' uniforms.[71] Other Chinese hired hands worked in his *stanitsa*. Jewish merchants operated stores in the bigger towns. And he likely had at least some interaction with Koreans as well. The "old settler" village of Blagoslovennoe just a few miles from Ekaterino-Nikol'sk was a Korean community. The peasants there were Orthodox, but they maintained their national language and customs and were in regular contact with their Cossack neighbors.[72]

In Harbin, which Ungern surely visited during his time on the Amur, he would have found something of the cosmopolitan feel that had surrounded him in St. Petersburg. Harbin, increasingly, was an "international city" of Russians and Chinese predominantly but also of Japanese and smaller communities of Europeans and Americans—a "Manchurian Petersburg," the "Moscow of Asia."[73] Even in Blagoveshchensk, by comparison a far less cosmopolitan place, people of various nationalities and faiths lived separately but together, as they did in so many of the empire's borderland towns.[74]

In fact, when we look back to the world Ungern knew on the Amur, two different imperial realities seem blurred together. On the one hand, we see state policy tightening up and national anxiety rising. We detect the beginnings of a more explicitly racial colonial order, with Russians at the top and "yellows" below. Yet we also see the persistence of older and much more tolerant or at least practical habits of multinational cohabitation and interaction. The arrival of a modern border regime on the river was redrawing the old frontier, but the older ways of cross-cultural interaction along the Amur, much as in the Trans-Baikal and many other places around the edges of the country, were not disappearing as much as adapting and adjusting.

The empire, at once old and new, had numerous shortcomings, but even on its easternmost and, in some respects, least certain border, it was not doomed to fall apart. On February 21, 1913, echoing celebrations across the country, the entire active-duty force of the Amur Cossacks assembled in Blagoveshchensk to mark the three hundredth anniversary of the Romanov dynasty. After a service in the Annunciation Cathedral, the city's grandest church, the Cossacks, dressed in their great coats and papakhas, lined up to parade down Blagoveshchensk Street (now Pioneer Street) toward the Amur embankment. "Cossacks!" the Host commander told his men, "Remember this historic day....Prove yourselves worthy of your ancestors who so gloriously served our great Russian state and the mighty tsars and emperors of the Romanov House."[75]

Surely no one in that parade, least of all young lieutenant Ungern, could have imagined that the great dynasty they were celebrating would be swept away just four years later.

CHAPTER 6

KOBDO

Oh. the jewel in the lotus!
—*Karandavyuha Sutra*

"In Search of Bold Deeds"

Six months after the parade in Blagoveshchensk and over 1,000 miles away, the young merchant Aleksei Burdukov was making ready to leave the central Mongolian town of Uliastai (now: Uliasutai) for his base in Kobdo (Mongolian: Khovd; Chinese: Kebuduo), a Chinese trading and garrison town in the far western part of the country. Just as he was about to set out, however, he was stopped by the local Russian consul, who asked him to wait: another Russian had just arrived, an officer from the Amur Cossacks, who was also heading in the same direction. Trips between Mongolian towns tended to be slow-going, with little company along the way other than the Mongol escorts who helped relay riders from one horse station to the next. Perhaps the extra wait would be worth it? The officer seemed like he would make an "interesting traveling companion."[1]

To come across Ungern in Mongolia in 1913 is something of a surprise. We expect him here later, of course, but not now, and perhaps because of this, most accounts of his life tend to gloss over this earlier episode in the country, treating it as little more than a prelude to the *real* Mongolian experience to follow during the civil war. On the face of it, this is logical enough—the civil war is indeed what Ungern is remembered for. But this approach also reflects our inclination to emphasize the dramatic moments in life, when, in reality, the less dramatic ones are no less important. Rather than straight lines leading up to momentous turns or breaks, most lives unfold as loops or spirals with uncharted detours and returns across already covered ground that become straightened out only in retrospect. Ungern, it turns out, had not one but two extended experiences in Mongolia. The most momentous of them came in 1920–1921, but the first and less dramatic one was now, in the late summer of 1913 and extending perhaps into 1914 as well.

And in this moment, the most important thing was not what would come later but rather what had just happened. Just a month or so before we find him in Uliastai, Ungern made a great change: he resigned from the army. We know this from his letter of resignation, which is housed today in the Russian State Military Historical Archive in Moscow. In the letter, addressed, as convention required, to the tsar, he cites "difficult family circumstances" as the cause but offers no details, and, given that the same phrase appears in most of the other resignation letters in the folder, it's likely that this was little more than boilerplate.[2] The only thing that seems clear from the file is that he was eager to leave the Amur.

Like any able-bodied officer resigning from the service, Ungern was required to register with the reserves. Most men in this position simply requested an assignment with their current regiment. Ungern, however, asked to rejoin the Trans-Baikal Cossacks, which meant that he would serve with them rather than the *Amurtsy* in the event of a general mobilization. He also seems to have been intent on leaving the region as quickly as possible. By piecing together information in the file, we know that he must have been present at the Host HQ in Blagoveshchensk in July 1913—this is where he signed his letter, which in turn means, given the great distance he had to cross to get to Uliastai, that he probably left for Mongolia either right then or very shortly thereafter, certainly well before his resignation request would be able to wend its way through the military system.[3]

What explains this curious turn in Ungern's story? Why the seemingly abrupt resignation from the army followed by the rapid departure for Mongolia? Why even go to Mongolia at all? Our best source for answering these questions, it turns out, is Burdukov, the merchant from Kobdo, who describes meeting Ungern in his memoirs. Burdukov is far from a perfect witness, however. For one, he wrote his memoirs many years later, well after the meeting occurred. More important, in the interval, he experienced a second, more meaningful encounter, not with Ungern directly but with his men, who arrested him and his family during the period of the Mongolian campaign under orders from Ungern to shoot them as "socialist sympathizers." (Burdukov was indeed helping the Reds at the time.) The family managed to escape, but it seems clear judging from some of the language of his account that the episode left a mark (understandably!) on his recollections of the earlier meeting.

Finally, the memoirs were published in the USSR in the 1960s, under Soviet censorship. This means that Burdukov couldn't have offered a gentler view of Ungern even if he had wanted to (and we can assume he did not).[4]

Still, even with these limitations, the memoirs are a remarkable source. Not only do they allow us our only view of Ungern by someone who actually knew him at the time but they are also vivid and direct, full of the ordinary stuff of life that we almost never find in more formal materials: the passing flux of moods and first impressions, petty annoyances, unfinished conversations. Reading the memoirs, Ungern truly comes to life, even if just for a moment, in the smallest of glimpses.

Burdukov's first recollection of seeing him was outside the consul's house tending to his horse. Though he had just ridden in to Uliastai on the last leg of a long relay from the capital Urga (Chinese: Kulun; Mongolian: Khüree), he told Burdukov he was ready to press on for Kobdo right away.

> He was sunburned and scruffy, with . . . the blank, dark eyes of a madman. The blondish beard he had grown on the road made him look about thirty years old. His uniform was unbelievably filthy, with worn trousers and holes in the tops of his boots. He had a sword and pistol at his side. A [Mongol] postal rider (*ulachi*) carried his rifle. The pack on his horse was empty—all he seemed to have with him was a small canvas road bag with a bundle sticking out from one end.
>
> To see a Russian officer riding across Mongolia like this . . . with no bedding or supplies or even a change of clothes left a truly strange impression.[5]

Riding hard, including at night, the two men completed the difficult 280-mile leg to Kobdo in less than three days. In Burdukov's description of the journey, Ungern comes off as both imperious and eccentric, arguing with and even whipping the Mongol riders who helped the pair along the way, yet also tireless in the saddle and gifted with an uncanny feel for the land. One evening when the party was lost, Ungern apparently saved the group by sniffing the air and then pointing into the blackness toward what he said would be a settlement. The group moved on and a short time later found the huts. Burdukov also recalled how Ungern used a small notebook to jot down Mongolian words as they rode, repeating them out loud to himself to learn the language. Burdukov spoke fluent Mongolian, so we can imagine the back-and-forth of a long grammar lesson as the two riders swayed their way through the valleys.

At some point in the midst of all this, Ungern told the merchant the information we want to know. His reason for leaving the Far East, it turns out, was straightforward: he was bored. Life on the Amur had been "suffocating." All the officers on the river were dying from routine. What he craved instead was a life of action like that of his ancestors, the Baltic knights. He relayed the story

6.1. Entrance to the Russian consulate, Uliastai. The merchant Aleksei Burdukov recalled meeting
Ungern outside this gate in the summer of 1913. Reproduced from Hermann Consten,
Weideplätze der Mongolen im Reiche der Chalcha (Berlin, 1920), vol. 2, pl. 28.

of the "400-verst" trek he made through the wilderness when he first came to the Amur, but the impression he gave Burdukov was that this feat was no longer enough—he wanted something more. So, after learning from the papers that a war was on in Kobdo, "he decided to resign from the army and race out [there] to volunteer."

As they traveled along, Ungern pressed Burdukov for information on the situation around Kobdo, about the clashes with the Chinese, and especially about Dambijantsan, the self-declared "Princely Holy One" (Mongolian: Noyon Khutagt) and de facto strongman of the region whose units he hoped to join. "The thing that interested Ungern," Burdukov writes, "was the experience of war rather than the ideas or causes behind it." "It was the fight that mattered most to him....He kept repeating that eighteen generations of his ancestors had fallen in battle and that this, too, would be his fate."[6]

Though the plan to volunteer in Kobdo was unusual, Ungern does not seem to have been especially self-conscious about it. He apparently carried a letter of introduction with him that Burdukov remembered seeing at the consul's house before they left Uliastai: "Such-and-such a regiment of the Amur Host hereby affirms that the bearer of this letter, Senior Lieutenant Roman Feodorovich Ungern-Sternberg, has resigned from active duty of his own accord and is now proceeding to the west in search of bold deeds'" (*v poiske podvigov*).[7]

The details of Burdukov's account are impossible to prove, of course, including the letter, which sounds almost too perfectly stereotypical to be true. All we know for sure based on evidence from the time is that Ungern resigned from the army and quickly left the Amur. Yet the overall gist of the story seems to capture something nonetheless, especially the impression we get of Ungern as an uncommon person, an adventurer in search of outsized experiences. It's fair to assume that most people in Ungern's time (including Burdukov) did not choose—or have the means—to "drop out of the continuity of life" to pursue "bold deeds."[8] (Most people in our day do not do this kind of thing either.) In this sense, Ungern was indeed out of the ordinary.

Yet for all this, like even the most unusual people, he was still a product of his times, and taking a wider view, it's clear there were multiple models of adventure for him to draw on in the world around him. The great boom of European and American imperialism that coincided with his coming of age also marked the onset of an era of mass culture that commodified adventure and turned it into the kind of commonplace one read about in the papers or saw in a skit at the concert hall. This was the era of the polar explorer and the Boy Scout, and of military adventurers, fictional and real, including eccentric insubordinates like the British officer Francis Younghusband, who disobeyed their orders yet still managed to do the right thing for king and country (in Younghusband's case, by "conquering" Tibet).[9] The Russians had heroes of their own and a similar "energizing myth of adventure."[10]

That Mongolia would be the site of Ungern's escapade was also appropriate because it was precisely the kind of place where this sort of thing was supposed to occur. Everything about the country seemed mysterious and unapproachable. Indeed, one could say that Mongolia's greatest attribute for the European world at the time was precisely its utter farawayness, the fact that it appeared as far off as anything could be, lost in time as much as distance, like Timbuktu or Tibet, both of which were also emerging as the latest remotest places of the Western imagination.[11] In this sense, the *real* Mongolia mattered less than the one you saw with your eyes shut: a vastness of sands and steppes, of plodding camel caravans and nomads "unchanged since the days of Genghis Khan." Depending on one's view, the country appeared either hopelessly primitive or reassuringly pure, but either way, it seemed the utter opposite of the modern world.

In fact, most European representations of Mongolia blended these stereotypes, creating an exotic image that managed to be at once evocative and revolting, inspiring and foul. This sense of things comes across in countless depictions from the period, though perhaps the best single distillation I have found is the now forgotten travelogue of Beatrix Bulstrode, the wife of a British diplomat in China who traveled to Mongolia from Beijing just a few months after Ungern. Bulstrode declares her exotic credo on the very first page—she has come to Mongolia, she writes, out of "a fascination for the unknown, a deep love of the picturesque, and [the] inherent desire to revert awhile to the primitive." And from there, she goes on to provide exactly what her readers would have expected: colorful scenes of "gloomy temples," boundless skies, "extraordinarily picturesque" horsemen, and the "jolt, joggle, bang-joggle, bang, jolt" of "truly impossible roads."[12]

Russia shared a border of some 2,000 miles with Mongolia, and the tsarist subjects who made their lives in the country (a few hundred mostly merchant "colonists" like Burdukov) far outnumbered the other Europeans and Westerners living there. As a result, it's fair to assume that the Russians were positioned to know the country far better than other Europeans. But this was not necessarily saying much. Basic knowledge—even an elementary awareness—of Mongolia within the Russian public was close to nil in the early 1900s, and this was true not only of the remote worlds of St. Petersburg and Moscow but even of Irkutsk, which sat far closer to the country and had long served as the regional headquarters of Russo-Mongolian relations.

Indeed, if educated Russians in Ungern's time thought about Mongolia at all, it tended to be in the same exotic vein as other Europeans, reflecting a similar mixture of revulsion and attraction, condescension and pity. There were individual variations, to be sure. As we saw earlier, Russian Asianist intellectuals felt a certain kinship with the Mongols, or at least with the idealized Mongols of their imagination, whereas Russian scholars—in particular, philologists and specialists on Buddhism—could be respectful and tolerant of

Mongol culture. Burdukov, an avid student of Mongolian life, is an example of a Russian who truly cared about the country and tried to understand it on its own terms.[13] But on the whole it's hard to imagine an ordinary Mongol of the time being able to tell much of a difference between a stereotypically French or British attitude, for example, and a Russian one. As one Russian writer put it, slipping into the common vocabulary, "though Mongolia lies at our very doorstep, for us no less than the Europeans, she remains a mystery."[14]

Buddhas East and West

Ungern's journey to Kobdo took place at a time of rising interest in Buddhism in Western societies. Buddhist circles had appeared in European and American cities by the 1890s. ("It's not uncommon nowadays to hear a New Yorker say he's a Buddhist," one American journalist wrote at the time.) And by the early 1900s, "God-seeking" intellectuals and other curious professionals were organizing similar societies in St. Petersburg and Moscow. Scholarship on Buddhism, Russian scholarship in particular, also ticked upward, as did diatribes against the religion by Christian churches.[15] Indeed, if there was anything a typical educated Russian/Westerner knew about Mongolia in the early 1900s it was probably that it was a Buddhist country, which, in keeping with the exotic stereotype of the age, meant that it was either alluring or heathenish, or both at the same time.[16]

The Mongols' conversion to Buddhism unfolded in phases, first in the era of the Mongol Empire and then more profoundly during the so-called second conversion of the sixteenth and seventeenth centuries. In each case, Tibet provided the model. Monks, known as lamas, many of them from Tibet ("lama" is a Tibetan word for "teacher"), arrived in the country to spread the new religion, and over time the faith entrenched itself, much as it had in Tibet, by melding with pre-Buddhist animist traditions and building up a veneration for the so-called Three Jewels: the Buddha and his lineages of incarnate lamas (teachers whose spirit was constantly reborn); the Buddha's law, known as the *dharma;* and the community of the enlightened (*sangha*), which effectively meant the monks and the monasteries.[17]

By the late Qing era, the influence of the Buddhist "church" in Mongolia was enormous, reaching into virtually every aspect of society. Estimates from the early 1900s suggest that over 40 percent of Mongolian men were lamas, and over a thousand small monasteries and some seven hundred large ones covered the country, the greatest of them presiding over their own expansive pasturages and serf-like populations (the shabi). The base of the population was made up of nomads who grazed their herds on tribal and monastery lands while also practicing limited agriculture. The elite, meanwhile, consisted of the tribal khans and banner chiefs (see below) as well as some fifty *khutuktus,* the "high incarnations," the most esteemed of the incarnate lamas who functioned in effect as the country's ecclesiastical aristocracy.[18]

Russians with a professional interest in Buddhism resided in either the Orthodox Church or in academia. By and large, the Church was hostile, seeing Buddhism not only as a regrettable "delusion" but also as a rival for the souls of potential converts among the Buryats and the Kalmyks, another Mongol people living within the empire whose migrations had taken them farther west to the shores of the Caspian Sea. Scholars, meanwhile, tended to be more sympathetic and tolerant of a space for Buddhism in Russian life, including a number of professors who made a point of training Buryat graduate students and developing contacts among lamas in Mongolia as well as the Trans-Baikal.[19]

For educated Russians outside the Church and the universities, the rising interest in Buddhism in the fin de siècle era is harder to define. Though reflecting the far eastern turn that affected so much of the country's high culture and foreign policy at the time, it also seems to have been driven, much as it was in Europe, less by Asia in a direct sense than by a general disquiet about the modern age. The same disorienting changes that led scholars like Gustav Le Bon to foresee a future of irrational crowds made others question their faith and seek new sources of spiritual sustenance. To many of these questioners, Buddhism offered things they couldn't find in the Christianity they knew, and because the religion was so strikingly different, it was easy to approach as a kind of spiritual salad bar: a place to pick and choose what one wanted, while leaving off the rest. In that sense, the "Buddha's way" that most Russians knew had little to do with the various Buddhisms actually lived by millions of Buddhists in Buddhist cultures but instead amounted to a quintessential exotic product: a cultural form exported from one context into another and completely refashioned in the process.

Indeed, for most of the Europeans and Westerners inclined to experiment with Buddhism in Ungern's time, the urge rarely culminated in the adoption of a Buddhist lifestyle or becoming Buddhist in a comprehensive sense (though some did indeed do this). The norm instead was eclecticism, a mixing and matching of Buddhist cosmology with Christian and even unchristian spiritualist or occult beliefs that then became mashed together in various hybrid forms. To people interested in this sort of spiritual blending, rather than an end in itself, Buddhism functioned more as a portal, a great front hall that one moved through on the way to deeper religious awareness.

By far the most influential group to embrace this view was the Theosophical Society, whose creed envisioned a blending of Eastern and Western religion—in particular, Christianity and Buddhism—within "a spiritual conception of the universe" that was also, as they saw it, wholly scientific.[20] All the peoples of the world were one, as were all the world's faiths, each of which expressed the reality of a single root of "divine wisdom" (Theosophia) that was founded in logic and therefore explainable through reason. By the early 1900s, the Society had grown from humble roots into a worldwide organization with chapters on multiple continents, including cities throughout European Russia.[21] Some of its Christian followers considered themselves Buddhists or something close: the Society's eccentric founder, a Russian émigré named Helen Blavatsky (Elena Blavatskaia), for example, described herself as a "Buddhist pantheist."[22]

Theosophy's popularity with the Western and Russian publics of the day lay in the fact that it seemed to bring everything together, providing a comforting intellectual-spiritual distillation of the European-dominated global moment of the late nineteenth century. Theosophists were the kind of broad-minded people who were able to revere the deep wisdom of "Eastern religion" while still acknowledging the authority of science. They harmonized ancient truths and current realities, combined "Eastern spirit" with "Western mind."

They also prided themselves in being the absolute opposite of intolerant imperialists: rather than dismissing "the East" as foul or backward, they sought to learn from it. Asia was the teacher, they were the students. Of course, at the same time, they were no less ethnocentric in their way. Like the Russian Asianists, for example, who managed to identify with Asia while at the same time supporting tsarist colonial expansion, the Theosophists embraced Buddhism even as they refashioned it into a product for their own consumption.[23]

It's not clear whether Ungern had any connections to Theosophy. We have no evidence that he attended even a single Society meeting, though he might have in St. Petersburg when he was finishing his cadet training, since numerous officers in the city were Society members. Some of the religious views that we hear from him by the time of the Mongolian campaign indeed ring with the sound of the movement, in particular his apparently easygoing embrace of Buddhism and mystical Christianity. At a minimum, it seems likely that he was influenced by the spiritual restlessness that lay behind Theosophy and other movements like it at the time, but again we don't have proof, only possibilities.

During his service in the Trans-Baikal, Ungern had lived cheek-to-jowl with the Mongol world. It's fair to assume, then, that well before he made the unusual decision to resign from the army and head for Kobdo, he already knew the country in a way that a passing visitor like Bulstrode, for example, never could. Yet could he have known it *without* exoticism? After all, he, too, was a foreigner approaching things from the outside in, and the exotic, with its relentless insistence on the contrasts of wonder and revulsion, was the frame everyone used. Surely he, too, was going to Mongolia, at least in part, because it was the seeming opposite of everything he knew best, including the polished worlds of his youth and the depressing sameness of the army's rules and routines. Mongolia was different. It was a realm beyond, the kind of place that made you special just by getting there.

The Amorphous Country

In 1913, much as today, the Mongol lands were divided into two basic parts. In the south, running up against the provinces of northern China, was the region the Qing knew as Inner Mongolia—"inner" because it lay closer to Beijing and "China proper." Today this region makes up the Inner Mongolian Autonomous Region of the People's Republic of China. The Mongols there included Chahars and Barguts and other tribes. Farther north, beyond Inner Mongolia, lay Outer Mongolia. Here one found various tribes as well: Tuvans and other Western Mongol groups in places like Kobdo, and the Khalkha Mongols, the largest group, in the center and east. Much of this vast area today makes up the independent state of Mongolia (Mongolian: *Mongol uls*). For well over two hundred years, the two halves of the Mongol lands had been part of the Qing Empire, but in 1911, in the midst of the turmoil and opportunity of the Chinese Revolution, the Mongols of Outer Mongolia declared their independence.

Ungern's arrival in 1913 coincided with a great sea change in the Mongols' historical relationships. The Manchus began their rule over Mongol territory at the time of their conquest of China in the 1600s. The lands of Inner Mongolia were incorporated earliest and most firmly into the new Qing state, but both parts were ultimately ruled in similar fashion. To divide the Mongols from each other, while tying them to the empire, the Qing organized them into autonomous military-administrative groupings known as banners.[24] The various Mongol tribal leaders (*khans*) who led the banners received titles and privileges confirmed by a colonial office in Beijing, and they were expected to defend the empire's northern frontiers. But otherwise they were largely left to themselves.

As a result, the Mongols' Buddhist faith flourished (within bounds) under Qing sponsorship. Their nomadic way of life was respected. Reflecting their special place within the imperial system, Mongolian became one of the official languages of court proclamations (along with Manchu and Chinese). The Mongols were even allowed their own chief political and spiritual leader—the Jibzundamba Khutuktu, also known as the Bogd Gegeen, or simply the Bogd (or Bogda), meaning "the Holy Brilliance," or "the Holy One"—the most supreme of the khutuktus whose revered status in both Outer and Inner Mongolia was comparable to that of the Dalai Lama in Tibet. Much as in most of Manchuria, ethnic Chinese (Han) agricultural settlement in the Mongol lands was prohibited.[25]

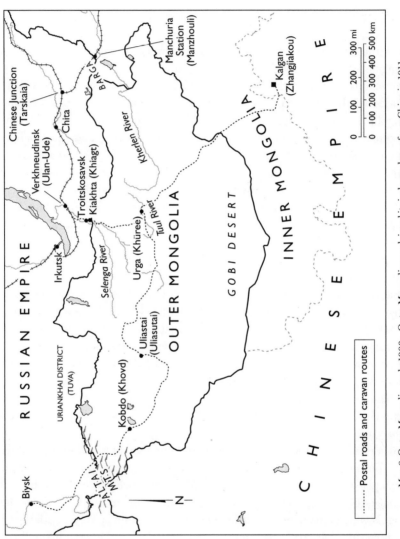

Map 6. Outer Mongolia, early 1900s. Outer Mongolia proclaimed its independence from China in 1911, but the boundaries of the Mongol lands were never as clear-cut as this map suggests. Different Mongol groups lived on either side of the Chinese, Russian, and Mongol borders.

RUSSIAN EMPIRE

Biysk

Irkutsk

Verkhneudinsk
(Ulan-Ude)

Chinese Junction
(Tarskaia)

Chita

BARGA

Manchuria
Station
(Manzhouli)

Troitskosavsk
Kiakhta (Khiagt)

Selenga River

Kherlen River

URIANKHAI DISTRICT
(TUVA)

Urga (Khüree)

Tuul River

Uliastai
(Uliasutai)

Kobdo (Khovd)

ALTAI MTS.

OUTER MONGOLIA

GOBI DESERT

INNER MONGOLIA

Kalgan
(Zhangjiakou)

CHINESE EMPIRE

N

------- Postal roads and caravan routes

0   100   200   300 mi
0 100 200 300 400 500 km

In the early 1900s, however, the Qing abruptly changed their approach. Reeling from the destruction and cost of the Boxer Rebellion and a new round of foreign military intervention (including the Russian-led occupation of most of northern Manchuria), the government launched what it called the New Policies (*xin zheng*). The basic objective of the new program was to save the dynasty, and this applied as much to frontier regions (like the Mongol lands) as it did to "China proper." The dynamics in each case were different, however. In Chinese areas, the thrust of the new measures amounted to the adoption of Westernizing reforms ("to blend together the best of what is Chinese and what is foreign"). The army was modernized. Weights and measures were standardized. Legal codes were revised. Foot-binding was banned. Chinese students left to study in Japan and the "western ocean powers." The "examination hell" of the old civil service system was abolished. The court spoke of creating a constitutional order and of unifying "the Manchus, Han, Mongols, Muslims, and Tibetans as one citizenry."[26]

In the "barbarian places" "beyond the Great Wall," however, the most obvious manifestation of the New Policies was the "re-imperialization" of the state through the support of large-scale Han colonization.[27] When Ungern served on the Amur, he saw the effects of this policy across the river in the thickening settlements of Heilongjiang. In the Mongol lands, including parts of Outer Mongolia, a similar process got underway. Colonization bureaus were opened. Han settlers received seeds and plots. And, along with this, the Qing began reorganizing the terms of Mongol military service and expanding the presence of the central government, reducing the autonomy that Mongol elites saw as their entitlement. The ethnic Chinese merchants who controlled most of the petty trade in Mongol areas received additional privileges. Their prices rose. Mongol indebtedness increased.

In Outer Mongolia, where Mongol identification with Qing power was more tenuous than Inner Mongolia, resentments over these developments rapidly eroded relations with the Qing authorities. By the summer of 1911, Mongol khans and influential lamas were meeting in secret to plot a way out from under the Qing thumb. Then in late December of that year, against the backdrop of a deepening anti-Qing rebellion in "China proper" and anti-Chinese riots in the Chinese administration's head town of Urga, they seized the moment and declared independence.[28]

To lead their new state, the Mongol notables agreed on the person of the then current Bogda, the Eighth Jibzundamba Khutuktu, a forty-two-year-old Tibetan-born lama revered throughout the country as the living Buddha. In a great ceremony held in Urga (now proclaimed as the Mongol capital) under the spans of a towering nomadic tent (*ger*) wrapped in yellow silk, the Bogda assumed the formal title of Bogd Khagan (Holy Emperor) and became in effect a theocratic monarch, like "the popes of medieval Christendom," according to one European contemporary. To inaugurate the new dynasty, he adopted the Buddhist and (unintentionally) populist-sounding reign name of "Elevated by the Many" (*Olnoo Örgögdsön*).[29]

The Mongolian Revolution of 1911 was a cautionary tale of the perils of imperial reform in a national age. The policies the Qing were pursuing—administrative standardization, military modernization, intensive borderland development, and the formation of a more integrated society—were broadly similar to those underway in many other states at the time, including tsarist Russia. Both the Romanov and the Qing, much like the other old dynastic houses of Eurasia (the Ottomans, the Habsburgs, the Qajars of Persia), found themselves faced with the same dangerous challenge. They had to strengthen and improve their states in order to compete with their foreign rivals. Yet to strengthen their states, they had to push through rapid and disruptive changes, including adjustments to the old balances between regions and peoples that had guaranteed the relative stability of their empires for centuries.

These changes gave rise to resentments as well as huge expenses and higher taxes, which in turn only increased the danger facing the governments. The Qing succumbed first, unable to overcome the compounding pressure. As one Chinese reformer put it, "The ruler is like a boat; the people are like the water. The water can support the boat; it can also overturn the boat."[30] The tsarist boat would go under a few years later, capsized by a similar list of troubles but even more by the special disaster of World War I.

In the summer of 1913 in Mongolia, however, the fates of the two countries seemed pointed in opposite directions. The Mongolian Revolution had been a rejection not just of Qing rule but of Chinese power more generally. The Bogda's government allowed Chinese merchants to remain in Mongolia—in fact, Chinese firms continued to dominate trade throughout the country—but Chinese officials and military units were forced to leave, and Han colonization offices were closed. To fill the vacuum left by the Chinese, while also providing the counterweight they hoped would keep them from coming back, the Mongols turned to the Russians. A delegation of khans and lamas traveled to St. Petersburg in the summer before the country declared independence to seek the tsar's protection. Then, as the Chinese went out, Russians came in: Russian soldiers (Cossacks from the Trans-Baikal Host, mostly), Russian advisers for the new army and ministries, Russian companies, Russian churchmen dreaming of new frontiers for Orthodoxy, and also Russian money in the form of generous loans to support the new regime. Along the Amur the Chinese loomed as a "yellow peril"; in Mongolia their setback became Russia's neocolonial opportunity.[31]

The imposition of this sort of influence over Mongolia proved how deeply late tsarist Russia was enmeshed in the imperial world of its time. In the early twentieth century, outside of Europe and the Americas, very few of today's states existed as independent countries. Instead the world resembled an orb of empires—overseas empires like Britain, France, Spain, Germany, and Japan; European and Asian/Middle Eastern continental empires; and the expanding continental and maritime "imperial republic" of the United States. Historians rightly draw distinctions between these various types of imperial states. Yet the differences between them inevitably blur at the edges.

In fact, if we consider the great empires of the day in terms of how they ruled, we see, regardless of how we might categorize them, that most were highly internally diverse, exerting their power over their varied peoples and territories not in one unbending way but rather in many. One of the great sources of tension in the age, as we have seen, was the trend toward diminishing this internal variation, though even as this general movement unfolded, empires never stopped being profoundly varied.

As one of the longest lived and most successful of empires, Russia expanded and ruled through constant adaptation, over time as well as space. In the non-Russian territories that made up their western borders (the Baltic provinces, Poland, "Little Russia" [Ukraine]), the tsars ruled very much in keeping with the general traditions of European multiethnic states. The country's expansion south toward the Black and Caspian seas and eastward into Siberia, however, was more like the European conquest and colonization of the Americas, South Africa, and Australia. The "pacification" of the Caucasus resembled the imposition of French power in Algeria. Russian rule in Central Asia shared much in common with British rule in India; and the CER's "concession" in Manchuria followed the pattern of the other foreign powers that carved out "spheres of influence" in China or Persia in the same period. Russia's leaders recognized these comparisons and participated in an active exchange of strategies and expertise with their imperial rivals and allies.

In their approach to newly independent Mongolia, the Russians adapted again, drawing on the latest iterations of international imperialist practice. Stopping short of formally taking over the country, they used their money and specialists to obtain the sort of influence over Mongolian affairs that effectively amounted to the same thing. This was the essence of the neocolonial arrangement—a modus operandi of colonial power without direct colonial control that increasingly defined US relations with the states of Central America and the Caribbean in the same period as well as the systems of "informal rule" that British and French "imperial agents" had established in parts of Africa.

To the architects of tsarist policy in Mongolia, this sort of informal imperialism made perfect sense. As they saw it, Russia was entitled to special influence and authority in the country, and the Mongolians, as poor, naïve "children of nature," needed their guidance. As Viktor Liuba, the Russian consul in Urga, stated in a cable to his superiors in St. Petersburg in early 1912, "In the eyes of the Mongol, we are now *the* 'elder brother'. No political favors or anything our officials or commercial people might have done could ever have brought about a more favorable situation than the one we see before us today. It would be a cruel shame (*bylo by zhestoko stydno*) if we did not make use of this opportunity to secure the position for ourselves in Mongolia that we so rightly deserve."[32]

After independence, Chinese silver taels (*liang*) began to disappear from Mongolian markets, replaced by Russian rubles. Russian merchants described Mongol customers bowing to the portraits of Nicholas II that hung in their shops. Notables in Urga requested a new Russian school for their children, and the Bogda himself displayed his Russophilia by ordering the construction of a boxy, two-story, Russian-style residence on the grounds of one of his Tibeto-Sino-Mongolian palaces.[33] (The model for the house was the main building of the Urga consulate.) One Russian visitor stated matter-of-factly: "The Mongols look to Russia today with enormous hope. They long for our support in every way."[34]

The meteoric rise of Russian influence in Mongolia immediately led to questions about the best overall direction for Russian policy. Some statesmen and commentators urged going after the greatest possible gains, arguing for the establishment of a Russian protectorate over Mongolia, even outright annexation. This tended to be the view of a number of influential military advisers and of the Ministry of Finance. But the view in the Ministry of Foreign Affairs was much more cautious. In fact, Russia's official diplomatic position from the start was to advise the Mongolians *against* declaring independence and to seek instead an expanded form of autonomy within China.

After the Russo-Japanese War, the overriding concern of tsarist foreign policy in East Asia was to head off the possibility of another Far Eastern war by coming to terms with Japan over spheres of influence. Supporting Mongolian independence risked upsetting those arrangements because the goal of the Khalkha leaders was to unite all the Mongol peoples of China, including groups in other banner regions of Outer Mongolia, such as Kobdo and Tuva in the west, and the lands of Inner Mongolia, including territories such as Barga that lay east of the "Peking meridian" and thus fell (by secret agreement) within Japan's sphere of influence. A pro-independence position also meant increasing tension with China since the new republican rulers, like the Qing, continued to consider all of Mongolia—Outer and Inner—as an integral part of the Chinese state.[35]

In the immediate aftermath of the Mongolians' declaration of independence, the tsarist government sent mixed signals (apparently on purpose) to the Bogda and his entourage, de facto acknowledging the existence of their new state on the one hand yet on the other stopping short of providing formal recognition. Ultimately, however, the Russian line became one of pushing their Mongolian "client" to drop its ambitions for sovereignty as Russian diplomats called for the country to revert to being part of the Chinese state, though with the important new condition that Beijing would provide Mongolia with guarantees of absolute autonomy, which in turn would be backed up by the Russians who would serve, in effect, as the honest brokers mediating the new relationship.

Chinese colonists and garrisons would be banned from autonomous Mongolia. The Bogda and his counselors would be free to make their own economic decisions and partnerships. Russia would receive special privileges, including a secret railway concession and permission to retain a consular guard that was only slightly smaller than the one allowed the Chinese high commissioner.[36] Meanwhile, the Russians also worked to undermine any sort of larger Mongol unity by effectively annexing part of Outer Mongolia for themselves—the far western region of Uriankhai in the Altay Mountains, which is today Tuva, one of the autonomous republics of the Russian Federation—and agreeing to a separate autonomous status within China for the eastern region of Barga (Mongolian: Khölön Buir; Chinese: Hulunbuer) bordering the area where Ungern had served on the Argun.[37] St. Petersburg cautiously supported Urga by pressuring the Chinese to abandon western Mongolia and upholding the idea that Kobdo should become part of the new Mongolian state, but that was about as far as Russian policy would go.

The overall outline of Outer Mongolia's autonomy became formalized in a series of agreements, the most important being the so-called Tripartite Treaty signed by Russia, China, and Mongolia in the historic Sino-Russian border town of Kiakhta in June 1915. The Russians saw the treaty as a happy achievement, given they were by then fighting the Great War in Europe and were desperate to avoid any extra obligations in Asia. Not surprisingly, the Chinese and the Mongolians saw the agreement in much dimmer terms, though for different reasons.[38]

What the treaty meant, though, for the moment at least, was that the would-be independent state of Mongolia formally ceased to exist, its disappearance seeming proof of the view neatly stated by a British journalist at the time that the country was "an amorphous state" without the power "to stand alone."[39] In an age of empires, surrounded by empires, Mongolia could only survive on its own if at least one of its larger neighbors—either Russia or China—allowed it to, and, for the time being, neither of them would.

Red Goat Hill

Kobdo today is known as Khovd, a small provincial center of about thirty thousand people that sits in the middle of a rocky plain ringed by hills and snow-capped mountains in the far western corner of Mongolia. With the exception of its moonscape surroundings, Khovd looks much like any other Mongolian town of its size. A collection of drab Soviet-era low-rises occupies the center.

On the outskirts are the stacks of slumbering factories and neighborhoods of round-domed gers—Mongolian tents, known in English as yurts—each of them sitting behind its own wall or fence, like houses on lots. Somewhat farther out of town lies the city airport whose single waiting room comes to life for the two or three flights a week that shuttle back and forth from the capital of Ulaan-baatar (formally Urga), located some 900 miles to the east.[40]

To find echoes of what Khovd was like in Ungern's time, we have to head into the town center, to the broad street lined with gnarled poplars that runs away from the main square. The trees, planted during the Qing era, lead us past a series of dilapidated, whitewashed houses, some built in the Russian style with low eves and ornately carved window frames. After a short walk, we reach the end of the street and find ourselves facing Khovd's only noteworthy landmark from the Qing period: the crumbling earthen walls of the old fortress that once marked the town's importance as a military outpost of the Chinese Empire. Though eroded by time, the dusty brown walls still tower some twelve feet high, dwarfing us as we stand beneath them.

The best view of the fortress is from a high point not far away, a jagged crag known as Red Goat Hill that rises up just behind the site. Climbing just part way up the hill, one can clearly make out the square-like perimeter of the fortress below. Today the space is barren, just a vast vacant lot of dirt and brush, but in its day the fort was home to the residence of the Qing provincial governor (*amban*), Buddhist and Chinese temples, a mosque, and tents and barracks for a peacetime garrison of about one hundred soldiers. Just behind the fort runs the Buyant River, whose lazy flow turns the surrounding area in the spring into lush, green pasture. Just outside the fort would have been a trading town of Chinese shops, huddled around earth-brick courtyards. Under the Qing, the fort lay at the center of a small but vibrant commercial world. The Altay region of southwestern Siberia was close by, as was the northeastern tip of the Qing-controlled territories of Central Asia (Xinjiang, or Eastern Turkestan). Wares from these regions made their way by caravan to Kobdo and from there to Urga and eventually to the markets of northern and central China. Most Kobdo merchants, Chinese and Russians alike, also conducted a local trade with nomads in the surrounding valleys.[41]

When Outer Mongolia declared independence, most of the Qing authorities and their troops responded peacefully and left the country, often by passing through Russian territory. The Chinese governor in Kobdo, however, refused to recognize the new Mongolian regime and reinforced his garrison. In response, in August 1912, the Mongols organized an assault on the fortress. A large painting of the battle hangs in the modest but pleasant building of the Khovd Provincial Museum just off the street with the poplars, not far from the fort itself. In it, we see the Mongols rushing against the fort, swords drawn, hoisting yellow banners, a color of royalty in China and of evocative spiritual

6.2. Mongol fighters, Kobdo, 1913. Reproduced from Hermann Consten, *Weideplätze der Mongolen im Reiche der Chalcha* (Berlin, 1920), vol. 2, pl. 41.

power in Tibetan and Mongolian Buddhism. The onslaught devastated the fortress and most of the town. After intense fighting, the Chinese surrendered and the amban and his remaining men were escorted, under Russian protection, back to China via Siberia.[42]

The situation remained tense during the following year amid fears that the Chinese might try to retake the town. Taking advantage of the general instability, Kazakh raiders plundered caravans and seized hostages passing to and from the Russian border. Meanwhile, different clan leaders among the Mongols vied between themselves for influence, clashing occasionally. The Urga government claimed to be in charge, but in fact the "true master of Kobdo district" was Dambiijantsan, also known as Ja Lama, a charismatic and notoriously brutal "renegade monk" who, having proven himself in the assault against the Qing, was rewarded for his efforts with a title by the Bogda, and then used his renown to establish himself as a semi-official warlord in the region. The Russian authorities considered him an outlaw, though like many outlaws, he had a romantic, even legendary aura, which explains why Ungern had heard of him and brought him up in his discussions with Burdukov. Still today nomads in the valleys outside of Khovd will show you where Ja Lama's men made their camps as well as the execution stones where he "inflicted all kinds of lawlessness and suffering."[43]

By the time Ungern reached Kobdo in late August 1913, the only figure of authority left in the town was the Russian consul Liuba, who had recently transferred from his former post in Urga. Kobdo had all but emptied out after the fighting, and Liuba described the town in the spring of 1913 as "a depressing vision of destruction and emptiness."

> Our small consular staff, a Cossack guard of fifty-three men, about fifteen merchants from Biisk [in Western Siberia], roughly fifty homeless and unemployed Chinese merchants, and three Central Asians (*sarty*) are huddled into the few standing houses that remain in the town. With the exception of ten to twelve lamas, there are no Mongols anywhere in the vicinity. In the trenches and ditches that were built around the town during the siege, in the outlying Chinese temples, and even in a few of the courtyards in the very center of the town, one can see the bodies of more than six hundred Chinese killed during the fighting and the aftermath. Most of the corpses remain above ground, covered with little more than a heaping of dirt. The outskirts of the town... are littered with the carcasses of horses, camels, dogs.... There is talk of moving the town to a new location.... In the meantime I have made it clear to the Mongolian authorities that they must clean the city and properly bury the dead.[44]

The situation in Kobdo reflected the challenges that the Russians faced as neocolonial sponsors. The world of empires worked best when the empires involved could depend on each other for stability. The breakdown of Chinese power was thus at once a gift and a problem for the Russians. Tsarist advisers had trained some of the Mongolian units that stormed the Kobdo fortress, but the instructors themselves were ordered to steer clear of the hostilities for fear of upsetting the Chinese. Officials in St. Petersburg grew nervous when they learned that some Mongols were spreading rumors that Russian officers had led the attack.[45]

At the same time, the Russians had little faith in the Mongols as a military deterrent, so even as they savored the Chinese withdrawal, they found themselves forced to fill the vacuum. Liuba reported some fifty Cossacks on hand in April 1913, but by late summer, the number had swelled to over three hundred, with more positioned still farther west, closer to the Russian border.[46] Almost all of these men were from the Trans-Baikal Host. In addition, the Russians sent a civilian topographical expedition to survey the area, while military teams scoured the valleys to spy on the Chinese. One of the scouts was Boris Rezukhin, a young officer of the Trans-Baikal Host and friend of Ungern's who would later serve under his command in Mongolia during the civil war.[47]

Just as the Russians wondered whether the Mongols would be able to maintain their independence in military terms, they also doubted their ability to run their own government. According to one of his superiors, Liuba, for one, was completely dismissive of the viability of Mongolian independence, seeing it as little more than a historical accident. In his view, the Mongols were "a race of people on the path to extinction, incapable of progress, doomed to be swallowed up by their neighbors."[48] His consular reports from 1913 brim with complaints about the incompetence of the Mongol authorities, including frustration with the fact that the newly appointed governor of the region preferred to live in his yurt outside of Kobdo rather than move into the town.[49] All of this meant that Mongolian independence, as perceived by the Russians, seemed as much a burden as it did an opportunity, a temptation that was also a headache and vice versa.

Adding to the challenge, as Russian officials saw it, was the nature of the Russian presence in the country. By the early twentieth century, views of colonization in Russia were ambivalent. On the one hand, there was clear enthusiasm for what seemed like a "grand and unstoppable process" of imperial settlement as well as enormous pride in the achievement of Russian power in Asia. We feel this energy and optimism coursing through much of the writing on the Great Siberian Migration, for example. But this confidence coexisted with a range of nagging anxieties and hesitations—concerns that Russian Cossacks and peasants had become too "nativized" in the Trans-Baikal, for example, or that Russian colonists in the Far East were doomed to be undone by the Chinese, who seemed both far more numerous and much harder workers. Some Russian observers voiced gloomy fears that the empire had overreached itself in "the East" and that the Russians there were not up to the task of transforming the cultures living around them.

In regard to the Russians in Mongolia, many Russian observers had similar concerns. The scholar Grigory Potanin, for example, concluded in the 1870s that local Russians had virtually no influence on the Mongols, and by the early 1900s a new generation of observers were making equally dim observations.[50] The petty traders and their families who made up the lion's share of the Russian diaspora tended to live in tents like the Mongols, usually near postal horse relay stations. The men among them often married Mongolian women. They knew Mongolian fluently.[51] But if anything, as outside observers saw it, the Russians in the country had adopted far more from their neighbors than they had given in return. And the business community as a whole, in particular the so-called Russian colony (*koloniia*) in Urga, was seen in an especially dark light. There, too, many Russian colonists lived among the Mongols rather than in the formal Russian area around the consulate, and officials routinely described them as petty and inward-looking, far more interested in squabbling among themselves and squeezing the most they could from their Mongolian customers than in supporting the "Russian cause."

Liuba, for example, was almost as dismissive of the Russians in Kobdo as he was of the Mongols. As he saw it, the local merchants were people of "low culture with a distinct lack of respect for the official representatives [of our government]"—that is, in this case, Liuba himself.[52] Their overall economic position was also weak. Though despised by the local population, the Chinese controlled a far greater share of the Mongolian market, and Western companies were beginning to arrive in the country as well.[53]

Some voices rose up to defend the Russian merchants, of course. As big firms from Moscow and Siberia began to invest in new opportunities in Mongolia in the early 1910s, their representatives blamed their country's weak economic presence less on the supposedly lackluster Russian merchants than on the diplomats of the Foreign Ministry, who, in their view, showed an "utter disregard" for Russian business. (The new businessmen were joined in this view by incoming neocolonial advisers from the Ministry of Trade and Industry who also looked down on the diplomats.)[54] But even pro-business advocates had to admit that the Russian trader who duped and overcharged his customers made a dismal ambassador. "Our Siberian merchants built the Russian cause in Mongolia," wrote one pair of businessmen in 1911, "yet at the same time, our standing among the Mongols suffers because of them."[55]

Indeed, in a curious twist that was very much in keeping with the broader paradoxes of the tsarist empire, some of the most committed champions of the "Russian cause" in Mongolia in the 1910s were not even Russian at all. Much of the work of promoting close ties with Russia and expanding Russian influence in the country was done by Buryats—in particular, by Russianized Buryat officials and scholars who joined the new retinue of advisers surrounding the Bogda's government. The linguist-economist (and socialist) Elbek-Dorzhi Rinchino worked on economic issues. The folklorist and literary scholar Tsyben

Zhamtsarano helped to produce the first Mongolian-language newspapers, printed in Urga in a newly established Russo-Mongolian printing shop.[56] Another Russianized Buryat, a man of an earlier generation, the influential lama and Russian-Tibetan go-between Avgan Dorzhiev, led the drive to build a Buddhist Lamaist temple in St. Petersburg. The Bogda presided as a guest of honor at the opening in 1913.[57]

The Buryat intellectuals' motivation for joining the effort to create "the new Mongolia" was different from that of broader tsarist policy, though it was shaped by a similar sort of paternalism. Like native colonial elites in other empires, they saw themselves as champions and protectors of the nation. As men who had grown up in yurts but gone on to universities, they had no doubt that they were the special ones who truly understood the modern world—the world of legal codes and private property, suffragettes and telephones, budgets and microscopes. It was thus only natural, as they saw it, that their backward Mongol cousins would turn to them as leaders and counselors.

In just a few years, when the Russian Empire would crack apart in revolution and civil war, intellectuals like Rinchino and Zhamstarano would find themselves forced to choose between the conflicting allegiances of empire and nation. Many hours would pass in smoky rooms debating how to get along with the warring Russian constituencies around them, while trying to bring about autonomy or even independence for the Buryats, including the possibility of uniting with the Mongols of Outer and Inner Mongolia to form a larger, pan-Mongolian state. And as they did all of this, they would find themselves drawn into one devil's bargain after another—first with the Reds, then with the Whites, then with the Reds again, hoping in each case to turn their vulnerable in-betweenness to their advantage.

In quasi-independent Mongolia before the Russian Revolution, however, things were simpler. For all of the uncertainty of Mongolia's new path, the context, for the Buryat intellectuals at least, was still a familiar one in which intermediaries like themselves had room to advance their own cause, while serving their imperial patrons as well. As Prince Esper Ukhtomsky, a confidant of Emperor Nicholas, put it: "For two centuries the members of this native race [i.e., the Buryats—WS] have shown themselves to be excellent and faithful subjects. Among them are many, to a large extent Russianized, who are fully qualified and well-suited to represent us. It is not time for Russia to take advantage of this circumstance?"[58]

Commander of the Whole Mongolian Cavalry!

According to Burdukov, when he and Ungern arrived in Kobdo after the three-day relay from Uliastai, Ungern met up with his friend Rezukhin from the Trans-Baikal Host. The next day, Burdukov saw him again and by this time he had changed into a spotless Trans-Baikal uniform that he had borrowed from Rezukhin to make a good impression on Consul Liuba and the commander of the Cossack detachment. The merchant next tells us that Ungern asked the two officials for permission to serve in one of the local Mongol units and that they flatly rejected his request. At this point the references to Ungern break off as the baron, according to Burdukov, leaves Kobdo and returns to Russia.[59]

General Petr von Wrangel, the famous leader of the White armies who happened to serve as one of Ungern's commanders a few years later during the Great War, offers a different version of the Kobdo episode that has been far more widely repeated. In the brief page or so that he devotes to Ungern in his memoirs, Wrangel notes that Ungern spent his time in Kobdo "commanding the Mongolian cavalry and fighting for Mongolian independence." An early English translation of the memoirs puts it more grandly still: "and there he was, commander of the whole cavalry force of Mongolia!"[60]

Wrangel had no firsthand knowledge to support this claim, of course, since he met Ungern only several years later. Perhaps Ungern told him something about Kobdo during the war, or perhaps the general was simply repeating a story he heard from others. In any case, it's clear that he didn't know Ungern well because a number of the details he relays about him are wrong.[61] Yet if Wrangel's story recurs so often in the histories we write about Ungern, it is surely because it fits so well with the myth of the "mad baron" that has grown up around him, while at the same time suiting our image of Mongolia as the kind of exotic place where a "mad baron" might go. As in so many other tales of empire from the period, the "natives" in the story have nothing better to do, it seems, than to be led by a mysterious foreigner.

The only direct evidence we have of Ungern's time in Kobdo jibes much more with Burdukov's less dramatic version of events. In a cable dated August 27, 1913, Liuba wrote to St. Petersburg that "a certain Senior Lieutenant Ungern-Sternberg of the Amur Cossack Host, at present in the reserves, has arrived here [in Kobdo] by way of Urga and has expressed a desire to serve with the Mongols, in Bair's unit or that of another commander, without pay if necessary. I informed him that I cannot [make such a recommendation] without obtaining prior approval from the imperial government. Our [Cossack] detachment commander here disapproves [of the idea]. Instructions requested."[62]

It's not clear that Liuba ever got a direct reply. All we find in the Foreign Ministry archives are two contradictory documents from the following month, one a memo from an undersecretary to the Foreign Minister arguing that it might indeed be useful to assign a Russian officer as a liaison to the informal Mongol bands around Kobdo, the other a telegram from the head consul in Urga stating that he had already refused Ungern's request on the matter—one

Ungern presumably made to him in person when he passed through the capital earlier in the summer[63]

In the end, did Ungern serve with any of the fighters near Kobdo? Like so much about his life, it is hard to say. He may have, though in that case we might expect to find some trace of him in the reports that Liuba and other diplomats filed from Kobdo over the following months. Instead, he disappears from view. The next time we see him is a year later and a world away, on the marshy edges of East Prussia, beneath the first salvos of World War I.

CHAPTER 7

WAR LAND

"Ah God! How pretty war is
With its songs and its rests."
—APOLLINAIRE. "L'Adieu du Cavalier" (1918)

The Imperial Cauldron

One of the myths of World War I is that it began with an outpouring of happy unanimity on all sides. "As never before, thousands and hundreds of thousands felt. . . that they belonged together," the Austrian writer Stefan Zweig recalled about the times in Vienna. In St. Petersburg, the Russian nationalist Vasilii Rozanov recorded something similar in his diary: "We will act as one, we will forget all our divisions, all our family quarrels." "Everywhere," he added, "there is an excitement for unity, a joy in feeling united."[1]

In reality, despite these impressions, reactions to the war were mixed almost everywhere. One could indeed find throngs of enthusiastic, cap-throwing patriots, like the crowd that gathered in St. Petersburg's Palace Square on August 2, 1914 to hear Tsar Nicholas announce that the war with Germany had begun. (Shortly after the tsar's speech, some of these patriots left the square and joined another crowd that ransacked the German embassy just a short walk away.)[2] Yet it was just as common to find Russians with misgivings about what lay ahead, including thousands of reservists who rioted at conscription offices around the country.[3] The Russian and Ukrainian peasants who made up well over 80 percent of the tsarist army also appear to have greeted the war with resignation as well as patriotism, and the government's decision to ban alcohol sales with the start of mobilization didn't help. "They've closed all the taverns," went one peasant rhyme, "Such is our tale of woe/ No more beer or vodka/ It's off to war we go."[4]

We don't know where Ungern was when he learned that about the mobilization—some writers say Estland, others St. Petersburg, Chita, or Mongolia.[5] But wherever he was, given his personality, we can assume he was one of the thousands of young men across Europe who indeed "rushed to the colors," or, like Hitler, sank to their knees with happiness at the news.[6] It was the summer of 1914. He was twenty-seven years old. He had left the army just a year before precisely because things had seemed too peaceful. Now the great event had come. He must have been elated.

We know, at least, that he took quick steps to be involved. Rather than wait to fight with the Trans-Baikal forces that would have to come all the way from Siberia, he enrolled with a Cossack regiment from the Don that was heading more rapidly to the front.[7] In a letter to one of his aunts in November 1914, he sounds lighthearted. After thanking her for the gift of a silk shirt and chocolate, he tells her that he has just been put up for a St. George's Cross.

> Last [month] in Prussia my patrol was surrounded, and we managed to jump the German wire only at the last minute. By the time they figured out what was happening and started shooting, we were already out of range. We got out all our wounded. The only trophies we left behind for the Prussians were a few injured horses. They must have been quite annoyed [about that].[8]

The Russian Empire thus found itself at war for the second time in less than a decade, though now, like the expanding universe that the physicists were beginning to uncover, the scale seemed infinite. By the time Ungern's patrol was racing away from the Germans, it was already clear that the new war would dwarf the conflict with Japan ten years before. Some 250,000 Russian troops would die even before the year was out. Over seven million of the tsar's subjects would be mobilized in 1914 alone, over eighteen million by the fall of 1917.[9] The debacle with Japan humbled the autocracy. The terrible weight of World War I would press down and destroy it.

Ungern wrote his anti-German letter in German, which is a small reminder of the many complexities that were about to come to the surface. We tend to think of World War I as a contest between well-defined enemies. The Central Powers fight the Entente. Austrians go up against Serbs, Germans against Frenchmen, British against Turks. But the reality was much more confusing. The war unfolded in fact as a titanic bloodletting between diverse and overlapping empires, especially in the eastern half of Europe that saw dramatic swings along frequently changing fronts. Every army from the Baltic to the Caucasus was, to varying degrees, a multinational force, and the lands they fought over were divided frontiers with densely mixed populations. Nations and ethnicities found themselves split down the middle by the war, as did thousands of families.

7.1. Ungern's great uncle, General Paul (Pavel) von Rennenkampf. Rennenkampf commanded
the first army corps that Ungern served under in fall 1914. Reproduced from
the Library of Congress, LC-B2-3202-2.

The transnational German nobles, for example, fought on all sides. The first major campaign on the eastern front was the Russian invasion of East Prussia that began in August 1914. One of the leading commanders was Ungern's relative, General Paul von Rennenkampf, the same von Rennenkampf who had led the suppression of the "Chita Republic" in the Trans-Baikal during the Revolution of 1905. His counterpart on the German side was General Hermann von François, the German descendant of a French protestant family from Luxemburg. The Great War in the east thus began with a Franco-German pitted against a Germano-Russian.[10] In the drowsy Prussian towns that tsarist forces occupied at the start of the campaign, they ripped down German army announcements and put up their own, in German, under Rennenkampf's signature. A casual reader might have assumed that one German general had simply come to replace another.[11]

Other divides around the front lines were still more confusing. Split between Austria, Germany, and Russia since the eighteenth century, Poles were drummed into the armies of all three belligerents. Ukrainians fought for Austria and Russia, Armenians for Russia and Turkey. Hoping to turn the national patchwork to its advantage, every side tried to use ethnic allegiances against the other. The Germans and Habsburgs formed Polish units to fight the Russians, whereas the Russians pledged, once the war was over, to make Poland "free in its faith, language, and self-government." The Russian army also assured the other "Peoples of Austria-Hungary" (in announcements in nine languages) that the driving goal of their fight was to uphold "the fulfillment of [all] national aspirations." The Habsburgs sent out similar pledges to Ukrainian-speakers in Russian territory. The Russian viceroy of the Caucasus organized Armenian detachments to fight the Turks. Meanwhile, the Ottomans established an anti-Russian Georgian Legion made up of tsarist POWs and appealed to Muslim coreligionists in Russia to abandon their homeland and join a Holy War against the tsar.[12]

The "liberationist hyperbole" that roared so loudly during the war years reflected the obvious fact that everyone knew that minority nationalism was a time bomb waiting to destroy the imperial order.[13] Now that the fight was on, the key was to make sure that the bomb went off in the other emperor's empire rather than one's own. In fact, even before the war, all the rivals of the region had realized this and had tried to manipulate minority nationalism in their neighbor's territory as best they could. (The Russian-Austrian maneuvering over the Ukrainians of eastern Galicia is a case in point.)[14] At the same time, the empires also clamped down on minority nationalist movements active on their own territory, though this sometimes meant, ironically, not rooting out these movements altogether but rather selectively promoting one group's agenda against another's.

In Russia, this complicated approach unfolded under the broad banner of Russification, which, as we've seen, was the government's earnest if uneven attempt to modernize the empire by reinforcing the power of the state and making diversity more workable from the state's point of view. In the Ottoman Empire, this agenda took the form of Ottomanization; in the Kaiserreich, of Germanization; whereas Magyarization unfolded in the Hungarian part of the Habsburg Empire. (A telling exception to the general rule was the Austrian half of the Habsburg Empire where, for a variety of reasons, no comparable process of Austrianization ever quite took hold.)[15] Of all these imperial-nationalist programs, the German course was arguably the most rigorously national in content, in part, at least, because the German state was by far the most ethnically homogenous of the empires. But all the empires, to a degree, drew from the same imperial-nationalist playbook, borrowing and adapting from one another as circumstances allowed.

Thus, by the time the Great War began, all the multinational belligerents of the eastern front had become nationalizing states, not just the zealous "new" German Empire of the Prussians but the old dynastic empires of the Ottomans, Habsburgs, and Romanovs as well. In the process, each of these older states shed some of the supranational ambiguity that had been a mainstay of their success for centuries. Given that none of them survived the war, one could argue—as many historians have—that they were undone by this momentous transformation. Threatened by the bomb of minority nationalism, the old empires responded by becoming ever more nationalist themselves, which only made things worse, and, once the war began, the trigger slipped altogether, destroying them all.[16] In this scenario, World War I emerges as a death knell for imperialism because its ultimate effect was to discredit empire itself as a political form.

7.2. Treaty of Brest-Litovsk, March 1918. The new Soviet government signed this treaty to extricate itself from the Great War. The five languages here—German, Hungarian, Bulgarian, Turkish, and Russian—are a reminder of the complexities of the war on the eastern front. Reproduced from http://en.wikipedia.org/wiki/File:Traktat_brzeski_1918.jpg.

But did things really happen this way? Looking at the situation from a different angle, one could argue that the great imperial states of the region came to an end not because they were undone by modern nationalism but because of the simple fact that they lost the war. Imperial Germany and the Ottoman Empire were dismembered by postwar treaties, whereas Austria-Hungary split into national parts just before the armistice. The Russian Empire, meanwhile, unraveled as a result of the revolutions of 1917, whose most important short-term consequence was to effectively knock the country out of the fight against the Central Powers, which in turn drastically reduced the state's ability to hold onto its territory. In the Russian case, this unraveling was in fact promoted by the new leadership—the Bolsheviks—who took charge of the country in the midst of social and military collapse and soon agreed to give up huge swaths of territory as part of a devil's bargain to hold onto power, biding their time until what they believed was the inevitable coming of world revolution.[17]

Indeed, it's impossible to claim that World War I tolled the bell for empire because the states that won the war actually saw their empires grow. Great Britain, France, and Italy took over the lands of their enemies in the Middle East, East Africa, and the eastern Mediterranean. Imperial Japan, which played the tune of the war better than anyone, also grew at war's end by asserting its rights to Germany's "sphere of influence" in China and seizing the country's possessions in the Pacific.[18] If tsarist Russia or even the relatively weaker Ottoman and Habsburg states had won the war or had managed to work their way out of it at a more advantageous point, it is hard to imagine that they would have collapsed. The old dynastic empires before the war were at once strong *and* weak. It seems too generous to call them "going concerns,"[19] but they were all at least muddling through in regard to their national problems. If they dissolved in the cauldron of the war, it was because the power of their states broke down, not because nationalism ripped them apart.[20]

But for all this, the war nonetheless left a profound mark on the relationship *between* nationality and empire. It ratcheted up the feeling that stood behind the seemingly simple act of pronouncing oneself a Pole, a Frenchman, or a Turk, while dramatically raising the stakes that came from choosing—or being forced to choose—one of these identities. At the same time, the war exacerbated divisions *within* national and imperial communities. The conflict made clear, in fact, what was already obvious to thousands of Europeans (and others) well before the war: that there were multiple ways of being national, some of which involved being transnational or imperial at the same time, and vice versa. For example, one might be a national imperialist, or an anti-imperial nationalist, or a socialist who supported one's emperor, or a socialist who did not, while remaining a Russian, a Georgian, a Lithuanian, a Muslim, or a Catholic (not to mention a Franco-German or a Germano-Russian). For many, the onslaught of the war brought these disparate visions and hyphenated identities to a murderous breaking point.

Since so much was at stake, by far the worst effects were felt by the minority groups in between—the people who found themselves living on either side of the front and appeared most likely to have mixed allegiances. During the war, government on all sides of the battle lines became the purview of the high commands. The Russian *stavka* ran the Russian borderlands. The Germans set up special military governments to oversee the territories they occupied in Russian Poland and in White Russia and the Baltic—what they referred to as *Das Land der Oberost* (the Upper East). In every case, the generals ruled their zones on the basis of an unforgiving standard of "maximum solutions" and "military necessity." Some peoples were considered friendly and favored, others as "hostile" or "unreliable," and punished accordingly. Nuances melted away.[21]

The Ottoman Armenians became the greatest casualties of this Manichean logic. In the aftermath of shattering losses against the Russians in late 1914 and early 1915, the Young Turk government determined that the large concentration of Armenians living near the Caucasus Front were helping the Russians (some Armenians were indeed doing this) and had to be deported. Emergency orders went out. Expulsions quickly followed, accompanied by mass executions and pogroms carried out by Ottoman troops and Kurdish irregulars. Between these murders and the deaths that came with the relocations, at least one million Armenians perished in the genocide.[22] The American ambassador to the empire, Henry Morgenthau, came away from a meeting with the Young Turk leader Mehmet Talat (Talat Pasha) convinced that the government's goal was the total destruction of the Armenians in Eastern Anatolia. "It's the saddest thing I've ever read or heard....Instead of contenting themselves with punishing [the Armenian rebels], [the Young Turks] think they must annihilate the entire race."[23]

The Jews of Eastern Europe also suffered disproportionately. Like the Armenians, they found themselves on opposite sides of the war zone, divided largely between the Habsburg region of Galicia (now southern Poland and western Ukraine) in the west and the Russian Empire in the east, in particular in so-called Pale of Jewish Settlement (*cherta evreiskoi osedlosti*), a vast swath of territory that today includes Lithuania, Belarus, western Ukraine, and Moldova. The intense Judeophobia of the Russian court and General Staff combined with the Jews' vulnerable position close to the border made it easy to assume, once hostilities began, that the Jews would side with the Germans and Austrians. The joint German-Austrian high command fanned these expectations by distributing leaflets to Polish Jews telling them that the German army was coming to deliver them from "Russian slavery." Articles with a similar message appeared in the German press.[24] The consequences for Jews on every side—and in particular in the Russian Empire—were horrific.

As they marched toward Habsburg territory at the onset of the war, Russian troops evicted Russian Jews from the border area, often by simply driving them over to the Habsburg side. Then, once across the frontier, they unleashed a wave of anti-Jewish pogroms, frequently with the full approval of their officers. (Jews in Austrian Galicia were also abused by their Ukrainian and Polish neighbors.)[25] Then, as the war shifted and the Russians found themselves thrown back onto their own territory six months later during the "Great Retreat" of spring 1915, the *stavka* ordered larger and more coordinated deportations. In May of that year, some 150,000 Russian Jews were expelled from Kovno [Kaunas] province alone in less than two weeks, with similar totals for other provinces. Army orders spoke of "Jews and suspect individuals" in the same breath, as if the two categories were interchangeable. Words such as "cleansing" and "purging" (*chistka, ochishchenie*) raced across the telegraphs. Lootings, beatings, and rape were common. Though the anti-Jewish atrocities did not amount to genocide, some Russian officers nonetheless spoke positively of resolving the "Jewish question" "in the Turkish manner."[26]

Given what we know of Ungern's movements during the war, he almost certainly witnessed some of these expulsions or, at the very least, their aftermath—columns of refugees, torched villages, ransacked synagogues. Cossack units were notorious for their involvement in anti-Jewish violence. Of the fifty-four pogroms recorded in Lithuania and Belorussia between April and October 1915, for example, more than 80 percent were ignited by the appearance of a Cossack unit.[27] Just a few years later in Mongolia, we see Ungern sanctioning pogroms and openly ordering the summary execution of Jews, so it is fair to assume, though we have no evidence to prove it, that he was already an anti-Semite by the war years.

Certainly by this time, of all the prejudices that surrounded him, anti-Semitism would have seemed wholly ordinary and unremarkable. To the Germano-Russian aristocrats of the empire, Jews were the ultimate "people apart." This was especially true of the poor, Yiddish-speaking, "shtetl Jews" of the Pale, most of whom the nobles rarely saw. But even the "modern" Russian and German-speaking Jews of St. Petersburg and Reval seemed different—the rich bankers and factory owners with their trimmed beards and gold timepieces who circulated in "society" yet kept to their own mysterious "Oriental" faith. By Ungern's youth, both cities were home to new Moorish-style synagogues whose ornate Eastern motifs seemed all the more proof of the Jews' abiding otherness.[28]

For the Russian officer corps, however, the Jews existed less in a world apart than not at all. The long-standing bar against their service in the corps meant that only a tiny handful of Jews—all of them Christian converts—were officers at the time the war began, and the rules against Jews serving in the corps were if anything tightening up. Secret instructions issued before the war went so far as to prohibit even converted Jews from becoming officers. This new development suggested that Jewishness was coming to be seen as a matter of biology rather than just one of culture or faith. Well before the Bolshevik Revolution, it was a commonplace for conservatives—including conservative officers—to describe Jews as unpatriotic, unsuited for military service, and generally politically unreliable. The Jews were the liberals, the democrats, the socialists, the revolutionaries—precisely the kind of stateless (rootless?) cosmopolitans you'd expect to sell out their country for a few rubles or a socialist slogan (or both). The fears and hysterias of the war intensified this crude anti-Semitism and allowed it to be enlisted in the service of ethnic cleansing.[29]

Of course, one of the ironies of Ungern's situation is that, like the Jews who were being abused and dispossessed around him, he, too, had been turned by the war into a member of a pariah community. As soon as the conflict began, Russian Germans joined Jews and Poles as the most suspect of all the empire's nationalities. And like the Jews, the empire's Germans found themselves deported en masse from the war zones—some two hundred thousand in the first months of the conflict and tens of thousands more in the years that followed. The Russian press regularly depicted Russian Germans as the enemy within. "No [Russian] Germans can be trusted," wrote General Nikolai Polivanov in 1916, in a cheap booklet meant for mass consumption: "They are spies and active collaborators, and the spies aren't just a few, isolated individuals, but virtually every member of the German population."[30] Anti-Germanism flowed thickly through Russian life. The German-sounding Saint Petersburg was changed to Petrograd. German stores were boycotted, and Russian Germans were searched and harassed. Fearing reprisals, they stopped speaking German in public.[31]

Anti-German paranoia in the Baltic was especially intense. Russian papers ran stories of treasonous barons signalling to German planes from their castles and building earthworks on their estates as fortifications for German troops. In October 1917, when a German naval squadron overwhelmed the Russian batteries on the Ungern-Sternbergs' ancestral island of Dagö/Hiiumaa, rumors spread that the island's Germans spilled out of their homes to welcome their "liberators."[32]

Anecdotes of this sort only confirmed the presumption that Baltic Germans, and in particular the nobles among them, looked down on the Russians and had been inclined to side with the enemy from the beginning. A Russian visitor to Reval in the fall of 1914 was struck by what he saw as a complete lack of patriotism on the part of the Germans of the town. "No, the Germans of Estland don't care much for us [Russian] barbarians around here, they simply don't care for us."[33] Meanwhile, as the anti-German temperature climbed, German nobles in the Baltic made repeated protests of their loyalty to the Council of Ministers and other state bodies, though the effect was minimal. Shortly after the war began, in conjunction with deportations around the front, the government launched a sweeping campaign to counteract what was described as "German dominance" throughout the empire (*nemetskoe zasil'e*). By 1916 a state commission was created to direct the fight. Laws stripped the barons of their privileges.[34]

Though anti-German resentments had helped to shape the Russification program in the Baltic from the start, the white heat of the war was altering the equation. The conflict was putting an end to one of the oldest presumptions of the Russian imperial order—that the Baltic barons were the loyal servants of the throne.

Prince of the Trenches

Ungern fought in the Great War for almost three years on all the Russian fronts, but we see him first in the East Prussian campaign. In an entry dated September 3, 1914, in a file in the Military Historical Archive in Moscow, he appears reporting for duty with the 34th Don Cossack Regiment, a mixed cavalry and infantry force of about a thousand men fighting in the Third Corps of the Russian First Army.[35] The regiment had entered East Prussia at the start of the Russian invasion a month earlier, but by the time Ungern arrived, virtually the entire First Army had been thrown back onto Russian territory by a sweeping German counterattack. The first place we see him is Bal'verzhishki (Yiddish: Balbirishok; Lithuanian: Balbieriškis), a mixed Jewish-Lithuanian village of about two thousand people located on the Neiman River, not far from Kovno (Kaunas) in what is today southwestern Lithuania. The village then was a jumble of mostly worn wooden buildings anchored by a humble market square and surrounded on all sides by a landscape of birch and pine woods interspersed with lakes and marshland. Just a few miles to the east lay the German Empire. We find Ungern leading reconnaissance patrols near the settlement.[36]

The pattern of fighting around Bal'verzhishki was similar to what Ungern would see over the rest of the war: a give-and-take of attack, counterattack, advance, retreat, then relative stability for a period as the armies dug into their trenches and held their lines. Between the start of the war and late 1916, he was wounded five times and earned five commendations, including the St. George's Cross, the Russian army's highest honor for valor. His military record shows us his movements. First, the Russo-German border in southern Lithuania, then north-central Poland facing the German advance on Warsaw, then back up into Lithuania during the "Great Retreat," then south to the Carpathians in what is now western Ukraine in the fall of 1916, and by the spring of 1917, northern Persia, the most southern and eastern Russian front of the war.

The war that he experienced was both intense and ordinary at the same time. The daily reports that fill his companies' field books—many of them scratched out on tattered scraps of paper—are crammed with lists of men killed

N

Reval
Petrograd
Riga
1914 1915
EAST PRUSSIA Vilnius
Balbieriškis
GERMAN EMPIRE 1915
1915 Warsaw 1916
POLAND RUSSIAN EMPIRE
1915
GALICIA 1916
Kiev
HABSBURG EMPIRE Czernowitz (Chernivtsi)
1916
Carpathian 1916
Mountains 1916

SERBIA
RUMANIA
BULGARIA
BLACK SEA Caucasus Mountains CASPIAN
SEA
Tiflis (Tbilisi)
Constantinople 1914 1914–15
GREECE Erzurum 1914–15
1914–15
Lake Van 1914–15 Julfa 1914–15
OTTOMAN EMPIRE 1914 Tabriz
Urmia Lake
Urmia

Tehran

PERSIA

0 100 200 300 400 mi
0   200   400   600 km

Map 7. The Russian fronts of World War I. The Great War in Eastern Europe and the Middle East was a war
of uncertainty defined by ever-shifting front lines and the mass movement of millions of troops and civilians.
Ungern fought all across the Russian zones of the conflict, from East Prussia to northern Persia.

or wounded, horses lost, rations or weapons undelivered, leaves granted or denied, descriptions of periods of shelling, attacking, pausing, regrouping. Enemy strength is gleaned from prisoners and helpful civilians. Requests go out for money and supplies. The physical location of the companies is usually noted either as a geographical coordinate or a hill number or by the name of a village or geographical feature: Unerzhizh (Unierzyż), Mziavo (Mdzewo), Strzhegovo (Strzegowo), Einary, Sarata-Iuzhnaia, the Dil Pass in the "eastern Carpathians" (*lesisty Karpaty*). We can guess that the places were unfamiliar to the Russian officers because their names often appear differently from one report to the next.[37]

In December 1914 Ungern transferred from the 34th Don to the 1st Nerchinsk Regiment of the Trans-Baikal Cossacks.[38] In doing this he returned to the world he had known before the war and at the same time fulfilled his original reserve assignment to serve with the Trans-Baikal Host. The 1st Nerchinsk would remain his home regiment for most of the rest of the conflict. During the war, it fell under the command of the Ussuri Horse Division, a special cavalry force made up of selected Cossack regiments from the Far East.[39] For a period of about six months beginning in fall 1915, Ungern served in a special partisan-like detachment that operated deep behind enemy lines.[40]

The grind of the war took an enormous toll. By the fall of 1916, facing the Austrians in the Carpathians, Ungern's commander described the condition of the Ussuri Division as "desperate." "After nearly three and a half months of uninterrupted fighting, at times against superior enemy forces, in mountainous terrain with no roads, exclusively on foot, with irregular rations and often without any feed at all for the horses, our force . . . has reached a dismal state." He added, "We have run out of reinforcements."[41] Enemy trenches at some points lay just fifty yards away. Every day brought shelling, sniper fire, raids. By the spring of 1917, roughly two and a half years into the war, the division reported that "170 percent of its officers and 200 percent of its dragoons and Cossacks" were lost.[42] The division thus found itself destroyed in the war not once but twice. First its entire prewar fighting strength was killed off. Then the men called up to replace these casualties were wiped out in turn.

This merciless arithmetic, reproduced many times over across the army, set the stage for all the calamities that followed. The titanic violence that began in 1914—of soldiers against soldiers, soldiers against civilians, states against "internal enemies"—gave rise to the violence of the Russian Revolution and Civil War. The Great War did not cause the revolution—given all the tensions and complexities of the empire, a revolution may well have occurred in Russia anyway. But the war guaranteed that whatever revolution did occur would be especially violent. Indeed, the revolutionary year of 1917 turned out to be, above all, the year of the soldier. Soldiers were the decisive players in the overthrow of the monarchy in Petrograd. Mutineers, deserters, and garrison troops helped to decide the Bolshevik takeover that followed in October. Naturally, all these men carried the Great War with them into the revolution and then from there into the civil war. The result was a bloody continuum. The brutality of one war became the bloodline of the next.

Hundreds of thousands of fighting men were shattered by this experience. Life at the front made them numb, soulless. The military doctor Lev Naumovich Voitolovskii remembered an exchange with a young soldier in the Carpathians in early 1915: "I don't feel anything anymore, not fear, not joy. It's as if I'm dead. People are all around, drinking and hollering, and I'm just empty. . . . Before all of this, I could never have done these things. . . . But now I feel nothing for people."[43] Yet others had an opposite reaction. They took energy from the war and seemed to thrive on its urgency and violence.[44] The young German officer Ernst Jünger glorified these men as "princes of the trenches," the fighters who combined "red-hot courage with cool intelligence."

> They are the men who, in the whirlwind of destruction, clear a magazine jam with a sure hand, who hurl smoking grenades back at the enemy, who, in the midst of the life and death struggle, read [the enemy's] intentions in his eyes.[45]

Though Jünger was describing an ideal type rather than a single person, Ungern seems to fit this profile. For most of the war, we see him in only the barest of terms—a name on lists of men wounded or promoted or receiving commendations.[46] But in some pages in the archives, he steps into fuller view.

April 1915, north of Warsaw, for example, we find him leading a raid on a German trench. According to fellow officer, who recorded the action in his field book, Ungern and his men began crawling toward the trench shortly after midnight. As they reached the first line of wire about 25 yards from the position, the Germans opened fire. At this point,

> Officer Ungern-Sternberg leapt to his feet before the wire and called out loudly in German, "You there, what's gotten into you? Stop your shooting. It's your own men!" After this, the firing died down and a voice called out from the trench, "Who goes there?" When we called back, "It's us!" the Germans started shooting again. Then officer Ungern-Sternberg, still standing at full height, called out a second time: "You swine! Hold your fire! Your nerves are getting to you! You're shooting your own people!"

After this, having fallen for the ruse, the Germans began crawling out of the trench to cut the wire. Ungern's men then opened fire and, after an intense firefight, took over the position.[47]

The stress of actions like this must have affected him. One hint of this is the only other time we get a clear view of him during the war—in late November 1916, when he was court-martialed for "conduct unbecoming an officer" while on leave in what is now the Ukrainian town of Chernivtsi (Russian: Chernovtsy;

German: Czernowitz) not far from the Carpathian front. The documents, neatly arranged in a thin file at the Russian State Military Historical Archive in Moscow, tell the outlines of a story that must have happened countless times during the war years: Ungern and an officer friend arrive at a hotel in Chernivtsi in the middle of the night looking for a room. Ungern is drunk. The doorman tells them the hotel is full, an argument ensues, and Ungern loses his temper. He takes a swipe at the doorman and ends up smashing a window. He then heads to the town commandant's office where he curses out the junior officer on watch and strikes him across the head with his sheathed saber. At this point, he passes out in a chair and is arrested a short time later.

In a deposition from the following morning, he admits to everything and (partially at least) apologizes. Taking his wartime record into account, the military court of the Eighth Army holds a speedy trial and sentences him to two months in the stockade.[48]

This is the impulsive Ungern we've come to know. But the incident also helps us appreciate the changes produced by the war. At the Naval College and in his earlier service, Ungern's brashness had been a problem, but now it had become, if not acceptable, at least more usable, more ordinary. In its way, the war was allowing Ungern to fit in, making room for his anger and violence, as it would for the rage of millions of other men like him across Europe, seeding the hatreds and resentments that would grow up so thickly in the postwar years. The incident in Chernivtsi, in fact, shows us how Ungern had fused with the war, and equally how the war, in turn, had fused with him. Even court-martialed and sentenced to the stockade, he remained an epitome of the war that the empire needed to wage, an example of the bold fighter that Russia seemed to require.

We hear this in the character references sent in by his commanders prior to the trial, all of which praise him as a remarkable officer. One officer described his wartime service as a "feat of uninterrupted heroism performed for the glory of Russia." Another called him an inspiration to his men, all of whom "dearly love him." Baron Petr von Wrangel, Ungern's regimental commander for a period in 1916, noted simply "he is an outstanding officer of unforgettable bravery," adding later in his memoirs: "From the beginning of the German-Russian war . . . he performed miraculous acts of courage."[49]

When the conflict began, the first heroes on the Russian side, like their counterparts in other armies, were celebrated for their jaunty bravery. War was still sport. Cossacks dressed in colorful uniforms and rode into battle armed with lances (*piki*), like medieval bogatyrs.[50] In the early going, Ungern himself seems to have embraced this carefree definition of valor. We hear hints of it, for example, in the letter he sent to his aunt in the first autumn of the war. But by the time of the court-martial, he had become the personification of a different sort of hero: the front-line officer (*frontovik*) tempered with the selfless hardness (*tverdost'*) that remorseless slaughter required.

It's tempting to think that some of the motivation for Ungern's bravery came from having to prove himself as a German.[51] One wonders what he thought of the imperial ambiguities of the war raging around him. Some Baltic Germans admitted to "heaviness in [their] hearts" at having to fight against fellow Germans and sought assignments to the Caucasus where they could face the Turks instead.[52] Though occasional press stories extolled Russian German soldiers, the norm was suspicion for anyone with German connections—military men and civilians alike. The officer corps was especially vulnerable in this respect because of its heavy percentage of Germans, especially at the highest ranks. When the war began, over 16 percent of Russian generals had German surnames. Fearing a backlash, the *stavka* issued a secret order requiring Russian German officers to be deployed to the front as much as possible in order to prove their patriotism.[53] There, too, though, resentments roiled. "Our regiment commander, Colonel Shleger, is not Russian," wrote one group of infantrymen shortly after the February Revolution, "he is German." "He does us much harm and sends many people to their deaths."[54]

Yet for all this, no coordinated witch hunt against German officers ever occurred. The tsarist army remained an imperial institution to the end, with all of its attendant contradictions. The names of men killed in action read like a tour of the empire's peoples—Russians, Ukrainians, Germans, Georgians, Tatars, Poles, Estonians, Armenians, Buryats.[55] Ironically, despite the fierce anti-Semitism of the military establishment, some half million Jews fought in the ranks during the war, and over a million Muslims.[56]

As the war stretched bloodily on and the General Staff needed ever more men, the exemptions granted to different ethnic groups gradually fell away. In 1915, Buryats, Yakuts, and Muslims from the North Caucasus were called up. Then in the summer of 1916, the government introduced a labor draft among Kazakh and Kyrgyz nomads in Russian Turkestan, which, because of clumsy mishandling and the accumulated abuses of Russian colonialism, became the trigger for the last great imperial uprising of the tsarist era. Railways were attacked. Russian settlements were torched. Martial law was imposed. Troops were sent in. In the violence, ten thousand Russians died, whereas casualties among the nomads may have numbered in the hundreds of thousands.[57] Among the major ethnic groups of the empire, only the Finns managed to avoid conscription.

The most significant change that took place during the war in terms of the army's role as an imperial institution was the creation of national units— that is, special regiments composed of members of a single ethnic/national or religious group. Ungern would later be involved in organizing such units, which began in earnest after the February Revolution and reflected the wider "mobilization of nationality" that grew to define Russian life during the war years. Yet even the introduction of ethnic regiments did not in itself spell the end of an older vision of the army as a tool of integration that could bind non-Russians to the empire. The new national units were supposed to fight *for* the empire rather than against it, or at least that was the intention. The empire, many presumed, would change—indeed, many Russians were convinced that it *had* to. But few expected it to disappear.

In fact, expectations of a great change of some sort had become rife during the war years. Historians today often describe World War I as the debut of "the modern age" or the true dawn of the twentieth century. In doing this, though, they are in a sense simply repeating the people of the time, who themselves tended to load the war with portentous meaning. The twenty or so years that preceded the conflict were an "era of acceleration" that brought confusing inconsistencies. On the one hand, Europe's influence expanded exponentially around the world. On the other, its sway became fragile and contested. New powers appeared— Japan and the United States. And new technologies and ideologies seemed to be challenging the old, predictable relationships between East and West, rich and poor, young and old, women and men, colonizers and colonized.[58] The effect for many Europeans was a sense of uncertainty and flux. In 1905, the conservative Austrian novelist and poet Hugo von Hofmannsthal described his age as a "time of sliding" (*das Gleitende*). "What previous generations believed to be fixed is in fact *das Gleitende*." As Hoffmansthal saw it, the key attributes of the era were "multiplicity and indeterminacy."[59] Even the homely peasants in a story by Chekhov described the times as an "age of nerves."[60]

On one level, the war itself was the ultimate expression of this nervousness. Yet to many it also appeared as the great watershed that would bring the uncertainty to an end. Like the proverbial moment of medical crisis when the patient either gets better or dies, the conflict seemed to be pushing an entire age to its tipping point. In Russia, this sense of looming change was pervasive. By the third year of the war, with the country reeling from enormous losses and dislocations, everyone seemed to agree that something had to change. Workers and soldiers clamored for food and peace. Feminists wanted women's citizenship. The Duma wanted a new government. The government wanted a new Duma (in fact, Nicholas disbanded it shortly before he was overthrown). Some nationalist intellectuals clamored for outright independence for their peoples. Others argued for the exact opposite—a renewal of the imperial compact that would rally the empire behind a vision of "supranational, statewide patriotism" and pave the way to a "Greater Russia" based on democracy, liberty, and "the friendship of peoples" (*druzhba narodov*).[61]

For millions of imperial subjects, the war thus became a metaphor for justifying and explaining the inevitability of a great transformation. "We are moving to a higher level of world life," wrote Anna Kamenskaia, the president of the Russian Theosophical Society, in late 1916. "The old, embittered, egotistical, isolated world is dying. The utilitarian, materialist culture is falling apart."[62] Like other Theosophists, Kamenskaia saw the war as a "cleansing fire," "a cosmic event of occult significance" whose destruction seemed to be ushering in a new age.

7.3. The February Revolution in Petrograd. Soldiers played a critical role in the upheaval that overthrew the tsar. The banner here proclaims "Down with the Monarchy!" Reproduced from the Library of Congress, LC-USZ62-17014.

The first great transformation, as it turned out, occurred just a few months after Kamenskaia's article. In February 1917, a series of strikes and bread riots in Petrograd turned masses of hungry and cold people into the streets. At first, the "disturbances," as they were described by the authorities, were ordinary— the sort of thing that the government had weathered before. But on the third day, the garrison troops sent to put down the unrest mutinied, and from that point on, the capital slipped into open revolt. Huge crowds engulfed the city. Red banners appeared. Calls went out to end the war and the monarchy. Duma leaders gathered in anticipation of taking power. In a reprise of 1905, a soldiers' and workers' soviet appeared.

By March 2, with the situation spiraling out of control and fears growing that the seeming unstoppable chaos in the capital would spread to the front, Tsar Nicholas made the fateful decision to abdicate, ceding the crown to his younger brother, Grand Prince Michael. When Michael refused the throne the next day, the deed was done. In little over a week, the spontaneous tumult of the February Revolution produced the change that everyone had assumed would happen yet had never quite expected. The tsarist era was over.

CHAPTER 8

THE ATAMAN'S DOMAIN

"We gonna fight your brother.
Raise hell."
—THE CLASH, "Death or Glory"

All Coherence Gone

It's not clear where Ungern was when the February Revolution began. The Bolsheviks claimed that he was still in the stockade and was then freed shortly thereafter in the wave of amnesties that followed the revolution, but given his short sentence, it's more likely he had already been released by the time the monarchy fell. (We don't know the location of the jail either.) Judging from the published summary of his trial in Novonikolaevsk, he seems to have told the tribunal that the army sent him to Vladivostok after his release (presumably for reserve service), but whether he actually reached the city at the time is unclear.[1] All we know for certain is that shortly after the overthrow of the tsar he made his way back to the war.

We know this thanks to Grigorii Semenov, another young officer of the Trans-Baikal Cossacks who was soon to become Ataman Semenov, warlord of the Trans-Baikal. The two men met and became close during the war, developing an unlikely friendship of opposites. Whereas Ungern was tall, thin, and brooding, Semenov was garrulous and vain, with the squat, broad build of a wrestler. His background was also far more modest, having grown up in a middling Cossack family on the Mongolian border and graduated from a second-tier officer's school in the provinces. (It's hard to imagine quotes from Virgil running across the front of the Semenov family homestead.)

Yet like Ungern, Semenov was brash and completely devoted to the romantic ideal of the officer-warrior. He had served in the Russian consular guard in Urga at the time of the Mongolian Revolution of 1911 and got himself into trouble there with his bold actions. He then earned a St. George's Cross during the war. In the memoirs he wrote in Japanese-controlled Manchuria in the 1930s, he describes a close bond with Ungern, and the feeling was apparently mutual, at least until they parted ways during the Mongolian campaign. We have copies of two letters Ungern sent to Semenov during the civil war. In both he uses the familiar form of "you" (*ty*) and addresses him as "Semën" (Simon), an affectionate play on his last name.[2]

Drawing on Semenov's memoirs, we can place the two men together in the spring of 1917 near the town of Urmia (Persian: Orūmīyeh), in what is today northwestern Iran, not far from the country's border with Turkey. Urmia then was one of the strategic lynchpins of the war in Persia, the southernmost of the Russian fronts, a world away from the humid marshes of East Prussia where Ungern had begun the war. The two men found themselves there in the same regiment facing the Ottomans.[3]

Though the war in Persia was relatively quiet at the time, the Russian army was falling apart. Instead of the clarity and unity many had hoped for, the revolution had brought just the opposite. Two centers of power formed in the vacuum left by the end of the monarchy. One was the formal heir to the Duma, the liberal and moderate Provisional Government—called "provisional" because it was supposed to hold power only until the election of a Constituent Assembly, the much-awaited revolutionary parliament that would determine the empire's future. The other was the Petrograd Soviet, whose several thousand mostly workers' and soldiers' deputies divided their sympathies between a range of socialist parties.

Though the two bodies began the year by convening in the same faded yellow palace in central Petrograd, the distance between them could not have been greater. The ministers of the Provisional Government took power based on what they understood as the proper order of things. Looking into the future, they saw the liberal-democratic Russia that they had always assumed was waiting to happen: an orderly society led by responsible men in bowler hats and tabbed collars, with open elections and a free judiciary. The Soviet, by contrast, drew its authority from the street and the trenches and was far less reserved. Each group was revolutionary, but the revolutions they represented were different.

The impact of the division on the army was enormous. As a rule, officers—especially career officers—identified with the Provisional Government as the legitimate successor to the tsar. Soldiers, by contrast, instinctively supported the more radical views of the Soviet. The most important document of the February Revolution, Order No. 1, issued as the Soviet's first official decree on March 1, 1917, highlighted this divide. Soldiers were instructed to form committees and take charge of the weapons in their units. They were to address their officers simply as "sir" (*gospodin*) rather than the lofty "your Excellency" that had been customary before. Officers, meanwhile, were required to adopt the polite form of "you" when speaking to their men. As General Krymov, a former commander of Ungern's, stated to his division in early April 1917, the revolution had created "new conditions of life." In keeping with the times, officers would now have to start "looking at things from the soldiers' point of view" (*poiti soldatam na vstrechu*).[4]

Soldiers, however, increasingly saw the revolution in terms that even sympathetic officers couldn't understand. Interpreting the Soviet's platform of "Peace Without Annexations and Indemnities" as a call to stop fighting altogether, entire units refused to go on the offensive or even move at all. "We'll hold the front, but we won't attack," was a common refrain. Other soldiers responded to the "new conditions" by deserting and leaving for home. (This was especially true of garrison soldiers in the rear—desertion at the front was less common.) Some 900,000 Russian soldiers were taken prisoner in 1917, some by willingly crossing over to the enemy side.[5]

To most officers, the army appeared to be disintegrating around them. "By May," Supreme Commander General Aleksei Brusilov remembered, "troops on every front were in a state of complete insubordination."[6] The most despised officers found themselves lynched, arrested, or hounded from their regiments. Some committed suicide. Many were disoriented to the point of not quite believing what was going on. As a delegation from the Duma reported in March after completing a tour of the front, "Many [officers] asked us, 'Couldn't you have waited to talk with the army before starting the revolution?'"[7] Semenov recalled a revolutionary holiday in Urmia that spring that began with "a political rally and the usual demagogic speeches" and ended with "all the units [of the division] marching through town carrying red banners and other revolutionary symbols." He added: "It was a disgusting sight."[8]

Semenov blamed the breakdown on his superiors who seemed too bewildered to take action. But the irony is that just as "soldier power" was driving the radicalism of the revolution, it was also creating opportunities for conservative junior officers like Semenov and Ungern who would go on to reject it.[9] In February 1917 Semenov was twenty-six, Ungern thirty-one, yet within just a few years both would command thousands of men. By May 1919 Semenov had been elected ataman (commander) of the Trans-Baikal Host (up to that point Host atamans had been appointed by the tsar). He then awarded himself medals and promotions to suit his new status. Ungern, meanwhile, rose from lieutenant colonel (*esaul*) at the time of his court-martial in late 1916 to colonel, then major general in November 1918, and lieutenant general in 1921, promoted each time by Semenov.[10]

Such was the dizzying change that became normal in abnormal times. As the old regime crumbled, opportunities abounded amid the confusion. The whole country seemed to be looking for something: "a symbol of political authority," according to Pavel' Miliukov, the leader of the main liberal party; "a name," according to General Anton Denikin, one of the tsarist commanders who would go on to oppose the Bolsheviks in the civil war. Lenin, the Bolshevik leader, had bluntly stated his opinion as early as 1905: "Revolution is war"—a war of "the people" against "the people's oppressors." There was no room for sentimentality. Politics was a matter of "Who whom?" (*Kto kogo?*)—that is, who would destroy whom in the remorseless struggle for power.[11]

As 1917 progressed, the bitter logic fueling the struggle intensified. The divide between the Provisional Government and the Petrograd Soviet was only the most obvious of the many fault lines running through imperial politics. Neutral ground increasingly slipped away. Individuals found themselves forced to pick their allegiances, if they hadn't already. And once they did, they then had to decide how far they would go.

In this revolution of a million personal choices, Ungern's politics were undoubtedly conservative from the start. Given his elite upbringing and education, we can assume that he would have been much less sympathetic to the soldiers' protests for democracy than the so-called officers of the people (*ofitsery naroda*), the noncoms from more humble backgrounds who came up during the war and now constituted the great majority of the officer corps.[12]

Indeed, to most conservatives in 1917, the word *demokratiia* was a slur, a cruel joke played out on the country by revolutionaries who were nothing more than charlatans whipping up the mob with their senseless slogans about perfect equality. Not surprisingly, the most hated of these demagogues were the Bolsheviks, the most radical of the socialists whose support among soldiers and workers grew over the year as the war went on. "The Bolsheviks are the true symbol of the Russian people," wrote a conservative professor from Moscow in the summer of 1917. "A mixture of stupidity, vulgarity, uncultured willfulness, lack of principle, hooliganism."[13]

If we take the February Revolution as the spontaneous outpouring of a genuine desire on the part of millions of Russians—at least right at that moment—to choose democracy over autocracy, to conservatives like Ungern the very idea of such a choice would have seemed preposterous. The autocracy stood for order, stability, history, divine grace, the greatness of Russian power. How could one simply *choose* to do away with it? Wasn't this the madness of 1905 all over again, another fit of collective hysteria, just as the scholar Le Bon had predicted?

In fact, Ungern's conservatism seems to have been based on a fairly straightforward conservative principle: old ways are better than new ones, in part, at least, precisely because they are old. That is, if a country's beliefs and practices endure for generations, on some level it is because they should. This means they are just, natural, in keeping with God's intentions. Of the venerable traditions, Ungern seems to have revered monarchy the most, seeing it as the lynchpin of all the others. In one of the interrogations the Reds conducted after his capture, he describes the ideal monarch as a kind of benevolent father figure, the "first democrat of the state" whose role is to mediate between the aristocracy and the peasantry, the two essential "class groups" of society.[14] (Ungern's societal ideal seems to have resembled a feudal pyramid, with the king at the top, served by his aristocrats, and the peasants below, serving their lords.)

The dry characterization of the tsar as the "first democrat" of the state and a would-be mediator between "class groups" may have been just for the Bolsheviks' benefit, however. The sociological phrasing makes one wonder, in fact, whether his interrogators didn't just insert their own vocabulary in this instance, translating his monarchism into their own terms. All we know for certain is that when he described his views before his capture, his language was far more vivid. As he wrote to a Mongol ally in April 1921,

> In your deep wisdom Your Highness surely sees the great danger posed to the foundations of human culture by the destructive teachings [of the revolutionaries], and you must know that there is only one way to fight against this evil—by restoring the rule of the emperors (*vosstanovlenie tsarei*). This alone can safeguard religion and return faith to the world.[15]

Other statements from the period echo the same view: the world is sick with revolution and the only cure is complete political and moral regeneration. The states of the past were powerful, Ungern writes to another correspondent in 1921, "because [they were ruled by] kings and ... aristocrats." "And we aristocrats have but one idea, one cause that drives us: to return the emperors (*tsari*) to their thrones."[16]

Yet, for all this, Ungern's first political decision of 1917, paradoxically, may well have been to support Nicholas II's removal, or at least to accept it. Semenov recalled that the young officers he knew on the Persian front tended to go along with the abdication.[17] By then faith in Nicholas's leadership had largely evaporated, and the hope was that a new ruler would restore confidence and get the country back behind the war.

Thus, for Ungern, disillusionment with the revolution may have come somewhat later, as it became clear that Grand Prince Michael had indeed refused the throne and that the country would remain without a tsar at least until elections could be held for the Constituent Assembly. We can imagine his dismay deepening as the army continued to disintegrate. It was precisely this sinking feeling that would drive thousands of conservatively inclined officers to create the anti-Bolshevik White Army—and the broader White cause—after the Bolshevik takeover. The revolution, it seemed, was stripping them of everything: their regiments, their authority, even their epaulettes, which the most radical soldiers hated as symbols of the old order and impatiently tore from their commanders' uniforms. (In keeping with this sentiment, the Provisional Government quickly drew up new codes for officers' uniforms *without* epaulettes.)[18] All but decimated by the war, the old officer corps was now being finished off by the revolution.

We have no direct evidence of when or how exactly Ungern turned against the new politics around him, but Semenov's memoirs suggest that something had happened by the spring. As he tells it, sometime in April he and Ungern decided to approach their commanders with a plan to form new units of "native volunteers." The rationale was simple: Russian soldiers at the front were sick of the war and corrupted by the ongoing erosion of discipline. "Alien" volunteers would give the soldiers a "moral example" that would reenergize them, in effect shaming them into action. Having grown up on the Mongolian border, Semenov spoke fluent Buryat and Mongolian. He would urge Buryat elders at home to send their sons to Persia to form a "Buryat national unit." Ungern, meanwhile, would focus on training local Assyrian Christians.[19] (The two men were posted at the time in the Assyrian village of Gulpashan, located just east of Urmia.)

The Assyrian dimension of the plan grew out of the ethnic violence that surrounded the Russians on the Persian front. In the years leading up to the war, Persia, like the Qing Empire, though nominally independent, had become a de facto colony, carved up between Britain and Russia, each of which retained a "sphere of influence" in Persian territory.[20] In their area of control, which covered the entire north of the country, the Russians pursued the same neocolonial agenda they had adopted in their other quasi-colonies of northern Manchuria and Outer Mongolia, building roads and railroads, and sending in colonists and military advisers. Meanwhile, Cossack regiments also arrived to help prop up the ailing Qajar dynasty and suppress antigovernment rebels.[21]

The small Christian population around Urmia, mostly Assyrians and Armenians, welcomed the rise in Russian influence, some to the point of joining a pro-Russian militia. Meanwhile, the far more numerous Muslim Azeris and Kurds around them tended to sympathize with the Ottomans, who, like the British and the Russians, also took advantage of the weakness of the Persian government to move their troops into the country.[22]

The Great War ignited this combustible mix of ethnic resentment and international rivalry into a bloody explosion. The Ottomans, who joined the war on the German side in October 1914, invaded northern Persia to drive out the Russians in early 1915. As the Russians retreated, some Persian Assyrians helped them by trying to fend off the Turks. This then became a pretext for the Ottomans and their local Muslim supporters to pursue the wholesale destruction of the local Assyrian population, which continued until the Russians were able to reoccupy the region several months later.[23]

The Assyrian aspect of Ungern and Semenov's plan drew on this bitter legacy. At the same time, the idea of creating national units was fully in keeping with the broader trends of the war. As we've seen, ethnicity was a key factor of the fighting on the eastern front from the very start, and the Russians, like others, had long since introduced ethnically based units as part of the war effort, with the Latvian Rifles created in 1915 being perhaps the best-known example. At the same time, for most of the war, Russian generals balked at going too far with the "ethnicization" of the army. Though just as eager as their rivals to exploit the power of ethnic solidarity, they worried that national units might backfire and encourage national separatism. Ethnic formations also seemed to contradict the Russification ideal that still defined military service and the imperial order more generally. As a result, few units of this sort were created prior to the end of the old regime.

The February Revolution, however, transformed the situation completely. With the autocracy gone, the idea that non-Russians would fight in the name of their non-Russian identity suddenly appeared democratic rather than dangerous, and ethnic units multiplied rapidly. Within months, Georgian, Armenian, Estonian, Finnish, and Lithuanian detachments were formed. Muslims called for a regiment of their own. Even Ukrainian units appeared, something inconceivable under the old order since the imperial government had not even recognized the Ukrainians as a nation.[24]

A new vision of imperial community appeared to be forming. Though once repressed, the non-Russians were now free, and because of this, they would surely fight eagerly both for themselves and for the country as a whole, which explains why the idea of ethnic units suddenly became so popular with everyone on all sides, the non-Russian intellectuals as well as the Provisional Government. Many of the slogans of 1917—"For an Autonomous Estonia in a Free Russia!" "A Free Armenia for a Free Russia!" and other variations on this theme—reflect this sense of the revolution as a moment of imperial renewal.[25] The old empire of Russification had ended, but not necessarily the possibility of empire itself.

Ungern and Semenov's work in Persia was a tiny part of this complicated search to reorganize the empire. Not surprisingly, like so many other plans for minority nationalism envisioned by outsiders, theirs rested on the presumption that they would switch on national passions for their purposes, in this case, to defeat the enemy, and then switch them off just as easily when they were done. Of course, in the real world, as opposed to the world of planners, things rarely work this neatly. In the case of the Persian experiment, however, it's impossible to say what might have been because the plans ended so quickly. Semenov's efforts to drum up recruits for a Buryat unit failed because he was too far away—at least, this is the explanation he offers in his memoirs. Meanwhile, even though Ungern (in Semenov's view) "succeeded brilliantly" in training

Assyrian partisans, the force was far too small to have any effect on army morale, which continued to disintegrate.[26]

Yet for all this, the episode in Persia appears to have been a watershed for Ungern personally. From this moment forward, the short remainder of his life would be tied both to the politics of leading ethnic troops and to Semenov, who would soon become his commander and one of the unlikely leaders of the anti-Bolshevik struggle in Eastern Siberia.

Ungern started down this path within just a few months. In the summer of 1917, Semenov was elected to represent his regiment at the Second Trans-Baikal Cossack Congress in Chita. En route to the congress he visited Petrograd, where he convinced the War Ministry to let him use his time in Siberia to resume recruiting a native regiment.[27] At some point during the late summer or early fall, as best we can tell, he then called Ungern to join him. By October, Ungern was in Chita.[28]

A little over 3,000 miles separate northwestern Persia from the Trans-Baikal. In 1917, the effective distance between the two regions was greater still—closer to 4,000 miles—because the easiest train connections at the time forced one to travel north for 1,000 miles from Urmia through the Caucasus all the way to Moscow before then turning east along the Trans-Siberian. Like so much about Ungern's life, we have no evidence to tell us how he actually made the journey. The records of his regiment's service in Persia have been lost. According to at least one source, he was in Reval when Semenov called him to Siberia.[29] If this was the case, he would have left Urmia initially for the Baltic.

Yet regardless of exactly how he did it, we know that at some point he had to have crossed the full distance from Persia to the Baikal. Imagining for a moment that he made the trip in one go, we can follow the stages: First, leaving Gulpashan, he would have headed east by horse or motor car to the shores of Lake Urmia, a vast saltwater pool lying just a few miles beyond Urmia town. Above the lake would have soared the myriad birds that migrate there regularly through the year—pelicans, flamingoes, gulls, ibises. Crossing the water on an army steamer, he would have made his way to the Russian-built railhead on the eastern side and then traveled north from there by train to the Russian frontier at Julfa. Outside the windows he would have seen a bare but beautiful country of rolling brown hills, dotted with Muslim villages. (Julfa today sits on the border between Iran and Azerbaijan.)[30]

More contrasts would have followed as he crossed into Russian territory: the snow-capped peaks of the eastern Caucasus, the thick pointy Georgian Orthodox steeples of Tiflis, the dry steppes of the Kuban and the northern Caucasus, the greener woods and fields of central Russia, bustling, dusty Moscow, more of the central Russian countryside, the great railway bridge spanning the Volga at Syzran, the Urals, and finally Siberia, with its oddly coupled halves—the west, a seemingly endless carpet of pine and birch forest; the east much hillier and rolling, cinched at the center by the deep blue clasp of Lake Baikal.

In the summer and early fall of 1917, this immense space, all of it controlled or influenced by the Russian state, could still be crossed as a single piece. From Julfa to Chita, the trains would have been waved on by stationmasters wearing the same orange-red peaked caps, standing under the same columns and clocks. Every station of any size would have sold Russian-language newspapers. Each train would have run on Petrograd time.

But Ungern's journey was taking place at precisely the moment when this interconnected space was beginning to break apart, and the early signs of the trouble would have been all around him: bands of "soldier-deserters" tramping the roads, refugees and orphans crowded onto the station platforms, angry newspaper headlines denouncing the Provisional Government or the Petrograd Soviet and calling for this or that form of national autonomy.[31] The revolution was a proverbial moment of truth, not just because it exposed the fierce social and political cleavages that were beginning to tear the country apart but also because it revealed its glaring weaknesses as an imperial system.

Like all vast and diverse political units, the Russian Empire was held together by state power, or, more often than not, by the *myth* of state power. Yet in 1917, under the combined pressures of revolution, war, and economic misery, the state thinned to the point of irrelevance, and even the myth evaporated. As one of the ministers of the Provisional Government remembered, "the entire administration, the police, all of it became completely disorganized.... The [Bolshevik] coup became possible...because the very presumption of the existence of authority had disappeared."[32] In fact, the Provisional Government directly contributed to this disappearance because it dismantled the institutions of the old regime before providing viable new ones to replace them. The geographical corollary to the story followed a similar dynamic: the center fractured and weakened, the parts divided into their own bitter camps, and territories started falling away.

The erosion of the state's control over its territory began during the war. Within a year of the start of the conflict, the tsarist government lost all of Russian Poland, and large parts of what are today Lithuania and Belarus, to German occupation—over 15 percent of the prewar territory of European Russia.[33] For months during late 1916, it then lost control over large parts of Turkestan as the region erupted in a massive anticolonial revolt. The breakdown then accelerated dramatically over the course of 1917.

Within months of the February Revolution, Ukrainian leaders began pushing for independence. Cossacks on the Don established their own military government. Calls for autonomy—and, in some cases, for full secession—rose up from the Baltic and the Caucasus. Successive cabinets of the Provisional Government tried to hold the line by talking about federalism and proposing one version or another of a "united and indivisible Russia" (*edinaia i nedelimaia Rossiia*), but the effects were minimal. "Old Russia," as the socialist journalist John Reed put it in the summer of 1917, "was rapidly breaking up."[34]

The overthrow of the Provisional Government in October drove this process further. As radicals reaching for the holy grail of world revolution, the Bolsheviks saw modern imperialism as little more than a mask hiding the sinister exploitation of the bourgeoisie. They thus stood for the end of empires everywhere, including Russia. As Lenin put it in 1916, "Man will advance toward the inevitable merging of nations (*sliianie natsii*) only through a transitional period of complete freedom for all oppressed peoples (*natsii*)."[35]

Indeed, though socialists rather than nationalists, the Bolsheviks recognized the revolutionary power of national grievance and sought to take advantage of it during the upheaval. Thus one of the first decrees they issued after taking power denounced the Provisional Government for inciting "national enmity" and granted the right to "free self-determination" to the "peoples of Russia," adding that this meant "even to the point of separation and the formation of an independent state."[36] Within just a few months of the declaration, President Woodrow Wilson would emerge as the leading icon of national self-determination thanks to his enshrining the idea in his famous Fourteen Points, but, technically speaking, Lenin and his comrades got there first.[37]

Overall, though, it was more what the Bolsheviks were doing than what they were saying that drove the final nail into the empire's coffin. The simple fact of their seizing power injected so much new instability into the already unstable imperial system that the national leaderships in the borderlands—especially in areas already under German occupation—concluded it was time to get out altogether. In December 1917, Finland, already practically independent, formally seceded. Within a few months, Estonia, Latvia, Lithuania, and "the People's Republic of Belarus" followed suit. Georgia, Armenia, and Azerbaijan left at the same time, initially as fellow members of a combined Trans-Caucasian Federation and slightly later as states of their own.[38]

Meanwhile, in addition to inviting the peoples of the empire to secede, the Bolsheviks also declared a unilateral end to the "imperialist war," and this, too, had a dramatic territorial effect. Now with truly no reason to stay in their trenches, Russian soldiers all along the empire's fronts began deserting in droves. Yet the Central Powers kept fighting, as did the rest of the Entente, and so, not surprisingly, as the Russians "spontaneously demobilized" and left their positions, both their enemies and their former allies moved in to fill the gap.[39] Thus the Romanians, previously allied with Russia, took over the tsarist province of Bessarabia, and the Germans advanced through Ukraine and the Baltic region, trumpeting their support for independence as they went. Meanwhile, the Turks reclaimed eastern Anatolia and moved into the Caucasus, and the British swallowed up Russia's zone in Persia.

The final blow to what was left of the empire's coherence came with the civil war that erupted across the country after the Bolshevik takeover. The basic territorial effect of the war was to split Russia into two parts: one Red, the other White, the former controlled by the Bolsheviks, the latter by their opponents. Though the divide between Reds and Whites shifted confusingly over time, for much of the civil war, the Reds' base was the middle of the country: the industrial and agricultural heartland of central European Russia, including the two capitals of Moscow and Petrograd. The Whites, meanwhile, controlled the old imperial periphery, claiming a broad collar of territory from the Baltic, Ukraine, and southern Russia in the west to Siberia and Turkestan in the east.

This divide between a Red middle and a White periphery was only the most obvious way in which the civil war sundered the empire, however. In fact, without a meaningful center to hold it together, the country quickly devolved into a bewildering patchwork of zones and sovereignties. Towns, villages, and even factory floors declared themselves separate republics. Cossack Hosts created their own quasi-independent states in the south and east. White Siberia announced its "temporary secession" until the Reds in Moscow could be unseated. Polish troops invaded from the west (the Polish-Soviet War of 1920). Meanwhile, in the north, south, and east, the British, French, American, and Japanese carved out military occupation zones staffed by their troops, which they sent to Russia to assist the Whites, hoping, in the process, to draw the country back into the war with Germany.[40]

Overall, compared with "White Russia," "Red Russia" was more territorially coherent, but both were essentially fragile creations. The empire had disintegrated. The center was gone. Yet the most important point about the empire's collapse was that it unfolded differently in different places. Some territories were indeed lost for good—Finland, the Baltic provinces, Poland. But overall the old tsarist state simply fell apart too quickly for most of its former territories to disentangle themselves from their prior habits and connections. Instead, the habits persisted, and, as a result, all the leaders in the civil war, the anti-imperialist Bolsheviks included, found themselves working within a postimperial framework in which empire remained the norm.

Indeed, in addition to its many other dimensions, it is useful to see the civil war as a war to gather up the broken pieces of the tsarist state and recreate a meaningful imperial center, whether that center actually called itself an empire or not. In a sense, then, it was all but certain that the order that would succeed the old empire would be large and multinational. The great question was *whose* large and multinational order it would be.

"People of the Stanitsas! The Time Has Come!"

Ungern's base for most of the civil war was the small garrison town of Dauria located on the Trans-Baikal Railway not far from the upper reaches of the

Argun River where he had served as a young officer some ten years before. Little more than a train stop, the settlement consisted of brick barracks and an armory dating from the time of the war with Japan, some stables, a telegraph office, a church, and a few Cossack homesteads. During the Great War, Austrian and Turkish POWs had been kept here. Beyond the settlement, meanwhile, was a vastness of prairie: a giant, bumpy carpet of grassy hills dotted, as the seasons allowed, with herds of horse and the round domes of Buryat and Mongol yurts.[41]

Today the town seems as unremarkable as it was in Ungern's time. Blocks of forlorn, Soviet-era apartments make up the center where the old barracks used to be. Across from the station, sagging wooden houses stare back at the passing trains. The nomads are gone, but the prairie is still there, the same enormity of horizon and isolation. Chita, the capital of the Trans-Baikal oblast', is a twelve-hour train ride to the north, while the Russo-Chinese border lies about an hour away in the other direction. Because of the closeness of the border and the fact that there was always so much army around, the town was off limits to outsiders during the Soviet period, Soviets and foreigners alike.

Dauria is important in our story because it is here that we begin to see Ungern more clearly than at any earlier point. The Mongolian campaign is just ahead, so we find writers alluding to this immediate pre-campaign period in their memoirs. And there are new sources from Ungern himself—a clutch of letters he wrote to Semenov and others as well as the paperwork of the Asiatic Division, his military command in the town.

Though his private world remains almost as unknowable as before, we nonetheless see something of who he has become by this moment. Traits that will loom large in Mongolia—his casual harshness and fervid anticommunism, for example—are already apparent. We hear echoes of the cult of death and duty that was common among White officers at the time, especially as the tide of the civil war turned against them. It is also in Dauria that we first learn of his apparent discomfort around women, this despite the fact that this was also, ironically, the period of his only marriage, a political union concluded in the summer of 1919 with the daughter of a Manchu commander from northern China.[42]

One of the traits we will see in Mongolia, however—his murderous anti-Semitism—is less visible. The reason for this is probably that, while in Dauria, he remained under Semenov's command, and Semenov, unlike many other White leaders, was not anti-Semitic, at least not overtly so. His army included a special Jewish regiment. He gave orders to his officials to tear down anti-Semitic broadsheets when they appeared at the Chita train station. His favorite mistress, Maria Sharaban (Mashka), was a Jewish cabaret singer.[43] Thus, while it is likely that Ungern was already an anti-Semite by this time, he was not yet in a position to act much on his prejudice. Instead, his assignment was to run the Russo-Manchurian border for the ataman. Everything else was secondary.

For most of the period between mid-1918 and 1920, Siberia was ruled by the Whites under the nominal authority of the war hero and former polar explorer Admiral Aleksandr Kolchak, who made his headquarters in Omsk in the western part of the region. Kolchak was recognized by the allies and the White generals fighting in European Russia as the supreme ruler (*verkhovnyi pravitel'*) of the anti-Bolshevik opposition, but even in Siberia, ironically, despite his lofty title, his influence was minimal.[44] Instead, the true "men of power" in the region, and throughout Eastern Siberia and the Far East in particular, were regional Cossack leaders known collectively as the atamans.

The reason for Kolchak's relative powerlessness over the atamans was a simple question of carrots and sticks: he had little to offer to keep them in line and was too far away to make them pay when they defied his instructions. Moreover, virtually his entire war effort depended on supplies coming to Western Siberia from the east along the Trans-Siberian, that is, through the atamans' domains, which meant that he needed them more than they needed him. As a result, the Cossack leaders formally deferred to Omsk but in practice did largely as they pleased. Often they barely even bothered deferring.[45]

Of the atamans, Semenov was the most ambitious and, for a period at least, the most successful. Beginning in December 1917, he committed himself to open resistance against the Bolsheviks by turning the regiment he and Ungern had begun assembling for the fight against the Germans into a force to fight the Reds instead. Given that Bolshevik-controlled Soviets had succeeded in taking over the Trans-Baikal in the early aftermath of the October Revolution, Semenov was forced to establish his first base outside the country, in the town of Manchuria Station, the first stop on the CER. By August of the next year, however, after having gradually retaken the border area around Manchuria Station (including Dauria) over the preceding months, he succeeded in taking Chita, and from then until the fall of 1920 when he was forced to flee by a new Red advance, he turned the city into the capital of his own informal anti-Bolshevik kingdom. His court opened for business at The Select, Chita's plushest hotel not far from the central train station.[46]

The guiding ideology of the ataman's regime was state reconstruction. Like most of his counterparts in the military wing of the White movement (including Kolchak, whom he loathed), Semenov was a devoté of *gosudarstvennost'*—a term that loosely translates as "state power" or "state tradition" but that also expresses a special reverence for the state as the essential root of order and meaning in social life. The Bolsheviks had purposefully destroyed Russia's *gosudarstvennost'*. As such, they were the ultimate *anti*-patriots. Semenov, meanwhile, in his own eyes at least, was the opposite—the great state restorer.

As he declared in a broadsheet issued in late 1917, "People of the Stanitsas! Rise up.... The time has come! Hurry to the rescue of your motherland, tattered and betrayed by traitors!" "My administration," he noted with similar patriotic verve two years later, "is designed to expand beyond the local level

8.1. Ataman Grigorii Semenov with General William S. Graves, Commander of the American
Expeditionary Force Siberia, 1918. Semenov tried to curry favor with the Americans but his
greatest patrons by far were the Japanese. Reproduced from the National Archives and
Records Administration, Washington, D.C., Photograph No. 111-SC-75800.

at a moment's notice." That is, as Semenov saw it, the Trans-Baikal was just
the beginning. His anti-Bolshevik kingdom in Chita was merely the first small
fraction of a broader whole. The motherland would be restored from the Trans-
Baikal, one region at a time.[47]

The most remarkable feature of this agenda of national reclamation was
its point of origin. As a frontier project pursued from the edges rather than
the center, Semenov's plan ran against the grain of centuries of political life.
Since its inception, the Russian Empire, like all empires, had operated on
the presumption that power resided in the center and flowed from there out-
ward toward the periphery. This was the practical reality—and mesmerizing
ideology—of imperial rule. Yet now, with the empire falling apart, there was
room to imagine power moving in the opposite direction, from the periphery
back toward the center. The periphery, from the periphery's perspective, had
become a power center of its own.

In the Trans-Baikal, the great manifestation of this change was the revival
of the older ways of the frontier. Semenov anchored his power in his home
constituency, the Trans-Baikal Cossacks, the "people of the stanitsas." But his

ambitions went well beyond to include northern Manchuria and Mongolia as well. Indeed, Semenov's image-makers carefully cultivated the ataman's profile as a leader (*vozhd'*) with ties extending to all the peoples of the frontier, regardless of the borders that separated them. "Grigorii Mikhailovich speaks fluent Buryat, Mongol, and Kalmyk, and even a little English," went one of his cheap propaganda pamphlets printed in Harbin. "The Chinese of Manchuria respect him.... The Mongols see [him] as one of their own."[48]

The pamphleteer added that the "best and truest friend of the ataman's brigade" was imperial Japan, which was undoubtedly correct, at least in the early going. At the highpoint of their involvement in the Russian Civil War, the Japanese deployed some six thousand men in and around Chita (out of over seventy thousand in Siberia altogether, most of whom were stationed on the Amur and points farther east) and supplied Semenov with weapons, funds, and logistical support.[49] (The other allies also initially supported Semenov, but then backed off when they realized how much his policies were undermining Kolchak.) Newspapers in Chita politely informed their readers of the schedules for Japanese artillery practice. Bookstores advertised "affordable and useful" Japanese phrasebooks. The Japanese in turn handed out sacks of flour to the city poor on the emperor's birthday.[50]

Developments across the border had similar effects. In the aftermath of the overthrow of the Qing in the 1911 Revolution, China entered its own tumultuous period of collapse and disintegration. In Outer Mongolia, as we've seen, the Mongol notables of Urga used the moment to expel the Chinese *ambans* and declare independence. Similar developments occurred in Tibet. Meanwhile, across the rest of the old Qing Empire, as the center faltered, provincial military governors (*dujun*)—known to their critics as warlords (*junfa*)—filled the vacuum. Soon the entire country divided into criminal-military fiefdoms.[51]

Yet much in the Russian case, even as the Chinese Empire splintered, the acceptance of empire by another name carried on. For Chinese intellectuals and warlords alike, the idea that non-Han peoples might be allowed to separate from China under the banner of nationalism or any other cause was simply "not on the agenda."[52] As if to prove this, the flag that the republicans flew—the nationalist flag—consisted of five horizontal stripes, red, yellow, blue, white, and black, symbolizing the so-called five races living together in harmony, whose benevolent cohabitation was supposed to continue under the new post-Qing order. And a basic continuity with the old empire was visible, too, in the very persistence of a republican government, which, like the Qing order it replaced, remained centered in Beijing and was never dismantled by the warlords despite the fact that they could have easily done so. Indeed, the warlords were not anti-imperial as much as anti-Qing. Rather than rejecting the imperial state, they simply redefined it in national terms and used the vision of unity to justify their power.[53]

We see this clearly in Manchuria and Outer Mongolia where regional strongmen expanded their own influence while at the same time identifying with Beijing and the cause of Chinese sovereignty. In each case, they took advantage of Russian disarray. In Outer Mongolia, with no effective Russian counterweight to protect Mongol autonomy and worried about what Semenov might do along the border, they forced the Mongols to invite Chinese troops to return to Urga. By late fall 1919, the Kiakhta Treaty was abrogated, and the warlord general Xu Shuzheng magnanimously allowed the Bogda to recognize the error of his ways and pledge his return to the national family.[54] Meanwhile in Manchuria, the so-called old marshal, Zhang Zuolin, directed a takeover of the CER.[55]

The Chinese strongmen like Xu and Zhang, whose power filled the vacuum of the Sino-Russian border in the late 1910s, shared much in common with their Russian counterparts. Like Semenov and the other atamans of the Far East, the warlords on the Chinese side were, for the most part, former military men who used the instability of the frontier to establish their authority, while at the same time drawing some of their legitimacy from the sheltering idea of the state—though in their case it was the Chinese republican state centered in Beijing. Like Semenov, they also had to come to terms with the Japanese, especially in central and southern Manchuria.[56]

Perhaps the most important distinction between warlordism on the Russian and Chinese sides was simply that the Chinese warlords, by and large, were more successful. Semenov remained at most a regional figure and was forced out of the Trans-Baikal by the Reds after less than two years in Chita. Ungern's rule in Mongolia was briefer still and his sweeping plans for imperial restoration never even began to be implemented. By contrast, Zhang controlled most of Manchuria for well over a decade and presided over a large army that made him a central player in national politics.[57] Xu's influence was more fleeting—he had to give up his position in Urga when a new ruling clique took over in Beijing in the summer of 1920. The practical effects of his removal for the Mongols, however, were minor since he was simply replaced by a new Chinese "high commissioner for Mongolia," the warlord General Chen Yi. It was Chen who would be in charge in Urga when Ungern took the town in February 1921.[58]

With the Trans-Baikal, Outer Mongolia, and northern Manchuria each under their own form of warlord rule, guns, goods, people, and disease (in particular, typhus and influenza) coursed back and forth between them. The CER continued to serve as the principal link tying Manchuria to the Trans-Baikal. By comparison, Outer Mongolia, without a railway to connect it to either Russia or China/Manchuria, remained more remote. Yet even there, the outside world came in with the telegraph and the camel caravans. Refugees and White soldiers forced out of Russia dribbled into the country from the Altay and Eastern Siberia. Meanwhile, Chinese traders and troops shifted up from the south

The roughly simultaneous collapse of the Russian and Chinese empires thus ushered in a new dynamic along their mutual border. Passport checks and quarantines continued, but as the power that had created these controls broke down, the border's meaning as a would-be dividing line eroded as well. In fact, for the warlords, each in different ways, it was often more useful to *weaken* borders than to reinforce them. And in any case the idea of diluting the border only really made sense in those parts of the zone where there was a semblance of a border to begin with. Much as earlier, most of the border area remained largely uncontrolled. With so much open country of steppes and hills, anyone aiming to cross between Russia and China/Mongolia could do so easily enough.

Ungern's civil war was fought in this environment. As best we can tell, like many officers in the White movement, he saw the fight as part of a broad continuum with the war against Germany. In April 1920, for example, in response to the accusation by a civilian official that he was illegally using convict labor at Dauria, Ungern retorted that the tsarist government had started this practice during the "German war" and it only made sense to do the same now because "the war now continues." Much like the fight against Germany, the struggle against the Bolsheviks required the same "practical measures to defend the motherland."[59]

We can see how this logic would have made sense to him. What had changed, really, from one war to the next? In the Great War, he had fought Germans, Austrians, and Turks. The fronts and the enemies were different now, of course, but the war—the actual fighting—for him had never stopped, and this was true for most of the men around him as well, Red and White alike. As the professor and politician Peter Struve wrote in late 1919, "the world war formally ended with...the armistice....In reality, however, everything we have experienced from that point onward, and continue to experience, is a continuation and transformation of the world war."[60]

But the presumption of a seamless continuity between the two conflicts holds only to a point, and Ungern would have known this, too. In operational terms, the fighting in the country around Dauria saw few of the pitched battles that defined the war on the eastern front or even the civil war as it was fought in other parts of Russia, including Western Siberia. Instead, it was a guerilla war of identity checks, detentions, beatings, executions, and occasional raids and skirmishes. For most of the conflict, the immediate enemy was the Red partisans—"Bolshevized" peasants and Cossacks, deserters from the White armies, students, "professional" radicals. Located well behind the front lines, Ungern did not face a formal Red Army force until the end of the Mongolian campaign when he led an assault back into Russian territory at Kiakhta and was roundly defeated.

The frame of the war was also different. For all the complexity and confusion of the Great War, the typical enemy was a foreign soldier, a man with a gun in a

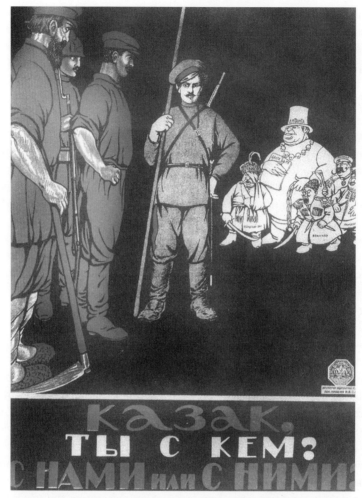

8.2. Dmitrii Moor, "Cossack, Whose Side Are You On? Ours or Theirs?" (1920).
This Bolshevik poster underscores the stark choice that faced countless Cossack
communities during the civil war. Given the pitiless zero-sum logic of the
conflict, the side you chose could determine everything. Reproduced
from *Chasovye otechestva: Iz istorii rossiiskogo kazachestva;
katalog vystavki* (St. Petersburg, 2006), 166, n. 322.

different uniform, speaking another language, firing from the other side of the
barbed wire. Now, however, the enemy was closer in, and more insidious because
of it. There was no clear front dividing "us" from "them." Partisans didn't wear
uniforms. Bolshevism was a creed one could hide if one had to. Indeed, as one
would expect in a civil war, the forces of the Whites and Reds shared a similar
social makeup—they were each made up overwhelmingly of peasant soldiers.
In the Trans-Baikal, Buryats, Tungus, and Russians fought on both sides.
Allegiances among the Cossacks were split roughly down the middle.

Finally, the civil war was also far more murderous and socially destructive than even the cataclysm of the Great War had been. Over two million Russian subjects died in World War I. Of these deaths, the large majority were military casualties. By comparison, during the revolution and civil war period (1917–1922), perhaps as many as seven times that number were lost—around fourteen to fifteen million people—and only a small minority were formal combatants.[61] One obvious explanation for the far greater scale and ratio of noncombatant deaths in the civil war is that the empire as a whole, rather than just one part of it, had become the battlefield. Staggering numbers of lives were lost to famine and disease. Another is that the Great War undermined the morality of the army and the population at large, allowing for even more butchery. But the horrendous violence and suffering of the civil war were also driven by the special ideological ferocity of the conflict.

Reds and Whites alike understood the war in millenarian terms that justified maximum violence. The logic of the times was that the moment of ultimate reckonings had arrived. The revolution must either prevail or perish, Russia would either survive or cease to be. Each side, in effect, imagined itself leading a crusade against the apocalypse, armed with a sword of unforgiving righteousness.[62] We are pure, our cause is just. Our enemy, meanwhile, is evil incarnate. To defeat him is not enough. He must be destroyed as well.[63]

This mentality took practical form in one of the most significant innovations of the war: the Red Terror—a complex of institutions and policies designed by the Bolsheviks to root out and destroy the opposition. Full-fledged, state-directed terror was necessary, as the Bolsheviks saw it, because the real enemy was not the White armies and their laughably reactionary commanders. It was the entire ethos and structure of imperial society. Terror was thus the sculptor's chisel, the tool that would cut out undesirables and carve the stone of a purer political community. To lead the fight, the party created a new organization, the Extraordinary Commission for the Struggle against Sabotage and Counter-Revolution, known by its Russian acronym as the Cheka, the first incarnation of the various political polices of the Soviet era. As one Cheka man wrote in 1918,

> Our war is not [a fight] against individuals. . . . When you get a hold of a suspect, don't start by searching for evidence of his actions or statements against Soviet power. The first question you need to ask is what class he belongs to, his background, upbringing, education, or profession. These questions should determine the fate of the accused. This is the essence and logic of the Red Terror.["64]

The White equivalent—the so-called White Terror—was less centralized (in part because there was less of a White center) but just as extreme. Both sides identified entire groups as unredeemable and lived by a worldview of guilt by association. Villages were torched for being either Red or White. Mass killings of POWs and "sympathizers" were common.[65]

In the Trans-Baikal, much as elsewhere, the basic requirement for success in this dismal contest lay in the ability to mobilize resources. For both sides, this meant effectively seizing men and supplies and living off the land. Detachments thus went into villages and took what they needed, at gunpoint if necessary. They also "confiscated" cargo trains or took "fees" and "gifts" to let them pass through. Given the back-and-forth of the war, residents often found themselves victimized not once but several times over. A report by the pro-White Buryat Duma in 1919, for example, complained that Buryats in the Selenga area were requisitioned and dragooned "from the Left" by the Reds shortly after the Bolshevik takeover and then "from the Right" by Semenov's Cossacks after they flushed out the Reds.[66]

Yet the other key to success in the Trans-Baikal, one often overlooked by historians, lay in the mobilization of the frontier itself. As we have seen, the civil war produced the final sundering of the empire that had begun with the Great War and the February Revolution. Power now devolved completely, becoming regional, even local in form—Semenov's rise to power in the Trans-Baikal was a perfect example of this process. But in borderland places like the Trans-Baikal, this process of devolution did stop at undoing the state; it also opened up and energized the frontier. The fates of the imperial state and of the frontier were thus inversely intertwined. As the former lost its power, the power of the latter rose to fill the vacuum. The side that would come out ahead in the Trans-Baikal, at least in part, would be the one that best captured and exploited this new frontier dynamic.

Ungern's experience in Dauria placed him in the very heart of this process. Like the war around him, he moved easily from one side of the border to the other, from the Trans-Baikal to northern Manchuria and the Mongol lands and back again. (He also apparently spent time in Beijing.)[67] We thus see him conducting business all across the zone: meeting with followers of the former Chinese president and would-be emperor Yuan Shikai in Chita; negotiating to buy horses from Buryat nomads on the Aga steppe; communicating with agents in Urga, Hailar, and Harbin; overseeing the gold mines at Nerchinsk.[68] A bandit leader from Barga named Fushengge apparently moved his men to Dauria because of Ungern's entreaties.[69] His cross-cultural marriage, too, was an act of frontier politics.

Violence—or the threat of violence—infused all these relationships. Dauria became the site of an infamous detention center (*gauptvakhta*) where Ungern oversaw beatings and interrogations of anyone who seemed ideologically suspect, Russians as well as foreigners. Many of the unfortunates who ended up at the facility were later hauled away and shot on the barren knolls that surround the town. ("To the hills!" [*v sopki*] was Ungern's euphemism for the executions.)[70] Only the thinnest crust of formality lay over these operations.

According to one witness from the times, the entire "military judicial section" at Dauria consisted of a single legal affairs officer charged with drafting paperwork on the executions.[71]

The Asiatic Division, Ungern's command in the town, offers perhaps the best window on the violent frontier revival that coursed around him in this moment. From the start of their fight against the Bolsheviks, Semenov and Ungern were deeply involved in organizing native units, continuing the work they had begun in Persia. But the urgency of the moment quickly led them to accept all comers, not just non-Russians. The result was the creation of mixed forces.

The first of these was the Special Manchurian Detachment (*Osobyi Manch'zhurskii Otriad,* or *OMO*), so-called because it was headquartered in Manchuria Station, Semenov's initial base of operations. Later, with the support of native anti-Bolshevik organizations, like the pro-Semenov Buryat Duma, new Buryat and Tungus regiments were formed as well as a mixed force eventually known as the Asiatic Mounted Brigade (*Aziatskaia Konnaia Brigada*), which Semenov placed under Ungern's command at Dauria beginning in late 1918. The Asiatic Division, created in February 1920, was meant to replace and expand the brigade and, on paper at least, was divided into separate Tatar, Mongol, and Buryat regiments.[72]

In practice, the diversity of the division was greater still, consisting of Russians, Ukrainians, Bashkirs, Tatars, Buryats, Tungus, Mongols (mostly from Chahars and Barguts, including Fushengge's men), and various and sundry former Austrian and Ottoman POWs who had been detained in the Trans-Baikal during the Great War. By the time of the Mongolian campaign, with the addition of Khalkha Mongols, Tibetans, and a small group of Japanese volunteers, Ungern told his interrogators that the division consisted of "about sixteen nationalities," though this may have been an underestimation.[73]

In terms of structure, the division was a hybrid, a cross between the old ways of the imperial army and the new national modes of organization brought up during the Great War. Paperwork was done in Russian, but in name at least, the force was divided into non-Russian regiments, with Russian and non-Russian officers as well as an Orthodox priest, a mullah, and lamas to cater to its varied believers. Officers were required to attend Mongolian language classes (and Ungern punished them when they didn't). Division offices were closed on Buddhist, Muslim, and Orthodox holidays.[74]

It is from Dauria that we also have our earliest description of Ungern in the improvised Russo-Mongolian uniform he would wear more frequently in Mongolia and then at his trial: a *deel* outfitted with the epaulettes of Semenov's army, another fusion of the old and the new, of the imperial army and the reviving frontier.[75]

In the spring of 1920, the division counted some 105 officers, 1,233 cavalry, and 365 infantry.[76] Its primary responsibility was to protect the border sector of the Trans-Baikal Railway, which served as the essential windpipe of Semenov's regime. Units were posted along the line and in nearby Cossack stanitsas. They conducted patrols, repaired bridges and sections of track destroyed in partisan attacks, deployed armored trains. Away from the line itself they also reconnoitered the border and hunted down "Red bands" in the countryside.

To supply the division, Ungern seized whatever he could: money and jewelry from passengers in transit, goods from warehouses and cargo trains, grain, livestock. Items of value were then resold to Russian and Chinese suppliers in Hailar and Harbin, often on credit, which then increased the pressure for new requisitions, and the cycle resumed. "Money was always in short supply in the division," wrote Ungern's logistics commander in Manchuria Station.[77] And whenever cash ran out, desertions increased. Criminality was thus essential to Ungern's command. If he didn't steal, his division might disappear, which meant that he stole constantly.

Russian authorities in the CER towns of northern Manchuria as well as the civilian government in Chita complained bitterly about the requisitions and other abuses at Dauria. Investigations were launched. But the protests had little effect. As one journalist put it, the Trans-Baikal at the time was "ruled by the saber."[78] Without a saber, there was little one could do.

For the better part of two years, Ungern held sway as "Semenov's right-hand man" in the rump state that the ataman cobbled together in the Trans-Baikal. Cossack officers like Ungern dominated Semenov's regime (with Semenov himself presiding as Cossack Number One), which was to be expected since the Cossacks made up the obvious military core of the region. But the broader society of the Trans-Baikal was far more diverse, both ethnically and socially, which meant that the ataman's rule always rested on a precarious balance of constituencies and interests. (Cossacks made up only about one-third of the population of the region in 1916.)[79] As a result, Semenov's "stateness," another awkward approximation of the term *gosudarstvennost'*, was always thin and contingent.

We feel this thinness in the ataman's decrees, which poured forth from Chita in the hundreds. Roughly half of them amounted to bombastic sermons about the need for "law and order" and "the salvation of the motherland" (with the word "STATE" [GOSUDARSTVO] frequently spelled out in capital letters). The other half, meanwhile, were orders of all sorts: to soldiers on leave to salute their superiors, to officers to behave themselves and stop bossing around civilians, to the public to ignore "nefarious rumors," to businesses and organizations to surrender this or that piece of property for "military needs."[80] Reading the pronouncements, one quickly gets the impression of a military kleptocracy bullying a largely unresponsive society.

Semenov must have had at least an inkling of this himself—reports told him that the population saw his government as corrupt and inconsistent. "The people are tired of war and struggle," wrote one official. "They do not understand the meaning of the government's measures."[81] Colonel Aleksei Budberg, who served briefly under Kolchak in Omsk, perhaps said it best when he described warlords like Semenov as the greatest albatrosses weighing down the White movement. "The abuses of the atamans (*atamanshchina*) are doing more to help the Bolsheviks than any of the sermonizing...by Lenin and Trotsky."[82]

For a time Semenov did well enough, both because of the combined effects of Japanese support and Kolchak's ineffectiveness, on the one hand, and his own talent—and ruthlessness—as a frontier politician on the other. But as the war turned against the Whites in Siberia, his regime began to waver. Beginning in late 1919, a Red Army surge along the Trans-Siberian took one White city after another: first Omsk, then Novonikolaevsk, then Irkutsk, where Kolchak was arrested and executed in February 1920. By April the Reds could have continued eastward to the Trans-Baikal, but the Politburo in Moscow decided to halt the offensive temporarily, both because men and materiel were needed for the war with Poland in the west and in order to create a new regional state, the so-called Far Eastern Republic (*Dal'nevostochnaia Respublika*), known as the DVR, to act as a "buffer" between Soviet Russia and the Japanese.

To create the new regime, the Bolsheviks followed the necessary legal fictions. First the DVR announced its independence, declaring the Trans-Baikal town of Verkhneudinsk, now Ulan-Ude, as its capital. Moscow then recognized the new state shortly thereafter.[83]

Within just a few months, however, the whole raison d'être for the buffer in the Trans-Baikal fell away as Tokyo abruptly—and unluckily for Semenov—decided to withdraw its forces from Chita and concentrate instead on the Amur and Vladivostok. Without the Japanese to intimidate the Reds and shore up their positions, the Whites' ability to hold on to the region crumbled quickly, and by October Red Army and DVR troops marched into Chita.[84]

Semenov fled the city just before the Reds' arrival, repairing by biplane to Dauria, where the Whites dug trenches around the town and managed to hold out for another month. By the time the noose tightened around Dauria, however, Ungern was no longer there. He had already crossed into Mongolia and was making his first attack on Urga. What historians call "the Mongolian campaign" had begun.

CHAPTER 9

URGA

"A pure offering for Geser.
Who has become leader of the army."
—MONGOLIAN PRAYER TO GESER-KHAN, protective deity of warriors and herds

The Mongolian Campaign

The Mongolian campaign is the best-documented period of Ungern's life. We find him everywhere now: in Mongolian, Chinese, and Japanese documents, Western diplomatic cables, Red Army and Comintern reports, orders from the Asiatic Division, newspapers, memoirs. Most striking of all, some of the new sources are personal, the kind that take us into his thoughts, in particular a handful of letters and the curious Order No. 15 that date from his time in power in Urga as well as the lengthy interrogation transcripts compiled by the Bolsheviks after his capture. The result is a dramatic shift in the story we can tell. Ungern entered Mongolia in the fall of 1920 and died less than a year later. Yet it's here, as the end of his life begins, that he finally comes into view.

Still, even with this remarkable change, there is much that we are able to reconstruct. Part of the problem lies in the complexity of the Mongolian war with its shifting groups of Mongols, Chinese, and Russians, including Russian Buryats, fighting each other in changing combinations. No log exists of Ungern's movements, so we can't always tell where he is, and, much as in Dauria, the cloying partisanship that sticks to almost everything we read from the period makes it difficult to trust what we're hearing.

Perhaps most important, this is also where we meet the historians. Ninety-nine percent of the scholarship on Ungern focuses on just this brief period of his life, with the result that, in addition to the unavoidable limitations of the sources, we now have to contend with the shortcomings of our histories. As an enemy of Soviet power, Ungern's profile in Russian and Mongolian writing during the communist period was purposefully distorted, whereas writing in the West, while less formally censored, often reduced him to a brutal and exotic caricature. (Some of it still does, in particular the writing of non-academic historians.) Even the more complex picture of Ungern that has emerged in the last decade thanks to the efforts of Sergei Kuz′min and other Russian and Mongolian specialists is inevitably incomplete in certain respects, as is my own study. Thus for all that we see more of Ungern in Mongolia, we don't necessarily see him better. Having an abundance of materials turns out to be as challenging in its way as having too few.

The term "Mongolian campaign" is a reminder of some of the complexities of the situation. Though accepted today as shorthand for the ten months between the fall of 1920 and the summer of 1921 when the Asiatic Division was operating in the country, the term didn't carry such a clear-cut meaning at the time. Ungern never coined a name for the war he fought in Mongolia, nor did his enemies. Instead, the naming process unfolded later as memoirists and historians began summarizing and sorting out events, reorganizing and tidying them up in the process. In this sense, much like any historical period agreed on in retrospect, the "campaign" at bottom is an abstraction, a box carved out of time to create significance and order. It has more to do with us than with Ungern.

It's also a loaded term, or at least one that suggests a particular point of view. Campaigns are intentional; they occur for a reason. If we accept that Ungern's time in Mongolia was a "campaign," it follows that we accept that he, too, had a reason for being there, perhaps even a master plan guiding his every step. Numerous contemporaries as well as later historians have indeed seen things this way. The Bolsheviks concluded right from the start that the campaign was the realization of a well-coordinated script concocted in concert with Semenov and the Japanese. Semenov, meanwhile, agreed, at least in part, boasting in his memoirs that the decision to go into Mongolia had been his idea. If things ended badly, he claimed, it was only because Ungern broke with the original plan after taking Urga and was eventually undone by his own excesses and miscalculations.[1]

As we look into things more closely, however, premeditated scenarios like this seem somewhat less convincing. In fact, there is no consensus in the sources as to how exactly the campaign came about—only a general agreement that it seems to have begun in either very late September or very early October 1920 when Ungern led the Asiatic Division across the Mongolian border not far from the Cossack *stanitsa* of Aksha some 180 miles west of Dauria. When his Red interrogators later asked him why he did this, he described the move as all but accidental—"a product of happenstance and fate" (*sluchainostiu i sud'boi*).[2]

His original intention, he said, had nothing to do with Mongolia. Instead, the idea was to move the division west to the opposite side of the Trans-Baikal in order to cut off the Red advance on Chita. This was the plan he had agreed on with Semenov, and he, Ungern, was simply doing his part to follow through when he learned in late September, mistakenly it turns out, that the ataman had left Chita and that the Reds had already taken the city. (In fact, Chita fell in late October.)[3] At this point, assuming the original plan was moot, and with his force reduced by desertions and stripped of field guns that he'd been forced to abandon in the rough terrain of the Yablonovy Mountains, he made a tactical decision to change course and move south into Mongolian territory. Semenov, he insisted, knew nothing about it.[4]

In other words, if we are to believe Ungern, he did not go to Mongolia with a "campaign" in mind, at least not one with all the meanings that would eventually be built into it. Instead, what we are calling a "campaign" only became one later, as events unfolded.[5]

The accounts left by Ungern's officers are contradictory. Some suggest that he intended to establish himself in Mongolia all along, whereas others appear to support his more contingent version of events. It is also possible that the decision to enter Mongolia, originally at least, was itself part of a plan to redeploy to the west, in this case, by making an end-around through Mongolian territory before cutting back into Russia with an attack on the strategic frontier town of Kiakhta, which at this point was held by the Reds.[6] A Japanese report from May 1921 describes shipments of weapons hidden near Urga in anticipation of Ungern's arrival, one delivered in the summer of 1919, the other in August 1920, suggesting that the decision to move into Mongolia was planned in advance, though whether these caches were meant to support an attack on Urga is unclear.[7] Meanwhile, a Chinese official on the CER reported to Beijing in October 1920 that Ungern had moved his soldiers to Aksha and that this was "very suspicious." The same official repeated the account of a Chinese merchant from Urga who relayed hearing as early as July that a "Russian army" near the border had plans to attack the capital.[8]

Again, as usual when it comes to Ungern's life, all we know with relative certainty is not what he may have been thinking or planning to do but rather what he did, which in this instance was to cross the border near Aksha and then make his way to the upper reaches of the Kerülen (Kherlen) River some 50 miles to the south where there was fodder and pasture. Judging from his comments to his interrogators, his force at the time consisted of about eight hundred men with, one assumes, roughly the same number of horses and a train of carts, covered wagons, and pack animals following behind.[9]

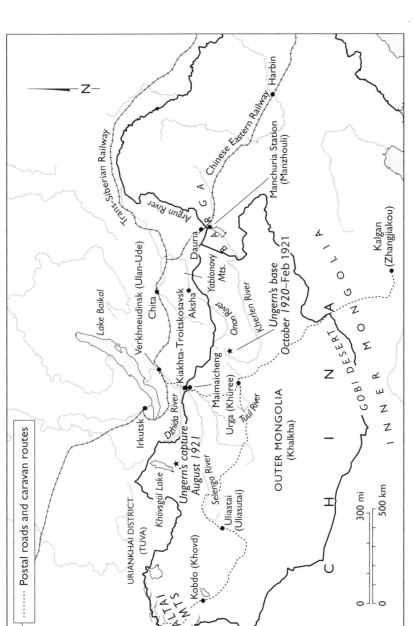

Map 8. The Trans-Baikal and Outer Mongolia, ca. 1917–1921

N

Trans-Siberian Railway

Lake Baikal

Irkutsk

Verkhneudinsk (Ulan-Ude)

Chita

Kiakhta-Troitskosavsk

Aksha

Dzhida River

Selenga River

Dauria

Argun River

Yablonovy Mts.

Onon River

A R G A

Chinese Eastern Railway

Harbin

Manchuria Station (Manzhouli)

Kherlen River

Ungern's base October 1920–Feb 1921

Maimaicheng

Urga (Khüree)

Tuul River

Ungern's capture August 1921

Khövsgöl Lake

URIANKHAI DISTRICT (TUVA)

Uliastai (Uliasutai)

OUTER MONGOLIA (Khalkha)

GOBI DESERT

MONGOLIA

INNER MONGOLIA

Kalgan (Zhangjiakou)

Kobdo (Khovd)

ALTAI MTS.

C H I N A

------- Postal roads and caravan routes

300 mi

500 km

0

0

As for what to call the act of entering Mongolia, this, too, is a key moment of interpretation. In documents written from the vantage of Moscow, Irkutsk, Beijing, and Urga, as well as in the accounts of historians, the event is usually described as an "invasion," but, much like "campaign," this term carries presumptions that don't fit the situation, or at least not entirely.[10] On the one hand, there seems no denying that Ungern "invaded" Mongolia inasmuch as he led a military force out of one country and into another. Yet seen another way, the situation on the border was so fluid and indeterminate at the time, it's hard to argue that he or anyone else could have invaded Mongolia in the traditional sense of the word.

As we saw earlier, the Russian and Chinese empires began tightening their shared frontier in Mongolia and Manchuria in the late nineteenth century. Checkpoints and inspections appeared. Passes were issued. Yet even then, the practical effects of the change were uneven and, in many places, simply invisible. Now, some twenty years later, with the empires that had created the border having themselves fallen apart, the line between them had faded as well. The vision of the border as a sovereign divide persisted in government sources—we hear it in High Commissioner Chen Yi's correspondence with the Chinese government in Beijing, for example, as well as in Sovnarkom's declarations from Moscow.[11] But the situation on the border itself was far less clear.

Movement across the border was ordinary business, the stuff of everyday life. Fighting between Reds and Whites routinely leeched into Mongolia from the Russian side. Chinese troops moved into the Russian border town of Kiakhta to protect Chinese shops. Buryat lamas and pilgrims, Bolshevik operatives, White couriers, Chinese agents, and Cossack consular guards shuttled back and forth, as did newly minted Mongolian communists, fresh from founding their Mongolian People's Party in Urga with Bolshevik support. Russian merchants bought up stock in Mongolia and drove the herds to the border for sale on the Siberian market. Meanwhile nomads flew from one side to the other whenever trouble appeared.[12] And Ungern would have been fully familiar with this dynamic since these were the same comings and goings that had surrounded him at Dauria.

Thus, if we take our starting point from the frontier rather than from how the frontier appeared in the eyes of some faraway center, it is hard to interpret the border crossing itself as an "invasion." The unraveling of the Qing and Romanov empires changed the meaning of the great line that ran between them, leading to two immediate consequences: first, a resurgence of the nonstate world of the frontier, that is, of the mesh of transborder connections that had always operated independent of the state's control, including even after the border began to tighten in the late nineteenth century; and second, the opening of a new field of political imagination. Along with chaos and violence, the breakdown of the states along their shared border also created opportunity. Multiple projects would now rise up: Red, White, Mongolian, Japanese, Chinese, each offering its own solution to the basic dilemma of the postimperial moment—the great question of whether to bend borders forward into new shapes or back into old ones.

It's not clear when Ungern decided to add his restorationist project to the mix, but the turning point, from a practical point of view, was *not* his decision to cross into Mongolia, since this sort of thing was relatively familiar. Instead the more meaningful moment was his decision shortly thereafter to attack Urga. Though close to the border, Urga was not, formally speaking, a border town, and as the capital of the country, it had special meaning both as the center of Khalkha religion and politics and the focal point of the Chinese republicans and their claims to the country. Attacking it thus meant taking things beyond a purely frontier framework. Urga could not be *just* a military objective, it had to be a political one as well.

In the memoir he published twenty years later in Shanghai, Ungern's aide-de-camp, A. S. Makeev, claimed that Ungern made the decision to move on Urga in the heat of the moment, after learning from Mongol informants that the Chinese commander there had arrested a group of White officers and their families and thrown them in the town's notorious Qing-era jail.[13] Whether this was indeed the main motivation, there were others. The town offered weapons, supplies, and shelter for the coming winter, as well as cash and gold, most of it locked up in the vaults of the town's Russian and Chinese banks. Most important, it was home to potential recruits and allies, including Mongol lamas and notables, most notably the Bogda, who despised the Chinese, as well as sympathetic Russians, including White officers and former tsarist officials, who despised the Bolsheviks.

Urga was also understood as enemy territory, a "Red town," as Makeev put it, because the leadership of the Russian colony there included socialists who were perceived as actively aiding the Bolsheviks.[14] (A number of them were indeed doing this.) Meanwhile, the Chinese republicans who ran the town overall were also Reds, at least as far as Ungern was concerned. In letters he later sent from the town, he described Sun Yat-sen, the nationalist leader and first Great President of the Chinese Republic, as "that famous revolutionary-Bolshevik," and denounced the republicans in general in similar terms.[15] In a war of absolutes, Urga was thus more than "Red" enough to be a target. The fact that it happened to be in another country was secondary. The revolutionary scourge had no respect for borders. It followed that the fight *against* the scourge had to be borderless as well.

"Your Good Deed Shall Shine across the World"

Urga (now Ulaanbaatar) sits in a wide valley surrounded by low mountains in north-central Mongolia. The Russian border at Kiakhta lies a little less than

200 miles to the north, the Hulunbuir region of Chinese Inner Mongolia and the northernmost part of the old CER is about 600 miles to the northeast, while the historic crossing to northern China at Kalgan (Chinese today: Zhangji-akou), on the other side of the Gobi, is 600 miles to the south. Today the city sprawls in every direction, creeping up the hillsides, and is home to well over a million people, close to half of Mongolia's population. In 1920, it was far smaller, perhaps just sixty or so thousand, not including the Chinese garrison, which counted an additional seven or eight thousand soldiers.[16]

In physical terms, the town then was less a single center than a loosely intertwined chain of settlements strung out for some 5 miles along the north bank of the Tuul River. At the western end were two interconnecting monastic districts: the so-called western monastic district of Gandan, with its great monastery tower housing a 90-foot-high copper statue of the miracle-producing bodhisattva Janraisig raised in 1912 to celebrate Mongolian independence, and just to the east, the "eastern monastic city" of Züün Khüree, the administrative heart of the Mongol town and the location of the former residence of the Qing amban. (Khüree, renamed Niislel Khüree, or "monastic capital" after independence, was also the Mongol name for Urga as a whole.) Far on the eastern end several miles away from the monastic districts was the Chinese quarter, literally the "trading town" (Chinese: Maimaicheng; Russian: Maimaichen); and, finally, roughly halfway between Maimaicheng and the monasteries, on a small rise, sat the Russian settlement, centered around the large compound of the old tsarist consulate.[17]

9.1. Urga, early 1900s, Gandan Monastery and gers. Courtesy National
Central Archives of Mongolia, Ulaanbaatar.

9.2. The Russian consulate in Urga, early 1900s. Reproduced from *Moskovskaia torgovaia ekspeditsiia v Mongolii* (Moscow, 1912), 32.

With the exception of the Gandan complex and a handful of other buildings, much of old Urga is gone today. The sprawl of modern Ulaanbaatar has long since eaten up the wooden neighborhoods that Ungern would have known. Countless temples—perhaps as many as a hundred—were torn down by the communists who came to power after his removal. Only one of the Bogda's four palaces remains. But a large painting in the city's historical museum helps us imagine what the town looked like before these great changes. Drawn from an illustrated map of 1913, the canvas displays the once separate districts: Maimaicheng, with its narrow streets coiled behind a high, mud-brick wall; the crowded temples and ger courtyards of Gandan and Züün Khüree; the Russian section, dotted with Siberian-style log cottages facing each other along a broad street. The museum itself sits not far from the old consular district in a handsome, European-style mansion that used to be the home of a wealthy Buryat merchant.[18]

Most Western and Russian accounts of the town describe it according to the predictable exotic contrasts: a combination of gleaming temples and miserable shacks, fragrant incense and spitting camels. In a description by the American "dinosaur hunter" Roy Chapman Andrews, for example, Urga comes across as a "dizzying chaos of conflicting architecture":

Three races [i.e., Mongols, Chinese, and Russians—WS] have met here and each maintains its own customs and way of life. High above the city, dominant and overpowering, stands the great temple of the Living Buddha, surrounded by the pill-box dwellings of fifteen thousand lamas. On the street are Mongols in half a dozen different tribal dresses. Tibetan pilgrims, Manchu Tartars, and camel drivers from Turkestan eat, drink, and gamble with Chinese from civilized Peking."[19]

Andrews also points out less appealing aspects: piles of waste in the streets, the dismal jail with its coffin-like punishment boxes, and the packs of dogs that roamed the town feeding on whatever they pleased, including the bodies of the dead that the Mongols laid out for burial at the edge of the steppe.[20]

Yet if Urga was a site of "barbaric splendor" for foreigners like Andrews, to the Mongols it was mostly a place of business—of the spirit as well as the purse. For pilgrims, it was a holy destination, for lamas, a center of learning; while nomads came to buy and sell, trading their animal goods for the wares and cloth they found in the Chinese shops. As a rule, they settled their purchases in kind or by credit, their paper money having become all but worthless in the turmoil of recent years. (When available, silver coins, including old tsarist coinage and Mexican silver dollars, also passed as currency.) Prices were high, so debts and resentments tended to run high as well.

In all, Ungern made three attempts to take the city. The first two, in late October and early November 1920, were fought off by the Chinese and almost undid the division. To regroup, Ungern withdrew to the Kerülen and used the winter to resupply with guns and matériel run in from Manchuria, while parlaying with the leaders of Mongol clans for more fighters and collecting new Russian recruits from the stragglers reaching Mongolia from White Siberia. Then in early February 1921, with his total force built up to about five thousand men, he attacked again and this time, after intense but brief resistance, largely in Maimaicheng, the Chinese withdrew and the division took the town.[21]

Looking back now, it seems clear the attack had two basic goals. The first and most obvious was to destroy or drive out the Chinese garrison; the second was to lay the groundwork of a new political compact, though the two goals were in fact never separate. Community building went hand-in-hand with the attack, and vice versa.

Ungern's first move, ordered two days before the main assault, was to "rescue" the Bogda, who had been arrested by the Chinese after the attacks a few months earlier and was being held under guard in his winter palace near the Tuul. (This is the palace that still stands today.) The raid unfolded in broad daylight and both embarrassed and unsettled the Chinese, who saw it as a bad omen and apparently began partially withdrawing even before the formal assault began. Dmitrii Pershin, a former tsarist official, recalled looking out from his home in Urga that day to see men moving across the slopes of the Holy

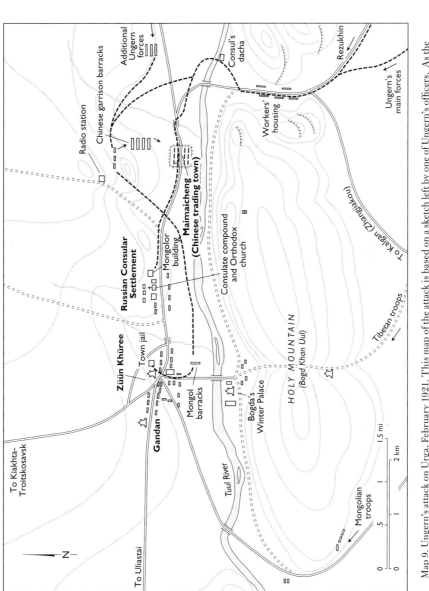

Map 9. Ungern's attack on Urga, February 1921. This map of the attack is based on a sketch left by one of Ungern's officers. As the Asiatic Division and Ungern's Mongol allies assaulted the town from the east and south, most of the Chinese garrison fled north in the direction of Kiakhta.

Mountain south of the town. Though he didn't know it at the time, these were Ungern's troops, including a detachment of Tibetan cavalry, making their way down to the Bogda's palace.[22]

With the Bogda freed, Ungern's legitimacy among the Mongols grew, and the looming battle for the town assumed even more the mantle of a would-be war of national liberation. In apparent fulfillment of this expectation, within a month of taking over, Ungern oversaw an elaborate reinstallation of the Bogda as the national ruler. In return, the Bogda honored him with the rank of khan, the title of Great Hero General, Builder of the State, and the privilege of wearing a three-eyed peacock plume in his Manchu-style velvet cap, a symbol of the highest nobility.[23] This is also when we first hear of him wearing the special orangey-gold deel he would later wear at his trial. (Other men in his command received honors as well.) "You have taken Urga," one Mongol leader wrote to him not long after the ceremony. "Your good deed shall shine across the world like the rays of the sun."[24]

We also see the overlapping of military and political objectives in the attack itself, which unfolded, in effect, as a rout bound up within two interlocking pogroms, one of Ungern's men against suspected Russian socialists and Jews and the other of Mongols against the Chinese, in particular Chinese merchants. The pogrom led by the Mongols appears to have been largely spontaneous, built out of the fury and possibility of the moment, and it apparently angered Ungern, since the enemy, as he saw it, was the Chinese republican garrison rather than the Chinese in general. Numerous witnesses from the time remember seeing Mongolian looters strung up on his orders for stealing from Chinese shops.[25]

By contrast, he did nothing to stop the violence against the Jews and Reds since this terror was planned. Before launching the attack, Ungern had instructed his men to "eliminate" any Jews and Reds they found in Urga and apparently made it clear that, once they took the town, they would have their so-called three legal days (*tri zakonnykh dnia*) to plunder as they saw fit. (This three-day license was a practice already well-known by the time from the western theaters of the war.)[26]

Given that numerous men in the division were Cossacks from the Trans-Baikal, they were familiar with Urga from visits over the years. They knew the houses of the Jewish families and, for good measure, carried lists of local "sympathizers" provided by informants as well as names from the town's Russian newspaper. The head of the Russian town council (*uprava*) was a socialist schoolteacher named Sheineman. Some of the town's most visible merchants were Jews. When the storm began, a few managed to hide or flee (including Sheineman). Others were beaten and summarily executed, the women raped. Refugees who managed to escape north to Kiakhta put the number of "Russians, Buryats, and Jews" killed in the pogrom at "more than three hundred." Another report described Jews as "slaughtered...to a person" (*perebito...pogolovno*).[27] (By way of comparison, Chinese accounts suggest that some three thousand Chinese were killed in the attack, soldiers and towns-people alike.)[28]

Pershin writes in his account of the campaign that the violence against the Jews continued even beyond the third day. Sent to meet with Ungern as a spokesman for the Russian colony, he recalls Ungern summarily cutting him off when he raised the issue of the ongoing murders, making it clear that the topic was not open for discussion.[29] One socialist who managed to escape gave an interview describing how Ungern's men hunted down entire Jewish house-holds, slaughtering even their farm animals. "This minor, almost unbelievable fact," the Bolshevik reporter noted, "reveals the true depths of the Ungernites' depravity (*ozverenie*)."[30]

What caused this pogrom? The prevailing view of the Russian sources and much of the historical writing is that it was the product of Ungern's personal anti-Semitism, which, by now at least, had become obvious. In addition to comments by witnesses like Pershin, we find proof of his hatred in some of the letters from Urga, which brim with descriptions of Jews as "a terrible evil...a parasite eating away at the world." In a note to a fellow White commander on the Amur, he writes that they should be exterminated without pity, to the last person: "neither men nor women, not even a family should remain." Like other anti-Semites in the White military leadership (and beyond), he appears to have seen socialists and Jews as essentially interchangeable. When asked by his interrogators after his capture why he hated them so much, he replied simply: "they caused the revolution."[31]

His influence on this question apparently extended to the Bogda as well, who issued a decree later that spring describing "the majority of the Red Par-ty" (that is, the Bolsheviks) as consisting of "Hebrews, also known as Jews, who...are intent merely on robbery, and therefore not to be trusted."[32]

Yet even accepting that Ungern was an extreme anti-Semite, describing the pogrom as the result of his personal prejudice is at best a partial explanation. The roots of the horror in Urga lay in groups and institutions as well as indi-viduals. If we take a broader view, it is more accurate to say that Ungern came to the town not with his private hatred alone but also with the accumulated habits of intolerance and violence that had been playing out in Russia for the preced-ing seven years, and it was this set of violent presumptions and practices that provided, in effect, the essential toolkit for the pogrom.

As we have seen, anti-Jewish violence was integral to the Russian military's experience of the Great War. As the war then morphed into the turmoil of the revolution and civil war, this storm intensified. During the "pogrom year" of 1919, for example, some thirteen hundred anti-Jewish riots and massacres exploded across Ukraine, the overwhelming share led by Whites and other

Urga   175

anti-Bolshevik forces, many of them war veterans. In the process, at least fifty thousand Jews were killed, far more than during the Great War. The pogrom that became the ultimate "symbol of those terrible years"—the slaughter of some sixteen hundred Jews in the Ukrainian shtetl of Proskuriv in just a few hours in February 1919—was explicitly ordered from above, and others were as well.[33]

Ungern, in this sense, was simply repeating familiar practices. He had fought in the Great War, as had many of the men in his division. As he left the front and traveled east, he performed the kind of "violent migration" that helped to spread the norms of the war fronts to the rest of the empire.[34] Just as official anti-Semitism had been a cultural pathology uniting the country's disparate regions prior to the war, the pogrom violence of the imperial army became a similar dark link after the war ended. By 1921, for millions of men in uniform, Jews everywhere had become national enemies, traitors who needed to be taught a lesson.[35] That hardly any of them lived in the east, in particular in the Trans-Baikal and Mongolia, did not change the equation.

Anti-Semitic tracts, like the *Protocols of the Elders of Zion,* appeared in Siberia just as they did in the west. Though far fewer than in European Russia, pogroms also occurred "beyond the Urals" during the war years.[36] By the time of the civil war, Jews in eastern Siberia—locals as well as refugees—were certainly aware of the volatile prejudices around them. In Manchuria Station, for example, the members of a local Jewish organization reported an incident in October 1919 when a drunken White officer stumbled off a train, shouting "Beat the Yids! Save Russia!" and anti-Semitic references appeared regularly in the White Siberian press.[37] Though far less common than in White Siberia, anti-Jewish hatred and violence occurred in Red-controlled areas as well.[38]

At the same time, like so many other massacres, the rampages in Urga, although shaped by wider phenomena, were deeply rooted in their own surroundings. Even before Ungern's arrival, the town was brimming with tensions: between Mongol notables and commoners, Mongols and Chinese, Chinese and Russians, and between the bitterly divided members of the Russian colony whose size had swollen in the preceding years with refugees from the civil war.

Tensions in the town were greater still because *all* the communities, not just the Russians, were split by their own internal resentments. In the time since Ungern's first assaults, the Chinese authorities, by way of reprisal, had arrested scores of Russians and Mongol leaders presumed to have pro-Russian sympathies. An American report described threats from the Chinese garrison commander to kill every white person in the town if there was another attack.[39] Chinese troops defiled the great monastery at Gandan. Food and fuel dwindled, then largely disappeared.[40] The town began to freeze.

Meanwhile, Ungern's force had also changed. Back in Dauria, the division had at least the trappings of a regular army corps: there were roll calls, drills, inspections, a quartermaster's office collecting chits and issuing supplies. Now it functioned more like a band of irregulars. After four winter months in the field, the troops were ill with scurvy, their uniforms in rags. To defend against desertions, Ungern imposed a harsh regimen of beatings and other improvised punishments for even minor violations or indiscretions, on occasion doing the beating himself, using a short Mongolian horsewhip (*tashur*) that he apparently always carried on his person. We read of offenders being forced to stand for hours on frozen rivers, their bodies slowly numbing from exposure. Makeev tells of a man strung up from a tree branch over a bonfire and burned to death.[41]

Imagining how Ungern's men might have been thinking, it's easy to believe that what Urga meant to them by February was simple deliverance—the prospect of a roof and a bed and the chance to seize whatever they could as payback for their deprivations. According to one of the division's Japanese soldiers later interrogated by Japanese officials in Manchuria, the men were exhausted, ready for plunder and rape. "The six months since we left Dauria were difficult, we wanted to take valuable things; this was justified. We wanted to have sex—white people with whites, yellows with yellows."[42] Prior to the attack, Ungern apparently told the men that they could keep two-thirds of the spoils, with the other third going to the division.[43]

Meanwhile, the Mongols who joined the attack must have looked forward to getting even with the Chinese who had requisitioned their herds and gouged them in their shops. Similar riots had exploded a decade earlier at the time of Mongolia's aborted attempt at independence. And the Mongols brought their own sense of urgency to the moment.

As early as the 1890s, the Bogda had prophesized that the Mongols would continue to suffer as long as the Chinese remained in the country: "If a Mongol wears a white hat and Chinese boots and lives like the Chinese, he will die together with the Chinese. Now here are the lands where the Chinese disappeared…and they are rich. The prosperous age of our Mongols will certainly commence." It must have been easy to see Ungern's arrival as the tipping point, the long-awaited moment for completing the unfinished business of 1911.[44]

In other words, the mayhem and bloodshed that erupted in Urga was a dagger's tip sharpened from all sides. The imperial order that had structured the relations between groups—however imperfectly—was gone, and the warlord politics of the frontier, led in this instance by Ungern and his Mongolian allies, was rising to take its place. What exploded in Urga, was a manifestation of postempire violence, terror in the imperial rubble. Without the misery, hatred, and statelessness so integral to the moment, it is hard to imagine the massacres raging as they did, of Jews, socialists, and Chinese alike.

Ungern thus caused the pogrom but not as it has usually been told, by simply ordering it into being. Instead, the brutality unfolded on prepared ground, ideologically and socially. The violence, in this sense, reflected at once structure and spontaneity, and was, like so much of the cruelty of the civil war, as intentional as it was elemental. From the letters he later wrote from the town, we know that he saw his victory as a turning point. The enemies of decency and tradition had finally received their due. Their destruction was not murder but justice. The great rectification had begun.

"I Will Gladly Die for Monarchy"

Once in control, Ungern moved to consolidate his position by pursuing the main Chinese force fleeing north from Urga toward the Russian border at Kiakhta, cutting down other enemy forces farther west and south, and contacting White detachments throughout the country to have them round up suspected Jews and socialists. (Eventually the dragnet would ensnare the merchant Aleksei Burdukov and his family, who were arrested—and almost shot—near Uliastai, about 600 miles west of Urga.) Meanwhile, after his restoration in early March, the Bogda made Ungern commander of the army.

Urga, too, was put back into working order. Roads and bridges were repaired, telegraphs rehung. Workers reopened the printing press at the Russian consulate, along with the electricity plant, radio station, and a tannery whose Jewish owner had been murdered in the pogrom. To pay for the reconstruction, Ungern went directly to the source, seizing gold and valuables from the Russian and Chinese banks in the town. By the spring, the Bogda's government began issuing bonds to raise still more cash (the locals called them *barony*).[45]

Meanwhile, the Asiatic Division confiscated cars, cannons, rifles, and machine guns from the warehouses of the Chinese garrison, and able-bodied men in the town who didn't volunteer right away found themselves quickly "mobilized"—that is, drummed into the force, including Mongols, Buryats, Tungus, Russians, and Chinese POWs. In the old Red Army archive in Moscow one can still read the high-sounding pledge slips the new recruits were expected to sign, promising to serve the division "in Mongolia and beyond."[46]

Ungern's other work was expressly political. In Urga proper, the most important political task was to build a reliable relationship with the Bogda. Ungern would later tell the Reds that he met the Mongolian leader on only three occasions and that he (Ungern) had no personal influence on the new Mongolian government.[47] At the same time, even accepting that this might be true, it is clear that the two men were bound to each other—the Bogda to Ungern as his kingmaker, and Ungern to him in turn as the guarantor for his legitimacy as warlord. In addition, Ungern also had to watch over the political situation in the city more generally. He thus set up a security office to flush out spies and "unreliables," while also handing out posts to ex-tsarist technocrats still living in the town.

His broader political activity, however, was to continue assembling the new community he needed to support the war. The great weapon of the cause was the division, which by now, with the addition of new Mongol, Chinese, and Tibetan troops, was even more diverse than before. The former official Pershin offered this description of Ungern's men shortly after they entered the town:

> All around were Cossacks, horses, carts, and still more Cossacks dressed in the most varied outfits—you couldn't call them uniforms. The only thing that made it clear they were Cossacks were their tall sheep's wool hats (*papakhi*) and their sabers and rifles.
>
> And the faces, God only knows the different types! Such a mixture of different races and tribes, from Russians from European Russia and Siberia to Bashkirs, Kazakhs (*kirgizy*), Tatars, and Buryats....
>
> "We've got all kinds," one of Ungern's men [told me], and that seemed to say it all.[48]

Jews may have been the only group excluded from the force, though even this prohibition was not absolute. One of the division's agents was a Chinese-speaking Jewish Christian convert from Manchuria named L'ev Vol'fovich, and his brother, also a baptized Jew, apparently served in the ranks. Ungern likewise took steps to protect at least some Jews in Urga, issuing special passes to guarantee their "safekeeping."[49]

At the same time, the division, at bottom, was just a tool, a means for creating and defending the community rather than the community itself. We see the wider membership Ungern had in mind in his letters. Indeed the letters, some twenty-seven or so altogether, all of them seized when the Red Army and their Mongol allies moved against him later in the summer, are surely the most revealing materials of his life, more still than his candid interrogation records or Order No. 15, if only because in the letters we hear him speaking privately and without duress. Roughly a fifth of the letters are practical notes or short commands dashed off to subordinates (like Vol'fovich) in Manchuria and elsewhere, but the rest are longer missives, some running to several tightly typed pages, that went out to a range of partners and prospective allies—Mongolian khans and khutukhtus, Chinese strongmen, White commanders, Kazakh leaders, and his Russian "agent" in Beijing.[50]

From these longer writings, what we see, in effect, is that Ungern's overarching goal in Mongolia amounted to resolving the problem of postempire by doing away with the "post" part of the equation—that is, for him, the answer to the conundrum of what to do with the mangled borders around him was to return them to the shape they had had before. The old empires had been savagely undone by revolution, the obvious thing now, then, was to rebuild them. At the same time, perhaps reflecting (but not acknowledging) the new imagination made possible by the revolution, he also proposed an important innovation. The centerpiece of the agenda, his "idée fixe" according to his interrogators, was to create what he called a "central Mongolian state" (*seredinnoe mongol'skoe gosudarstvo*) that would stretch over most of the steppe region of Central Eurasia, from roughly the western edges of Manchuria to the Caspian Sea. The only real analogue for this sort of state was the Mongol Empire of the thirteenth and fourteenth centuries, which then gave rise to the idea that Ungern imagined himself as a new Genghis Khan. (He indeed makes a few references to the great khan in his letters but not to himself in Genghis' role.)[51]

This vision of a Mongolian megastate was at odds with a number of the other plans of the moment. Before its fall, the Kolchak government's answer to the "Mongolian question" was to leave things alone and continue abiding by the Kiakhta Treaty of 1915, which confirmed Mongolia as an autonomous region within China and gave Russia, implicitly at least, special influence in Mongolian affairs. The Bolsheviks, by contrast, rejected the Kiakhta Treaty (much as they did every other tsarist agreement) and set their eyes on world revolution, though in the case of China and Mongolia, initially at least, this translated into contradictory overtures supporting both Chinese sovereignty and Mongolian "freedom." Most Chinese republicans, meanwhile, were inclined to see the chaos in Russia as a useful opportunity to reassert themselves in Mongolia and either scale back or simply eliminate the autonomy they had been forced to concede in 1915, turning Mongolia, in effect, into something closer to an ordinary Chinese province.

Yet whereas it contrasted with these approaches, Ungern's pan-Mongolian vision was nonetheless very much in step with the thinking of many Mongols, who tended to assume that it was only common sense for the various Mongol ethnic groups—Khalkhas, Oirats, Barguts, Chahars, and depending on the observer, the Tuvans and Buryats as well—to live together in a single state. This idea had its roots in the beginnings of Mongolian nationalism in the late Qing period. Indeed, part of the energy that fueled the drive for Mongolian independence was the vision of creating a "Greater Mongolia" (Mongolian: *yeke Monggol uls*) that would gather the Mongols under a single tent by tearing down the supposedly artificial divisions that outsiders like the Qing and the Russians had erected between them. Such expansive thinking was quite ordinary at the time, a Mongolian analogue to the visions of "greater" Britains, Polands, or Finlands that we find on the opposite end of the continent in the same period. Ungern's birthplace of Graz had been an early center of Pan-Germanism, the German variant of this idea.[52]

In the heady rush of Mongolian independence in 1911, the Bogda's government had hoped to achieve at least a limited version of Greater Mongolia by claiming all the Mongol territories formerly ruled by the Qing (that is, both Inner and Outer Mongolia), but the effort failed almost immediately, in part because of the opposition of the Chinese, which was to be expected, but also to the Mongols' own divisions and mutual resentments, which tended to be greater than the nationalists cared to admit, and, perhaps most of all, to the tsarist government, which favored stability and therefore supported only the creation of a (relatively) limited Mongolia rather than a greater one.

Despite these setbacks, however, the pan-Mongolian idea lived on and resurfaced again in the turmoil of the Russian Revolution and Civil War when a group of some sixteen Inner Mongolian and Buryat leaders took advantage of a series of meetings sponsored by Semenov and the Japanese in early 1919 to declare the founding of a new pan-Mongolian state. Unlike the Mongolia defined by the Kiakhta Treaty, this new version, as the founders saw it, was to be truly independent. They thus announced the formation of a government, replete with ministerial posts divided among representatives of the various Mongol groups as well as plans in time to create a parliament. They dispatched a delegation to the Paris Peace Conference to make the case for foreign recognition. The Japanese agreed to provide a loan. (Officers from the emperor's Siberian Army were present at the meetings.) Meanwhile, Semenov pledged to organize a military force for the new state, receiving the title of prince and an appointment as chief state adviser in return.[53]

Like the first attempt at a pan-Mongolian union, however, this one failed all but right away, and for similar reasons. The most obvious was that the Khalkhas, the largest of the Mongol groups, refused to participate. Though invited to the meetings, the autonomous government in Urga balked at joining the initiative in part, it seems, because they were worried about how the Chinese would respond but also because they saw themselves as the rightful leaders of the Mongol world rather than the Buryats or the Mongols of Inner Mongolia. Meeting with Chen Yi in March 1919, the Mongolian foreign minister tried to underscore the Khalkhas' loyalty by showing him Semenov's telegrams and dismissing the whole project as a Russian provocation: "The Russians do not like it when the Mongols and Chinese are on intimate terms."[54] Though the lamas who made up one part of the Urga government were broadly sympathetic to the goal of independence, the nobles who made up the other were hesitant since they saw the new state as a likely threat to their privileges.

There was also intense international opposition to the pan-Mongolian idea in the surrounding neighborhood. Both the Kolchak government and the Bolsheviks opposed the initiative, since they each saw the new state as little more than a thinly veiled attempt by the Japanese to advance their plans against Siberia. (One of the few things Kolchak and the Bolsheviks shared in common was a vigorous disgust for Semenov and Japan.) Ironically, though, even the Japanese themselves soon backed away from the new state as they began drawing down their Siberian Expedition and repositioning their emphasis on Manchuria. In one clear sign of the new chill, the delegation that was supposed to go to Paris traveled first to Tokyo and found itself stalled there by the Japanese authorities. The leaders of the new Mongolia never got to meet President Wilson.[55]

By far the most important opposition, however, came from the republican Chinese leadership, which, as it turned out, took little comfort from the fact that the Khalkhas chose not to participate in the pan-Mongolia meetings and quickly used what they saw as the "collusion" between the "bandit" Semenov, Japan, and "the Mongols of our country" as a justification to do what they wanted to do anyway, which was to unilaterally scrap the Kiakhta Treaty and cancel Mongolia's autonomy.

In July 1919 the first Chinese troops returned to Urga led by General Xu. By August the Mongolian government formally requested additional Chinese assistance against a possible attack by Semenov's forces. Then in November the Bogda dutifully bowed to the portrait of the Great President in a ceremony in Urga and was granted a new title and seal by the Chinese authorities. The cancellation was complete.[56] The paper-based creation of one Mongolia thus led directly to the undoing of another. By the fall of 1919 no Mongolian state appeared on the map at all, autonomous, independent, or otherwise.

Was Ungern a pan-Mongolist bent on recreating the stillborn Greater Mongolia of 1919? To the Bolsheviks, he certainly was, and they therefore quickly concluded that everything he was doing necessarily related back to a grand plan coordinated with Semenov and the Japanese. (The charge that he collaborated with Japan would become the first one leveled against him at his trial.) Indeed, to be fair to the Reds, it is impossible to conceive that Ungern did *not* know about the Greater Mongolia platform. The meeting of February–March 1919 where Inner Mongol and Buryat enthusiasts announced the creation of their new state took place in Chita, not far from Semenov's headquarters, and a similar meeting was held in Dauria a few weeks before. It's unclear whether Ungern attended either event, but he would have known the participants.[57] In fact, shortly after the Chita conference, the "government" of the new Mongolian union relocated to Dauria, which means that even if he did not participate in the meetings, he would have been well aware of the goings-on.[58] Like Semenov, it's also clear that Ungern saw the Mongols as the Whites' natural allies in the struggle against the Reds and as essentially a single people, downplaying their various internal divides.[59] In at least one letter, he speaks directly of the need to "unify the Mongols."[60]

Yet his political goals were nonetheless different from those of Semenov and his various Mongol and Buryat supporters, not to mention the Japanese military in Siberia, so to describe him as a pan-Mongolist in the way the Bolsheviks meant it is ultimately misleading. (He also repeatedly denied that he had any meaningful contact with the Japanese, and materials from the Japanese archives seem to bear this out.)[61] That is, Ungern was indeed a pan-Mongolist, but pan-Mongolism was a big tent with ample room for multiple interpretations.

The Buryat intellectuals who joined the cause in 1919, for example, were nationalists who saw an independent pan-Mongolian state as the best way at the time to secure their quest for Buryat autonomy. They were not pro-Semenov as much as pro-Buryat, and a number of them would later switch their allegiances to the Bolsheviks once it seemed clear that the Reds were more likely to advance their goals. In fact, some of them had already worked with the Bolsheviks earlier in the civil war before switching to Semenov's camp after he took over in the Trans-Baikal.[62]

Meanwhile, the various mostly Khalkha Mongols who formed the early core of the Mongolian People's Party were also inclined to think in pan-Mongolist terms. The MPP's first party platform, drawn up in March 1921, declared that whereas the party's initial objective was to restore the autonomy of Outer Mongolia, the eventual goal was "the union of all the Mongolian tribes in a single self-governing state."[63] The author of the platform was Tsyben Zhamtsarano, a Buryat scholar who had made the same crooked ideological journey described above, starting off as an official with the tsarist mission in Urga, then allying himself, at least nominally, with Semenov through the Semenov-affiliated Buryat Duma, and finally moving over to the Red Mongols and their Bolshevik patrons.

Pan-Mongolism was thus a borderland product, and like the people who created it, could be made to pivot in a variety of directions. Ungern's version of the ideology was more proof of this fact. Its distinction was simply its deep conservatism: rather than embracing a dream of Mongol unity as a way out of empire, he turned the ideal on its head and supported the return of the Qing by arguing, in effect, that the best way to guarantee the unity of the Mongols was for them to live as before under the rule of Chinese emperor. Other participants in the pan-Mongolist meetings at Dauria and Chita had adopted a similar pro-Qing position, though they ultimately lost out in the discussions.[64]

If we accept Ungern's statements at face value, his abiding cause in Mongolia was "the restoration of the emperors" (*vosstanovlenie tsarei*). In that respect, he was committed to driving out the Chinese republicans and restoring the Bogda, all of which the pan-Mongolists in Chita would have supported. But unlike them, he had no interest in creating an independent Mongolia, much less a parliamentary order. Instead, his "central Mongolian state" seems to have been intended as an intermediary form, a way station on the road to the promised land of a Qing restoration. The Bogda, as he saw him, was not an independent ruler as much as an imperial subcontractor, a would-be cross-continental echo to the Baltic barons. Just as the German lords had presided over their domains for the tsar, the Bogda would preside over his for the Manchu Khan, which, in Ungern's view, was the very purpose of the Bogdas and how they had always operated before.

As he noted in one of his letters, "for Mongolia to seek to secede from China" was an "empty dream" (*pustaia mechta*). Instead, the "great...task" of the moment needed to be "the reestablishment of the [rule of] the lawful emperor"—that is, the resurrection of the Qing Dynasty and the return of the

Mongols to their traditional place within the imperial order.[65] He made the point more directly to his Bolshevik interrogators:

> QUESTION: How did your support for Mongolian independence affect your dealings with monarchist circles in China?
>
> ANSWER: I never conceived of sovereign independence (*suverenitet*) for the Mongols....I saw their destiny only in terms of [their] subordination to the Manchu khans on the basis of so-called Manchu customary law, which would have allowed them [another sort of] independence [i.e., autonomy within the Chinese Empire—WS]. The Mongol elite would have been perfectly happy with this. As I saw it, the Manchus needed to hold sway over a ring [of territories]: Mongolia, Tibet, China, as well as [the nomadic areas of] Siberia and...Central Asia. My entire correspondence with the outside world was directed toward this goal.[66]

Indeed, if we are to describe Ungern's period in Mongolia as a "campaign" in the full sense of the word, and it had definitely become one by the time he took Urga, then this was the vision at the heart of it: the search for a sweeping imperial restoration that would begin in Mongolia but then move from there to the rest of the former Qing world and, in time, to Russia and Europe. In this scenario, the return of the Qing was crucial because they were the rightful historical overlords of both Mongolia and China.

To most Chinese and Mongolian nationalists, this was an absurd notion. In their view, the Qing were Manchu outsiders, a dynasty of foreign conquerors, alien to the Han and the Mongols alike. But Ungern seems to have seen the Qing more like they saw themselves—that is, as rulers who operated at once in two registers, as "sovereigns of China" on the one hand and as "Central Asian khans" on the other. Seen in this way, they provided the necessary link that tied China to the steppe and therefore, by extension, the only legitimate basis for the return to order.[67]

The stages of Ungern's plan were fuzzy. In fact, to describe his thinking as a "plan" is perhaps to give it more coherence than it deserves since few details were worked out. In that sense, what he was proposing was closer to an idea, a balloon tethered to unfolding events. Mongolia came first in the sequence of restorations, surely at least in part because it was close by. It was also by far the easiest throne for him to restore, given the relative weakness of the Chinese republicans in the country and the size of the military force he could organize against them. He could also be reasonably sure that a wide range of Mongols would support him, since he was well aware of their veneration for the Bogda and their grievances against the Chinese and especially the Urga garrison.

As for the next stages, they are harder to make out. The letters have little to say about how Ungern imagined restoring the Qing. In fact, he seems to sidestep the issue, focusing instead on persuading his correspondents to support the overall goal and to make contacts with monarchists they know in China rather than going into detail about how exactly his idea would become a reality. It is possible he believed that all that was needed was to renew the compact between the emperor and his regional elites, the presumption being that the rest of the old imperial machinery would simply snap back into place after that. There is some evidence that he imagined a military offensive would be required. But without more material it is hard to say what he was thinking.

As for Russia, its place in his reasoning is also contradictory. On the one hand, he seems to have felt, initially at least, that the likelihood of restoring the monarchy there was farther off than in China. Much as in Europe, the sickness of revolution in Russia, as he saw it, had gone too deep. As he wrote to a Mongol correspondent in early March,

> To think right now of restoring the emperors of Europe is impossible because of the rot that has taken hold of European learning and hence of the [European] peoples themselves, who have been driven mad by socialist ideas. So, for the time being, one has to restore the Middle Kingdom (*Sredinnoe tsarstvo*) and all the peoples within it, stretching to the Caspian Sea, and only after that can one think of beginning to bring back the Russian monarchy, assuming, that is, that the [Russian] people come to their senses [about this], but if they don't, then they [i.e., the Russians] will have to be conquered.[68]

Yet by May he had changed course entirely and had begun organizing a campaign against the Reds in Siberia under the banner of restoring the monarchy—the campaign that would lead to his capture and execution. Not only did he decide to do this well before his goals in the "Middle Kingdom" were achieved, but he was also making the turn to Russia so quickly that it's hard to see how "the Russian people," given how much they'd been "corrupted" by revolution, could possibly have had the time to "come to their senses" and join the cause.

In fact, as he later told his interrogators, his decision to begin a campaign against the Reds in the spring seems to have been driven more by immediate practical concerns than by any shift in the ideological landscape. His former logistics officer at Manchuria Station described him in October 1920 as a "man of action" (*chelovek zhivogo dela*). He was impatient, dismissive of paperwork and procedure, inclined to reach decisions quickly and never look back.[69] Here this same impetuousness seems to be in play: indeed, in this instance, his monarchism and restlessness appear to work together, pulling him first one way then the next, initially toward China, then back toward the Trans-Baikal.

Indeed, Ungern's overall persona in the letters seems to fit with what we know of him so far. The image throughout is that of the dedicated servitor-aristocrat, the selfless knight committed to sacrificing himself for the sake of honor, justice, and tradition. At the same time, he also comes across (whether intentionally or not) as a paternalist and know-it-all. In one letter to a Mongol ally, for example, he advises him to put aside whatever concerns he might have that bringing back the Qing will mean, in effect, reestablishing a system that favors China. In fact, this won't happen. The Mongol peoples, the Tibetans, and others will all be autonomous, though just *how* they'll become autonomous, he doesn't quite explain. "I've done all that I can," he adds, referring to the feat of taking Urga. "Now your turn has come."[70]

The letters also brim with practical operational advice on military matters large and small as well as commentary on the international context of the moment, all information presumably unsolicited.[71] He seems to have seen himself as someone who understood things better than the people he was talking to, in particular his would-be Mongol allies. Many of the letters are dotted with the kind of patronizing asides one might expect to hear from an overbearing sibling: "Now remember," "Don't forget," "You must surely realize...."

If Ungern's self-image is predictably positive, the portrait of his enemies is understandably the opposite: they are the "supporters of evil," "followers of the black Satan," the peddlers of "the destructive Bolshevik religion" and, more generally, of "the revolutionary teachings of the West that have caused such harm to mankind."[72] From the letters, it's clear too that the real enemy in his view is not so much the individuals who spout the awful teachings or even the groups—most obviously, the Jews—who seem predisposed to them, but rather radicalism itself. The ultimate curse is the mentality of revolution, which he sees as an infection (*zaraza*) "worse than cholera and the plague" with the power to insinuate itself into any culture.[73] The fighters for the right, therefore, have to remain ever vigilant, ready to spring into action on all fronts, at any time, in every direction.

The great divide as Ungern sees it is thus not between peoples or even classes but between the revolutionaries and everyone else. In a letter to a Chinese leader, for example, he writes that it pains him to think that the Chinese might see him as an enemy. "Knowing me, of course, you must understand perfectly well that I would never seek war with the Chinese." He goes on to explain that attacking the republicans in Urga was a matter of principle. The duty of every "honest warrior" (*chestnyi voin*) is to fight against all revolutionaries "regardless of nationality," since they are "nothing more than evil spirits in human form."[74]

In the same vein, in another letter to a Mongol correspondent he stresses that, though his wife is a Manchu, this does not make him beholden to the Manchus as a group. Instead, he supports the restoration of the Qing because he is an aristocrat, and aristocrats are the "loyal servants of kings."[75] His cause is selfless and universal—a goal pursued for the world rather than for the good of a single nation or class, and certainly not for himself. Thus in another letter to the same Chinese leader mentioned above, he writes simply: "Personally, I need nothing (*Lichno mne nichego ne nado*). I will gladly die for the restoration of the monarchy, if not in my own state than in another."[76]

Yet the writings from Urga also reveal sides of Ungern that seem new, or, more likely, were already part of his character but have been invisible to us because we haven't had the sources. His anti-Semitism is one; another is his spirituality, which comes through both in the letters as well as the remembrances of people who knew him at the time, all of whom describe him as inclined to eclectic and mystical religious views. There are reports that he "converted" to Buddhism, though what seems more likely is that he combined faiths, mixing and matching the elements that spoke to him the same way numerous people did in his time, the Theosophists included, searching for satisfaction in the deep logic of religion rather than within the bounds of a single tradition.

One of the interrogation teams described his spiritual "profile" in the following terms:

> Believes in God. As a Protestant, understands God as good and evil as the opposite of God (*Kak protestant, po-svoemu schitaet Boga, kak dobro, protivo-postavliaet emu zlo*). Describes himself as a fatalist and believes strongly in destiny. Infected with mysticism and assigns great importance to [the role of] Buddhism in the fate of peoples. Sees himself as called to the struggle for justice and morality in accordance with the teachings of the Gospels.[77]

Semenov had a similar view: "By nature the baron was a great mystic....As he saw it, God was the source of pure reason and of the highest knowledge, the Beginning of all beginnings....'One must feel God in one's heart,' he would always say."[78]

We sense this mysticism especially strongly in Ungern's view of the war, which he casts as an apocalyptic contest of good against evil, "brother...against brother, son against father," godlessness against God. Yet at the same time, like a mystic seer, he senses the immanence of salvation. In a number of letters, he writes that "a light is coming from the East," explaining that what he means by this is "the restoration of the emperors," which by extension seems to mean the return of everything good and decent that has been defiled by the revolution: faith, truth, kindness, tradition.[79] "I know and believe that a light shall come from the East and bring happiness to all mankind."[80]

The Bogda's return to power is thus about much more than politics. A great moral drama is unfolding, carrying the world to a turning point. "Look at the West," he writes in the draft of a letter to Kazakh leaders:

> Look at its past full of fire and blood and the vicious, savage struggle of man against God. The West has given man science, wisdom, and power, yet it has also brought godlessness, immorality, treason, the abnegation of truth and

goodness....There, in the West, the destruction of entire empires (*tsarstva*) has begun. Whole nations are being led to their deaths.[81]

The East, by contrast, is home to peoples (in particular, the Mongols and the Chinese) who still respect the virtues of tradition, which is precisely why "the salvation of the world" will begin with them. In this sense, for all of its unavoidable ideological noise, the fight is essentially a moral struggle, a contest over beliefs and principles and the way one should live. "True success," he writes in a letter to the Mongol leader Yegüzer Khutuktu:

> shall come when we take up the ideas of truth, honor, and goodness, and act not out of petty economic or material interests or on the basis of financial calculations but rather in the name of the immutable, eternal values of the purity and sacredness of religion and the creative power of the Bogd Khan and the Manchu Khan.[82]

The imperial tide that Ungern imagined as beginning in Mongolia was thus at least two things at once: a military-political solution to the problem of imperial collapse and a spiritual crusade. It was also, at least on the face of it, curiously at odds with itself. The empires of Russia and China were gone, and it was the chaos of their unraveling that gave power to the nonstate frontier, which in turn gave power to him. Yet, as he plotted the future from his command post in Urga, his vision was to reestablish the empires, which meant, in effect, putting the genie of the frontier back in the bottle, forcing it to serve the imperial idea rather than work against it. The wide-ranging diplomatic offensive that he pursued in his letters can be read as his attempt to negotiate this complicated political reversal.

Yet looked at in another way, there was a logic to what he was proposing and even to how he was going about it. The multiethnic, multiconfessional Asiatic Division, like the Trans-Baikal Cossack Host that made up its core, was indeed a frontier institution. But, like the Host, the division was also a creation of empire, just as Ungern himself was both a frontier product and a scion of the imperial establishment. So repackaging the frontier to serve the imperial order was not in itself an implausible prospect. The need to "tame" the frontier and harness it to the interests of a higher power was the challenge that faced all the actors of the borderland, regardless of their ideological differences, from Chinese warlords like Xu, Chen, and Zhang to the Bogda and his government, the Buryat pan-Mongolists, as well as the Bolsheviks and their Red Mongol allies. This had also been Semenov's challenge as he envisioned his own mission of state reconstruction rolling forth from Chita.

Nor was Ungern's idea of restoring the Qing and, in time, the Romanovs as farfetched as it now seems in retrospect. Monarchists in eastern Russia and across the growing anti-Bolshevik emigration continued to imagine restoring the tsar.[83] In late 1920 in Western Siberia, where Ungern would soon be tried and shot, Red reports described anti-Bolshevik units fighting under the banner of "Tsar Michael," and there were other indications of pro-monarchist sympathies in the region as well.[84]

Meanwhile, in China two attempts at imperial restoration had already taken place. In late 1915, the second Great President of the Republic, the former general Yuan Shikai, concluding that being president, even Great President, was not lofty enough, declared himself emperor, creating the Hongxian dynasty (sometimes rendered in English as the dynasty of the Glorious Constitution) and replacing the republic with what he called the Empire of China (*Zhonghua diguo*).[85] Two years later another Chinese general made an attempt to restore the Qing, putting the boy emperor Puyi back on the throne. Both of these restorations were brief—the second one lasted just twelve days. But they are proof that the idea of imperial rule in China remained plausible. Even the much-discredited Qing continued to have their supporters, including some among the Mongols.[86]

Indeed, at the very time that Ungern was trying to promote the power of the Qing from his base in Urga, 700 miles away in Beijing Puyi continued to make his home in the great palace of the Forbidden City, where the leaders of the new China had allowed him to stay after the Qing abdication and even after the aborted restoration of 1917. Living alongside him were 470 eunuchs and 100 "palace ladies" whose upkeep was assured by the generous "Articles for the Favorable Treatment of the Qing House" that had been drawn up by the republican government shortly after the 1911 revolution.[87]

One of the remarkable effects of revolutions is the ability to make themselves seem inevitable. The old regime had rotted to bits and was fated to fall. The people were oppressed and had to rise. Modern revolutionaries are the master editors of time, eliminating contingency and replacing it with the rock-hard certainty of their version of progress. But when we step around what the revolutionaries are telling us and move back into the moment of revolution itself, rather than solid ground, what we usually find is confusion and unpredictability. The world might indeed be tipping into something new, but it might just as readily be about to move sidewise or slip back in the other direction.

This was Ungern's situation in Urga. The defining quality of the moment was its unsettledness. Nothing was certain. All futures were possible, including ones that replayed the past. The empires around him had unraveled, but the important point was that they had *just* unraveled. How hard, then, could it be to rewind the clock and put them back together again?

CHAPTER 10

KIAKHTA

I pray thee, this once, O God, that I may be avenged of the Philistines
for my two eyes.
—JUDGES 16:28

The Kingdom of Tea

Kiakhta sits among rolling hills in the southern part of Russia's Buryat Autonomous Republic. With its worn apartment blocks and shady streets lined with sagging log houses, it feels much like the other small towns of the region. Even the fact that the local Lenin statue happens to stand across from an old nineteenth-century church and that both the cathedral and the "genius of the revolution" seem to have gotten a fresh coat of paint in recent years is not terribly unusual, since this is the kind of ideological disconnect one finds all over Russia today. The only remarkable thing about Kiakhta is what it used to be. Just beyond the town lies the Mongolian border, and for most of the eighteenth and nineteenth centuries this unassuming place was the Russian Empire's only official gateway to China.

In late May 1921, in what turned out to be the most important decision of his life, Ungern led the Asiatic Division out of Urga to launch a campaign against the Reds in Siberia, which he began by attacking Kiakhta. The attack failed and, as a result, the division spent the next two months in the field, moving between northern Mongolia and the southern Trans-Baikal, advancing as far into Russia as the Buddhist monastery at Goose Lake on the way to Verkhneudinsk (now: Ulan-Ude), before being forced to turn back again, this time deeper into Mongolia.

In a sense, the defeat at Kiakhta marked the beginning of the end for the division since the debacle was the first sign that the Red Army force they were facing was far stronger than Ungern had expected. By August, with their prospects dimming, resentments increased and some officers decided to mutiny. General Boris Rezukhin, Ungern's second-in-command and his service mate from his days with the Trans-Baikal Host, was killed first. Then the officers made an attempt on Ungern. He managed to escape, but was captured by the Reds shortly thereafter.

Ungern began his assault on Siberia with Kiakhta because it was the obvious way into Russia from the Mongolian side. One of the country's few roads linked Urga to Kiakhta, continuing north from there to Verkhneudinsk and Lake Baikal. Still today the town is the only major crossing point for motor traffic between the two countries for hundreds of miles. There was no railroad in Ungern's time. Though the tsarist government considered building a Baikal-Urga spur to connect Mongolia to the Trans-Siberian, the line did not materialize until the 1940s, and, ironically, even then, it was laid in such a way as to bypass Kiakhta. Instead of running through the town, the line's closest stop is Naushki, a sleepy border post about 20 miles to the west.

The road and the railroad are useful ways to think about Kiakhta's story. In an age when roads were rare, the one that passed through Kiakhta brought the town trade, wealth, and importance. Then as the railway age began, the Trans-Siberian was laid farther east, pointing towards Manchuria and beyond it, to the Pacific, rather than to Mongolia, and the absence of the train left the town behind.

Even before Kiakhta was a town, however, it was a political decision. Relations between Russia and China began in the late 1600s when the two empires first ran into each other on the Amur River, with the Qing proving to be the stronger of the powers at the time (see chapter 5). Between the 1680s and 1720s, the states then signed a series of treaties that established a framework of relations that would last well into the 1800s. At the heart of the arrangement was Kiakhta-Maimaicheng, twin towns to be built opposite each other on either side of the border, Kiakhta on the Russian, Maimaicheng on the Chinese, where the two empires agreed that they would do their business.

Kiakhta was composed, in fact, of two settlements: Troitskosavsk, which was the site of the original Russian fort on the Kiakhta River, and Kiakhta proper, founded slightly later farther down the river bank and directly on the border. (Reflecting its two constituent parts, Kiakhta's name flip-flopped over the years. During the period of the revolution, it was officially known as Troitskosavsk, though everyone in the region was well aware of its two components and referred to them separately.)[1] The Chinese, meanwhile, built their settlement right across from Kiakhta proper, on their side of the border. When the explorer Johann Gmelin visited in the 1730s, he described just a short stretch of dirt road and two painted customs posts separating the towns.[2]

Though diplomats and travelers passed through Kiakhta-Maimaicheng, the most important traffic by far was trade, a fact underscored by the name the Chinese gave to their settlement: Maimaicheng means "trading town" in Chinese and was the generic term the Qing used for all their merchant colonies in Mongolia. (Hence the Maimaicheng in Urga, Kobdo, and other towns.) The Mongols called the local Maimaicheng Övör Hiagt, or South Kiakhta.

The principal Russian goods of trade were fur, then later cloth and fabric of different sorts, whereas the major Chinese export was tea, which arrived in Kiakhta by camel caravan from China proper before then being transported to Irkutsk, Moscow, and the fairs of central Russia. Given its role as a key relay point of the so-called Great Tea Road (*velikii chainyi put'*), Kiakhta became fantastically rich, a "kingdom of tea" ruled by a clutch of tea barons who larded the town with handsome stone houses and a small but vibrant cultural establishment. By the early twentieth century, even after its fortunes had started to decline, the town boasted eight schools, a library, and a branch of the Russian Geographical Society.[3]

Much as elsewhere along the Russo-Chinese border, interactions between the different communities were routine. Upon signing their contracts, Chinese and Russian merchants would host and toast each other in the Russian-based pidgin that was the town's lingua franca. (Mongols and Buryats also served as interpreters for the respective sides since they understood each other easily, while the Buryats knew Russian and the Mongols Chinese.) A number of Chinese firms had offices or stalls in Kiakhta. Qing and tsarist authorities worked together to fight fires, pursue burglars, and collect custom duties. Conversions and intermarriages between Russians and Chinese, though not the norm, were also not unheard of. Meanwhile, Chinese, Mongols, and Buryats from the surrounding countryside, many of them Cossacks, would come to Kiakhta to tour the small museum attached to the Geographical Society. (We know this thanks to the museum staff, who began keeping track of their visitors in the early 1900s.)[4]

Transborder connections continued during the period of the Russian Revolution, such that the Kiakhta Ungern would have known was a place where the business of upheaval, much like the tea trade, moved back and forth. Thus just as Ungern took his force into Mongolia, Chinese troops stationed in Maimaicheng entered Kiakhta to protect the interests of Chinese merchants during the to-and-fro of the fighting. (Kiakhta, like many other Trans-Baikal towns, changed hands between Reds and Whites several times during the conflict.)

Later, in the wake of Ungern's storming of Urga in February 1921, two-thirds of the Chinese garrison and thousands of refugees fled north to Maimaicheng along the Urga-Kiakhta road, throwing the town into panic, with much of the chaos flowing from there into Kiakhta. According to Red reports, Chinese authorities requested entry visas, arms, and supplies, as well as permission to use the telegraph to send wires to Beijing via Chita. The Chinese,

10.1. The border at Kiakhta-Maimaicheng. The view here is from the Russian side. Maimaicheng
is in the distance. Courtesy National Central Archives of Mongolia, Ulaanbaatar.

meanwhile, gave the Reds permission to deploy troops up to 15 miles inside Mongolia "in order to fight off the Whites."[5] We know that the Soviet representative in Kiakhta met at least once in Maimaicheng in February with Chen Yi, the Chinese high official who had been chased out of Urga by Ungern's attack, and there may have been other meetings as well.[6]

Shortly after reaching Maimaicheng, Chen cabled Beijing to tell the government that "White bandits" had taken Urga. He and his superiors in the capital then agreed in a series of telegrams that the best way to handle this setback was to cooperate with the "Red party" (*Hong dang*) for the time being, while insisting on respect for Chinese sovereignty (*zhuquan*) and doing what they could to check attempts by the Reds to exploit their weakness.[7] Chinese materials prove that Chen's men and the Reds were indeed in regular contact over the following months. It was from the Reds, for example, that Chen, and later Beijing, first learned that an "illegal government" had been set up in Urga by the "bandit party" (*fei dang*) (that is, by Ungern and his Mongol allies) and that "the Baron" (Chinese: *Ba long*) had become "commander in chief."[8]

At the same time, it's clear that the Reds' closest connections in Kiakhta were not with the Chinese but rather with the Mongol radicals who rejected them and wanted to replace Chinese rule with "a democratic government that unites the people."[9] Anti-Chinese radicals began to meet in secret in Urga in 1919, where some of them also made contact with Bolshevik operatives, leading to the founding of a Mongolian People's Party shortly thereafter, followed quickly by a visit to Russia for "consultations." At this point, however, the radicals were nationalists much more than communists, and consequently they cooperated not only with the Bolsheviks but also with members of the Bogda's government, drawn together by a common resentment of the Chinese and by a shared sense that the best way to check China, much as before, was through Russian assistance.

After Ungern's takeover, however, a number of the radicals, much like Chen and his Chinese soldiers, found themselves forced to flee to Kiakhta, and once on Red-controlled territory their agenda changed. Now rather than working with the Bogda's government, they used the occasion of their first party congress to announce the formation of a government of their own, while at the same time committing themselves to throwing out not only the Chinese but Ungern as well. Sükhbaatar, the young commander who would become the party's most charismatic leader, was in Kiakhta at the time, along with Choibalsan, who would later emerge in the 1930s as "Mongolia's answer to Stalin."[10] By March, the MPP confirmed their new course by attacking the Chinese in Maimaicheng and destroying the town, which they then quickly renamed Altanbulag, or Golden Spring in Mongolian. Almost simultaneously they relocated their provisional government to the new site. (The entire operation at this point consisted of three gers.) Meanwhile, at least eight thousand desperate Chinese refugees flooded into Kiakhta.[11]

That the first thing the Red Mongols did from Kiakhta was launch an attack on Maimaicheng is not surprising. Everything about the two towns was close, in distance if not in culture. The border between them had real significance in that it underscored more than anywhere the formal separation that was supposed to exist between the empires of Russia and China. Here indeed were customs houses and border guards as well as the rest of the border-making machinery that the nineteenth-century tsars and the Qing had begun to put together and that we now expect to see at international crossing points. But from the start the border at Kiakhta-Maimaicheng was meant to connect as much as to divide, and this function of connection never went away, even as Whites changed to Reds and governments rose and fell around it. As Chen wrote in one of his telegrams to Beijing, the border at Kiakhta was "just a street." There was no way to stop people from moving across it, in particular during a crisis.[12]

Thus though the Soviets would later take credit for showing the Mongolians the path to socialist revolution, and the Mongolian communists, for their part, would politely acknowledge the Russians' assistance while celebrating their own heroes, the forgotten player in the equation was the location itself.[13] Kiakhta was the logistical and political hub of the border world, a place that united as well as separated. One could imagine building things there and going farther, which is why the town became Ungern's destination as well.

"The Time Has Come to Get to Work"

The decision to launch a spring campaign seems to have been motivated by a combination of factors. For one, it was almost certainly something that Ungern had been planning to do from the start. Informants told Red agents as early as November 1920 that he intended to use Mongolia as a base for "attacking the border areas [and] seizing major points such as Kiakhta and others."[14] In February, shortly after taking Urga, he himself told a Chinese ally that: "All my efforts are directed to the north, where I shall move to break through to Russia as soon as possible."[15]

A campaign against Siberia made sense in other ways. For one, Ungern knew that he was vulnerable to attack in Urga, if not by the Reds then by the Chinese. As it turned out, only a week or so after he moved out for Kiakhta, the Chinese president issued a special decree (*Zheng Meng ling*) ordering Zhang Zuolin to lead a campaign to reclaim Mongolia for the republic. (The order also came with a lofty title for Zhang and other inducements.) The campaign never developed, however, in part because other Chinese warlords, in particular in Inner Mongolia, were wary of the effects that a rise in Zhang's power would have on their own positions, but also, it seems, because Zhang himself was not especially interested. Once the Reds entered Mongolia in June in response to Ungern's attack, Zhang used the development as an excuse to table his preparations for the campaign, informing the president that the Red intervention had resolved the "bandit problem" and the Mongolian question was now best approached as an international issue to be settled through negotiations.[16]

By the spring it had also become clear to Ungern that his supplies were running short and that relations with the Mongols were likely to worsen as a result. As he told the interrogators in Novonikolaevsk a week before the trial, his men were starting to get into trouble:

> AFANAS'EV: In your statements to the 5th Army, you indicated that you began to see signs of a breakdown in discipline (*razlozhenie*) among your troops. What signs exactly? . . .
>
> UNGERN: . . . Cases of drunkenness, robberies—just a few cases, but enough to show that [the men] had stayed put for too long.
>
> BEZHANOV: You said that you decided to launch the attack on Soviet Russia in order to raise the spirits of your troops. Why did you determine that you needed to raise their spirits?
>
> UNGERN: In general, it is always good for troops to be active. If there is work to do, then there won't be demoralization.

He added that the "refugees" serving in the division (presumably a reference to the Russian recruits he had mobilized in Urga and earlier) had little interest in fighting the Chinese. "They wanted to move against Soviet Russia, to get back to their homes" (*opiat' na svoiu storonu*).[17]

As for the political situation, in that respect, too, the timing seemed good, or at least as good as any. In a letter to his agent in Beijing sent just before the campaign, Ungern sounds confident. The work of uniting the Mongols is moving ahead. He has made contact with Kazakh leaders and expects to find additional allies among "people of influence" in Tibet and Chinese Turkestan. The "central Mongolian empire" has not materialized, and the Qing are not yet restored, but he plans to return to Mongolia after the Russian offensive to resume these great objectives.[18] In the meantime, as he later told his interrogators, his attack against the Reds would ignite a "powder keg" of popular resentment in Siberia that would carry things further. The scattered White units still operating there would come together. A great army would form.[19]

Indeed, perhaps what best explains the decision to launch the Siberian offensive is this sense of a great cause waiting to happen. Ungern lived in risk, and more risk meant greater opportunity. In a sense, he never stopped being an officer of the Great War, where the best men were the ones who went forward despite the odds. He told his interrogators that he never planned to make a stand in Urga—he didn't know how to fight from a defensive position.[20] As he wrote a week before the campaign to a khan in western Mongolia, "The Russians have done all they can in Khalkha. It's time now for them to go home—there is still much to do in the fight against the Bolsheviks. The time has come to get to work (*brat'sia za delo*)."[21]

The daughter of a former tsarist official in Urga, another Russian German, remembers how her father tried to convince Ungern to stay in Urga: "He said to him, 'Where will you go? Here you have fodder for the horses, everything, whereas out there they will destroy you (*razob'iut*).' But Ungern wouldn't listen and went all the same."[22]

This expectation of a great moment to come appears especially strongly in the most famous document of the campaign: the so-called Order No. 15, a cross between a combat order and a spiritual-political manifesto that Ungern issued on the day his troops marched out of Urga toward Siberia. The order is well-known in part because it was intended to be: Ungern had it printed for distribution to the division as well as other White forces across Mongolia and later admitted that he assumed it would be read by the "general population" as well. After his death, it was then published and cited many times over by émigré writers as well as the Bolsheviks, who seized on it to underscore his credentials as a class enemy, while exposing his anti-Semitism, apocalyptic mysticism, and ruthlessness as a commander, all of which are indeed on full display in the document.[23] As a result, the order quickly emerged as the ultimate calling card for his image as the "mad baron" and has generally been treated this way ever since.

With its blend of operational instructions and Christian prophecy, the order is undeniably strange—the kind of thing a "mad baron" might write. ("Highly unorthodox for a combat order" was the way one of the Red interrogators put it.)[24] This impression is reinforced by the language of the text, which veers from lofty and intensely emotional in some passages to "military-bureaucratic" and crudely folksy in others. Ungern later explained that two men actually wrote the order for him, one an officer on his staff and the other Ferdinand Ossendowski, a civil war refugee, science-fiction writer, geology professor, and mystic (among other things), who was likely responsible for the document's more evocative passages.[25]

Yet, for all of its eccentricity, perhaps the most striking thing about the order is how typical it is—typical of Ungern but also of the war around him. The righteous tone matches what we hear in his letters, and a number of elements echo the writings of other members of the anti-Bolshevik opposition, including the reference to Christian eschatology, which was a common motif in conservative responses to the revolution. Indeed, stripped of its anti-Semitism and biblical quotations and with the ideology turned around, the order might even pass as a document of the Reds. Certainly the extremism it represents belonged to both sides. The Bolsheviks were no less determined than the Whites to eradicate their enemies, and just as convinced in their fashion that a millenarian moment was at hand.

Indeed, if there is something distinctive about the order, it's less the extremism or the mysticism than the incompleteness. Ungern boldly declares the beginning of a great campaign to defeat the Reds and restore the monarchy but offers no practical political plan or even much of a military roadmap. He claims that everything has been well thought through, but it hasn't really. Like the restoration of the Qing, this grand undertaking seems to hang in the air. It will happen because it must. The details, apparently, will be worked out in the doing.

Order No. 15

The full title of the document is "Order Directed to Russian Units Operating on the Territory of Soviet Siberia, No. 15." The number is the first hint of something unusual: it's out of sequence. There are no orders fourteen or sixteen. Ungern reportedly chose the number fifteen because of its mystical qualities. The title is also inaccurate inasmuch as the primary audience for the order appears to have been Ungern's men in Urga and especially the other White forces in Mongolia rather than any units already operating in Siberia. In fact, it's not clear that any Whites in Siberia ever saw the document. (Ungern later admitted that he did not have contact with such forces at the time.) Given this, the order is best viewed as a declaration of faith, a wish uttered to the future rather than a practical plan of action addressing the here and now.

Several versions of the order exist in the Russian archives. The ones I've seen are copies that were prepared in Red Army or party offices for forwarding elsewhere, and, as a result, slight differences appear between them: missing words, shuffled formats. Overall, however, the basic text is consistent and reflects the original, which Ungern had printed at the press of the former tsarist consulate in Urga. The copy I cite here, from the State Archive of the Russian Federation in Moscow, runs to five densely typed pages, replete with erratic punctuation and scratched out lines. (We can almost see the clerk typing too quickly.) A brief note at the bottom of the text tells us that this particular copy was prepared by one of the offices of the Fifth Army, the Red Army force whose units tracked and then defeated Ungern in Mongolia.[26]

The document begins with a brief preamble in which Ungern introduces himself as the commander of the Asiatic Division and announces that he is writing to "all Russian units ready to fight the Reds in Russia." The text then falls into two sections followed by a conclusion, with each section organized around a succession of numbered points.

The first section lays out the basic case for the campaign, which is to restore the monarchy by bringing back "Emperor Michael," the brother of the late Tsar Nicholas, to whom Nicholas abdicated during the February Revolution but who then quickly declined the throne. Ungern doesn't discuss Michael much, presumably because he had few details to offer, but he describes him as the "legitimate master of the Russian land," implying that returning him to the throne is a lawful act and therefore the right thing to do. At the same time, the more explicit argument is that the country simply needs him to survive. The Bolsheviks have destroyed Russia, gutting the Russians' faith and goodness and wrecking everything they believe in. To save them now, they need leaders they can trust—"names . . . known, cherished, and honored by all." As the lawful tsar and father of the people, the implication here is that Michael is the only "name" possible.

Ungern then explains that the campaign to deliver Michael to the throne will unfold as a military operation led from Mongolia, where the Asiatic Division together with Mongol troops have recently restored the "rightful rule" of the Bogda and expelled the "illegitimate" Chinese "revolutionary Bolsheviks." Given that Mongolia is now a base for White forces, it is a "natural" starting point for this new effort. He goes on to claim that he is acting on Semenov's orders and that his offensive will be bolstered by a coming assault to be led by Semenov himself in the Ussuri region with possible help from the Japanese. The success of the campaign is guaranteed, he writes matter-of-factly, because "it has been drawn up on the basis of a broad and well-considered political plan."

The second section of the order lays out what White units in Siberia are to do as the campaign proceeds, with a special stress on issues of logistics and organization. Smaller units should be ready to combine with larger ones and place themselves under the authority of commanders Ungern has appointed to the various sectors of the front. Units must maintain their strength as they go forward, mobilizing men and then releasing and replacing them with new recruits as the offensive advances. All able-bodied men are to fight on the front lines, with no "shameful" hiding at the rear. Collaboration with "foreign allies" is discouraged since the foreigners "carry the same revolutionary disease" as the Bolsheviks. Unit commanders must appoint civilian officials to run the areas they "liberate" and do their utmost to get Red units to defect, while also being careful to "confiscate" supplies only from households that were not previously "requisitioned" by the Reds. (The idea being, it seems, that considerate confiscators confiscate only once.)

The order also underscores the need for absolute discipline, spelling out severe consequences for failure or insubordination. As Ungern writes in point 5 of section 2: "Given that distances are too great for me to enforce discipline (*karat'*) myself, sector and unit commanders will be responsible for eliminating all tensions and conflicts in their forces. A fish rots from the head. Let them remember that future generations will either praise or curse their names."

The most widely cited passages state this code more harshly. Point 9 notes simply that "commissars, communists, and Jews are to be eliminated (*unichtozhat'*) together with their families." The following point then explains that the fight against the Reds has to be utterly unforgiving. The horrors of the present moment were inconceivable in the past therefore the norms that applied in "former times" are irrelevant. "Today only one form of punishment is acceptable—death by varying degrees. The old ways of justice based on 'truth and mercy' have changed. Now 'truth and merciless severity' must prevail. The evil that has come to earth to destroy the divine in the soul of man must be ripped out root and branch (*dolzhno byt' vyrvano s kornem*)."

The final part of the order then resumes this cosmological theme. Peace, Ungern writes, is "heaven's greatest gift." Yet socialism, though purporting to stand for peace, in fact stands for the opposite, since "the very logic of socialism is struggle." It follows from this that the socialists are the ones to blame for the current conflict and, extrapolating further, that the conflict is in fact the fateful battle between good and evil that Christians know will mark the end of the world. As if to prove this, he cites three verses from the Book of Daniel that describe the battle, including the decisive turning point when Daniel prophesizes that "Grand Prince" Michael—that is, Archangel Michael—will appear to save his people. God will then deliver the believers, while the wicked will perish.

10.2. Banner of the Asiatic Division. Ungern's force carried this standard as they left Urga for the Russian border in May 1921. The reverse side shows the face of Christ and the inscription "God Is with Us." Reproduced from S. L. Kuz'min, *Istoriia Barona Ungerna: opyt rekonstruktsii* (Moscow, 2011), insert.

"And from the time . . . that the abomination that maketh desolate is set up, there shall pass a thousand two hundred and ninety days. Blessed is he that waiteth and cometh to the thousand three hundred and thirty days."

Given that the order appeared just as the spring campaign began, we have no information to tell us what Ungern thought about it prior to the offensive. In his statements to his interrogators after his capture, however, he takes full responsibility for the document. His only regret, he says, is that the text omitted "the most important question"—the "movement (*dvizhenie*) of the yellow race."[27] At the same time, he downplays the importance of the order overall, telling the interrogators that it was designed essentially as an internal document with two limited goals: (1) to convince the Whites in Mongolia that the coming attack was part of a wider offensive, thus making them more likely to sign on; and (2) to bolster his authority with his regional commanders. This is why he claimed to be under Semenov's command when in fact he had not been in contact with Semenov for months by this point. (At least this was what he told the interrogators.) He also claimed that he assumed the order would have little effect. As he put it elliptically in one exchange, "Fate plays the part, an order is nothing but paper."[28]

We don't know much about how Whites in Mongolia reacted to the document, except that impressions seem to have varied. Colonel Aleksandr Kaigorodov, for example, one of the commanders in the Kobdo region, apparently disregarded it.[29] Andrei Shubin, a low-ranking officer also near Kobdo, confided to his Bolshevik captors that he read the text but "couldn't figure it out" (*ne razobralsia*).[30] The division's doctor in Urga interpreted it as "the product of a diseased brain."[31] By contrast, an officer based in Uliastai recalled that when the order reached his unit, his commander seized on it as a pretext to launch a new crackdown against "socialist sympathizers," while local Russian loyalists quickly held church services to bless the return of the tsar.[32]

Ungern's troops, meanwhile, left Urga the day the order came out, May 21, 1921, filing out of town in the direction of the Kiakhta road, the riders dressed in dark-blue deels with epaulettes, each regiment with its own banner, and Ungern's convoy bearing the campaign standard: a square yellow flag emblazoned on one side with an image of the face of Christ and the words "God is with Us" and on the other with a cursive monogram of the initials "M II," standing for Michael the Second, that is, the future Emperor Michael. A band played at the front of the procession and camel-drawn cannon brought up the rear.[33]

The main fighting force that left Urga that day, divided into two commands under Ungern and Rezukhin, numbered some 3,600 men. The combined total of the smaller units based in central and western Mongolia amounted to perhaps another 1,700. Meanwhile, 150 soldiers plus additional support personnel remained behind to oversee the capital.[34]

Tied and Bound

The offensive against Red Siberia lasted three months, roughly a third of the duration of the Mongolian campaign overall. In retrospect, the operation had little chance of success. Ungern's force was too small, with poor communications and intelligence, and, as he confessed to his interrogators, he had no expectation of advancing far without local support.[35] When this support failed to materialize, his options were limited.

At the same time, the campaign did not crumble all at once. After the defeat at Kiakhta in early June, Ungern experienced a number of victories, even managing to advance to within some 40 miles of Verkhneudinsk, the capital of the DVR. In their counterattack and pursuit, the Reds faced the same challenges he did in terms of terrain and supply. After Kiakhta, most of the campaign for both sides amounted to a question of searching and hoping, either for a breakthrough or for the enemy.

Much as with the rest of the Mongolian campaign, the attack involved multiple players: White units, Red partisans, regular Red Army detachments, DVR army units, Mongols siding with Ungern, others siding against him. His arrival also became the occasion for the settling of scores between local communities in the mixed Buryat and Russian lands on the Trans-Baikal side.[36] Ironically, the most important act of the offensive had nothing to do with him: on July 6, with the Asiatic Division hundreds of miles away to the north, a Red Army and Red Mongol force ignored them entirely and entered Urga.

There was no resistance—the small force that Ungern had left in the capital fled before the Reds arrived. Shortly thereafter the newcomers established a pro-Communist government, retaining the Bogda as the nominal head of state but arresting his "reactionary" ministers.[37] As one Red Army writer put it, capturing the irony of the moment, "Ungern wanted to move against us, but the opposite occurred: we moved against him."[38]

The fighting between Ungern and the Reds was concentrated in the hills and valleys around the border zone west of Kiakhta, and the movement back and forth across the border by both sides seems all the more confirmation that the line was only what one made of it. Practically speaking, outside of Kiakhta there was no line. One knew which country one was in by the natural or human landmarks of the area: a hilltop, a village, a familiar valley of gers and horses. The maps available to both sides, based on tsarist surveys from before the Great War, showed the run of the border, but their reliability was questionable, and they added nothing to the force of the border as a boundary in any case.[39]

At the same time, the Reds and Ungern seem to have thought about the border differently, and this, in turn, reflected an important difference between them. When Ungern moved into Mongolia the preceding fall, there is no evidence that he regarded crossing the line as a meaningful act: he simply moved over it. Given the tactical military context of the frontier, which seems to have been the only context affecting him at the time, the line mattered less than the zone around it, and within the zone this sort of crossing was ordinary. The Reds, however, were operating in at least two contexts. Partisans and DVR troops on the ground treated the border much as Ungern did: if they needed to cross one way or the other to find supplies or to escape or prepare an ambush, they did so. But the Red leadership in Moscow and places like Novonikolaevsk and Irkutsk saw the border as a line of sovereignty between states, which meant that they approached it with a different set of calculations.

In fact, the Red approach to the border reflects not only the differences between the views of the central commands versus those of the frontier but also the complexity of Red foreign policy. The civil war turned Sovnarkom into a pragmatic if ruthless government, and by the summer of 1921 the commissars were already fully versed in the practical arts of state survival. They had signed treaties, including with powers they loathed, recognized foreign governments, and confirmed trade protocols. And they had redrawn their own borders on several occasions in the see-saw of the conflict, both at their own initiative, which was the case with the creation of the DVR, and under duress, such as after the war with Poland in the Treaty of Riga signed in March 1921. The very fact that the Bolsheviks had created their own state—known by 1918 as the Russian Socialist Federated Soviet Republic—was proof of a certain adjustment to the realities of international politics.[40] They had to think about respecting the borders of other states because they had borders of their own.

Yet, on the other hand, the RSFSR was not an ordinary state: it was the world's only socialist country and "the cradle of world revolution," which necessarily influenced the way the Bolsheviks viewed the border question. Indeed, the early party leadership was convinced from the moment they seized power in Petrograd that the ne plus ultra of their cause was to spread communism on a global scale with the goal of creating what would ultimately be a borderless world of international proletarian harmony. As a result, they viewed the existing state order with disgust and were committed to overthrowing it.

The clearest proof of this was the Third Communist International, or Comintern, an umbrella for the communist parties of the world that was founded in Moscow in 1919 to take on the nitty-gritty work of world revolution. Soon calls went out for the establishment of a world federation of Soviet republics, and fiery exhortations envisioned a "civil war around the world . . . under the banner of Soviet power."[41] Borders were going to figure in the story but only insofar as they served the needs of the "toiling masses." The rule of "capital" was finished. As the Comintern leader Grigorii Zinov'ev remarked at a gathering of radicals from the colonial world in Baku in 1920, "The tinkle of the chairman's bell on this platform is the funeral knell for the world bourgeoisie."[42]

All of this naturally created complications for Bolshevik policy in places like Mongolia. Should the Soviets send in troops to pursue Ungern or simply arm the Mongolian party and wait things out? Should they support Mongolian independence or merely autonomy within China, with special protections provided by Moscow? (This scenario envisioned, in effect, a return to the terms of the Kiakhta Treaty, though in a Soviet framework.) Was world revolution better advanced by favoring the Mongols or the Chinese, by respecting borders or by rearranging them? Or was it possible to somehow do all of this at the same time?

By February, with Ungern having taken Urga, these questions returned to the fore with new intensity, and the Soviet leadership ultimately settled on trying to have their cake and eat it too by waiting for the right moment when they would be able to intervene in the country by invitation, thus helping the Red Mongols while at the same time justifying themselves to Beijing. Party and state officials in the border area were told not to cross the border for the time being, and to be appropriately accommodating to the panicked Chinese authorities who were now in Kiakhta-Maimaicheng. In the meantime, arms and instructors were provided to the Mongol revolutionaries who already had received permission to move back and forth across the border, and the Red Army was instructed to set up a special mounted partisan force that was expected in time to move across the border as well.[43] Meanwhile, the foreign minister of the DVR informed the Chinese government that if they didn't do something about Ungern, the DVR and Russian Federation would take steps on their own.

Some Soviet sources suggest that the Reds would have attacked Ungern in the spring even without his assault on Kiakhta, though the assault had the unintended effect of making the politics of the situation all the easier. The DVR government was instructed to immediately request the assistance of the Red Army, since Kiakhta was on DVR territory. The Mongolian Provisional Government in Altanbulag (formerly Maimaicheng) quickly followed suit by inviting the Red Army to enter Mongolia. Boris Shumiatskii, the leading Comintern official on the border, wrote at the end of August from Irkutsk when everything was done that the Soviet plan from the start (which he took credit for as his own idea) had been to "draw the enemy to our borders." Ungern had hoped to lure the Soviets into Mongolia to confront him at Urga, but they had wisely resisted this temptation and instead "prepared the Red Mongols," so that when he came up to the border he would find himself trapped, caught between the Red Army in front of him and the Red Mongols behind.[44]

Documents from the moment of the campaign itself, however, show a far messier picture, full of errors, difficulty, and confusion, on the Reds' side as well as Ungern's. After the failure at Kiakhta, Ungern moved west into the valley of the Selenga River on the Mongolian side, and from there crossed the border to try to move up toward Verkhneudinsk. Skirmishes and battles followed. According to Red reports and some memoir accounts, Ungern destroyed a number of Buryat and Russian settlements and executed villagers suspected of supporting the Red side. The harsh discipline toward his subordinates that had long been a part of his military style continued with regular beatings and occasional executions, of officers as well as men. The Red senior command, meanwhile, was divided by its own disagreements, and confusion in the field led to at least one case of Red partisans battling a Red Army unit for hours before finding out they were fighting their own side.[45]

The hilly and in parts swampy terrain made reconnaissance and supply difficult for both sides. Ungern's ability to coordinate his operations was hampered by the fact that he had to rely solely on riders to deliver messages between his detachments and had no overall picture of Red movements. The Reds, meanwhile, could communicate through their HQ, while also using biplanes, which the Whites apparently saw frequently and mistook, at first at least, for Japanese machines, leading to wild presumptions that the imperial army had already made its way to the Trans-Baikal and perhaps even to Chita. (In fact, there were no Japanese units were anywhere near the region at this point.)

Not surprisingly, both sides also made use of what we would now call psychological warfare, sending or dropping leaflets to urge defections. One of Ungern's sheets read: "Soldiers of the Red Army! Aren't you ashamed to be fighting against truth, justice, and order? Where are the commissar hooligans leading you, those hired-hands (*naimiti*) of the Yids? They promised you bread and peace but all you've gotten is war and hunger! Come to your senses and cross over to fight with us before it's too late. With us are God and Baron Ungern!"[46]

Meanwhile, the Reds responded in kind, playing up their own nationalist argument: "To all the Russian soldiers and officers serving under Baron Ungern,...Ungern is one of the blackest of the generals of the old tsarist army...and a hireling of Japan.... He is holding you, Russian soldiers, our countrymen by spirit and blood, in thrall, under the illusion that he can break the ironclad Red Army of the Soviet Republic.... In the name of the working people, we say to you, honest Russian soldiers, born and raised on Russian soil: reflect on your situation, look at your past, return to your native Russia where a happy welcome awaits you as well as forgiveness for all that you have done against your brothers and fathers." The leaflet went on to promise that anyone who defected voluntarily would enjoy "the full rights of a citizen of the RSFSR," while the rest would have to contend with "the fearsome might of the people's fury."[47]

It's impossible to know the effect of these attempts at persuasion. All we can say for certain is that resentments grew among Ungern's officers. When Ungern realized that he could not count on a large uprising in the Trans-Baikal and that the Red force he was facing was stronger and better disciplined than he expected, he chose to turn back to Mongolia. The about-face would have been clear proof to the men that the campaign had failed. He told his interrogators that his plan then changed to moving his force westward to the Tuva/Uriankhai region, where he could expect to link up with other White forces and continue the fight. A number of his officers, however, wanted to go in the opposite direction, to Manchuria and the Russian Far East, back to their homes or at least to places they knew. Presumably their confidence in Ungern's leadership had also eroded, given the setbacks and his various abuses over the preceding months. They coordinated a plan to split off and lead the men to the east.

First they approached Rezukhin, but he apparently refused to go along with the mutiny, so they killed him and continued their preparations to split off and move out. Then two days later, learning that Ungern was expecting to meet with Rezukhin soon and that the murder was likely to be found out, they decided to seize the moment and eliminate Ungern as well. A party made a nighttime ride to his camp, where they fired and threw grenades into what they thought

10.3. Khatanbaatar Magsarjav in a Red Army cap, early 1920s. One of
the heroes of the siege of Kobdo, Magsarjav initially sided with
Ungern before later switching to the Reds. Ungern's captor,
Bishrelt Gün Sündüi, explained that he decided to turn
against the baron because of Magsarjav's example.
From a postcard in the author's collection.

was his tent. As it turned out, however, the tent belonged to his orderlies; his
own was nearby. According to what Ungern later told his interrogators, when
the firing started, he assumed it was a Red raid. It wasn't until he raced out of
his tent and ran straight into a machine gun that he realized what was going on.
He had had no inkling of a mutiny before the attack began.

Events then raced forward. Ungern managed to escape on his horse, hiding in the woods in the dark. By morning, he found his way to his Mongol
company, which he saw as his most loyal unit, and together they began heading west. But then, suddenly, after riding with them for just a few miles, the
Mongols jumped him and tied him up. The Mongol commander of the group,

Bishrelt Gün Sündüi, later became a local folk hero because of his exploits. In the account he provided to Mongolian officials, he explained that he decided to capture Ungern because he had heard the Mongol Provisional Government's call for Mongol patriots to rise up "to liberate our [country] from the oppression of foreigners," and he knew that the great commander Khatanbaatar Magjarsav, once an ally of Ungern's and a member of the Bogda's government, had already switched sides. In his telling, he, Sündüi, tricked Ungern by asking him for a light as they were riding. Then, as the Baron looked away and began searching for a match, he tackled him off his horse. A short time later he found a Red detachment and handed his captive over as a trophy.[48]

The version of events provided by the Red Partisan commander Petr Shchetinkin is different, though it seems more credible as Shchetinkin had no reason to alter the particulars of Ungern's capture and was otherwise quite frank in admitting the difficulties and mistakes of the Reds' campaign. Sündüi, by contrast, had every motivation to embellish the circumstances in retrospect since he had fought for Ungern and needed to make up for this by proving his bona fides to the communist authorities.[49]

According to Shchetinkin's account, his partisan unit happened to be operating not far from Ungern's forces when they captured a White officer who told them about the mutiny just two nights earlier.

> Interrogating the prisoner to obtain Ungern's exact location, I then directed my unit to Ungern's camp intending to take advantage of the disarray among his men and capture him. On the way there, twelve Mongol bandits were apprehended, though they were unable to provide additional information. Continuing on, we captured another noncom, a Buryat, who told us that Ungern was tied up and was being taken by his Mongol company to Rezukhin's headquarters. At that time, a party of seventeen men that I had sent ahead came across a group of about thirty men with horses who were standing around and seemed preoccupied with something. The squad charged the group and quickly surrounded and disarmed them.
>
> Among the prisoners was Baron Ungern. As our scouts were charging at the group, still tied and bound, [Ungern] called out: "The Reds are coming! Spread out!" The Mongols became confused and paralyzed with surprise, which allowed them all to be taken without casualties. At this moment, I arrived with the rest of the unit. Briefly interrogating Ungern, I dispatched an escort of twenty men to transport him and the rest of the prisoners to the 104th Brigade HQ. I instructed the men to shoot Ungern if the bandits made any attempt to free him.[50]

This was the morning of August 20, 1921, in what is today the eastern end of Khövsgöl province in north-central Mongolia.[51] The area around is a beautiful rolling carpet of low, wooded hills interspersed with stretches of prairie. The landscape has surely changed since Ungern and the partisans were here because nothing stays the same, but it can't have changed very much. Ulaanbaatar is a long day's drive away, Kiakhta perhaps slightly longer because the route is less direct. The Russian border lies about 50 miles to the north, just beyond the horizon.

CHAPTER 11

RED SIBERIA

You can't make soup out of promises.
—FRANCIS SPUFFORD. *Red Plenty*

The Siberian Chicago

Ungern would have known from the moment he was captured that he was going to be shot. He later admitted to his interrogators that he tried to take his life on two occasions, first, as soon as he saw the Reds, by reaching for the poison he always kept in the lining of his deel, but it had fallen out of the garment, then later on the way to Kiakhta by trying to hang himself with a pair of horses' reins. (They were too thick.) Suicide was a gruesome practice of the civil war on both sides, in particular among officers, since it was simply assumed that they would be executed and probably tortured beforehand, which Ungern knew well enough because he had ordered such things himself.[1]

The story from here to the end follows a predictable sequence: the interrogations, then the trial and the execution. Compared with the rest of Ungern's life, even the well-documented period of the Mongolian campaign, this last month is the easiest of all for us to reconstruct. He was under constant scrutiny during this period, his location recorded, on some days, to the minute. In the interrogation transcripts and the trial, we hear him speaking directly, in what seems a natural, unfiltered way. But of course, the irony is that this is surely the least natural time to observe him. Everything now is scripted, he playing his part as prisoner, his captors playing theirs. And the sources are from the Reds' side, which means that we see only what they were inclined to record. Though candid and revealing, the materials have their own worldview, and some things simply don't appear.

The very last part of the story, the execution, for one, is not recorded, or at least the records are not available. The Russian FSB in Moscow and Novosibirsk claim that their archives have no files on the matter, which is possible, though it is also possible that they are not interested in showing them to historians. We know the execution occurred—the party leadership in Novonikolaevsk confirmed it in a telegram sent to Moscow the day after the trial.[2] But we have no documents to tell us where or when exactly the event took place, or how, though there are a number of stories, including that Ungern bit into his St. Georges' Cross before he was shot in order to keep it from the Bolsheviks.[3]

Most executions in Novonikolaevsk took place at night on the outskirts of town or in the basement of the provincial Cheka headquarters. The bodies were then either burned or buried in unmarked graves. Some were thrown in the river. By this time, it was common to "finish" victims with a single shot to the back of the head, though machine guns or firing squads were occasionally used. A special unit within the Cheka office conducted the executions.[4] When Ungern arrived in Novonikolaevsk at 1 o'clock in the morning on September 7, he was handed into the custody of Ivan Pavlunovskii, the chief of the Novonikolaevsk Cheka. Pavlunovskii was almost certainly involved in the execution.[5] It is possible that members of the revolutionary tribunal were there as well, since this, too, was not unprecedented. In a pamphlet published shortly after the event, Ungern's prosecutor Emelian Iaroslavskii states matter-of-factly that the execution took place in Novonikolaevsk on the day of the trial.[6] Was Iaroslavskii there? It is hard to say, as the execution is not mentioned in his papers.[7]

Perhaps the most interesting thing *not* in the materials, however, is what Ungern thought of what he was seeing around him. During the twenty-five days between his capture and the execution, he undertook the last great journey of his life, a transit of some 1,500 miles across the middle of Siberia. First Shchetinkin's men transported him out of Mongolia to the brigade HQ at Torei, a small village on the Russian side of the border in what is today the south-central part of the Buryat Republic. From there he was moved by cart down the valley of the Dzhida River to Kiakhta, from Kiakhta north by boat along the Selenga to Verkhneudinsk, and from there farther north and west by train, first to Irkutsk and then from Irkutsk to Novonikolaevsk.

We know that he was closely guarded along the way, including during visits to the restroom.[8] He would have spent much of the journey locked up or otherwise shut away in rooms with his interrogators. Yet he must have been able to see at least something of the country around him. At Verkhneudinsk we know that his boat delivered him to the main pier, while the Reds in Irkutsk apparently showed him around town in a motor car.[9]

11.1. Ob Railway Bridge under construction, 1890s. This massive bridge became the raison d'être for Novonikolaevsk (now Novosibirsk), which quickly mushroomed into one of the great railway boomtowns of the empire. Reproduced from Vladimir Grinevich and Iurii Mandrikian (comps.), *Novo-Nikolaevsk 1893–1926* (Novosibirsk, 2006), no page number indicated.

He had been to every town he was moving through before, at least in passing, even Novonikolaevsk, since it was a major relay point on the Trans-Siberian. Would the country have seemed any different to him now? Did it feel strange to be moving so deeply into Russia? His interrogators described him as being drawn to "Eastern culture in every respect, including the food." When they asked him at one point whether he remembered if an event in Mongolia had occurred in February or earlier, he answered that it was hard for him to say since his practice at the time had been to count months according to the lunar calendar, like the Chinese and Mongolians.[10] Yet now, with every mile toward Novonikolaevsk, the world of the lunar calendar was slipping away.

The Bolsheviks seized power in Petrograd and much of central Russia in the late fall/early winter of 1917 and, though the degree of their control shifted over time, they ruled the center for the full duration of the war. In most of the rest of the country, however, their authority waxed and waned before finally prevailing, creating different timelines of power in different places. In Siberia the "Red surge" ran from west to east, with western towns coming under communist control sooner, eastern ones later. Ungern's journey from east to west was thus taking him not only against the grain of the Bolshevik advance but also deeper into the revolution, from the Trans-Baikal where the Reds' power was relatively new, to Novonikolaevsk, where they had been in control since late 1919.

Novonikolaevsk, Ungern's last stop, was indeed, in some respects, the center of the Siberian revolution. Sitting on the southern course of the Ob River roughly halfway between Moscow and the Pacific Ocean and just north of the rich uplands of the Altay, it was both the largest city on the Trans-Siberian and Siberia's unofficial capital, home to the two overlapping institutions that the Bolsheviks used to govern the region: the Siberian Bureau (Sibbiuro), the chief party organ, and the Siberian Revolutionary Committee (Sibrevkom), the chief government body, both of which had recently relocated from Omsk.[11] In the late tsarist era, the city had been a railroad boomtown, a bustling "Siberian Chicago" that seemed to embody all the energy and promise of tsarist modernization. In 1921 it was imagined as the heart of a new "Red Siberia."

The challenge of this prospect was enormous, however, because of the effects of the war. Between 1918 and 1919 the city changed hands twice, first as the Whites pushed out the Bolsheviks, then as the Bolsheviks forced out the Whites. During the White period, Red partisans fought a back-country war that was met by mass White reprisals. When the Reds took over, they faced a more diverse range of partisan opponents and responded with even more violence. The impact on the city was catastrophic. Between 1914 and 1921, starting with the mobilization for the Great War and then following with everything else, at least a third of the population either died or left.[12] The nadir was the winter of 1919/20 when the Red Army drove out Kolchak's forces in the midst of a typhus outbreak that killed thousands, if not tens of thousands, of people. The newly arrived Red authorities organized burial teams to stack frozen bodies in mass graves. Everything in the city closed. "This is not an epidemic, it is an extinction," wrote one official.[13]

By the time Ungern reached Novonikolaevsk the worst of the war in the surrounding region was over. The fall of 1921 was a tipping point of sorts. The Reds had eliminated the partisan movement in most of Western Siberia with brute force earlier in the year, and the civil war as a whole was ending. The last of a number of peasant uprisings in central Russia had been crushed. A peace treaty had been signed with Poland. All the White armies in European Russia had been driven out. The Red Army had begun to demobilize. With the exception of the Japanese in the Far East, the allies had withdrawn their forces and left the country.

The greatest proof of the turn in the war was the Bolsheviks' decision in March 1921 to announce a change in course, what they called the New Economic Policy (NEP). An armed uprising at the naval base of Kronstadt near Petrograd that month had convinced the leadership that if they didn't abandon the most extreme economic practices of "war communism" they risked losing important constituencies, like Red soldiers and sailors. They thus declared an end to requisitioning and lifted the ban on private trade. Some of the country's old capitalist ways were allowed to resume. In 1920 Trotsky candidly admitted that "we robbed all of Russia to defeat the Whites." The turn to the NEP in early 1921 was, in effect, the party's recognition that the plundering had to stop, at least temporarily. Lenin called it a "strategic retreat."[14]

The result of this shift was a complicated situation. The Bolsheviks remained committed to the vision of a new society based on the "expropriation of the expropriators," the rule of the working class, and the immanence of world revolution, yet, at the same time, they also allowed aspects of old capitalist society to reappear—in particular, money, markets, and floating prices, as well as so-called bourgeois specialists and former people (that is, people of former privilege), who were now sought out for their expertise and capital. The Red revolution was thus turning ever so slightly pink, still pointed down the road to socialism but in a semi-capitalist car.

The many contradictions of this situation were visible in Novonikolaevsk. On the one hand, the revolution remained as righteous and rigid as ever. Streets continued to be renamed "in the spirit of the times." Workers' and Red Army clubs held lectures and food drives. "Voluntary Saturdays" (*subbotniki*) were organized to exhort citizens to clean up the town and unload railway cars. The party faithful were reminded to "remain vigilant" because "capital is still alive" and enemies were everywhere, including among the communists themselves: "Saboteurs and counter-revolutionaries have no place in Soviet organizations. They must be ripped out like bad teeth." Meanwhile, the new Bolshevik idiom of unpronounceable acronyms continued stamping itself mercilessly onto the city. Sibbiuro and Sibrevkom occupied the commanding heights, but there were many others: Sibdal'torg, Rezinotrest, Neftesindikat, Sibmedtorg.[15]

And yet, all one had to do was look around to see the many aspects of the new order that didn't add up, all the hypocrisies and shortcomings. In the old days there had been bourgeois "exploiters," now there were "NEP men" doing the same thing, flaunting the "easy money" they were making from the return of the market. "Equality between the sexes," while much proclaimed, was barely visible "in the way we actually live." Only two thousand apartments in a city of some seventy thousand people had indoor plumbing and electricity. Thousands of residents in the city proper were living in dugouts or basements. There were still burned-out buildings and ruined railway cars, scores of homeless orphans, refugees from a disastrous famine on the Volga, crime.[16] If Novonikolaevsk was the capital of the new Siberia, and the capital looked like this, what of the rest of it?

A pamphlet published in the city the following year on the occasion of the fifth anniversary of the October Revolution captured some of the unsettledness of the moment: "So as you see, the current state of affairs is rather mixed up and complicated. What is Soviet Russia? What is Soviet power? What lies ahead?"[17]

"The Trial Will Have Great Political Significance"

As soon as Ungern reached Kiakhta, Boris Shumiatskii, the highest-ranking Comintern official on the Mongolian border, a member of the 5th Army's Revolutionary Military Council and a member of the Sibbiuro, sent a wire to

Moscow confirming his capture. Another telegraph followed a few days later from Ivan Smirnov, the head of Sibrevkom, informing Lenin and Trotsky that Ungern was being escorted under heavy guard to Novonikolaevsk, where he was to be tried for treason, and requesting their view of the situation. "The trial," Smirnov added, "will have great political significance."[18] The Politburo wrote back on August 29, passing on Lenin's instructions: "Devote special attention to this matter. Determine the reliability (*solidnost'*) of the charges and, if they are reliable, of which there seems little doubt, hold a public trial, conduct it with maximum speed, and shoot him."[19]

Lenin's instructions are a reminder that there were, in fact, two realities in Bolshevik Russia in the fall of 1921. One was everyday life in places like postwar Novonikolaevsk, with all of its ambiguity and contradiction. The other was the marble-smooth world of party ideology. The two realities affected each other, but they were also distinct. The social reality of the revolution was determined by the messiness of history and experience. The party's ideological reality, by contrast, was rooted in absolutes. The world might *seem* ambiguous, but this was an illusion. Ungern was going to be executed by people who, like him, knew how to look beyond the mirage to see the deeper essence of things.

As Lenin suggested, the trial was not about guilt or innocence. That could be determined by checking the "reliability" of the charges. Instead, the trial was a political event, which was the only reason to make it public. Moving quickly was also important, presumably because there was no need to keep someone like Ungern around for long. Even the use of the verb "to shoot" is revealing. Shooting was efficient. It fit with the need to move quickly. The word was also a common term of the Bolshevik wartime lexicon, reflecting their view that the struggle underway was a fight to the death and that reformism was a mirage.[20] The more we shoot, the logic went, the fewer will remain to sabotage the revolution. "Enemies of the people" do not change their spots. They have to be eliminated.[21]

Perhaps the most revealing point of this exchange of telegraphs, however, is that both the leadership in Siberia and in Moscow assumed that a trial was necessary and that it would work in their favor. The political trials that the Bolsheviks had conducted right after they took power produced lighter verdicts than many had expected, in large part, party leaders concluded, because the proceedings had been poorly prepared. On other occasions, they decided against holding trials altogether, most obviously when they ordered the summary execution of Tsar Nicholas and his family in Ekaterinburg in the summer of 1918 and Kolchak in the winter of 1920.[22] Though few people knew it at the time, including Ungern, Grand Prince Michael had been murdered without a trial in 1918 as well.[23]

The Bolsheviks knew from their own experience in the revolutionary underground that high-profile trials could be problematic: one had to worry about defendants speaking out, judges reaching their own conclusions, the audience. In this case, the presumption seems to have been that Ungern was a low-risk affair. There was little popular affection for the "Semenovites," especially in Western Siberia, and therefore little chance of things backfiring. Compared with the earliest political trials, things were better organized now, with less left to chance. The best proof of this was that Siberian authorities had held a far more complicated trial of high-ranking former Kolchak officials to great effect (as they saw it) the previous year in Omsk.[24] Finally, the leadership in Novonikolaevsk, if not Moscow, already knew that Ungern was cooperating with his interrogators, so one could assume that he, too, would play his role. His case was thus a good one all around for what Lenin called a "model trial" (*obratsovyi protsess*): a proceeding meant to deliver swift and severe "proletarian justice," while educating "the masses" at the same time.[25]

This idea of impacting "the masses" was perhaps the most important thing. At one point, the Politburo proposed moving the affair to Moscow, but Sibbiuro succeeded in convincing them to keep it in Novonikolaevsk, arguing that "the struggle against Ungern" had unfolded in Siberia and that therefore keeping the trial in the region would have "more effect on society" than it would in the capital. (They added that people in Moscow knew about Ungern only from the papers.)[26] The journey to Novonikolaevsk thus became an interval of preparation: the interrogators would complete their questioning of Ungern along the way to confirm the charges, while Sibbiuro would use the time to make arrangements for the final drama.

In all, we have records relating to six interrogation sessions held in three locations—Kiakhta-Troitskosavsk, Irkutsk, and Novonikolaevsk—each conducted by a different team.[27] Two of the interrogations were recorded verbatim, the others summarized. The questions range from detailed queries on military tactics and supply to general points about Ungern's network of contacts and his political and religious views. The interrogators refer periodically to the letters as well as Order No. 15. In Irkutsk they took photographs, including the one that would become the most reproduced, of him seated in his deel and Mongolian boots, his cap on his lap, staring calmly into the camera.

Ungern spoke candidly about his actions and plans, objecting to only a few particulars in the interrogators' rendition of events, so the two sessions for which we have verbatim transcripts feel more like interviews than inquisitions. The impression one gets from the exchanges is that Ungern saw most of what he was describing as self-evident: the harsh nature of the war, his interpretation of God, the Jews, the Mongols, politics. Meanwhile, the Red interrogators seem to have seen him as cooperative but strangely detached, unaffected by the violence he talked about, fatalistic, mystical. At a minimum these are the general traits they emphasize in their summaries. The interrogation materials were then forwarded to Novonikolaevsk along with Ungern himself.[28]

The organization of the trial reflected the same sort of practical efficiency. Sibbiuro met in closed session on September 6 to appoint a five-man revolutionary tribunal to preside over the event.[29] Revolutionary tribunals were the early Soviet state's equivalent of political courts. They multiplied rapidly and chaotically over the civil war years, spreading throughout the levels of government and the army and charged with handling every variety of antistate crime—from profiteering, sabotage, and embezzlement to open revolt against the government. In the process, they became the most visible public face of the Red Terror, processing hundreds of cases and thousands of death sentences in Western Siberia alone.[30] They worked closely with the Cheka and the police (*militsiia*). In fact, tribunals often included men with Cheka connections.

Four of the five members of Ungern's tribunal were party officials. The fifth was a railway worker selected as a "worker representative," though, in this case, he was also a party member. V. E. Oparin, the tribunal chairman, was a key figure in the tribunal apparatus in Western Siberia with a background as a military political officer, which was also typical of tribunal cadres.[31] Soviet law permitted tribunals to determine their own procedures for a given case. At the meeting on September 6, Sibbiuro appointed a defender for Ungern and Iaroslavskii as the prosecutor. (Iaroslavskii was himself a Sibbiuro member.) A team was also appointed to draw up "a plan" for the trial, which was then approved a few days later. (The plan itself is not in the Sibbiuro files, however.)[32] Meanwhile, Ungern's capture and relay to Novonikolaevsk continued to be talked up in the press and on propaganda boats, all of it also encouraged by the Siberian party leadership.[33]

In a fitting choice for a show trial, the venue chosen for the event was the Pine Tree Theater *(Teatr "Sosnovka")*, located in a park by the same name close to the Ob. The theater no longer exists, having been torn down some years ago, the park around it paved over to make way for a factory complex. But in its time it was a long, rectangular, wooden building, a typical summer theater, the kind found in public gardens around the empire and Europe in the fin de siècle, and it was probably picked for the trial because of its size. On the day of the event, September 15, a Thursday, a large crowd of "thousands of workers and Red Army soldiers" crammed into the stuffy, poorly lit hall. Tickets were apparently given out in advance to the army as well as party and government offices. Perhaps to help prepare for the event, Sibbiuro let its staff off early the day before.[34]

We don't have a good description of how the stage was arranged, but we know that the members of the tribunal sat behind a table covered in red felt, and that both they and Iaroslavskii wore standard revolutionary dress: plain tunics, leather jackets, knee-high boots, Red Army overcoats. (It's not clear what the public defender was wearing, but he is described as "former jury court attorney Bogoliubov," so he may have come to the event in more appropriately bourgeois attire.) Photos show clutter next to the stage, including what looks like a panel mimicking a sign that used to hang outside one of Semenov's train-car offices on the Trans-Siberian: "No report, no entry." (*Bez doklada ne vkhodit'*). Ungern. meanwhile, appeared in his deel, along with his cap, epaulettes, and St. George's Cross. The trial began at noon and ended at 5:20 pm with the reading of the verdict.[35]

The Revolutionary Classroom

Since Ungern was going to be shot anyway, the point of the trial was to set up the execution in the right way—that is, to put it in the necessary ideological context while at the same time keeping people interested, since the event was also a spectacle. The single most important thing was to underscore the clear divide between the accusers and the accused, which meant exposing Ungern's personal crimes but also their larger meaning. Ungern stood for a way of life that was antidemocratic, reactionary, corrupt, exploitative, deceitful, delusional, murderous, and disloyal. The Soviet order, naturally, was the opposite. Outside the Pine Tree Theater, Novonikolaevsk was a busy and disorganized place in the midst of a still unsettled revolution, but the court was a zone of clarity.

Our only view of the trial comes from *Soviet Siberia* (*Sovetskaia Sibir'*), the official newspaper of Sibrevkom, which printed redacted transcripts of the proceedings as well as a descriptive commentary in the days after the event. We cannot be sure that the trial followed Sibbiuro's plan, since we don't know it, and the newspaper could easily have smoothed over rough edges and added embellishments. But the content is at least consistent with the interrogations, which makes the material credible. More than anything, though, the transcripts give us a view of what the organizers *wanted* the trial to look like, which is itself revealing, both for what they include and what they leave out.[36]

The proceedings began with the appropriate solemnity, the audience rising to stand as the members of the tribunal took their seats on the stage. Once Ungern was brought out, Chairman Oparin asked him to state his party and rank. The chairman then read the indictment that had been drawn up by Pavlunovskii, the Cheka chief, concluding with the three charges that were the basis for the trial:

1. Aiding and abetting the expansionist plans of Japan by attempting to create a Central Asiatic state and seeking to overthrow the DVR in the Trans-Baikal.
2. Seeking to overthrow Soviet power in Russia, and Siberia in particular, with the intention of restoring the monarchy by placing Mikhail Romanov on the throne.

3. Committing mass atrocities and torture (*zverskie massovye ubiistva i pytki*) against: (a) peasants and workers, (b) communists, (c) state workers (*sovetskie rabotniki*), (d) Jews, who were slaughtered to a person (*vyrezalis' pogolovno*), (e) children, and (f) Chinese revolutionaries, etc.[37]

Ungern pled guilty to all three counts, with the exception of the association with Japan, and the trial then followed a straightforward course of questions, answers, brief recesses, and final statements. No witnesses were called, presumably because the plan excluded them, though witness testimony was read out loud to the court in one instance. At one point in the proceedings, Defense Counsel Bogoliubov requested that the judges submit Ungern to a mental examination in order to consider a possible insanity plea, but this motion was denied and Ungern himself rejected the idea. He also declined to make a final statement.

The key figure in the trial, arguably more important that Ungern himself, was the prosecutor, Iaroslavskii. The prosecutors' primary role in all the show trials of the era was "to hurl the truth" at the accused, while at the same time educating the audience about the deeper meaning of the crimes at hand.[38] As a result, they tended to hold the floor in the proceedings, with the best of them managing to be at once grandiloquent and sneering toward their prey. Judging from the performance reflected in the transcripts, Iaroslavskii had a special talent for this work, and the party seems to have appreciated his skills, since he went on to become one of the master ideologues of the regime, leading the charge in the state's antireligious campaigns of the 1920s and 1930s. His ashes today still lie in the hallowed precinct of the Kremlin Wall in Moscow, tucked between two lesser-known communists not far from Lenin's tomb.[39]

Iaroslavskii was, in effect, the teacher in this particular revolutionary classroom, so he sculpted the lesson. He did this in part with his questioning, which moved through each of the charges, going over the violence of the Mongolian campaign as well as Ungern's political plans and his links with other Whites, the Bogda, Zhang Zuolin, and his (supposed) collaboration with the Japanese. One example is the following exchange:

PROSECUTOR: When you occupied Urga, were there murders and robberies?

UNGERN: Yes, first troops fought against troops, but then the Mongol residents began fighting with the Chinese.

PROSECUTOR: Did you issue an order to stop searches that were not approved against everyone except Jews? What did you mean by this? Did you want to destroy all Jews?

UNGERN: Yes, I declared the Jews as outside the law.

11.2. Iaroslavskii and the Revolutionary Tribunal. Note Iaroslavskii's plain revolutionary garb and the carafe of water on his table, presumably placed there because he was going to be speaking a lot. The members of the tribunal sit in the foreground. Though we can't see him, Ungern would have been just off camera to the left, directly across from Iaroslavskii. Courtesy State Central Museum of Contemporary History, Moscow.

PROSECUTOR: Who ordered the workers of Tsentrosoiuz to be killed?

UNGERN: I did.

PROSECUTOR: Why?

UNGERN: Because they worked for the Soviet government.[40]

The lesson's full meaning crystallized in the final statement, however, where Iaroslavskii used Ungern to offer a sweeping indictment of what Russia had been and what it would still be, if it weren't for the Bolsheviks.[41]

The Russia of yesterday, as Iaroslavskii put it, was a "country of nobles" where barons and dukes ruled the land. They were able to order people about and beat them as they pleased, while fawning over the tsars and reaping all the benefits, hiring themselves out as required. But then the revolution came and took away their ill-gotten gains and privileges and gave the land back to the "peasant masses," and the nobles couldn't stand this, so they rose up against Soviet power.

The lords started the Great War and every other war, so they gladly stepped into the fight with the revolutionaries. Like all religious people, they had no qualms using God to justify their crimes or to embrace the vilest sort of anti-Semitism, not only because it was convenient to blame the Jews for the revolution but also because they—the aristocrats—cynically wanted to use "national hatred" to try to control "the people." Finally, they were happy to sell their services to "foreign interventionists" and anyone else, since their blood had long since "mixed with the blood of the money bag" and, in the case of nobles like Ungern at least, it's unclear how Russian they were to begin with. As Iaroslavskii put it, "We know very well that there has never been a greater species of exploiters than the Baltic barons. They are parasites who literally latched themselves to the body of Russia and then sucked on [it] for centuries."

The central point of Iaroslavskii's indictment was thus that Ungern's crime was at bottom a crime of origins. He was not mentally unsound but rather the ultimate representative of his class, doing the things that people like him could not help but do. If Ungern were able to design the future, he would impose a "military dictatorship," restore the Romanovs, strip the peasants of their land, and deny "the people" any say in government. The tribunal had to deliver the death penalty because this could not be allowed to happen. The nobility had "outlived itself." Ungern had to be executed so that "all the barons, wherever they might be, will know that they too one day will meet [his] fate."

The Family Reunion

Perhaps because it was not especially relevant to Iaroslavskii's lesson, Mongolia did not figure much in the trial, neither in the exchanges nor the final statements. It makes more of an appearance in the narrative commentary on the proceedings that appeared in *Soviet Siberia* a few days afterward. The piece was written by Ivan Maiskii, who was noted at the time as an expert on Mongolia and later went on to prominence as the Soviet ambassador to Great Britain in the 1930s and World War II.[42] Yet even Maiskii's article treats Mongolia largely as a prop for the show, a backward, medieval country of princes and khutuktus where one would expect to see a bizarre, mystical "thirteenth-century baron" like Ungern. As Maiskii puts it, describing Ungern's vision of his Mongolian empire, "What foolishness to speak of Genghis Khan in the age of Lenin."[43]

Novonikolaevsk was a gritty railway town in the middle of Siberia with an overwhelmingly ethnically Russian population. Mongolia and the Trans-Baikal frontier were a world away, even more in culture than in miles. As a result, one can only imagine the exotic impression Ungern must have made there in his deel. In fact, it's likely that his handlers kept him in the cloak for the trial precisely because it was another useful way to underscore the great contrast of the day: the unvarnished, direct, methodical justice of the Workers' and Peasants' State on the one hand versus the outmoded, pathetic eccentricity of the old regime on the other.

Yet for all the Bolsheviks' insistence on difference, we can also see the trial as its own dark version of a family reunion. Ungern and the Bolsheviks were not the same. There is no one-to-one equivalency. The ideological differences between them were profound, and the Bolsheviks prevailed in the war against Ungern in part because of the appeal of their ideology and even more because of how they used it. But the differences between them were not the black-and-white contrasts of Red and White propaganda, but rather the differences of siblings. The irony of the Red-White contest, like all civil wars, was that its seemingly starkly opposite protagonists were the product of a single home, in this case the Russian Empire, which shaped both sides.

The trial offers, in fact, its own small window on the way that the empire framed the revolutionary crisis. The Bolsheviks, like Ungern, were imperial people with diverse ethnic backgrounds and long-standing habits of mobility and cross-cultural combination. Just as he was a cosmopolitan shaped by his upbringing in the aristocracy and the officer corps, they were shaped by the cosmopolitan mores of the revolutionary underground and the emerging Soviet establishment. Just as he seems to have been hardened by the Great War and the revolution and civil war that followed, they were as well. In fact, both sides were shaped all the more by the disintegration of the imperial home and the specific ways in which it fell apart. Indeed, perhaps the most profound difference between them was how they responded to the collapse. The Bolsheviks found a way out, Ungern did not.

Most of the leading members of the party had spent years in transit around the empire and abroad, usually in Europe, either as organizers in the underground or in exile. They were polyglots who knew multiple languages, and many had non-Russian backgrounds. Joseph Stalin, for example, was Georgian. Feliks Dzerzhinskii (Dzierżyński), the first head of the Cheka, was Polish (as was the Mongol expert Maiskii mentioned above, whose birth name was Jan Lachowiecki). Trotsky was the most famous Jew in the party and, as a result, the most frequently vilified in anti-Bolshevik anti-Semitic propaganda, but there were numerous others, including Shumiatskii, the party official who interrogated Ungern in Kiakhta, and the prosecutor Iaroslavskii, who was born Minei Izraelevich Gubel'man and adopted his "battle name" after spending time in the underground in Iaroslavl'.[44]

Like Ungern, who was eager to support "the restoration of the emperors" in any country and took his counterrevolution abroad, the Bolsheviks were committed to doing the same with their interpretation of revolutionary socialism. As Trotsky put it, "I am not a Jew, I am an internationalist."[45] Like Ungern, they crafted their military instrument—the Red Army—into a multinational force,

11.3. Ungern in his cap at the trial. Courtesy
State Archive of Novosibirsk Oblast.

and like him, they were ready to conquer all that they could of the old Russian Empire to ensure that as much of it as practical came under their rule. Ungern aimed to complete a Siberian reconquista from the east. The Red Army had made just this sort of advance from the west. The English socialist Bertrand Russell, who visited Soviet Russia in the spring of 1920, noted, in fact, that the Red "re-conquest of Asiatic Russia" had made the Bolsheviks flush with "what is essentially an imperialist feeling," though he acknowledged that they themselves would have indignantly denied the idea.[46] (Russell also compared the leaders of the party to "British public school types," which they presumably would not have liked either.)

What is perhaps most similar about Ungern and the Bolsheviks, however, is that they both assumed that there was something self-evident about combining peoples and territories within large conglomerations. The Russian empire had fallen apart, but the vast multinational space left in its wake was seen as a territory that needed to be kept together under a single political order. Indeed, for all that Ungern supported the old regime and his enemies despised it, they seemed to agree that most if not all the peoples of the old state should continue to live together in some sort of common home. The key question was what the home should look like.

For Ungern, the lynchpin was the monarchy. Loyalty to the emperor created a pyramid of allegiances that in turn guaranteed the unity of the state. Thus all one had to do was to restore the emperor and unity would follow. Empires were the source of peace and stability—bigger was thus better in an obvious sense. The Bolsheviks, by contrast, saw the old empire as a grotesque hypocrisy built on Russification and colonial oppression. A basic goal of the revolution was thus to destroy this system and replace it with another. Yet they too, like Ungern, assumed that bigger was better.

Even Lenin's principled support for the right to self-determination was not an endorsement of the power to use that right. Instead, it was more a question of appealing to the psychology of the offended party, in this case, the non-Russians. Once they knew they had the right to leave, Lenin argued, they would, in fact, choose to stay because they would see the obvious benefits of life under the new socialist order. "We demand the freedom of self-determination," he wrote in 1913, "not because we dream...of the ideal of small states, but on the contrary, because we desire large states and a rapprochement, even a merging of nations. [But this rapprochement can be achieved] only on a truly democratic, truly international basis, which is unthinkable without the freedom of secession."[47]

When inserted into the zero-sum calculus of the civil war, this logic had two important consequences. The first was that it allowed the Bolsheviks to conclude that anyone supporting national independence was obviously an enemy, since true socialists knew that the path to world revolution ran through solidarity rather than separation. And second, the same logic, by extension, justified the Bolsheviks' reconquest of the empire's borderlands in the name of Soviet power, which was presented not only as the radical refutation of the old tsarist order but also as the only solution to the eternal problem of weaker or smaller peoples being dominated by larger or more powerful ones.

As Stalin put it in a speech to the 10th Party Congress in March 1921, "It is obvious that the only political order (*rezhim*) capable of resolving the national question—that is, the only political order able to create the conditions that will guarantee the peaceful development and fraternal cooperation of diverse peoples and tribes—is the system (*rezhim*) of Soviet power, the system of the dictatorship of the proletariat."[48]

Stalin's point, in fact, underscored the greatest of all the divides between Ungern and the Bolsheviks in the political arena: the Reds appreciated the power of the "national question" and used it to their advantage; Ungern, as best we can tell, did not. Though he commanded a multinational force and conducted international diplomacy, he seems to have viewed nationality as a secondary issue. According to his political credo, the link that mattered most was the one between the emperor and his servitors, which was not a bond of nationality but of dynastic allegiance. Thus when he called on Mongol and Kazakh leaders to do right by their peoples, what he meant was for them—the elites—to renew their ties to the Qing. It was this bond of ruler and aristocrat that would make things better, not anything having to do with the nation.

In this sense, Ungern was operating within a very old system of political values, one that even the conservative tsarist empire had started to question as it cut its complicated imperial path through the national age. Indeed, all the great multinational empires of Europe were forced to engage with the power of nationality in Ungern's time, yet he himself seems to have been at once both affected by this great trend and curiously outside of it. He commanded a military force organized around the national principle, with Buryat and Tatar regiments, for example. Yet his larger political vision did not emphasize nationality. Rather than nations, he saw the world in terms of a more abstract conflict between East and West, "whites" and "yellows," revolution and tradition.

The only seemingly nationalist ideology he embraced was anti-Semitism, though even in this area he was curiously nonnational. Most conservative Russian anti-Semites couched their hatred of the Jews in an ideology of Russian patriotism, following the logic of: I am a Russian patriot, therefore I hate the Jews. Ungern, by contrast, seems to have hated them because he hated the revolution.[49]

Unlike Kolchak and other White generals, he was not a Russian state nationalist, so he seems to have been uninterested in the common White preoccupation with a "United and Indivisible Russia."[50] Yet what is more interesting is that he was not a non-Russian nationalist either. In this respect, he was quite different from Semenov, who seems to have instinctively understood the national politics of the Trans-Baikal frontier, in particular the grievances of the Buryats, and, for a time, was able to use them to his advantage—his sponsorship of the heavily Buryat-influenced pan-Mongolianist platform of 1919 is a case in point. Ungern took advantage of Mongol grievances as well, of course, but he seems to have seen them through the lens of his own antirevolutionary glasses, interpreting Mongol resentment as a reaction to the overbearing rule of the Chinese republicans rather than seeing it as the expression of a deeper anticolonial grievance against Chinese power in general, including the rule of the Qing.

The Bolsheviks, by comparison, were far more attuned to the political implications of nationality in the upheaval of the revolution. As we saw, as soon as they took power, they issued a Declaration of the Rights of the Peoples of Russia, granting non-Russian groups autonomy and the right of secession, which they followed shortly thereafter with the establishment of a Commissariat for the Nationalities (abbreviated as Narkomnats, with Stalin as its first commissar). For its part, the Far Eastern Republic, Ungern's immediate territorial opponent, likewise inaugurated a Ministry of Nationalities a month before Ungern's division left Urga for Kiakhta and premised its nationality policy on the idea of "broad autonomy" for minority groups.[51] The Reds in general also made a point of exploiting the link between national grievance and anti-White sentiment whenever they could, including in the fight against Ungern.

Knowing that he and other Whites in Mongolia had Muslim troops, for example, the Comintern ordered Turkic-language flyers to be drawn up promising amnesty to the Muslims if they defected.[52] Red authorities worked closely with Red Buryats to get Buryats in Ungern's force to cross over. When the Red Army and DVR troops moved into Mongolia later in June 1921, they likewise prepared the ground for national support by issuing a statement "to the Mongolian people," explaining that they were intervening with the sole purpose of destroying "our common enemy, the bloodthirsty tsarist general Baron Ungern," and promising that they would leave as soon as they were done. (Knowing the Mongols' resentments over White requisitions, they also pledged that Red troops would pay "immediately and in full for whatever you sell to them.")[53]

This sensitivity to popular national sentiment and the readiness to use it in the revolutionary struggle helped the Bolsheviks enormously. Winning the war as well as the peace required mobilization, and national feeling was a key weapon for the cause. Most Bolsheviks, even those with non-Russian backgrounds, at least at this early stage, disdained nationalism, but they were willing to hitch national concerns to their socialist objectives. It was this kind of practical thinking that would lead a little over a year after Ungern's execution to the creation of the Union of Soviet Socialist Republics, a multinational creation explicitly designed to be anti-imperial yet that proved to be at once radically different and curiously continuous with the empire it was replacing.[54]

Unlike the old empire, the new USSR was premised on the recognition and promotion of minority national cultures and based on an administrative structure that linked nationality to territory, granting many (though not all) peoples of the state what, in theory, was their own political unit, from a handful of large, so-called "union-level republics" to scores of smaller, subunion entities as well. (One example of the latter was the Buryat-Mongol Autonomous Republic, carved out of the Trans-Baikal in 1922.) In this respect, the USSR was the ultimate anti-Russification state, a political form crafted to address all the resentments against overweening Russian power that had fueled the anti-imperial rage of 1917. The Bolsheviks even dropped the word "Russia" from the name of the state. Yet like the old empire, the new one was also authoritarian, hierarchical, rigidly centralized, and dominated by Russian culture, in addition, not coincidentally, to presiding over almost exactly the same territory.[55] Thus much stayed the same even as much changed as well.

Ungern might have created a non-Russification empire himself if he had had the chance. Not being a Russian nationalist of any variety, it's unlikely he would have been tempted by Russification as a solution to the imperial problem. Instead his worldview seems closer to that of the almost eternal

Emperor Franz-Joseph, the monarch of his first homeland, whose reign unfolded in an age of nationalism but who convinced himself (and other true believers
as well) that his empire could survive anyway. With a just king presiding above
the peoples, the thinking went, the peoples would have no reason not to stay together. One of the great ironies of Ungern's situation is that the new Bolshevik
model seems to have borrowed something from this approach as well, with the
party simply standing in for the king, but the key difference was that Ungern,
the unreconstructed Habsburg, discounted the power of minority nationalism,
whereas the Soviets understood its crucial importance.

Indeed, what the creation of the USSR proved quite clearly was that the
Bolsheviks were pragmatic politicians, at once ideologues and bureaucrats.
During the civil war, they consolidated their power and defeated their enemies
by building and staffing institutions: the Red Army, the Comintern, the revolutionary tribunals, the party itself, among many others. In his final statement,
Iaroslavskii mocked Ungern for his lack of political organization. "And what's
his political system? He doesn't have one. Nothing at all, except to bring back
the beating stick (*palka*) and put Mikhail Romanov on the throne."[56] The public defender Bogoliubov tried to turn this weakness to Ungern's advantage by
claiming that precisely because Ungern was a complete "nonentity" as a political leader, he posed no real threat to the revolution and should therefore be
spared.[57]

These claims are exaggerations: Ungern did have a politics, but his only
structure was the Asiatic Division. He had no party, no government, no statis-
tics. He dispatched letters to would-be allies, but it's not clear that he created
much of a patronage network or distributed extensive largesse or protection,
the way warlords have to do if they are going to get very far. His propaganda
machine was not, in fact, a machine. Unlike the Bolsheviks and other Whites,
he had no newspapers or propaganda boats. In fact, the division seems to have
done almost no propaganda work at all, with the exception of Ungern's own
letter-writing campaign and his murky Order No. 15.[58] It's true that Urga was
relatively isolated and that his time for building institutions in Mongolia was
limited. But his statements suggest that he also wasn't much interested. "A government can always be found," he said in one of his interrogations (*pravitel'stvo
vsegda naidetsia*), implying that the war was the important thing; political
structures were secondary.[59] By contrast, the Bolsheviks knew that the political structures *were* the war.

Indeed, it was their commitment to institution building that gave the Reds
the advantage to achieve in the end what Ungern could not, which was to re-
direct the energy of the frontier and force it to serve a higher power. When
the state structures of the Russian and Chinese empires unraveled, the borderlands between them unraveled as well. Like Semenov and Zhang, Ungern rode
the wave of this disintegration, in fact, he rode it all the way to Urga. But he was

ultimately much less successful than Zhang and even less successful than the mostly unsuccessful Semenov in institutionalizing the chaos that gave him his power. The Bolsheviks fought with the same ruthlessness and extremism as he did, but they also organized party cells, implemented programs, indoctrinated an army, and adopted a state-centered language of territorial sovereignty, class interests, and national liberation, all of which allowed them to impose themselves on the frontier in a way that Ungern never could. In effect, the Bolsheviks fought Ungern with the pitilessness of a wartime government, whereas he fought them with pitilessness alone, which necessarily limited what he could achieve.

In the end, he was killed by this difference. Pavlunovskii, the Cheka chief, was a relative newcomer to Novonikolaevsk, as were most of the other communist leaders in the city, sent from place to place by the party the same way that the old tsarist ministries and the army used to move their officials around the empire. Like those institutions, his Siberian Cheka formed a link in a great chain of offices that operated throughout the country down to the county level, and was run by a multinational workforce made up of Russians, Jews, Latvians, Poles, Ukrainians, and others. The head of the execution detail in Novonikolaevsk in this period was Pavlunovskii's assistant, a Jew named Evreinov.[60] Ungern was probably shot by just one man, perhaps Evreinov, standing right behind him, but in a larger sense he was shot by a system, a system his enemies had begun to build but he had not.

CONCLUSION

Everything begins in mysticism but ends in politics
—CHARLES PÉGUY. *Notre Jeunesse*

After Ungern's capture, the Asiatic Division broke into smaller and smaller parts. Some of the men reached Manchuria and were arrested by the Chinese. Some took refuge in the pro-White Russian mission in Beijing. Others were captured by the Reds in Mongolia. The Reds and their Mongol allies continued fighting small White forces in the western part of the country for the next several months, defeating the last of them by early 1922, some of whom were then later tried in Novonikolaevsk in a reprise of the Ungern trial.

A number of the people who figured in Ungern's life had complicated fates. Shchetinkin, the Red partisan commander who oversaw his capture, became a military adviser in Mongolia and died there in an accident in the late 1920s. The merchant Burdukov left the country and had a second career teaching Mongolian in Leningrad before being swept up in the Stalinist purges and dying in the camps. This happened to others as well. A number of the Buryat intellectuals who supported the pan-Mongolist movement were arrested and shot in the 1930s. Smirnov, the head of Sibrevkom, was tried in one of the great show trials in Moscow in the same period. Pavlunovskii, the Cheka chief in Novonikolaevsk, was executed in 1940. Of the prominent communists associated with Ungern, only Iarovslavskii and Maiskii survived the Stalinist repressions, though each had their troubles. The Soviets ultimately got Semenov as well, arresting him in his home in Japanese-occupied Manchuria at the end of

World War II. From there he was taken back to Moscow, where he was tried and hanged in 1946.

As for Mongolia, after Ungern's death the country began its journey as a nominally independent Soviet satellite, similar to what the countries of Eastern Europe would become after World War II. The country declared its independence on the day before Ungern's trial—the 13th day of the 8th moon of the 11th year of the Bogda's reign (that is, September 14, 1921). As long as he was alive, the now almost completely blind great lama remained the country's titular constitutional monarch, but after his death in 1924 the last vestiges of the old order were scrapped and Mongolia became a people's republic.

Since 1991 Russian and other historians have made much of the fact that without Ungern, Mongolia today, much like Inner Mongolia, might still be a part of China. Without the Mongolian campaign, the argument goes, the Soviets would not have intervened in the country and, without their protection, the Red Mongols would never have been able to achieve independence. There is some truth to this view, though, like most outsider perspectives, it (unintentionally or not) overstates the role of foreigners and reduces the contributions of the Mongols themselves to their own history. It also glosses over the inconsistencies of Soviet policy, which for years after Ungern's defeat zigzagged between supporting Mongolian independence and acknowledging Chinese claims to the country.

Though the degree of his responsibility for Mongolia's independence is debatable, it is fitting that if Ungern is known much today, it is almost exclusively in relation to this last chapter in his life. It was undeniably the Mongolian campaign that made him into a visible and influential figure, while also offering all the elements of a gripping story: violence, mysticism, exoticism, vast ambition followed by abject failure, plus, last but not least, the sources that allow historians to put the story together.

Yet at the same time, the focus on the Mongolian campaign alone has tended to obscure the fact that Ungern's life overall was much less about Mongolia than about the Russian Empire and its awkward combinations of peoples, spaces, and questions. He did not magically materialize in Urga as the "mad baron." Instead he was carried there by the currents of tsarist imperial life, including the chaotic maelstrom of the empire's unraveling. The campaign in that sense was not an exceptional moment as much as part of a larger flow, a dynamic at once bigger than Ungern and also more interesting.

Every historian has an approach to the past that then shapes the picture he or she creates. In this book, my goal has been to use Ungern's life to offer a tableau of the Russian Empire. On the face of it, this is a doomed proposition because no single life could possibly encompass the fullness of the terrain, but then again, every painting leaves something out. The important thing is what ends up in the frame.

What we see in the frame of Ungern's life is a view of the late tsarist world as a series of interconnected questions and spaces: social and geographical, political and cultural; a puzzle in which each piece, while different, is similar enough to the next that they fit together and, in this way, piece by piece create a larger whole. Though Ungern is not representative, his life has the virtue of taking us into many of the great issues of his time—modernization, Russification, nationalism, imperialism, war, revolution, imperial collapse, and, though it was not the one he wanted, the beginnings of imperial regeneration as well. Because he lived in so many places, he allows us to see more pieces of the puzzle than most. Indeed, following him across the empire's expanses, we're reminded of what a staggering proposition the Russian Empire was. Somehow it had to hold together Estland and the Trans-Baikal, St. Petersburg and the Amur, a German border and a Mongolian one.

One of the clues to how Russia's rulers did this for so long lies in the way the puzzle was put together: rigid in some respects but loose and adaptive in others. The empire was built on violence and exploitation but also on recurring accommodations between the center and its various peripheries that ultimately produced what could be called a kind of laissez-faire imperialism. Once certain basic obligations were met, the tsars were not especially interested in changing the peoples and places they ruled. The result was a great deal of de facto autonomy and, flowing from this, considerable stability as well. A persistent gap existed in the workings of the empire, a useful space between the arrogance of imperial proclamations and the practical reality of leaving good enough alone. The empire's success lived in this gap, which, though it varied from place to place and changed over time, nonetheless shaped the broader dynamic of Russian rule for centuries.

Ungern's life coincided, however, with a time of profound transition. Around the time of his birth, a great squeeze began as the empire's parts became increasingly pushed together in the uneven rush of modernization, changing the old imperial gap in the process. One reflection of this was Russification, which unfolded as the government's imperfect attempt to create and enforce what it saw as a more manageable and efficient form of imperial diversity. Another was the remarkable if checkered achievement of the Trans-Siberian and the country's turn toward East Asia. Still another was the wrenching upheaval of 1905. Ungern was a member of a generation that saw connectedness, standardization, possibility, and frustration all rise dramatically, each in equal measure.

The great squeeze of the late imperial era brought new pressures to bear on the empire, but it nonetheless held together. The ties binding its disparate parts were as physical as they were mental: trains and telegraphs, but also prejudices, like anti-Semitism, and comforts, like the sense of a common home created by circulating currents of people, including peasant colonists, merchants, revolutionaries, governors, and army officers like Ungern. A steady transimperial flow of goods, people, fears, and temptations also increasingly tied the empire to its various neighbors: the European empires, including the Ottomans, on one end, and the Qing on the other.

Every location of Ungern's life up to the time of the Great War reveals something of the flux and indeterminacy of the time: the presence of unresolved grievances and clumsy policies as well as old hierarchies that seemed to have outlived their usefulness. But it is reading too much into these shortcomings to say that the empire was fated to come apart. The imperial plaster was hardly smooth, but the cracks that were appearing were also a reflection of the dynamic change and possibility that were a part of the time. The prehistory of the collapse turns out to have been quite short. The tsarist government entered World War I and quickly took on pressures that it could barely handle. Then when the regime was overthrown in the midst of the enormous crisis of the war, the bonds that held the country together indeed weakened and broke, but what we also see by following Ungern's experience is how contingent and tenuous many of these breaks turned out to be. The country fell apart in some ways yet held together in others.

One of the great questions of the revolution and civil war turned on what Russia would look like when it was all over—which peoples and territories would be a part of it and how the new puzzle would fit together. Fighting in the interconnected borderlands of the Trans-Baikal and Outer Mongolia, Ungern found himself in the midst of the creative destruction that was, in effect, working out the answer to this conundrum. As we have seen, there was a certain logic to the fact that the Russian Revolution would spill across its borders in such liminal places, because one of the revolution's basic effects was to destroy the state that had created the borders in the first place. The state's boundaries were also inherently porous in the best of circumstances, with multiple connections tying the peoples on either side. That the empires on the other side of the line happened to be falling apart at the same time only intensified the confusion and violence.

In places like the Trans-Baikal, the civil war thus turned very quickly into a bitter contest to secure multiethnic and transborder allegiances and to imagine and then create new states or communities out of the imperial debris. Victory would go to the side that managed to capture the chaos and channel it toward something more permanent, something bigger. The Bolsheviks ultimately proposed the blueprint of a new multinational order that they promised would be the absolute opposite of everything that had come before. Ungern, meanwhile, offered a return to the empire of old where everyone knew their place under a just tsar. The Bolsheviks won; Ungern, very obviously, did not.

I've argued here that his failure stemmed, at least in part, from his inadequacies as a politician, but one could add, in his defense, that this was perhaps to be expected. Iaroslavskii mocked him at the trial as a pathetic lackey of the old regime who found himself without a master and was unmoored because of it. If we strip away the righteous hyperbole, the charge has something to it. The age-old talent of the nobility lay in holding onto power rather than regaining it. Their enemies, the Bolsheviks, by contrast, were professionally dedicated to seizing power. In this sense, the war between them was a battle of opposites, a struggle of antipodes with mismatching skill sets.

Yet in other ways, Ungern's opponents were very much like him, just as ruthless and intolerant in their extremism as he was, just as righteous, and, not surprisingly because they all came from the same place, just as much the products of the empire's diverse and far-flung society. By the end of his life, Ungern's great cause was the restoration of the imperial order. In a very basic sense, this was a quest to resurrect his own calling, to recreate a world where people like him could be useful again. Empires depend on cosmopolitan servitors, and the Russian Empire, among many others, had a long history of cultivating and rewarding them. Indeed, for the better part of two centuries, the Baltic barons were perhaps the most distinguished and coddled representatives of the form.

The Bolsheviks, by contrast, were intent on destroying the tsarist elite, including the barons, but, ironically, they also needed people like them—that is, people who knew multiple languages and moved easily between cultures, and, in fact, the party leadership reproduced a cosmopolitan milieu that was curiously similar to that of the lords of the old regime. Like the barons and dukes they despised, they agreed that most of the peoples of the empire should continue to live together in a common home and they saw a clear historical logic behind the melding of nations and territories into large combinations. In fact, it was precisely because such combinations were going to shape the world of the future that revolutionary cosmopolitanism seemed both so natural and so important. In seizing power, the Bolsheviks had helped to crack the empire apart, of course, but, as they saw it, the empire that had to go was the imperial order of the old regime and its echo in the empire of the Provisional Government. By contrast, the creation of an empire redefined as a pseudo-federalist, centralized multinational state, founded on a "correct" understanding of socialism and nationality, and monopolized by the party, was perfectly fine. In fact, building this sort of empire was absolutely necessary.

The Reds prevailed in the civil war for many reasons, but one of them was because they turned out to be much better than their opponents at negotiating the terrain of the empire's collapse. In fact, they did this so well, using a combination of military acumen, repression, and diplomacy, that they were able to reassemble much of the old imperial puzzle and impose their new order on top of it. As they went about this work, which included defeating, pillorying, and then executing Ungern, while also repackaging the power of the non-state frontier that he briefly represented, they prided themselves in the fact that what they were doing had nothing to do with empire: they were the liberators, the anti-imperialists, the people on the right side of history, whereas men like Ungern were the sorry old face of imperialism itself. But what seems clearer now is that both sides, Ungern and the Bolsheviks, were functioning within a world still covered by empire's shadow and therefore still guided by its presumptions and behaviors. One aimed to reset the broken clock of the empire to an earlier time, the other to replace it with a new one, rename it, and take it into the future.

Did Ungern ever think about any of these ironies and similarities? In writing this book, I have often asked myself an even more basic question: What did he think of himself? After a life spent moving between places and cultures, their influences gradually adding up to who he became, which of our more familiar categories would he have listed on his vita: German, Russian, European, Asian, Eurasian? None of them on their own seem quite right. He turns out to be as difficult to place in our registers as his cloak, which was sewn from a number of worlds at once. Perhaps we should just say that he belonged to the tsarist empire and leave it at that.

ACKNOWLEDGMENTS

Many institutions generously offered me time, hospitality, research assistance, or funding (or all three) to pursue my work on this book: the Taft Research Center of the University of Cincinnati, the University Research Council (also of UC), the National Council for Eurasian and East European Research, the Kennan Institute of the Woodrow Wilson International Center for Scholars in Washington D.C., the Fulbright Program sponsored by the Bureau of Education and Cultural Affairs of the US Department of State, the Slavic Research Center of Hokkaido University, the American Center for Mongolian Studies in Ulaanbaatar, the Institute of Qing History of the People's University in Beijing, and the Institute of Modern History of Academia Sinica in Taipei, Taiwan.

Many kind individuals helped me in the places I visited for my research. Of these, I'd especially like to thank: Herwig Höller in Graz; William Godsey and Todd Heidt in Vienna; Brad Woodworth and Karsten Brüggemann in Tallinn and Tartu; Urmas Selirand in Kärdla; Enno Alliksaar in Järvakandi; Chen Peng, Qiang Guangmei, Hu Xiangyu, James Palmer, and Huang Xingtao in Beijing; Yu Miin-ling and Huang Ko-wu in Taipei; Narantsetseg B. and Mergensanaa L. in Ulanbaatar; Irina Lukka in Helsinki; Uyama Tomohiko and Naganawa Norihiro in Sapporo; Ekaterina Kosiakova in Novosibirsk; Ekaterina Mel'nikova and Boris Mironov in St. Petersburg; Aleksei Kozulin in Ulan-Ude; and Tatiana Leonova and Nadezhda Barabanova in Moscow.

I simply could not have completed my work without the special generosity of two colleagues and friends in Moscow who found materials for me in archives and helped me with countless hours of their time and advice: Yuri Nikiforov and Mikhail Myagkov.

Many other colleagues and friends either read drafts of chapters or were kind enough to offer their support, knowledge, linguistic expertise, or counsel at different stages of the project. Of these, I'd especially like to thank Brad

Woodworth, Doug Smith, Charles King, Peter Holquist, Chia Yin Hsu, David Schimmelpenninck van der Oye, Christopher Kaplonski, Brian Baumann, Ekaterina Pravilova, Loretta Kim, Stephen Norris, Paul du Quenoy, Jane Burbank, Peter Perdue, David McDonald, Laurie Manchester, Austin Jersild, Sören Urbansky, Ronny Rönnqvist, Victor Zatsepine, Toivo Raun, Vladimir Shishkin, David Wolff, Glennys Young, Valerie Kivelson, Sean Pollock, and Liubov' Fadeeva. I am grateful to my current and former colleagues at the University of Cincinnati for their helpful critiques, textual assistance, and general encouragement along the way, especially Maura O'Connor, Barbara Ramusack, Hilda Smith, Tom Sakmyster, Sigrun Haude, Todd Herzog, Annulla Linders, Tom Lorman, Hsing-yi Kao, Manbun Kwan, Kate Sorrels, and Ross Dickinson. Hope Earls, the only Hope I've ever known, deserves special recognition for never ceasing to badger me (gently) to get "the thing" done and for looking the other way while I ate her crackers.

Thanks to my wonderful Chinese teachers who bravely endured my faulty tones: Lili Zhang and especially Jade Lin.

I remain forever in debt to my teachers of Russian and the empire's history: Ben Eklof, David Ransel, Alex Rabinowitch, Hiro Kuromiya, Toivo Raun, and Alfred Rieber.

John Ackerman at Cornell has been supportive from the start. I'm grateful for his confidence in me and his editorial mastery. My thanks, too, to Karen Laun, senior production editor at the Press, who provided wonderful help to get the manuscript into final form and has the patience of a bodhisattva. I thank Bill Nelson for his superb maps.

Finally, it's customary for authors to end their acknowledgments by thanking their families, and in most cases the thanks are for their loved ones having put up with them, the implication being that they—the authors—were either cranky, absent, or generally impossible during most of the time they were writing the book. In my case, I'm relieved to report that Betsy, Frank, Nick, and Emma, not to mention Akbar, Geronimo Carlos, the fish (blessed of memory), my sisters, parents, aunts, uncles, cousins, and in-laws all tell me that I actually wasn't too bad, but going on past precedent, I know they're just being polite. In fact, I'm sure that I was impossible—if not all the time, then at least frequently, but they were just the opposite, especially Betsy, who, despite having every reason to throttle me, was lovely in every way. I thank her very deeply. This book is dedicated to her.

ABBREVIATIONS

Archives

AVPRI   Arkhiv vneshnei politiki Rossiiskoi imperii (Moscow, Russia)

EAA   Eesti Ajalooarhiiv (Tartu, Estonia)

GAChO   Gosudarstvennyi arkhiv Chitinskoi oblasti (Chita, Russia)

GAKhO   Gosudarstvennyi arkhiv Khabarovskoi oblasti (Khabarovsk, Russia)

GANO   Gosudarstvennyi arkhiv Novosibirskoi oblasti (Novosibirsk, Russia)

GARF   Gosudarstvennyi arkhiv Rossiiskoi Federatsii (Moscow, Russia)

Hoover   Hoover Institution Archives, Hoover Institution for War and Peace (Stanford, Calif.)

NARB   Natsional'nyi arkhiv Respubliki Buriatii (Ulan-Ude, Russia)

RGAVMF   Rossiiskii gosudarstvennyi arkhiv voenno-morskogo flota (St. Petersburg, Russia)

RGIADV   Rossiiskii gosudarstvennyi istoricheskii arkhiv Dal'nego Vostoka (Vladivostok, Russia)

RGVA   Rossiiskii gosudarstvennyi voennyi arkhiv (Moscow, Russia)

RGVIA   Rossisskii gosudarstvennyi voenno-istoricheskii arkhiv (Moscow, Russia)

Archival Abbreviations

f.   fond (holding)

b.   back (reverse side of page)

d.   delo (file)

l.   list (page)

ll.   listy (pages)

n.   nimistu (register)

op.   opis′ (register)

s.   säilik (file)

l.   lehekülg (page)

Publications

AHR   *American Historical Review*

FzOG   *Forschungen zur Osteuropäischen Geschichte*

JfGO   *Jahrbücher für Geschichte Osteuropas*

JMH   *Journal of Modern History*

Kritika   *Kritika: Explorations in Russian and Eurasian History*

Kuz′min,   S. L. Kuz′min, *Baron Ungern v istochnikakh i dokumentakh*
Baron Ungern   (Moscow, 2004)

Kuz′min, *Istoriia*   S. L. Kuz′min, *Istoriia Barona Ungerna: Opyt rekonstruktsii*
Barona Ungerna   (Moscow, 2011)

Nachrichten   *Nachrichten über das Geschlecht Ungern-Sternberg*

OI   *Otechestvennaia istoriia*

SEER   *Slavonic and East European Review*

SR   *Slavic Review*

RR   *Russian Review*

VI   *Voprosy istorii*

neof. ch.   neofitsial′naia chast′ (unofficial section)

NOTES

Introduction

1. *Tsentral'nyi muzei vooruzhennykh sil,* Material Objects Collection (*veshchovoi fond*), n.2/2926.

2. Norman Davies, *Vanished Kingdoms: The History of Half-Forgotten Europe* (London, 2011).

3. For a range of works that use individual lives to open up a perspective on imperial connections in Russia and elsewhere, see Michael Khodarkovsky, *Bitter Choices: Loyalty and Betrayal in the Russian Conquest of the North Caucasus* (Ithaca, 2011); Francis W. Wcislo, *Tales of Imperial Russia: The Life and Times of Sergei Witte, 1849–1915* (New York, 2011); David Lambert and Alan Lester (eds.), *Colonial Lives across the British Empire: Imperial Careering in the Long Nineteenth Century* (New York, 2006); Linda Colley, *Captives: Britain, Empire, and the World, 1600–1850* (New York, 2004); Miles Ogborn, *Global Lives: Britain and the World, 1550–1800* (New York, 2008); Fredrik Lindström, *Empire and Identity: Biographies of the Austrian State Problem in the Late Habsburg Empire* (West Lafayette, Ind., 2008); Timothy Snyder, *The Red Prince: The Secret Lives of a Habsburg Duke* (New York, 2010); Robert Bickers, *Empire Made Me: An Englishman Adrift in Shanghai* (New York, 2004); David Ransel, *A Russian Merchant's Tale: The Life and Adventures of Ivan Alekseevich Tolchënov, Based on His Diary* (Bloomington, Ind., 2009); and Steven M. Norris and Willard Sunderland (eds.), *Russia's People of Empire: Life Stories from Eurasia, 1500 to the Present* (Bloomington, Ind., 2012). A revealing book that uses the same approach to open up different social questions is Peter Gay, *Schnitzler's Century: The Making of Middle-Class Culture, 1815–1914* (New York, 2002).

4. For an argument underscoring the differences between the genres, see Jill Lepore, "Historians Who Love Too Much: Reflections on Microhistory and Biography," *Journal of American History* 88, no. 1 (2001), 133. For an opposite view stressing the overlap between microhistory and biography, see Barbara Caine, *Biography and History* (Basingstoke, Eng., 2010), 52–53.

5. Many are the evocative treatments of Ungern. For a range of excerpted sources and popular historical and literary works, see Chen Zhaoxiang, "Bai E nanjue xiechi Wai Meng nao duli," *Wanbao wen cui,* 1 (2012), 26–27; O. Batsaikhan, "Baron Ungern—Mongol ulsyn

baatar bolokh n'," http://www.tsahimurtuu.mn/index.php/2012-03-05-03-28-33/86-news/
article/759-archive-story-552 (last accessed: May 2012); A. Zhukov, *Oprichnyi Baron* (Ulan-
Ude, 2011); Leonid Iuzefovich, *Samoderzhets pustyni: Baron R. F. Ungern-Shternberg i mir v
kotorom on zhil* (1993; rev. ed.: Moscow, 2010); James Palmer, *The Bloody White Baron: The
Extraordinary Story of a Russian Nobleman Who Became the Last Khan of Mongolia* (New York,
2011); n.a., *Baron Ungern von Sternberg: Der letzte Kriegsgott* ([Preetz], 2007); Ronny Rönnqvist, *Baron Ungern, Mongoliets härskare* (Helsinki, 2006); Érik Sablé, *Ungern* (Series: Qui
suis-je?) (Paris, 2006); A. V. Shishov, *Ungern: Demon mongol'skikh stepei; Roman* (Moscow,
2005); Vasilii Tsvetkov, "Na sopkakh Mongolii: Beloe delo Barona Ungerna," *Rodina,* no. 1
(2005), 49–57; Mikhail Demidenko, *Put' v Shambalu: Baron Ungern, belyi rytsar' Tibeta* (Moscow, 2004); Rhys Hughes, "The Brutal Buddha:ºBaron von Ungern-Sternberg," in Hughes,
A New Universal History of Infamy (Tallahassee, Fla., 2004), 23–32; Nicholas J. Middleton,
The Bloody Baron: The Wicked Dictator of the East (London, 2001); Olev Remsu, *Kindralleitnant Robert Roman Ungern-Sternberg: Hiiumaa parun, kellel oli maailma suurim varandus ning kes tahtis vallutada Euroopa* (Pärnu, 1999); José Luis Ontiveros, "Ungern-Khan,"
in Ontiveros, *El Húsar Negro* (Mexico City, 1999), 77–90; Jean Mabire, *Ungern: L'héritier
blanc de Gengis Khan* (Rouen, 1997); Jean Mabire, *Ungern, le dieu de la guerre: La chevauchée
du general-baron Roman Feodorovitch von Ungern-Sternberg, du Golfe de Finlande au désert
de Gobi* (Paris, 1987); N. N. Kniaz'ev, *Legendarnyi baron* (Harbin, 1942); Vladimir Pozner,
Bloody Baron: The Story of Ungern-Sternberg (New York, 1938); and Berndt Krauthoff, *Ich Befehl!: Kampf und Tragödie des Barons Ungern-Sternberg* (Bremen [1938]). For a recent popular
treatment of twentieth-century Russia that repeats the exotic and brutal caricature, see Rachel
Polonsky, *Molotov's Magic Lantern: Travels in Russian History* (New York, 2010), 338–42.

6. David McCullough, "Climbing into Another Head," in Marie Arana (ed.), *The Writing
Life: Writers on How They Think and Work; A Collection from the Washington Post Book World*
(New York, 2003), 163–67.

7. In recent years, Russian historians have produced impressive academic studies of Ungern, in particular Sergei Kuz'min, who edited two volumes of documents and memoirs related (mostly) to the Mongolian campaign and authored his own six-hundred-page interpretive
study. Though my approach to Ungern's story is quite different, I have benefited greatly from
these works. See S. L. Kuz'min, *Istoriia Barona Ungerna: Opyt rekonstruktsii* (Moscow, 2011);
S. L. Kuz'min (ed. and comp), *Baron Ungern v dokumentakh i memuarakh* (Moscow, 2004);
and S. L. Kuz'min (comp.), *Legendarnyi baron: Neizvestnye stranitsy grazhdanskoi voiny* (Moscow, 2004). See also E. A. Belov, *Baron Ungern fon Shternberg: Biografiia, ideologiia, voennye
pokhody, 1920–1921* (Moscow, 2003). A range of other historians have produced valuable studies of Ungern and the campaign. I cite these works in the chapters relating to the civil war period.

Chapter 1

1. Evangelische Pfarrgemeinde Graz-Heilandskirche, Taufbuch (baptismal register), n.5
(1881–1888), 171. In the register, Nikolai is spelled "Nikolay" and "Max" appears with a period after the "x," suggesting that this was probably an abbreviation for Maximilian, though
in the genealogy books, the name tends to appear as "Max" as well. The register also clearly
indicates that Ungern was born in 1886, though his birth year often appears as 1885 because
the Julian calendar used by the Russian Empire in the nineteenth century was twelve days
behind the Gregorian calendar used in the Habsburg Empire and other central and western
European states.

2. *Grazer Geschäfts- und Adreß-kalender für das Schaltjahr 1886: Ausschießlich nach amtlichen Quellen redigirt* (Graz, 1886), 63.

3. Sokratis Dimitriou, "Die Grazer Stadtentwicklung 1850 bis 1914," in Dimitriou (ed.), *Stadterweiterung von Graz: Gründerzeit* (Graz, 1979), 10–11. On Geidorf's history, see Edith Münzer, *Als die Stadt noch am Land war: Grazer Bezirke erzählen; St. Leonhard, Geidorf, Jakomini* (Graz, 1978), 59–112.

4. On late medieval German colonial settlements like Graz, see Robert Bartlett, *The Making of Europe: Conquest, Colonization, and Cultural Change, 950–1350* (Princeton, N.J., 1993), 167–196. For Graz's early history, see Franz Popelka, *Geschichte der Stadt Graz*, 2 vols. (Graz, 1959–1960); and Walter Brunner et al. (eds.), *Geschichte der Stadt Graz*, vol. 1 (Graz, 2003). On the origin of the name of the city, see Popelka, *Geschichte*, 1: 41–46.

5. For population figures and changes in the city, see Dimitriou, "Grazer Stadtentwicklung 1850 bis 1914," 17, 20, 22, 24; William H. Hubbard, "Politics and Society in the Central European City: Graz, Austria, 1861–1918," *Canadian Journal of History/Annales canadiennes d'histoire* 5, no. 1 (1970), 26; and Ulrike Schuster, *Verlorenes Graz: Eine Spurensuche im 19. und 20. Jahrhundert nach demolierten Bauwerken und Denkmalen der Steierischen Landeshauptstadt* (Vienna, 1997), 46–47, 52–54.

6. See *Special-Orts-Repertorium der im Österreichischen Reichsrathe vertretenen Königsreiche und Länder*, vol. 4, *Steiermark* (Vienna, 1883).

7. A Prussian jingle repeated by aristocrats in the eighteenth century neatly sums up this relationship: "The king's sway depends on our say" ("Und der König absolut, wenn er unseren Willen tut"). See Lother Höbelt, "The Discrete Charm of the Old Regime," *Austrian History Yearbook* 27 (1996), 291.

8. Jonathan Powis, *Aristocracy* (Oxford, 1984), 91.

9. Matthew Arnold, *Culture and Anarchy: An Essay in Political and Social Criticism* (New Haven, Conn., 1994; original 1869 text, edited and introduction by Samuel Lipman, essays by Maurice Cowling, Gerald Gradd, Samuel Lipman, and Steven Marcus), 56. See also Antony Taylor, *Lords of Misrule: Hostility to Aristocracy in Late Nineteenth- and Early Twentieth-Century Britain* (Basingstoke, 2004).

10. William D. Godsey, "Nobles and Modernity," *German History* 20, no. 4 (2002), 507.

11. On noble identities in this period, see Anthony L. Cardoza, *Aristocrats in Bourgeois Italy: The Piedmontese Nobility, 1861–1930* (New York, 1997); Dominic Lieven, *The Aristocracy in Europe, 1815–1914* (New York, 1992); Ellis Watson, *Aristocracy and the Modern World* (Basingstoke, 2006); David Cannadine, *The Decline and Fall of the British Aristocracy* (New Haven, Conn., 1990); and Eagle Glassheim, *Noble Nationalists: The Transformation of the Bohemian Aristocracy* (Cambridge, Mass., 2005).

12. This is the basic argument advanced in Arno J. Mayer, *The Persistence of the Old Regime* (New York, 1981). For more recent reflections on how European nobles and nobilities adapted to the challenges of modern politics, see also Jörn Leonhard and Christian Wieland, "Noble Identities from the Sixteenth to the Twentieth Centuries: European Aristocratic Cultures in Law, Politics, and Aesthetics," in Jörn Leonhard and Christian Wieland (eds.), *What Makes the Nobility Noble? Comparative Perspectives from the Sixteenth to the Twentieth Century* (Göttingen, 2011), 14–15.

13. Nora Fugger, *The Glory of the Habsburgs: The Memoirs of Princess Fugger* (London, 1932), 6. For a sense of the great imperial capital in the 1880s, see Frederic Morton, *A Nervous Splendor: Vienna, 1888/1889* (New York, 1980).

14. P. K. Rosegger et al., *Wanderrungen durch Steiermark und Kärnten* (Stuttgart, n.d.), 95–96; Victor Tissot, *Vienne et la vie viennoise* (13th ed.; Paris, 1878), 96; and K. Baedeker, *Süd-Deutschland und Oesterreich: Handbuch für Reisende* (Leipzig, 1884), 417.

15. Brunner, et al., *Geschichte der Stadt Graz,* vol. 2, 466, 488–91.

16. *Grazer Zeitung,* January 4, 1886, front page; *Tagespost (Abendblatt),* January 11, 1886, no page number indicated.

17. On Ungern's attempt to obtain an Austrian visa, see *GARF,* f.9427, op.1, d.392, l.47; "Doprosy R. F. Ungerna 1 i 2 sentiabria 1921 g. v Irkutske," Kuz'min, *Baron Ungern,* 210.

18. The villas of Geidorf were the newest statement of taste. "You must see my Villa," ran a contemporary poem, "I'll ask you for your view/I'm sure you'll soon agree/My architect's a genius, too." See *Landhaus und Villa in Niederösterreich, 1840–1914* (Vienna, 1982), 69. On the villas of Geidorf, see Anita Pieber, "Villen und Gartenanlagen in Graz Geidorf 1840–1900" (Master's thesis, Karl-Franzens University, Graz, 1999).

19. For a roughly contemporary description of the town, see A. von Lorent, *Wimpffen am Neckar: Geschichtlich und topographlich nach historischen Mittheilungen und archäoligischen Studien dargestellt* (Stuttgart, 1870). The town today is known as Bad Wimpfen.

20. "Statistik der landtäflichen Güter," in Franz Günther, *Der österreichische Grossgrundbesitz: Nachschlage-Buch über Eigenthums- und Besitzstand aller landtäflichen Güter Oesterreichs* (Vienna, 1873) n.163, l.313. For "Alpen" as mountain pasture, see Nicholas Shoumatoff and Nina Shoumatoff, *The Alps: Europe's Mountain Heart* (Ann Arbor, Mich., 2001), 117.

21. William Godsey, "Quarterings and Kinship: The Social Composition of the Habsburg Aristocracy in the Dualist Era," *JMH* 71, no. 1 (1999), 56–104; Hannes Stekl, "Zwischen Machtverlust und Selbstbehauptung: Österreichs Hocharistokratie vom 18. bis ins 20. Jahrhundert," in Hans-Ulrich Wehler (ed.), *Europäischer Adel 1750–1950* (Göttingen, 1990), 146, 163; and Glassheim, *Noble Nationalists,* 21–22. Gudula Walterskirchen concludes that the late Habsburg *Hochadel* was composed of "about 180 families, with something like 11,000 family members." See *Der vergeborgene Stand: Adel in Österreich heute* (Vienna, 1999), 13.

22. Ernst Hanisch, *Der lange Schatten des Staates: Österreichische Gesellschaftsgeschichte im 20. Jahrhundert* (Vienna, 1994), 87. Anti-baronial prejudice in the late nineteenth century stemmed from the fact that many of Austria's highest nobles at the time saw the title of "baron" as a cheapened rank since many barons were not true bluebloods but rather rich parvenus from the bourgeois class who had bought their titles—the Barons Rothschild, for example, who dared to be Jewish as well as rich. On the land question: Sophie Charlotte's family's holdings in Steiermark totaled 251 *Joche* (approximately 356 acres). By contrast, in 1913, the largest landlords in the province in owned over 86,000. See Roman Sandgruber, *Österreichische Agrarstatistik, 1750–1918* (Vienna, 1978), 237.

23. *Genealogisches Handbuch des Adels* (1952), vol. 4, 457–58, 477–79. For debates surrounding the origin of the family name, see Michael von Taube, *Ungern-Sternberg: Ursprung und Anfänge des Geschlechts in Livland* (Tartu, 1940), 8–29.

24. For the list, see Carl Arvid von Klingspor (ed.), *Baltisches Wappenbuch* (Stockholm, 1883), 43–44.

25. Heide Whelan, *Adapting to Modernity: Family, Caste, and Capitalism among the Baltic German Nobility* (Cologne, 1999), 143. The Baltic nobility's marriage market changed somewhat over the late nineteenth century, however, as more nobles formed mixed marriages with nonnoble spouses and foreigners, including Russians (281–82).

26. Wasson, *Aristocracy and the Modern World,* 25.

27. Mayer, *Persistence of the Old Regime,* 82.

28. For expressions of the nobles' powerful attachment to their manors and "local homelands," see Glassheim, *Noble Nationalists,* 17; and Cardoza, *Aristocrats in Bourgeois Italy,* 122–24.

29. This is the sensible brief definition of the term "transnational" offered by Sven Beckert. See his remarks in "AHR Conversation: On Transnational History," *AHR* 111, no. 5 (2006), 1445.

30. Anthony Pagden, "Europe: Conceptualizing a Continent," in Padgen, *The Idea of Europe: From Antiquity to the European Union* (New York, 2002), 52, 54.

31. On transnational Germans and the challenges of defining "a social entity which one can call a German society" in the late nineteenth and early twentieth centuries, see Edward Ross Dickinson, "Germans or Europeans? Moral Reform and Sex Reform before World War I" (Unpublished paper, 2007); Ute Frevert, "Europeanizing Germany's Twentieth Century," *History and Memory* 17, nos. 1/2 (2005), 89–94; and Philipp Ther, "Beyond the Nation: The Relational Basis of a Comparative History of Germany and Europe," *Central European History* 36, no. 1 (2003), 56–57. On regional identities in European history, see Celia Applegate, "A Europe of Regions: Reflections on the Historiography of Sub-National Places in Modern Times," *AHR* 104, no. 4 (1999), 1157–82.

32. Evangelische Pfarrgemeinde Graz-Heilandskirche, Taufbuch, n.5 (1881–1888), l.171.

33. Otto von Taube, *Das Buch der Keyserlinge: An der Grenze Zweier Welten; Lebenserinnerungen aus einem Geschlecht* (1937; repr.: Berlin, 1944), 59.

34. Quote from Benedict Anderson, *Imagined Communities: Reflections on the Origins and Spread of Nationalism* (rev. ed.; New York, 1991), 85. On "nationalizing states," see Rogers Brubaker, *Nationalism Reframed: Nationhood and the National Question in the New Europe* (New York, 1996), 79–106.

35. Johann Gottfried Herder, "Auch eine Philosophie der Geschichte zur Bildung der Menschheit: Beitrag zu vielen Beiträgen des Jahrhunderts (1774)," in *Sämtliche Werke* (Hildesheim, 1967), vol. 5, 509.

36. Abigail Green, *Fatherlands: State-Building and Nationhood in Nineteenth-Century Germany* (New York, 2001); Philipp Ther, "Imperial Instead of National History: Positioning Modern German History on the Map of European Empires," in Alexei Miller and Alfred J. Rieber (eds.) *Imperial Rule* (New York, 2004), 47–66; Roger Chickering, *We Men Who Feel Most German: A Cultural Study of the Pan-German League, 1886–1914* (Boston, 1984); Howard Sargeant, "Diasporic Citizens: Germans Abroad in the Framing of German Citizenship Law," in Krista O'Donnell et al. (eds.), *The Heimat Abroad: The Boundaries of Germanness* (Ann Arbor, Mich., 2005), 17–39, esp. 24–25; and Annemarie H. Sammartino, *The Impossible Border: Germany and the East, 1914–1922* (Ithaca, 2010), 4–5, 18–24.

37. Alan Sked, *The Decline and Fall of the Habsburg Empire, 1815–1918* (2nd ed.; Harlow, Eng., 2001), 335 (table). In 1880 the exact percentage of German speakers in Cisleithania was 36.8 percent.

38. Daniel L. Unowsky, *The Pomp and Politics of Patriotism: Imperial Celebrations in Habsburg Austria, 1848–1916* (West Lafayette, Ind., 2005), 2; and Pieter M. Judson, "When Is a Diaspora Not a Diaspora? Rethinking Nation-Centered Narratives about Germans in Habsburg East Central Europe," in O'Donnell et al., *Heimat Abroad*, 224.

39. Timothy Snyder, *The Red Prince: The Secret Lives of a Habsburg Archduke* (New York, 2009), 27.

40. "The National Status of the Individual," in Robert A. Kann, *The Multinational Empire: Nationalism and National Reform in the Habsburg Monarchy, 1848–1918* (New York, 1950), vol. 2, appendix 3, 310. As one historian puts it, "The Austrian solution chosen in 1867 was not to recognize national groups as carriers of collective political rights but instead to recognize nationality as an individual quality." See Fredrik Lindström, *Empire and Identity: Biographies of the Austrian State Problem in the Late Habsburg Empire* (West Lafayette, Ind., 2008), 8.

41. Barbara Jelavich, *Modern Austria: Empire and Republic, 1815–1986* (New York, 1987), 81–82.

42. Pieter M. Judson, *Guardians of the Nation: Activists on the Language Frontiers of Imperial Austria* (Cambridge, Mass., 2006), 14–15.

43. Sidney Whitman, *The Realm of the Habsburgs* (London, 1893), 23, 25–26.

44. Hubbard, "Politics and Society in the Central European City," 40.

45. Manfred Hirschegger, "Die Grazer 'Tagespost' von 1880. bis 1890: Ein Beitrag zur steierischen Pressegeschichte" (PhD diss., Graz University, 1981), 158; and Hubbard, "Politics and Society in the Central European City," 40–44; P. K. Rosegger, *Das Volksleben in Steiermark in Character- und Sittenbilden* (Vienna, 1881), 29–38.

46. *Tagespost (Abendblatt)*, September 11, 1884, no page number indicated.

47. Glassheim, *Noble Nationalists*, 24, 29.

48. Vasilii Rosanov, "Kosmopolitizm i natsionalizm," in *Natsiia i imperiia v russkoi mysli nachala xx veka* (Moscow, 2004), 133–34. Rozanov published this piece in 1911. The quotes in the original are reversed.

49. On Constantin, see *EAA*, f.1674, n.2, s.207, l.40(b); Evangelische Pfarrgemeinde Graz-Heilandskirche, Taufbuch, n.5 (1881–1888), 291.

Chapter 2

1. For a brief survey of the history of the property, see Alo Särg, *Hiiumaa mõisad ja mõisnikud* (Tallinn, 2006), 21.

2. This description of the factory (German name: Dagö-Kertel Tuchfabrik) is drawn from the grandfather's obituary, which appeared in the *Revaler Beobachter* on January 19, 1898. A clipping is held in the Ungern-Sternberg family holding in *EAA*, f.854, n.1, s.1080, between pages 22 and 23. For an Estonian obituary, see *Valgus* (January 27, 1898), 1. For photos of the factory and a snapshot of some of Ungern's relatives sitting on the veranda of the Kärdla house in the 1890s and early 1900s, see Toomas Karjahärm (comp.), *Vana Hiiumaa: Ehitised ja inimesed* (n.p., 2013), 44-46.

3. On early German conquest and Christianization in what would become Estonia, see Eric Christiansen, *The Northern Crusades: The Baltic and the Catholic Frontier, 1100–1525* (Minneapolis, Minn., 1980),105–9; Tiina Kala, "The Incorporation of the Northern Baltic Lands into the Western Christian World," in Alan V. Murray (ed.), *Crusade and Conversion on the Baltic Frontier, 1150–1500* (Aldershot, Eng., 2001), 3–20; and Robert Bartlett, *The Making of Europe: Conquest, Colonization, and Cultural Change, 950–1350* (Princeton, N.J., 1993), 191–96.

4. David Kirby, *Northern Europe in the Early Modern Period: The Baltic World, 1492–1772* (New York, 1990), 24–26; Toivo U. Raun, *Estonia and the Estonians* (2nd rev. ed.; Stanford, Calif., 2001), 19–21, 45–48.

5. On the various careers of Baltic German noblemen, see Whelan, *Adapting to Modernity,* 190–98.

6. For the published account of his survey, see F. R. Ungern-Shternberg, *O vinodelii na iuzhnom beregu Kryma* (St. Petersburg, 1888).

7. For Theodor's biographical details, see Constantin von Ungern-Sternberg, *Nachrichten über das Geschlecht Ungern-Sternberg,* pt. 2 (2d ed.; Reval, 1902), 54 (entry E.287); *EAA*, f.1674, n.2, s.207, l.40(b). For an example of Theodor's scholarship on the Caucasus, see Th. von Ungern-Sternberg, *Die Orographie des Kaukasus in Beziehung zur alten Kultur in*

Vorder-Asien (St. Petersburg, 1891). Theodor also provides a brief autobiographical statement in the appendix to his published doctoral thesis: *Untersuchungen über den finnlaendischen Rapakiwi-Granit* (Leipzig, 1882), 45–46.

8. *EAA*, f.1674, n.2, s.207, l.40(b); See also Constantin von Ungern-Sternberg, *Nachrichten*, 34.

9. Shortly after the couple's marriage, Theodor purchased the estate of Waldau (Valtu), one of the grandest manors in all of Estland, but had to sell the property just three years later because of money problems. For a photograph and brief description of the estate, see Ants Hein (comp.), *Eesti mõisad: 250 fotot aastaist, 1860–1939* (Tallinn, 2004), 194.

10. Otto von Taube, *Im alten Estland: Kinderheitserinnerungen* (Stuttgart, n.d.), 74, 274. Taube's grandfather, the renowned naturalist Count Alexander von Keyserling, also considered Ungern's mother "thoroughly enchanting." See Helene von Taube (ed.), *Graf Alexander Keyserling: Ein Lebensbild aus seinen Briefen und Tagebüchern* (Berlin, 1902), vol. 2, 308–9, 361.

11. Theophile von Bodisco, *Versunkene Welten: Erinnerungen einer estländischen Dame* (Henning von Wistinghausen, ed.) (Weissenhorn, 1997), 198.

12. For the file, see *EAA*, f.1187, n.2, s.1801.

13. On divorce among the Baltic Germans in this period, see Whelan, *Adapting to Modernity*, 122–23. By comparison, Orthodox authorities had much stricter regulations on divorce. See Barbara Alpern Engel, "In the Name of the Tsar: Competing Legalities and Marital Conflict in Late Imperial Russia," *JMH* 77, no. 1 (2005), 74–75, 82–83.

14. *EAA*, f.1187, n.2, s.1801, no pagination indicated.

15. *EAA*, f.1187, n.2, s.1801, no pagination indicated.

16. According to the papers in the file, Theodor appears to have initially requested that he receive full custody of the children once they reached the age of twelve, but, for unknown reasons, he then withdrew this request just a month later. See *EAA*, f.1187, n.2, s.1801, no pagination indicated.

17. "Baron von Ungern-Sternberg," *St. Peterburger Zeitung*, July 29 (August 10) 1897, 3; *EAA*, f.860, n.1, s.1672, ll.1–16; *Genealogisches Handbuch der baltischen Ritterschaften: Estland*, vol. 1 (Görlitz, n.d.), 465.

18. "Totenliste," *Revaler Beobachter*, November 7 (November 20) 1907, 3; "Kirchlicher Anzeiger," *Revalsche Zeitung*, November 10 (November 23) 1907, 3.

19. B. Erdmann, "Einige Glossen über baltische Lebensformen," *Baltische Monatsschrift* 75 (1913), 412. Russian lords saw their manors in similar ways. On the meanings of the estate in Russian noble culture, see Priscilla Roosevelt, *Life on the Russian Country Estate: A Social and Cultural History* (New Haven, Conn., 1995); and John Randolph, *The House in the Garden: The Bakunin Family and the Romance of Russian Idealism* (Ithaca, 2006), 37–38, 56–63.

20. Raun, *Estonia and the Estonians*, 45–51, 68–70; Jerome Blum, *The End of the Old Order in Rural Europe* (Princeton, N.J., 1978), 228–31.

21. Toivo Raun, "The Estonians," in Edward C. Thaden (ed.), *Russification in the Baltic Provinces and Finland, 1855–1914* (Princeton, N.J., 1981), 288–89, 292–93; Whelan, *Adapting to Modernity*, 24. Over time the term *saks* came to refer to any wealthy or educated person, including Russians or Estonians. See Raun, "Estonians," 293; and Bradley D. Woodworth, "Civil Society and Nationality in the Multiethnic Russian Empire: Tallinn/Reval, 1860–1914" (PhD. diss., Indiana University, 2003), 26

22. On the operations at Jerwakant, see *Adres-kalendar' estliandskoi gubernii na 1893 god* (Revel', 1893), 103; and *Adressbuch baltischer Landwirthe* (Reval, 1899), 35, 46. The glass factory still exists today—AS Järvakandi Klaas. It produces most of the beer bottles on the Estonian market.

23. *Spisok naselennykh mest estliandskoi gubernii k 1912-mu godu* (Revel', 1913), 14.

24. Taube, *Im alten Estland,* 30–33.

25. Whelan, *Adapting to Modernity,* 246–50.

26. Otto von Taube, *Stationen auf dem Wege: Erinnerungen an meine Werdezeit vor 1914* (Heidelberg, 1969), 366. For additional information on the Jerwakant manor, see Heinz Pirang, *Das baltische Herrenhaus* (1928; repr,: Riga, 1977) vol. 2, 35–36; Hubertus Neuschäffer, *Schlösser und Herrenhäuser in Estland* (Pöln, 1993), 93–94; and Hein, *Eesti mõisad,* 176. For photographs of the estate today, see also Alo Särg, *Raplamaa mõisad ja mõisnikud* (Tallinn, 2007), 50–54.

27. On *Kultur* and *Bildung,* see Wolf Lepennies, *The Seduction of Culture in German History* (Princeton, N.J., 2006), 4–5; Hans-Georg Betz, "Elites and Class Structure," in Eva Kolinsky and Wilfried van der Will (eds.), *The Cambridge Companion to Modern German Culture* (New York, 1998), 73–74; and Whelan, *Adapting to Modernity,* 181–83.

28. Taube, *Im alten Estland,* 120.

29. Whelan, *Adapting to Modernity,* 38–39; David Kirby, *The Baltic World, 1772–1993: Europe's Northern Periphery in an Age of Change* (New York, 1995), 178.

30. Haltzel, "Baltic Germans," 143–44.

31. Twenty different Ungern-Sternbergs attended the elite German-language middle and high school in Reval, the Cathedral School (*Domschule*), between the 1860s and its closing in 1893. Ungern would almost certainly have been sent there had it still been open during his school-age years. See Bernhard Haller (comp.), *Album der estländischen Ritter- und Domschule zu Reval vom 12. Januar 1859 bis 18. Juni 1892* (Reval, 1893).

32. Raun, *Estonia and the Estonians,* 59–62; Bradley D. Woodworth, "Administrative Reform and Social Policy in the Baltic Cities of the Russian Empire: Riga and Reval, 1870–1914," *Jahrbüch für Europäische Verwaltungsgeschichte* 16 (2004), 114–36; Arved von Taube, Erik Thomson, and Michael Garleff, "Die Deutschbalten—Schicksal und Erbe einer eigenständigen Gemeinschaft," in Wilfried Schlau (ed.), *Die Deutschbalten* (Munich, 1995), 64. Dorpat University was renamed Iur'ev University. Today it is the University of Tartu.

33. Aleksei Miller, *Imperiia Romanovykh i natsionalizm: Esse po metodologii istoricheskogo issledovaniia* (Moscow, 2006), 93; Renate Bridenthal, "Germans from Russia: The Political Network of a Double Diaspora," in O'Donnell et al., *Heimat Abroad,* 188.

34. "Zapiska pomozhnika uezdnogo nachal'nika (okolo 1898 g.)," in Toomas Kar'iakhiarm [Karjahärm] (comp.), *Imperskaia politika Rossii v Pribaltike v nachale xx veka: Sbornik dokumentov i materialov* (Tartu, 2000), 11; "Ob etnograficheskom sostave naseleniia Pribaltiiskogo kraia," *Estliandskie gubernskie vedomosti,* May 19, 1888, neof. ch., 76.

35. On "state simplification," see James C. Scott, "State Simplifications: Nature, Science, People," in Ian Shapiro and Russell Hardin (eds.), *Political Order* (New York, 1996), 42–85. On the need to understand Russifications in the plural rather than the singular, see Miller, *Imperiia Romanovykh i natsionalizm,* 54–77. See also Andreas Kappeler's comments on the contradictions of Russification policies in "The Ambiguities of Russification," *Kritika* 5, no. 2 (2004), 291–97.

36. A. Vorotin, *Printsipy pribalitiiskoi zhizni* (Revel', 1891), foreword, no page number indicated.

37. Gert von Pistohlkors, "Die Ostseeprovinzen unter russischer Herrschaft (1710/95–1914)," in von Pistohlkors (ed.), *Deutsche Geschichte im Osten Europas: Baltische Länder* (Berlin, 1994), 365; Fanny von Anrep, *Briefe einer Livländerin aus den Jahren 1873–1909* (Gertrud Westermann, ed.) (Landshut, 1990), 68.

38. Wilhelm von Wrangell, *Die estländische Ritterschaft, ihre Ritterschaftshauptmänner und Landräte* (Limberg/Lahn, 1967), 131; Pistohlkors, "Ostseeprovinzen unter russischer Herrschaft," 365; Haltzel, "Baltic Germans," 177.

39. Taube, *Graf Alexander Keyserling*, vol. 2, 599.

40. Whelan, *Adapting to Modernity*, 228–30; Woodworth, "Civil Society," 190.

41. For a description of Reval's old Upper Town in the 1880s, see P. P. Semenov (ed.), *Zhivopisnaia Rossiia: Otechestvo nashe v ego zemel'nom, istoricheskom, plemennom, ekonomicheskom i bytvovom znachenii*, vol. 2, pt.1, *Severo-zapadnye okrainy Rossii i velikoe kniazhestvo Finliandii* (St. Petersburg and Moscow, 1882), 219–22.

42. On the Nevsky Cathedral, see Mari Isoaho, *The Image of Alexander Nevskiy in Medieval Russia: Warrior and Saint* (Leiden, 2006), 67, 77; and Frithjof Benjamin Schenk, *Aleksandr Nevskij: Heiliger-Fürst-Nationalheld; eine Erinnerungsfigur im russischen kulturellen Gedächtnis (1263–2000)* (Cologne, 2004), 212–13. The church was completed in 1900. For the broader Russian transformation of the Domberg/Toompea, see Karsten Brüggemann, "Wie der Revaler Domberg zum Moskauer Kreml wurde: Zur lokalen Repräsentation imperialer Herrschaft im späten Zarenreich," in Jörg Baberowski, David Feest, and Christoph Gumb (eds.), *Imperiale Herrschaft in der Provinz: Repräsentationen politischer Macht im späten Zarenreich* (Frankfurt, 2008), 172–95.

43. The quote is drawn from *Illustrirter Führer durch Reval und seine Umgebungen* (Reval, 1901), 21.

44. N. A. Troinitskii (ed.), *Pervaia vseobshchaia perepis' naseleniia Rossiiskoi imperii 1897 g.* (St. Petersburg, 1905), vol. 49, 42–43. The census of 1897 counted not nationality but rather "native language." According to this measure, self-declared German speakers and Russian speakers each made up approximately 16 percent of Reval's population. The great majority of the rest indicated Estonian as their "native language."

45. For the history of the school, see G. F. Bauer, *Stareishaia gimnaziia v Rossii: Ocherki iz proshlogo Revel'skoi gimnazii imperatora Nikolaia I* (Revel', 1910); Endel Laul, *Tallinna 1. Keskkool, 1631–1981: NSV Liidu vanima keskkooli minevik ja tänapäev* (Tallinn, 1981); and Woodworth, "Civil Society," 268, 270, 285, 289–91. The school is still active today in the same building. For the most recent history of the institution, see *Gustav Adolfi Gümnaasium 375* (Tallinn, 2006).

46. *EAA*, f.101, n.1, s.93, no pagination indicated. These figures roughly correlate to the breakdown for the school as a whole, whose total enrollment in 1902 was 384 students. See *EAA*, f.101, n.1, s.36, no pagination indicated.

47. On the principal and his patriotic credentials, see S. G. Isakov (comp.), *Russkie obshchestvennye i kul'turnye deiateli v Estonii: Materially k biograficheskomu slovariu* (2d rev. ed.; Tallinn, 1996) vol. 1, 138; G. Ianchevetskii (ed. and comp.), *Venok na mogilu: Stati posviashchennye pamiati byvshego estliandskogo gubernatora kniazia S. V. Shakhovskogo* (Revel', 1896). For overviews of the teaching staff and lists of teachers, see Bauer, *Stareishaia gimnaziia v Rossii*, 54–59; and Laul, *Tallinna 1. Keskkool, 1631–1981*, 95–99.

48. For the student code of conduct and Ungern's schedule and curriculum, see *EAA*, f.101, n.1, s.469, l.102–4(b); and *EAA*, f.101, n.1, s.485, no pagination indicated. The quoted phrases are from Antonio Gramsci, "On Education," in Gramsci, *Selections from the Prison Notebooks* (Quintin Hoare and Geoffrey Nowell Smith, eds. and trans.) (New York, 1971), 37; and James C. McClelland, *Autocrats and Academics: Education, Culture, and Society in Tsarist Russia* (Chicago, 1979), 26–27. For the school's general curriculum in the very early 1900s, see Laul, *Tallinna 1. Keskkool, 1631–1981*, 77.

49. Jean-Jacques Rousseau, "Considérations sur le gouvernement de Pologne et sur sa réformation projettée," in Rousseau, *Oeuvres complètes* (Paris, 1964), vol. 3, 966.

50. On language and religious instruction at the school in 1902–1903, see *EAA*, f.101, n.1, s.485, no pagination.

51. *EAA*, f.101, n.1, s.36, no pagination indicated.

52. Shakovskoi's quote appears in *Iz arkhiva S. V. Shakovskogo: Materially dlia istorii nedavnego proshlogo Pribaltiiskoi okrainy, 1885–1894 gg.* (St. Petersburg, 1909), vol. 1, xxvi. The quote, in a slightly different translation, also appears in Woodworth, "Civil Society," 188.

53. For Ungern's grades and conduct, see *EAA*, f.101, n.1, s.93, 94, and 95. None of these files are paginated.

54. Nils von Ungern-Sternberg (comp.), *De Hungaria: Ungern-Sternberg zu Pürkel; ein Geschlecht im Wandel der Zeiten* (Bamberg, 1979), 185; [Arved von Ungern-Sternberg], "Roman Baron Ungern-Sternberg: Lebensgeschichte," *EAA*, f.1423, n.1, s.192, l.14.

55. Bodisco, *Versunkene Welten*, 298.

56. On street signs and mixed speech, see Woodworth, "Civil Society," 197; and Alfred Schönfeldt, "Deutsche Sprache und gesellschaftliche Ordnung im Baltikum," in Walther Mitzka (ed.), *Wortgeographie und Gesellschaft* (Berlin, 1968), 669.

57. "Rech' G. Ministra Iustitsii I. V. Murav'eva, proiznesennaia 29 sentiabria 1895 goda na obede ot Revel'skogo obshchestva," *Revel'skie izvestiia*, October 3, 1895, 1.

58. *EAA*, f.101, n.1, s.1266, l.4.

Chapter 3

1. I borrow this term from Catherine Edwards and Greg Woolf, "Cosmopolis: Rome as World City," in Edwards and Woolf (eds.), *Rome the Cosmopolis* (New York, 2003), 1–3. See also James Cracraft, "Saint Petersburg: The Russian Cosmopolis," in Cynthia Hyla Whittaker (ed.), *Russia Engages the World, 1453–1825* (Cambridge, Mass., 2003), 24–49.

2. On the diversity and distribution of the city's non-Russian population in the early twentieth century, see *Mnogonatsional'nyi Peterburg: Istoriia, religii, narody* (St. Petersburg, 2003), 26, 54–71; T. M. Smirnova, *Natsional'nost'-Piterskie: Natsional'nye men'shinstva Peterburga i Leningradskoi oblasti v xx veke* (St. Petersburg, 2002), 62–63; James H. Bater, *St. Petersburg: Industrialization and Change* (Montreal, 1976), 376–78; Benjamin Nathans, *Beyond the Pale: The Jewish Encounter with Late Imperial Russia* (Berkeley and Los Angeles, 2002), 113–20; and Steven Duke, "Multiethnic St. Petersburg: The Late Imperial Period," in Helena Goscilo and Stephen M. Norris (eds.), *Preserving Petersburg: History, Memory, Nostalgia* (Bloomington, Ind., 2008), 142–63.

3. Boris V. Anan'ich and Sergei G. Beliaev, "St. Petersburg: Banking Center of the Russian Empire," in William Craft Brumfield, et al. (eds.), *Commerce in Russian Urban Culture, 1861–1914* (Washington, D.C., 2001), 15–16; Smirnova, *National'nost'-Piterskie*, 119–30.

4. *RGAVMF*, f.432, Register of Names (*imennoi ukazatel'*); *Ves' Peterburg na 1903 god* (St. Petersburg, 1903), 674.

5. On admission requirements, see *RGAVMF*, f.432, op.1, d.7103, ll.67–67(b).

6. *RGAVMF*, f.432, op.1, d.7135, ll.98–99. For a description by one of Ungern's fellow students of preparing for and then taking the school's nerve-wracking entrance exams, see G. K. Graf, *Moriaki (ôcherki iz zhizni morskikh ofitserov)* (Navarre, 1930), 5–8.

7. On the history of the school, see A. Krotov, *Morskoi kadetskii korpus: Kratkii istoricheskii ocherk s illiustratsiiami* (St. Petersburg, 1901).

8. The building is currently the home of the Peter the Great Naval College and the Naval Institute of St. Petersburg.

9. For a copy of the invitation to the ball of 1903, see *RGAVMF*, f.432, op.1, d.7200, l.14.

10. A. Iu. Emelin (comp.), *Morskoi kadetskii korpus v vospominaniiakh vospitannikov* (St. Petersburg, 2003), 71.

11. David Alan Rich, *The Tsar's Colonels: Professionalism, Strategy, and Subversion in Late Imperial Russia* (Cambridge, Mass., 1998), 31. On military education in the cadet schools in the late imperial decades, see Dietrich Beyrau, *Militär und Gesellschaft im Vorrevolutionären Russland* (Cologne-Vienna, 1984), 370–71; V. M. Krilov, *Kadetskie korpusa i rossiiskie kadety* (St. Petersburg, 1998), 51–53; and Iu. Galushko and A. Kolesnikov, *Shkola rossiiskogo ofitserstva: Istoricheskii spravochnik* (Moscow, 1993), 73–174. On the tradition of intense devotion to the tsar within the military, see Hans-Peter Stein, "Der Offizier des russischen Heeres im Zeitabschnitt zwischen Reform und Revolution (1861–1905)," *FzOG* 13 (1967), 467–73.

12. *RGAVMF*, f.432, op.1, d.7217, l.92(b).

13. Graf, *Moriaki*, 67; Emilin, *Morskoi kadetskii korpus*, 75, n.5.

14. *RGVIA*, f.499, op.1, d.1238, l.5. The quoted phrase is from the army law (*polozhenie*) of 1888.

15. P. A. Zaionchkovskii, *Samoderzhavie i russkaia armiia na rubezhe xix–xx stoletii, 1881–1903* (Moscow, 1973), 199; Mark von Hagen, "Confronting Backwardness: Dilemmas of Soviet Officer Education in the Interwar Years, 1918–1941," in Elliott V. Converse III (ed.), *Forging the Sword: Selecting, Educating, and Training Cadets and Junior Officers in the Modern World* (Chicago, 1998), 86, 96, n.15; Walter M. Pintner, "The Nobility and the Officer Corps in the Nineteenth Century," in Eric Lohr and Marshall Poe (eds.), *The Military and Society in Russia, 1450–1917* (Leiden, 2002), 250–51. Stein estimates approximately 75 percent of officers were Russian Orthodox. See "Offizier des russischen Heeres," 462–63.

16. *RGAVMF*, f.432, op.1, d.7189, ll.6–7. Ungern was in cadet regiment no. 1.

17. Zaionchkovskii, *Samoderzhavie i russkaia armiia*, 199–200.

18. Ibid., 201, n.133. N. A. Mashkin, *Vysshaia voennaia shkola rossiiskoi imperii xix–nachala xx veka* (Moscow, 1997), 152. A tiny number of Jews were promoted to officer by serving for long periods as noncommissioned officers. An even smaller number received special promotions approved by the tsar. On these cases as well as the general restrictions against Jews in the officer corps, see Nathans, *Beyond the Pale*, 28–29, 182; Yuri Slezkine, *The Jewish Century* (Princeton, N.J., 2004), 124–27; Joshua A. Sanborn, *Drafting the Russian Nation: Military Conscription, Total War, and Mass Politics, 1905–1925* (DeKalb, Ill., 2003), 116–17; D. Raskin, "Evrei v sostave rossiiskogo ofitserskogo korpusa v xix–nachale xx veka," in D. A. El'iashevich (ed.), *Evrei v Rossii: Istoriia i kul'tura; Sbornik nauchnykh trudov* (St. Petersburg, 1998), 170–74; Iokhanan Petrovskii-Shtern, *Evrei v russkoi armii, 1827–1914* (Moscow, 2003), 319–24. It is worth noting that the Russian military was not alone in restricting the service of Jews as officers. See Stein, "Offizier des russischen Heeres," 459–60.

19. For this incident, see *RGAVMF*, f.432, op.1, d.7288, l.13. For the commandant's remarks on the geographical diversity of the students, see *RGAVMF*, f.432, op.1, d.7217, l.92(b).

20. For references to student-officer relations and views, see *RGAVMF*, f.432, op.1, d.7217, l.92; and *RGAVMF*, f.432, op.1, d.7217, l.13. See also *RGAVMF*, f.432, op.1, d.7137, l.2(b). On the various degrees of "confinement" faced by rule-breaking cadets, see *RGAVMF*, f.432, op.1, d.7135, l.136.

21. *RGAVMF*, f.432, op.2, d.2162, ll.3(b)–4; *RGAVMF*, f.432, op.1, d.7293, ll.238–40.

22. *RGAVMF,* f.432, op.2, d.2162, ll.5(b)–7(b). Ungern's dismal record was all the more impressively bad for beating the otherwise unrivaled delinquent in his class, a certain Nikolai Zadler, who accumulated a total of eighty-one infractions between October 1899 and November 1905. Between 1903 and early 1905, when the two were going head-to-head, Ungern outdid Zadler by fifteen demerits. For Zadler's record, see *RGAVMF,* f.432, op.1, d.7191, ll.108–11(b).

23. *RGAVMF,* f.432, op.2, d.2162, l.6.

24. *RGAVMF,* f.432, op.1, d.7260, l.3.

25. This quotation from the petition appears in Walter Sablinsky, *The Road to Bloody Sunday: Father Gapon and the St. Petersburg Massacre of 1905* (Princeton, N.J., 1976), 188.

26. *RGAVMF,* f.432, op.1, d.7340, ll.6, 10.

27. On the tsar's visit, see *RGAVMF,* f.432, op.1, d.7217, l.23. For the tsar's own brief description, see *Dnevnik imperatora Nikolaia II, 1890–1906 gg.* (Moscow, 1991), 137. For a contemporary description of patriotic fanfare in the country (and St. Petersburg in particular) during the early months of the war, see *Russko-iaponskaia voina i nashi geroi* (Moscow, 1904), 17–21.

28. *RGAVMF,* f.432, op.2, d.2162, l.11.

29. Cited in Yoshihisa Tak Matsusaka, *The Making of Japanese Manchuria, 1904–1932* (Cambridge, Mass., 2001), 24. See also Peter Duus, *The Abacus and the Sword: The Japanese Penetration of Korea, 1895–1910* (Berkeley and Los Angeles, 1995), 64.

30. On the building of the CER, see Sören Urbansky, *Kolonialer Wettstreit: Russland, China, Japan und die Ostchinesische Eisenbahn* (Frankfurt, 2008), 37–53; Chia Yin Hsu, "A Tale of Two Railroads: 'Yellow Labor,' Agrarian Colonization, and the Making of Russianness at the Far Eastern Frontier, 1890s–1910s," *Ab Imperio,* no. 3 (2006), 221–28; N. E. Ablova, "Rossiia i russkie v Man'chzhurii v kontse xix–nachale xx vv.," in O. R. Airapetov (ed.), *Russko-iaponskaia voina, 1904–1905: Vzgliad cherez stoletie* (Moscow, 2004), 185–89; and S. C. M. Paine, "The Chinese Eastern Railway from the First Sino-Japanese War until the Russo-Japanese War," in Bruce A. Elleman and Stephen Kotkin (eds.), *Manchurian Railways and the Opening of China: An International History* (Armonk, N.Y., 2010), 19–21, 26–28.

31. See Steven G. Marks, *Road to Power: The Trans-Siberian Railroad and the Colonization of Asian Russia, 1850–1917* (Ithaca, 1991).

32. Quoted in Marks, *Road to Power,* 204. For broader criticisms of Russia's railway system from the period, see O. N. Eliutin, "'Zolotoi vek' zheleznodorozhnogo stroitel'stva v Rossii i ego posledstviia," *VI,* no. 2 (2004), 47–57. On the Circum-Baikal railway that became operational in late 1904, see L. G. Kolotilo and V. G. Andrienko, *Transbaikal'skii perekrestok: Problemy transportnykh putei i zheleznodorozhnoi paromnoi perepravy cherez ozero Baikal na rubezhe xix–xx vv.* (St. Petersburg, 2005), 234–36.

33. D. W. Meinig, *The Shaping of America: A Geographical Perspective on 500 Years of History,* vol. 3, *Transcontinental America, 1850–1915* (New Haven, Conn., 1998), 4–28, 327–47.

34. A. N. Kulomzin, *Le Transsibérien* (Paris, 1904), 311; Claudia Weiss, "Representing the Empire: The Meaning of Siberia for Russian Imperial Identity," *Nationalities Papers* 35, no. 3 (2007), 445–46.

35. Willard Sunderland, "The 'Colonization Question': Visions of Colonization in Late Imperial Russia," *JfGO* 48, no. 2 (2000), 210–32; A. V. Remnev, "Samoderzhavie i Sibir' v kontse xix–nachale xx veka: Problemy regional'nogo upravleniia," *OI,* no. 2 (1994), 65.

36. Michael D. Gordin, "Measure of All the Russias: Metrology and Governance in the Russian Empire," *Kritika* 4, no. 4 (2003), 784.

37. See, for example, *Karta sledovaniia skorykh soglasovannykh ot Moskvy do Dal'niago i obratno* (1903), reprinted here.

38. I borrow this phrase from Stephen Kern, *The Culture of Time and Space, 1880–1918* (Cambridge, Mass., 1983), 1–2.

39. V. I. Godunov, *Istoriia 91-ogo pekhotnogo Dvinskogo polka, 1805–1905 gg.* (Iur'ev, 1905), 318–19. See also V. I. Godunov, *Kratkii ocherk istorii 91-ogo pekhotnogo Dvinskogo polka (dlia nizhnykh chinov)* (Revel', 1905), 95.

40. Godunov, *Kratkii ocherk*, 95.

41. Ungern's regiment was posted near the city of Tieling, Liaoning Province, about 50 miles northeast of Mukden (Shenyang).

42. *Kratkaia istoriia 12-ogo pekhotnogo velikolutskogo polka* (Moscow, 1911), 282.

43. Ibid., 287.

44. David Wolff, *To the Harbin Station: The Liberal Alternative in Russian Manchuria, 1898–1914* (Stanford, Calif., 1999), 27–41. For Chinese understandings of the "alienated corridor," see Blaine R. Chiasson, *Administering the Colonizer: Manchuria's Russians under Chinese Rule, 1918–1929* (Vancouver, B.C., 2010), 22–23.

45. For descriptions of the Manchurian landscape in this general period, see Francis Edward Younghusband, *The Heart of a Continent: A Narrative of Travels in Manchuria, Across the Gobi Desert, Through the Himalayas, the Pamirs, and Chitral, 1884–1894* (New York, 1896), 5–7, 22–25. On Qing policies supporting Han colonization in Manchuria, see James Reardon-Anderson, *Reluctant Pioneers: China's Expansion Northward, 1644–1937* (Stanford, Calif., 2005), 78–83. Descriptions of climate and geography for central and southern Manchuria, then and now, appear in *Russko-iaponskaia voina, 1904–1905 gg.* (St. Petersburg, 1910), vol. 1, 101–28; and Zhao Songqiao, *Physical Geography of China* (New York, 1986), 97–101.

46. Ablova, "Rossiia i russkie v Man'chzhurii," 210. See also Albova, *KVZhD i rossiiskaia emigratsiia v Kitae: Mezhdunarodnye i politicheskie aspekty istorii (pervaia polovina xx v.)* (Moscow, 2005), 79.

47. Harbin's population on the eve of the war was likely around forty thousand; two-thirds were Chinese, the rest mostly Russians. During the war the city's population swelled enormously, reaching perhaps one hundred thousand people. By 1907 it had fallen to approximately fifty thousand. For these figures, see R. K. I. Quested, *"Matey Imperialists"? The Tsarist Russians in Manchuria, 1895–1917* (Hong Kong, 1982), 221. On life in Harbin in this period, see Wolff, *To the Harbin Station*, 115–45; Eva-Maria Stolberg, *Sibirien: Russlands "Wilder Osten"; Mythos und soziale Realität im 19. und 20. Jahrhundert* (Stuttgart, 2009), 213–20; and Ablova, *KVZhD i rossiiskaia emigratsiia v Kitae*, 57–80. On Harbin as a "dual city," see James H. Carter, *Creating a Chinese Harbin: Nationalism in an International City, 1916–1932* (Ithaca, 2002), 21–24.

48. Reardon-Anderson, *Reluctant Pioneers*, 72–84, 112–13; David Wolff, "Bean There: Toward a Soy-Based History of Northeast Asia," in Thomas Lahusen (ed.), *Harbin and Manchuria: Place, Space, and Identity* (Durham, N.C., 2001), 244–45. On Manchuria's ambiguous image as both un-Chinese and Chinese at the same time in the late Qing period, see Mark C. Elliott, "The Limits of Tartary: Manchuria in Imperial and National Geographies," *Journal of Asian Studies* 59, no. 3 (2000), 603–46; and Li Narangoa, "The Power of Imagination: Whose Northeast and Whose Manchuria?" *Inner Asia* 4, no. 1 (2002), 4–5.

49. Wolfgang Seuberlich, *Zur Verwaltungsgeschichte der Mandschurei (1644–1930)* (Hartmut Walraveng, ed.) (Wiesbaden, 2001), 76–77.

50. Alexander Lukin, *The Bear Watches the Dragon: Russia's Perceptions of China and the Evolution of Russian-Chinese Relations since the Eighteenth Century* (Armonk, N.Y., 2003), 3–74.

51. George M. Fredrickson, *Racism: A Short History* (Princeton, N.J., 2002), 1–2, 99–101.

52. On the "yellow peril" ideology in Western writing and its influence on Russian commentary and reporting up to and during the war, see Michael Keevak, *Becoming Yellow: A Short History of Racial Thinking* (Princeton, N.J., 2011), 124–44; Heinz Gollwitzer, *Die Gelbe Gefahr: Geschichte eines Schlagworts; Studien zum imperialistischen Denken* (Göttingen, 1962), 107, 109–11; Milan Hauner, *What Is Asia to Us? Russia's Asian Heartland Yesterday and Today* (Boston, 1990), 49–52; David Schimmelpenninck van der Oye, *Toward the Rising Sun: Russian Ideologies of Empire and the Path to War with Japan* (DeKalb, Ill., 2001), 82–86, 92–103; Marlène Laruelle, "'Zheltaia opasnost'' v rabotakh russikikh natsionalistov nachala veka," in Airapetov, *Russko-iaponskaia voina, 1904–1905,* 579–91; Richard Austin Thompson, *The Yellow Peril, 1890–1924* (New York, 1978); and Louise McReynolds, *The News under Russia's Old Regime: The Development of a Mass-Circulation Press* (Princeton, N.J., 1991), 191.

53. On Asianism, see David Schimmelpenninck van der Oye, *Russian Orientalism: Asia in the Russian Mind from Peter the Great to the Emigration* (New Haven, Conn., 2010), 234–35.

54. E. E. Ukhtomskii, *K sobytiiam v Kitae: Ob otnosheniiakh Zapada i Rossii k vostoku* (St. Petersburg, 1900), 82. A personal confidant of Tsar Nicholas and the first director of the Russo-Chinese Bank, Ukhtomskii proved this point himself by "getting along" with the Qing foreign minister and negotiating the initial agreement to build the CER. On Ukhtomskii, see Schimmelpenninck, *Toward the Rising Sun,* 42–60; and Marlène Laruelle, *Mythe aryen et rêve imperial dans la Russie du xixème siècle* (Paris, 2005), 156–68.

55. For a reference to Ungern's Asian inclinations by his interrogators, see "Dopros R. F. Ungerna 27 avgusta 1921 g. v Troitskosavske," in Kuz'min, *Baron Ungern,* 201.

56. Oswald Spengler, *The Decline of the West* (New York, 1946), vol.1, 16. In contrast to Ungern, though, Spengler saw Russia as a "civilization" distinct from the West (the initial volume of Spengler's work first appeared in German in 1918); and Ezra Pound, "Hugh Selwyn Mauberley," in Pound, *Selected Poems* (New York, 1957), 61.

57. Keith Stevens, "Between Scylla and Charybdis: China and the Chinese during the Russo-Japanese War, 1904–1905," *Journal of the Hong Kong Branch of the Royal Asiatic Society* 43 (2003), 136. On varying Russian policies and attitudes toward the Chinese during the war, see Quested, *"Matey" Imperialists?,* 139–41. On Qing neutrality and Chinese villages destroyed in the battle zones, see Yang Chuang, Gao Fei, and Feng Yujun, *Bainian Zhong E guanxi* (Beijing, 2006), 43–44; and *Sha E qin Hua shi* (2nd ed.; Beijing, 2007), 307, 310–12.

58. For soldiers' or more generally popular views of the Chinese and Japanese, see Richard Stites, "Russian Representations of the Japanese Enemy," in John W. Steinberg et al. (eds.), *The Russo-Japanese War in Global Perspective: World War Zero* (Leiden, 2005), 404–8; and Stephen M. Norris, *A War of Images: Russian Popular Prints, Wartime Culture, and National Identity, 1812–1945* (DeKalb, Ill., 2006), 109–15. On Chinese as "unchristians" and soldiers' suspicions of their support of the Japanese as well as descriptions of looting, see F. I. Shikuts, *Dnevnik soldata v russko-iaponskuiu voinu* (Moscow, 2003), 11, 38.

59. Wolff, *To the Harbin Station,* 38. The original saying is "50 versts" rather than 50 miles.

60. *RGVIA,* f.319, op.1, d.630, ll.174, 186.

61. On the burning of Jerwakant, see Lui Pikkov, "1905. aasta Raplamaal," in Hans Treimann and Tiina Treimann (eds.), *Rännud Raplamaa minevikku: Koduloolisi uurimusi ja mälestusi* ([Rapla], 2006), 197–214; and *EAA,* f. 3654, n. 1, s. 54, l. 249–50. On the death and destruction of 1905–1906 in the Baltic, see Whelan, *Adapting to Modernity,* 1, 309–10. On Ungern's family's escape from the burning manor, see Bodisco, *Versunkene Welten,* 251; and von Taube, *Im alten Estland,* 19.

62. For a range of criticisms of officer education in this period, see M. Galkin, "Offitserskii vopros," *Voina i mir,* no. 7 (1906), 5, 8–10, 14–15, 21; S-er, "V zashchitu voennykh

uchilishch i o zhelatel'nykh v nikh reformakh," *Voina i mir,* no. 7 (1907), 166; "Neobkhodi-maia mera dlia podgotovki molodykh ofitserov," *Razvedchik,* no. 863 (1907), 255; and A. P., "Neskol'ko myslei ob ulushchenii ofitserskogo sostava nashei armii," *Ofitserskaia zhizn',* nos. 127/28 (1908), 390.

63. V. Permskii, "Nuzhdy voennogo obrazovaniia," *Razvedchik,* no. 867 (1907), 316.

64. Gal'kin, *Novyi put' sovremennogo ofitsera* (St. Petersburg, 1907), 15, 75.

65. The quoted phrase appears in L. L. Tol'stoi, *Pamiatka russkogo ofitsera* (St. Petersburg, 1907), 8.

66. Gregory Vitarbo, "Nationality Policy and the Russian Imperial Officer Corps, 1905–1914," *SR* 66, no. 4 (2007), 691–92. On the increasing importance of ethnic na-tionalism within the army in the 1905–1914 period, see also Sanborn, *Drafting the Rus-sian Nation,* 72–73; and Mark von Hagen, "The Levée en masse from Russian Empire to Soviet Union, 1874–1938," in Daniel Moran and Arthur Waldron (eds.), *The People in Arms: Military Myth and National Mobilization since the French Revolution* (New York, 2003), 165–67.

67. A. I. Denikin, *Put' russkogo ofitsera* (New York, 1953), 282. This view of interethnic harmony was less prevalent among Polish officers. See Mark von Hagen, "The Limits of Re-form: The Multiethnic Imperial Army Confronts Nationalism, 1874–1917," in David Schim-melpenninck and Bruce W. Menning (eds.), *Reforming the Tsar's Army: Military Innovation from Peter the Great to the Revolution* (Washington, D.C., 2004), 45.

68. *RGVIA,* f.319, op.1, d.492, ll.159–60, 163. The street's name was changed after the October Revolution and today is Red Cadet Street (ul. Krasnogo Kursanta). In enrolling in his new military institute, Ungern may have had help from his step-uncle, Baron Barthold von Hoyningen-Huene, a career military officer and member of the elite Horse Guard Regiment. See Ronny Rönnqvist, *Baron Ungern, Mongoliets härskare* (Helsinki, 2006), 22, 145.

69. Applicants could be from any social estate, but the overwhelming majority (70 per-cent) of the yunkers in Ungern's period were the sons of officers and civil servants. Roughly a quarter were hereditary nobles. Most young men admitted were between the ages of nineteen and twenty-one. See *RGVIA,* f.319, op.1, d.628, l.27. On the role of the institutes within the empire's system of military education, see Galushko and Kolesnikov, *Shkola russkogo ofitserstva,* 140–52.

70. For descriptions of the institute, see A. N. Petrov (ed.), *Istoricheskii ocherk Pavlovsk-ogo voennogo uchilishcha, Pavlovskogo kadetskogo korpusa i imperatorskogo voenno-sirotskogo doma, 1798–1898 gg.* (St. Petersburg, 1898); and "Pamiatka Pavlovskogo voennogo uchilish-cha, 1863–1913," *Pedagogicheskii sbornik,* no. 10 (1913), 324–42.

71. P. N. Krasnov, *Pavlony: 1-e Voennoe Pavlovskoe Uchilishche pol veka tomu nazad; Vospo-minaniia* (Paris, 1943), 31–32.

72. For a description of life in the summer camp around Ungern's time, see Vladimir Tru-betskoi, *Zapiski kirasira* (Moscow, 1991), 139–57. Krasnoe Selo was a popular spot with the Romanovs. On Tsar Nicholas's fondness for the camp, see Richard Wortman, "Moscow and Petersburg: The Problem of Political Center in Tsarist Russia, 1881–1914," in Sean Wilentz (ed.), *Rites of Power: Symbolism, Ritual, and Politics since the Middle Ages* (Philadelphia, Penn., 1985), 250. On the larger military culture and display of the capital, see V. V. Lapin et al., eds., *Voennaia stolitsa rossiiskoi imperii v fotografiiakh kontsa xix–nachala xx veka* (St. Peters-burg, 2004).

73. His best subject was French, where he earned a perfect twelve out of twelve points. He performed worst in artillery, tactics, and mechanics, where he ended up with scores of just 50 percent (i.e., six points out of twelve). *RGVIA,* f.319, op.1 (vol.1), d.630, ll.120, 348(b).

74. For such incidents, see *RGVIA,* f.319, op.1 (vol.1), d.627, ll.d. 21–22, 37.

75. In 1908, of the 403 yunkers enrolled at the school, 375 were Orthodox, 15 were Catholics, 9 were Lutherans, and 4 were Muslims. The entire officer staff was Orthodox, though some of the enlisted men who served on campus were Catholic and one was Jewish. See *RGVIA*, f.319, op.1, d.628, l.27; and f.319, op.1, d.597, ll.27(b)–30(b).

76. For the reference to *okraintsy,* see M. M., "Bud'te russkimi," *Okrainy Rossii* no. 12 (March 21, 1909), 179.

77. *RGVIA*, f.319, op.1 (vol.1), d.630, l.120. Let history record that the valedictorian, a certain Ushakov, graduated with the stunning overall score of 11.35 points out of 12. Ungern, by comparison, ended up with a 7.7.

78. Rönnqvist, *Baron Ungern, Mongoliets härskare,* 25.

79. *RGVIA*, f.319, op.1, d.630, l.247(b). The original posting was with the 2nd Siberian Cossack Regiment with quarters in the town of Dzharkent.

80. According to family accounts, Ungern did indeed make the decision himself and used personal connections to obtain the change. See the information in Rönnqvist, *Baron Ungern, Mongoliets härskare,* 25. There is no explanation for the change in the archives, however.

81. *RGVIA*, f.319, op.1, d.630, ll.247(b)–248.

Chapter 4

1. Dmitri Mendeleev, *K poznaniiu Rossii: S prilozheniem karty Rossii* (St. Petersburg, 1906), 108–9.

2. For example, *Karta Rossiiskoi imperii i sopredel'nykh s neiu gosudarstv* (E. A. Koverskii, comp.) (sometime after 1902). Also compare the two maps of European versus Asian Russia published by the War Department Printing House in the early years of the century: *Karta Evropeiskoi Rossii s pokazaniem zheleznykh dorog i parakhodnykh soobshchenii* (1910) and *Karta Aziatskoi Rossii s pokazaniem zheleznykh dorog i parakhodnykh soobshchenii* (1907).

3. On images of masculinity in Europe in this period, see George L. Mosse, *The Image of Man: The Creation of Modern Masculinity* (New York, 1996), 77–106.

4. "Chertezhnaia rospis' pritokov r. Leny v ee verknem techenii, pashennykh mest, rastoianii mezhdu ustiiami rek, so svedeniiami o mestnom naselenii [1640/1641]," in G. N. Rumiantsev and S. B. Okun' (comps.), *Sbornik dokumentov po istorii Buriatii: xvii vek* (Ulan-Ude, 1960), vol. 1, 36. "Beasts of the sea" is presumably a reference to the nerpa, the Baikal freshwater seal.

5. On the Russian conquest of the region and Siberia more generally in this period, see N. N. Stepanov, "Prisoedinenie Vostochnoi Sibiri v xvii v. i tungusskie plemena," in *Russkoe naselenie Pomor'ia i Sibiri (period feodalizma)* (Moscow, 1973), 106–24; W. Bruce Lincoln, *The Conquest of a Continent: Siberia and the Russians* (1994; repr.: Ithaca, 2007), 41–72; Yuri Slezkine, *Arctic Mirrors: Russia and the Small Peoples of the North* (Ithaca, 1994), 11–45. Tungus was the name given in the tsarist period to the broadly distributed ethnic group known today as the Evenks.

6. The Daurs (common alternative spelling: Dahurs) were a Mongol people concentrated near the Argun River and Upper Amur. On the early use of the term "Dauria" to refer to the Trans-Baikal region, see T. V. Fedotova, *Slovar' toponimov Zabaikal'ia* (Chita, 2003), 38; and V. F. Balabanov, *Istoriia zemli Daurskoi* (Chita, 2003), 21.

7. For demographic information and comparisons regarding the size of the Trans-Baikal region (*zabaikal'skaia oblast'*), see A. V. Kozulin, *Demograficheskie protsessy v Zabaikal'e*

(konets xix–nachalo xx veka) (Ulan-Ude, 2004), 169; N. I. Razumov, *Zabaikal'e: Svod materialov vysochaishe uchrezhdennoi kommissii dlia izsledovaniia mestnogo zemlevladeniia i zemlepol'zovaniia, pod predsedatel'stvom stats-sekretaria Kulomzina* (St. Petersburg, 1899), 1; and *Sibir' i velikaia sibirskaia zhelznaia doroga* (2nd rev. ed.; St. Petersburg, 1896), 36.

8. On fin de siècle interests in Asia, see Schimmelpenninck, *Toward the Rising Sun;* Schimmelpenninck, *Russian Orientalism,* 210–23; Jane Ashton Sharp, *Russian Modernism between East and West: Natal'ia Goncharova and the Moscow Avant-Garde* (New York, 2006), 20–40; and I. I. Rodigina, *"Drugaia Rossiia": Obraz Sibiri v russkoi zhurnal'noi presse vtoroi polovine xix–nachala xx veka* (Novosibirsk, 2006).

9. Weiss, "Representing the Empire", 444; Stolberg, *Sibirien,* 95–100; Sunderland, "'Colonization Question,'" 210–32.

10. The quoted phrases are drawn from "Zur Lage," *Baltische Monatsschrift* 19, no. 1 (1870), 8.

11. For a few of these connections, see Nils von Ungern-Sternberg, "Der mongolisch-mandschurische Raum im Kräftespiel des Fernen Ostens," *Baltische Monatsschrift* 37 (1890), 449–57; Max von Wimpffen, *Kritische Worte über den Buddhismus* (Vienna, 1891); Edmund Russow, *Alexander Graf Keyserling* (Reval, 1892); Robert Graf von Keyserling, *Vom Japanischen Meer zum Ural: Eine Wanderung durch Sibirien* (Breslau, 1898); Hermann Graf von Keyserling, *Über die innere Beziehung zwischen den Kulturproblemen des Orients und Okzidents: Eine Botschaft an die Völker des Ostens* (Jena, 1913); von Taube, *Buch der Keyserlinge;* and Al'fred Keiserling, *Vospominaniia o russkoi sluzhbe* (Moscow, 2001). General Paul von Rennenkampf was the brother of Ungern's paternal grandmother, Natalie von Rennenkampf.

12. Shane O'Rourke, *The Cossacks* (Manchester, 2007); and Robert H. McNeal, *Tsar and Cossack, 1855–1914* (New York, 1987).

13. This figure represents the total population of the Cossack estate within the empire, which included adult men past their service age as well as women and children. The number of active duty Cossacks at the time was roughly five hundred thousand. See *Otchet glavnogo upravleniia kazach'ikh voisk za 1908 god* (St. Petersburg, 1909), 15.

14. For general overviews of the history of the Trans-Baikal Host, see F. Shulunov, *K istorii Buriat-Mongol'skogo kazachestva (kratkii ocherk)* (Ulan-Ude, 1936); L. V. Sambueva, *Buriatskoe i evenkiiskoe kazachestvo na strazhe otechestva: Vtoraia chetvert' xviii–pervaia polovina xix vv.* (Ulan-Ude, 2003); V. I. Vasil'evskii, *Zabaikal'skoe kazach'e voisko: Kratkii istoricheskii ocherk* (Moscow, 2000); "Zabaikal'skoe voiskovoe kazach'e obshchestvo: Iz istorii zabaikal'skikh kazakov," in *Rossiiskoe kazachestvo: Nauchno-spravochnoe izdanie* (Moscow, 2003), 349–81; V. B. Bazarzhapov, *Buriaty na sluzhbe otechestva (xviii–xx vv.)* (Ulan-Ude, 2005), 17–32; and Nikolai Smirnov, *Zabaikal'skoe kazachestvo* (Moscow, 2008).

15. Slezkine, *Arctic Mirrors,* 13–22; Stepanov, "Prisoedinenie Vostochnoi Sibiri," 108–10.

16. On the outposts in the Trans-Baikal, see A. R. Artem'ev, *Goroda i ostrogi Zabaikal'ia i Priamur'ia vo vtoroi polovine xvii–xviii vv.* (Vladivostok, 1999), 40–94.

17. On the early twentieth-century campaigns, the best account is Smirnov, *Zabaikal'skoe kazachestvo,* 78–321.

18. G-n, "'Pasynki'—zabaikal'tsy," *Sibirskie voprosy,* no. 1 (1907), 76.

19. *RGVIA,* f.1553, op.1, d.16, l.20–34.

20. McNeal, *Tsar and Cossack,* 154–218, 219–22.

21. See Judith Deutsch Kornblatt, *The Cossack Hero in Russian Literature: A Study in Cultural Mythology* (Madison, Wisc., 1992), 3–96; Vladimir Kemenev, *Vasily Surikov, 1848–1916* (Bournemouth, Eng., 1997), 95–119, 135–41; and Richard Stites, *Russian*

Popular Culture: Entertainment and Society since 1900 (New York, 1992), 18, 31. The film came out in October 1908, a few months after Ungern moved to the Trans-Baikal.

22. N. Putintsev, "Nashi kazach'i voiska (neobkhodimost' izucheniia ikh trekhvekovogo istoricheskogo proshlogo," *Voennyi sbornik,* no. 1 (January 1900), 47.

23. S. Grekov, "Forma odezhdy dlia kazakov," *Ofitserskaia zhizn',* no. 105 (1908), 76; I. Stol'ianov, "Kazach'ii golovnoi ubor," *Razvedchik,* no. 932 (1908), 583. Cossacks in the Caucasus were also issued a special cloak (the *cherkeska*), such as the one Ungern posed in as a boy in the tourist photo from Tiflis. For a full description of the Cossack uniform, see V. K. Shenk, *Pravila nosheniia form odezhdy ofitersami vsekh rodov oruzhiia i grazhdanskimi chinami Voennogo Vedomstva* (St. Petersburg, 1910), table no. 31, 80–81.

24. M. Khoroshkhin and E. Putilov, *Zabakail'skaia kazach'ia knizhka* (St. Petersburg, 1893), ii.

25. For Ungern's assignment, see *RGVIA,* f.319, op.1, d.630, l.252; *RGVIA,* f.1553, op.1, d.10, l.123. I take July 27 as the date of Ungern's arrival in Chita, because of the duty order for his posting, which was issued on that day from host headquarters.

26. On Tsagan-Oluevskaya, see *Otchet o sostoianii Zabaikal'skogo kazach'ego voiska za 1908 god* (Chita, 1909), appendix 2, ii–iii. Tsagan-Oluevskaya took its name from the Tsagan-Olui, a shallow wash that cuts through the valley of the *stanitsa.* Ust'-Narynsk is today part of the village of Brusilovka, located some 30 miles east of Zabaikal'sk. In 2002, the village had a population of 273 people. On Brusilovka today, see the entry in the on-line version of the *Enstiklopediia Zabaikal'ia,* http://ez.chita.ru/encycl/concepts/?id=142 (last accessed: September 2013).

27. Ust'-Narynsk does not appear on a map of the Trans-Baikal Region published in 1909. See *Karta Zabaikal'skoi oblasti, putei soobshcheniia, vazhneishikh poselenii i pereselencheskikh uchastkov* (A. I. Popov, comp,) (Chita, 1909). To reach his post, Ungern would have traveled by train from Chita, taking the so-called Chinese spur off of the main Trans-Siberian down to the border and the crossing into Manchuria. In 1903, the travel time from Chita to the border was about sixteen hours. See M. E. Storzh, *Raspisanie khoda poezdov, ili illiustrirovannyi sputnik passazhira po Zabaikal'skoi zheleznoi doroge (s 15 oktiabria 1903 g. po 18 aprelia)* (Irkutsk, 1903), 43–44.

28. This description appears in "Po Zabaikal'iu," in A. Kruber et al. (comps.), *Aziatskaia Rossiia: Illiustrirovannyi geograficheskii sbornik* (Moscow, 1905), 488.

29. *Otchet glavnogo upravleniia kazach'ikh voisk za 1908 god* (St. Petersburg, 1909), 2–3.

30. The Trans-Baikal Cossacks were leaders among Cossack hosts in having the most horses per capita. In 1903 the host counted 233,372 horses, that is, a roughly 2:1 horse to male Cossack rider ratio. Sector 2, Ungern's sector, had the most horses of all, with an average of 3.5 horses per Cossack. See O. I. Sergeev, *Kazachestvo na russkom Dal'nem Vostoke v xvii–xix vv.* (Moscow, 1983),77.

31. For these and other descriptions and names of horses, many of them from Ungern's sector, see *RGVIA,* f.1553, op.1, d.10, ll.52, 57–57(b), 80, 86, 94, 99, 111.

32. For general works on these two ethnicities and their interrelationship during the tsarist period, see L. L. Abaeva and N. L. Zhukovskaia (eds.), *Buriaty* (Moscow, 2004), 57–61; A. S. Shubin, *Kratkii ocherk etnicheskoi istorii evenkov Zabaikal'ia xvii–xx vv.* (Ulan-Ude, 1973), 32–50; and T. V. Uvarova, *Nerchinskie evenki v xviii–xx vekakh* (Moscow, 2005), 66–73, 124–37. Contemporary ethnographers refer to the Tungus who lived near Ungern's sector as the "Nerchinsk Evenks" after the nearby mining town of Nerchinsk.

33. *Otchet glavnogo upravleniia kazach'ikh voisk za 1908 god,* 21. The vast majority of the non-Russian Cossacks were Buryats (some 88 percent). See S. Patkanov, *O priroste inorodcheskogo naseleniia Sibiri: Statisticheskie materialy dlia osveshcheniia voprosa o vymiranii pervobytnykh plemen* (St. Petersburg, 1911), 84.

34. For descriptions of these contacts and borrowings, see K. D. Loginovskii, "O byte kazakov vostochnogo Zabaikal'ia," *Zhivaia starina* 12, no. 2 (1902), 182–200; K. El'nitskii, *Inorodtsy Sibiri i sredneaziatskikh vladenii Rossii: Etnograficheskii ocherk* (St. Petersburg, 1910), 39; *Vsia Chita i Zabaikal'e s otdelom Priamur'ia v raione postroiki Amurskoi zheleznoi dorogi* (Chita, 1910), 82; A. V. Konstantinov and N. N. Konstantinova, *Istoriia Zabaikal'ia (s drevneishikh vremen do 1917 goda)* (Chita, 2002), 216; O. V. Buraeva, *Etnokul'turnoe vzaimodeistvie narodov Baikal'skogo regiona v xvii–nachale xx vv.* (Ulan-Ude, 2005), 194–95. For a glossary of local "Trans-Baikal words," see G. M. Osokin, *Na granitse Mongolii: Ocherki i materialy k etnografii iugo-zapadnogo Zabaikal'ia* (St. Petersburg, 1906), 281–92.

35. P. T. Matsokin, "O vlianii lamaizma na kul'turnoe razvitie buriat Zabaikal'ia," *Vestnik Azii*, no. 8 (February 1911), 90.

36. Razumov, *Zabaikal'e*, 41–42.

37. *Aziatskaia Rossiia* (St. Petersburg, 1914), vol. 1, 185; Remezov, *Zabaikal'e*, 42; Buraeva, *Etnokul'turnoe vzaimodeistvie*, 184–85; A. G. Iankov, "Sibiriaki—karymy: K voprosu o sibirskoi identichnosti," in A. O. Boronoev (ed.), *Sibir': Problemy sibirskoi identichnosti* (St. Petersburg, 2003), 99; and G. G. Ermak, *Semeinyi i khoziaistvennyi byt kazakov iuga Dal'nego Vostoka Rossii: Vtoraia polovina xix–nachalo xx veka* (Vladivostok, 2004), 43.

38. For descriptions of the border operations at Manchuria Station, see V. Soldatov, *Zheleznodorozhnye poselki po Zabaikal'skoi linii* (St. Petersburg, 1912), vol. 5, pt. 2, 309–12; and Urbansky, *Kolonialer Wettstreit*, 55–56.

39. On the development of modern border regimes and the various presumptions and practices that justify and accompany them, see Michel Foucault, "Governmentality," in Graham Burchell et al. (eds.), *The Foucault Effect: Studies in Governmentality* (Chicago, 1991), 87–104; Michael Baud and Willem Van Schendel, "Toward a Comparative History of Borderlands," *Journal of World History* 8, no. 2 (1997), 211–42, esp. 214–15; John Torpey, *The Invention of the Passport: Surveillance, Citizenship, and the State* (New York, 2000); Erika Lee, *At America's Gates: Chinese Immigration during the Exclusion Era, 1882–1943* (Chapel Hill, N.C., 2003); and several of the essays in Jane Caplan and John Torpey (eds.), *Documenting Individual Identity: The Development of State Practices in the Modern World* (Princeton, N.J., 2001). The quoted phrase is from Geert Mak, *In Europe: Travels through the Twentieth Century* (New York, 2008), 155.

40. N. N. Smirnov, *Zabaikal'skie kazaki v otnosheniiakh Rossii s Kitaem i Mongoliei* (Volgograd, 1999), 144–59; D. P. Raiskii, "Snosheniia zabaikal'skikh krest'ian i kazakov s Mongoliei i Manchzhuriei," *Russkii vestnik* 274 (August 1901), 585–94; Viktoriia Baliabina, *Argunei: Zabaikal'skaia starina* (Irkutsk, 1988), 32–34. On the Chinese military settlements, see Gao Qiang, "Shi lun Qing mo Min chu dongbei jun tun shi bian," *Qiqihaer daxue xuebao (Zhexue shehui kexue ban)*, no. 6 (2011), 6–9; and Xushu Ming, "Qing mo Heilongjiang yimin yu nongye kaifa," *Qing shi yanjiu*, no. 2 (1991), 21–25, esp. 21–22.

41. For the broadening parameters of the term *inorodtsy* in the last decades of the empire, see John W. Slocum, "Who, and When, Were the Inorodtsy? The Evolution of the Category of 'Aliens' in Imperial Russia," *RR* 57, no. 2 (1998), 185–87.

42. On the concerns prompted by too much borrowing from "aliens" in this period, see Willard Sunderland, "Russians into Iakuts? 'Going Native' and Problems of Russian National Identity in the Siberian North, 1870s–1914," *SR* 55, no. 4 (1996), 806–25.

43. Slezkine, *Jewish Century*, 110, 115–16.

44. The quoted phrase is drawn from A. I. Termen, *Sredi Buriat Irkutskoi i Zabaikal'skoi oblasti: Ocherki i vpechatleniia* (St. Petersburg, 1912), 1.

45. The steppe councils of the Western Buryats were closed slightly earlier in 1901. On the developments mentioned here, see S. Iu. Darzhaev, *Stepnye dumy: Organy samoupravleniia*

buriat v rossiiskom gosudarstve: 1822–1904 (Ulan-Ude, 2001), 65–67; G. R. Galdanova et al. (eds.), *Lamaizm v Buriatii xviii–nachala xx veka: Strukhtura i sotsial'naia rol' kul'turnoi sistemy* (Novosibirsk, 1983), 32–33; and Dittmar Schorkowitz, "The Orthodox Church, Lamaism, and Shamanism among the Buriats and Kalmyks, 1825–1925," in Robert P. Geraci and Michael Khodarkovsky (eds.), *Of Religion and Empire: Missions, Conversions, and Tolerance in Tsarist Russia* (Ithaca, 2001), 218–22; and Robert W. Montgomery, "Buriat Social and Political Activisim in the 1905 Revolution," *Sibirica* 10, no. 3 (2011), 2–4.

46. For these references, see Tsyben Zhamtsarano, *Putevye dnevniki, 1903–1907 gg.* (Ulan-Ude, 2001), 201, 221; and M. Bogdanov, "Buriatskoe 'vozrozhdenie,'" *Sibirskie voprosy*, no. 3 (1907), 38–49. On Buryat politics in 1905, see Montgomery, "Buriat Social and Political Activisim," 1–28, esp. 5–16.

47. *NARB*, f.131, op.1, d.259, l.5.

48. Donald W. Treadgold, *The Great Siberian Migration: Government and Peasant in Resettlement from Emancipation to the First World War* (Princeton, N.J., 1957), 34; *Sibir' v sostave rossiiskoi imperii* (Moscow, 2007), 50.

49. Siberia's population grew at an average rate of 3.3 percent between 1897 and 1914. The next highest growth (2.47 percent) was in the North Caucasus, where there was also continuing new settlement. See B. N. Mironov, *Sotsial'naia istoriia Rossii perioda imperii (xviii–nachalo xx v.)* (St. Petersburg, 1999), 23.

50. *P. A. Stolypin: Perepiska* (Moscow, 2004), 62.

51. See, for example, *Zabaikal'skie oblastnye vedomosti*, no. 92 (2 September 1909), 1; and no. 108 (16 October 1909), 1. For an example of a settlement map, see Alberto Masoero, "Territorial Colonization in Late Imperial Russia: Stages in the Evolution of a Concept," *Kritika* 14, no. 1 (2013), 79.

52. *Kolonizatsiia Sibiri v sviazi s obshchim pereselencheskim voprosom* (St. Petersburg, 1900), 372.

53. N. M.Iadrintsev, *Sibir' kak koloniia v geograficheskom, etnograficheskom i istoricheskom otnosheniiakh* (2nd ed.; St. Petersburg, 1892; repr.: Novosibirsk, 2003), 185.

54. By way of illustration, in 1908, only 5 students out of 403 in Ungern's military institute were "of the Cossack estate." See *RGVIA*, f.319, op.1, d.628, l.27. On Cossack officer training, see McNeal, *Tsar and Cossack*, 62–65.

55. L. Domozhirov, "L'gota kazach'ikh ofitserov," *Voennyi sbornik*, no. 8 (1908), 104. For a similar complaint and references to "native-born" and "non-native Cossacks," see also K. Kuznetsov, "O kazach'ikh shtabnykh ofitserov," *Vestnik konnitsy*, no. 21 (1909), 969–71; and St. Skorokhovod, "Otkrytoe pis'mo," *Vestnik konnitsy*, no. 1 (1909), 24–25.

56. John Bushnell, "The Tsarist Officer Corps, 1881–1914: Customs, Duties, Inefficiency," *AHR* 86, no. 4 (1981), 762.

57. For a description of traditional Buryat and Mongol tea preparation, see Sharon Hudgins, "Raw Liver, Singed Sheep's Head, and Boiled Stomach Pudding: Encounters with Traditional Buryat Cuisine," *Sibirica* 3, no. 2 (2003), 132–34.

58. *RGVIA*, f.400, op.11, d.499, l.19. The event occurred on 22 September 1908 at a place called "St. Sobolino." This may refer to a Cossack settlement or a train stop. On the Chinese border bandits, see Dmitrii Ershov, *Khunkhuzy: Neob"iavlennaia voina; Etnicheskii banditizm na Dal'nem Vostoke* (Moscow, 2010), 9–37.

59. See, for example, *RGVIA*, f.5285, op.1, d.171, ll.210(b), 388(b), 444; and f.5285, op.1, d.172, ll.139, 165. The paperwork on the debts is confusing, so my calculation of Ungern's total debt of 85 rubles by the time he left the Host in early 1910 may be somewhat short. He might have owed as much as 135. In either case, the sum was significant—according to host records,

a horse at the time cost 60 rubles—though judging from the files, Ungern did indeed pay the money back.

60. Bernice Glatzer Rosenthal, *New Myth, New World: From Nietzsche to Stalin* (University Park, Penn., 2002), 19.

61. I. S. Simonov, "Chto chitaiut starshie vospitanniki nashikh kadetskikh korpusov," *Pedagogicheskii sbornik,* no. 7 (1905), 32. The most popular author among the cadets was Turgenev, followed closely by Tolstoy and Pushkin. The highest-ranking "foreign" writer was the Polish historical novelist Henryk Sienkiewicz.

62. *RGVIA,* f.1553, op.1, d.10, ll.23–23(b). Le Bon's work first appeared in French in 1899. On Le Bon, see Robert A. Nye, *The Origins of Crowd Psychology: Gustave Le Bon and the Crisis of Mass Democracy in the Third Republic* (London, 1975); and the introduction by John L. Stanley to Gustave Le Bon, *The Psychology of Socialism* (John L. Stanley, ed.) (New Brunswick, N.J., 1982), v–xxxvi. The Russian edition being recommended by the military district was Gustav Le Bon, *Psikhologiia sotsializma* (St. Petersburg, 1908).

63. *RGVIA,* f.1553, op.1, d.10, l.23.

64. On 1905 in the Trans-Baikal, see Konstantinov and Konstantinova, *Istoriia Zabaikal'ia,* 231–34; V. G. Izgachev (ed.), *Revoliutsionnoe dvizhenie v Zabaikal'e 1905–1907 gg.: Sbornik dokumentov i materialov k piatidesiatiletiiu pervoi russkoi revoliutsii* (Chita, 1955). On socialist and revolutionary sympathies within the Host, see Sergeev, *Kazachestvo na russkom Dal'nem Vostoke v xvii–xix vv.,* 121.

65. For the quotations reproduced here, see Gustave Le Bon, *Psychologie des foules* (Paris, 1895; repr.: Paris, 2003), 14. *The Crowd* is the common English title of the work.

66. These points are summarized in heated prose near the end of the book. See Le Bon, *Psychologie du socialisme* (Paris, 1899), 474–77.

67. Ibid., 42.

68. Ibid., 468.

Chapter 5

1. For a brief discussion of the various versions of the duel, see S. L. Kuz'min, "Deiatel'nost' barona R. F. fon Ungern-Shternberga i ego rol' v istorii," in Kuz'min, *Baron Ungern,* 8. For the interrogators' mention of the scar, see "Doprosy R. F. Ungerna 1 i 2 sentiabria 1921 v g. Irkutske," 210.

2. On the trek, see Kuz'min, "Deiatel'nost' barona R. F. fon Ungern-Shternberga," 8; Iuzefovich, *Samoderzhets pustyni,* 20–21; and Pozner, *Bloody Baron,* among others. For a description of the Greater Khingan range in this period, see E. Osadchii, "V gorakh Bol'shogo Khingana: Zametki okhotnika," in M. N. Levitskii (ed.), *V trushchobakh Man'chzhurii i nashikh vostochnykh okrain: Sbornik ocherkov, rasskazov i vospominanii voennykh topografov* (Odessa, 1910), 501–13.

3. The earliest witness who seems to have heard the story from Ungern firsthand is Aleksei Burdukov, a Russian merchant who met Ungern in 1913, but Burdukov did not write down his recollections until many years later. For more on Burdukov, see chapter 6.

4. See *RGVIA,* f.400, op.11, d.499, l.19(b).

5. This discussion draws on Peter Kenez, "A Profile of the Prerevolutionary Officer Corps," *California Slavic Studies* (Berkeley and Los Angeles, 1973), vol. 7, 121–58.

6. The reference to "Slavic expansiveness" is from N. N. Portugalov, "Ofitsery," *Ofitserskaia zhizn',* no. 209 (1910), 1620. For a detailed picture of the officer milieu with vivid descriptions of wine, women, song, and graft, see John Bushnell, "The Tsarist Officer Corps,

1881–1914: Customs, Duties, Inefficiency," *AHR* 86, no. 4 (1981), 753–80. On marriage in the officer corps in Ungern's time, see V. Klokchaev, *Brak ofitserov: Zakonopolozheniia glavneishikh gosudarstv zapada; Istoriia razvitiia i sovremennoe polozhenie voprosa v Rossii; Kriticheskii ocherk* (St. Petersburg, 1907). Officers in the Cossack Hosts had to abide by the same rules on marriage that applied to regular army officers. See Klokchaev, *Brak ofitserov,* 65–67.

7. For an insightful discussion on this issue, see Catriona Kelly, "The Education of the Will: Advice Literature, *Zakal,* and Manliness in Early Twentieth-Century Russia," in Barbara Evans Clements et al. (eds.), *Russian Masculinities in History and Culture* (New York, 2002), 137–38.

8. Bushnell, "Tsarist Officer Corps," 760–61; and Paul Robinson, "Courts of Honour in the Late Imperial Russian Army," *SEER* 84, no. 4 (2006), 722–24. For the dueling code, see Durasov, *Duel'nyi kodeks* (St. Petersburg, 1908), 14–15. (Duels between officers could be with swords or pistols.) On dueling more generally in Russian and European culture, see V. G. Kiernan, *The Duel in European History: Honour in the Reign of the Aristocracy* (New York, 1988); and Irina Reifman, *Ritualized Violence Russian Style: The Duel in Russian Culture and Literature* (Stanford, Calif., 1999).

9. *RGVIA,* f.5288, op.1, d.62, l.2–2(b).

10. These quotes describing the qualities and military readiness of the Cossacks are drawn from an order from the Trans-Baikal Host from 1908. See *RGVIA,* f.1553, op.1, d.10, ll.154–154(b).

11. L. Domozhirov, "L'gota kazach'ikh ofitserov," *Voennyi sbornik,* no. 8 (August 1908), 109.

12. *RGVIA,* f.400, op.11, d.499, l.27(b). The report is also printed in Kuz'min, *Baron Ungern,* 53.

13. The origins of the name "Amur" are obscure, though the word seems to derive from the languages of indigenous Tungusic and Mongol peoples on the river. On various theories surrounding the origins of the term, see Victor Zatsepine, "The Amur: As River, as Border," in Diana Lary (ed.), *The Chinese State at the Borders* (Vancouver, B.C., 2007), 152; and Valerii Pavlik, *Dolgii put' na Amur: Erofei Khabarov i ego "voisko"* (Khabarovsk, 2004), 110–12. The dragon was the symbol of the Chinese emperors. Zatsepine notes that the color black, which is associated with the name of the Amur in Manchu (*Sakhalian-Ula*—Black River) as well as other regional languages, seems to be an allusion to the "river's black soil and its dark, clean water."

14. For descriptions of the river around Ungern's time, see Aleksandr Kirillov, *Geografichesko-statisticheskii slovar' Amurskoi i Primorskoi oblastei* (Blagoveshchensk, 1894), 48–51; G. E. Grum-Grzhimailo, *Opisanie Amurskoi oblasti* (St. Petersburg, 1894); "Po Amuru do Khabarovska," in A. Kruber et al. (comps.), *Aziatskaia Rossiia: Illiustrirovannyi geograficheskii sbornik* (Moscow, 1905), 564–75; and A. I. Karpov, *Reka Amur s ego pritokami kak put' soobshcheniia; Amurskii liman i ego farvartery s kartoiu rek Amurskogo basseina* (St. Petersburg, 1909).

15. *Obzor Amurskoi oblasti za 1911 g.* (Blagoveshchensk, 1912), 4, 24; *Pamiatnaia knizhka Amurskoi oblasti na 1914 g.* (n.p., 1914), 175.

16. Fridtjof Nansen, *Through Siberia: The Land of the Future* (London, 1914), 390. For one reference to tigers in the vicinity, see V. F. Dukhovskaia, *Iz moikh vospominanii* (n.p., 1901), 451–52.

17. On attempts to establish Russian power on the Amur and early views of the region up to the late seventeenth century, see Stephan, *Russian Far East,* 26–32; Mark Bassin, "Expansion and Colonialism on the Eastern Frontier: Views of Siberia and the Far East in Pre-Petrine Russia," *Journal of Historical Geography* 14, no. 1 (1988), 12–15; and A. I. Alekseev, *Osvoenie russkimi liud'mi Dal'nego Vostoka i Russkoi Ameriki do kontsa xix veka* (Moscow, 1982).

18. For the early history of the Jurchens and the creation of the Qing Empire, see Pamela Kyle Crossley, *The Manchus* (Malden, Mass., 1997); and William T. Rowe, *China's Last Empire: The Great Qing* (Cambridge, Mass., 2009), 11–30.

19. On the peoples of the region in the seventeenth century, see Robert H. G. Lee, *The Manchurian Frontier in Ch'ing History* (Cambridge, Mass., 1970), 14–16; and James Forsyth, *A History of the Peoples of Siberia: Russia's North Asian Colony, 1581–1990* (New York, 1992), 103.

20. Lo-shu Fu (comp.), *A Documentary Chronicle of Sino-Western R|elations (1644–1820)* (Tuscon, Ariz., 1966), vol. 1, 94–95. The pinyin for *lo-ch'a* is *luocha*. For the Chinese text of Kangxi's instructions, see Jiang Zhaocheng and Wang Rigen, *Kangxi zhuan* (Beijing, 2011), 215–16. For a discussion of Chinese images of Europeans (Russians included) as "hairy barbarians," see Frank Dikötter, "Hairy Barbarians, Furry Primates, and Wild Men: Medical Science and Cultural Representations of Hair in China," in Alf Hiltebeitel and Barbara D. Miller (eds.), *Hair: Its Power and Meaning in Asian Cultures* (Albany, 1998), 52–54.

21. Stephan, *Russian Far East*, 30–32; V. S. Miasnikov, *Imperiia Tsin i russkoe gosudarstvo v xvii veke* (Moscow, 1980), 207–57; and *Sha E qin Hua shi*, vol. 1. For a multidimensional perspective on Qing-Russian relations and the Nerchinsk Treaty of 1689, see Peter C. Perdue, *China Marches West: The Qing Conquest of Central Eurasia* (Cambridge, Mass., 2005), 161–73.

22. The best treatment of Russia's "Amur question" in the mid-nineteenth century is Mark Bassin, *Imperial Visions: Nationalist Imagination and Geographical Expansion in the Russian Far East* (New York, 1999).

23. For this comparison, see Stephen R. Platt, *Autumn in the Heavenly Kingdom: China, the West, and the Epic Story of the Taiping Civil War* (New York, 2012), 211.

24. On the surface area surrendered to the Russians and the establishment of the new border, see Lee, *Manchurian Frontier in Ch'ing History*, 5. The quoted phrase is from the memo of the Chinese diplomat who negotiated the Treaty of Aigun with the Russians in 1858. See S. C. M. Paine, *Imperial Rivals: China, Russia, and Their Disputed Frontier* (Armonk, N.Y., 1996), 69. On the evolution of the Sino-Russian border in this region, see also *Sha E qin Hua shi*, vol. 2.

25. Murav'ev is still very much a Russian national hero. The giant statue of the count that towers over the Amur at Khabarovsk appears on the current 5,000-ruble banknote.

26. B. K. Kukel', "Iz epokhi prisoedineniia Priamurskogo kraia," in N. P. Matkhanova (ed.), *Graf N. N. Murav'ev-Amurskii v vospominaniiakh sovremennikov* (Novosibirsk, 1998), 232. Kukel' was one of Murav'ev's assistants. For more on Murav'ev and his plans for the region, see Bassin, *Imperial Visions*, 106–35.

27. The law establishing the Host was confirmed in 1860, though the initial decree on the founding dates to December 1858 and one could argue that the force was effectively established in 1857 when Murav'ev dispatched the first Trans-Baikal families to the Amur. To settle the matter once and for all, in 1913, all three Far Eastern Hosts (the Trans-Baikal, the Amur, and the Ussuri) were permitted to date their origins to the seventeenth century. See *Stoletie voennogo ministerstva: 1802–1902*, vol. 11, *Glavnoe upravlenie kazach'ikh voisk: Istoricheskii ocherk* (St. Petersburg, 1902), pt. 1, 390–91; and Oleg Agafonov, *Kazach'i voiska rossiiskoi imperii: Panteon otechestvennoi slavy* (Moscow and Kaliningrad, 1995), 296.

28. This story is related by one of the Count's clerks. See R. K. Bogdanov, "Vospominaniia Amurskogo kazaka o proshlom s 1849 po 1880 god," *Zapiski Priamurskogo otdela imperatorskogo russkogo geograficheskogo obshchestva* 5, no. 3 (1900), 62. Following the flow of the river, the right bank is the southern side, the left bank the north.

29. The name of the Chinese settlement that became Blagoveshchensk is Hailanpao, which is still used as the Chinese name for the city today. On the founding and renaming, see Shen Jian, "Hailanpao de E ming shiyi," *Eluosi yanjiu,* no. 5 (2010), 135–38.

30. This description of early Cossack settlers on the Ussuri is drawn from G. T. Murov, *Liudi i nravy Dal'nego Vostoka: Ot Vladivostoka do Khabarovska* (Tomsk, 1901), 149.

31. *Otchet glavnogo upravleniia kazach'ikh voisk za 1908 god* (St. Petersburg, 1909), 15.

32. Ekaterino-Nikol'sk today is part of the Jewish Autonomous Region, a district carved out of the Far East in the Stalin era as a "Palestine" for Soviet Jews (its original name was the Jewish National District, though it was also known simply by the name of its head town, Birobidzhan). Jews currently make up only a little over 1 percent of the region's population, but Ekaterino-Nikol'sk celebrated its 150th anniversary in the summer of 2008 with a concert of "Cossack, Russian, and Jewish songs." For the anniversary celebration, see www.edinoros.ru/news for June 10, 2008 (last checked: October 2008). For a reference to Ekaterino-Nikol'sk as the "Fair Lady of the Amur," see Kirillov, *Geografichesko-statisticheskii slovar',* 150.

33. *Materialy statistiko-ekonomicheskogo obsledovaniia kazach'ego i krest'ianskogo khoziaistva Amurskoi oblasti* (St. Petersburg, 1912), vol. 1, pt. 1, 158–63, 175–78, 182.

34. See "Karta zaseleniia Amurskoi oblasti sostavlena po materialam karty Amurskogo pereselencheskogo raiona izdaniia Pereselencheskogo Upravleniia, zheleznodorozhnoi karty M.P.S. i dr. (1909)," included in P. F. Unterberger, *Priamurskii Krai, 1906–1910: Ocherk* (St. Petersburg, 1912).

35. For an example of the training activities, see *RGVIA,* f.5288, op.1, d.70, l.60.

36. *RGVIA,* f.400, op.11, d.499, l.20.

37. *RGVIA,* f.5288, op.1, d.1, l.37. The quoted phrases are reversed in the original.

38. On Chinese workers registering in Ekaterino-Nikol'sk, see *RGIADV,* f.704, op.1, d.1052, l.52(b). On the flow of Chinese migrants and trade across the Amur in Amur oblast' more generally in this period, see Qi Xuejun and Han Laixing, "Mingguo shiqi de Heihe yu Hailanpao bianjing maoyi," *Heihe Xuekan,* no. 4 (1989), 51, 53; and Zhacaiping Changsheng [Victor Zatsepine], "Huaren dui Eluosi yuandong chengshi fazhan de gongxian," *Xiboliya yanjiu* 34, no. 4 (2007), 59–63. On the liquor trade, see V. V. Sinichenko, "Kontrabanda spirta i narkotikov na russko-kitaiskoi granitse (vtoraia polovina xix–nachalo xx vekov)," http://mion.isu.ru/pub/power/2.html (last consulted: September 28, 2008). According to information compiled by the Russian Ministry of Finance in 1913, illegally imported alcohol represented some 90 percent of all Russian contraband seizures, and the steady flow of the traffic was a simple matter of price. Legal alcohol, either made on the Russian side or imported with duty from China, cost 15 to 27 rubles per *vedro* (approx. 3.2 US gallons), whereas liquor smuggled in from the Chinese side of the river cost five times less. See N. A. Beliaeva et al., *Dal'nevostochnaia kontrabanda kak istoricheskoe iavlenie (Bor'ba s kontrabandoi na Dal'nem Vostoke Rossii vo vtoroi polovine xix–pervoi tret'i xx veka)* (Vladivostok, 2010), 71, 74.

39. For references to these points, *see RGIADV,* f.702, op.4, d.725, ll.40–40(b), 346–346(b). On the *honghuzi,* see Mark Gamsa, "How a Republic of Chinese Red Beards Was Invented in Paris," *Modern Asian Studies* 36, no. 2 (2002), 993–1010; and Phil Billingsley, *Bandits in Republican China* (Stanford, Calif., 1988).

40. *RGIADV,* f.704, op.1, d.1052, ll.19–20, 27–30.

41. The entire native population of the area in 1922 was estimated to be approximately twenty-seven thousand people, with an additional fifteen thousand Chinese colonists. Christopher P. Atwood, *Young Mongols and Vigilantes in Inner Mongolia's Interregnum Decades, 1911–1931* (Leiden, 2002), vol.1, 114, 120.

42. Population growth in the two more southerly Manchurian provinces of Jilin and Shengjing (after 1907 renamed Fengtian; now: Liaoning), which were much more populated to begin with, was almost as great. For these figures, see Reardon-Anderson, *Reluctant Pioneers*, 82.

43. For references to these developments, see "Evakuatsiia russkikh raboch'ikh iz Priamuria," *Priamurskie vedomosti*, no. 1758 (September 22, 1911), 5; N. I. Dubinina, "Rol' Amurskoi Ekspeditsii (1909–1910) v izuchenii Dal'nego Vostoka Rossii," in D. P. Bolotin and A. P. Zabiiako (eds.), *Rossiia i Kitai na dal'nevostochnykh rubezhakh:Materialy konferentsii* (Blagoveshchensk, 2001), vol. 1, 346–53; and *Istoriia Dal'nego Vostoka SSSR v epokhu feodalizma i kapitalizma, xvii v.–fevral' 1917 g.* (Moscow, 1991), 309.

44. "Po Amuru do Khabarovska," 570–71.

45. Sin-San, "S Amura," *Okrainy Rossii*, nos. 36/37 (1910), 527.

46. Ibid., 528.

47. On the presumptions of American imperialism in Asia in this period, see Stuart Creighton Miller, *Benevolent Assimilation: The American Conquest of the Philippines, 1899-1903* (New Haven, Conn., 1984); and Paul A. Kramer, *The Blood of Government: Race, Empire, the United States, and the Philippines* (Chapel Hill, N.C., 2006).

48. Waves, floods, and deluges were common terms used to describe the rise of Chinese colonization in Manchuria. For the quotation, see V. I. Nemirovich-Danchenko, *V tsarstve zheltogo drakona (v 1908-m godu)* (Petrograd, 1915), 8.

49. *RGIADV*, f.702, op.1, d.713, l.4(b). This quotation appears in the military governor's annual report for 1911.

50. K. D.,"Nastoiashchee i budushchee Priamur'ia," *Okrainy Rossii*, nos. 33/34 (1909), 480. See also D. I., "Pereselenie ili kolonizatsiia," *Okrainy Rossii*, no. 42 (1912), 579.

51. *RGIADV*, f.702, op.3, d.347, pt.1, l.216.

52. These percentages are based on official calculations. The true number of Chinese living on Russian territory was likely considerably higher. See Larin, *Kitaitsy v Rossii*, 13–15. The Japanese were also described as "yellows," but almost all the Japanese in the empire lived not in the Amur region but in the neighboring Maritime region (*Primorskaia oblast'*), which fronted the Sea of Japan. The Maritime region was also home to more Koreans and Chinese than the Amur. Larin, *Kitaitsy v Rossii*, 14–15.

53. Prasenjit Duara, "Nationalists among Transnationals: Overseas Chinese and the Idea of China, 1900-1911," in Aihwa Ong and Donald M. Nonini (eds.), *Ungrounded Empires: The Cultural Politics of Modern Chinese Transnationalism* (New York, 1997), 43; and Philip A. Kuhn, *Chinese among Others: Emigration in Modern Times* (Lanham, Md., 2008), 138, 240–43. On the establishment of Chinese migrant communities in the Russian Far East in this period, see V. Datsyshen, "Formirovanie kitaiskoi obshchiny v rossiiskoi imperii (vtoraia polovina xix v.)," *Diaspory*, nos. 2/3 (2001), 42–44.

54. These quotes are drawn from M. Kh. Chasovoi, *Ugroza sibirskomu vostoku* (St. Petersburg, 1910), 95; and A. Tatishchev, "Amurskaia oblast' v kolonizatsionnom otnoshenii," *Voprosy kolonizatsii* 5 (1909), 210.

55. Cited in Anatolii Remnev, *Rossiia Dal'nego Vostoka: Imperskaia geografiia vlasti xix–nachala xx vekov* (Omsk, 2004), 439.

56. Unterberger, *Priamurskii krai*, 86.

57. *Priamur'e: Fakty, tsifry, nabliudeniia, sobrany na Dal'nem Vostoke sotrudnikami obshchezemskoi organizatsii* (Moscow, 1909), 159.

58. On the legislation restricting Chinese migrants, see Hsu, "A Tale of Two Railroads," 238–40; O. A. Timofeev, *Rossiisko-kitaiskie otnosheniia v Priamur'e (seredina*

xix nachalo xx vv.) (Blagoveshchensk, 2003), 79–82; and F. V. Solov'ev, *Kitaiskoe otkhod-nichestvo na Dal'nem Vostoke Rossii v epokhu kapitalizma (1861–1917 gg.)* (Moscow, 1989), 40–43.

59. Remnev, *Rossiia Dal'nego Vostoka,* 478, 483.

60. V. M. Kabuzan, *Dal'nevostochnyi krai v xvii–nachale xx vv. (1640–1917): Istoriko-demograficheskii ocherk* (Moscow, 1985), 13, 44. The levels of new arrivals dipped in the following years, however, and the overall share of settlers in the Far East versus the total number of settlers in the empire in general remained quite small—less than 8 percent. See Kabuzan, *Dal'nevostochnyi krai,* 103, 113.

61. Kabuzan, *Dal'nevostochnyi krai,* 155–56. The overall number of Chinese migrants remained high, however, because of illegal—or nonregistered—migration. In fact, because of the pressing need for labor, the Russian government repealed some of its own restrictions against Chinese migrant workers and within just a few years, the Great War paved the way to a "period of unbridled Chinese migration into Russia." See Vladimir Datsyshen, "Historical and Contemporary Trends of Chinese Labor Migration into Siberia," in Felix B. Chang and Sunnie T. Rucker-Chang (eds.), *Chinese Migrants in Russia, Central Asia, and Eastern Europe* (New York, 2012), 23–25.

62. E. I. Nesterova, "Atlantida gorodskogo masshtaba: Kitaiskie kvartaly v dal'nevostochnykh gorodakh (konets xix–nachalo xx v.)," *Etnograficheskoe obozrenie,* n.4 (2008), 49; Idem, "Stranitsy istorii sozdaniia kitaiskikh kvartalov v russkikh dal'nevostochnykh gorodakh v kontse xix–nachale xx vv." in Bolotin and Zabiiako (eds.), *Rossiia i Kitai na dal'nevostochnykh rubezhakh,* vol. 2, 57–62; Tat'iana Sorokina, "Kitaiskie kvartaly dal'nevostochnykh gorodov (konets xix–nachalo xx v.)," *Diaspory,* nos. 2/3 (2001), 54–74.

63. *Otchet ob organizatsii protivochumnykh i protivokholernykh meropriatii na vodnykh putiiakh Amurskogo basseina v navigatsii 1911 goda* (Kazan', 1912), 8, 26–27, 53. For a thorough treatment of the epidemic of 1910–1911, see Mark Gamsa, "The Epidemic of Pneumonic Plague in Manchuria, 1910–1911," *Past & Present,* no. 190 (2006), 147–83.

64. Larin, *Kitaitsy v Rossii,* 20–21.

65. On the violence at Blagoveshchensk and a comparable but smaller massacre in the nearby area of the Sixty-Four Villages (*Liu shi si tun*), see V., "Blagoveshchenskaia 'utopiia'," *Vestnik Evropy* 45 (1910), 231–41; Lewis H. Siegelbaum, "Another Yellow Peril: Chinese Migrants in the Russian Far East and the Russian Reaction Before 1917," *Modern Asian Studies* 12, no. 2 (1978), 318–19; Viktor Diatlov, "Blagoveshchenskaia 'utopiia': Iz istorii materializatsii fobii," in Sergei Panarin (ed.), *Evraziia: Liudi i mify* (Moscow, 2003), 123–41; *Sha E qin Hua shi,* vol. 4, pt. 1, 151–59; and Victor Zatsepine, "The Blagoveshchensk Massacre of 1900: The Sino-Russian War and Global Imperialism," in James Flath and Norman Smith (eds.), *Beyond Suffering: Recounting War in Modern China* (Vancouver, B.C., 2011), 107–29.

66. The Harbin synagogue was opened in 1907. On Jews in the Russian Far East and Harbin, see Viktoriia Romanova, "Rossiiskie Evrei v Kharbine," *Diaspory,* no. 1 (1999), 115–42; David Wolff, *To the Harbin Station: The Liberal Alternative in Russian Manchuria, 1898–1914* (Stanford, Calif., 1999), 96–114.

67. On the new restrictions on Jewish settlement in Siberia and the Far East, see L. V. Kal'mina and L. V. Kuras, *Evreiskaia obshchina v zapadnom Zabaikal'e (60-e gody xix veka–fevral' 1917 goda)* (Ulan-Ude, 1999), 32–36; Viktoriia Romanova, *Vlast' i Evrei na Dal'nem Vostoke Rossii: Istoriia vzaimootnoshenii (vtoraia polovina xix v.–20-e gody xx v.)* (Krasnoiarsk, 2001), 77–78.

68. According to the imperial census of 1897, there were even fewer Jews in the Amur region itself—just 0.33 percent of the population, a total of 394 individuals. On policies toward Jews in the Far East during Gondatti's governor-generalship (1911–1917), see Romanova, *Vlast' i Evrei,* 81–114. A number of Jews deported from the Amur and Maritime regions simply moved to Harbin, which one Jewish newspaper referred to in 1912 as the empire's new "Pale of Settlement" and which always had far more Jews (in relative and absolute terms) than any of the cities in the Russian Far East. See Romanova, "Rossiiskie Evrei v Kharbine," 120. For more on Gondatti's administration in the Amur region, see N. I. Dubinina, *Priamurskii general-gubernator N. L. Gondatti* (Khabarovsk, 1997).

69. Eric Lohr, *Russian Citizenship: From Empire to Soviet Union* (Cambridge, Mass., 2012), 72–73. As Lohr notes, however, given the heavy dependence on Chinese labor, anti-Chinese restrictions in the Amur region were often skirted in practice, including by the government, which issued scores of exemptions to Russian firms in need of Chinese workers.

70. On "de-Polonizing energy," see *Zapadnye okrainy Rossiiskoi imperii* (Moscow, 2006), 261.

71. *RGVIA,* f.5288, op.1, d.1, ll.167(b), 181, 210(b).

72. Grum-Grzhimailo,*Opisanie Amurskoi oblasti,* 408–14. For an overview of Bogoslovennoe, see Ross King, "Bogoslovennoe: Korean Village on the Amur, 1871–1937," *Review of Korean Studies* 4, no. 2 (2001), 133–76, esp. 148–52 for information on the village during the 1910s.

73. Officers in the Amur Military District often went to Harbin for R&R. See E. Kh. Nilus (comp.), *Istoricheskii obzor Kitaiskoi vostochnoi zheleznoi dorogi (1896–1923 gg.)* (Harbin, 1923), 510. One historian counts fifty-three nationalities in Harbin in 1913. See Olga Bakich, "Émigré Identity: The Case of Harbin," in Lahusen, *Harbin and Manchuria,* 53–54. For a contemporary reference to Harbin as an "international city" and the city's nicknames, see Nikolai Shteinfeld, *My i iapontsy v Man'chzhurii* (Harbin, 1913), 4; and Wolff, *To the Harbin Station,* 46.

74. *Obzor Amurskoi oblasti za 1911 g.,* 3.

75. *RGVIA,* f.5288, op.1, d.1, l.103.

Chapter 6

1. A. V. Burdukov, *V staroi i novoi Mongolii: Vospominaniia, pis'ma* (Moscow, 1969), 100. Burdukov was thirty years old in 1913.

2. *RGVIA,* f.400, op.11, d.499, l.14.

3. *RGVIA,* f.400, op.11, d.499, l.37. Formal approval of Ungern's resignation and his new reserve status took about four months, though, technically speaking, the case wasn't fully settled until almost a year later, in June 1914, when he finally paid the necessary filing fee of 1 ruble 50 kopecks. See *RGVIA,* f.400, op.11, d.499, l.39.

4. The memoirs were published posthumously by his daughter. See her foreword to his writings: T. A. Burdukova, "A. V. Burdukov (biografiia)," in Burdukov, *V staroi i novoi Mongolii,* 8–21.

5. Burdukov, *V staroi i novoi Mongolii,* 100. Ungern was, in fact, twenty-eight at the time.

6. Ibid., 101.

7. Ibid., 100.

8. The reference to adventure as the act of leaving the continuity of life is drawn from the sociologist Georg Simmel's famous description of the "adventurer type." See "The Adventurer,"

in Simmel, *On Individuality and Social Forms: Selected Writings* (Donald N. Levine, ed.) (Chicago, 1971), 187–98.

9. For reflections on the place of adventurers and explorers in Western popular culture in this period, see Beau Riffenburgh, *The Myth of the Explorer: The Press, Sensationalism, and Geographical Discovery* (New York, 1994); and Felix Driver, *Geography Militant: Cultures of Exploration and Empire* (Malden, Mass., 2001). For a popular biography of Younghusband whose title says it all, see Patrick French, *Younghusband: The Last Great Imperial Adventurer* (London, 1994).

10. On the mystique of explorers and military men and the broader pull of adventure stories in Russian culture in this period, see Donald Rayfield, *The Dream of Lhasa: The Life of Nicholai Przhevalskii, Explorer of Central Asia* (London, 1976); Daniel Brower, "Imperial Russia and Its Orient: The Renown of Nikolai Przhevalskii," *RR* 53, no. 3 (1994), 367–81; Tatiana Shaumian, *Tibet: The Great Game and Tsarist Russia* (New Delhi, 2000), 17–18; and Schimmelpenninck, *Toward the Rising Sun,* 24–41. The reference to the "energizing myth of adventure" is borrowed from Martin Green, *Dreams of Adventure, Deeds of Empire* (New York, 1979), 27.

11. For discussions on the exotic imagery of Tibet and Timbuktu, see Orville Schell, *Virtual Tibet: Searching for Shangri-La from the Himalayas to Hollywood* (New York, 2000), 15–30; Peter Bishop, *The Myth of Shangri-La: Tibet, Travel Writing, and the Western Creation of Sacred Landscape* (London, 1989); and Anthony Sattin, *The Gates of Africa: Death, Discovery, and the Search for Timbuktu* (New York, 2005).

12. Beatrix Bulstrode, *A Tour in Mongolia* (New York, 1920), 1, 56–57, 78, 97, 116, 129.

13. Though from a modest background, Burdukov taught himself literary as well as spoken Mongolian and became a well-regarded expert on Mongolian life, writing numerous articles about the country for the Siberian press and corresponding with Russian Mongolianists in St. Petersburg. For more on his life, see E. M. Darevskaia, *Sibir' i Mongoliia: Ocherki russko-mongol'skikh sviazei v kontse xix–nachale xx vekov* (Irkutsk, 1994), 240–55.

14. I. F. Molodykh, *Selenga v predelakh Mongolii: Kratkii ocherk o rabotakh Mongol'skoi ekspeditsii 1919 goda* (Irkutsk, 1920), 3. For another contemporary comment on how little most Russians knew about Mongolia in this period, see Burdukov, *V staroi i novoi Mongolii,* 334.

15. For references to these issues, see Thomas A. Tweed, *The American Encounter with Buddhism, 1844–1912: Victorian Culture and the Limits of Dissent* (Chapel Hill, N.C., 2000); Lawrence Sutin, *All Is Change: The Two-Thousand-Year Journey of Buddhism to the West* (New York, 2006), 171–201; Douglas T. McGetchin, *Indology, Indomania, and Orientalism: Ancient India's Rebirth in Modern Germany* (Madison, N.J., 2009), 120–40; J. J. Clarke, *Oriental Enlightenment: The Encounter between Asian and Western Thought* (New York, 1997), 74–75, 87–89; Roger-Pol Droit, *The Cult of Nothingness: The Philosophers and the Buddha* (Chapel Hill, N.C., 2003), 156–57; John Snelling, *Buddhism in Russia: The Story of Avgan Dorzhiev, Lhasa's Emissary to the Tsar* (Shaftesbury, Eng., 1993), 9–10; and A. I. Andreev, *Khram Buddy v severnoi stolitse* (St. Petersburg, 2004), 18–20. On the renaissance of Orientalist scholarship in Russia in this period, including Buddhist studies, see T. V. Ermakova, *Buddiiskii mir glazami rossiiskikh issledovatelei XIX–pervoi treti XX veka* (St. Petersburg: Nauka, 1998), 249–75; Vera Tolz, *Russia's Own Orient: The Politics of Identity and Oriental Studies in the Late Imperial and Soviet Periods* (New York, 2011), 10–17; and Schimmelpenninck, *Russian Orientalism,* 171–98.

16. For various examples highlighting the exotic draw and revulsion of Buddhism in the fin de siècle, see Donald S. Lopez, Jr., *Prisoners of Shangri-La: Tibetan Buddhism and the West* (Chicago, 1998), 3–5, 31–42, 49–52.

17. For a brief overview of the history of Buddhism in Mongolia, see Michael K. Jerryson, *Mongolian Buddhism: The Rise and Fall of the Sangha* (Chiang Mai, Thailand, 2007), 11–34.

18. On the hierarchies that defined Mongolian society during the Qing and autonomous periods, see C. R. Bawden, *The Modern History of Mongolia* (New York, 1968), 14, 137–38, 157–58. Khutuktu in contemporary (Cyrillic-script) Mongolian is transliterated as khutagt.

19. Dittmar Schorkowitz, "The Orthodox Church, Lamaism, and Shamanism among the Buriats and Kalmyks, 1825–1925," in Robert P. Geraci and Michael Khodarkovsky (eds.), *Of Religion and Empire: Missions, Conversions, and Tolerance in Tsarist Russia* (Ithaca, 2001), 218–22; and Vera Tolz, "Imperial Scholars and Minority Nationalisms in Late Imperial and Early Soviet Russia," *Kritika* 10, no. 2 (2009), 275–79.

20. This quote is from Annie Besant, "In Defense of Theosophy: A Lecture Delivered in St. James Great Hall London," reprinted in Aidan A. Kelly (ed.), *Theosophy,* vol. 2, *Controversial and Polemical Pamphlets* (New York, 1990), 5

21. On Theosophy in Russia, see Maria Carlson, *"No Religion Higher Than Truth": A History of the Theosophical Movement in Russia, 1875–1902* (Princeton, N.J., 1993); and Carlson, "Fashionable Occultism: Spiritualism, Theosophy, Freemasonry, and Hermeticism in Fin-de-Siècle Russia," in Bernice Glatzer Rosenthal (ed.), *The Occult in Russian and Soviet Culture* (Ithaca, 1997), 139–43. On Theosophy in general, see Sutin, *All Is Change,* 171–201; Clarke, *Oriental Enlightenment,* 89–92; and Peter Washington, *Madame Blavatsky's Baboon: A History of the Mystics, Mediums, and Misfits Who Brought Spiritualism to America* (New York, 1995).

22. *The Letters of H.P. Blavatsky,* Vol. 1, *1861-1879* (John Algeo, ed.) (Wheaton, Ill., 2003), 370.

23. On the relationship between Theosophy and imperialism, see Joy Dixon, "Ancient Wisdom, Modern Motherhood: Theosophy and the Colonial Syncretic," in Antoinette Burton (ed.), *Gender, Sexuality, and Colonial Modernities* (New York, 1999), 193–94; and Gauri Viswanathan, *Outside the Fold: Conversion, Modernity, and Belief* (Princeton, N.J., 1998), 196–203.

24. On the Qing conquest and incorporation of the Mongol lands, see Peter C. Perdue, *China Marches West: The Qing Conquest of Central Eurasia* (Cambridge, Mass., 2004), 133–299; and Pamela Kyle Crossley, "Making Mongols," in Pamele Kyle Crossley et al. (eds.), *Empire at the Margins: Culture, Ethnicity, and Frontier in Early Modern China* (Berkeley and Los Angeles, 2006), 58–82.

25. On the Qing policies mentioned here, see Johan Elverskog, *Our Great Qing: The Mongols, Buddhism, and the State in Late Imperial China* (Honolulu, 2006); T. D. Skrynnikova, *Lamaistskaia tserkov' i gosudarstvo: Vneshniaia Mongoliia xvi–nachalo xx veka* (Novosibirsk, 1988), 42–79; and Sechin Jagchid, "The Manchu Ch'ing Policy toward Mongolian Religion," in Walter Heissig (ed.), *Tractata Altaica: Denis Sinor Sexaginario Optime de Rebus Altaicis Merito Dedicata* (Wiesbaden, 1976), 301–19. Another translation of Bogd Gegeen is "Brilliant Light." See Jerryson, *Mongolian Buddhism,* 22.

26. On the late Qing reforms, see William T. Rowe, *China's Last Empire: The Great Qing* (Cambridge, Mass, 2009), 255–62; and Ichisada Miyazaki, *China's Examination Hell: The Civil Service Examination in Imperial China* (New York, 1976), 124–27. The goal of blending together "the best of what is Chinese and what is foreign" comes from the Reform Edict of the Empress Dowager Cixi issued in 1900. See Rowe, *China's Last Empire,* 256. The quote on the need to create a united citizenry is drawn from a late Qing text. See Edward J. M. Rhoads, *Manchus and Han: Ethnic Relations and Political Power in Late Qing and Early Republican China, 1861–1928* (Seattle, 2000), 294.

27. On "re-imperialization," see Rhoads, *Manchus and Han,* 286–87.

28. Urgunge Onon and D. Pritchatt, *Asia's First Modern Revolution: Mongolia Proclaims Its Independence in 1911* (Leiden, 1997); and Tatsuo Nakami, "A Protest against the Concept of the 'Middle Kingdom': The Mongols and the 1911 Revolution," in Eto Shinkichi and Harold Z. Schiffrin (eds.), *The 1911 Revolution in China: Interpretive Essays* (Tokyo, 1984), 129–49, esp. 136–37.

29. On the Bogda's life and the enthronement of 1911, see Emgent Ookhnoi Batsaikhan, *Bogdo Jebtsundamba Khutuktu, the Last King of Mongolia: Mongolia's National Revolution of 1911* (Ulaanbaatar, 2009), 189–203; Tachibana Makoto, *Mongolyn martagdsan tuukh: Bogd Khaant zasgiin gazar (1911–1921)* (Ulaanbaatar, 2011), 31–54. On the day of the Bogda's enthronement as marking the true beginning of Mongolia's twentieth century, see Christopher Kaplonski, "Introduction" (Part 5), in David Sneath and Christopher Kaplonski (eds.), *The History of Mongolia*, vol. 3, *The Qing Period, Twentieth-Century Mongolia* (Folkstone, Eng., 2010), 851. For the comparison to the papacy, see Frans August Larson, *Larson, Duke of Mongolia* (Boston, 1930), 111. One Mongol expert refers to the government created after the 1911 revolution as a "curious blend of church and state." See Larry William Moses, *The Political Role of Mongol Buddhism* (Bloomington, Ind., 1977), 148. On the Buddhist as well as unintentional democratic allusions of the Bogda's reign name, see Bawden, *Modern History of Mongolia,* 195–96.

30. The quoted saying appears in an essay by the reformer Zheng Guanying (1842–1922/23). See Frederic Wakeman, Jr., *The Fall of Imperial China* (New York, 1979), 209.

31. On these developments, see Sh. Sandag, "Politicheskoe i ekonomicheskoe polozhenie vneshnei Mongolii v kontse xix–nachale xx v.," *Mongol'skii sbornik: Ekonomika, istoriia, arkheologiia* (Moscow, 1959), 126–38; B. Shirendyb, *Mongoliia na rubezhe xix–xx vekov (istoriia sot'sial'no-ekonomicheskogo razvitiia)* (Ulan Bator, 1963), 84–89, 101–4; E. I. Lishtovannyi, *Istoricheskie vzaimootnosheniia Sibiri i Mongolii: Kul'tura i obshchestvo (xix v.–30-e gg. xx v.)* (Ulan-Ude, 1988), 66, 92–93; E. M. Dar'evskaia, "Russkii sovetnik pravitel'stva Mongolii S. A. Kozin," in *Vostok i Rossiia: Vzgliad iz Sibiri: Materialy i tezisy dokladov k nauchno-prakticheskoi konferentsii, Irkutsk, 16–18 maia 1996 g.* (Irkutsk, 1996), 155–60; and Aileen Friesen, "Fulfilling God's Plan: The Russian Orthodox Church and the East in the Early Twentieth Century" (unpublished paper, 2013).

32. *AVPRI,* Kitaiskii stol, op.491, 1911, d.566, l.50.

33. On these matters, see S. G. Luzianin, "Rossiia i Khalkha Mongoliia: Opyt ekonomicheskoi i politicheskoi integratsii (nachalo xx v.–1917 g.)," in *Rossiia i vostok: Problem vzaimodeistviia* (Cheliabinsk, 1995), 81; A. D. Kornakov, "Po povodu provozglasheniia Mongolami nezavisimosti," *Trudy Troitskosavskogo-Kiakhtinskogo otdeleniia Priamurskogo otdela imperatorskogo russkogo geograficheskogo obshchestva* 15, no. 2 (1912), 24; I. I. Lomakina, *Mongol'skaia stolitsa, staraia i novaia (i uchast'e Rossii v ee sud'be)* (Moscow, 2006), 48–49. In the early 1900s, Mongols (like Tibetans) tended to incorporate well-known foreign political rulers into their godly pantheon or revere them as bodhisattvas, that is, buddhas who chose to remain within the world to spread enlightenment. It was also common for Mongol and Tibetan Buddhists to refer to the Russian ruler as "the white tsar," drawing on the association between the color white and the direction west in Central Eurasian cosmology. See Marlène Laruelle, "'The White Tsar': Romantic Imperialism in Russia's Legitimizing of Conquering the East," *Acta Slavica Iaponica* 25 (2008), 113.

34. A. P. Svechnikov, *Russkie v Mongolii: Nabliudeniia i vyvody; Sbornik rabot otnositel'no Mongolii (Khalkhi)* (St. Petersburg, 1912), 10.

35. E. A. Belov, *Rossiia i Kitai v nachale xx veka: Russko-kitaiskie protivorechiia v 1911–1915 gg.* (Moscow, 1917), 39–401; Paine, *Imperial Rivals,* 272–76; and Xiaoyuan Liu, *Reins*

of Liberation: An Entangled History of Mongolian Independence, Chinese Territoriality, and Great Power Hegemony, 1911–1950 (Washington, D.C. and Stanford, Calif., 2006), 20–21. On the shifting agreements reached between Russia and Japan over the Mongol lands and Manchuria in 1907, 1910, and 1912, see Peter Berton, *Russo-Japanese Relations, 1905–1917: From Enemies to Allies* (New York, 2012), 2–7. On the ambitions of the Bogda's government to unify Inner and Outer Mongolia, including a short-lived military campaign organized against Chinese-controlled Inner Mongolia in the summer and fall of 1913, see two articles by Tatsuo Nakami: "Babujab and His Uprising: Re-examining the Inner Mongol Struggle for Indepen-dence," *The Memoirs of the Toyo Bunko* (The Oriental Library), no. 57 (1999), 140–41; and "A Protest against the Concept of the 'Middle Kingdom,'" 136, 142.

36. On Russian policy toward Mongolia in this period, see Iu. V. Kuz'min, "Russko-Mongol'skie otnosheniia v 1911–1912 godakh i pozitsiia obshchestvennykh krugov Rossii," in Edward H. Kaplan and Donald W. Whisenhunt (eds.), *Opuscala Altaica: Essays Presented in Honor of Henry Schwarz* (Bellingham, Wash., 1994), 393–407; Belov, *Rossiia i Kitai v nachale xx veka*, 156–57; and Paine, *Imperial Rivals*, 287–98. The senior Chinese official in Outer Mongolia as established by the Kiakhta Treaty, the *duhu shi*, often translated as high commis-sioner, was granted a guard of 200, while the head Russian consul in Urga was allowed 150 and the lesser Russian consuls in other towns, 50. See Sow-Theng Leong, *Sino-Soviet Diplomatic Relations, 1917–1926* (Honolulu, 1976), 73; and Zhang Qixiong, *Wai Meng Zhuquan guishu jiaoshe 1911–1916* (Taibei, 1995), 240–41.

37. Belov, *Rossiia i Kitai v nachale xx veka*, 167–80; Onon and Pritchatt, *Asia's First Mod-ern Revolution*, 41–58; Leong, *Sino-Soviet Diplomatic Relations*, 73; and T. Nakami, Ts. Bat-bayar, and J. Boldbataar, "Mongolia," in Chahryar Adle et al. (eds.), *History of the Civilizations of Central Asia*, vol. 6, *Towards the Contemporary Period: From the Mid-Nineteenth to the End of the Twentieth Century* (Paris, 2005), 348–53.

38. On the Kiakhta Treaty, see Belov, *Rossiia i Kitai v nachale xx veka*, 154–66; Paine, *Im-perial Rivals*, 298–305; Morris Rossabi, "Sino-Mongol Border: From Conflict to Precarious Resolution," in Bruce A. Elleman, Stephen Kotkin, and Clive Schofield (eds.), *Beijing's Power and China's Borders: Twenty Neighbors in Asia* (Armonk, N.Y., 2012), 171–72; and Makoto, *Mongolyn martagdsan tuukh*, 345–74. For Chinese assessments (which are still negative, for PRC historians and those in Taiwan alike), see, for example, Chen Chunhua (comp.), *Eguo waijiao wen shu xuan yi: Guan yu Menggu wenti* (Harbin, 1991), 4; *Sha E qin Hua shi*, vol. 4, pt. 2, 199–200; and Zhang, *Wai Meng Zhuquan guishu jiaoshe 1911–1916*, 254–61, 306, 309.

39. "Russia and Mongolia," *The North China Herald,* January 20, 1912, 149.

40. For most travelers coming from Ulaanbaatar, taking the plane is by far the easiest way to get to Khovd, given that the drive from the capital along the "joggle-bang, jolt" of Mongo-lian roads takes at least three days. Kobdo, the old Russian name for Khovd, is based on the name of the town in literary Mongolian. My thanks to Brian Baumann for this information.

41. For a description of the fort and the nearby trading town, see A. Chuets [Burdukov], "Gorod Kobdo," *Sibirskaia zhizn'* (February 17, 1912); Liu Guojun, "19 shiji mo Kebuduo maimaicheng ji lü Meng shang," *Wenshi yuekan*, no. 7 (2007), 42–43. On the historical back-ground of Qing power and relations with Russia in the Kobdo region, see B. Niamdorzh, *Khovdyn khiazgaar 1911–1919 on* (Ulaanbaatar, 2006), 17–51; and D. Gongor, *Khovdyn khuraangui tuukh* (Ulaanbaatar, 2006), 69–88.

42 On the battle and the immediate aftermath from various perspectives, see Belov, *Rossiia i Kitai v nachale xx veka*, 133–35; V. A. Moiseev, *Rossiia i Kitai v Tsentral'noi Azii (vtoraia polovina xix v.–1917 g.)* (Barnaul, 2003), 272–75; V. L. Uspenskii, "Zhurnal 'Mon-gol Sonin Bichig' o sobytiiakh v Mongolii v 1911–1912 godakh," in S. Luvsanvandan (ed.),

Aktual'nye problemy sovremennogo mongolovedeniia (Ulan Bator, 1987), 74; Niamdorzh, *Khovdyn khiazgaar*, 52–104; *Sha E qin Hua shi*, vol. 4, pt. 2, 127–30; and Zhang, *Wai Meng Zhuquan guishu jiaoshe 1911–1916*, 72–73;. For recollections of the battle by a Mongol contemporary, see Owen Lattimore and Fujiko Isono (eds.), *The Diluv Khutagt: Memoirs and Autobiography of a Mongol Buddhist Reincarnation in Religion and Revolution* (Wiesbaden, 1982), 72–75.

43. Dambiijantsan was not a Mongol from Outer Mongolia but rather a Kalmyk from southern Russia. On his unusual story, with details on how his head ended up in a jar of formaldehyde in a St. Petersburg museum, see Inessa Lomakina, *Golova Dzha-Lamy* (Ulan-Ude and St. Petersburg, 1993); and Lomakina, *Groznye makhakaly vostoka* (Moscow, 2004). See also John Gaunt, "Mongolia's Renegade Monk: The Career of Dambijantsan," *Journal of the Anglo-Mongolian Society* 10 (1987), 27–41. A Russian diplomat present in Kobdo during the siege noted that the Mongol fighters revered Dambiijantsan as the reincarnated spirit of Amursana, a leader of western Mongol resistance against the Qing in the eighteenth century, but added condescendingly that he was in fact nothing but a "typical Kalmyk with an ugly and cunning appearance." *AVPRI*, Kitaiskii stol, op.491, 1912, d.634, l.35(b). The description of Ja Lama's cruelty is taken from the recollections of a prominent lama. See Lattimore and Isono, *Diluv Khutagt*, 76.

44. *AVPRI*, Kitaiskii stol, op.491, 1912, d.639, l.48. For similar descriptions of the town from the same period, see Chuets [Burdukov], "Po nezavisimoi Mongolii: g. Kobdo i ego okrestnosti (putevye zametki)," *Sibirskaia zhizn'* (December 6, 1912); and H. G. C. Perry-Ascough and R. B. Otter-Barry, *With the Russians in Mongolia* (London, [1913]), 222–23.

45. On these issues, see *AVPRI*, Kitaiskii stol, op.491, 1912, d.100a, ll.59, 71–71(b); and Kitaiskii stol, op.491, 1912, d.632, l.185.

46. On the arrival of additional Cossack forces over the summer, see Liuba's report from 9 July 1913, *AVPRI*, Kitaiskii stol, op.491, 1912, d.639, l.111.

47. On Rezukhin's work in Mongolia, see *AVPRI*, Kitaiskii stol, op.491, 1912–13, d.631, ll.24, 40, 45, 77, 98, 108–9.

48. I. Ia. Khorostovets, *Ot Chingis Khana do sovetskoi respubliki: Kratkaia istoriia Mongolii s obosbym uchetom noveishego vremeni* (German ed., 1926; Ulan Bator, 2004), 203. Khorostovets was a senior Russian diplomat dispatched to Mongolia in 1912 to work out the terms of the new Russo-Mongolian relationship.

49. *AVPRI*, Kitaiskii stol, op.491, 1912, d.639, ll.122(b), 133(b), 182. The German traveler Hermann Consten described Liuba as an overbearing "workaholic" who treated the Mongols arrogantly and was roundly disliked. See his *Weideplätze der Mongolen im Reiche der Chalcha* (Berlin, 1920) vol.2, 10.

50. *Pis'ma G. N. Potanina* (Irkutsk, 1989), vol. 3, 64.

51. See, for example, the comments in A.P. Benningsen, *Neskol'ko dannykh o sovremennoi Mongolii* (St. Petersburg, 1912), 16.

52. *AVPRI*, Kitaiskii stol, op.491, 1912, d.639, ll.36–37(b).

53. For generally dim views of Russian merchants in Mongolia as well as comments on the overall situation of trade and foreign influence in the country, see B. Gur'ev, "Russkaia torgovlia v zapadnoi Mongolii," *Vestnik Azii*, no. 10 (October 1911), 48–49; "Russkie dela v Mongolii," *Dal'nii vostok*, no. 33 (August 17, 1913), 9–12; V. Tomlin, *Mongoliia i ee sovremennoe znachenie dlia Rossii* (Moscow, 1913), 14; A. P. Boloban, *Mongolii v ee sovremennom torgovo-ekonomicheskom otnoshenii: Otchet agenta ministerstva torgovli i promyshlennosti v Mongolii A. P. Bolobana za 1912–1913 god* (Petrograd, 1914), 103, 135; I. M. Maiskii, *Mongoliia nakanune revoliutsii* (2d rev. ed; Moscow, 1960), 91–92; N. E. Edinarkhova, "Russkie v Mongolii: Obraz

zhizni i tipy povedeniia," in *Diaspory v istoricheskom vremeni i prostranstve; Natsional'naia situatsiia v vostochnoi Sibiri; Tezisy dokladov mezhdunarodnoi nauchno-prakticheskoi konferentsii 6–8 oktiabria 1994 g.* (Irkutsk, 1994), 121–23; and Edinarkhova, "Russkie kuptsy v Mongolii," *Vostok,* no. 1 (1996), 76–89.

54. On these points, see *Moskovskaia torgovaia ekspeditsiia v Mongoliiu* (Moscow, 1912), 276–77; and Svechnikov, *Russkie v Mongolii,* 28.

55. M. I. Bogolepov and M. N. Sobelev, *Ocherki Russko-Mongol'skoi torgovli: Ekspeditsiia v Mongoliiu 1910 goda* (Tomsk, 1911), 4.

56. On Buryats in government circles in Mongolia and the modernizing reforms mentioned here, Robert A. Rupen, "The Buriat Intelligentsia," *The Far Eastern Quarterly* 15, no. 3 (1956), 383–98; Maiskii, *Mongoliia nakanune revoliutsii,* 93–94; B. V. Bazarov and L. B. Zhabaeva, *Buriatskie natsional'nye demokraty i obshchestvenno-politicheskaia mysl' mongol'skikh narodov v pervoi treti xx veka* (Ulan-Ude, 2008), 60–68; Shirendyb, *Mongoliia na rubezhe xix–xx vekov,* 106–7; Lishtovannyi, *Istoricheskoe vzaimootnosheniia Sibiri i Mongolii,* 36–37, 65–66, 78–79, 92–93, 96–97; and György Kara, *Books of the Mongolian Nomads: More Than Eight Centuries of Writing Mongolian* (Bloomington, Ind., 2005), 183–84.

57. On Dorzhiev, see Snelling, *Buddhism in Russia.* On the temple: A. I. Andreev, "Iz istorii peterburgskogo buddiiskogo khrama," *Orient* 1 (1992), 6–26; and Schimmelpenninck, *Russian Orientalism,* 171–73.

58. Esper Oukhtomsky, "The English in Tibet: A Russian View," *The North American Review* 174 (1904), 28.

59. Burdukov, *V staroi i novoi Mongolii,* 102.

60. P. N. Wrangel [Vrangel'], *Vospominaniia generala barona P. N. Vrangelia* (Moscow, 1992), vol. 1, 12; Wrangel, *The Memoirs of General Wrangel: The Last Commander-in-Chief of the Russian National Army* (Sophie Goulston, trans.) (London, 1929), 7.

61. For example, Wrangel describes Ungern's mother as a widow rather than a divorcée, that he was wounded and received a St. George's Cross in the war with Japan, and that he had his duel while on the Amur and then spent a year wandering "in the wilderness" between Vladivostok and Harbin. See Wrangel, *Vospominaniia,* vol. 1, 12. For some additional context on Wrangel's wartime service and his recollections of Ungern, see Entoni Kroner (Anthony Kröner), *Belaia armiia, chernyi baron: Zhizn' generala Petra Vrangelia* (Moscow, 2011), 75–77.

62. *AVPRI,* Kitaiskii stol, op.491, 1912, d.639, l.168. Bair was a local Mongol leader actively cooperating at the time with Liuba and the Cossack command, which may explain why Ungern suggested an assignment with his force. By contrast, Russian impressions of Dambiijantsan by this point were wholly negative. For Liuba's assessment of Bair as a leader with the potential to offer "considerable services" to the Russians, see another telegram from the same day: *AVPRI,* Kitaiskii stol, op.491, 1912, d.639, l.168.

63. For these two texts, see Kuz'min, *Istoriia barona Ungerna,* 427.

Chapter 7

1. Stefan Zweig, *The World of Yesterday* (Lincoln, Neb., 1964), 223; V. V. Rozanov, *Poslednie list'ia* (A.N. Nikoliukin, ed.) (Moscow, 2000), 255. For evocations of unity in Germany at the war's outset, see also Modris Eksteins, *Rites of Spring: The Great War and the Birth of the Modern Age* (Boston, 1989), 192–93. Eksteins quotes the playwright Ernst Toller, who later became bitterly opposed to the war, as claiming in 1914: "The nation recognizes no races anymore; all speak one language, all defend one mother, Deutschland."

2. Eric Lohr, *Nationalizing the Russian Empire: The Campaign against Enemy Aliens during World War I* (Cambridge, Mass., 2003), 13. On the reverent crowd that listened to the tsar, see Richard S. Wortman, *Scenarios of Power: Myth and Ceremony in Russian Monarchy* (Princeton, N.J., 1995), vol. 2, 510; and Sir Bernard Pares, *The Fall of the Russian Monarchy: A Study of the Evidence* (1939; New York, 1961), 187–88. For the divided reception of the war across European societies, see Adrian Gregory, *The Last Great War: British Society and the First World War* (New York, 2008), 9–39; Jeffrey Verhey, *The Spirit of 1914: Militarism, Myth, and Mobilization in Germany* (New York, 2000); and Jean-Jacques Becker, *1914: Comment les français sont entrés dans la guerre* (Paris, 1977).

3. Joshua A. Sanborn, *Drafting the Russian Nation: Military Conscription, Total War, and Mass Politics, 1905–1925* (DeKalb, Ill., 2003), 30–31; and Allan K. Wildman, *The End of the Russian Imperial Army: The Old Army and the Soldiers' Revolt (March–April 1917)* (Princeton, N.J., 1980), 77–79.

4. V. I. Simakov, *Chastushki: Izdany po zapisiam 1914–1915 g.* (Petrograd, 1915), 5. The Russian original reads: "Kak na nashe nyne gore/Vse kazenki na zapore/Net ni piva, ni vina/Tol'ko s Germaniei voina!" For a discussion of the myth of general enthusiasm for the start of the war, see Niall Ferguson, *The Pity of War* (New York, 1999), 174–211. On the wartime prohibition of alcohol and the mood of peasant soldiers, see Patricia Herlihy, *Alcoholic Empire: Vodka and Politics in Late Imperial Russia* (New York, 2002), 139–40; Wildman, *End of the Russian Imperial Army,* 77–78; and O. S. Porshneva, "Rossiiskii krest'ianin v pervoi mirovoi voine (1914–fevral' 1917)," in I. V. Narskii and O. Iu. Nikonova (eds.), *Chelovek i voina: Voina kak iavlenie kul'tury* (Moscow, 2001), 195–96. See also Leonid Heretz, *Russia on the Eve of Modernity: Popular Religion and Traditional Culture under the Last Tsars* (New York, 2008), 193–200.

5. For varying accounts of Ungern's location when the mobilization began, see Rönnqvist, *Baron Ungern, Mongoliets härskare,* 33; Kuz'min, *Istoriia Barona Ungerna,* 65; Vladimir Pozner, *Bloody Baron: The Story of Ungern-Sternberg* (New York, 1938), 54; and N. N. Kniaz'ev, "Legendarnyi Baron," in S. L. Kuz'min (comp.), *Legendarnyi baron: Neizvestnye stranitsy grazhdanskoi voiny* (Moscow, 2004), 16.

6. Mosse, *Image of Man,* 107; James J. Sheehan, *Where Have All the Soldiers Gone? The Transformation of Modern Europe* (Boston, 2008), 60–61. For a skeptical view of Hitler's much ballyhooed moment of joy in the summer of 1914, see Thomas Weber, *Hitler's First War: Adolf Hitler, the Men of the List Regiment, and the First World War* (New York, 2010), 11–27.

7. It's often claimed that Ungern used family connections to arrange his new assignment. His great uncle, Pavel (Paul) von Rennenkampf, was the commander of the First Army at the time, so this is entirely possible. The Don regiment's papers indicate only his enlistment, there is no additional information. Ronny Rönnqvist claims that Ungern signed up with an Uhlan regiment in the Second Army, using the connections of another relative, but there is no evidence of this in Ungern's military record. See Rönnqvist, *Baron Ungern, Mongoliets härskare,* 33.

8. Nils von Ungern-Sternberg, *De Hungaria,* 281. Based on the rough dating alluded to in the letter, the incident that earned Ungern the St. George's Cross seems to be the one described in the official army account submitted for the commendation. See *RGVIA,* f.400, op.12, d.26975, ll.524–29. The account dates from February 1915 but the incident is noted as having occurred on September 22, 1914.

9. For these figures from 1914, see Peter Gatrell, "Poor Russia, Poor Show: Mobilising a Backward Economy," in Stephen Broadberry and Mark Harrison (eds.), *The Economics of World War I* (New York, 2005), 250; and Gatrell, *Russia's First World War: A Social and Economic History* (New York, 2005), 1, 22.

10. On the generals of the East Prussian battles in August 1914, see Dennis E. Showalter, *Tannenberg: Clash of Empires, 1914* (Washington, D.C., 2004); and A. M. Zaionchkovskii, *Pervaia mirovaia voina* (St. Petersburg, 2002), pt. 1.

11. For some of these broadsheets, see *Beiträge zum Einfall der Russen in Ostpreussen 1914: Aus der Russenzeit in Insterburg* (Insterburg, 1914).

12. For these efforts and texts, see "Odezwa W. Ksiecia Mikolaja," in *Odbudowa państwowości polskiej: Najważniejsze dokumenty 1912–styczeń1924* (Warsaw-Cracow, 1924), 27; "Vozzvanie Verkhovnogo Glavnokomanduiushchego: Narody Avstro-Vengri," in *God voiny: s 19-ogo iiulia 1914 g. po 19-oe iiulia 1915 g.* (Moscow, 1915), 13–14; Von Hagen, "Limits of Reform," 48, 52; Norman Davies, *God's Playground: A History of Poland*, vol. 2, *1795–Present* (New York, 2005), 282; Michael A. Reynolds, *Shattering Empires: The Clash and Collapse of the Ottoman and Russian Empires, 1908–1918* (New York, 2011), 121–23, 130–33; A. O. Arutiunian, *Kavkazskii front, 1914–1917 gg.* (Erevan, 1971), 291–335; Stanford J. Shaw, *The Ottoman Empire in World War I*, vol. 1, *Prelude to War* (Ankara, 2006), 385, 414–16; and Hakan Kırımlı, "The Activities of the Union for the Liberation of Ukraine in the Ottoman Empire during the First World War," *Middle Eastern Studies* 34, no. 4 (1998), 177–200.

13. The term "liberationist hyperbole" is drawn from Von Hagen, "Limits of Reform," 48.

14. Paul Robert Magocsi, "Galicia: A European Land," in Paul Robert Magocsi and Christopher Hann (eds.), *Galicia: A Multicultured Land* (Toronto, 2005), 12–15; Anna Veronika Wendland, *Die Russophilen in Galizien: Ukrainische Konservativen zwischen Österreich und Russland, 1848–1915* (Vienna, 2001); and S. A. Nikitin, *Slavianskie komitety v Rossii, 1858–1876* (Moscow, 1960).

15. On the complexities of Austrian nationalism and pro-German politics in late Habsburg Austria, see Barbara Jelavich, *Modern Austria: Empire and Republic, 1815–1986* (New York, 1987), 81–82; and Pieter M. Judson, *Guardians of the Nation: Activists on the Language Frontiers of Imperial Austria* (Cambridge, Mass., 2006).

16. For the most eloquent recent statement of this general argument, see Aviel Roshwald, *Ethnic Nationalism and the Fall of Empires: Central Europe, Russia, and the Middle East, 1914–1923* (New York, 2001).

17. This was the bargain at the heart of the Treaty of Brest-Litovsk, which the Bolshevik government signed with the Germans in March 1918. Lenin traded land for peace, hoping that the land would come back later. On Brest-Litovsk, see Robert Service, *Spies and Commissars: The Early Years of the Russian Revolution* (New York, 2012), 95–105.

18. Frederick Dickinson, *War and National Reinvention: Japan in the Great War, 1914–1919* (Cambridge, Mass., 1999); and Sven Saaler, "The Construction of Regionalism in Modern Japan: Kodera Kenkichi and his 'Treatise on Greater Asianism'," *Modern Asian Studies* 41, no. 6 (2007), 1261–94, esp. 1281–87. See also Xu Guoqi, *China and the Great War: China's Pursuit of a New National Identity and Internationalization* (New York, 2005), esp. 258–77.

19. This is Aviel Roshwald's description, *Ethnic Nationalism and the Fall of Empires*, 33.

20. This is a contested question for historians of the Habsburg Empire, some of whom argue that the empire fell apart as a result of "external factors"—that is, losing the war—and others that the principal reason was nationalism within the empire. See Mark Cornwall, "Disintegration and Defeat: The Austro-Hungarian Revolution," in Mark Cornwall (ed.), *The Last Years of Austria-Hungary: A Multi-National Experiment in Early Twentieth-Century Europe* (rev. ed.; Exeter, Eng., 2002), 167–96, in particular 168.

21. On these issues, see Isabel V. Hull, *Absolute Destruction: Military Culture and the Practices of War in Imperial Germany* (Ithaca, 2005), 226–62; Vejas Gabriel Liulevicius, *War Land on the Eastern Front: Culture, National Identity, and German Occupation in World War*

I (New York, 2000); Mark von Hagen, *War in a European Borderland: Occupations and Occupation Plans in Galicia and Ukraine, 1914–1918* (Seattle, 2007); A. Iu. Bakhturina, *Okrainy rossiiskoi imperii: Gosudarstvennoe upravlenie i natsional'naia politika v gody pervoi mirovoi voiny* (Moscow, 2004); and Sammartino, *Impossible Border,* 24–37.

22. The war wasn't alone to blame, of course. The grounds for the intolerance and extremism of the genocide were laid earlier, but the war was the trigger that allowed the spiral of violence to unfold. See Hans-Lukas Kieser, *Der verpasste Friede: Mission, Ethnie und Staat in der Ostprovinzen Türkei, 1839–1938* (Zurich, 2000), 339–44; Donald Bloxham, *The Great Game of Genocide: Imperialism, Nationalism, and the Destruction of the Ottoman Armenians* (New York, 2005), 69–96; Aaron Rodrique, "L'état impérial ottoman et les politiques de deportation," in Bertrand Badie and Yves Déloye (eds.), *Le temps de l'état: Mélanges en l'honneur de Pierre Birnbaum* (Paris 2007), 185–202; and Ronald Grigor Suny, "The Holocaust before the Holocaust: Reflections on the Armenian Genocide," in Hans-Lukas Kieser and Dominik J. Schaller (eds.), *Der Völkermord an der Armeniern und die Shoah* (Zurich, 2002), 83–100.

23. Cited in Norman M. Naimark, *Fires of Hatred: Ethnic Cleansing in Twentieth-Century Europe* (Cambridge, Mass., 2001), 38. The quotation comes from a letter Morganthau wrote to Rabbi Steven Wise in October 1915.

24. Steven E. Aschheim, *Brothers and Strangers: The East European Jew in German and German-Jewish Consciousness, 1800–1923* (1982; repr.: Madison, Wisc. [1999]), 139–43, 157–60; Oleg Budnitskii, *Russian Jews between the Reds and the Whites, 1917–1920,* trans. Timothy J. Portice (Philadelphia, 2012), 136–38.

25. Alexander V. Prusin, *Nationalizing a Borderland: War, Ethnicity, and Anti-Jewish Violence in East Galicia, 1914–1920* (Tuscaloosa, Ala., 2005), 24–32; Marsha Rozenblit, *Reconstructing a National Identity: The Jews of Habsburg Austria during World War I* (New York, 2001), 50, 52.

26. Lohr, *Nationalizing the Russian Empire,* 17–22, 138; Prusin, *Nationalizing a Borderland,* 48–62; and Peter Holquist, "La violence de l'armée russe à l'encontre des Juifs en 1915: Causes et limites," in John Horne (ed.), *Vers la guerre totale: Le tournant de 1914–1915* (Paris, 2010), 208, 210–11, 218.

27. Eric Lohr, "The Russian Army and the Jews: Mass Deportation, Hostages, and Violence during World War I," *RR* 60, no. 3 (2001), 416.

28. On the Moorish revival in late nineteenth-century synagogue architecture, see Ivan Davidson Kalmar, "Moorish Style: Orientalism, the Jews, and Synagogue Architecture," *Jewish Social Studies* 7, no. 3 (2001), 68–100; and Carol Herselle Krinsky, *Synagogues of Europe: Architecture, History, Meaning* (New York, 1985), 81–85. On debates over the style of the St. Petersburg synagogue, see Benjamin Nathans, *Beyond the Pale: The Jewish Encounter with Late Imperial Russia* (Berkeley and Los Angeles, 2002), 155; and Michael Stanislawski, *For Whom Do I Toil? Judah Leib Gordon and the Crisis of Russian Jewry* (New York, 1988), 131–32. For a broad overview of Jews in Europe during the war years, see David Vital, *A People Apart: The Jews in Europe, 1789–1939* (New York, 1999), 647–702.

29. Iokhanan Petrovskii-Shtern, *Evrei v russkoi armii, 1827–1914* (Moscow, 2003), 343–44, 351–54; and Sanborn, *Drafting the Russian Nation,* 69. By ethnic cleansing, I mean "the intention... to remove a people and often all traces of them from a given territory." See Naimark, *Fires of Hatred,* 3.

30. For this quote, see N. D. Polivanov, *O nemetskom zasilii* (2nd ed.; Petrograd, 1916), 1–2. On the deportations of Russian Germans and anti-German sentiment, see Lohr, *Nationalizing the Russian Empire,* 32–54, 129–37. On spy mania in Russia during the war, see William

C. Fuller, Jr., *The Foe Within: Fantasies of Treason and the End of Imperial Russia* (Ithaca, 2006), 150–83.

31. See, for example, Siegfried von Bremen, "Erinnerungen," in Henning von Wistinghausen (ed.), *Zwischen Reval und St. Petersburg: Erinnerungen von Estländern aus zwei Jahrhunderten* (Weissenhorn, 1993), 221. On restrictions facing Russian Germans in the war zone, see Sammartino, *Impossible Border*, 33–34.

32. On anti-German fears and paranoia in the Baltic, see Bakhturina, *Okrainy rossiiskoi imperii*, 78–116; Michael B. Barrett, *Operation Albion: The German Conquest of the Baltic Islands* (Bloomington, Ind., 2008), 180–86, 227.

33. A. Rennikov, *V strane chudes: Pravda o pribaltiiskikh nemtsakh* (2nd ed.; Petrograd, 1915), 232.

34. I. G. Sobolev, *Bor'ba s "nemetskim zasil'em" v Rossii v gody pervoi mirovoi voiny* (St. Petersburg, 2004), 25–28, 50–66.

35. In early September 1914, the "fighting strength" of the regiment was indicated as 21 officers and 942 "bayonets." See *Vostochno-Prusskaia operatsiia* (Moscow, 1939), 494.

36. The note on Ungern's reporting for duty appears in *RGVIA*, f.5088, op.1, d.38, l.45. On the sorties, see *RGVIA*, f.5088, op.1, d.5, ll.1–1(b), also ll.3–4, 5–9. Ungern began his service in the regiment in Fourth Company (*sotnia*). At the time of the war, Bal'verzhishki was located in Mariampol' district, Suvalki (Suwałki) province.

37. For these aspects of life at the front as well as references to Ungern, see the field books in *RGVIA*, f.5281, op.1, d.25, ll.1–4; f.5281, op.1, d.1; f.5281, op.1, d.2, ll.23, 30(b), 34(b); f.5281, op.1, d.59, ll.7–7(b); and f.5282, op.1, d.22, ll.6(b)–9.

38. Exactly how Ungern transferred remains unclear. Reports submitted by his Don regiment on December 30 and 31, 1914 indicate that he was sent on a week-long assignment (*komandirovka*) to Petrograd for horseshoes on November 12 and never came back, meaning that he effectively went AWOL. Yet we know that this is also the time when he transferred to the Trans-Baikal regiment. See *RGVIA*, f.5088, op.1, d.38, ll.103(b)–104.

39. Vasil'evskii, *Zabaikal'skoe kazach'e voisko*, 31–32. For a history of the First Nerchinsk published prior to the war, see A. E. Makovkin, *1-i Nerchinskii polk Zabaikal'skogo kazach'ego voiska, 1898–1906 gg.: Istoricheskii ocherk* (St. Petersburg, 1907).

40. On Ungern's behind-the-lines service, see Ol'ga Khoroshilova, *Voiskovye partizany velikoi voiny* (St. Petersburg, 2002), 78, 85, 96, 98–101, 104, 132. For materials relating to these "partisan" units, see *RGVIA*, f.2007, op.1, d.66 and d.67. A service record dating from late 1916 indicates that he served with the special unit from September 1915 to April 1916.

41. *RGVIA*, f.3532, op.1, d.218, ll.1–3.

42. *RGVIA*, f.3532, op.1, d.216, l.360.

43. L. Voitolovskii, *Vskhodil krovavyi mars: Po sledam voiny* (Moscow, 1998), 239–40.

44. For a discussion of "the joy of war" as part of the experience of World War I, see Ferguson, *Pity of War*, 357–66; and Alan Kramer, *Dynamic of Destruction: Culture and Mass Killing in the First World War* (New York, 2007), 232–33. On fear and excitement wrapped together (*Angstlust*), see the discussion in Jan Plamper, "Fear: Soldiers and Emotion in Early Twentieth-Century Russian Military Psychology," *SR* 68, no. 2 (2009), 264.

45. Ernst Jünger, *Der Kampf als inneres Erlebnis* (2nd. rev. ed.; Berlin, 1926), 75–76. Jünger uses the term "princes of the trenches" in his wartime diary. See *The Storm of Steel: From the Diary of a German Storm-Troop Officer on the Western Front* (London, 1929), 235.

46. For lists and other brief references to Ungern in the war, see "Ob"iavlennye v vysochaishem prikaze 12-ogo noiabria," *Russkii invalid*, no. 271 (November 24, 1915), 3; "Ot

osobogo otdeleniia glavnogo shtaba po sboru svedenii o poteriiakh v deistvuiushchikh armiiakh," *Russkii invalid,* no. 231 (August 29, 1916), 2; "Ob"iavleniia v vysochaishem prikaze 4-ogo sentiabria," *Russkii invalid,* no. 252 (September 21, 1916), 2; "Vysochaishiia nagrady ob"iavlennye v vysochaishem prikaze 1-ogo dekabria," *Russkii invalid,* no. 343 (December 23, 1916), 1; *RGVIA,* f.400, op.12, d.26975, ll.525–29 (on Ungern's first St. George's Cross).

47. *RGVIA,* f.5282, op.1, d.26, ll.6(b)–9. The Russian press occasionally featured stories of Russian officers—presumably Russian Germans—who used their knowledge of German to deceive the enemy. For one example, see "Russkii ofitser," *Voina,* no. 10 (1914), 11.

48. *RGVIA,* f.2137, op.1, d.138, ll.40–41 (b). The court's verdict is also published in Kuz'min, *Baron Ungern,* 63–65. Emelian Iaroslavskii, the prosecutor at Ungern's trial in 1921, stated that Ungern had been sentenced to three years at his court-martial, presumably either because the Reds honestly got the sentence wrong or wanted to make Ungern look as bad as possible. See "Sud nad Baronom Ungernon," *Sovetskaia Sibir',* no. 201 [561] (September 18, 1921), 3; and [E.] Iaroslavskii, *Baron Roman Ungern-fon-Shternberg* (Petrograd, 1922), 2.

49. *RGVIA,* f.2137, op.1, d.138, ll.11, 30–31; Wrangel, *Vospominaniia,* vol. 1, 12–13. This is also where Wrangel recounts what he knew of Ungern's adventure in Kobdo.

50. On jaunty images of bravery, in particular in relation to Kuz'ma Kriuchkov, the winner of the war's first St. George's Cross, see Hubertus F. Jahn, *Patriotic Culture in Russia during World War I* (Ithaca, 1995), 23–24; and Stephen M. Norris, *A War of Images: Russian Popular Prints, Wartime Culture, and National Identity, 1812–1945* (DeKalb, Ill., 2006), 140–41. Lances were also used by German and some British cavalry forces during the war.

51. Family accounts relate that Ungern was exposed to at least one incident of anti-German prejudice from a Russian commanding officer. There may have been others. See, for example, [Arved von Ungern-Sternberg] "Roman Baron von Ungern-Sternberg: Lebensgeschichte," *EAA,* f.1423, n.1, s.192, l.16–17.

52. See, for example, Bremen, "Erinnerungen," 221.

53. On Germans on the General Staff and secret rulings, see P. A. Zaionchkovskii, "Russkii ofitserskii korpus nakanune pervoi mirovoi voiny," in *P. A. Zaionchkovskii, 1904–1983 gg.: Stat'i, publikatsii i vospominaniia o nem* (Moscow, 1998), 31.

54. O. N. Chaadaeva (ed.), *Soldatskie pis'ma 1917 goda* (Moscow-Leningrad, 1927), 24. For more on such sentiments, see Von Hagen, "Limits of Reform," 49.

55. See, for example, the names that appear in just one issue of the army's paper: *Russkii invalid,* no. 106 (1915), 3–6.

56. Zvi Gitelman, *A Century of Ambivalence: The Jews of Russia and the Soviet Union, 1881 to the Present* (2nd rev. ed.; Bloomington, Ind., 2001), 55; Robert D. Crews, *For Prophet and Tsar: Islam and Empire in Russia and Central Asia* (Cambridge, Mass., 2006), 351. Even before the war began, Russian military planners had begun examining the possibility of extending the draft to numerous previously exempted groups, including most Muslim peoples. On this, see Tomohiko Uyama, "A Particularist Empire: The Russian Policies of Christianization and Military Conscription in Central Asia," in Uyama (ed.), *Empire, Islam, and Politics in Central Eurasia* (Sapporo, 2007), 52–53.

57. Some 100,000 to 200,000 nomads, "perhaps still more," are estimated to have been killed during the uprising, with as many as 250,000 forced to flee the empire, mostly by crossing the Chinese border. For these figures and an analysis of the revolt, see Jörn Happel, *Nomadische Lebeswelten und zarische Politik: Der Aufstand in Zentralasien 1916* (Stuttgart, 2010), 15, 55–182.

58. C. A. Bayly, *The Birth of the Modern World, 1780–1914: Global Connections and Comparisons* (Malden, Mass., 2004), 451–87.

59. Cited in Carl E. Schorske, *Fin-de-Siècle Vienna: Politics and Culture* (New York, 1980), 19.

60. Anton Chekhov, "On Official Duty," in *The Chekhov Omnibus: Selected Stories* (London, 1994), 503.

61. For these issues, see N. N. Ardashev, *Velikaia voina i zhenshchiny russkie* (Moscow, 1915), 14–15; Melissa K. Stockdale, "'My Death for the Motherland Is Happiness': Women, Patriotism, and Soldiering in Russia's Great War," *AHR* 109, no. 1 (2004), 78–116; and Tsyoshi Hasegawa, *The February Revolution, Petrograd 1917* (Seattle, 1981), 145–211. The quoted phrases appear in "Natsional'nyi vopros v Rossii," in L. S. Kozlovskii (ed.), *Voina i Pol'sha: Pol'skii vopros v russkoi pol'skoi pechati* (Moscow, 1914), 1; and N. A. Gredeskul', *Rossiia i ee narody: "Velikaia Rossiia" kak programma razresheniia natsional'nogo voprosa v Rossii* (Petrograd, 1916), 5, 6–7, 66–68. See also E. N. Trubetskoi, *Otechestvennaia voina i eia dukhovnyi smysl* (Moscow, 1915), 9, 20.

62. Cited in Carlson, *"No Religion Higher Than Truth,"* 78.

Chapter 8

1. "Sud nad Baronom Ungernom-fon-Shternberg," *Sovetskaia Sibir'*, no. 199 [559] (September 16, 1921), 1. The prosecution at the Novonikolaevsk trial also contended that he was released from prison after the February Revolution. See Iaroslavskii, *Baron Roman Ungern-fon-Shternberg*, 2. Sergei Kuz'min suggests a release in early 1917, before the February events. See Kuz'min, *Istoriia Barona Ungerna*, 69.

2. See, for example, his letters to Semenov from April 4 and June 27, 1918 in *RGVA*, f.39454, op.1, d.1, ll.1 and 2.

3. Semenov does not tell us when Ungern arrived in Urmia, but it could not have been later than March 1917. They served together in the Host's Third Verkhneudinsk Regiment, named after the town of Verkhneudinsk, today: Ulan-Ude, the capital of the Russian Federation's Buryat Republic. See Ataman Semenov, *O sebe: Vospominaniia, mysli i vyvody* (Moscow, 2002), 76. The Russians organized their operations in Persia as part of what they called the Caucasus front (*Kavkazskii front*), a huge area running some 600 miles from the eastern corner of the Black Sea to the southern Caspian. Total Russian army strength in this theater in early 1917 was approximately 220,000 men and officers. For a description of the scope of the front in early 1917, see Arutiunian, *Kavkazskii front, 1914–1917 gg.*, 257–58; and A. V. Shishov, "Kavkazskii front," in V. L. Mal'kov (ed.), *Pervaia mirovaia voina: Prolog xx veka* (Moscow, 1998), 586.

4. *RGVIA*, f.5281, op.1, d.81, l.6 (b). Krymov was commander of the Ussuri Mounted Division. By the time this order was issued, Ungern was already serving in Persia and had left Krymov's command.

5. Wildman, *End of the Russian Imperial Army*, 115, 362–71; Gatrell, *Russia's First World War*, 66.

6. Aleksei Alekseevich Brusilov, *Moi vospominaniia: Vospominaniia, memuary* (Minsk, 2003), 276.

7. "Vyderzhki iz dokladov chlenov Gosudarstvennoi Dumy N. O. Ianushkevicha i F. D. Filonenko (zaslushany Vremennym Komitetom Gosudarstvennoi Dumy v zasedanii 13 marta 1917 g.)," in N. E. Kakurin (comp.), *Razlozhenie armii v 1917 godu* (Moscow and Leningrad, 1925), 47.

8. Semenov, *O sebe*, 72.

9. On "soldier power," see Wildman, *End of the Russian Imperial Army,* 159–201.

10. Kuz′min, "Deiatel′nost′ barona R.F. fon Ungern-Shternberga i ego rol′ v istorii," 13, 23. Ungern's final promotion may have been his own idea since it appears to date to the period right after his taking of Urga when his relationship with Semenov had become at best unclear.

11. For these references, see Jane Burbank, *Intelligentsia and Revolution: Russian Views of Bolshevism, 1917–1922* (New York, 1986), 171; Pavel Zyrianov, *Admiral Kolchak: Verkhovnyi pravitel′ Rossii* (Moscow, 2006), 345; and James Ryan, "'Revolution Is War': The Development of the Thought of V. I. Lenin on Violence, 1899–1907," *SEER* 89, no. 2 (2011), 270.

12. As a result of the mobilization and accelerated graduation from officer schools, the imperial army counted approximately 125,000 officers when the war began. Some 220,000 men then became officers during the war years, the great majority from nonnoble backgrounds. See I. N. Grebenkin, "Ofitserstvo rossiiskoi armii v gody pervoi mirovoi voiny," *VI,* no. 2 (2010), 52–53.

13. I. V. Got′e, *Time of Troubles: The Diary of Iurii Vladimirovich Got′e; Moscow, July 8, 1917 to July 23, 1922* (Terence Emmons, ed. and trans.) (Princeton, N.J., 1988), 28. One didn't have to be a conservative to have this view. Skeptical socialists like Maksim Gorky saw the Bolsheviks and "the people" in much the same light. See Gorky, *Untimely Thoughts: Essays on Revolution, Culture, and the Bolsheviks, 1917–1918* (Mark D. Steinberg, ed.; Herman Ermolaev, trans.) (New Haven, Conn., 1995).

14. "Doprosy R. F. Ungerna 1 i 2 sentiabria 1921 g. v Irkutske," 218.

15. "Vtoroe pis′mo R. F. Ungerna Tsende-Gunu," in Kuz′min, *Baron Ungern,* 143.

16. Quotes from "Pis′mo R. F. Ungerna nachal′niku otdel′nogo otriada voisk, deistvuiushchikh v provintsii Tsitsikar," and "Pervoe pis′mo R. F. Ungerna Palta-vanu," in Kuz′min, *Baron Ungern,* 145, 132.

17. Semenov, *O sebe,* 66–67. On the discrediting of the monarchy before and after the overthrow of the tsar and the political weakness of monarchists in 1917, see Matthew Rendle, *Defenders of the Motherland: The Tsarist Elite in Revolutionary Russia* (New York, 2010), 56–57; and Orlando Figes and Boris Kolonitskii, *Interpreting the Russian Revolution: The Languages and Symbols of 1917* (New Haven, Conn., 1999), 9–29.

18. On the politics of epaulettes during the revolutionary year, see B. I. Kolonitskii, *Pogony i bor′ba za vlast′ v 1917 godu* (St. Petersburg, 2001). On the response of officers to the February Revolution and the deepening political crisis, see Rendle, *Defenders of the Motherland,* 115–56.

19. Semenov, *O sebe,* 75.

20. Russia and Great Britain formalized their effective division of Persia in the so-called Anglo-Russian Convention of 1907. The Persians were informed of the agreement only after the fact. See Jennifer Siegel, *Endgame: Britain, Russia, and the Final Struggle for Central Asia* (New York, 2002), 18–19; and Guive Mirfendereski, *A Diplomatic History of the Caspian Sea: Treaties, Diaries, and Other Stories* (New York, 2001), 85–93.

21. On Russian policies in Persia prior to the war, see P. N. Strelianov (Kalabukhov), *Kazaki v Persii, 1909–1918* (Moscow, 2007); and Siegel, *Endgame,* 9, 33–35, 57–59, 63–65, 86–87, 110–13, 117–29. The Russians expressed their dim view of Persia's international status in a jingle from the times: "A chicken is not a bird/Persia is not a foreign country" (*kuritsa ne ptitsa/Persiia ne zagranitsa*). Firuz Kazemzadeh, *Russia and Britain in Persia, 1864–1914: A Study in Imperialism* (New Haven, Conn., 1968), 676.

22. On the ethnoreligious mosaic of the Urmia region before and during the war, see Florence Hellot-Bellier, "La première guerre mondiale à l'ouest du lac d'Urumiye," in Oliver Bast (ed.), *La Perse et la grande guerre* (Tehran, 2002), 329–52.

23. In addition to the atrocities against Assyrian Christians in Persia, the Turkish army and government also organized and condoned massacres of Assyrians in Ottoman territory (far eastern Anatolia, Hakkari district, Van province). On these events and policies, see Michael A. Reynolds, *Shattering Empires: The Clash and Collapse of the Ottoman and Russian Empires, 1908–1918* (New York, 2011), 117–18, 126–27; M. S. Lazarev, *Kurdskii vopros (1891–1917)* (Moscow, 1972), 293–95, 303–12; Donald Bloxham, *The Great Game of Genocide: Imperialism, Nationalism, and the Destruction of the Ottoman Armenians* (New York, 2005), 97–98; and Gabriele Yonan, *Ein vergessener Holocaust: Die Vernichtung der christlichen Assyrer in der Türkei* (Göttingen, 1989), 111–12. Estimates of the dead vary. Bloxham suggests that at least seven thousand Assyrians were massacred in Persia in early 1915, with many more fleeing as refugees. Yet the Assyrian delegation to the Paris Peace Conference in 1919 claimed 250,000 deaths over the course of the war, though, according to David Gaunt, this estimate may be too low. See Gaunt, "The Ottoman Treatment of the Assyrians," in Ronald Grigor Suny, Fatma Müge Göçek, and Norman M. Naimark (eds.), *A Question of Genocide: Armenians and Turks at the End of Empire* (New York, 2011), 244–45.

24. Sanborn, *Drafting the Russian Nation*, 80–81; Gatrell, *Russia's First World War*, 183–84; "Formirovanie natsional'nykh chastei," in Kakurin, *Razlozhenie armii v 1917 godu*, 78–85.

25. For a photo of Estonian soldiers carrying a banner with this slogan, see Rex A. Wade, *The Russian Revolution, 1917* (2nd ed.; New York, 2005), 161.

26. Semenov, *O sebe*, 76.

27. Ibid., 81–86.

28. We know that Ungern was in Chita in October 1917, based on his testimony at his trial. See "Sud nad Baronom Ungernom," *Sovetskaia Sibir'*, no. 200 [560] (September 17, 1921), 4.

29. Kuz'min, "Deiatel'nost' barona R.F. fon Ungern-Shternberga i ego rol' v istorii," 12.

30. For descriptions of the Urmia region close to the time of Ungern's service, see Viktor Shklovsky, *A Sentimental Journey: Memoirs, 1917–1922* (Ithaca, 1984), 82–87. To be more precise, Julfa today sits on the border between Iran and the Nakhichevan Autonomous Region, a landlocked enclave of Azerbaijan wedged between Iran and Armenia. In fact, there are twos Julfas, one on the Azeri side, the other across from it in Iran, with the Aras River running between them.

31. Sarah Badcock, *Politics and the People in Revolutionary Russia: A Provincial History* (New York, 2007); and Joshua Sanborn, "Unsettling the Empire: Violent Migrations and Social Disaster in Russia during World War I," *JMH* 77, no. 2 (2005), 290–324.

32. V. Nabokov, *Vremennoe pravitel'stvo (vospominaniia)* (1924; repr.: Moscow, 1991), 40–41.

33. Gatrell, "Poor Russia, Poor Show," 239.

34. John Reed, *Ten Days That Shook the World* (1919; New York, 1981), 48.

35. V. I. Lenin, "Sotsialisticheskaia revoliutsiia i pravo natsii na samoopredelenie," in *Polnoe sobranie sochinenii* (5th ed.; Moscow, 1969), vol. 27, 256. See also Terry Martin, *The Affirmative Action Empire: Nations and Nationalisms in the Soviet Union, 1923–1939* (Ithaca, 2001), 5.

36. "Declaration of the Rights of the Peoples of Russia," in Robert V. Daniels (ed.), *A Documentary History of Communism in Russia: From Lenin to Gorbachev* (Hanover, N.H., 1993), 66–67.

37. Erez Manela, *The Wilsonian Moment: Self-Determination and the International Origins of Anticolonial Nationalism* (New York, 2007), 6–7.

38. On the imperial disintegration in 1917, see Ronald Grigor Suny, *The Revenge of the Past: Nationalism, Revolution, and the Collapse of the Soviet Union* (Stanford, Calif., 1993),

20–83; and Richard Pipes, *The Formation of the Soviet Union: Communism and Nationalism, 1917–1923* (2nd ed.; Cambridge, Mass., 1997), 50–113.

39. The reference to "spontaneous demobilization" is drawn from N.N. Golovin, *Voennye usiliia Rossii v mirovoi voine* (Paris, 1939; reprint: Moscow, 2001), 353.

40. On the territorial confusion and fragmentation of the period, with references to the developments cited here, see Donald J. Raleigh, *Experiencing Russia's Civil War: Politics, Society, and Revolutionary Culture in Saratov, 1917–1922* (Princeton, N.J., 2002), 9, 74–106; Evan Mawdsley, *The Russian Civil War* (2nd ed.; New York, 2007), 26–29, 45–55, 70; Stephen Watrous, "The Regionalist Conception of Siberia, 1860–1920," in Galya Diment and Yuri Slezkine (eds.), *Between Heaven and Hell: The Myth of Siberia in Russian Culture* (New York, 1993), 129; and Suny, *Revenge of the Past,* 20–83.

41. For an early description of Dauria before the civil war, see V. Soldatov, *Zheleznodorozhnye poselki po Zabaikal'skoi linii* (St. Petersburg, 1912), vol. 5, pt. 2, 308. For descriptions during the revolutionary years, see Golubev, *Vospominaniia,* manuscript, *Hoover,* 12; and V. I. Shaiditskii, "Na sluzbe otechestva," in Kuzmin, *Baron Ungern,* 278.

42. The wedding apparently took place in an Orthodox church in Harbin, though I've found no direct evidence to confirm this or even his wife's name, which varies between different memoirs and genealogical books. Often she is simply referred to as a "Manchu princess." On sources and stories related to the marriage, see Kuz'min, *Istoriia Barona Ungerna,* 94–95. One writer suggests that Ungern may also have had a relationship with a certain Maria von Ekse during the war and that she bore him three children. See Rönnqvist, *Baron Ungern, Mongoliets härskare,* 116–17.

43. For these and other references, see *GAChO,* f.334, op.2, d.125, l.45–47 (on removing anti-Semitic sheets at the train station); Jamie Bisher, *White Terror: Cossack Warlords of the Trans-Siberian* (New York, 2005), 136–37; L. V. Kuras, "Ataman Semenov i 'evreiskii vopros,'" in *Istoriia "beloi" Sibiri: Tezisy vtoroi nauchnoi konferentsii (4–5 fevralia 1997 g.)* (Kemerovo, 1997), 46–48; and "Ob"iavlenie," *Russkii vostok,* no. 45, March 5 (February 20), 1919, 1 (on the formation of a Jewish regiment). Semenov was not above making anti-Semitic insinuations when it suited him, however. See a decree he wrote in response to the "treasonous action" of the Jewish regiment in Nerchink on Easter Sunday 1920: V. I. Vasilevskii (comp.), *Ataman Semenov: Voprosy gosudarstvennogo stroitel'stva; Sbornik dokumentov i materialov* (Chita, 2002), 93.

44. Kolchak's power was limited even in Omsk where nongovernment "right-wing groups" operated largely as they saw fit and "the supreme ruler himself was no more than a figurehead." See Vladimir N. Brovkin, *Behind the Front Lines of the Civil War: Political Parties and Social Movements in Russia, 1918–1923* (Princeton, N.J., 1994), 196.

45. On the Whites in Siberia, see Jonathan D. Smele, *Civil War in Siberia: The Anti-Bolshevik Government of Admiral Kolchak, 1918–1920* (New York, 1996); and N. G. O. Pereira, *White Siberia: The Politics of Civil War* (Buffalo, 1996). On the civil war in the Russian Far East, including the power of Cossack leaders in the region, see the summary in Stephan, *Russian Far East,* 117–40.

46. Though Semenov received visitors and conducted business at The Select, his private residence was the *style moderne* mansion of the architect Gavril Nikitin located nearby. Chita had two train stations, one east of downtown, the other in the downtown proper. The Select was closer to the latter on Amur Street, one of town's main thoroughfares. See V. Lobanov, *Staraia Chita: Dokumental'nyi rasskaz* (2d rev. ed.; Chita, 2003), 123–25, 142–43. When Semenov's troops withdrew from Chita in October 1920, they blew up the hotel, which was then rebuilt in 1931. For a photo of The Select today, see Valerii Nemerov, *Progulki po staroi Chite* (Chita, 2010), 34.

47. For these quotes, see "Vozzvanie G. M. Semenova k stanichnikam o bor'be s bolshevi-kami," in Vasilevskii, *Ataman Semenov*, 6; and "Glavnokomanduiushchii Ataman Semenov o zadachakh momenta," *Kazach'e ekho*, no. 41 (February 18 [5], 1920), 1.

48. These quotes are drawn from the manuscript of a booklet about Semenov published in Harbin in 1919. See *GAChO*, f.329, op.1, d.78, ll.20(b), 25(b).

49. On Japanese troop numbers, see B. M. Shereshevskii, *Razgrom Semenovshchiny (aprel'-noiabr' 1920 g.)* (Novosibirsk, 1966), 96; and Reiko Tanaka, "Imperial Dilemma: The Japanese Intervention in Siberia, 1918–1922" (PhD diss., University of Cambridge, 2003), 10, 14.

50. For example, *Kazach'e ekho*, no. 44 (April 25 [12], 1920), 4 (ad for Russian-Japanese phrase books); "Obrashchenie generala Ooba," *Iz shtaba otd. Vostochno-Sibirskoi Armii*, no. 1 (April 10, 1919), 1 (on Japan's good intentions in Siberia); and *Russkii vostok*, no. 34 (18 [5] February, 1919), 2 (warning to Chita residents about Japanese artillery practice).

51. For an overview of the warlord era, see Diana Lary, *China's Republic* (New York, 2007), 45–80. See also her "Warlord Studies," *Modern China*, 6, no. 4 (1980), 439–70.

52. See Peter Zarrow, "Social and Political Developments: The Making of the Twentieth-Century Chinese State," in Kam Louie (ed.), *The Cambridge Companion to Modern Chinese Culture* (New York, 2008), 26.

53. On the persistence of the central government in Beijing and the contested politics of warlord rule, see Jonathan D. Spence, *The Search for Modern China* (New York, 1990), 289; Arthur Waldron, *From War to Nationalism: China's Turning Point, 1924–1925* (New York, 1995), 37–38; Xiaoyuan Liu, *Frontier Passages: Ethnopolitics and the Rise of Chinese Communism, 1921–1945* (Washington, D.C. and Stanford, Calif., 200?), 21–24; Leong, *Sino-Soviet Diplomatic Relations, 1917–1926*, 61–62.

54. Xu Shuzheng's haughty speech to a great council of Mongolian khans in 1919 was recalled by a Mongolian notable. See Lattimore and Isono, *Diluv Khutagt*, 99. On Chinese moves to end Mongolian autonomy, see Belov, *Rossiia i Mongoliia (1911–1919 gg.)*, 180–83; and Zhang Qixiong, *Shou fu Wai Meng zhuquan, 1917–1920* (Taibei, 1998), 75–114.

55. James H. Carter, *Creating a Chinese Harbin: Nationalism in an International City, 1916–1932* (Ithaca, 2002), 107–15; and Asada Musafumi, "The China-Russia-Japan Military Balance in Manchuria, 1906–1918," *Modern Asia Studies* 44, no. 6 (2010), 1307–8.

56. Many Chinese warlords, formally at least, were state representatives with military or civilian titles given to them by the republican government in Beijing. (Zhang's title, for example, was Inspector-General of the Three Eastern Provinces.) Beijing's practical power to control them, however, was limited overall and sometimes simply nonexistent. For the suggestion that Ungern and Chinese warlords were operating in similar environments, see Paul du Quenoy, "Warlordism à la russe: Baron von Ungern-Sternberg's Anti-Bolshevik Crusade, 1917–1921," *Revolutionary Russia* 16, no. 2 (2003), 21.

57. Zhang was finally undone in 1928 when he crossed the Japanese, who then got back at him by blowing up his train car. On Zhang, see David Bonavia, *China's Warlords* (Hong Kong and New York, 1995), 60–84; Matsusaka, *Making of Japanese Manchuria, 1904–1932*, 258–66; Gavan McCormack, *Chang Tso-lin in Northeast China, 1911–1928: China, Japan, and the Manchurian Idea* (Stanford, Calif., 1977); and G. S. Karetina, *Chzhan Tsolin' i politicheskaia bor'ba v Kitae v 20-e gody xx v.* (Moscow, 1984).

58. On Xu and Chen, see Zhang, *Shou fu Wai Meng zhuquan*, 109–13. Chen had held the post of senior official in Mongolia earlier as well, from 1917 to the fall of 1919.

59. *GAChO*, f.329, op.1, d.29, l.46(b).

60. Quoted in Peter Holquist, *Making War, Forging Revolution: Russia's Continuum of Crisis, 1914–1921* (Cambridge, Mass., 2002), 2. On the White military leadership's conviction

that the civil war was simply a continuation of the European war with a new enemy, see S. I. Konstantinov, "Vlianie vzaimosviazi mirovoi i grazhdanskoi voin na psikhologicheskii raskol rossiiskogo obshchestva," in I. V. Narskii and O. Iu. Nikonova (eds.), *Chelovek i voina: Voina kak iavlenie kul'tury* (Moscow, 2001), 182.

61. For these figures, see Gatrell, *Russia's First World War,* 246–47; Mawdsley, *Russian Civil War,* 287. These totals are only approximations, however. One expert suggests that 1.3 million Russian soldiers died in World War I but notes that other estimates run to twice that number. See William C. Fuller, Jr., "The Imperial Army," in Dominic Lieven (ed.), *The Cambridge History of Russia,* vol. 2, *Imperial Russia, 1689–1917* (New York, 2006), 552.

62. On the competing apocalyptic visions at the heart of the war, see the reflections of the philosopher Fedor Stepun, *Byvshee i nesbyvsheesia* (Moscow and St. Petersburg, 1995), 459.

63. On the mutual demonization of Reds and Whites and the justification for violence, see Aleksei Litvin, *Krasnyi i belyi terror v Rossii, 1918–1922 gg.* (Moscow, 2004); Leonid Heretz, "The Psychology of the White Movement," in Vladimir N. Brovkin (ed.), *The Bolsheviks in Russian Society: The Revolution and the Civil War* (New Haven, Conn., 1997), 111–12; and Igor Narskii, "Konstruirovanie mifa o grazhdanskoi voine v rannei sovetskoi Rossii (na primere Urala v 1917–1922 gg.)," in Iuliia Khmelevskaia (comp.), *Rossiia i voina v xx stoletii: Vzgliad iz udaliaiushcheisia perpektivy* (Moscow, 2005), 79–85.

64. *VChK upolnomochena soobshchit' … 1918 g.* (Moscow, 2004), 275–76. This statement appeared in the Cheka publication *Krasnyi terror* (Red Terror) in November 1918.

65. Peter Holquist, "State Violence as Technique: The Logic of Violence in Soviet Totalitarianism," in Amir Weiner (ed.), *Landscaping the Human Garden: Twentieth-Century Population Management in a Comparative Framework* (Stanford, Calif., 2003), 25; and Brovkin, *Behind the Front Lines of the Civil War,* 204–6.

66. *NARB,* f.R-483, op.1, d.31, l.103.

67. In a letter written during the Mongolian campaign, Ungern states that he spent eight months in Beijing. It's not clear when, however. See "Pis'mo R. F. Ungerna Naiman-vanu," in Kuz'min, *Baron Ungern,* 129.

68. *NARB,* f.R-305, op.1, d.13, ll.1, 8, 9 (on purchasing horses); *GAChO,* f.334, op.1, d.113, l.19 (on meeting with the Chinese delegation); "Khronika," *Russkii vostok,* no. 29, February 9 [January 27], 1919, 1 (on overseeing Nerchinsk mines).

69. On Fushengge at Dauria, see the information in Chinese reports from 1919 in *Zhong E guanxi shiliao: Wai Menggu (Zhonghua Minguo liu nian zhi ba nian)* [1919] (Taibei, 1959) document no. 14, 314–15.

70. For a reference to this euphemism, see the statements of Major General Kazachikhin, Ungern's director of logistics at Manchuria Station: *RGVA,* f.16, op.3, d.222, l.56. An early Soviet account of the abuses at Dauria describes an area near the settlement known as "the valley of death" where many of the victims were buried. See Stepan Seryshev, "Vooruzhennaia bor'ba za vlast' sovetov na Dal'nem Vostoke," *Revoliutsiia na Dal'nem Vostoke* (Petrograd, 1923), 80.

71. V. I. Shaiditskii, "Na sluzhbe otechestva," in Kuz'min, *Baron Ungern,* 279.

72. For a copy of the order creating the division, dated February 5, 1920, see *GAChO,* f.329, op.1, d.13, l.168. On the shifting names and structures of these various units, see Kuz'min, "Deiatel'nost' barona R.F. fon Ungern-Shternberga i ego rol' v istorii," 13–14.

73. "Dopros R. F. Ungerna 7 sentiabria 1921 g. [v Novonikolaevske]," in Kuz'min, *Baron Ungern,* 229.

74. On the multinational profile of the division in Dauria, see Kuz'min, *Istoriia Barona Ungerna,* 84–86.

75. A. A. Karevskii, "K voprosu o simvolike Aziatskoi Konnoi Divizii," in *Kazachestvo Rossii v belom dvizhenii* (Almanakh *Belaia gvardiia*, no. 8) (Moscow, 2005), 185–92; Kuz'min, *Istoriia Barona Ungerna*, 84.

76. Kuz'min, "Deiatel'nost' barona R.F. fon Ungern-Shternberga i ego rol' v istorii," 14.

77. *RGVA*, f.16, op.3, d.222, l.57.

78. Ludovic-H. Grondijs, *La guerre en Russie et en Sibérie* (Paris, 1922), 447.

79. V. V. Alekseev (ed.), *Istoriia kazachestva Aziatskoi Rossii* (Ekaterinburg, 1995), vol. 2, 101.

80. For examples, see *GAKhK*, f.959, op.1, d.4, ll.4–4(b), 5, 6; f.959, op.1, d.2a, ll.303, 358; and Vasilevskii, *Ataman Semenov*,14, 19, 28-29, 31-32, 34.

81. For a sampling of these reports, see *GAChO*, f.334, op.2, d.113, ll.6–7(b), 29–29(b); f.334, op.2, d.138, ll.8, 18–18(b), 24–24(b), 25–25(b), 36. The quotes here are drawn from a report submitted to the head of the Trans-Baikal region by the Nerchinsk district head on November 24, 1919: *GAChO*, f.334, op.2, d.113, ll.6, 7(b). Complaints of depredations by the Asiatic Division also reached Semenov from various "local residents," and he issued at least one stern decree in May 1919 ordering them to stop their abuses, but it's not clear that his intervention changed very much. See Vasilevskii, *Ataman Semenov*, 24.

82. Aleksei Budberg, *Dnevnik belogvardeitsa: Vospominaniia, memuary* (Minsk and Moscow, 2001), 16.

83. As a local publication put it frankly at the time, the DVR was a "somewhat unusual state formation... called into being by the special circumstances of the global political moment" (*mirovaia politicheskaia kon'iunktura*). See *Po rodnomu kraiu: Kratkii ocherk Dal'ne-Vostochnoi Respubliki i Zabaikal'ia (sbornik stat'ei i materialov)* (Verkhneudinsk, 1922), 15.

84. Shereshevskii, *Razgrom Semenovshchiny*, 223. On the Far Eastern Republic, "three times the size of France but with a population of just two million people," see Dittmar Dahlmann, *Sibirien, vom 16. Jahrhundert bis zur Gegenwart* (Paderborn, 2009), 235; and Stephan, *Russian Far East*, 141-55.

Chapter 9

1. Semenov, in fact, went further, claiming not only that he planned Ungern's initial foray into Mongolia but also that he concocted a ruse to hide the scheme from the Reds, the Chinese, and his own HQ by claiming (falsely) that Ungern had broken from his command and gone off on his own. See Semenov, *O sebe*, 248-53.

2. "Doprosy R. F. Ungerna 1 i 2 sentiabria 1921 g. v Irkutske," 211.

3. To say that the city "fell" is something of an exaggeration: in fact, Semenov and his forces simply left—Semenov himself departing by biplane for Dauria on October 20—and the Reds entered the city unopposed on October 22. See Shereshevskii, *Razgrom Semenovshchiny*, 223.

4. "Doprosy R. F. Ungerna 1 i 2 sentiabria 1921 g. v Irkutske," 211.

5. This interpretation is also shared by Thomas E. Ewing, *Between the Hammer and the Anvil? Chinese and Russian Policies in Outer Mongolia, 1911-1921* (Bloomington, Ind., 1980), 196; A. S. Kruchinin, "'Mongol'skii pokhod' Barona Ungerna: K voprosu o podlinnykh tseliakh i putiakh ikh realizatsii," *Vestnik molodykh uchenykh* (seriia: Istoricheskie nauki), no. 1 (2002), 65–71; and Kuz'min, "Deiatel'nost' barona R. F. fon Ungerna-Shternberga i ego rol' v istorii," 17.

6. Ungern hints that this might have been in the case in a letter written from Urga to a potential Chinese ally. See "Pis'mo R. F. Ungerna Chuan Kuniu 16 fevralia 1921 g.," Kuz'min, *Baron Ungern*, 100.

7. The report by Chief of Staff of the Siberian Expeditionary Army Isomura Toshi is described in Leong, *Sino-Soviet Diplomatic Relations, 1917–1926,* 165–66.

8. *Zhong E guanxi shiliao (Zhong dong tie lu, dongbei bianfang, wai menggu) (Minguo jiu nian)* [1920] (Taibei, 1969), Section on Outer Mongolia (Wai Menggu), document no. 71, 44–45. The date of the telegram is October 13, 1920, by which time Ungern was already in the country.

9. "Dopros R. F. Ungerna 27 avgusta 1921 g. v Troitskosavske" and "Doprosy R. F. Ungerna 1 i 2 sentiabria 1921 g. v Irkutske," 201, 211.

10. For references to "invasion" in scholarly works, see, for example, Yang Chuang, Gao Fei, and Feng Yujun, *Bai nian Zhong E guanxi* (Beijing, 2006), 57; *Sha E qin Hua shi,* vol. 4, pt. 2, 276–77; Li Bin, "Shi shu enqin fan meng suo yinfa de zhi feng maodun dou zheng," *Nan dou xue tan (renwen shehui kexue xue bao),* no. 5 (2002), 14; Baabar, *Twentieth-Century Mongolia* (Christopher Kaplonski, ed.) (Knapwell, Eng., 1999), 207, 209–10. Official Chinese materials from the period use the verb *qinrao* to describe Ungern's actions, which translates as "invade and harass." See, for example, *Zhong E guanxi shiliao (dongbei bianfang, Wai Menggu) (Minguo shi nian)* [1921] (Taibei, 1975), Section on Outer Mongolia (Wai Menggu), document no. 29, 13.

11. Chen Yi had replaced Xu Shuzheng as Beijing's leading official in Outer Mongolia in the summer of 1920. For concerns about the integrity of the Mongolian border in Chinese materials from the summer and fall to early winter of 1920, see *Zhong E guanxi shiliao* [1920], Section on Outer Mongolia (Wai Menggu), document no. 49, 29–34; no. 92, 62; no. 100, 66; and no. 103, 67. There are more references to the need to protect Chinese "sovereignty" (*zhuquan*) after Ungern's capture of Urga in February 1921 and the entry of Red troops in Mongolia later that summer. See, for example, *Zhong E guanxi shiliao* [1921], Section on Outer Mongolia (Wai Menggu), document no. 45, 23; no. 189, 107; and no. 193, 110.

12. On the traffic around the border, see Fujiko Isono, "Soviet Russia and the Mongolian Revolution of 1921," *Past & Present,* no. 83 (1979), 123–25, 128–29; Darevskaia, *Sibir' i Mongoliia,* 287–350; Anthony B. Chan, *Arming the Chinese: The Western Armaments Trade in Warlord China, 1920–1928* (Vancouver, 1982), 123–25 (on White mercenaries working for Chinese warlords); Gregor Benton, *Chinese Migrants and Internationalism: Forgotten Histories, 1917–1945* (New York, 2007), 23, 25, 27–29; *AVPRI,* f. Urga consulate, op.732, 1919–1920, d.26, ll.33, 78, 256–57 (on Red clashes with Semenov's men on Mongolian territory, requisitions, Buryats crossing border); *NARB,* f.R-483, op.1, d.38, ll.2(b)–3 (on Mongolian lamas regularly visiting temples in Russian Buryat lands, Russians buying stock and other goods in Mongolia, Buryats taking their herds to Mongol territory to escape Reds); Belov, *Rossiia i Mongoliia,* 174–75, 205 (n.27); *Zhong E guanxi shiliao* [1920], Section on Outer Mongolia (Wai Menggu), document no. 62, 40 (on Russians in Outer Mongolia making political contacts with Mongols); no. 100, 66 (on Red "incursions" into Mongolia).

13. A. S. Makeev, *Bog voiny Baron Ungern: Vospominaniia byvshego ad"iutanta Nachal'nika Aziatskoi Konnoi Divizii* (Shanghai, 1934), 21–22.

14. On the divisions in the Russian colony during the revolution, see E. M. Darevskaia, "Fevral'skaia revoliutsiia v Rossii i russkaia koloniia v Urge," *Trudy Irkutskogo gosudarstvennogo universiteta* 25, no. 1 (1958), 23–48. For Makeev's quote, see Makeev, *Bog voiny Baron Ungern,* 34. On the Whites' view of Urga as a "Red town," see also Ungern's casual quip to his interrogators that "the Reds were in Urga before they were in Russia," which appears in "Dopros R. F. Ungerna 7 sentiabria 1921 g. [v Novonikolaevske]," 233.

15. "Vtoroe pis'mo R. F. Ungerna Palta-vanu," in Kuz'min, *Baron Ungern,* 133. The letter cited dates from April 27, 1921. Great President of the Republic (*Minguo da zongtong*) was the formal title of the Chinese presidency in the post-Qing era.

16. One of Ungern's officers estimated the population of the town in late 1920 at approximately sixty-five thousand, with close to half made up of lamas. See M. G. Tornovskii, "Sobytiia v Mongolii-Khalkhe v 1920–1921 godakh: Voenno-istoricheskii ocherk (vospominaniia)," in Kuz'min, *Legendarnyi baron*, 180. Estimates of the size of the garrison range as high as sixteen thousand (Tornovskii's guess is twelve thousand to fifteen thousand). For more estimates, see Kuz'min, "Deiatel'nost' barona R. F. fon Ungern-Shternberga i ego rol' v istorii," 19.

17. The consulate's importance to the local Russians was underscored by the fact that they referred to the whole quarter as "the consulate" or the "consular town" (*konsul'stvo, konsul'skii poselok*). The Mongols called it the "consular hill" (*konsulyn denj*) or simply *konsul*. As for Urga, other names that one finds for the city are Da Khüree/Ikh Khüree, with "da" and "ikh" meaning "great" or "large" in Chinese and Mongolian, respectively, and Bogdiin Khüree, referring to the city as the seat of the Bogda. "Urga" is derived from the Mongolian Örgöö, meaning "palace" or "residence," referring to the Bogda's residence. The most common Chinese name for the town, Kulun, derives from a Mongol word for an enclosed area. For a detailed description of the layout of Urga, see Szusza Majer and Krizstina Teleki, "Monasteries and Temples of Bogdiin Kh'ree, Ikh Kh'ree or Urga, the Old Capital City of Mongolia in the First Part of the Twentieth Century" (Unpublished paper, 2006), esp. 30–40.

18. The area of Ulaanbaatar that used to be the Russian consular town is still known as the Russian district (*Oros mikroraion*). On the map that provides the basis for the painting in the museum, see Majer and Teleki, "Monasteries and Temples of Bogdiin Kh'ree," 7.

19. Roy Chapman Andrews, *Under a Lucky Star: A Lifetime of Adventure* (Garden City, N.Y., 1945), 151. Andrews first visited Mongolia in 1917, though his most celebrated expeditions took place in 1922–1925. The "great temple of the Living Buddha" described in this passage is probably a reference to the imposing gold-roofed temple complex that surrounded the Bogda's yellow palace in Züün Khüree, all of which was destroyed during the antireligious campaigns of the late 1930s.

20. Like many Eurasian nomadic peoples, Mongols traditionally practiced open-air or "sky" burials. For references to the issues cited here, see Andrews, *Under a Lucky Star*, 150–52, 161. Like most Western and Russian observers, Beatrix Bulstrode also describes the burials and the roaming dogs. See Bulstrode, *A Tour in Mongolia* (New York, 1920), 205–6.

21. According to a Red Army intelligence report, the early-morning assault unfolded so quickly that scores of Chinese soldiers were caught in their beds and ended up fleeing "before they could even get their clothes on." *RGVA*, f.16, op.3, d.214, l.37. The report is dated February 8, 1921. Despite Chen's request for more troops to reinforce the Urga garrison, the Beijing government was unable to force the warlords it depended on to commit their men to the cause. On this, see Li, "Shi shu enqin fan meng suo yinfa de zhi feng maodun dou zheng," 14.

22. "D. P. Pershin, "Baron Ungern, Urga i Altan Bulak," *GARF*, f.5873, op.1, d.5, l.53. For the quotation in the published memoir, see D. P. Pershin, *Baron Ungern, Urga i Altan-Bulak* (Samara, 1999), 107.

23. "Ukaz Bogdo-gegena o prisvoenii R. F. Ungernu i ego spodvizhnikam mongol'skikh titulov i stepenei," in Kuz'min, *Baron Ungern*, 91.

24. *RGVA*, f.39454, op.1, d.9, l.23. The letter is undated.

25. For references to Ungern's punishment of Mongols as well as his own men caught looting Chinese shops, see *Tales of an Old Lama* (C. R. Bawden, trans. and ed.) (Tring, UK, 1997), 67; and Makeev, *Bog voiny Baron Ungern*, 39. One memoir writer recalls that Ungern raced through a lunch being offered to him by some grateful Russians on the day of the attack in order to personally put down the anti-Chinese riots. See K. I. Lavrent'ev, "Vziatie g. Urgi baronom Ungernom," in Kuz'min, *Baron Ungern*, 318. By contrast, Chinese sources contend that

Ungern approved of the attacks on Chinese merchants. See, for example, *Zuijin shi nian Zhong E zhi jiao she* (Shen Yunlong, series ed.) (1923; repr.: Taibei, n.d.), 169.

26. On the practice of the "three legal days," see N. I. Shtif, *Pogromy na Ukraine (period dobrovol'cheskoi armii)* (Berlin, 1922), 20.

27. On the pogrom, see Romanova, *Vlast' i Evrei na Dal'nem Vostoke Rossii,* 152; Darevskaia, *Sibir' i Mongoliia,* 340. Perhaps the most vivid eyewitness account of the pogrom I have read is by Boris Volkov, a White officer who was living in Urga at the time. See Volkov, "Ob Ungerne," Boris N. Volkov Papers, *Hoover.* For the Red reports, see *RGVA,* f.16, op.3, d.219, ll.50, 67. By adding up and comparing various accounts of the murders, Sergei Kuz'min suggests a total of between 100 and 120 Russian victims. See Kuz'min, *Istoriia Barona Ungerna,* 415.

28. *Sha E qin Hua shi,* vol. 4, pt. 2, 279. For contemporary Chinese descriptions of the assault and its aftermath, see *Zhong E guanxi shiliao* [1921], Section on Outer Mongolia (Wai Menggu), no. 26, 11; Chen Chong Zu (ed.), *Wai Meng Gu jin shi shi* (Shanghai, 1922), chap. 3, pt. 9, 47–49; and *Zuijin shi nian Zhong E zhi jiao she,* 169.

29. Pershin, "Baron Ungern, Urga i Altan Bulak," *GARF,* f.5873, op.1, d.5, l.53, ll.64–64(b); and Pershin, *Baron Ungern, Urga i Altan-Bulak,* 125.

30. "Ungernovshchina: Beseda s g. Makstenek," *Dal'ne-vostochnyi telegraf,* no. 20 (August 26, 1921), 2. For a White officer's recollection of such family murders during the pogrom, see K. I. Lavrent'ev, "Vziatie g. Urgi baronom Ungernom v 1921 godu," *Hoover,* 17.

31. For these references to Ungern's letters, see *RGVA,* f.39454, op.1, d.9, ll.16–17, 13; *RGVA,* f.16, op.3, d.222, ll.21–21(b). On Jews as the cause of the revolution, see "Dopros R. F. Ungerna 27 avgusta 1921 g. v Troitskosavske," 204. One officer remembered that Ungern frequently denounced "Yids, Americans, and socialists" in the same breath. See Volkov, "Ob Ungerne," 57.

32. The Mongolian specialist C. R. Bawden describes this as the "first and perhaps only …deliberate expression of anti-Semitism …in Mongolian history." For Bawden's comments and the translation cited here, see Bawden, *Modern History of Mongolia,* 232–33. For the full decree, see "Sükhbaataryg bogdod baraalkhuulakhyg shaardsan bichig (1921)," in *1921 Ony Ardyn Khuv'sgalyn Tüükhend Kholbogdokh Barimt Bichgüüd 1917–1921* (Ulaanbaatar, 1957), 113.

33. Henry Abramson, *A Prayer for the Government: Ukrainians and Jews in Revolutionary Times, 1917–1920* (Cambridge, Mass., 1999), 122, 126–31; L. V. Miliakova, "Vvedenie," in Miliakova (ed.), *Kniga pogromov: Pogromy na Ukraine, v Belorussii i evropeiskoi chasti Rossii v period grazhdanskoi voiny, 1918–1922 gg.; Sbornik dokumentov* (Moscow, 2007), xv. For fifty thousand as the "minimum credible estimate" of Jewish murders during the civil war years, see John Klier, "Pogroms," in Gershon David Hundert (ed.), *The Yivo Encyclopedia of Jews in Eastern Europe* (New Haven, Conn, 2008), vol. 2, 1380. High estimates run to two hundred thousand Jewish deaths.

34. On the crucial role of "violent migrations" in shaping the violence of the revolutionary period, see Sanborn, "Unsettling the Empire," 290–324.

35. Eric Lohr, "1915 and the War Pogrom Paradigm in the Russian Empire," and Vladimir P. Buldakov, "Freedom, Shortages, Violence: The Origins of the 'Revolutionary Anti-Jewish Pogrom' in Russia, 1917–1918," in Jonathan Dekel-Chen, David Gaunt, Natan M. Meir, and Israel Bartal (eds.), *Anti-Jewish Violence: Rethinking the Pogrom in East European History* (Bloomington, Ind., 2010), 41–51 and 74–91.

36. Lilia Kalmina, "The Possibility of the Impossible: Pogroms in Eastern Siberia," in Dekel-Chen, Gaunt, Meir, and Bartal, *Anti-Jewish Violence,* 131–43; and Oleg Budnitskii, "Jews, Pogroms, and the White Movement: A Historiographical Critique," *Kritika* 2, no. 4 (2001), 769.

On a reprinting of the *Protocols* in White-controlled Novonikolaevsk in 1919, see E. E. Kolosov, *Sibir' pri Kolchake: Vospominaniia, materialy, dokumenty* (Petrograd, 1923), 107.

37. V. A. Samodelkin, "Antisemitskaia propaganda v Sibirskoi armii (po dokumentam Natsional'nogo Soveta evreev Sibiri i Urala," in *Istoriia "beloi" Sibiri: Tezisy nauchnoi konferentsii (7–8 fevralia 1995 g.)* (Kemerovo, 1995), 57.

38. The most disturbing proof of this is the case of a Red-supported pogrom that took place in the Far Eastern town of Nikolaevsk-on-the-Amur in May 1920. On this event, see Romanova, *Vlast' i Evrei na Dal'nem Vostoke Rossii;* Budnitskii, *Russian Jews between the Reds and the Whites,* 119–20; and I. V. Nam, *Natsional'nye men'shinstva Sibiri i Dal'nego Vostoka na istoricheskom perelome (1917–1922)* (Tomsk, 2009), 410–11.

39. James Boyd, "'A Very, Quiet Outspoken, Pleasant Gentleman [*sic*]': The United States Military Attaché's Reports on Baron von Ungern-Sternberg, March 1921," *Inner Asia* 12 (2010), 373.

40. For descriptions of life in Urga between Ungern's attacks, see Lattimore and Isono, *Diluv Khutagt,* 107; Sluchainyi, "V osazhdennoi Urge," *Hoover,* Boris N. Volkov collection, box 3, folder 9, 101–10.

41. Makeev, *Bog voiny Baron Ungern,* 28–29. See also Dmitri Alioshin, *Asian Odyssey* (New York, 1940), 183–85, 219–29. On scurvy, see [No first name indicated] Golubev, "Vospominaniia," Golubev history, *Hoover,* 116.

42. S. L. Kuz'min, O. Batsaikhan, K. Nunami, and M. Tachibana, "Baron Ungern i Iaponiia," *Vostok,* no. 5 (2009), 121. My translation here is based on a Russian translation of the original Japanese.

43. See the memoir by the officer Sergei Lavrov, "Sobytiia v Mongolii-Khalkhe v 1920–1921 godakh," *Hoover,* 36. Sergei Kuz'min has determined that the true author of this account is Mikhail Tornovskii (Lavrov is a misattribution.) For a reprint of the memoir, see Tornovskii, "Sobytiia v Mongolii-Khalkhe v 1920–1921 godakh," 168–323, reference to 222.

44. For the prophecy here, see Alice Sárközi, *Political Prophecies in Mongolia in the Seventeenth to Twentieth Centuries* (Wiesbaden, 1992), 131. See also Andrei Znamenski, *Red Shambhala: Magic, Prophecy, and Geopolitics in the Heart of Asia* (Wheaton, Ill., 2011), 27. On the prophetic role of the khutuktus in Mongolian religion and politics, see Caroline Humphrey, "Remembering an 'Enemy': The Bogd Khaan in Twentieth-Century Mongolia," in Rubie S. Watson (ed.), *Memory, History, and Opposition under State Socialism* (Santa Fe, 1994), 31–32.

45. For a Red report on the bonds, see *RGASPI,* f.495, op.152, d.15, l.9. For a brief discussion and reproductions of the bills, see Martha Avery, *The Tea Road: China and Russia Meet across the Steppe* (Beijing, 2003), 95–96; and Ts. Batsaikhan and A. Puntsog, *Mongoliin möngön temdeg* (Ulaanbaatar, 1998), 27.

46. "Usloviia naima dobrovol'tsev v Aziatskuiu diviziiu v 1921 g.," in Kuz'min, *Baron Ungern,* 149–50.

47. "Dopros R. F. Ungerna 27 avgusta 1921 g. v Troitskosavske," 202.

48. D. P. Pershin, "Baron Ungern, Urga i Altan Bulak," *GARF,* f.5873, op.1, d.5, ll.62–62(b); and Pershin, *Baron Ungern, Urga i Altan-Bulak,* 123.

49. On Jews serving as agents and in other capacities, see Kuz'min, *Istoriia Barona Ungerna,* 398-99. Vol'fovich apparently felt close enough to Ungern to sign his letters as "Lyova," a diminuitive form of his first name. See "Pis'mo L. Vol'fovicha R. F. Ungernu ot 24 noiabria 1920 g.," Kuz'min, *Baron Ungern,* 88–89.

50. My count of the letters is based on the copies in Kuz'min, *Baron Ungern,* 119–83. In addition to letters sent by Ungern, Kuz'min's collection includes a smaller number of letters

written to him by others, as well as what appears to be a forged letter sent to the Siberian leader Vasilii Anuchin, who apparently faked the letter himself "to elevate his political prestige." On the forgery, see Kuz'min, *Istoriia Barona Ungerna,* 5.

51. The casual presumption that Ungern represented a twentieth-century version of Genghis Khan quickly became part of his myth, both pro and contra. For the clearest proof of this, see Mabire, *Ungern: L'heritier blanc de Gengis Khan.*

52. Duncan Bell, *The Idea of Greater Britain: Empire and the Future of World Order, 1860–1900* (Princeton, N.J., 2007); Chickering, *We Men Who Feel Most German;* Piotr Okulewicz, *Koncepcja "miedzymorza" w myśli i praktyce politycznej obozu Józefa Piłsudskiego w latach 1918–1926* (Poznan, 2001); and David Kirby, *A Concise History of Finland* (New York, 2006), 201–2.

53. On the pan-Mongolian plans of 1919, see Ewing, *Between the Hammer and the Anvil?,* 117–28; Uradyn E. Bulag and Caroline Humphrey, "Some Diverse Representations of the Pan-Mongolian Movement in Dauria," *Inner Asia: Occasional Papers of the Mongolia and Inner Asia Studies Unit,* no. 1 (1996), 1–23; Uradyn E. Bulag, *Nationalism and Hybridity in Mongolia* (New York, 1998), 81–83; Christopher P. Atwood, *Young Mongols and Vigilantes in Inner Mongolia's Interregnum Decades, 1911–1931* (Leiden, 2002), vol. 1, 135–37; and Bazarov and Zhabaeva, *Buriatskie natsional'nye demokraty,* 140–62. On the presence of Japanese officers at the pan-Mongolian meetings, see James Boyd, *Japanese-Mongolian Relations, 1873–1945: Faith, Race, and Strategy* (Folkestone, Eng., 2011), 91.

54. These are the minister's words as recorded by Chen in his telegram to Beijing shortly after the meeting. See *Zhong E guanxi shiliao: Wai Menggu (Zhonghua Minguo liu nian zhi ba nian)* (Taibei, 1959) document no. 55, 343.

55. The Japanese may also have backed away from the plan because they saw the new state as likely to give Semenov more leverage, thus making him harder to control. For this idea, see Zhang, *Shou fu Wai Meng zhuquan (1917–1920),* 62–63.

56. On the ceremony, see Zhang, *Shou fu Wai Meng zhuquan,* 118–21.

57. No period sources I have seen indicate that Ungern was involved in the pan-Mongolian sessions, which also included an initial gathering in Verkhneudinsk. A cryptic announcement in a Chita newspaper from late February 1919 states that he was on two-month leave at the time of the Chita and Dauria meetings, which might suggest that he was not even in the area, though when exactly his leave began and where he went is unclear. See "Khronika," *Russkii vostok,* February 26, 1919, 4. Various writers contend that he spent an extended time in Beijing during this period.

58. The leaders of the new would-be Greater Mongolia planned to establish their government headquarters in Hailar but because the town was under Zhang Zuolin's control at the time, they opted to relocate temporarily to Dauria. See Bazarov and Zhabaeva, *Buriatskie national'nye demokraty,* 151.

59. "Vtoroe pis'mo R. F. Ungerna Iugotszur-khutukhte," in Kuz'min, *Baron Ungern,* 169

60. See, for example, "Pis'mo R. F. Ungerna K. Gregori 20 maia 1921 g.," in Kuz'min, *Baron Ungern,* 159.

61. Historians come down somewhat differently on the question of Japanese support for the Mongolian campaign. While it's clear that the Reds greatly exaggerated the nature of Ungern's ties to the Japanese, Kuz'min tends to dismiss the existence of ties altogether, while the Japanese specialist James Boyd argues that, despite the fact that Tokyo officially cut off aid to Semenov (and presumably Ungern as well) beginning in May 1919, aid in at least some form nonetheless continued through the period of the Mongolian campaign. In November 1921, a Japanese Foreign Ministry report extolled "the proud Japanese participation in Ungern's army." For these

different views, see Kuz'min et al., "Baron Ungern i Iaponiia;" Kuz'min, *Istoriia Barona Ungerna*, 401–5; and Boyd, *Japanese-Mongolian Relations*, 96–98.

62. On the dilemmas facing Buryat nationalists during this period, see Bazarov and Zhabaeva, *Buriatskie natsional'nye demokraty*, 140–42.

63. Rupen, "Buriat Intelligentsia," 389.

64. One leader involved in the pan-Mongolian movement who declared his support for a Qing restoration was Fushengge, the bandit leader from Barga who based his men at Ungern's headquarters at Dauria. Fushengge's pro-Qing stance contributed to a split in the movement and he was ultimately killed in an assault by Semenov's troops in the fall of 1919. See Atwood, *Young Mongols and Vigilantes*, vol. 1, 137; and Bulag and Humphrey, "Some Diverse Representations of the Pan-Mongolian Movement in Dauria," 10.

65. *RGVA*, f.39454, op.1, d.9, l.104; "Pervoe pis'mo R. F. Ungerna Iugotszur-khutukhte," Kuz'min, *Baron Ungern*, 123.

66. "Dopros Ungerna, byvshego nachal'nika 1-i Aziatskoi konnoi divizii, proizvedennyi 29 avgusta v g. Troitskosavske," Kuz'min, *Baron Ungern*, 207.

67. Ungern's view of the Qing in this respect seems much in sync with the approaches of recent scholarship on the Qing—often described as the new Qing history—that emphasizes the complexity of the Manchus as both a Chinese and an Inner Asian dynasty. On this see Mark C. Elliott, "Les Mandchous et la définition de la nation," *Annales* 61, no. 6 (2006), 1447–77, esp. pp.1453–59. The quotes here are from Elliott, not Ungern.

68. *RGVA*, f.39454, op.1, d.9, l.29.

69. *RGVA*, f.16, op.3, d.222, l.56. The officer offered this description in a report sent to White authorities conducting an investigation of illegal requisitions carried out at Manchuria Station. The statement was then either given to or intercepted by the Red Army.

70. "Pervoe pis'mo R. F. Ungerna Palta-vanu," in Kuz'min, *Baron Ungern*, 131.

71. I say "presumably" here because we have few letters sent to Ungern by other people. It's possible that some letters sent to him were lost or destroyed, though it's also possible that many of his would-be correspondents simply never wrote back. In the interrogations, Ungern suggests that this was the case. See, for example, "Doprosy R. F. Ungerna 29 avgusta 1921 v g. Troitskosavske," in Kuz'min, *Baron Ungern*, 207.

72. "Vtoroe pis'mo R. F. Ungerna Palta-vanu," "Pis'mo R. F. Ungerna Naiden-vanu 10 aprelia 1921 g.," and "Vtoroe pis'mo R. F. Ungerna Tsende-gunu," in Kuz'min, *Baron Ungern*, 133, 141, and 143, respectively.

73. For this reference, see "[Pis'mo R. F. Ungerna] nachal'niku otdel'nogo otriada voisk, deistvuiushchikh v provintsii Tsitsikar," in Kuz'min, *Baron Ungern*, 145.

74. *RGVA*, notes, 7; also "Pis'mo R. F. Ungerna Chzhan Kuniu 16 fevralia 1921," in Kuz'min, *Baron Ungern*, 101.

75. "Pervoe pis'mo R. F. Ungerna Palta-vanu," 132. Ungern and his wife began living separately soon after their wedding, he at Dauria, she at Manchuria Station, and the marriage apparently ended within a year. See Kuz'min, *Istoriia Barona Ungerna*, 95–96.

76. "Pis'mo R. F. Ungerna Chzhan Kuniu 2 marta 1921 g.," Kuz'min, *Baron Ungern*, 102.

77. The last line in this section of the report reads: "Does not view his cruelty and terror as contradicting the Gospels. Speaks calmly of shootings, murders, executions of various degrees and all manner of punishments." See "Doprosy R. F. Ungerna 1 i 2 sentiabria 1921 g. v Irkutske," 210.

78. Semenov, *O Sebe*, 139–40, 141.

79. For this phrase and similar variants, see the following letters: "Pervoe pis'mo R. F. Ungerna Iugotszur-khutukhte," "Pis'mo R. F. Ungerna Aru-Kharchiin-vanu," "Pis'mo R. F. Ungerna Naiman-vanu," "Pis'mo R. F. Ungerna nachal'niku otdel'nogo otriada voisk deistvuiushchikh

v provintsii Tsitsikar," and "Pis'mo R. F. Ungerna Li Chzhuanuiu," in Kuz'min, *Baron Ungern,* 125, 128, 129, 145, and 146, respectively.

80. "Pervoe pis'mo R. F. Ungerna Tsende-gunu," in Kuz'min, *Baron Ungern,* 135.

81. "Proekt pis'ma predsedatelia Soveta ministrov Mongolii kazakham," in Kuz'min, *Baron Ungern,* 163.

82. "Vtoroe pis'mo R. F. Ungerna Iugutszur-khutukhte," in Kuz'min, *Baron Ungern,* 169.

83. On Russian monarchists in this period, see Burbank, *Intelligentsia and Revolution,* 170–89. One of Ungern's correspondents during his time in Urga was General Viktorin Molchanov, a White commander and monarchist based in the Amur region. On Molchanov, see Iu. A. Pavlov, "General V. M. Molchanov: Zhizn' i sud'ba," in *Iz istorii grazhdanskoi voiny na Dal'nem Vostoke (1918–1922 gg.): Sbornik nauchnykh stat'ei* (Khabarovsk, 2002), 77–83.

84. V. I. Shishkin, "Kratkii obzor voenno-politicheskogo polozheniia Sibiri na fronte voisk vnutrennei sluzhby Sibiri," in Shishkin (ed.), *Sibirskaia Vandeia: Vooruzhennoe soprotivlenie kommunisticheskomu rezhimu v 1920 godu* (Novosibirsk, 1997), 700.

85. On Yuan and the brief rule of the Hongxian dynasty, see Jonathan Spence, *The Search for Modern China* (New York, 1990), 281–87; Ernest P. Young, *The Presidency of Yuan Shih-k'ai: Liberalism and Dictatorship in Early Republican China* (Ann Arbor, Mich., 1977); and Immanuel C. Y. Hsü, *The Rise of Modern China* (6th ed.; New York, 2000), 478–82.

86. On the fleeting Qing restoration and support for the Qing in Inner Mongolia and Barga, see Spence, *Search for Modern China,* 287–88; Hsü, *The Rise of Modern China,* 483; Johan Elverskog, *Our Great Qing: The Mongols, Buddhism, and the State in Late Imperial China* (Honolulu, 2006), 6; Bulag and Humphrey, "Some Diverse Representations of the Pan-Mongolian Movement in Dauria," 10; and Henry Serruys, "An Imperial Restoration in Ordos, 1916–1917," *Études mongoles et sibériennes,* no. 16 (1985), 51–59.

87. Puyi remained in the inner court of the Forbidden City until his ultimate eviction in 1924. He then returned to prominence as a puppet ruler for the Japanese in Manchuria [Manchukuo] during World War II. On his removal from the palace, see Waldron, *From War to Nationalism,* 209.

Chapter 10

1. Troitskosavsk and Kiakhta were close to a third small center, the village of Ust'-Kiakhta, located at the confluence of the Kiakhta and the much larger Selenga River, which flows north to Lake Baikal. On the succession of names, see Dany Savelli, "Kiakhta, ou l'épaisseur de la frontière," *Une Russie plurielle: Confins et profondeurs* (Special edition of *Études mongoles et sibériennes, centrasiatiques et tibétaines,* vols. 38–39, 2007–2008), 272–73.

2. Johann G. Gmelin, *Expedition ins unbekannte Sibirien* (Dittmar Dahlmann, ed.) (Sigmaringen, 1999), 157.

3. For a short overview of Kiakhta's history, see Savelli, "Kiakhta, ou l'épaisseur de la frontière," 271–338. On the founding, see Clifford C. M. Foust, *Muscovite and Mandarin: Russia's Trade with China and Its Setting, 1727–1805* (Chapel Hill, N.C., 1969). "The kingdom of tea" (*tsarstvo chaia* and its equivalent in other languages) was a common term used to describe Kiakhta in European and Russian writing of the 1800s.

4. For the history of merchant relations in Kiakhta-Maimaicheng and some of the details mentioned here, see Deng Jiugang, *Cha ye zhi lu: Ou Ya shangdao xing shuai san ban nian* (Hohot, 2000), 84–92; Savelli, "Kiakhta, ou l'épaisseur de la frontière," 284–86, 306; Alexandre Petrov, "Les Chinois à Kiakhta (1728–1917)," in *Une Russie plurielle,* 361–91; T. S. Aiusheeva,

"Uchebnye zavedeniia Troitskosavska-Kiakhty," in V. E. Gulgonov (ed.), *Kiakhta: Stranitsy istorii* (Ulan-Ude, 1999), 30–36; Dieter Stem, "Myths and Facts about the Kiakhta Trade Pidgin," in Eva-Marie Stolberg (ed.), *The Siberian Saga: A History of Russia's Wild East* (Frankfurt, 2005), 63–72.

5. *RGVA,* f.16, op.3, d.214, l.37; *RGVA,* f.16, op.3, d.24, l.55. For reports of refugees, see *GANO,* f.R-1, op.2a, d.11, l.98; *RGVA,* f.16, op.3, d.219, l.46; and A. Narvskii, "Zamysli bandita Ungerna," *Krasnoe Pribaikal'e,* no. 24 [33], February 27, 1921, 1.

6. On one of these meetings, see *RGVA,* f.16, op.3, d.219, l.46.

7. For telegrams between Chen and Beijing to this effect, see *Zhong E guanxi shiliao* [1921], Section on Outer Mongolia (Wai Menggu), document no. 15, 7–8; no. 26, 11; and no. 29, 13. These telegrams were exchanged in late February–early March 1921. In addition to the terms "Red party" and "White party," the Chinese also referred to the Reds and Whites as the "new party" and the "old party," respectively.

8. *Zhong E guanxi shiliao* [1921], Section on Outer Mongolia (Wai menggu), document no. 60, 28–29. Chen sent this telegram from Manzhouli (Manchuria Station) on March 29, 1921. We don't find Ungern referred to by name (Chinese: Enqin 恩琴) in Chinese cables until the following month.

9. This quote appears in a speech by the Mongolian revolutionary Soliin Danzan from March 1921. See Ewing, *Between the Hammer and the Anvil?,* 233.

10. Kaplonski, "Introduction" (Part 5), 852.

11. Altanbulag today sits close to where Maimacheng once did, just across the border from Kiakhta. On the Mongol attack on the town, see Bawden, *Modern History of Mongolia,* 230–31. On the refugees from Maimaicheng, see *Zhong E guanxi shiliao* [1921], Section on Outer Mongolia (Wai Menggu), document no. 48, 24; no. 54, 26; and no. 58, 2, 7–28.

12. *Zhong E guanxi shiliao* [1921], Section on Outer Mongolia (Wai Menggu), document no. 15, 7.

13. The party line in Mongolia during the socialist period was to describe the 1921 revolution as "a joint undertaking of the Mongolian and the Soviet people." See Tatsuo Nakami, "New Trends in the Study of Modern Mongolian History: What Effect Have Political and Social Changes Had on Historical Research?" *Acta Asiatica,* no. 76 (1999), 24.

14. *RGASPI,* f.495, op.152, d.3, l.24.

15. *RGVA,* f.39454, op.1. d.9, l.25.

16. On these and other aborted Chinese plans to attack Ungern, see Li Bin, "Shi shu Enqin fan meng suo yin fa de Zhi Feng maodun duozheng," 14–18. The title of the president's order was the Order of the Mongolian Expedition. For all of the concern about the possibility of a new Chinese assault, Ungern nonetheless confided to a Mongolian ally in April that he had learned from "radio and newspaper intercepts" that Zhang was apparently refusing to commit troops to a Mongolian campaign and that "China was not in a position at the moment to send a force against Khalkha." See "Pis'mo R.F. Ungerna Naiden-vanu 10 aprelia 1921 g.," 141.

17. *RGVA,* f.16, op.3, d.222, l.2; "Dopros R. F. Ungerna 7 sentiabria 1921 g. [v Novonikolaevske]," 220. Ungern also discussed his concern about supplies and increased exactions from the Mongols in the other interrogations. See, for example, Kuz'min, "Dopros R. F. Ungerna 27 avgusta 1921 g. v Troitskosavske," 202.

18. *RGVA,* f.39454, op.1, d.9, ll.16–17; "Pis'mo R. F. Ungerna K. Gregori 20 maia 1921 g.," 159–60.

19. *RGVA,* f.16, op.3, d.222, l.2; and *RGVA,* f.39454, op.1, d.9, l.17; Kuz'min, "Pis'mo R. F. Ungerna K. Gregori 20 maia 1921 g.," and "Dopros R. F. Ungerna 7 sentiabria 1921 [v Novonikolaevske]," 160 and 220, respectively.

20. "Dopros R.F. Ungerna 27 avgusta 1921 g. v Troitskosavske," 204.

21. "Pis'mo R. F. Ungerna Tszasaktu-khanu 15 maia 1921," in Kuz'min, *Baron Ungern*, 165.

22. I. P. Vitte, quoted in Kuz'min, *Istoriia barona Ungerna*, 237.

23. For an early Soviet publication of the order that lays out the Soviet view of what it reveals about Ungern, see *Revoliutsiia na Dal'nem Vostoke* (Petrograd, 1923), vol. 1, 429–33.

24. "Dopros R. F. Ungerna 7 sentiabria 1921 [v Novonikolaevske]," 231.

25. Ossendowski's memoir of his civil war experience, including the period he spent in Mongolia, did much to popularize Ungern's image as the "mad baron" in the West (Ossendowski described him as a "bloody storm of avenging karma"). Since he was known for florid prose, delusions of grandeur, and an interest in selling books, the memoir was panned by critics as unreliable, though recent reassessments suggest that the descriptions of his meetings with Ungern are valuable nonetheless. See Ferdinand Ossendowski, *Beasts, Men, and Gods* (New York, 1922); Louis de Maistre, *Dans les coulisses de l'Agartha: L'extraordinaire mission de Ferdinand Anton Ossendowski en Mongolie* (Milan, 2010), 9–10; and S. L. Kuz'min and L. Iu. Reit, "Zapiski F. A. Ossendovskogo kak istochnik ob istorii Mongolii," *Vostok*, no. 5 (2008), 97–110.

26. See *GARF*, f.9431, op.1, d.40, l.3(b), complete text: ll.1–3(b). The quotes that follow are from this copy of the order. For photographs of the sheets of the original version of the order, replete with the seal of the headquarters of the Asiatic Division on the last page, see Kuz'min, *Legendarnyi baron*, photo insert, no page indicated. For a recent printed version, see "Prikaz R. F. Ungerna No. 15 o nastuplenii na Sibir'," in Kuz'min, *Baron Ungern*, 169–73.

27. "Doprosy R. F. Ungerna 1 i 2 sentiabria 1921 g. v Irkutske," 213.

28. "Dopros R. F. Ungerna 7 sentiabria 1921 g. [v Novonikolaevske]," 231.

29. "Dopros R. F. Ungerna 27 avgusta 1921 g. v Troitskosavske," 202.

30. *RGVA*, f.16, op.3, d.222, l.24.

31. N. M. Riabukhin (Ribo), "The Story of Baron Ungern-Sternberg Told by His Staff Physician," *Hoover*, 12. M. G. Tornovskii, an officer serving in Urga, recalled that he and his fellow officers found the order "overly long, shrouded in mysticism (*tumanno-misticheskii*), and hard to understand." See Tornovskii, "Sobytiia v Mongolii-Khalkhe v 1920–1921 godakh," 248.

32. K. Noskov, *Avantiura, ili chernyi dlia belykh v Mongolii 1921-i god* (Harbin, 1930), 28–33.

33. For descriptions, see Makeev, *Bog Voiny Baron Ungern*, 57–59; and Tornovskii, "Sobytiia v Mongolii-Khalkhe v 1920–1921 godakh," 255. The combination of Christ's face and the motto "God is with Us" appear on numerous Russian regimental banners, including of the Trans-Baikal Host, which was likely the inspiration for this particular flag. Judging from other descriptions, the troops also carried a Russian tricolor emblazoned with Michael's monogram.

34. For these figures, see Kuz'min, *Istoriia Barona Ungerna*, 240–41.

35. See, for example, "Doprosy R. F. Ungerna 1 i 2 sentiabria 1921 g. v Irkutske" and "Dopros R. F. Ungerna 7 sentiabria 1921 g. [v Novonikolaevske]," 213 and 231, respectively.

36. For a vivid description of these tensions and conflicts, see the report of the DVR commission that investigated the effects of Ungern's attack on DVR territory: *NARB*, R-476, op.1, d.47, ll.17–21.

37. Technically speaking, the "old Mongolian government" (with the exception of the Bogda) was not overthrown but rather voluntarily "resigned... in the interests of progress and improving the welfare of the people." See the official Soviet communiqué in *RGASPI*, f.495, op.152, d.15, l.8.

38. *Krasnaia armiia RFSFR: 23 fevralia 1918–23 fevralia 1922; Iubileinyi sbornik* (Moscow, n.d.), 24.

39. For Red Army comments on the poor quality of topographical maps of the border, see M. Kriuchkov, "Kartografiia Mongolii," *Krasnaia armiia na vostoke*, no. 1 (November 1921),

36–39. Kuz'min notes that the Asiatic Division used maps only inconsistently during the campaign (*ot sluchaia k sluchaiu*). See Kuz'min, *Istoriia Barona Ungerna,* 247.

40. The RSFSR also had a number of unofficial names that were used enough to become official in every other respect: Sovetskaia Rossiia, Respublika Sovetov, Strana Sovetov. In White usage, Red-controlled Russia tended to be referred to dismissively as Sovdepia, a play on the words "Soviet" and "deputies."

41. For this quote, see "Second Congress of the Communist International, Manifesto, International Relations after Versailles," http://www.marxists.org/history/international/comintern/2nd-congress/manifesto (last accessed: May 2012).

42. See the translated transcript of the meeting at "Baku Congress of the Peoples of the East: Seventh Session," http://www.marxists.org/history/international/comintern/baku/ch07 (last accessed: May 2012).

43. On the formation of this partisan force, see "Bor'ba russkogo i Mongol'skogo narodov protiv belogvardeiskikh band Ungerna," *Istoricheskii arkhiv,* no. 4 (1957), 73; and A. N. Kislov, *Razgrom Ungerna (O boevom sodruzhestve sovetskogo i mongol'skogo narodov)* (Moscow, 1964), 29. On the other issues mentioned here, see "Mandat vydannii D. Sukhe-Batoru nachal'nikom Troitskosavskogo pogranichnogo otriada na pravo peresecheniia granitsy i poluchenii pomoshchi so storony grazhdanskikh i voennykh organizatsii RSFSR," in *Sovetsko-Mongol'skie otnosheniia, 1921–1974: Dokumenty i materialy* (Moscow and Ulaanbaatar, 1975), vol. 1, 1.

44. Shumiatskii's vision of the plan appears in a letter to the Commissar of Foreign Affairs Grigorii Chicherin. See *RGASPI,* f.495, op.152, d.9, ll.10–11. In another letter to Chicherin, Shumiatskii exaggerates the size of Ungern's force and offers an ecstatic description of what his defeat means for Bolshevik possibilities in Far East. See Kuz'min, "G. V. Chicherinu, 10.11.1921 g.," in Kuz'min, *Baron Ungern,* 188–89. On Shumiatskii's wide-ranging work in Siberia during the civil war, see A. P. Iakushina, "Boris Zakarovich Shumiatskii (1886–1943)," *Istoriia SSSR,* no. 2 (1969), 118–23. On the politics between Moscow, the DVR, and Mongolia related to the Red Army entering the fight against Ungern, see Kuz'min, *Istoriia Barona Ungerna,* 253–54.

45. For details on some of the in-fighting and confusion of the campaign on the Red side, see "Bor'ba russkogo i Mongol'skogo narodov protiv belogvardeiskikh band Ungerna," 77; and *RGVA,* f.16, op.1, d.34, ll. 121–22, 123–23(b). Clear proof of the frustration: the Red high command immediately investigated the officer who let Ungern slip away after the Kiakhta battle and ultimately reassigned him to military school. On this, see Kislov, *Razgrom Ungerna,* 88.

46. Cited in A. P. Efimenko, "K biografii barona R. F. Ungerna-Shternberga," *Arkhiv naslediia-2003: Nauchnyi sbornik* (Moscow, 2005), 310.

47. *NARB,* f.R-305, op.1, d.20, l.4. This sheet is dated July 7 [1921].

48. For a Russian translation of Sündüi's statement, see "Obstoiatel'stva pleneniia R. F. Ungerna," in Kuz'min, *Baron Ungern,* 194–97. For more on Sündüi's version of the event, see Kuz'min, *Istoriia Barona Ungerna,* 283–85.

49. Another argument against Sündüi's version of events is that the Reds detained him and took him over to the Russian side for questioning along with Ungern. He was only released several days later in Kiakhta.

50. Shchetinkin's report dates from September 1, 1921. For the passage quoted here, see "Bor'ba russkogo i Mongol'skogo narodov protiv belogvardeiskikh band Ungerna," 79–80. For an earlier report in which he documents some of the challenges of the Red campaign, including poor equipment and a lack of food for his men, see *RGVA,* f.185, op.3, d.761, ll.21–21(b).

51. The exact date of Ungern's capture is unclear; August 19, 20, 21, and 22 are suggested by different accounts. I side with August 20 because it is the date indicated in Shchetinkin's report.

Chapter 11

1. In his first recorded interrogation at Kiakhta (Troitskosavsk), Ungern acknowledges ordering the execution of Red officers during the summer campaign. See "Dopros R. F. Ungerna 27 avgusta 1921 g. v Troitskosavske," 205.

2. The telegram was addressed to Vyacheslav Molotov of the party's Central Committee. *GANO*, f.1, op.2, d.151, l.28. A handwritten draft of the telegram appears on the preceding page.

3. For allusions to stories of the execution that appeared in émigré memoirs, see Kuz'min, *Istoriia Barona Ungerna*, 302.

4. On the locations and techniques of executions, see A. G. Tepliakov, *Protsedura: Ispolneniia smertnykh prigovorov v 1920–1930-kh godakh* (Moscow, 2007), 5, 15, 21–23, 30–31, 37–38 passim. On Cheka executions in general, see also George Leggett, *The Cheka: Lenin's Political Police; The All-Russian Extraordinary Commission for Combatting Counter-Revolution and Sabotage (December 1917 to February 1922)* (New York, 1981), 198–99.

5. On Ungern being passed to Pavlunovskii, see the telegram in *RGVA*, f.16, op.1, d.37, l.332; as well as what appears to be Pavlunovskii's signed receipt: *RGVA*, f.16, op.1, d.37, l.327. The telegram is reprinted in "O dostavke R. F. Ungerna v Novonikolaevske, doprose i podgotovke suda," in Kuz'min, *Baron Ungern*, 234.

6. Iaroslavskii, *Baron Roman Ungern-fon-Shternberg*, 16.

7. For a voluminous holding of Iaroslavskii's papers, see *RGASPI*, f.89, op.1–11.

8. Guards on the boat journey from Kiakhta to Verkhneudinsk, for example, had orders to send one unarmed man into the WC along with Ungern and post another armed one outside the door. See *RGVA*, f.16, op.1, d.37, l.337.

9. On Ungern's arrival at the pier, see "Ungern v Verkhneudinske," *Dal'ne-Vostochnyi Telegraf*, no. 26 (September 2, 1921), 1. The authorities were worried that a local mob might try to seize Ungern, so they later moved the boat to a village across the river. On this and the driving tour of Irkutsk, see Kuz'min, *Istoriia Barona Ungerna*, 295.

10. "Dopros R. F. Ungerna 27 avgusta 1921 g. v Troitskosavske" and "Dopros R. F. Ungerna 7 sentiabria 1921 g. [v Novonikolaevske]," 201, 222.

11. The relocation to Novonikolaevsk was announced in the spring of 1921, with the move itself following in the summer. On Sibrevkom as the "master of Siberia," see A. G., "Novonikolaevsk—Stolitsa Sibiri," *Delo revoliutsii*, no. 60 (March 16, 1921), 1. The Siberian Bureau reported to the Central Committee of the Russian Communist Party in Moscow, the Siberian Revolutionary Committee reported to Sovnarkom. On the Sibrevkom-Sibbiuro relationship and the establishment of these bodies, see V. I. Shishkin, *Revoliutsionnye komitety Sibiri v gody grazhdanskoi voiny (avgust 1919–mart 1921 g.)* (Novosibirsk, 1978), 10–110.

12. For the impact of the revolution and civil war on Novonikolaevsk and the surrounding region, see V. T. Shuklentsov, *Grazhdanskaia voina na territorii Novosibirskoi oblasti* (Novosibirsk, 1970); and V. G. Kokoulin, *Novonikolaevsk v gody revoliutsii, grazhdanskoi voiny i "voennogo kommunizma" (fevral' 1917–mart 1921 g.)* (Novosibirsk, 2010).

13. *Sibirskii revoliutsionnyi komitet (Sibrevkom) avgust 1919–dekabr' 1925: Sbornik dokumentov i materialov* (Novosibirsk, 1959), no. 288, 486. This quote is from an official in Tomsk, though the description applies to Novonikolaevsk as well. On the typhus epidemic, see E. I. Kosiakova, "Epidemiia tifa v Novonikolaevske nachala 1920-kh gg. kak aspekt ekstremal'noi povsednevnosti," http://sib-subethnos.narod.ru/p2005/kosykova.htm (last accessed: May 2013); and *Istoriia goroda Novonikolaevsk-Novosibirsk: Istoricheskie ocherki* (Novosibirsk,

2005), vol. 1, 124. On conditions in the city in general at the time of the Red takeover, see Kokoulin, *Novonikolaevsk v gody revoliutsii,* 192–98.

14. The quote from Trotsky appears in K. Radek, "Lev Trotskii," in *A. Lunacharskii, K. Radek i L. Trotskii, siluety: Politicheskie portrety* (Moscow, 1991), 356. On the introduction of NEP, including what the policy change meant in Lenin's thinking, see Roger W. Pethybridge, *One Step Backward, Two Steps Forward: Soviet Society and Politics in the New Economic Policy* (New York, 1990).

15. On the issues mentioned here, see L. M. Goriushkin (ed.), *Novonikolaevsk-Novosibirsk: Sobytiia, liudi; 1893–1993* (Novosibirsk, 1993), 123–24; *Istoriia goroda Novonikolaevsk-Novosibirsk,* vol. 1, 30, vol. 2, 126; Shishkin, *Sibirskaia Vandeia,* 351–52; and M. Krekova, "Bud vsegda na cheku," *Politrabotnik Sibiri,* no. 2 (December 31, 1920), 6. Shortly after Ungern's trial, the provincial authorities proposed renaming the city as Krasnoobsk—Red Town on the Ob—and debates about renaming continued until 1925 when the city was renamed Novosibirsk. See Goriushkin, *Novonikolaevsk-Novosibirsk,* 127.

16. *Ves' Novonikolaevsk: Adresno-spravochnaia kniga za 1924–1925 god* (Novonikolaevsk, 1924), section 1, 51 (on the "terrible housing shortage"); *Istoriia goroda Novonikolaevsk-Novosibirsk,* vol. 2, 125, 166, 173, 180–81; and Shuklentsov, *Grazhdanskaia voina na territorii Novosibirskoi oblasti.*

17. G. Bergman, *Piat' let vlasti raboch'ikh i krest'ian* (Novonikolaevsk, 1922), 4.

18. The Politburo records that include Smirnov's telegram are in *RGASPI,* f.17, op.3, d.195, l.1; and reproduced in "Reshenie Politbiuro TsK RKP(b) o sude nad R. F. Ungernom," in Kuz'min, *Baron Ungern,* 198.

19. Lenin's instructions were dictated by telephone to the Politburo. See "Reshenie Politbiuro TsK RKP(b) o sude nad R. F. Ungernom," 198–99. They also appear in Lenin's collected works: "Predlozhenie v Politbiuro TsK RKP(b) o predanii sudu Ungerna," in Lenin, *Polnoe sobranie sochinenii,* vol. 44, 110.

20. On Lenin's frequent use of the verb, see Litvin, *Krasnyi i belyi terror v Rossii,* 64–65.

21. On the term "enemies of the people" in the revolutionary and civil war period, see Leggett, *Cheka,* 13–14. For the broader rhetoric of vilification used to describe the Whites during the civil war, see Volkov, *"Gidra kontrrevoliutsii,"* 39–81.

22. On the executions of the tsarist family and Kolchak, see Mark D. Steinberg and Vladimir M. Khrustalev, *The Fall of the Romanovs: Political Dreams and Personal Struggles in a Time of Revolution* (New Haven, Conn., 1995), 277–366; and Zyrianov, *Admiral Kolchak,* 575–78. For an example of an early political trial that did not turn out as the party organizers had expected, see Adele Lindenmeyr, "The First Soviet Political Trial: Countess Sofia Panina before the Petrograd Revolutionary Tribunal," *RR* 60, no. 4 (2001), 505–25.

23. See the documents in "Sud'ba Mikhaila Romanova," *VI,* no. 9 (1990), 149–63.

24. On the trial, known as the "Trial of the Kolchak Ministers," see the introduction and documents in V. I. Shishkin (ed.), *Protsess nad kolchakovskimi ministrami, mai 1920* (Moscow, 2003). For an early Soviet treatment, see N. Raivid and V. Bykov (eds.), *Kolchakovshchina: Sbornik* (Ekaterinburg, 1924), 146–64. The chairman of the tribunal at the ministers' trial was Pavlunovskii.

25. V. I. Lenin, "O zadachakh Narkomiusta v usloviiakh novoi ekonomicheskoi politiki: Pis'mo k D. I. Kurskomu," in *Polnoe sobranie sochinenii,* vol. 44, 397, 399. On show trials in the early Soviet period, see Marc Jensen, *A Show Trial under Lenin: The Trial of the Socialist Revolutionaries, Moscow, 1922* (The Hague, 1982); Julie A. Cassady, *The Enemy on Trial: Early Soviet Courts on Stage and Screen* (DeKalb, Ill., 2000); Elizabeth A. Wood, "The Trial of Lenin: Legitimating the Revolution through Political Theater, 1920–1923," *RR* 61, no. 2

(2002), 235–48; and Robert Argenbright, "Marking NEP's Slippery Path: The Krasnosh-chekov Show Trial," *RR* 61, no. 2 (2002), 249–75. On the trial in 1918 of Roman Malinovskii, a Bolshevik accused of betraying the party, see Igal Halfin, *Intimate Enemies: Demonizing the Bolshevik Opposition, 1918–1928* (Pittsburgh, 2007), 1–17.

26. *GANO,* f.1, op.3, d.23, l.69.

27. The interrogation teams appear to have included at least three men. The transcript of the session in Novonikolaevsk, for example, indicates seven men in the room in addition to Ungern, six of whom asked questions. See "Dopros R. F. Ungerna 7 sentiabria 1921 g. [v Novonikolaevske]," 220.

28. On the relay of the materials, see, for example, "Raport o preprovozhdenii plennogo R. F. Ungerna," in Kuz'min, *Baron Ungern,* 219.

29. *GANO,* f.1, op.3, d.23, l.70

30. On the creation of the tribunals, see Leggett, *Cheka,* 172–73. On the tribunal network in Siberia, see Mikhail Sergeevich Pivovarov, "Revoliutsionnye tribunaly v Sibiri (noiabr' 1919–ianvar' 1923 g.)" (PhD diss. abstract [avtoreferat]); Kemerovo, 2007).

31. Pivovarov, "Revoliutsionnye tribunaly v Sibiri," 16. The summary of the trial describes Oparin as the chairman (*predsedatel'*) of the Predsibotdel of the Verkhtrib VTsIK.

32. *GANO,* f.1, op.3, d.23, l.70. For the meeting confirming the worker's representative on the tribunal, see *GANO,* f.1, op.3, d.23, l.71. Since the trial was a family affair with no divide between the prosecution and the judges, Iaroslavskii and Oparin were both appointed to the team that was to come up with the "plan for the trial," as was the Cheka chief Pavlunovskii.

33. On Sibbiuro's recommendation to publicize Ungern's capture and trial, see *GANO,* f.1, op.3, d.21, l.57. For a few examples of stories in the Red Siberian press on Ungern in late August and early September, see "Ungernovshchina," *Dal'nevostochnii Telegraf,* no. 20 (August 26, 1921), 2; "Ungern vziat v plen," *Dal'nevostochnii Telegraf,* no. 20 (August 26, 1921), 1; "Ungern v Verkhneudinske," 1; and "Na Dal'nem Vostoke," *Sovetskaia Sibir',* no. 186 (September 1, 1921), 2. His relay to Novonikolaevsk was also followed in the White press in the Russian Far East. See "Dostavka Barona Ungerna v Irkutsk," *Russkaia armiia,* no. 33 (September 16, 1921), 2. The Red Siberian as well as the central press began printing reports on the summer campaign and excerpts from his letters beginning in June 1921. For some examples of this coverage, see "Mongoliia," *Pribaikal'e,* June 3, 1921, 1; "Chernye Tuchi," *Pribaikal'e,* June 12, 1921, 1; Fomenko, "Vozvanie polkovogo kollektiva krest'ianam, raboch'im i boitsam," *Krasnoe Pribaikal'e,* no. 60 [69] (June 15, 1921), 1; V. S-v, "Na bor'bu s Baronom," *Krasnoe Pribaikal'e,* no. 60 [69] (June 15, 1921), 2; "Bor'ba s Ungernom," *Krasnoe Pribaikal'e,* no. 63 [72] (June 24, 1921), 2; "Krovavyi pir belobanditov," *Krasnoe Pribaikal'e,* no. 69 [78] (July 15, 1921), 1; "Koshmarnye dni Mongolii i Primongol'ia (materialy o belobanditakh i ikh zver-stvakh," *Vlast' truda* [Irkutsk], no. 507 [383] (July 24, 1921), 1; and "Polozhenie v Mongolii," *Pravda,* no. 189 (August 27, 1921), 1. On propaganda boats (and trains), see Peter Kenez, *The Birth of the Propaganda State: Soviet Methods of Mass Mobilization, 1917–1929* (New York, 1985), 58–62.

34. *GANO,* f.1, op.2, d.147, l.13. The description of the large crowd is from the telegram sent from the Sibbiuro the next day confirming Ungern's execution. See GANO, f.1, op.2, d.151. For brief listing of the Pine Tree Theater, see *Ves' Novonikolaevsk,* section 10, 3. Ironi-cally, the theater's 1921 season began in June with a production of a play by Grigorii Ge entitled *The Execution (Kazn'),* which began after public remarks on the difference between bourgeois and proletarian art and the singing of the "Internationale." For a review, see St. K.-ts., "Otkry-tie sada 'Sosnovka,'" *Delo revoliutsii,* no. 124 (June 3, 1921), 2.

35. I am relying on the time indicated in the newspaper on the day following the trial. By contrast, at the bottom of the verdict itself, which was printed in the newspaper five days later,

the time of its delivery is indicated as 3:15 pm Moscow time, which would have been 6:15 pm in Novonikolaevsk according to the time zone system adopted by the Soviet government in 1919. Compare "Sud nad baronom Ungernom fon Shternberg," *Sovietskaia Sibir'*, no. 199 [559] (September 16, 1921), 1; and "Sud nad baronom Ungernom fon Shternberg," *Sovietskaia Sibir'*, no. 202 [562] (September 20, 1921), 4. These materials are also reprinted in "Khod suda nad R. F. Ungernom v Novonikolaevske 15 sentiabria 1921 g.," in Kuz'min, *Baron Ungern*, 245, 263.

36. For an analysis of the trial as political theater, see Paul du Quenoy, "Perfecting the Show Trial: The Case of Baron von Ungern-Sternberg," *Revolutionary Russia* 19, no. 1 (2006), 79–93.

37. "Sud nad baronom Ungernom fon Shternberg," no.199 [559] (September 16, 1921), 1. For the full text of the indictment, see "Sud nad baronom Ungernom: Zakliuchenie po delu," *Sovetskaia Sibir'*, no. 197 [557] (September 14, 1921), 1.

38. On the role of the prosecutor and the court in general "hurling the truth" at the accused in early Soviet political trials, see Jensen, *A Show Trial under Lenin*, 186.

39. On Iaroslavskii, see P. S. Fateev, *Emelian Mikhailovich Iaroslavskii* (Moscow, 1980); and V. T. Agalakov, *Emelian Iaroslavskii v Sibiri* (Irkutsk, 1964). While Iaroslavskii was undoubtedly skilled at this line of work, he clearly had an advantage in making himself look good at Ungern's trial since he was both a member of the Sibbiuro team that organized the proceedings and the editor of *Sovetskaia Sibir'*, which printed them.

40. "Sud nad Baronom Ungernom," *Sovetskaia Sibir'*, no. 200 [560] (September 17, 1921), 4.

41. For this and the quotes that follow from Iaroslavskii's final statement, see "Sud nad baronom Ungernom-fon-Shternberg: Rech' obnivitelia t. Iaroslavskogo," *Sovetskaia Sibir'*, no. 201 [561] (September 18, 1921), 3. The final statement also appears in "Khod suda nad R. F. Ungernom v Novonikolaevske 15 sentiabria 1921 g.," 250–55.

42. I. Maiskii, "Sud nad Ungernom," *Sovetskaia Sibir'*, no. 202 [562] (September 20, 1921), 2–3. On Maiskii's work on Mongolia and its influence, see T. I. Iusupova, *Mongol'skaia komissiia Akademii nauk: Istoriia sozdaniia i deiatel'nosti, 1925–1953* (St. Petersburg, 2006), 28; and Lishtovannyi, *Istoricheskoe vzaimootnosheniia Sibiri i Mongolii,* 66–67. On Maiskii in general, see Gabriel Gorodetsky, "Maiskii, Ivan Mikhailovich," in Gershon David Hundert (ed.), *The Yivo Encyclopedia of Jews in Eastern Europe* (New Haven, 2008), vol. 1, 1118–19. Maiskii continued to be consulted as a Mongolian expert after the trial. See, for example, a piece he published just a few months later: I. Maiskii, "Mongoliia," *Zhizn' natsional'nostei*, no. 80 [128] (December 1921), 4.

43. Maiskii, "Sud nad Ungernon," 3.

44. On Iaroslavskii's nom de guerre, see Agalakov, *Emelian Iaroslavskii v Sibiri*, 6. Maiskii appears to have grown up in a Russified Jewish family, though he denied his Jewish ancestry. See Gorodetsky, "Maiskii, Ivan Mikhailovich," 1118.

45. Cited in Liliana Riga, "Ethnonationalism, Assimilation, and the Social Worlds of the Jewish Bolsheviks in Fin-de-Siècle Tsarist Russia," *Comparative Studies in Society and History* 48, no. 4 (2006), 782.

46. Bertrand Russell, "Impressions of Bolshevik Russia [1920]," in Russell, *Uncertain Paths to Freedom: Russia and China, 1919–1922* (Richard A. Rempel and Beryl Haslam, eds., with assistance from Andrew Bone and Albert C. Lewis) (New York, 2000), 182, 180. Even if the Bolsheviks rarely described their civil war victories in terms of imperial conquests, the idea of conquering was part of their self-image and rhetoric. On this, see Shelia Fitzpatrick, *The Russian Revolution* (2nd ed.; New York, 1994), 103 (on Lenin's reference to Russia as a "conquered nation" and the communists as "conquerors"); and Jörg Baberowski, "Zivilisation der Gewalt: Die kulturellen Ursprünge des Stalinismus," *Öffentlichen Vorlesungen*

(Humboldt University, Berlin, 2003), vol. 136, 6, http://edoc.hu-berlin.de (last consulted: March 2012).

47. Cited in Pipes, *Formation of the Soviet Union,* 45.

48. *Protokoly s"ezdov i konferentsii vsesoiuznoi kommunisticheskoi partii (b): Desiatyi s"ezd RKP(b); mart 1921 g.* (Moscow, 1933), 187.

49. On the patriotic logic of far rightist anti-Semitism, see Hans Rogger, "Was There a Russian Fascism? The Union of the Russian People," in Rogger, *Jewish Policies and Right-Wing Politics in Imperial Russia* (Berkeley and Los Angeles, 1986), 212–32. See also Peter Kenez, "Pogroms and White Ideology in the Russian Civil War," in John Klier and Shlomo Lambroza (eds.), *Pogroms: Anti-Jewish Violence in Modern Russian History* (New York, 1992), 293–313. On the relationship between nationalism and anti-Semitism more generally, see the case studies in Klaus Holz, *Natsionaler Antisemitismus: Wissenssoziologie einer Weltanschauung* (Hamburg, 2001).

50. Ungern told his interrogators that he was not interested in this slogan because he didn't consider himself a Russian patriot. See "Doprosy R. F. Ungerna 1 i 2 sentiabria 1921 g. v Irkutske," 213.

51. Nam, *Natsional'nye men'shinstva Sibiri i Dal'nego Vostoka,* 384–85. For a full overview of DVR nationality policies, see 383–430. Much as in the RSFSR, where Stalin, a Georgian, ran Narkomnats, the minister of the DVR's Ministry of Nationalities was a Latvian, Karl Ianovich Luks.

52. "Zapros Sibbiuro TsK RKP(b) na agitatsionnuiu literature dlia razlozheniia voisk barona Ungerna," and "Trebovanie B. Z. Shumiatskogo k Sibbiuro TsK RKP(b) ob organizatsii raboty po agitatsii sredi Bashkir, Tatar i Kazakhov v belogvardeiskikh chastiakh barona Ungerna," in *Dal'nevostochnaia politika Sovetskoi Rossii (1920–1922 gg.): Sbornik dokumentov sibirskogo biuro TsK RKP(b) i sibirskogo revoliutsionnogo komiteta* (Novosibirsk, 1996), 221, 225.

53. "Obrashchenie Revvoensoveta voisk Sibiri k mongol'skomu naseleniiu v sviazi s nastupleniem Krasnoi Armii na territoriiu Mongolii" (June 21, 1921), in *Sovetsko-Mongol'skie otnosheniia, 1921–1974,* vol. 1, 16. On the need to pay for local supplies, see the points stressed in a telegram Sibrevkom leader Smirnov sent to Lenin to report the Red Army's move into Mongolia in late June 1921: *GANO,* f.R-1, op.2, d.77, ll.224–224(b).

54. On the creation of the USSR, see "Deklaratsiia ob obrazovanii soiuza sovetskikh sotsialisticheskikh respublikh" and "Dogovor ob obrazovanii soiuza sovetskikh sotsialisticheskikh respublikh," dating to December 30, 1922. For the scanned originals of these documents from the Russian archives, see http://www.1000dokumente.de (last accessed: May 2012).

55. For the background to the formation of the USSR, see Terry Martin, "An Affirmative Action Empire: The Soviet Union as the Highest Stage of Imperialism," in Terry Martin and Ronald Grigor Suny (eds.), *A State of Nations: Empire and Nation-Making in the Age of Lenin and Stalin* (New York, 2001), 67–90; Francine Hirsch, *Empire of Nations: Ethnographic Knowledge and the Making of the Soviet Union* (Ithaca, 2005), 62–98; Ronald Grigor Suny, *The Revenge of the Past: Nationalism, Revolution, and the Collapse of the Soviet Union* (Stanford, Calif., 1993), 76–102; and Pipes, *Formation of the Soviet Union,* 242–93. For the decree establishing the "Mongol-Buryat Autonomous Region" in January 1922, see *Sibirskii revoliutsionnyi komitet,* 542–43.

56. "Sud nad baronom Ungernom-fon-Shternberg: Rech' obnivitelia t. Iaroslavskogo," 3.

57. "Rech' zashchitnika Bogoliubova," *Sovetskaia Sibir',* no. 202 [562] (September 20, 1921), 4.

58. In a letter to his agent in Beijing just before leaving Urga for the spring campaign, Ungern mentions the need to publish "a good newspaper [in China] agitating for the restoration of the

monarchy under the scepter of the Qing." Nothing came of this idea, however. See "Pis'mo R. F. Ungerna K. Gregori 20 maia 1921 g.," 160.

59. "Doprosy R. F. Ungerna 1 i 2 sentiabria 1921 g. v Irkutske," 213.

60. For the breakdown of the nationality of Cheka personnel in 1921, see Litvin, *Krasnyi i belyi terror v Rossii,* 73. Pavlunovskii was sent to Siberia from Moscow in 1920. S. A. Evreinov, whose official position was director of the Division of Secret Operations (*nachal'nik sekretnogo otdela*), was known for personally taking part in numerous executions along with a protégé of his named I. E. Bogdanov. For biographical sketches of Pavlunovskii as well as references to other Siberian communists as transplants to the region and details on the execution personnel in Novonikolaevsk, see Tepliakov, *Protsedura,* 21, 39. See also *Istoriia goroda Novonikolaevsk-Novosibirsk,* 121; Leggett, *Cheka,* 466; and Shishkin, *Protsess nad kolchakovskimi ministrami, mai 1920,* 461. Iaroslavskii was an exception to the non-Siberian norm among high-ranking Siberian party members, as he was originally from Chita.

BIBLIOGRAPHY

Archival and Unpublished Collections

Arkhiv vneshnei politiki Rossiiskoi imperii (Moscow, Russia)
Eesti Ajalooarhiiv (Tartu, Estonia)
Evangelische Pfarrgemeinde Graz-Heilandskirche (Graz, Austria) (Baptismal Registry)
Gosudarstvennyi arkhiv Chitinskoi oblasti (Chita, Russia)
Gosudarstvennyi arkhiv Khabarovskoi oblasti (Khabarovsk, Russia)
Gosudarstvennyi arkhiv Novosibirskoi oblasti (Novosibirsk, Russia)
Gosudarstvennyi arkhiv Rossiiskoi Federatsii (Moscow, Russia)
Hoover Institution Archives, Hoover Institution for War and Peace (Stanford, Calif.)
Natsional'nyi arkhiv Respubliki Buriatii (Ulan-Ude, Russia)
Rossiiskii gosudarstvennyi arkhiv voenno-morskogo flota (St. Petersburg, Russia)
Rossiiskii gosudarstvennyi istoricheskii arkhiv Dal'nego Vostoka (Vladivostok, Russia)
Rossiiskii gosudarstvennyi voennyi arkhiv (Moscow, Russia)
Rossisskii gosudarstvennyi voenno-istoricheskii arkhiv (Moscow, Russia)
Tsentral'nyi muzei vooruzhennykh sil (Moscow, Russia) (Material Objects Collections)

Historical Maps

Karta sledovaniia skorykh soglasovannykh ot Moskvy do Dal'niago i obratno (1903)
Karta Rossiiskoi imperii i sopredel'nykh s neiu gosudarstv (E. A. Koverskii, comp.) (after 1902)
Karta Evropeiskoi Rossii s pokazaniem zheleznykh dorog i parakhodnykh soobshchenii (1910)
Karta Aziatskoi Rossii s pokazaniem zheleznykh dorog i parakhodnykh soobshchenii (1907)
Karta Zabaikal'skoi oblasti, putei soobshcheniia, vazhneishikh poselenii i pereselencheskikh uchastkov (A. I. Popov, compiler; Chita, 1909)
Karta zaseleniia Amurskoi oblasti sostavlena po materialam karty Amurskogo pereselencheskogo raiona izdaniia Pereselencheskogo Upravleniia, zheleznodorozhnoi karty M.P.S. i dr (1909)

Published Primary Sources

Journal titles appear with the years consulted. Chinese sources are listed in simplified characters.

1921 Ony Ardyn Khuv'sgalyn Tüükhend Kholbogdokh Barimt Bichgüüd, 1917–1921 (Ulaanbaatar, 1957)

A. Lunacharskii, K. Radek i L. Trotskii, siluety: Politicheskie portrety (Moscow, 1991)

Adres-kalendar' estliandskoi gubernii na 1893 god (Revel', 1893)

Adressbuch baltischer Landwirthe (Reval, 1899)

Alioshin, Dmitri, *Asian Odyssey* (New York, 1940)

Andrews, Roy Chapman, *Under a Lucky Star: A Lifetime of Adventure* (Garden City, N.Y., 1945)

Anrep, Fanny, von, *Briefe einer Livländerin aus den Jahren 1873–1909* (Gertrud Westermann, ed.) (Landshut, 1990)

Ardashev, N. N., *Velikaia voina i zhenshchiny russkie* (Moscow, 1915)

Arnold, Matthew, *Culture and Anarchy: An Essay in Political and Social Criticism* (New Haven, Conn., 1994; original 1869 text, edited and introduction by Samuel Lipman, essays by Maurice Cowling, Gerald Gradd, Samuel Lipman, and Steven Marcus)

Aziatskaia Rossiia (St. Petersburg, 1914), 3 vols.

Baedeker, K., *Süd-Deutschland und Oesterreich: Handbuch für Reisende* (Leipzig, 1884)

Baltische Monatsschrift (1870, 1913)

Beiträge zum Einfall der Russen in Ostpreussen 1914: Aus der Russenzeit in Insterburg (Insterburg, 1914)

Benningsen, A. P., *Neskol'ko dannykh o sovremennoi Mongolii* (St. Petersburg, 1912)

Bergman, G., *Piat' let vlasti raboch'ikh i krest'ian* (Novonikolaevsk, 1922)

Besant, Annie, "In Defense of Theosophy: A Lecture Delivered in St. James Great Hall London," reprinted in Aidan A. Kelly (ed.), *Theosophy,* vol. 2, *Controversial and Polemical Pamphlets* (New York, 1990), 1–20

[Blavatsky, Helen], *The Letters of H.P. Blavatsky,* Vol. 1, *1861–1879* (John Algeo, ed.) (Wheaton, Ill., 2003)

Bodisco, Theophile, von, *Versunkene Welten: Erinnerungen einer estländischen Dame* (Henning von Wistinghausen, ed.) (Weissenhorn, 1997)

Bogdanov, R. K., "Vospominaniia amurskogo kazaka o proshlom s 1849 po 1880 god," *Zapiski Priamurskogo otdela imperatorskogo russkogo geograficheskogo obshchestva* 5, no. 3 (1900), 1–109

Bogolepov, M. I., and M. N. Sobelev, *Ocherki russko-mongol'skoi torgovli: Ekspeditsiia v Mongoliiu 1910 goda* (Tomsk, 1911)

Boloban, A. P., *Mongolii v ee sovremennom torgovo-ekonomicheskom otnoshenii: Otchet agenta ministerstva torgovli i promyshlennosti v Mongolii A. P. Bolobana za 1912–1913 god* (Petrograd, 1914)

"Bor'ba russkogo i mongol'skogo narodov protiv belogvardeiskikh band Ungerna," *Istoricheskii arkhiv,* no. 4 (1957), 71–81

Brusilov, Aleksei Alekseevich, *Moi vospominaniia: Vospominaniia, memuary* (Minsk, 2003)

Budberg, Aleksei, *Dnevnik belogvardeitsa: Vospominaniia, memuary* (Minsk and Moscow, 2001)

Bulstrode, Beatrix, *A Tour in Mongolia* (New York, 1920)

Burdukov, A. V., *V staroi i novoi Mongolii: Vospominaniia, pis'ma* (Moscow, 1969)

Chaadaeva, O. N. (ed.), *Soldatskie pis'ma 1917 goda* (Moscow-Leningrad, 1927)

Chasovoi, M. Kh., *Ugroza sibirskomu vostoku* (St. Petersburg, 1910)

Chekhov, Anton, *The Chekhov Omnibus: Selected Stories* (London, 1994)

Chen Chong Zu 陈崇祖 (ed.), *Wai Meng Gu jin shi shi* 外蒙古近世史 (Shanghai, 1922)

Chen Chunhua 陈春花 (comp.), *Eguo waijiao wenshu xuan yi: Guanyu Menggu wenti* 俄国外交文书选译: 关于蒙古问题 (Harbin, 1991)

"Chertezhnaia rospis' pritokov r. Leny v ee verknem techenii, pashennykh mest, rastoianii mezhdu ustiiami rek, so svedeniiami o mestnom naselenii [1640/1641]," in G. N. Rumiantsev and S. B. Okun' (comps.), *Sbornik dokumentov po istorii Buriatii: xvii vek* (Ulan-Ude, 1960), vol. 1, 34–37

Consten, Hermann, *Weideplätze der Mongolen im Reiche der Chalcha* (Berlin, 1919–1920) 2 vols.

Dal'nevostochnaia politika Sovetskoi Rossii (1920–1922 gg.): Sbornik dokumentov sibirskogo biuro TsK RKP(b) i sibirskogo revoliutsionnogo komiteta (Novosibirsk, 1996)

Daniels, Robert V. (ed.), *A Documentary History of Communism in Russia: From Lenin to Gorbachev* (Hanover, N.H., 1993)

Denikin, A. I., *Put' russkogo ofitsera* (New York, 1953)

Dnevnik imperatora Nikolaia II, 1890–1906 g.g. (Moscow, 1991)

Dukhovskaia, V. F., *Iz moikh vospominanii* (n.p., 1901)

Durasov [No first name indicated], *Duel'nyi kodeks* (St. Petersburg, 1908)

El'nitskii, K., *Inorodtsy Sibiri i sredneaziatskikh vladenii Rossii: Etnograficheskii ocherk* (St. Petersburg, 1910)

Fugger, Nora, *The Glory of the Habsburgs: The Memoirs of Princess Fugger* (London, 1932)

Gal'kin, M., *Novyi put' sovremennogo ofitsera* (St. Petersburg, 1907)

Genealogisches Handbuch des Adels (Limburg, 1951–1978), multiple volumes

Genealogisches Handbuch der baltischen Ritterschaften: Estland (Görlitz, n.d.), vol. 1

Gmelin, Johann G., *Expedition ins unbekannte Sibirien* (Dittmar Dahlmann, ed.) (Sigmaringen, 1999)

God voiny: s 19-ogo iiulia 1914 g. po 19-oe iiulia 1915 g. (Moscow, 1915)

Godunov, V. I., *Istoriia 91-ogo pekhotnogo dvinskogo polka, 1805–1905 gg.* (Iur'ev, 1905)

——, *Kratkii ocherk istorii 91-ogo pekhotnogo dvinskogo polka (dlia nizhnykh chinov)* (Revel', 1905)

Gorky, Maksim, *Untimely Thoughts: Essays on Revolution, Culture, and the Bolsheviks, 1917–1918* (ed. Mark D. Steinberg, trans. Herman Ermolaev) (New Haven, Conn., 1995)

Got'e, Iurii V., *Time of Troubles: The Diary of Iurii Vladimirovich Got'e; Moscow, July 8, 1917 to July 23, 1922* (ed. and trans. Terence Emmons) (Princeton, N.J., 1988)

Graf, G. K., *Moriaki (ocherki iz zhizni morskikh ofitserov)* (Navarre, 1930)

Grazer Geschäfts- und Adreß-kalender für das Schaltjahr 1886: Ausschließlich nach amtlichen Quellen redigirt (Graz, 1886)

Gredeskul', N. A., *Rossiia i ee narody: "Velikaia Rossiia" kak programma razresheniia natsional'nogo voprosa v Rossii* (Petrograd, 1916)

Grondijs, Ludovic-H., *La guerre en Russie et en Sibérie* (Paris, 1922)

Grum-Grzhimailo, G. E., *Opisanie amurskoi oblasti* (St. Petersburg, 1894)

Günther, Franz, *Der österreichische Grossgrundbesitz: Nachschlage-Buch über Eigenthums- und Besitzstand aller landtäflichen Güter Oesterreichs* (Vienna, 1873)

Gur'ev, B., "Russkaia torgovlia v zapadnoi Mongolii," *Vestnik Azii,* no. 10 (October 1911), 48–49

Haller, Bernhard (comp.), *Album der estländischen Ritter- und Domschule zu Reval vom 12. Januar 1859 bis 18. Juni 1892* (Reval, 1893)

Herder, Johann Gottfried, "Auch eine Philosophie der Geschichte zur Bildung der Menschheit: Beitrag zu vielen Beiträgen des Jahrhunderts (1774)," *Sämtliche Werke* (Hildesheim, 1967) vol. 5, 475–594

Iadrintsev, N. M., *Sibir' kak koloniia v geograficheskom, etnograficheskom i istoricheskom otnosheniiakh* (St. Petersburg, 1892)

Ianchevetskii G. (ed. and comp.), *Venok na mogilu: Stati posviashchennye pamiati byvshego estliandskogo gubernatora kniazia S. V. Shakhovskogo* (Revel', 1896)

Iaroslavskii, [Emelian], *Baron Roman Ungern-fon-Shternberg* (Petrograd, 1922)

Illustrirter Führer durch Reval und seine Umgebungen (Reval, 1901)

Iz arkhiva S. V. Shakovskogo: Materially dlia istorii nedavnego proshlogo Pribaltiiskoi okrainy, 1885–1894 gg. (St. Petersburg, 1909)

Jünger, Ernst, *Der Kampf als inneres Erlebnis* (2nd rev. ed.; Berlin, 1926)

——, *The Storm of Steel: From the Diary of a German Storm-Troop Officer on the Western Front* (London, 1929)

Kakurin, N. E. (comp.), *Razlozhenie armii v 1917 godu* (Moscow and Leningrad, 1925)

Kar'iakhiarm [Karjahärm], Toomas (comp.), *Imperskaia politika Rossii v Pribaltike v nachale xx veka: Sbornik dokumentov i materialov* (Tartu, 2000)

Karpov, A. I., *Reka Amur s ego pritokami kak put' soobshcheniia: Amurskii liman i ego farvartery s kartoiu rek amurskogo basseina* (St. Petersburg, 1909)

Keiserling [Keyserling], Al'fred, *Vospominaniia o russkoi sluzhbe* (Moscow, 2001)

Keyserling, Hermann, von, *Über die innere Beziehung zwischen den Kulturproblemen des Orients und Okzidents: Eine Botschaft an die Völker des Ostens* (Jena, 1913)

Keyserling, Robert, von, *Vom Japanischen Meer zum Ural: Eine Wanderung durch Sibirien* (Breslau, 1898)

Khoroshkhin, M., and E. Putilov, *Zabakail'skaia kazach'ia knizhka* (St. Petersburg, 1893)

Khorostovets, I. Ia., *Ot Chingis Khana do sovetskoi respubliki: Kratkaia istoriia Mongolii s osobym uchetom noveishego vremeni* (German ed., 1926; Ulan Bator, 2004)

Kirillov, Aleksandr, *Geografichesko-statisticheskii slovar' Amurskoi i Primorskoi oblastei* (Blagoveshchensk, 1894)

Klingspor, Carl Arvid, von (ed.), *Baltisches Wappenbuch* (Stockholm, 1883)

Klokchaev, V., *Brak ofitserov: Zakonopolozheniia glavneishikh gosudarstv zapada; Istoriia razvitiia i sovremennoe polozhenie voprosa v Rossii; Kriticheskii ocherk* (St. Petersburg, 1907)

Kolonizatsiia Sibiri v sviazi s obshchim pereselencheskim voprosom (St. Petersburg, 1900)

Kolosov, E. E., *Sibir' pri Kolchake: Vospominaniia, materialy, dokumenty* (Petrograd, 1923)

Kornakov, A. D., "Po povodu provozglasheniia Mongolami nezavisimosti," *Trudy Troitskosavskogo-Kiakhtinskogo otdeleniia Priamurskogo otdela imperatorskogo russkogo geograficheskogo obshchestva* 15, no. 2 (1912), 17–37

Kozlovskii, L. S. (ed.), *Voina i Pol'sha: Pol'skii vopros v russkoi-pol'skoi pechati* (Moscow, 1914)

Krasnaia armiia na vostoke (1921)

Krasnaia armiia RFSFR: 23 fevralia 1918–23 fevralia 1922; Iubileinyi sbornik (Moscow, n.d.)

Krasnov, P. N., *Pavlony: 1-e Voennoe Pavlovskoe Uchilishche pol veka tomu nazad; Vospominaniia* (Paris, 1943)

Kratkaia istoriia 12-ogo pekhotnogo velikolutskogo polka (Moscow, 1911)

Krotov, A., *Morskoi kadetskii korpus: Kratkii istoricheskii ocherk s illiustratsiiami* (St. Petersburg, 1901)

Kruber, A., et al. (comps.), *Aziatskaia Rossiia: Illiustrirovannyi geograficheskii sbornik* (Moscow, 1905)

Kukel', B. K., "Iz epokhi prisoedineniia Priamurskogo kraia," in N. P. Matkhanova (ed.), *Graf N. N. Murav'ev-Amurskii v vospominaniiakh sovremennikov* (Novosibirsk, 1998), 229–235.

Kulomzin, A. N., *Le Transsibérien* (Paris, 1904)

Kuz'min, S. L. (ed. and comp.), *Baron Ungern v dokumentakh i memuarakh* (Moscow, 2004)

———, *Legendarnyi baron: Neizvestnye stranitsy grazhdanskoi voiny* (Moscow, 2004)

Larson, Frans August, *Larson, Duke of Mongolia* (Boston, 1930)

Lattimore, Owen, and Fujiko Isono (eds.), *The Diluv Khutagt: Memoirs and Autobiography of a Mongol Buddhist Reincarnation in Religion and Revolution* (Wiesbaden, 1982)

Le Bon, Gustave, *Psychologie des foules* (Paris, 1895; reprint: Paris, 2003)

———, *Psychologie du socialisme* (Paris, 1899)

———, *Psikhologiia sotsializma* (St. Petersburg, 1908)

———, *The Psychology of Socialism* (ed. John L. Stanley) (New Brunswick, N.J., 1982)

Lenin, V. I., *Polnoe sobranie sochinenii* (5th ed.; Moscow, 1958–1965), 55 vols.

Levitskii, M. N. (ed.), *V trushchobakh Man'chzhurii i nashikh vostochnykh okrain: Sbornik ocherkov, rasskazov i vospominanii voennykh topografov* (Odessa, 1910)

Lorent, A., von, *Wimpffen am Neckar: Geschichtlich und topographlich nach historischen Mittheilungen und archäoligischen Studien dargestellt* (Stuttgart, 1870)

Makeev, A. S., *Bog voiny Baron Ungern: Vospominaniia byvshego ad"iutanta nachal'nika Aziatskoi Konnoi Divizii* (Shanghai, 1934)

Makovkin, A. E., *1-i Nerchinskii polk Zabaikal'skogo kazach'ego voiska, 1898–1906 gg.: Istoricheskii ocherk* (St. Petersburg, 1907)

Maiskii, I. M., *Mongoliia nakanune revoliutsii* (2d rev. ed; Moscow, 1960)

Materialy statistiko-ekonomicheskogo obsledovaniia kazach'ego i krest'ianskogo khoziaistva Amurskoi oblasti (St. Petersburg, 1912), 2 vols.

Mendeleev, D., *K poznaniiu Rossii: S prilozheniem karty Rossii* (St. Petersburg, 1906)

Molodykh, I. F., *Selenga v predelakh Mongolii: Kratkii ocherk o rabotakh mongol'skoi ekspeditsii 1919 goda* (Irkutsk, 1920)

Moskovskaia torgovaia ekspeditsiia v Mongolii (Moscow, 1912)

Murov, G. T., *Liudi i nravy Dal'nego Vostoka: Ot Vladivostoka do Khabarovska* (Tomsk, 1901)

Nabokov, V., *Vremennoe pravitel'stvo (vospominaniia)* (1924; reprint: Moscow, 1991)

Nansen, Fridtjof, *Through Siberia: The Land of the Future* (London, 1914)

Natsiia i imperiia v russkoi mysli nachala xx veka (Moscow, 2004)

Nemirovich-Danchenko, V. I., *V tsarstve zheltogo drakona (v 1908-m godu)* (Petrograd, 1915)

Nilus, E. Kh. (comp.), *Istoricheskii obzor kitaiskoi vostochnoi zheleznoi dorogi (1896–1923 gg.)* (Harbin, 1923)

Noskov, K., *Avantiura, ili chernyi dlia belykh v Mongolii 1921-i god* (Harbin, 1930)

Obzor Amurskoi oblasti za 1911 g. (Blagoveshchensk, 1912)

Odbudowa państwowości polskiej: Najważniejsze dokumenty, 1912–styczeń 1924 (Warsaw-Cracow, 1924)

Ofitserskaia zhizn' (1908, 1910)

Okrainy Rossii (1909, 1910, 1911, 1912)

Osokin, G. M., *Na granitse Mongolii: Ocherki i materialy k etnografii iugo-zapadnogo Zabaikal'ia* (St. Petersburg, 1906)

Ossendowski, Ferdinand, *Beasts, Men, and Gods* (New York, 1922)

Otchet glavnogo upravleniia kazach'ikh voisk za 1908 god (St. Petersburg, 1909)

Otchet o sostoianii Zabaikal'skogo kazach'ego voiska za 1908 god (Chita, 1909)

Otchet ob organizatsii protivochumnykh i protivokholernykh meropriatii na vodnykh putiiakh Amurskogo basseina v navigatsii 1911 goda (Kazan', 1912)

Oukhtomsky [Ukhtomskii], Esper, "The English in Tibet: A Russian View," *North American Review* 174 (1904), 24–29

P. A. Stolypin: Perepiska (Moscow, 2004)

"Pamiatka Pavlovskogo voennogo uchilishcha, 1863–1913," *Pedagogicheskii sbornik,* no. 10 (1913), 324–42

Pamiatnaia knizhka Amurskoi oblasti na 1914 g. (n.p., 1914)

Pares, Sir Bernard, *The Fall of the Russian Monarchy: A Study of the Evidence* (1939; New York, 2008)

Patkanov, S., *O priroste inorodcheskogo naseleniia Sibiri: Statisticheskie materialy dlia osveshcheniia voprosa o vymiranii pervobytnykh plemen* (St. Petersburg, 1911)

Pedagogicheskii sbornik (1905)

Perry-Ascough, H. G. C., and R. B. Otter-Barry, *With the Russians in Mongolia* (London, [1913])

Pershin, D. P., *Baron Ungern, Urga i Altan-Bulak* (Samara, 1999)

Petrov, A. N. (ed.), *Istoricheskii ocherk Pavlovskogo voennogo uchilishcha, Pavlovskogo kadetskogo korpusa i imperatorskogo voenno-sirotskogo doma, 1798–1898 gg.* (St. Petersburg, 1898)

Po rodnomu kraiu: Kratkii ocherk Dal'ne-Vostochnoi Respubliki i Zabaikal'ia (sbornik stat'ei i materialov) (Verkhneudinsk, 1922)

Politrabotnik Sibiri (1920)

Polivanov, N. D., *O nemetskom zasilii* (2nd ed.; Petrograd, 1916)

Potanin, G. N., *Pis'ma G. N. Potanina* (Irkutsk, 1977–1989), 3 vols.

Pound, Ezra, *Selected Poems* (New York, 1957)

Priamur'e: Fakty, tsifry, nabliudeniia, sobrany na Dal'nem Vostoke sotrudnikami obshchezemskoi organizatsii (Moscow, 1909)

Protokoly s''ezdov i konferentsii vsesoiuznoi kommunisticheskoi partii (b): Desiatyi s''ezd RKP(b); mart 1921 g. (Moscow, 1933)

Raivid, N., and V. Bykov (eds.), *Kolchakovshchina: Sbornik* (Ekaterinburg, 1924)

Razumov, N. I., *Zabaikal'e: Svod materialov vysochaishe uchrezhdennoi kommissii dlia izsledovaniia mestnogo zemlevladeniia i zemlepol'zovaniia, pod predsedatel'stvom stats-sekretaria Kulomzina* (St. Petersburg, 1899)

Razvedchik (1907, 1908)

Reed, John *Ten Days That Shook the World* (1919; New York, 1981)

Rennikov, A., *V strane chudes: Pravda o pribaltiiskikh nemtsakh* (2nd ed.; Petrograd, 1915)

Revoliutsiia na Dal'nem Vostoke (Petrograd, 1923), vol. 1

Rosegger, P. K., *Das Volksleben in Steiermark in Character- und Sittenbilden* (Vienna, 1881)

Rosegger, P. K., et al., *Wanderrungen durch Steiermark und Kärnten* (Stuttgart, n.d.)

Rousseau, Jean-Jacques, "Considérations sur le gouvernement de Pologne et sur sa réformation projettée," in Rousseau, *Oeuvres complètes* (Paris, 1964), vol. 3, 953–1041

Rozanov, V. V., *Poslednie list'ia* (A. N. Nikoliukin, ed.) (Moscow, 2000)

Russell, Betrand, *Uncertain Paths to Freedom: Russia and China, 1919–1922* (ed. Richard A. Rempel and Beryl Haslam, with assistance of Andrew Bone and Albert C. Lewis) (New York, 2000)

Russkii vestnik (1901)

"Russkie dela v Mongolii," *Dal'nii vostok*, no. 33 (August 17, 1913), 9–12

Russko-iaponskaia voina i nashi geroi (Moscow, 1904)

Russko-iaponskaia voina, 1904–1905 gg. (St. Petersburg, 1910), vol.1

Russow, Edmund, *Alexander Graf Keyserling* (Reval, 1892)

Sárközi, Alice, *Political Prophecies in Mongolia in the Seventeenth to Twentieth Centuries* (Wiesbaden, 1992)

Semenov, Ataman [Grigorii], *O sebe: Vospominaniia, mysli i vyvody* (Moscow, 2002)

Semenov, P. P. (ed.), *Zhivopisnaia Rossiia: Otechestvo nashe v ego zemel'nom, istoricheskom, plemennom, ekonomicheskom i bytvovom znachenii*, vol. 2, pt.1, *Severo-zapadnye okrainy Rossii i velikoe kniazhestvo Finliandii* (St. Petersburg and Moscow, 1882)

Shenk, V. K., *Pravila nosheniia form odezhdy ofitersami vsekh rodov oruzhiia i grazhdanskimi chinami Voennogo Vedomstva* (St. Petersburg, 1910)

Shikuts, F. I., *Dnevnik soldata v russko-iaponskuiu voinu* (Moscow, 2003)

Shishkin, V. I. (ed.), *Sibirskaia Vandeia: Vooruzhennoe soprotivlenie kommunisticheskomu rezhimu v 1920 godu* (Novosibirsk, 1997)

——, *Protsess nad kolchakovskimi ministrami, mai 1920* (Moscow, 2003)

Shklovsky, Viktor, *A Sentimental Journey: Memoirs, 1917–1922* (Ithaca, 1984)

Shtif, N. I., *Pogromy na Ukraine (period dobrovol'cheskoi armii)* (Berlin, 1922)

Sibir' i velikaia sibirskaia zhelznaia doroga (2nd rev. ed.; St. Petersburg, 1896)

Sibirskii revoliutsionnyi komitet (Sibrevkom) avgust 1919–dekabr' 1925: Sbornik dokumentov i materialov (Novosibirsk, 1959)

Sibirskie voprosy (1907)

Simakov, V. I., *Chastushki: Izdany po zapisiam 1914–1915 g.* (Petrograd, 1915)

Soldatov, V., *Zheleznodorozhnye poselki po Zabaikal'skoi linii* (St. Petersburg, 1912), vol. 5, pt. 2

Sovetsko-Mongol'skie otnosheniia, 1921–1974: Dokumenty i materialy (Moscow and Ulaanbaatar, 1975), 2 vols.

Special-Orts-Repertorium der im Österreichischen Reichsrathe vertretenen Königsreiche und Länder, vol. 4, *Steiermark* (Vienna, 1883)

Spengler, Oswald, *The Decline of the West* (New York, 1946–47), 2 vols. *Spisok naselennykh mest estliandskoi gubernii k 1912-mu godu* (Revel', 1913)

Stepun, Fedor, *Byvshee i nesbyvsheesia* (Moscow and St. Petersburg, 1995)

Stoletie voennogo ministerstva: 1802–1902, vol. 11, *Glavnoe upravlenie kazach'ikh voisk: Istoricheskii ocherk* (St. Petersburg, 1902)

Storzh, M. E., *Raspisanie khoda poezdov, ili illiustrirovannyi sputnik passazhira po Zabaikal'skoi zheleznoi doroge (s 15 oktiabria 1903 g. po 18 aprelia)* (Irkutsk, 1903)

"Sud'ba Mikhaila Romanova," *Voprosy istorii*, no. 9 (1990), 149–63

Svechnikov, A. P., *Russkie v Mongolii: Nabliudeniia i vyvody; Sbornik rabot otnositel'no Mongolii (Khalkhi)* (St. Petersburg, 1912)

Tales of an Old Lama (ed. and trans. C. R. Bawden) (Tring, UK, 1997)

Taube, Helene, von (ed.), *Graf Alexander Keyserling: Ein Lebensbild aus seinen Briefen und Tagebüchern* (Berlin, 1902), 2 vols.

Taube, Otto von, *Das Buch der Keyserlinge: An der Grenze Zweier Welten; Lebenserinnerungen aus einem Geschlecht* (1937; reprint: Berlin, 1944)

——, *Im alten Estland: Kinderheitserinnerungen* (Stuttgart, n.d.)

——, *Stationen auf dem Wege: Erinnerungen an meine Werdezeit vor 1914* (Heidelberg, 1969)

Termen, A. I., *Sredi Buriat Irkutskoi i Zabaikal'skoi oblasti: Ocherki i vpechatleniia* (St. Petersburg, 1912)

Tissot, Victor, *Vienne et la vie viennoise* (13th ed.; Paris, 1878)

Tol'stoi, L. L., *Pamiatka russkogo ofitsera* (St. Petersburg, 1907)

Tomlin, V., *Mongoliia i ee sovremennoe znachenie dlia Rossii* (Moscow, 1913)

Troinitskii, N. A. (ed.), *Pervaia vseobshchaia perepis' naseleniia Rossiiskoi imperii 1897 g.* (St. Petersburg, 1905), vol. 49

Trubetskoi, E. N., *Otechestvennaia voina i eia dukhovnyi smysl* (Moscow, 1915)

Trubetskoi, Vladimir, *Zapiski kirasira* (Moscow, 1991)

Ukhtomskii, E. E., *K sobytiiam v Kitae: Ob otnosheniiakh Zapada i Rossii k vostoku* (St. Petersburg, 1900)

Ungern-Sternberg, Constantin, von, *Nachrichten über das Geschlecht Ungern-Sternberg*, pt. 2 (2nd ed.; Reval, 1902)

Ungern-Sternberg, Th. (Theodor), von, *Untersuchungen über den finnlaendischen Rapakiwi-Granit* (Leipzig, 1882)

——, *O vinodelii na iuzhnom beregu Kryma* (St. Petersburg, 1888)

——, *Die Orographie des Kaukasus in Beziehung zur a alten Kultur in Vorder-Asien* (St. Petersburg, 1891)

Unterberger, P. F. *Priamurskii Krai, 1906–1910: Ocherk* (St. Petersburg, 1912)

Vasilevskii, V. I. (comp.), *Ataman Semenov: Voprosy gosudarstvennogo stroitel'stva; Sbornik dokumentov i materialov* (Chita, 2002)

VChK upolnomochena soobshchit'... 1918 g. (Moscow, 2004)

Vestnik Azii (1911)

Vestnik Evropy (1910)

Vestnik konnitsy (1909)

Ves' Novonikolaevsk: Adresno-spravochnaia kniga za 1924–1925 god (Novonikolaevsk, 1924)

Ves' Peterburg na 1903 god (St. Petersburg, 1903)

Vlast' truda (Irkutsk) (1921)

Voennyi sbornik (1900, 1908)

Voina (1914, 1915)

Voina i mir (1906, 1907)

Voitolovskii, L., *Vskhodil krovavyi mars: Po sledam voiny* (Moscow, 1998)

Voprosy kolonizatsii (1909)

Vorotin, A., *Printsipy pribalitiiskoi zhizni* (Revel', 1891)

Vsia Chita i Zabaikal'e s otdelom Priamur'ia v raione postroiki Amurskoi zheleznoi dorogi (Chita, 1910)

Whitman, Sidney, *The Realm of the Habsburgs* (London, 1893)

Wimpffen, Max, von, *Kritische Worte über den Buddhismus* (Vienna, 1891)

Wistinghausen, Henning, von (ed.), *Zwischen Reval und St. Petersburg: Erinnerungen von Estländern aus zwei Jahrhunderten* (Weissenhorn, 1993)

Wrangel [Vrangel'], P. N., *The Memoirs of General Wrangel: The Last Commander-in-Chief of the Russian National Army* (trans. Sophie Goulston) (London, 1929)

——, *Vospominaniia generala barona P. N. Vrangelia* (Moscow, 1992), 2 vols.

Younghusband, Francis Edward, *The Heart of a Continent: A Narrative of Travels in Manchuria, across the Gobi Desert, through the Himalayas, the Pamirs, and Hunza, 1884–1894* (London, 1904)

Zhamtsarano, Tsyben, *Putevye dnevniki, 1903–1907 gg.* (Ulan-Ude, 2001)

Zhivaia starina (1902)

Zhizn' natsional'nostei (1920, 1921)

Zhong E guanxi shiliao: Wai Menggu (Zhonghua Minguo liu nian zhi ba nian) [1919] 中俄关系史料：外蒙古 (中华民国六年至八年) (Taibei, 1959)

Zhong E guanxi shiliao (Zhong dong tie lu, dongbei bianfang, Wai Menggu) (Minguo jiu nian) [1920] 中俄关系史料 (中东铁路、东北边防、外蒙古) (民国九年) (Taibei, 1969)

Zhong E guanxi shiliao (dongbei bianfang, Wai Menggu) (Minguo shi nian) [1921] 中俄关系史料 (东北边防, 外蒙古) (民国十年) (Taibei, 1975)

Zuijin shi nian Zhong E zhi jiao she 最近十年中俄之交涉 (Shen Yunlong 沈云龙, series editor) (1923; reprint: Taibei, n.d.)

Zweig, Stefan, *The World of Yesterday* (Lincoln, Neb., 1964)

Secondary Sources

Abaeva, L. L., and N. L. Zhukovskaia (eds.), *Buriaty* (Moscow, 2004)

Ablova, N. E., "Rossiia i russkie v Man'chzhurii v kontse xix–nachale xx vv.," in Airapetov, *Russko-iaponskaia voina, 1904–1905* (Moscow, 2004), 183–213

——, *KVZhD i rossiiskaia emigratsiia v Kitae: Mezhdunarodnye i politicheskie aspekty istorii (pervaia polovina xx v.)* (Moscow, 2005)

Abramson, Henry, *A Prayer for the Government: Ukrainians and Jews in Revolutionary Times, 1917–1920* (Cambridge, Mass., 1999)

Agafonov, Oleg, *Kazach'i voiska rossiiskoi imperii: Panteon otechestvennoi slavy* (Moscow and Kaliningrad, 1995)

Agalakov, V. T., *Emelian Iaroslavskii v Sibiri* (Irkutsk, 1964)

"AHR Conversation: On Transnational History," *AHR* 111, no. 5 (2006), 1440–64

Airapetov, O. R. (ed), *Russko-iaponskaia voina, 1904–1905: Vzgliad cherez stoletie* (Moscow, 2004)

Aiusheeva, T. S., "Uchebnye zavedeniia Troitskosavska-Kiakhty," in V. E. Gulgonov (ed.), *Kiakhta: Stranitsy istorii* (Ulan-Ude, 1999), 30–36

Alekseev, A. I., *Osvoenie russkimi liud'mi Dal'nego Vostoka i Russkoi Ameriki do kontsa xix veka* (Moscow, 1982)

Alekseev, V. V. (ed.), *Istoriia kazachestva Aziatskoi Rossii* (Ekaterinburg, 1995), 3 vols.

Anan'ich, Boris V., and Sergei G. Beliaev, "St. Petersburg: Banking Center of the Russian Empire," in William Craft Brumfield, et al. (eds.), *Commerce in Russian Urban Culture, 1861–1914* (Washington, D.C., 2001), 9–20

Anderson, Benedict, *Imagined Communities: Reflections on the Origins and Spread of Nationalism* (rev. ed.; New York, 1991)

Andreev, A. I., "Iz istorii peterburgskogo buddiiskogo khrama," *Orient* 1 (1992), 6–26

——, *Khram Buddy v severnoi stolitse* (St. Petersburg, 2004)

Applegate, Celia, "A Europe of Regions: Reflections on the Historiography of Sub-National Places in Modern Times," *AHR* 104, no. 4 (1999), 1157–82

Argenbright, Robert, "Marking NEP's Slippery Path: The Krasnoshchekov Show Trial," *RR* 61, no. 2 (2002), 249–75.

Artem'ev, A. R., *Goroda i ostrogi Zabaikal'ia i Priamur'ia vo vtoroi polovine xvii–xviii vv.* (Vladivostok, 1999)

Arutiunian, A. O., *Kavkazskii front, 1914–1917 gg.* (Erevan, 1971)

Aschheim, Steven E., *Brothers and Strangers: The East European Jew in German and German-Jewish Consciousness, 1800–1923* (1982; reprint: Madison, Wisc. [1999])

Atwood, Christopher P., *Young Mongols and Vigilantes in Inner Mongolia's Interregnum Decades, 1911–1931* (Leiden, 2002), 2 vols.

Avery, Martha, *The Tea Road: China and Russia Meet across the Steppe* (Beijing, 2003)

Baabar, *Twentieth-Century Mongolia* (Christopher Kaplonski, ed.) (Knapwell, Eng., 1999)

Baberowski, Jörg, "Zivilisation der Gewalt: Die kulturellen Ursprünge des Stalinismus," *Öffentlichen Vorlesungen* (Berlin, 2003), vol. 136, http://edoc.hu-berlin.de/humboldt-vl/136/baberowski-joerg/PDF/baberowski.pdf

Badcock, Sarah, *Politics and the People in Revolutionary Russia: A Provincial History* (New York, 2007)

Bakhturina, A. Iu., *Okrainy rossiiskoi imperii: Gosudarstvennoe upravlenie i natsional' naia politika v gody pervoi mirovoi voiny* (Moscow, 2004)

Bakich, Olga, "Émigré Identity: The Case of Harbin," in Thomas Lahusen (ed.), *Harbin and Manchuria: Place, Space, and Identity* (Durham, N.C., 2001), 51–73

Balabanov, V. F., *Istoriia zemli Daurskoi* (Chita, 2003)

Baliabina, Viktoriia, *Argunei: Zabaikal'skaia starina* (Irkutsk, 1988)

Baron Ungern von Sternberg: Der letzte Kriegsgott ([Preetz], 2007)

Bartlett, Robert, *The Making of Europe: Conquest, Colonization, and Cultural Change, 950–1350* (Princeton, N.J., 1993)

Barrett, Michael B., *Operation Albion: The German Conquest of the Baltic Islands* (Bloomington, Ind., 2008)

Bassin, Mark, "Expansion and Colonialism on the Eastern Frontier: Views of Siberia and the Far East in Pre-Petrine Russia," *Journal of Historical Geography* 14, no. 1 (1988), 12–15

——, *Imperial Visions: Nationalist Imagination and Geographical Expansion in the Russian Far East* (New York, 1999)

Bater, James H., *St. Petersburg: Industrialization and Change* (Montreal, 1976)

Batsaikhan, Ookhnoi, "Baron Ungern—Mongol ulsyn baatar bolokh n'," http://www.tsahimurtuu.mn/index.php/2012-03-05-03-28-33/86-news/article/759-archive-story-552 (last accessed May 2012)

——, *Bogdo Jebtsundamba Khutuktu, the Last King of Mongolia: Mongolia's National Revolution of 1911* (Ulaanbaatar, 2009)

Batsaikhan, Ts., and A. Puntsog, *Mongoliin möngön temdeg* (Ulaanbaatar, 1998)

Baud, Michael, and Willem van Schendel, "Toward a Comparative History of Borderlands," *Journal of World History* 8, no. 2 (1997), 211–42

Bauer, G. F., *Stareishaia gimnaziia v Rossii: Ocherki iz proshlogo Revel'skoi gimnazii imperatora Nikolaia I* (Revel', 1910)

Bawden, C. R., *The Modern History of Mongolia* (2nd rev. ed.; London and New York, 1989)

Bayly, C. A., *The Birth of the Modern World, 1780–1914: Global Connections and Comparisons* (Malden, Mass., 2004)

Bazarov, B. V., and L. B. Zhabaeva, *Buriatskie natsional'nye demokraty i obshchestvenno-politicheskaia mysl' mongol'skikh narodov v pervoi treti xx veka* (Ulan-Ude, 2008)

Bazarzhapov, V. B., *Buriaty na sluzhbe otechestva (xviii–xx vv.)* (Ulan-Ude, 2005)

Becker, Jean-Jacques, *1914: Comment les français sont entrés dans la guerre* (Paris, 1977)

Bell, Duncan, *The Idea of Greater Britain: Empire and the Future of World Order, 1860–1900* (Princeton, N.J., 2007)

Beliaeva, N. A., et al., *Dal'nevostochnaia kontrabanda kak istoricheskoe iavlenie (Bor'ba s kontrabandoi na Dal'nem Vostoke Rossii vo vtoroi polovine xix–pervoi tret'i xx veka)* (Vladivostok, 2010)

Belov, E. A., *Rossiia i Kitai v nachale xx veka: Russko-kitaiskie protivorechiia v 1911–1915 gg.* (Moscow, 1917)

——, *Rossiia i Mongoliia (1911–1919 gg.)* (Moscow, 1999)

——, *Baron Ungern fon Shternberg: Biografiia, ideologiia, voennye pokhody, 1920–1921* (Moscow, 2003)

Benton, Gregor, *Chinese Migrants and Internationalism: Forgotten Histories, 1917–1945* (New York, 2007)

Betz, Hans-Georg, "Elites and Class Structure," in Eva Kolinsky and Wilfried van der Will (eds.), *The Cambridge Companion to Modern German Culture* (New York, 1998), 67–85

Beyrau, Detrich, *Militär und Gesellschaft im Vorrevolutionären Russland* (Cologne-Vienna, 1984)

Bickers, Robert, *Empire Made Me: An Englishman Adrift in Shanghai* (New York, 2004)

Billingsley, Phil, *Bandits in Republican China* (Stanford, Calif., 1988)

Bisher, Jamie, *White Terror: Cossack Warlords of the Trans-Siberian* (New York, 2005)

Bishop, Peter, *The Myth of Shangri-La: Tibet, Travel Writing, and the Western Creation of Sacred Landscape* (London, 1989)

Bloxham, Donald, *The Great Game of Genocide: Imperialism, Nationalism, and the Destruction of the Ottoman Armenians* (New York, 2005)

Blum, Jerome, *The End of the Old Order in Rural Europe* (Princeton, N.J., 1978)

Bolotin, D. P., and A. P. Zabiiako (eds.), *Rossiia i Kitai na dal'nevostochnykh rubezhakh: materialy konferentsii* (Blagoveshchensk, 2001–2002), 4 vols.

Bonavia, David, *China's Warlords* (Hong Kong and New York, 1995)

Boyd, James, "'A Very, Quiet Outspoken, Pleasant Gentleman [*sic*]': The United States Military Attaché's Reports on Baron von Ungern-Sternberg, March 1921," *Inner Asia* 12 (2010), 365–77

——, *Japanese-Mongolian Relations, 1873–1945: Faith, Race, and Strategy* (Folkestone, Eng., 2011)

Bridenthal, Renate, "Germans from Russia: The Political Network of a Double Diaspora," in O'Donnell et al., *Heimat Abroad,* 187–218

Brovkin, Vladimir N., *Behind the Front Lines of the Civil War: Political Parties and Social Movements in Russia, 1918–1923* (Princeton, N.J., 1994)

Brower, Daniel, "Imperial Russia and Its Orient: The Renown of Nikolai Przhevalskii," *RR* 53, no. 3 (1994), 367–81

Brubaker, Rogers, *Nationalism Reframed: Nationhood and the National Question in the New Europe* (New York, 1996)

Brüggemann, Karsten, "Wie der Revaler Domberg zum Moskauer Kreml wurde: Zur lokalen Repräsentation imperialer Herrschaft im späten Zarenreich," in Jörg Baberowski, David Feest, and Christoph Gumb (eds.), *Imperiale Herrschaft in der Provinz: Repräsentationen politischer Macht im späten Zarenreich* (Frankfurt, 2008), 172–95

Brunner, Walter, et al. (eds.), *Geschichte der Stadt Graz* (Graz, 2003), 4 vols.

Budnitskii, Oleg, "Jews, Pogroms, and the White Movement: A Historiographical Critique," *Kritika* 2, no. 4 (2001), 1–23

——, *Russian Jews between the Reds and the Whites, 1917–1920* (trans. Timothy J. Portice) (Philadelphia, 2012)

Bulag, Uradyn E., *Nationalism and Hybridity in Mongolia* (New York, 1998)

Bulag, Uradyn E. and Caroline Humphrey, "Some Diverse Representations of the Pan-Mongolian Movement in Dauria," *Inner Asia: Occasional Papers of the Mongolia and Inner Asia Studies Unit,* no. 1 (1996), 1–23

Buldakov, Vladimir P., "Freedom, Shortages, Violence: The Origins of the 'Revolutionary Anti-Jewish Pogrom' in Russia, 1917–1918," in Dekel-Chen, Gaunt, Meir, and Bartal, *Anti-Jewish Violence,* 74–91

Buraeva, O. V., *Etnokul'turnoe vzaimodeistvie narodov Baikal'skogo regiona v xvii–nachale xx vv.* (Ulan-Ude, 2005)

Burbank, Jane, *Intelligentsia and Revolution: Russian Views of Bolshevism, 1917–1922* (New York, 1986)

Bushnell, John, "The Tsarist Officer Corps, 1881–1914: Customs, Duties, Inefficiency," *AHR* 86, no. 4 (1981), 753–80

Caine, Barbara, *Biography and History* (Basingstoke, Eng., 2010)

Cannadine, David, *The Decline and Fall of the British Aristocracy* (New Haven, Conn., 1990)

Caplan, Jane, and John Torpey (eds.), *Documenting Individual Identity: The Development of State Practices in the Modern World* (Princeton, N.J., 2001)

Cardoza, Anthony L., *Aristocrats in Bourgeois Italy: The Piedmontese Nobility, 1861–1930* (New York, 1997)

Carlson, Maria, *"No Religion Higher Than Truth": A History of the Theosophical Movement in Russia, 1875–1902* (Princeton, N.J., 1993)

——, "Fashionable Occultism: Spiritualism, Theosophy, Freemasonry, and Hermeticism in Fin-de-Siècle Russia," in Bernice Glatzer Rosenthal (ed.), *The Occult in Russian and Soviet Culture* (Ithaca, 1997), 135–52

Carter, James H., *Creating a Chinese Harbin: Nationalism in an International City, 1916–1932* (Ithaca, 2002)

Cassady, Julie A., *The Enemy on Trial: Early Soviet Courts on Stage and Screen* (DeKalb, Ill., 2000)

Chan, Anthony B., *Arming the Chinese: The Western Armaments Trade in Warlord China, 1920–1928* (Vancouver, 1982)

Chen Zhaoxiang 陈肇祥, "Bai E nanjue xiechi Wai Meng nao duli" 白俄男爵挟持闹独立, Wanbao wen cui 晚报文萃, 1 (2012), 26–27

Chiasson, Blaine R., *Administering the Colonizer: Manchuria's Russians under Chinese Rule, 1918–1929* (Vancouver, 2010)

Chickering, Roger, *We Men Who Feel Most German: A Cultural Study of the Pan-German League, 1886–1914* (Boston, 1984)

Christiansen, Eric, *The Northern Crusades: The Baltic and the Catholic Frontier, 1100–1525* (Minneapolis, Minn., 1980)

Clarke, J. J., *Oriental Enlightenment: The Encounter between Asian and Western Thought* (New York, 1997)

Colley, Linda, *Captives: Britain, Empire, and the World, 1600–1850* (New York, 2004)

——, *The Ordeal of Elizabeth Marsh: A Woman in World History* (London, 2007)

Cornwall, Mark, "Disintegration and Defeat: The Austro-Hungarian Revolution," in Mark Cornwall (ed.), *The Last Years of Austria-Hungary: A Multi-National Experiment in Early Twentieth-Century Europe* (rev. ed.; Exeter, Eng., 2002), 167–96

Cracraft, James, "Saint Petersburg: The Russian Cosmopolis," in Cynthia Hyla Whittaker (ed.), *Russia Engages the World, 1453–1825* (Cambridge, Mass., 2003), 24–49

Crews, Robert D., *For Prophet and Tsar: Islam and Empire in Russia and Central Asia* (Cambridge, Mass., 2006)

Crossley, Pamela Kyle, *The Manchus* (Malden, Mass., 1997)

——, "Making Mongols," in Pamela Kyle Crossley et al. (eds.), *Empire at the Margins: Culture, Ethnicity, and Frontier in Early Modern China* (Berkeley and Los Angeles, 2006), 58–82

Dahlmann, Dittmar, *Sibirien, vom 16. Jahrhundert bis zur Gegenwart* (Paderborn, 2009)

Darevskaia, E. M., "Fevral'skaia revoliutsiia v Rossii i russkaia koloniia v Urge," *Trudy Irkutskogo gosudarstvennogo universiteta* 25, no. 1 (1958), 23–48

——, *Sibir' i Mongoliia: Ocherki russko-mongol'skikh sviazei v kontse xix–nachale xx vekov* (Irkutsk, 1994)

——, "Russkii sovetnik pravitel'stva Mongolii S. A. Kozin," in *Vostok i Rossiia: Vzgliad iz Sibiri: Materialy i tezisy dokladov k nauchno-prakticheskoi konferentsii, Irkutsk, 16–18 maia 1996 g.* (Irkutsk, 1996), 155–60

Darzhaev, S. Iu., *Stepnye dumy: Organy samoupravleniia buriat v rossiiskom gosudarstve: 1822–1904* (Ulan-Ude, 2001)

Datsyshen, Vladimir, "Formirovanie kitaiskoi obshchiny v rossiiskoi imperii (vtoraia polovina xix v.)," *Diaspory*, nos. 2/3 (2001), 36–53

——, "Historical and Contemporary Trends of Chinese Labor Migration into Siberia," in Felix B. Chang and Sunnie T. Rucker-Chang (eds.), *Chinese Migrants in Russia, Central Asia, and Eastern Europe* (New York, 2012), 19–40

Davies, Norman, *God's Playground: A History of Poland,* vol. 2, *1795–Present* (New York, 2005)

——, *Vanished Kingdoms: The History of Half-Forgotten Europe* (London, 2011)

Dekel-Chen, Jonathan, David Gaunt, Natan M. Meir, and Israel Bartal (eds.), *Anti-Jewish Violence: Rethinking the Pogrom in East European History* (Bloomington, Ind., 2010)

Demidenko, Mikhail, *Put' v Shambalu: Baron Ungern, belyi rytsar' Tibeta* (Moscow, 2004)

Deng Jiugang 邓九刚, *Cha ye zhi lu: Ou Ya shangdao xing shuai san ban nian* 茶叶之路: 欧亚商道兴衰三百年 (Hohot, 2000)

Diatlov, Viktor, "Blagoveshchenskaia 'utopiia': Iz istorii materializatsii fobii," in Sergei Panarin (ed.), *Evraziia: Liudi i mify* (Moscow, 2003), 123–41

Dickinson, Edward Ross, "Germans or Europeans? Moral Reform and Sex Reform before World War I" (Unpublished paper, 2007)

Dickinson, Frederick, *War and National Reinvention: Japan in the Great War, 1914–1919* (Cambridge, Mass., 1999)

Dikötter, Frank, "Hairy Barbarians, Furry Primates, and Wild Men: Medical Science and Cultural Representations of Hair in China," in Alf Hiltebeitel and Barbara D. Miller (eds.), *Hair: Its Power and Meaning in Asian Cultures* (Albany, 1998), 51–74

Dimitriou, Sokratis (ed.), *Stadterweiterung von Graz: Gründerzeit* (Graz and Vienna, 1979)

Dixon, Joy, "Ancient Wisdom, Modern Motherhood: Theosophy and the Colonial Syncretic," in Antoinette Burton (ed.), *Gender, Sexuality, and Colonial Modernities* (New York, 1999), 193–206

Driver, Felix, *Geography Militant: Cultures of Exploration and Empire* (Malden, Mass., 2001)

Droit, Roger-Pol, *The Cult of Nothingness: The Philosophers and the Buddha* (Chapel Hill, N.C., 2003)

Duara, Prasenjit, "Nationalists among Transnationals: Overseas Chinese and the Idea of China, 1900–1911," in Aihwa Ong and Donald M. Nonini (eds.), *Ungrounded Empires: The Cultural Politics of Modern Chinese Transnationalism* (New York, 1997), 39–60

Dubinina, N. I., *Priamurskii general-gubernator N. L. Gondatti* (Khabarovsk, 1997).

——, "Rol' Amurskoi ekspeditsii (1909–1910) v izuchenii Dal'nego Vostoka Rossii," in Bolotin and Zabiiako (eds.), *Rossiia i Kitai na dal'nevostochnykh rubezhakh*, vol. 1, 346–53

Duke, Steven, "Multiethnic St. Petersburg: The Late Imperial Period," in Helena Goscilo and Stephen M. Norris (eds.), *Preserving Petersburg: History, Memory, Nostalgia* (Bloomington, Ind., 2008), 142–63

Duus, Peter, *The Abacus and the Sword: The Japanese Penetration of Korea, 1895–1910* (Berkeley and Los Angeles, 1995)

Edinarkhova, N. E., "Russkie v Mongolii: Obraz zhizni i tipy povedeniia," in *Diaspory v istoricheskom vremeni i prostranstve; Natsional'naia situatsiia v vostochnoi Sibiri; Tezisy dokladov mezhdunarodnoi nauchno-prakticheskoi konferentsii 6–8 oktiabria 1994 g.* (Irkutsk, 1994), 121–23

——, "Russkie kuptsy v Mongolii," *Vostok*, no. 1 (1996), 76–89

Edwards, Catharine, and Greg Woolf, "Cosmopolis: Rome as World City," in Edwards and Woolf (eds.), *Rome the Cosmopolis* (New York, 2003), 120

Efimenko, A. P., "K biografii barona R. F. Ungerna-Shternberga," in *Arkhiv naslediia-2003: Nauchnyi sbornik* (Moscow, 2005), 276–314

Eksteins, Modris, *Rites of Spring: The Great War and the Birth of the Modern Age* (Boston, 1989)

Eliutin, O. N., "'Zolotoi vek' zheleznodorozhnogo stroitel'stva v Rossii i ego posledstviia," *VI*, no. 2 (2004), 47–57

Elliott, Mark C., "The Limits of Tartary: Manchuria in Imperial and National Geographies," *Journal of Asian Studies* 59, no. 3 (2000), 603–46

———, "Les Mandchous et la définition de la nation," *Annales* 61, no. 6 (2006), 1447–77

Elverskog, Johan, *Our Great Qing: The Mongols, Buddhism, and the State in Late Imperial China* (Honolulu, 2006)

Emelin, A. Iu. (comp.), *Morskoi kadetskii korpus v vospominaniiakh vospitannikov* (St. Petersburg, 2003)

Engel, Barbara Alpern, "In the Name of the Tsar: Competing Legalities and Marital Conflict in Late Imperial Russia," *JMH* 77, no. 1 (2005), 70–96

Enstiklopediia Zabaikal'ia: Chitinskaia oblast' (Novosibirsk, 2000–2006), 4 vols.

Ermak, G. G., *Semeinyi i khoziaistvennyi byt' kazakov iuga Dal'nego Vostoka Rossii: Vtoraia polovina xix–nachalo xx veka* (Vladivostok, 2004)

Ermakova, T. V., *Buddiiskii mir glazami rossiiskikh issledovatelei xix–pervoi treti xx veka* (St. Petersburg, 1998)

Ershov, Dmitrii, *Khunkhuzy: Neob'' iavlennaia voina; Etnicheskii banditizm na Dal'nem Vostoke* (Moscow, 2010)

Ewing, Thomas E., *Between the Hammer and the Anvil? Chinese and Russian Policies in Outer Mongolia, 1911–1921* (Bloomington, Ind., 1980)

Fateev, P. S., *Emelian Mikhailovich Iaroslavskii* (Moscow, 1980)

Fedotova, T. V., *Slovar' toponimov Zabaikal'ia* (Chita, 2003)

Ferguson, Niall, *The House of Rothschild: Money's Prophets, 1798–1848* (New York, 1998)

———, *The Pity of War* (New York, 1999)

Figes, Orlando, and Boris Kolonitskii, *Interpreting the Russian Revolution: The Languages and Symbols of 1917* (New Haven, Conn., 1999)

Fitzpatrick, Shelia, *The Russian Revolution* (2nd ed.; New York, 1994)

Forsyth, James, *A History of the Peoples of Siberia: Russia's North Asian Colony, 1581–1990* (New York, 1992)

Foucault, Michel, "Governmentality," in Graham Burchell, et al. (eds.), *The Foucault Effect: Studies in Governmentality* (Chicago, 1991), 87–104

Foust, Clifford C. M., *Muscovite and Mandarin: Russia's Trade with China and Its Setting, 1727–1805* (Chapel Hill, N.C., 1969)

Fredrickson, George M., *Racism: A Short History* (Princeton, N.J., 2002)

French, Patrick, *Younghusband: The Last Great Imperial Adventurer* (London, 1994)

Frevert, Ute, "Europeanizing Germany's Twentieth Century," *History and Memory* 17, nos. 1/2 (2005), 87–116

Friesen, Aileen, "Fulfilling God's Plan: The Russian Orthodox Church and the East in the Early Twentieth Century" (Unpublished paper, 2013)

Fu, Lo-shu (comp.), *A Documentary Chronicle of Sino-Western Relations (1644–1820)* (Tuscon, Ariz., 1966)

Fuller, William C., Jr., *The Foe Within: Fantasies of Treason and the End of Imperial Russia* (Ithaca, 2006)

———, "The Imperial Army," in Dominic Lieven (ed.), *The Cambridge History of Russia*, vol. 2, *Imperial Russia, 1689–1917* (New York, 2006), 530–53

Galdanova, G. R., et al. (eds.), *Lamaizm v Buriatii xviii–nachala xx veka: Strukhtura i sotsial'naia rol' kul'turnoi sistemy* (Novosibirsk, 1983)

Galushko, Iu., and A. Kolesnikov, *Shkola rossiiskogo ofitserstva: Istoricheskii spravochnik* (Moscow, 1993)

Gamsa, Mark, "How a Republic of Chinese Red Beards Was Invented in Paris," *Modern Asian Studies* 36, no. 2 (2002), 993–1010

——, "The Epidemic of Pneumonic Plague in Manchuria, 1910–1911," *Past & Present,* no. 190 (2006), 147–83

Gao Qiang 高强, "Shi lun Qing mo Min chu dongbei jun tun shi bian," 试论清末民初 东北军屯实边 *Qiqihaer daxue xuebao (Zhexue shehui kexue ban)* 齐齐哈尔大学学报 (哲学社会科学版), no. 6 (2011), 6–9

Gatrell, Peter, "Poor Russia, Poor Show: Mobilising a Backward Economy," in Stephen Broadberry and Mark Harrison (eds.), *The Economics of World War I* (New York, 2005), 235–75

——, *Russia's First World War: A Social and Economic History* (Harlow, Eng., 2005)

Gaunt, David, "The Ottoman Treatment of the Assyrians," in Ronald Grigor Suny and Fatma Müge Göçek (eds.), *A Question of Genocide: Armenians and Turks at the End of Empire* (New York, 2011), 244–59

Gaunt, John, "Mongolia's Renegade Monk: The Career of Dambijantsan," *Journal of the Anglo-Mongolian Society* 10 (1987), 27–41

Gay, Peter, *Schnitzler's Century: The Making of Middle-Class Culture, 1815–1914* (New York, 2002)

Gitelman, Zvi, *A Century of Ambivalence: The Jews of Russia and the Soviet Union, 1881 to the Present* (2nd rev. ed.; Bloomington, Ind., 2001)

Glassheim, Eagle, *Noble Nationalists: The Transformation of the Bohemian Aristocracy* (Cambridge, Mass., 2005)

Godsey, William D., "Quarterings and Kinship: The Social Composition of the Habsburg Aristocracy in the Dualist Era," *JMH* 71, no. 1 (1999), 56–104

——, "Nobles and Modernity," *German History* 20, no. 4 (2002), 504–21

Gollwitzer, Heinz, *Die Gelbe Gefahr: Geschichte eines Schlagworts; Studien zum imperialistischen Denken* (Göttingen, 1962)

Golovin, N. N., *Voennye usiliia Rossii v mirovoi voine* (Paris, 1939; reprint: Moscow, 2001)

Gongor, D., *Khovdyn khuraangui tuukh* (Ulaanbaatar, 2006)

Gordin, Michael D., "Measure of All the Russias: Metrology and Governance in the Russian Empire," *Kritika* 4, no. 4 (2003), 783–815

Goriushkin, L. M. (ed.), *Novonikolaevsk-Novosibirsk: Sobytiia, liudi, 1893–1993* (Novosibirsk, 1993)

Gorodetsky, Gabriel, "Maiskii, Ivan Mikhailovich," in Hundert, *Yivo Encyclopedia of Jews in Eastern Europe,* vol. 1, 1118–19

Gramsci, Antonio, *Selections from the Prison Notebooks* (eds. and trans. Quintin Hoare and Geoffrey Nowell Smith) (New York, 1971)

Grebenkin, I. N., "Ofitserstvo rossiiskoi armii v gody pervoi mirovoi voiny," *VI,* no. 2 (2010), 52–66

Green, Abigail, *Fatherlands: State-Building and Nationhood in Nineteenth-Century Germany* (New York, 2001)

Green, Martin, *Dreams of Adventure, Deeds of Empire* (New York, 1979)

Gregory, Adrian, *The Last Great War: British Society and the First World War* (New York, 2008)

Gustav Adolfi Gümnaasium 375 (Tallinn, 2006)

Halfin, Igal, *Intimate Enemies: Demonizing the Bolshevik Opposition, 1918–1928* (Pittsburgh, 2007)

Hanisch, Ernst, *Der lange Schatten des Staates: Österreichische Gesellschaftsgeschichte im 20. Jahrhundert* (Vienna, 1994)

Happel, Jörn, *Nomadische Lebebswelten und zarische Politik: Der Aufstand in Zentralasien 1916* (Stuttgart, 2010)

Hasegawa, Tsyoshi, *The February Revolution, Petrograd 1917* (Seattle, 1981)

Hauner, Milan, *What Is Asia to Us? Russia's Asian Heartland Yesterday and Today* (Boston, 1990)

Hein, Ants (comp.), *Eesti mõisad: 250 fotot aastaist, 1860–1939* (Tallinn, 2004)

Hellot-Bellier, Florence, "La première guerre mondiale à l'ouest du lac d'Urumiye," in Oliver Bast (ed.), *La Perse et la grande guerre* (Tehran, 2002), 329–52

Herlihy, Patricia, *Alcoholic Empire: Vodka and Politics in Late Imperial Russia* (New York, 2002)

Heretz, Leonid, "The Psychology of the White Movement," in Vladimir N. Brovkin (ed.), *The Bolsheviks in Russian Society: The Revolution and the Civil War* (New Haven, Conn., 1997), 105–21

——, *Russia on the Eve of Modernity: Popular Religion and Traditional Culture under the Last Tsars* (New York, 2008)

Hirsch, Francine, *Empire of Nations: Ethnographic Knowledge and the Making of the Soviet Union* (Ithaca, 2005)

Hirschegger, Manfred, "Die Grazer 'Tagespost' von 1880. bis 1890: Ein Beitrag zur steierischen Pressegeschichte" (PhD diss., Graz University, 1981)

Höbelt, Lother, "The Discrete Charm of the Old Regime," *Austrian History Yearbook* 27 (1996), 289–302

Holquist, Peter, *Making War, Forging Revolution: Russia's Continuum of Crisis, 1914–1921* (Cambridge, Mass., 2002)

——, "State Violence as Technique: The Logic of Violence in Soviet Totalitarianism," in Amir Weiner (ed.), *Landscaping the Human Garden: Twentieth-Century Population Management in a Comparative Framework* (Stanford, Calif., 2003), 19–45

——, "La violence de l'armée russe à l'encontre des Juifs en 1915: Causes et limites," in John Horne (ed.), *Vers la guerre totale: Le tournant de 1914–1915* (Paris, 2010), 191–219

Holz, Klaus, *Natsionaler Antisemitismus: Wissenssoziologie einer Weltanschauung* (Hamburg, 2001)

Hopkirk, Peter, *Setting the East Ablaze: Lenin's Dream of Empire in Asia* (New York, 1984)

Hsü, C. Y., *The Rise of Modern China* (6th ed.; New York, 2000)

Hsu, Chia Yin, "A Tale of Two Railroads: 'Yellow Labor,' Agrarian Colonization, and the Making of Russianness at the Far Eastern Frontier, 1890s–1910s," *Ab Imperio*, no. 3 (2006), 217–53

Hubbard, William H., "Politics and Society in the Central European City: Graz, Austria, 1861–1918," *Canadian Journal of History/Annales canadiennes d'histoire* 5, no. 1 (1970), 25–45

Hudgins, Sharon, "Raw Liver, Singed Sheep's Head, and Boiled Stomach Pudding: Encounters with Traditional Buryat Cuisine," *Sibirica* 3, no. 2 (2003), 131–52

Hughes, Rhys, "The Brutal Buddha: Baron von Ungern-Sternberg," in Hughes, *A New Universal History of Infamy* (Tallahassee, Fla., 2004), 23–32

Hull, Isabel V., *Absolute Destruction: Military Culture and the Practices of War in Imperial Germany* (Ithaca, 2005)

Humphrey, Caroline, "Remembering an 'Enemy': The Bogd Khaan in Twentieth-Century Mongolia," in Rubie S. Watson (ed.), *Memory, History, and Opposition under State Socialism* (Santa Fe, 1994), 21–44

Hundert, Gershon David (ed.), *The Yivo Encyclopedia of Jews in Eastern Europe* (New Haven, Conn., 2008), 2 vols.

Iakushina, A. P., "Boris Zakarovich Shumiatskii (1886–1943)," *Istoriia SSSR,* no. 2 (1969), 118–23

Iankov, A. G., "Sibiriaki—Karymy: K voprosu o sibirskoi identichnosti," in A. O. Boronoev (ed.), *Sibir': Problemy sibirskoi identichnosti* (St. Petersburg, 2003), 98–103

Isakov, S. G. (comp.), *Russkie obshchestvennye i kul'turnye deiateli v Estonii: Materially k biograficheskomu slovariu* (2d rev. ed.; Tallinn, 1996)

Isoaho, Mari, *The Image of Alexander Nevskiy in Medieval Russia: Warrior and Saint* (Leiden, 2006)

Isono, Fujiko, "Soviet Russia and the Mongolian Revolution of 1921," *Past & Present,* no. 83 (1979), 116–40

Istoriia Dal'nego Vostoka SSSR v epokhu feodalizma i kapitalizma, xvii v.-fevral' 1917 g. (Moscow, 1991)

Istoriia goroda Novonikolaevsk-Novosibirsk: Istoricheskie ocherki (Novosibirsk, 2005), 2 vols.Iusupova, T. I., *Mongol'skaia komissiia Akademii nauk: Istoriia sozdaniia i deiatel'nosti, 1925–1953* (St. Petersburg, 2006)

Iuzefovich, Leonid, *Samoderzhets pustyni: Baron R. F. Ungern- Shternberg i mir v kotorom on zhil (1993; rev ed.: Moscow, 2010)*

Izgachev, V. G. (ed.), *Revoliutsionnoe dvizhenie v Zabaikal'e, 1905–1907 gg.: Sbornik dokumentov i materialov k piatidesiatiletiiu pervoi russkoi revoliutsii* (Chita, 1955)

Jagchid, Sechin, "The Manchu Ch'ing Policy toward Mongolian Religion," in Walter Heissig (ed.), *Tractata Altaica: Denis Sinor Sexaginario Optime de Rebus Altaicis Merito Dedicata* (Wiesbaden, 1976), 301–19

Jahn, Hubertus F., *Patriotic Culture in Russia during World War I* (Ithaca, 1995)

Jelavich, Barbara, *Modern Austria: Empire and Republic, 1815–1986* (New York, 1987)

Jensen, Marc, *A Show Trial under Lenin: The Trial of the Socialist Revolutionaries, Moscow, 1922* (The Hague, 1982)

Jerryson, Michael K., *Mongolian Buddhism: The Rise and Fall of the Sangha* (Chiang Mai, Thailand, 2007)

Jiang Zhaocheng 蒋兆成 and Wang Rigen 王日根, *Kangxi zhuan* 康熙传 (Beijing, 2011)

Judson, Pieter M., *Guardians of the Nation: Activists on the Language Frontiers of Imperial Austria* (Cambridge, Mass., 2006)

——. "When Is a Diaspora Not a Diaspora? Rethinking Nation-Centered Narratives about Germans in Habsburg East Central Europe," in O'Donnell, Bridenthal, and Reagin (eds.), *Heimat Abroad,* 219–47

Kabuzan, V. M., *Dal'nevostochnyi krai v xvii–nachale xx vv. (1640–1917): Istoriko-demograficheskii ocherk* (Moscow, 1985)

Kala, Tiina, "The Incorporation of the Northern Baltic Lands into the Western Christian World," in Alan V. Murray (ed.), *Crusade and Conversion on the Baltic Frontier, 1150–1500* (Adershot, Eng., 2001), 3–20

Kalmar, Ivan Davidson, "Moorish Style: Orientalism, the Jews, and Synagogue Architecture," *Jewish Social Studies* 7, no. 3 (2001), 68–100

Kalmina, Lilia, "The Possibility of the Impossible: Pogroms in Eastern Siberia," in Dekel-Chen, Gaunt, Meir, and Bartal (eds.), *Anti-Jewish Violence*, 131–43

Kal'mina, L. V., and L. V. Kuras, *Evreiskaia obshchina v zapadnom Zabaikal'e (60-e gody xix veka–fevral' 1917 goda)* (Ulan-Ude, 1999)

Kann, Robert A., *The Multinational Empire: Nationalism and National Reform in the Habsburg Monarchy, 1848–1918* (New York, 1950), 2 vols.

Kappeler, Andreas, "The Ambiguities of Russification," *Kritika* 5, no. 2 (2004), 291–97

Kara, György, *Books of the Mongolian Nomads: More Than Eight Centuries of Writing Mongolian* (Bloomington, Ind., 2005)

Karjahärm, Toomas (comp.), *Vana Hiiumaa: Ehitised ja inimesed* (n.p., 2013)

——, *Vana Tallinn: Ehitised ja inimesed* (Tallinn, 2007)

Karetina, G. S., *Chzhan Tsolin' i politicheskaia bor'ba v Kitae v 20-e gody xx v.* (Moscow, 1984)

Karevskii, A. A., "K voprosu o simvolike Aziatskoi Konnoi Divizii," in *Kazachestvo Rossii v belom dvizhenii* (Moscow, 2005), 185–92

Kazemzadeh, Firuz, *Russia and Britain in Persia, 1864–1914: A Study in Imperialism* (New Haven, Conn., 1968)

Keevak, Michael, *Becoming Yellow: A Short History of Racial Thinking* (Princeton, N.J., 2011)

Kelly, Catriona, "The Education of the Will: Advice Literature, *Zakal,* and Manliness in Early Twentieth-Century Russia," in Barbara Evans Clements, et al. (eds.), *Russian Masculinities in History and Culture* (New York, 2002), 131–51

Kemenev, Vladimir, *Vasily Surikov, 1848–1916* (Bournemouth, Eng., 1997)

Kenez, Peter, "A Profile of the Prerevolutionary Officer Corps," *California Slavic Studies* (Berkeley and Los Angeles, 1973), vol. 7, 121–58

——, *The Birth of the Propaganda State: Soviet Methods of Mass Mobilization, 1917–1929* (New York, 1985)

——, "Pogroms and White Ideology in the Russian Civil War," in John Klier and Shlomo Lambroza (eds.), *Pogroms: Anti-Jewish Violence in Modern Russian History* (New York, 1992), 293–313

Kern, Stephen, *The Culture of Time and Space, 1880–1918* (Cambridge, Mass., 1983)

Khodarkovsky, Michael, *Bitter Choices: Loyalty and Betrayal in the Russian Conquest of the North Caucasus* (Ithaca, 2011)

Khoroshilova, Ol'ga, *Voiskovye partizany velikoi voiny* (St. Petersburg, 2002)

Kiernan, V. G., *The Duel in European History: Honour in the Reign of the Aristocracy* (New York, 1988)

Kieser, Hans-Lukas, *Der verpasste Friede: Mission, Ethnie und Staat in der Ostprovinszen Türkei, 1839–1938* (Zurich, 2000)

King, Ross, "Bogoslovennoe: Korean Village on the Amur, 1871–1937," *Review of Korean Studies* 4, no. 2 (2001), 133–76

Kirby, David, *A Concise History of Finland* (New York, 2006)

——, *Northern Europe in the Early Modern Period: The Baltic World, 1492–1772* (New York, 1990)

Kırımlı, Hakan, "The Activities of the Union for the Liberation of Ukraine in the Ottoman Empire during the First World War," *Middle Eastern Studies* 34, no. 4 (1998), 177–200

Kislov, A. N., *Razgrom Ungerna (O boevom sodruzhestve sovetskogo i mongol'skogo narodov)* (Moscow, 1964)

Klier, John, "Pogroms," in Hundert, *Yivo Encyclopedia of Jews in Eastern Europe*, vol. 2, 1375–1381

Kniaz'ev, N. N., *Legendarnyi baron* (Harbin, 1942)

Kokoulin, V. G., *Novonikolaevsk v gody revoliutsii, grazhdanskoi voiny i "voennogo kommunizma" (fevral' 1917–mart 1921 g.)* (Novosibirsk, 2010)

Kolonitskii, B. I., *Pogony i bor'ba za vlast' v 1917 godu* (St. Petersburg, 2001).

Kolotilo, L. G., and V. G. Andrienko, *Transbaikal'skii perekrestok: Problemy transportnykh putei i zheleznodorozhnoi paromnoi perepravy cherez ozero Baikal na rubezhe xix–xx vv.* (St. Petersburg, 2005)

Konstantinov, A. V., and N. N. Konstantinova, *Istoriia Zabaikal'ia (s drevneishikh vremen do 1917 goda)* (Chita, 2002)

Konstantinov, S. I., "Vliianie vzaimosviazi mirovoi i grazhdanskoi voin na psikhologicheskii raskol rossiiskogo obshchestva," in I. V. Narskii and O. Iu. Nikonova (eds.), *Chelovek i voina: Voina kak iavlenie kul'tury* (Moscow, 2001), 181–189

Kornblatt, Judith Deutsch, *The Cossack Hero in Russian Literature: A Study in Cultural Mythology* (Madison, Wisc., 1992)

Kosiakova, E. I., "Epidemiia tifa v Novonikolaevske nachala 1920-kh gg. kak aspekt ekstremal'noi povsednevnosti," http://sib-subethnos.narod.ru/p2005/kosykova.htm (last accessed May 2013)

Kozulin, A. V., *Demograficheskie protsessy v Zabaikal'e (konets xix–nachalo xx veka)* (Ulan-Ude, 2004)

Kramer, Alan, *Dynamic of Destruction: Culture and Mass Killing in the First World War* (New York, 2007)

Kramer, Paul A., *The Blood of Government: Race, Empire, the United States, and the Philippines* (Chapel Hill, N.C., 2006)

Krauthoff, Bernd, *Ich Befehl! Kampf und Tragödie des Barons Ungern-Sternberg* (Bremen, [1938])

Krilov, V. M., *Kadetskie korpusa i rossiiskie kadety* (St. Petersburg, 1998)

Krinsky, Carol Herselle, *Synagogues of Europe: Architecture, History, Meaning* (New York, 1985)

Kroner, Entoni (Anthony Kröner), *Belaia armiia, chernyi baron: Zhizn' generala Petra Vrangelia* (Moscow, 2011)

Kruchinin, A. S., "'Mongol'skii pokhod' Barona Ungerna: K voprosu o podlinnykh tseliakh i putiakh ikh realizatsii," *Vestnik molodykh uchenykh* (seriia: *Istoricheskie nauki*), no. 1 (2002), 65–71

Kuhn, Philip A., *Chinese among Others: Emigration in Modern Times* (Lanham, Md., 2008)

Kuras, L. V., "Ataman Semenov i 'evreiskii vopros,'" in *Istoriia "beloi" Sibiri: Tezisy vtoroi n nauchnoi konferentsii (4–5 fevralia 1997 g.)* (Kemerovo, 1997), 46–48

Kuz'min, Iu. V., "Russko-Mongol'skie otnosheniia v 1911–1912 godakh i pozitsiia obshchestvennykh krugov Rossii," in Edward H. Kaplan and Donald W. Whisenhunt (eds.), *Opuscala Altaica: Essays Presented in Honor of Henry Schwarz* (Bellingham, Wash., 1994), 393–407

Kuz'min, Iu.V., and K. Demberel, "Russkaia koloniia v Urge (1861–1920) v rossiiskoi istoriografii," in *Diaspory v istoricheskom vremeni i prostranstve; Natsional'naia situatsiia v Vostochnoi Sibdiri; Tezisy dokladov mezhdunarodnoi nauchno- prakticheskoi konferentsii 6–8 oktiabria 1994 g.* (Irkutsk, 1994), 117–21

Kuz'min, S. L., *Istoriia Barona Ungerna: Opyt rekonstruktsii* (Moscow, 2011)

——, O. Batsaikhan, K. Nunami, and M. Tachibana, "Baron Ungern i Iaponiia," *Vostok*, no. 5 (2009), 115–33

——, and L. Iu. Reit, "Zapiski F. A. Ossendovskogo kak istochnik ob istorii Mongolii," *Vostok*, no. 5 (2008), 97–110

Lambert, David, and Alan Lester (eds.), *Colonial Lives across the British Empire: Imperial Careering in the Long Nineteenth Century* (New York, 2006)

Landhaus und Villa in Niederösterreich, 1840–1914 (Vienna, 1982)

Lapin, V. V., et al., *Voennaia stolitsa rossiiskoi imperii v fotografiiakh kontsa xix–nachala xx veka* (St. Petersburg, 2004)

Larin, A. G., *Kitaitsy v Rossii* (Moscow, 2000)

Laruelle, Marlène, "'Zheltaia opasnost'' v rabotakh russikikh natsionalistov nachala veka," in Airapetov, *Russko-iaponskaia voina, 1904–1905,* 579–91

——, *Mythe aryen et rêve imperial dans la Russie du xixème siècle* (Paris, 2005)

——, "'The White Tsar': Romantic Imperialism in Russia's Legitimizing of Conquering the Far East," *Acta Slavica Iaponica* 25 (2008), 113–34

Lary, Diana, *China's Republic* (New York, 2007)

——, "Warlord Studies," *Modern China,* 6, no. 4 (1980), 439–70

Laul, Endel, *Tallinna 1. Keskkool, 1631–1981: NSV Liidu vanima keskkooli minevik ja tänapäev* (Tallinn, 1981)

Lazarev, M. S., *Kurdskii vopros (1891–1917)* (Moscow, 1972)

Lee, Erika, *At America's Gates: Chinese Immigration during the Exclusion Era, 1882–1943* (Chapel Hill, N.C., 2003)

Lee, Robert H. G., *The Manchurian Frontier in Ch'ing History* (Cambridge, Mass., 1970)

Leggett, George, *The Cheka: Lenin's Political Police; The All-Russian Extraordinary Commission for Combatting Counter-Revolution and Sabotage (December 1917 to February 1922)* (New York, 1981)

Lepennies, Wolf, *The Seduction of Culture in German History* (Princeton, N.J., 2006)

Lepore, Jill, "Historians Who Love Too Much: Reflections on Microhistory and Biography," *Journal of American History* 88, no. 1 (2001), 129–44.

Li Bin 李彬, "Shi shu Enqin fan meng suo yinfa de Zhi Feng maodun dou zheng," 试述恩琴犯蒙所引发的直奉矛盾斗争, *Nandou xuetan (renwen shehui kexue xue bao)* 南都学坛 (人文社会科学学报), no. 5 (2002), 14–18

Lieven, Dominic, *The Aristocracy in Europe, 1815–1914* (New York, 1992)

Lincoln, W. Bruce, *The Conquest of a Continent: Siberia and the Russians* (New York, 1994; reprint: Ithaca, 2007)

Lindenmeyr, Adele, "The First Soviet Political Trial: Countess Sofia Panina before the Petrograd Revolutionary Tribunal," *RR* 60, no. 4 (2001), 505–25

Lindström, Fredrik, *Empire and Identity: Biographies of the Austrian State Problem in the Late Habsburg Empire* (West Lafayette, Ind., 2008)

Lishtovannyi, E. I., *Istoricheskie vzaimootnosheniia Sibiri i Mongolii: Kul'tura i obshchestvo (xix v.–30-e gg. xx v.)* (Ulan-Ude, 1988)

Litvin, Aleksei, *Krasnyi i belyi terror v Rossii, 1918–1922 gg.* (Moscow, 2004)

Liu Guojun 刘国俊, "19 shiji mo Kebuduo maimaicheng ji lü Meng shang," 19 世纪末科布多买卖城及旅蒙商, *Wenshi yuekan* 文史月刊, no. 7 (2007), 42–43

Liu, Xiaoyuan, *Frontier Passages: Ethnopolitics and the Rise of Chinese Communism, 1921–1945* (Washington, D.C., 2004)

——, *Reins of Liberation: An Entangled History of Mongolian Independence, Chinese Territoriality, and Great Power Hegemony, 1911–1950* (Washington, D.C. and Stanford, Calif., 2006)

Liulevicius, Vejas Gabriel, *War Land on the Eastern Front: Culture, National Identity, and German Occupation in World War I* (New York, 2000)

Leong, Sow-Theng, *Sino-Soviet Diplomatic Relations, 1917–1926* (Honolulu, 1976)

Leonhard, Jörn, and Christian Wieland (eds.), *What Makes the Nobility Noble? Comparative Perspectives from the Sixteenth to the Twentieth Century* (Göttingen, 2011)

Lobanov, V., *Staraia Chita: Dokumental'nyi rasskaz* (2nd rev. ed.; Chita, 2003)

Lohr, Eric, "The Russian Army and the Jews: Mass Deportation, Hostages, and Violence during World War I," *RR* 60, no. 3 (2001), 404–19

——, *Nationalizing the Russian Empire: The Campaign against Enemy Aliens during World War I* (Cambridge, Mass., 2003)

——, "1915 and the War Pogrom Paradigm in the Russian Empire," in Dekel-Chen, Gaunt, Meir, and Bartal, *Anti-Jewish Violence,* 41–51

——, *Russian Citizenship: From Empire to Soviet Union* (Cambridge, Mass., 2012)

Lomakina, I. I., *Golova Dzha-Lamy* (Ulan-Ude and St. Petersburg, 1993)

——, *Groznye makhakaly vostoka* (Moscow, 2004)

——, *Mongol'skaia stolitsa, staraia i novaia (i uchast'e Rossii v ee sud'be)* (Moscow, 2006)

Lopez, Donald S., Jr., *Prisoners of Shangri-La: Tibetan Buddhism and the West* (Chicago, 1998)

Lukin, Alexander, *The Bear Watches the Dragon: Russia's Perceptions of China and the Evolution of Russian-Chinese Relations since the Eighteenth Century* (Armonk, N.Y., 2003)

Luzianin, S. G., "Rossiia i Khalkha Mongoliia: Opyt ekonomicheskoi i politicheskoi integratsii (nachalo xx v.–1917 g.)," in *Rossiia i vostok: Problem vzaimodeistviia* (Cheliabinsk, 1995), 79–81

Mabire, Jean, *Ungern, le dieu de la guerre: La chevauchée du general-baron Roman Feodorovitch von Ungern-Sternberg, du Golfe de Finlande au desert de Gobi* (Paris, 1987)

——, *Ungern: L'heritier blanc de Gengis Khan* (Rouen, 1997)

Magocsi, Paul Robert, "Galicia: A European Land," in Paul Robert Magocsi and Christopher Hann (eds.), *Galicia: A Multicultured Land* (Toronto, 2005), 3–21

Maistre, Louis, de, *Dans les coulisses de l'Agartha: L'extraordinaire mission de Ferdinand Anton Ossendowski en Mongolie* (Milan, 2010)

Majer, Szusza, and Krizstina Teleki, "Monasteries and Temples of Bogdiin Kh'ree, Ikh Kh'ree or Urga, the Old Capital City of Mongolia in the First Part of the Twentieth Century" (Unpublished paper, 2006)

Mak, Geert, *In Europe: Travels through the Twentieth Century* (New York, 2008)

Makoto, Tachibana, *Mongolyn martagdsan tuukh: Bogd Khaant zasgiin gazar (1911–1921)* (Ulaanbaatar, 2011)

Manela, Erez, *The Wilsonian Moment: Self-Determination and the International Origins of Anticolonial Nationalism* (New York, 2007)

Marks, Steven. G., *Road to Power: The Trans-Siberian Railroad and the Colonization of Asian Russia, 1850–1917* (Ithaca, 1991)

Martin, Terry, *The Affirmative Action Empire: Nations and Nationalisms in the Soviet Union, 1923–1939* (Ithaca, 2001)

——, "An Affirmative Action Empire: The Soviet Union as the Highest Stage of Imperialism," in Terry Martin and Ronald Grigor Suny (eds.), *A State of Nations: Empire and Nation-Making in the Age of Lenin and Stalin* (New York, 2001), 67–90

Mashkin, N. A., *Vysshaia voennaia shkola rossiiskoi imperii, xix–nachala xx veka* (Moscow, 1997)

Masoero, Alberto, "Territorial Colonization in Late Imperial Russia: Stages in the Evolution of a Concept," *Kritika* 14, no. 1 (2013), 59–91

Matsusaka, Yoshihisa Tak, *The Making of Japanese Manchuria, 1904–1932* (Cambridge, Mass., 2001)

Mawdsley, Evan, *The Russian Civil War* (2nd ed.; New York, 2007)

Mayer, Arno J., *The Persistence of the Old Regime* (New York, 1981)

McClelland, James C., *Autocrats and Academics: Education, Culture, and Society in Tsarist Russia* (Chicago, 1979)

McCormack, Gavan, *Chang Tso-lin in Northeast China, 1911–1928: China, Japan, and the Manchurian Idea* (Stanford, Calif., 1977)

McCullough, David, "Climbing into Another Head," in Marie Arana (ed.), *The Writing Life: Writers on How They Think and Work; A Collection from the Washington Post Book World* (New York, 2003), 163–67

McGetchin, Douglas T., *Indology, Indomania, and Orientalism: Ancient India's Rebirth in Modern Germany* (Madison, N.J., 2009)

McNeal, Robert H., *Tsar and Cossack, 1855–1914* (New York, 1987)

McReynolds, Louise, *The News under Russia's Old Regime: The Development of a Mass-Circulation Press* (Princeton, N.J., 1991)

Meinig, D. W., *The Shaping of America: A Geographical Perspective on 500 Years of History*, vol. 3, *Transcontinental America, 1850–1915* (New Haven, Conn., 1998)

Miasnikov, V. S., *Imperiia Tsin i russkoe gosudarstvo v xvii veke* (Moscow, 1980)

Michałowski, Witold St., *Testament Barona* (Warsaw, 1972)

Middleton, Nicholas J., *The Bloody Baron: The Wicked Dictator of the East* (London, 2001)

Miliakova, L. V. (ed.), *Kniga pogromov: Pogromy na Ukraine, v Belorussii i evropeiskoi chasti Rossii v period grazhdanskoi voiny, 1918–1922 gg.; Sbornik dokumentov* (Moscow, 2007)

Miller, Aleksei, *Imperiia Romanovykh i natsionalizm: Esse po metodologii istoricheskogo issledovaniia* (Moscow, 2006)

Miller, Alexei, and Alfred J. Rieber (eds.), *Imperial Rule* (New York, 2004)

Miller, Stuart Creighton, *Benevolent Assimilation: The American Conquest of the Philippines, 1899–1903* (New Haven, Conn., 1984)

Mirfendereski, Guive, *A Diplomatic History of the Caspian Sea: Treaties, Diaries, and Other Stories* (New York, 2001)

Mironov, B. N., *Sotsial'naia istoriia Rossii perioda imperii (xviii–nachalo xx v.)* (St. Petersburg, 1999)

Miyazaki, Ichisada, *China's Examination Hell: The Civil Service Examination in Imperial China* (New York, 1976)

Mnogonatsional'nyi Peterburg: Istoriia, religii, narody (St. Petersburg, 2003)

Moiseev, V. A., *Rossiia i Kitai v Tsentral'noi Azii (vtoraia polovina xix v.–1917 g.)* (Barnaul, 2003)

Montgomery, Robert W., "Buriat Social and Political Activism in the 1905 Revolution," *Sibirica* 10, no. 3 (2011), 1–28

Morton, Frederic, *A Nervous Splendor: Vienna, 1888/1889* (New York, 1980)

Moses, Larry William, *The Political Role of Mongol Buddhism* ([Bloomington, Ind.], 1977)

Mosse, George L., *The Image of Man: The Creation of Modern Masculinity* (New York, 1996)

Münzer, Edith, *Als die Stadt noch am Land war: Grazer Bezirke erzählen; St. Leonhard, Geidorf, Jakomini* (Graz, 1978)

Musafumi, Asada, "The China-Russia-Japan Military Balance in Manchuria, 1906–1918," *Modern Asia Studies* 44, no. 6 (2010), 1283–1311

Naimark, Norman M., *Fires of Hatred: Ethnic Cleansing in Twentieth-Century Europe* (Cambridge, Mass., 2001)

Nakami, Tatsuo, "A Protest against the Concept of the 'Middle Kingdom': The Mongols and the 1911 Revolution," in Eto Shinkichi and Harold Z. Schiffrin (eds.), *The 1911 Revolution in China: Interpretive Essays* (Tokyo, 1984), 129–49

——, "Babujab and His Uprising: Re-examining the Inner Mongol Struggle for Independence," *The Memoirs of the Toyo Bunko* (The Oriental Library), no. 57 (1999), 137–53

——, "New Trends in the Study of Modern Mongolian History: What Effect Have Political and Social Changes Had on Historical Research?" *Acta Asiatica*, no. 76 (1999), 7–39

——, Ts. Batbayar, and J. Boldbataar, "Mongolia," in Chahryar Adle, et al. (eds.), *History of the Civilizations of Central Asia*, vol. 6, *Towards the Contemporary Period: From the Mid-Nineteenth to the End of the Twentieth Century* (Paris, 2005), 336–67

Nam, I. V., *Natsional'nye men'shinstva Sibiri i Dal'nego Vostoka na istoricheskom perelome (1917–1922)* (Tomsk, 2009)

Narangoa, Li, "The Power of Imagination: Whose Northeast and Whose Manchuria?" *Inner Asia*, 4, no. 1 (2002), 3–25

Narskii, Igor, "Konstruirovanie mifa o grazhdanskoi voine v rannei sovetskoi Rossii (na primere, Urala v 1917–1922 gg.)," in Iuliia Khmelevskaia (comp.), *Rossiia i voina v xx stoletii: Vzgliad iz udaliaiushcheisia perpektivy* (Moscow, 2005), 79–85

Nathans, Benjamin, *Beyond the Pale: The Jewish Encounter with Late Imperial Russia* (Berkeley and Los Angeles, 2002)

Nemerov, Valerii, *Progulki po staroi Chite* (Chita, 2010)

Nesterova, E. I., "Stranitsy istorii sozdaniia kitaiskikh kvartalov v russkikh dal'nevostochnykh gorodakh v kontse xix–nachale xx vv." in Bolotin and Zabiiako (eds.), *Rossiia i Kitai na dal'nevostochnykh rubezhakh*, vol. 2, 57–62

——, "Atlantida gorodskogo masshtaba: Kitaiskie kvartaly v dal'nevostochnykh gorodakh (konets xix–nachalo xx v.)," *Etnograficheskoe obozrenie*, no. 4 (2008), 44–58

Neuschäffer, Hubertus, *Schlösser und Herrenhäuser in Estland* (Pöln, 1993)

Niamdorzh, B., *Khovdyn khiazgaar, 1911–1919 on* (Ulaanbaatar, 2006)

Nikitin, S. A., *Slavianskie komitety v Rossii, 1858–1876* (Moscow, 1960)

Norris, Stephen M., *A War of Images: Russian Popular Prints, Wartime Culture, and National Identity, 1812–1945* (DeKalb, Ill., 2006)

——, and Willard Sunderland (eds.), *Russia's People of Empire: Life Stories from Eurasia, 1500 to the Present* (Bloomington, Ind., 2012)

Nye, Robert A., *The Origins of Crowd Psychology: Gustave Le Bon and the Crisis of Mass Democracy in the Third Republic* (London, 1975)

O'Donnell, Krista, Renate Bridenthal, and Nancy Reagin (eds.), *The Heimat Abroad: The Boundaries of Germanness* (Ann Arbor, Mich., 2005)

Ogborn, Miles, *Global Lives: Britain and the World, 1550–1800* (New York, 2008)

Okulewicz, Piotr, *Koncepcja "miedzymorza" w myśli i praktyce politycznej obozu Józefa Piłsudskiego w latach 1918–1926* (Poznan, 2001)

Onon, Urgunge, and Derrick Pritchatt, *Asia's First Modern Revolution: Mongolia Proclaims Its Independence in 1911* (Leiden, 1997)

Ontiveros, José Luis, "Ungern-Khan," in Ontiveros, *El Húsar Negro* (Mexico City, 1999), 77–90

O'Rourke, Shane, *The Cossacks* (Manchester, 2007)

Pagden, Anthony, "Europe: Conceptualizing a Continent," in Pagden (ed.), *The Idea of Europe: From Antiquity to the European Union* (New York, 2002), 33–54

Paine, S. C. M., *Imperial Rivals: China, Russia, and Their Disputed Frontier* (Armonk, N.Y., 1996)

——, "The Chinese Eastern Railway from the First Sino-Japanese War until the Russo-Japanese War," in Bruce A. Elleman and Stephen Kotkin (eds.), *Manchurian Railways and the Opening of China: An International History* (Armonk, N.Y., 2010), 13–36

Palmer, James, *The Bloody White Baron: The Extraordinary Story of a Russian Nobleman Who Became the Last Khan of Mongolia* (New York, 2011)

Pares, Bernard, *The Fall of the Russian Monarchy: A Study of the Evidence* (1939; New York, 1961)

Pavlik, Valerii, *Dolgii put' na Amur: Erofei Khabarov i ego "voisko"* (Khabarovsk, 2004)

Pavlov, Iu. A., "General V. M. Molchanov: Zhizn' i sud'ba," in N. I. Ruban et al. (eds.), *Iz istorii grazhdanskoi voiny na Dal'nem Vostoke (1918–1922 gg.): Sbornik nauchnykh stat'ei* (Khabarovsk, 2002), 77–83

Perdue, Peter C., *China Marches West: The Qing Conquest of Central Eurasia* (Cambridge, Mass., 2005)

Pereira, N. G. O., *White Siberia: The Politics of Civil War* (Buffalo, 1996)

Pethybridge, Roger W., *One Step Backward, Two Steps Forward: Soviet Society and Politics in the New Economic Policy* (New York, 1990)

Petrov, Alexandre, "Les Chinois à Kiakhta (1728–1917)," in *Une Russie plurielle*, 361–91

Petrovskii-Shtern, Iokhanan, *Evrei v russkoi armii, 1827–1914* (Moscow, 2003)

Pieber, Anita, "Villen und Gartenanlagen in Graz Geidorf, 1840–1900" (Master's thesis, Karl-Franzens University, Graz, 1999)

Pikkov, Lui, "1905. aasta Raplamaal," in Hans Treimann and Tiina Treimann (eds.), *Rännud Raplamaa minevikku: Koduloolisi uurimusi ja mälestusi* ([Rapla], 2006), 197–214

Pintner, Walter M. "The Nobility and the Officer Corps in the Nineteenth Century," in Eric Lohr and Marshall Poe (eds.), *The Military and Society in Russia, 1450–1917* (Leiden, 2002), 241–52

Pipes, Richard, *The Formation of the Soviet Union: Communism and Nationalism, 1917–1923* (2nd ed.; Cambridge, Mass., 1997)

Pirang, Heinz, *Das baltische Herrenhaus* (1928; Riga, 1977), 3 vols.

Pistohlkors, Gert, von, "Die Ostseeprovinzen unter russischer Herrschaft (1710/95–1914)," in von Pistohlkors (ed.), *Deutsche Geschichte im Osten Europas: Baltische Länder* (Berlin, 1994), 266–450

Pivovarov, Mikhail Sergeevich, "Revoliutsionnye tribunaly v Sibiri (noiabr' 1919–ianvar' 1923 g.)" (PhD diss. abstract [avtoreferat]; Kemerovo, 2007)

Plamper, Jan, "Fear: Soldiers and Emotion in Early Twentieth-Century Russian Military Psychology," *SR* 68, no. 2 (2009), 259–83

Platt, Stephen R., *Autumn in the Heavenly Kingdom: China, the West, and the Epic Story of the Taiping Civil War* (New York, 2012)

Polonsky, Rachel, *Molotov's Magic Lantern: Travels in Russian History* (New York, 2010)

Popelka, Franz, *Geschichte der Stadt Graz* (Graz, 1959–1960), 2 vols.

Porshneva, O. S., "Rossiiskii krest'ianin v pervoi mirovoi voine (1914–fevral' 1917)," in I. V. Narskii and O. Iu Nikonova (eds.), *Chelovek i voina: Voina kak iavlenie kul'tury* (Moscow, 2001), 190–216

Powis, Jonathan, *Aristocracy* (Oxford, 1984)

Pozner, Vladimir, *Bloody Baron: The Story of Ungern-Sternberg* (New York, 1938)

Prusin, Alexander V., *Nationalizing a Borderland: War, Ethnicity, and Anti-Jewish Violence in East Galicia, 1914–1920* (Tuscaloosa, Ala., 2005)

Qi Xuejun 祁学俊 and Han Laixing 韩来兴, "Mingguo shiqi de Heihe yu Hailanpao bianjing maoyi," 民国时期的黑河与海兰泡边境贸易 *Heihe Xuekan* 黑河学刊, no. 4 (1989), 51–79

Quenoy, Paul, du, "Warlordism à la russe: Baron von Ungern-Sternberg's Anti-Bolshevik Crusade, 1917–1921," *Revolutionary Russia* 16, no. 2 (2003), 1–27

——, "Perfecting the Show Trial: The Case of Baron von Ungern-Sternberg," *Revolutionary Russia* 19, no. 1 (2006), 79–93

Quested, R. K. I., *"Matey Imperialists"? The Tsarist Russians in Manchuria, 1895–1917* (Hong Kong, 1982)

Raleigh, Donald J., *Experiencing Russia's Civil War: Politics, Society, and Revolutionary Culture in Saratov, 1917–1922* (Princeton, N.J., 2002)

Randolph, John, *The House in the Garden: The Bakunin Family and the Romance of Russian Idealism* (Ithaca, 2006)

Ransel, David, *A Russian Merchant's Tale: The Life and Adventures of Ivan Alekseevich Tolchënov, Based on His Diary* (Bloomington, Ind., 2009)

Raskin, D., "Evrei v sostave rossiiskogo ofitserskogo korpusa v xix–nachale xx veka," in D. A. El'iashevich (ed.), *Evrei v Rossii: Istoriia i kul'tura; Sbornik nauchnykh trudov* (St. Petersburg, 1998), 170–74

Raun, Toivo U., "The Estonians," in Edward C. Thaden (ed.), *Russification in the Baltic Provinces and Finland, 1855–1914* (Princeton, N.J., 1981), 287–354

——, *Estonia and the Estonians* (2nd rev. ed.; Stanford, Calif., 2001)

Rayfield, Donald, *The Dream of Lhasa: The Life of Nicholai Przhevalskii, Explorer of Central Asia* (London, 1976)

Reardon-Anderson, James, *Reluctant Pioneers: China's Expansion Northward, 1644–1937* (Stanford, Calif., 2005)

Reifman, Irina, *Ritualized Violence Russian Style: The Duel in Russian Culture and Literature* (Stanford, Calif, 1999)

Remnev, A. V., "Samoderzhavie i Sibir' v kontse xix–nachale xx veka: Problemy regional'nogo upravleniia," *OI*, no. 2 (1994), 60–73

——, *Rossiia Dal'nego Vostoka: Imperskaia geografiia vlasti, xix–nachala xx vekov* (Omsk, 2004)

Remsu, Olev, *Kindralleitnant Robert Roman Ungern-Sternberg: Hiiumaa parun, kellel oli maailma suurim varandus ning kes tahtis vallutada Euroopa* (Pärnu, 1999)

Rendle, Matthew, *Defenders of the Motherland: The Tsarist Elite in Revolutionary Russia* (New York, 2010)

Reynolds, Michael A., *Shattering Empires: The Clash and Collapse of the Ottoman and Russian Empires, 1908–1918* (New York, 2011)

Rhoads, Edward J. M., *Manchus and Han: Ethnic Relations and Political Power in Late Qing and Early Republican China, 1861–1928* (Seattle, 2000)

Rich, David Alan, *The Tsar's Colonels: Professionalism, Strategy, and Subversion in Late Imperial Russia* (Cambridge, Mass., 1998)

Riffenburgh, Beau, *The Myth of the Explorer: The Press, Sensationalism, and Geographical Discovery* (New York, 1994)

Riga, Liliana, "Ethnonationalism, Assimilation, and the Social Worlds of the Jewish Bolsheviks in Fin-de-Siècle Tsarist Russia," *Comparative Studies in Society and History* 48, no. 4 (2006), 762–97

Robinson, Paul, "Courts of Honour in the Late Imperial Russian Army," *SEER* 84, no. 4 (2006), 708–28

Rodigina, I. I., *"Drugaia Rossiia": Obraz Sibiri v russkoi zhurnal'noi presse vtoroi polovine xix–nachala xx veka* (Novosibirsk, 2006)

Rodrique, Aaron, "L'état impérial ottoman et les politiques de deportation," in Bertrand Badie and Yves Déloye (eds.), *Le temps de l'état: Mélanges en l'honneur de Pierre Birnbaum* (Paris 2007), 185–202

Rogger, Hans, *Jewish Policies and Right-Wing Politics in Imperial Russia* (Berkeley and Los Angeles, 1986)

Romanova, Viktoriia, "Rossiiskie Evrei v Kharbine," *Diaspory*, no. 1 (1999), 115–42

——, *Vlast' i Evrei na Dal'nem Vostoke Rossii: Istoriia vzaimootnoshenii (vtoraia polovina xix v.–20-e gody xx v.)* (Krasnoiarsk, 2001)

Rönnqvist, Ronny, *Baron Ungern, Mongoliets härskare* (Helsinki, 2006)

Roosevelt, Priscilla, *Life on the Russian Country Estate: A Social and Cultural History* (New Haven, Conn., 1995)

Rossabi, Morris, "Sino-Mongol Border: From Conflict to Precarious Resolution," in Bruce A. Elleman, Stephen Kotkin, and Clive Schofield (eds.), *Beijing's Power and China's Borders: Twenty Neighbors in Asia* (Armonk, N.Y., 2012), 169–89

Rossiiskoe kazachestvo: Nauchno-spravochnoe izdanie (Moscow, 2003)

Rosenthal, Bernice Glatzer, *New Myth, New World: From Nietzsche to Stalin* (University Park, Penn., 2002)

Roshwald, Aviel, *Ethnic Nationalism and the Fall of Empires: Central Europe, Russia, and the Middle East, 1914–1923* (New York, 2001)

Rothschild, Emma, *The Inner Life of Empires: An Eighteenth-Century History* (Princeton, N.J., 2011)

Rowe, William T., *China's Last Empire: The Great Qing* (Cambridge, Mass., 2009)

Rozenblit, Marsha, *Reconstructing a National Identity: The Jews of Habsburg Austria during World War I* (New York, 2001)

Rupen, Robert A., "The Buriat Intelligentsia," *The Far Eastern Quarterly* 15, no. 3 (1956), 383–98

Ryan, James, "'Revolution Is War': The Development of the Thought of V. I. Lenin on Violence, 1899–1907," *SEER* 89, no. 2 (2011), 248–73

Saaler, Sven, "The Construction of Regionalism in Modern Japan: Kodera Kenkichi and His 'Treatise on Greater Asianism,'" *Modern Asian Studies* 41, no. 6 (2007), 1261–94

Sablé, Erik, *Ungern* (Series: *Qui suis-je?*) (Paris, 2006)

Sablinsky, Walter, *The Road to Bloody Sunday: Father Gapon and the St. Petersburg Massacre of 1905* (Princeton, N.J., 1976)

Sambueva, L. V., *Buriatskoe i evenkiiskoe kazachestvo na strazhe otechestva: Vtoraia chetvert' xviii–pervaia polovina xix vv.* (Ulan-Ude, 2003)

Sammartino, Annemarie H., *The Impossible Border: Germany and the East, 1914–1922* (Ithaca, 2010)

Samodelkin, V. A., "Antisemitskaia propaganda v sibirskoi armii (po dokumentam Natsional'nogo Soveta Evreev, Sibiri i Urala," in *Istoriia "beloi" Sibiri: Tezisy nauchnoi konferentsii (7–8 fevralia 1995 g.)* (Kemerovo, 1995), 56–58

Sanborn, Joshua A., *Drafting the Russian Nation: Military Conscription, Total War, and Mass Politics, 1905–1925* (DeKalb, Ill., 2003)

——, "Unsettling the Empire: Violent Migrations and Social Disaster in Russia during World War I," *JMH* 77, no. 2 (2005), 290–324

Sandag, Sh., "Politicheskoe i ekonomicheskoe polozhenie vneshnei Mongolii v kontse xix–nachale xx v.," *Mongol'skii sbornik: Ekonomika, istoriia, arkheologiia* (Moscow, 1959), 126–38

Sandgruber, Roman, *Österreichische Agrarstatistik, 1750–1918* (Vienna, 1978)

Särg, Alo, *Hiiumaa mõisad ja mõisnikud* (Tallinn, 2006)

——, *Raplamaa mõisad ja mõisnikud* (Tallinn, 2007)

Sargeant, Howard. "Diasporic Citizens: Germans Abroad in the Framing of German Citizenship Law," in O'Donnell et al., *Heimat Abroad*, 17–39

Sattin, Anthony, *The Gates of Africa: Death, Discovery, and the Search for Timbuktu* (New York, 2005)

Savelli, Dany, "Kiakhta, ou l'épaisseur de la frontière," in *Une Russie plurielle*, 271–338

Schell, Orville, *Virtual Tibet: Searching for Shangri-La from the Himalayas to Hollywood* (New York, 2000)

Schenk, Frithjof Benjamin, *Aleksandr Nevskij: Heiliger-Fürst-Nationalheld; Eine Erinnerungsfigur im russischen kulturellen Gedächtnis (1263–2000)* (Cologne, 2004)

Schimmelpenninck van der Oye, David, *Toward the Rising Sun: Russian Ideologies of Empire and the Path to War with Japan* (DeKalb, Ill., 2001)

——, *Russian Orientalism: Asia in the Russian Mind from Peter the Great to the Emigration* (New Haven, Conn., 2010)

Schönfeldt, Alfred, "Deutsche Sprache und gesellschaftliche Ordnung im Baltikum," in Walther Mitzka (ed.), *Wortgeographie und Gesellschaft* (Berlin, 1968), 660–77

Schorkowitz, Dittmar, "The Orthodox Church, Lamaism, and Shamanism among the Buriats and Kalmyks, 1825–1925," in Robert P. Geraci and Michael Khodarkovsky (eds.), *Of Religion and Empire: Missions, Conversions, and Tolerance in Tsarist Russia* (Ithaca, 2001), 201–25

Schorske, Carl E., *Fin-de-Siècle Vienna: Politics and Culture* (New York, 1980)

Schuster, Ulrike, *Verlorenes Graz: Eine Spurensuche im 19. und 20. Jahrhundert nach demolierten Bauwerken und Denkmalen der Steierischen Landeshauptstadt* (Vienna, 1997)

Scott, James C., "State Simplifications: Nature, Science, People," in Ian Shapiro and Russell Hardin (eds.), *Political Order* (New York, 1996), 42–85

Serruys, Henry, "An Imperial Restoration in Ordos, 1916–1917," *Études mongoles et sibériennes*, no. 16 (1985), 51–59

Sergeev, O. I., *Kazachestvo na russkom Dal'nem Vostoke v xvii–xix vv.* (Moscow, 1983)

Service, Robert, *Spies and Commissars: The Early Years of the Russian Revolution* (New York, 2012)

Seuberlich, Wolfgang, *Zur Verwaltungsgeschichte der Mandschurei (1644–1930)* (Hartmut Walraveng, ed.) (Wiesbaden, 2001)

Sha E qin Hua shi 沙俄侵华史 (2nd ed; Beijing, 2007), 4 vols.

Sharp, Jane Ashton, *Russian Modernism between East and West: Natal'ia Goncharova and the Moscow Avant-Garde* (New York, 2006)

Shaumian, Tatiana, *Tibet: The Great Game and Tsarist Russia* (New Delhi, 2000)

Shaw, Stanford J., *The Ottoman Empire in World War I*, vol. 1, *Prelude to War* (Ankara, 2006)

Sheehan, James J., *Where Have All the Soldiers Gone? The Transformation of Modern Europe* (Boston, 2008)

Shen Jian 沈坚, "Hailanpao de E ming shiyi" 海兰泡的俄名释义, *Eluosi yanjiu* 俄罗斯研究, no. 5 (2010), 135–38

Shereshevskii, B. M., *Razgrom Semenovshchiny (aprel'–noiabr' 1920 g.)* (Novosibirsk, 1966)

Shirendyb, B., *Mongoliia na rubezhe xix–xx vekov: Storiia sotsial'no-ekonomicheskogo razvitiia)* (Ulan Bator, 1963)

Shishkin, V. I., *Revoliutsionnye komitety Sibiri v gody grazhdanskoi voiny (avgust 1919–mart 1921 g.)* (Novosibirsk, 1978)

Shishov, A. V., "Kavkazskii front," in V. L. Mal'kov (ed.), *Pervaia mirovaia voina: Prolog, xx veka* (Moscow, 1998), 578–588

——, *Ungern: Demon mongol'skikh stepei; Roman* (Moscow, 2005)

Shoumatoff, Nicholas, and Nina Shoumatoff, *The Alps: Europe's Mountain Heart* (Ann Arbor, Mich., 2001)

Showalter, Dennis E., *Tannenberg: Clash of Empires, 1914* (Washington, D.C., 2004)

Shubin, A. S., *Kratkii ocherk etnicheskoi istorii evenkov Zabaikal'ia xvii–xx vv.* (Ulan-Ude, 1973)

Shuklentsov, V. T., *Grazhdanskaia voina na territorii Novosibirskoi oblasti* (Novosibirsk, 1970)

Shulunov, F., *K istorii Buriat-Mongol'skogo kazachestva (kratkii ocherk)* (Ulan-Ude, 1936)

Sibir' v sostave rossiiskoi imperii (Moscow, 2007)

Siegel, Jennifer, *Endgame: Britain, Russia, and the Final Struggle for Central Asia* (New York, 2002)

Siegelbaum, Lewis H., "Another Yellow Peril: Chinese Migrants in the Russian Far East and the Russian Reaction before 1917," *Modern Asian Studies* 12, no. 2 (1978), 307–30

Simmel, Georg, *On Individuality and Social Forms: Selected Writings* (ed. Donald N. Levine) (Chicago, 1971)

Sinichenko, V. V., "Kontrabanda spirta i narkotikov na russko-kitaiskoi granitse (vtoraia polovina xix–nachalo xx vekov)," http://mion.isu.ru/pub/power/2.html (last accessed September 28, 2008)

Sked, Alan, *The Decline and Fall of the Habsburg Empire, 1815–1918* (2nd ed.; Harlow, Eng., 2001)

Skrynnikova, T. D., *Lamaistskaia tserkov' i gosudarstvo: Vneshniaia Mongoliia xvi–nachalo xx veka* (Novosibirsk, 1988)

Slezkine, Yuri, *Arctic Mirrors: Russia and the Small Peoples of the North* (Ithaca, 1994)

——, *The Jewish Century* (Princeton, N.J., 2004)

Slocum, John W., "Who, and When, Were the Inorodtsy? The Evolution of the Category of 'Aliens' in Imperial Russia," *RR* 57, no. 2 (1998), 173–90

Smele, Jonathan D., *Civil War in Siberia: The Anti-Bolshevik Government of Admiral Kolchak, 1918–1920* (New York, 1996)

Smirnov, Nikolai, *Zabaikal'skie kazaki v otnosheniiakh Rossii s kitaem i mongoliei* (Volgograd, 1999)

——, *Zabaikal'skoe kazachestvo* (Moscow, 2008)

Smirnova, T. M., *Natsional'nost'–Piterskie: Natsional'nye men'shinstva Peterburga i Leningradskoi oblasti v xx veke* (St. Petersburg, 2002)

Sneath, David, and Christopher Kaplonski (eds.), *The History of Mongolia,* vol. 3, *The Qing Period, Twentieth-Century Mongolia* (Folkstone, Eng., 2010)

Snelling, John, *Buddhism in Russia: The Story of Avgan Dorzhiev, Lhasa's Emissary to the Tsar* (Shaftesbury, Eng., 1993)

Snyder, Timothy, *The Red Prince: The Secret Lives of a Habsburg Duke* (New York, 2010)

Sobolev, I. G., *Bor'ba s "nemetskim zasil'em" v Rossii v gody pervoi mirovoi voiny* (St. Petersburg, 2004)

Solov'ev, F. V., *Kitaiskoe otkhodnichestvo na Dal'nem Vostoke Rossii v epokhu kapitalizma (1861–1917 gg.)* (Moscow, 1989)

Sorokina, Tatiana, "Kitaiskie kvartaly dal'nevostochnykh gorodov (konets xix–nachalo xx v.)," *Diaspory,* nos. 2/3 (2001), 54–74

Spence, Jonathan D., *The Search for Modern China* (New York, 1990)

Stanislawski, Michael, *For Whom Do I Toil? Judah Leib Gordon and the Crisis of Russian Jewry* (New York, 1988)

Stein, Hans-Peter, "Der Offizier des russischen Heeres im Zeitabschnitt zwischen Reform und Revolution (1861–1905)," *FzOG* 13 (1967), 346–507

Steinberg, Mark D., and Vladimir M. Khrustalev, *The Fall of the Romanovs: Political Dreams and Personal Struggles in a Time of Revolution* (New Haven, Conn., 1995)

Stekl, Hannes, "Zwischen Machtverlust und Selbstbehauptung: Österreichs Hocharistokratie vom 18. bis ins 20. Jahrhundert," in Hans-Ulrich Wehler (ed.), *Europäischer Adel, 1750–1950* (Göttingen, 1990), 144–65

Stem, Dieter, "Myths and Facts about the Kiakhta Trade Pidgin," in Eva-Marie Stolberg (ed.), *The Siberian Saga: A History of Russia's Wild East* (Frankfurt, 2005), 63–72

Stepanov, N. N., "Prisoedinenie Vostochnoi Sibiri v xvii v. i tungusskie plemena," in *Russkoe naselenie Pomor'ia i Sibiri (period feodalizma)* (Moscow, 1973), 106–24

Stephan, John J., *The Russian Far East: A History* (Stanford, Calif., 1994)

Stevens, Keith, "Between Scylla and Charybdis: China and the Chinese during the Russo-Japanese War, 1904–1905," *Journal of the Hong Kong Branch of the Royal Asiatic Society* 43 (2003), 127–62

Stites, Richard, *Russian Popular Culture: Entertainment and Society since 1900* (New York, 1992)

——, "Russian Representations of the Japanese Enemy," in John W. Steinberg, et al. (eds.), *The Russo-Japanese War in Global Perspective: World War Zero* (Leiden, 2005), 395–410

Stockdale, Melissa K., "'My Death for the Motherland Is Happiness': Women, Patriotism, and Soldiering in Russia's Great War," *AHR* 109, no. 1 (2004), 78–116

Stolberg, Eva-Maria, *Sibirien: Russlands "Wilder Osten"; Mythos und soziale Realität im 19. und 20. Jahrhundert* (Stuttgart, 2009)

Strelianov (Kalabukhov), P. N., *Kazaki v Persii, 1909–1918* (Moscow, 2007)

Sunderland, Willard, "Russians into Iakuts? 'Going Native' and Problems of Russian National Identity in the Siberian North, 1870s–1914," *SR* 55, no. 4 (1996), 806–25

——, "The 'Colonization Question': Visions of Colonization in Late Imperial Russia," *JfGO* 48, no. 2 (2000), 210–32

Suny, Ronald Grigor, "The Holocaust before the Holocaust: Reflections on the Armenian Genocide," in Hans-Lukas Kieser and Dominik J. Schaller (eds.), *Der Völkermord an der Armeniern und die Shoah* (Zurich, 2002), 83–100

——, *The Revenge of the Past: Nationalism, Revolution, and the Collapse of the Soviet Union* (Stanford, Calif., 1993)

——, Fatma Müge Göçek, and Norman M. Naimark (eds.), *A Question of Genocide: Armenians and Turks at the End of Empire* (New York, 2011)

Sutin, Lawrence, *All Is Change: The Two-Thousand-Year Journey of Buddhism to the West* (New York, 2006)

Tanaka, Reiko, "Imperial Dilemma: The Japanese Intervention in Siberia, 1918–1922" (PhD diss., University of Cambridge, 2003)

Taube, Arved, von, Erik Thomson, and Michael Garleff, "Die Deutschbalten— Schicksal und Erbe einer eigenständigen Gemeinschaft," in Wilfried Schlau (ed.), *Die Deutschbalten* (Munich, 1995), 51–115

Taube, Michael, von, *Ungern-Sternberg: Ursprung und Anfänge des Geschlechts in Livland* (Tartu, 1940)

Taylor, Antony, *Lords of Misrule: Hostility to Aristocracy in Late Nineteenth- and Early Twentieth-Century Britain* (Basingstoke, 2004)

Tepliakov, A. G., *Protsedura: Ispolneniia smertnykh prigovorov v 1920–1930-kh godakh* (Moscow, 2007)

Ther, Philipp, "Beyond the Nation: The Relational Basis of a Comparative History of Germany and Europe," *Central European History* 36, no. 1 (2003), 45–73

——. "Imperial Instead of National History: Positioning Modern German History on the Map of European Empires," in Miller and Rieber, *Imperial Rule*, 47–66

Thompson, Richard Austin, *The Yellow Peril, 1890–1924* (New York, 1978)

Timofeev, O. A., *Rossiisko-kitaiskie otnosheniia v Priamur'e (seredina xix–nachalo xx vv.)* (Blagoveshchensk, 2003)

Tolz, Vera, "Imperial Scholars and Minority Nationalisms in Late Imperial and Early Soviet Russia," *Kritika* 10, no. 2 (2009), 261–90

——, *Russia's Own Orient: The Politics of Identity and Oriental Studies in the Late Imperial and Soviet Periods* (New York, 2011)

Torpey, John, *The Invention of the Passport: Surveillance, Citizenship, and the State* (New York, 2000)

Treadgold, Donald W., *The Great Siberian Migration: Government and Peasant in Resettlement from Emancipation to the First World War* (Princeton, N.J., 1957)

Tsvetkov, Vasilii, "Na sopkakh Mongolii: Beloe delo Barona Ungerna," *Rodina*, no. 1 (2005), 49–57

Tweed, Thomas A., *The American Encounter with Buddhism, 1844–1912: Victorian Culture and the Limits of Dissent* (Chapel Hill, N.C., 2000)

Une Russie plurielle: Confins et profondeurs (Special edition of *Études mongoles et sibériennes, centrasiatiques et tibétaines*, vols. 38–39, 2007–2008)

Ungern-Sternberg, Nils, von (comp.), *De Hungaria: Ungern-Sternberg zu Pürkel; Ein Geschlecht im Wandel der Zeiten* (Bamberg, 1979)

Unowsky, Daniel L., *The Pomp and Politics of Patriotism: Imperial Celebrations in Habsburg Austria, 1848–1916* (West Lafayette, Ind., 2005)

Urbansky, Sören, *Kolonialer Wettstreit: Russland, China, Japan und die Ostchinesische Eisenbahn* (Frankfurt, 2008)

Uspenskii, V. L., "Zhurnal *Mongol Sonin Bichig* o sobytiiakh v Mongolii v 1911–1912 godakh," in S. Luvsanvandan (ed.), *Aktual'nye problemy sovremennogo mongolovedeniia* (Ulan Bator, 1987)

Uvarova, T. V., *Nerchinskie evenki v xviii–xx vekakh* (Moscow, 2005)

Uyama, Tomohiko, "A Particularist Empire: The Russian Policies of Christianization and Military Conscription in Central Asia," in Uyama (ed.), *Empire, Islam, and Politics in Central Eurasia* (Sapporo, 2007), 23–63

Vasil'evskii, V. I., *Zabaikal'skoe kazach'e voisko: Kratkii istoricheskii ocherk* (Moscow, 2000)

Verhey, Jeffrey, *The Spirit of 1914: Militarism, Myth, and Mobilization in Germany* (New York, 2000)

Viswanathan, Gauri, *Outside the Fold: Conversion, Modernity, and Belief* (Princeton, N.J., 1998)

Vital, David, *A People Apart: The Jews in Europe, 1789–1939* (New York, 1999)

Vitarbo, Gregory, "Nationality Policy and the Russian Imperial Officer Corps, 1905–1914," *SR* 66, no. 4 (2007), 682–701

Volkov, E. V., *"Gidra kontrrevoliutsii": Beloe dvizhenie v kul'turnoi pamiati sovetskogo obshchestva* (Cheliabinsk, 2008)

Von Hagen, Mark "Confronting Backwardness: Dilemmas of Soviet Officer Education in the Interwar Years, 1918–1941," in Elliott V. Converse III (ed.), *Forging the Sword: Selecting, Educating, and Training Cadets and Junior Officers in the Modern World* (Chicago, 1998), 82–98

——, "The Levée en masse from Russian Empire to Soviet Union, 1874–1938," in Daniel Moran and Arthur Waldron (eds.), *The People in Arms: Military Myth and National Mobilization since the French Revolution* (New York, 2003), 159–88

——, "The Limits of Reform: The Multiethnic Imperial Army Confronts Nationalism, 1874–1917," in David Schimmelpenninck and Bruce W. Menning (eds.), *Reforming the Tsar's Army: Military Innovation from Peter the Great to the Revolution* (Washington, D.C., 2004), 34–55

——, *War in a European Borderland: Occupations and Occupation Plans in Galicia and Ukraine, 1914–1918* (Seattle, 2007)

Vostochno-Prusskaia operatsiia (Moscow, 1939)

Wade, Rex A., *The Russian Revolution, 1917* (2nd ed.; New York, 2005)

Wakeman, Frederic, Jr., *The Fall of Imperial China* (New York, 1979)

Waldron, Arthur, *From War to Nationalism: China's Turning Point, 1924–1925* (New York, 1995)

Walterskirchen, Gudula, *Der vergeborgene Stand: Adel in Österreich heute* (Vienna, 1999)

Washington, Peter, *Madame Blavatsky's Baboon: A History of the Mystics, Mediums, and Misfits Who Brought Spiritualism to America* (New York, 1995)

Watrous, Stephen, "The Regionalist Conception of Siberia, 1860–1920," in Galya Diment and Yuri Slezkine (eds.), *Between Heaven and Hell: The Myth of Siberia in Russian Culture* (New York, 1993), 113–32

Watson, Ellis, *Aristocracy and the Modern World* (Basingstoke, Eng., 2006)

Wcislo, Francis W., *Tales of Imperial Russia: The Life and Times of Sergei Witte, 1849–1915* (New York, 2011)

Weber, Thomas, *Hitler's First War: Adolf Hitler, the Men of the List Regiment, and the First World War* (New York, 2010)

Weiss, Claudia, "Representing the Empire: The Meaning of Siberia for Russian Imperial Identity," *Nationalities Papers* 35, no. 3 (2007), 439–56

Wendland, Anna Veronika, *Die Russophilen in Galizien: Ukrainische Konservativen zwischen Österreich und Russland, 1848–1915* (Vienna, 2001)

Whelan, Heide, *Adapting to Modernity: Family, Caste, and Capitalism among the Baltic German Nobility* (Cologne, 1999)

Wildman, Allan K., *The End of the Russian Imperial Army: The Old Army and the Soldiers' Revolt (March–April 1917)* (Princeton, N.J., 1980)

Wolff, David, *To the Harbin Station: The Liberal Alternative in Russian Manchuria, 1898–1914* (Stanford, Calif., 1999)

——, "Bean There: Toward a Soy-Based History of Northeast Asia," in Thomas Lahusen (ed.), *Harbin and Manchuria: Place, Space, and Identity* (Durham, N.C., 2001), 241–52

Wood, Elizabeth A., "The Trial of Lenin: Legitimating the Revolution through Political Theater, 1920–1923," *RR* 61, no. 2 (2002), 235–48

Woodworth, Bradley D., "Civil Society and Nationality in the Multiethnic Russian Empire: Tallinn/Reval, 1860–1914" (PhD diss., Indiana University, 2003)

——, "Administrative Reform and Social Policy in the Baltic Cities of the Russian Empire: Riga and Reval, 1870–1914," *Jahrbüch für Europäische Verwaltungsgeschichte* 16 (2004), 114–36

Wortman, Richard S., "Moscow and Petersburg: The Problem of Political Center in Tsarist Russia, 1881–1914," in Sean Wilentz (ed.), *Rites of Power: Symbolism, Ritual, and Politics since the Middle Ages* (Philadelphia, Penn., 1985), 244–74

——, *Scenarios of Power: Myth and Ceremony in Russian Monarchy* (Princeton, N.J., 1995–2000), 2 vols.

Wrangell, Wilhelm, von, *Die estländische Ritterschaft, ihre Ritterschaftshauptmänner und Landräte* (Limberg/Lahn, 1967)

Xu Guoqi, *China and the Great War: China's Pursuit of a New National Identity and Internationalization* (New York, 2005)

Xu Shuming 许淑明, "Qing mo Heilongjiang yimin yu nongye kaifa," 请末黑龙江移民与农业开发 *Qing shi yanjiu* 清史研究, no. 2 (1991), 21–25

Yang Chuang 杨闯, Gao Fei 高飞, and Feng Yujun 冯玉军, *Bainian Zhong E guanxi* 百年中俄关系 (Beijing, 2006)

Yonan, Gabriele, *Ein vergessener Holocaust: Die Vernichtung der christlichen Assyrer in der Türkei* (Göttingen, 1989)

Young, Ernest P., *The Presidency of Yuan Shih-k'ai: Liberalism and Dictatorship in Early Republican China* (Ann Arbor, Mich., 1977)

Zaionchkovskii, A. M., *Pervaia mirovaia voina* (St. Petersburg, 2002)

Zaionchkovskii, P. A., S*amoderzhavie i russkaia armiia na rubezhe xix–xx stoletii, 1881–1903* (Moscow, 1973)

Zakharova, L. G., I. U. Kukushkin, and Terence Emmons (eds.), *P. A. Zaionchkovskii, 1904–1983 gg.: Stat'i, publikatsii i vospominaniia o nem* (Moscow, 1998)

Zapadnye okrainy rossiiskoi imperii (Moscow, 2006)

Zarrow, Peter, "Social and Political Developments: The Making of the Twentieth-Century Chinese State," in Kam Louie (ed.), *The Cambridge Companion to Modern Chinese Culture* (New York, 2008), 20–45

Zatsepine, Victor, "The Amur: As River, as Border," in Diana Lary (ed.), *The Chinese State at the Borders* (Vancouver, 2007), 151–61

——, "The Blagoveshchensk Massacre of 1900: The Sino-Russian War and Global Imperialism," in James Flath and Norman Smith (eds.), *Beyond Suffering: Recounting War in Modern China* (Vancouver, 2011), 107–29

Zhacaiping Changsheng 扎采平 常胜 [Victor Zatsepine], "Huaren dui Eluosi yuandong chengshi fazhan de gongxian," 华人对俄罗斯远东城市发展的贡献 *Xiboliya yanjiu* 西伯利亚研究 34, no. 4 (2007), 59–63

Zhang, Qixiong 张启雄, *Wai Meng zhuquan guishu jiaoshe, 1911–1916* 外蒙主权归属交涉 1911–1916 (Taibei, 1995)

——, *Shou fu Wai Meng zhuquan, 1917–1920* 收复外蒙主权 1917–1920 (Taibei, 1998)

Zhao Songqiao, *Physical Geography of China* (New York, 1986)

Zhukov, A., *Oprichnyi Baron* (Ulan-Ude, 2011)

Znamenski, Andrei, *Red Shambhala: Magic, Prophecy, and Geopolitics in the Heart of Asia* (Wheaton, Ill., 2011)

Zyrianov, Pavel, *Admiral Kolchak: Verkhovnyi pravitel' Rossii* (Moscow, 2006)

INDEX

Note: Page numbers followed by *f* indicate a figure.

Romanov Dynasty, 3–4; collapse of, 112, 140, 145, 198, 231, 278n17; executions by Bolsheviks of, 214, 295n22; Michael, Grand Prince of, 4, 140, 145, 189, 198–201; modernizing reforms by, 112; monarchist support of, 187–89, 223, 290n83; three-hundredth anniversary of, 99. *See also* Nicholas II
Rönnqvist, Ronny, 272n7
Rousseau, Jean-Jacques, 39
Rozanov, Vasilii, 24, 124
Russell, Bertrand, 222, 297n46
Russian Baltic region: annexation to Russia of, 19, 26; European-style rule in, 113; German nobility of, 17–20, 25–28, 31–35, 66–67, 132–33, 242n25, 274n30; German occupation of, 130; loyalty considerations in, 76–77; map of, 27f; provinces of, 26; Revolution of 1905 in, 59; Russia's loss of, 149–51; Russification in, 35–42, 246nn31–32, 246n35. *See also* Estland
Russian Empire, 229–33; abolition of serfdom in, 26, 32; adaptable imperialist approaches of, 113–15; annexation of the eastern Baltic region by, 19, 26; borders of, 8, 10–11, 62, 105, 157; collapse of, 7, 129, 141–44, 147–51, 226–27, 231–33; diversity of, 5–7, 66, 75–78, 257nn41–42; Duma of, 58–59, 62, 139–40, 142; East Asian foreign policy of, 114–15; eastward pull of, 51–52, 63–69, 77–78, 94, 230; European identity of, 43–44, 56–58, 252n56; exotic stereotypes of, 104–6, 171–72, 220, 265–66nn8–10; expansion into Mongolia of, 112–23, 268n35; German population of, 36, 44; Jewish segregation in, 97, 130–31, 265n68; linkages and connections within, 10; maps of, xv, 254n2; modernizing reforms in, 112; Persian policies of, 278nn20–21; railways of, 51–55, 64, 66, 250n32, 252n54; Russification policies of, 35–42, 44, 48, 127, 246nn31–32, 246n35; Turkestan uprising of 1916 against, 138, 276n58; Ungern's geographical framing of, 7–11
Russian Far East. *See* Eastern Siberia/Russian Far East
Russian Geographical Society, 192
Russian imperial army: breakdown following February Revolution of, 141–51; Cossack units of, 67–70; elite institutes of, 58–62, 79, 253n69, 253n72, 254n75, 254n77; ethnic units of, 138–39, 147–48, 276nn57–58; non-Russian officers of, 47–48, 60–62, 249n18, 253nn66–67, 254n75; officer corps of, 84–88, 259n6, 260n8, 278n12; peasant service in, 124–25, 272n4; political ideals of, 80–82; Russian German leadership of, 138, 276n51; Russification of, 60–62, 253nn66–67; size of, 84; social ideals of, 86–88,

144, 278n13; Ungern's resignation from, 101–4, 265n3, 265n8. *See also* Cossacks; World War I
Russianization, 44–45
Russian Revolutions: of 1905, 8, 32, 49–58, 58–59, 140; of February 1917, 8, 135, 140, 141–51; of October 1917, 8, 135, 153
Russian Socialist Federated Soviet Republic (RSFSR), 203–4, 293n40, 298n51
Russification, 127–28, 225–26, 230; in the Amur River region, 96–99; anti-Semitism and, 97–98; fear as basis for, 98; of the imperial army, 60–62, 253nn66–67; as imperial policy, 37, 44, 48, 147–48, 246n35; in the Russian Baltic region, 35–42, 246nn31–32; in Trans-Baikal, 75–78, 120–21, 257n45; Trans-Siberian Railway and, 51–53
Russo-Japanese War of 1904–1905, 50–55, 57, 59, 66, 94, 250n27; in Manchuria, 53–55, 80, 251n41; Qing neutrality during, 58, 252nn57–58; Trans-Baikal Host in, 68–69, 80

2nd Company of the 1st Argun Regiment, 70
Semenov, Ataman (Grigorii Mikhailovich), 7, 141–63, 226–27; arrest and execution of, 228–29; corruption of, 162–63, 283n81; goals in the Far East of, 155–63, 165, 181, 182, 273n1; indigenous regiments of, 148; language skills of, 155; on national movements, 224; Persian campaign of, 146–48, 277nn3–4, 279n23; personal traits of, 141–42, 187, 280n43; on revolution, 143; Ungern's letters to, 152; White Army leadership role of, 143, 152–53, 162–63, 165, 198–200, 280n46, 283n3
Shakhovskoi, Sergei, 41
Sharaban, Maria, 152
Shchetinkin, Petr, 207, 210, 228, 293n50
Shilka River, 84, 88
Shubin, Andrei, 201
Shumiatskii, Boris, 204, 213–14, 221, 293nn44–46
Sibbiuro, 212, 294n11
Siberia: indigenous nomadic peoples of, 64–65, 68, 72–73, 78, 168, 254n5; Red surge in, 211–13; Russian settlement of, 51–52, 64–68, 77–78, 119, 258n49; Trans-Baikal Host in, 67–70. *See also* Amur River region; Eastern Siberia; Novonikolaevsk; Trans-Baikal
Sibrevkom, 212, 294n11
Sienkiewicz, Henryk, 259n61
Simmel, Georg, 265n8
Sino-Japanese War of 1894–1895, 50
Slavic expansiveness, 84, 259n6
Smirnov, Ivan, 214, 228, 298n53
Snyder, Timothy, 22